ENCYCLOPEDIA

OF

GODS

ENCYCLOPEDIA
OF
GODS

Over 2,500 Deities of the World

MICHAEL JORDAN

Facts On File, Inc.

AN INFOBASE HOLDINGS COMPANY

ENCYCLOPEDIA OF GODS: Over 2,500 Deities of the World

Facts On File, Inc.
11 Penn Plaza
New York, NY 10001

Library of Congress Cataloging-in-Publication Data

Jordan, Michael
    Encyclopedia of gods: over 2,500 deities of the world / Michael
Jordan.
        p.   cm.
    Includes index.
    ISBN 0-8160-2909-1
    1. Gods—Encyclopedias.   I. Title.
BL473.J67   1993
291.2'11—dc20   92-46762

Printed in the United States of America

RRD VC 10 9 8 7 6 5 4 3 2

This book is printed on acid-free paper.

CONTENTS

INTRODUCTION

In compiling a book like *Encyclopedia of Gods,* one is struck both by the enormous number and variety of deities that occur in different religions around the world, and also by the way patterns repeat themselves—almost every culture has its creator gods, gods concerned with a locally important aspect of the weather, goddesses of fertility, gods whose duty it is to protect the home. The same mysteries have puzzled people on every continent, the same fears have beset them and they have all attempted to explain the mysteries and allay the fears in the same way—through the worship of gods.

We know, beyond reasonable doubt, that a world measured purely in spiritual dimensions has been identified for at least 60,000 years—it may have been present as an innate part of the human psyche since the very beginnings of consciousness. But why does the human spirit harbor such a need for gods?

The beginnings of an answer to this question may be found in the beliefs of the simplest cultures. Primitive peoples attribute to all of nature, everything that exists in a physical state, a spiritual identity that is ever-present but unseen, conjured or appeased by the special powers placed upon certain individuals of the tribe, the *shamans,* or wise ones. These spirits may be poorly defined, but they are endowed with human form and human habits: they walk, talk, enjoy sexual relations, exhibit anger, sorrow, joy, mischief and so on. Thus one finds in simple shamanistic faiths such characters as "cloud man" and "grass woman," "old man of rocks" and "reindeer child."

As this animistic style of religion develops, the rather vague ethereal spirits of clouds, rocks, trees, birds and animals become detached from their temporal "shells" and take on progressively more abstract associations. Thus we find a goddess of childbirth, a god of storms, a god of blacksmiths or sailors, even a deity concerned with the proper use of pots and pans. As the scope of their responsibilities broadens, the deities become more clearly defined, more "human" personalities. We come to know them

by their appearances, by their style of dress, by the attributes they carry. Yet some of their animistic traits persist, and they may still be identified in inanimate symbols and devices and be represented as animals or other living things. The social infrastructure of the spirit world may also closely mirror our own: thus deities become arranged in hierarchical orders known as pantheons and may be separated into groups, not only responsible for different areas of worldly control, but also directing their powers toward good or evil.

To explain the precise significance in our lives of gods and goddesses is more complicated because it may alter according to environment and according to the stage of social and economic development. Again it necessitates a return to the template provided in the most simple religions. Without the benefit of science, technology and history, the natural world is a puzzling and frightening place, steered by great invisible forces. If every object in nature has a spiritual identity, which may be considered to act as its protector or guardian, logic dictates that mankind's activities affect the object not only in its physical state but also in its spiritual dimension. Thus the approval of the relevant spirit must be obtained before the hunting of game, the felling of a tree, the commencement of a journey, the building of a house. Responsibility for our actions is taken from us and given into the hands of an all-powerful, if unseen, being.

The need to expiate our activities has persisted through the ages: the prime role of gods is still to protect, to steer, to govern the order of life and to provide answers to conundrums that science and the modern temporal world cannot resolve.

This encyclopedia contains more than 2,500 entries of deities derived from both ancient and contemporary cultures. It does not generally include personalities regarded as demigods, demons or mythical heroes. A demigod is defined here as a personality who was once mortal but has been elevated to the celestial ranks. Generally speaking, and it is certainly true of the occidental religions, gods are iconic figures whose "pedigree" belongs exclusively in the heavens. They are distinct and separate from humankind. In some religions, however, most notably Buddhism, all deities are perceived as having once been mortal beings whose pursuit of excellence and enlightenment has elevated them ever higher through a series of spheres or planes toward perfection. In the mythologies of other cultures, often of a tribal nature, there exist significant ancestral personalities who have clearly been deified and are treated entirely as gods and goddesses, e.g., the Sumerian god Dumuzi or the Norse god Balder. In such instances, personalities that might correctly be regarded as demigods have an entry here. It should be noted, therefore, that while Gautama Buddha is included, there are no entries for Jesus Christ or the prophet Muhammad.

Although certain cultures, such as those of Greece and Rome, will be well known to most readers, others will be less familiar, and some historical background may be useful.

The Sumerians were the first high civilization to inhabit Mesopotamia. Their style of cuneiform writing was only deciphered a few years ago and much of their history and circumstance is still not properly known. In the twenty-fourth century BC they were taken over by the Akkadians under Sargon and the style of writing changed to a Semitic cuneiform. The names of many deities changed at the same time. The Old Babylonian era began at about the end of the second millennium BC and was marked largely by the influence of the law-making king Hammurabi. With some interruptions, the influence of Babylon continued through the neo-Babylonian period of biblical notoriety, until roughly two hundred years before the birth of Christ. The Hittite Empire arose in the mountainous region of what is now Turkey and its period of influence was comparatively short-lived. The Hurrians, closely linked with the Hittite Empire, were less a compact culture than a loose-knit and widely traveled people who shared a common language. They influenced much cross- fertilization of cultures in the ancient Near East.

The demise of these ancient orders came in 539 BC when the Persians under Cyrus conquered Babylon.

Their hegemony was brief and was replaced by the Greek influences of Alexander the Great and his Macedonian Empire in the fourth century BC. The Romans under Pompey came in the first century BC. Muslim expansionism took over key areas of Syria-Palestine and Persia in the seventh century AD, introducing the new religion of Islam to an area that had seen strong, if short-lived, influence from Zoroastrianism.

In parallel with the Mesopotamian cultures, that of Egypt survived more or less intact from sometime before 3000 BC until the end of the Roman Empire period, though from the 1st century AD, under Roman provincial rule, the makeup of Egypt's religion becomes increasingly confused.

The classical religions of Greece and Rome supplanted those of the ancient world as the dominant occidental faiths. Greece was the pioneer and, although known properly from about 800 BC, coincidental with the rise of the city-states, her deities were probably well established in much earlier times, perhaps in the Mycenaean age, which began circa 1600 BC. Rome seems largely to have borrowed deities from Greece and renamed them. Her influence collapsed with the sack of Rome by the Visigoths in 410 AD.

Elsewhere in Europe the Celtic gods were probably taking substance as early as the late Bronze Age in central Europe (circa 900 BC), but they come under historical scrutiny only from about 400 BC. Celtic culture was effectively a spent force in Europe by the first century BC with the defeat of the Gaulish rebellion under Vercingetorix, but its influence continued in Ireland until Christianization in the fifth century AD. The Celts were never literate and names of deities are known only from Romano-Celtic inscriptions and the questionably accurate writings of Christian monks. The Vikings, with whom the Nordic Icelandic culture is most closely associated, began their major period of influence in the eighth century AD, but their deities are often modeled on older Germanic gods who probably held sway from at least the first or second centuries AD. Their culture is better recorded through the Icelandic Eddaic literature.

In India, Hinduism took shape perhaps as early as 1700 BC with the migration of Aryan people from the southern steppes of Russia into the subcontinent. The development of the two great epic poems, the *Rama-yana* and the *Mahabharata,* between 300 BC and 300 AD swelled the ranks of deities and the process of enlargement continued with the more recent literature of the Puranas and the development of Tantrism. Though now associated more with the Far East, Buddhism began in northern India with the teachings of Gautama Buddha in about 500 BC. It was introduced to China in the first century and to Japan as late as the sixth century AD.

Of the major Meso- and South American religions discussed, the earliest is that of the Mayans, the Yucatan peninsula of Mexico, whose civilization arose in the fourth century BC, reached its peak during the seventh century AD and then waned in influence as the Toltec Empire began to flourish. The Incas, though established on parts of the Pacific coast of Peru in the fifth century BC, did not begin serious cultural expansion for several hundred years and their brief empire period commenced in 1438 AD. The Aztecs, in Mexico, started their rise to prominence about a hundred years earlier but were largely contemporary with the Incas. These pre-Columbian cultures came to an abrupt end with the arrival of the conquistadores, Cortez conquering the Aztec capital in 1521 and Pizarro taking Peru twelve years later. Almost all their sacred literature was destroyed.

To assist in placing the various cultures in a chronological perspective, a chart is provided on pages xii–xii.

It is notoriously difficult to pinpoint the moment in time at which a personality or a title first becomes identifiable as a deity. Frequently a name is recognizable from a list or a text but it is not possible to say with certainty whether that word reflects an object of worship or some more secular notion. The word may, at first, refer only to a phenomenon, such as the sunrise. Eventually the term for sunrise is adopted as the proper name of a deity who is the apotheosis of that phenomenon, but precisely when that change in usage has taken place is unknown. With rare exceptions, deities do not emerge "overnight." They are slow to evolve, often deriving from the personality of an older god or goddess. Likewise they may be highly tenacious, their worship dwindling imperceptibly, sometimes over many centuries. Rarely is the period

of reverence for a deity, from "source to sink," clear-cut. Because of the once enormous number of animistic spirits, a process of merging or syncretization frequently takes place when deities who exhibit similar roles become redundant and join forces as a single personality. Obviously when cultures merged, some deities were also superseded. Sometimes a compound name may give a clue to this process, but often only the title of the dominant figure remains for the record.

Thus the chronology can never be precise and is frequently the subject of disagreement between scholars. Where dates are given for a "known period of worship," these are to be regarded as an approximate guide only.

Apart from the distinctions outlined below, the deities listed here are treated equably, though many of the entries in large pantheons such as those of Hinduism and Buddhism are probably on a level of importance equal to that of Christian saints.

Entries are in alphabetical order, without breakdown into ethnic or cultural groups, and each entry is listed under the name by which the deity is most commonly known. The modern geographical area of the world in which the deity is, or has been, recognized is given in [square brackets].

Two types of entry are employed in the encyclopedia. Entries for deities who may be regarded as being, or having been, of major significance within their cultural area are headed by **BOLD CAPITALS** and are given more detailed coverage in the text. The remainder are treated in less detail. In all cases the information includes the original cultural source. This may sometimes be reflected by a language, e.g., Sumerian; by a cultural movement, e.g., Babylonian, Hindu or Buddhist; or by a tribal identity, e.g., Yoruba or Navajo. It should be noted that the term "Akkadian-Babylonian" is taken to mean that period influenced by the Akkadian and Babylonian hegemonies, during which texts were composed in the Semitic Akkadian language.

Also included is the role of the deity in the pantheon—whether he or she is perceived as a creator, a god of concepts like fertility or death or taking more specific responsibility, such as for the well-being of a grain crop. His or her immediate genealogy is listed since gods and goddesses are invariably considered to have celestial parents, siblings and offspring. Mythology plays a significant role in sustaining religion and its personalities, particularly among the broad mass of cultures that are essentially non-literate. The deeds of spirit beings are recorded in word-of-mouth stories. When mythology plays a significant part in the understanding or makeup of the personality, its outlines may be included and the literary source identified. Information may be of use in recognizing a god or goddess from iconography, such as dress, symbols, sacred animals and other attributes is also provided when known, and art references are given. Attributes may be of particular importance in identifying deities from large and complex pantheons such as those found in Hinduism and Buddhism. These deities may appear in a number of physical forms or emanations in order to perform different roles, i.e., as an ascetic, a lover, a prince or a warrior. Sometimes variations are described as *avataras,* which may be best explained as reincarnations in which a divine being has been born into the world to save it from danger and to restore order during some particular moment of disruption.

Distinction is drawn between sky and astral personalities who are perceived to live in the regions above the temporal world and who are generally concerned with climate, weather, cosmic events and other such heavenly activities, and those associated with the earth and its well-being. Thus deities of fertility, agriculture, the sea, domestic affairs and death are generally earth-bound and are described as *chthonic.*

Two or more deities may be combined into a hybrid. Less than true syncretizations, such deities retain the hyphenated names of the original personalities. Generally such hybridized deities are not given space. This is particularly appropriate in the case of the Hindu pantheon where the effect would be to incorporate very large numbers of names representing little more than a fusion of two personalities detailed elsewhere in the encyclopedia. All significant *avataras,* or incarnations of a deity, are, however, included. In some cases we have no names for figures depicted in art, either because none are provided or because we cannot decipher them, but the iconic form is so well represented that academic circles have pro-

vided code letters, e.g., those Mayan gods listed as God A, God B and so on. When it is generally assumed that a code-named figure is the same as a fully identified deity, the code name may be noted at the end of an entry.

Where cross-references to other deities seem appropriate, they are included. Romans were particularly prone to adopt Greek and Celtic deities, retaining more or less all the original personality, but changing the name. Thus Zeus becomes Jupiter and Aphrodite is renamed Venus.

Because of the numbers involved, no attempt has been made to indicate that a god mentioned in another's entry has an entry of his or her own. But if the deity is named without explanation, as Seth in the story of Horus and vice versa, the readers will usually find that an entry exists for that deity.

When a name originates in a script form other than Roman, e.g., Sanskrit, the nearest phonetic equivalent is provided in the spelling. In many instances, particularly where there has been Greek influence, the name given is the Hellenized version. Where applicable, the word *Greek* appears in [square brackets] as part of a heading: this applies to a number of Hellenized Egyptian deities whose Greek-style names are more commonly used; the original Egyptian name is then given at the end of the entry. The reader should be aware that other reference sources may interpret phonetics differently and it is worth exploring possible alternative spellings if an entry is not immediately found. For illustration, the Greek god Asklepios may, in some other works, be entered as Asclepius. Spellings are generally those incorporated in the source reference works cited in the bibliography. There are exceptions: the Loeb translations of Greek authors, for instance, tend to use "Romanized" spellings. Wherever applicable, a literal English translation of the meaning is given and alternative names and spellings may also be included under "synonyms" or at the end of the entry. If a form of a name is specific to a certain language or culture, this is also stated.

It should be noted that in ancient Near Eastern pantheons, the sound *sh* is transcribed as *š*, and that in Baltic and some African languages, *sh* is transcribed as *s*. Generally, a *c* placed before the vowel sounds *e* or *i* is pronounced soft, like an *s*. In all cases *z* should be pronounced like the French *j* in *jardin*, though many people will prefer to employ the Anglicized pronunciation of names like Zeus.

Although *Encyclopedia of Gods* represents the most comprehensive worldwide listing of deities available in a single volume, it makes no claim to be exhaustive. Aside from the reservations already stated, the volume of potential entries would make this an unrealistic objective. The gods of Hatti (Hittite), for example, are described as being "in excess of 10,000." There are at least as many deities known to Japanese Shintoism. Many thousands more find their place in the Chinese pantheons. The volume therefore, includes those names that a student or enthusiast of iconography or mythology would reasonably need to explore and that a casual reader or traveler might encounter in texts or inscriptions.

One should always be aware that our present-day knowledge of the names and personalities of deities is strictly governed. In too many instances ethnologists have simply not bothered to investigate local faiths before they have been corrupted or obliterated by the more universal modern religions. Primitive societies have often been reluctant to speak the names of deities to outsiders for fear of divine—or missionary—reprisal. Thus there are accountable geographical gaps in what might otherwise be a more complete survey.

Chronology of the Principal Religions and Cultures covered in this book

CULTURE	3000 BC	2500	2000	1500	1000
SUMERIAN					
AKKADIAN-BABYLONIAN					
HITTITE-HURRIAN					
EGYPTIAN					
GREEK					
ROMAN					
JUDAISM					
CHRISTIAN					
ISLAMIC					
HINDU					
BUDDHIST					
INCA					
MAYAN					
AZTEC					
CELTIC					
NORDIC-ICELANDIC					

500 BC   0   500 AD   1000   1500   2000 AD

A

A-a
Sun goddess. Mesopotamian (Babylonian-Akkadian) and western Semitic. Consort of the sun god Šamaš. Also Aya.

A'aš
God of wisdom. Hittite and Hurrian. A deity derived from the Mesopotamian model of Enki/Ea. A'aš keeps the tablets of fate.

Abandinus
God of unknown affinities. Romano-Celtic (British). The name appears in an inscription at Godmanchester, Cambridge, England.

Abellio
Tree god. Romano-Celtic (Gallic). Known from inscriptions in the Garonne valley of southwestern France and thought to be associated with apple trees.

Abeona
Goddess of passage. Roman. Linked with the goddess Adeona, she is concerned with the safe going-out and coming-in of a child.

Abgal
1. Desert god. Pre-Islamic northern Arabian. Known from the Palmyrian desert regions as a tutelary god of Bedouins and camel drivers. 2. Minor attendant spirits. Mesopotamian (Sumerian). Associated with Enki and residing in the Abzu or primeval water.

Abhijit *(victorious)*
Minor goddess of fortune. Hindu (Puranic). A benevolent *naksatra* or astral deity; daughter of Daksa and consort of Candra (Soma).

Abhijnaraja
Physician god. Buddhist-Lamaist [Tibet]. Accounted among a series of *sMan-bla* (medicine *buddhas*). Typically depicted with stretched earlobes. Color: red.

Abhimukhi *(friendly disposed)*
Minor goddess. Buddhist (Vajrayana). One of twelve deified *bhumis* recognized as different spiritual spheres through which a disciple passes. Color: yellow. Attributes: book and staff.

Abnoba
Forest and river goddess. Romano-Celtic (Continental European). Known locally from the Black Forest region of Germany. The name "Avon," associated with many rivers, derives from her name.

Abonsam
Malevolent spirit. West African. Recognized by tribes in the Gold Coast, etc. Traditionally driven away in an annual expulsion ritual by firing guns and shouting loudly, emptying houses of furniture and beating the interiors with sticks, the *abonsam* was finally driven into the sea. The ritual was preceded by four weeks of total silence in the area.

Abu
Minor vegetation god. Mesopotamian (Sumerian). Said to have sprung from the head of the god Enki, thus symbolizing plants emerging from the earth's soil.

Abundantia
Minor fertility goddess. Roman. The personification of abundance. She continued in French my-

1

thology after the Roman occupation, as a lady who enters houses in the night, bringing prosperity.

Abzu
Primordial deity of underground waters, the "deep." Mesopotamian (Sumerian). His center of cult was at Eridu (southern Mesopotamia). He was replaced in Akkadian times by Apsu.

Ac Yanto *(our helper)*
God of white men. Mayan (classical Mesoamerican) [Mexico]. The brother of the creator god Hachacyum. Responsible for the creation of European immigrants, including their possessions and products.

Acacila
Animistic spirit. Aymara Indian [Peru and Bolivia—Titicaca Basin]. One of a group of vaguely defined beings who control the weather, including rain, hail and frost.

Acala *(immovable)*
1. Minor goddess. Buddhist (Vajrayana). One of twelve deified *bhumis* recognized as different spiritual spheres through which a disciple passes. Color: white. Attributes: staff on a lotus. 2. Tutelary god. Buddhist (Mahayana). Also a *dikpala* or guardian of the northeastern quarter. Color: blue. Attributes: jewel, lotus, staff and sword.

Acan
God of wine. Mayan (Yucatec, classical Mesoamerican) [Mexico]. Identified with the local brew, *balche,* made from fermented honey to which the bark of the *balche* tree has been added.

Acat
God of tattooers. Mayan (classical Mesoamerican) [Mexico].

Acca Larentia
Obscure mother goddess. Roman. Believed in some traditions to be the mother of the Lares, but also the mother of the god Hercules and the adopted mother of Romulus, the founder of Rome. She was celebrated in the *Larentalia* festival on December 23, which was also a feast of the dead.

Acchupta *(untouched)*
Goddess of learning. Jain [India]. One of sixteen *vidyadevi* headed by the goddess Sarasvati.

Acolmiztli *(shoulderlion)*
Minor chthonic underworld god. Aztec (classical Mesoamerican) [Mexico]. One of the deities collectively classed as the Mictlantecuhtli complex.

Acolnahuacatl
Minor chthonic underworld god. Aztec (classical Mesoamerican) [Mexico]. One of the deities collectively classed as the Mictlantecuhtli complex.

ADAD *(wind)*
Origin Mesopotamian (Babylonian-Akkadian). Weather god.

Known period of worship   circa 1900 BC or earlier to circa 200 BC.

Synonyms   Ramman (thunder); Iškur (Sumerian).

Center(s) of cult   Karakara and at Aleppo and Mari [Syria].

Art references   reliefs, stelae, glyptics, etc.

Literary sources   cuneiform texts including *Atrahasis,* inscriptions.

Adad is derived from the older (Sumerian) model of Iškur. At Mari [Syria] he enjoyed a major cult following. Occasionally the subject of a sacred marriage ceremony in parts of Mesopotamia and Syria. His father is the supreme sky god Anu. He is described as a benevolent giver of life in the fields but is also a more violent storm god. His name in Akkadian cuneiform means "wind." His animal is the bull. In human form he is depicted wearing horned headdress and tiered skirt or robe decorated with astral symbolism. He may carry a scimitar embellished with a single panther head and his symbol is the lightning fork often fixed upon a pair of pincers. See also Hadad [Syrian].

Adamas
Primordial creator being. Gnostic Christian (Nassene). Recognized locally in Phrygia [northwestern Turkey] as an androgynous force in the cosmos.

Adeona
Goddess of passage. Roman. See Abeona.

Adhimukticarya
Minor goddess. Buddhist (Vajrayana). One of twelve deified *bhumis* recognized as different spiritual spheres through which a disciple passes. Color: red. Attributes: red lotus and staff.

Adhimuktivasita   (control of confidence)
Minor goddess. Buddhist. One of a group of twelve *vasitas* or goddesses personifying the disciplines of spiritual regeneration. Color: white. Attribute: flower bud.

Adibuddha   (the primeval buddha)
The original *buddha.* Buddhist. The primordial force in the cosmos from whom the five *dhyanibuddhas* arose. The embodiment of the concept of emptiness. He is considered by some authorities to be identical with Vaharaja and Vajrasattva. His image, sitting on a lotus leaf, is often carried by other Buddhist deities. Epithets include Svabhava (self-creating), Svayambhu (self-enlightened).

Adidharma   (the primeval law)
Primordial goddess. Buddhist-Lamaist [Tibet]. Particularly worshiped in Lamaism, she is the *Sakti* of Adibuddha. Attributes: cup and knife.

Adikia
Goddess of injustice. Greek. An ugly figure who is depicted on the Kypselos Chest being throttled by the goddess of justice Dike.

Adimurti   (the primeval personification)
Form or *avatara* of the god Visnu. Hindu (Epic and Puranic). Probably very similar to Narayana. Conventionally depicted as Visnu seated on the coils of the serpent Sesa (Adisesa) and attended by two wives. Attributes: those of Visnu. Also Vaikunthanatha, Paramapathanatha.

Aditi   (the free one)
Archaic mother goddess. Hindu (Vedic). According to the *Rg Veda* Aditi is said to be the wife of Kasyapa or of Brahma and mother of the *Adityas,* a group of minor gods including Mitra, Aryaman, Bhaga, Varuna, Daksa and Anisa. No other consort is mentioned in the literature. She is also considered to be the mother of Hari. Other legends give her as the mother of the rain god Indra. No human physical features are drawn, though she is sometimes identified in the guise of a cow. Aditi is also perceived as a guardian goddess who brings prosperity and who can free her devotees from problems and clear away obstacles. She disappears largely from later Hindu traditions.

Aditya   (descendant of Aditi)
Collective name for sun gods. Hindu (Vedic and Puranic). These numbered six in Vedic times but later increased to twelve. The sons of the primordial goddess Aditi. Also an epithet for Surya. Attributes: two or more lotuses.

ADONIS   (lord)
Origin   Hellenic name adopted predominantly in Phoenician and Syrian culture and based on an old western Semitic deity [Lebanon and Syria]. Ferti¹ ₎ and vegetation god.

Known period of worship   circa 200 BC (Seleucid period) to circa 400 AD.

Synonyms   Adon (lord, Semitic).

Center(s) of cult   mainly at Berytus and Aphaca.

Art references   sculptures, plaques, votive stelae, glyptics, etc.

Literary sources   various literary texts (few inscriptions).

Adonis is modeled on the Mesopotamian dying vegetation god Dumuzi (Hebrew: Tammuz). He appears as a youthful deity. The river Adonis [Nahr Ibrahim] is sacred to him largely because its waters flow red after heavy winter rains, having become saturated with ferrous oxide. In Hellenic tradition he is the son of the mythical Cyprian king Cinyras and his mother is Myrrha. According to Hesiod he is also the son of Phoenix and Alphesiboea. He is the consort of Aphrodite. Tradition has it that he was killed by a boar during a hunting expedition and is condemned to the underworld for six months of each year, during which the earth's vegetation parches and dies under the summer sun and drought. He was honored in a spring festival when priests in effeminate costume gashed themselves with knives. Frequently depicted nude and sometimes carrying a lyre. Also Attis (Phrygian); Atunis (Etruscan).

Adrastea

Mountain goddess. Hellenized Phrygian [northwestern Turkey]. Probably derived from a local Anatolian mountain deity. Known from inscriptions in Greece from circa 400 BC as a deity who defends the righteous. It is uncertain whether she bears any link with the Celtic goddess Andraste.

Adro

Tutelary god. Lugbara [Lake Albert, East Africa]. The personification of grass fires and whirlwinds who, in antiquity, created mankind. Thought to live in the vicinity of rivers with many wives and children.

Aeacos

Chthonic underworld god. Greco-Roman. One of three judges of Hades assessing the souls of the dead entering the underworld (see also Minos and Rhadamanthos). Identified by Plato as the son of Zeus and Aigina. In the *Theogony* (Hesiod), Aeacos is also the consort of Psamathe and father of Phocos. Also Aiakos.

Aed

Chthonic underworld god. Celtic (Irish). Known from inscriptions. Aed mac Lir, son of Lir and

Aobh was, according to tradition, turned into a swan by his stepmother, Aoife.

AEGIR *(water)*

Origin   Icelandic (Nordic). God of the ocean.

Known period of worship   Viking period (circa 700 AD) but probably earlier, through to Christianization (circa 1100 AD).

Synonyms   none known.

Center(s) of cult   none known but probably enjoyed sanctuaries along the west coast of Norway and elsewhere in Nordic region.

Art references   runic inscriptions; reliefs in metal and stone.

Literary sources   Icelandic codices; *Prose Edda* (Snorri); *Historia Danica* (Saxo).

A lesser known Aesir god of Asgard concerned with the moods of the sea and their implications for mariners. The river Eider was known to the Vikings as "Aegir's Door." Aegir is also depicted in some poetry as the "ale brewer," perhaps an allusion to the caldrons of mead that were thought to come from under the sea (see also the Celtic deities Dagda and Gobniu). There are references in literature to Saxons sacrificing captives, probably to Aegir, before setting sail for home. Linked in uncertain manner to the goddess Ran, he was believed to have sired nine children, the waves of the sea, who were possibly giantesses.

AENGUS

Origin   Celtic (Irish). Of uncertain status.

Known period of worship   circa 500 BC or earlier until Christianization circa 400 AD.

Synonyms   Mac Oc; Aengus Oc.

Center(s) of cult   Brugh na Boinne (Valley of the Boyne).

Art references   various monumental carvings and inscriptions.

Literary sources   *Books of Invasions; Cycles of Kings.*

The son of the Dagda by "the wife of Elcmar" (one of the kings of Tara) who may have been the goddess Boann, Aengus lived in the Valley of the Boyne and was closely linked with the ancient funerary tumuli in the region. According to legend, Aengus fell in love with a maiden whose identity he sought in vain. As he wasted away, his father and mother made enquiries until they located Caer, daughter of the king of Cannaught, who lived on Loch Bel Dragon in the shape of a swan with 150 attendant swans. Aengus eventually found her and he also changed into a bird.

Aeolos

God of storms and winds. Greek. One of the sons of Poseidon, said to have presented the winds in a leather bag to the hero Odysseus, and to have given the sail to seafarers. According to legend his home was the Aeolian Island [Lipari Island]. In one legend he is married to Eos and is the father of six sons, the various directional winds. The hexagonal Temple of Winds, on each side of which is depicted a flying figure of one of the winds, and which is dedicated to Aeolos, still stands in Athens.

Aeolus

God of storms and winds. Roman. Derived from the Greek storm god Aeolos, he is the consort of Aurora and the father of six sons, Boreas the north wind, Corus the northwest wind, Aquilo the west wind, Notus the southwest wind, Eurus the east wind and Zephyrus the south wind.

Aequitas

Minor god. Roman. Spirit of fair dealing, known particularly from the second century BC.

Aericura

Chthonic underworld god. Romano-Celtic. Known only from inscriptions.

Aesculapius

God of healing. Roman. Developed from the Greek deity Asklepios and introduced into Rome in 293 BC as a plague god. Attributes include the *caduceus* (winged scepter), the symbol of modern medicine.

AESIR

Origin Icelandic (Nordic). The major race of sky gods in Norse religion.

Known period of worship Viking period (circa 700 AD) but developed earlier, until Christianization (circa 1100 AD) and in some instances beyond.

Synonyms none known.

Center(s) of cult throughout areas of Nordic influence, particularly at Uppsala in Sweden.

Art references engraving on stone and weapons; other art objects etc.

Literary sources Icelandic codices; *Prose Edda* (Snorri); *Historia Danica* (Saxo); various classical authors.

The twelve Aesir gods are headed by Othin, the All-Father (see also the Koryak Siberian deity Quikinn.a'qu) and probably are, in part, derived from a Germanic pantheon established in prehistory. The Aesir follow a common pattern whereby cultures establish a "senior" pantheon of great gods which usually number seven or twelve. Some of these are creator gods but do not necessarily include the archetypal founders of the cosmos. In mythology the Aesir exist in a realm known as Asgar [1] one of a number of heavens perceived in Nordic and Germanic lore. The gods live in great halls. Othin occupies Valaskjalf, roofed with silver, and in a separate building, Valhall, he assembles slain mortal heroes. These warriors will one day serve to defend Asgard in the final onslaught against the established order by the frost giants and other adversaries. The Aesir fought a primal battle with a rival group of gods, the Vanir. Their constant enemies, though, are the Frost Giants, the Midgard Serpent, a huge sea snake encircling the Nordic lands, and Fenrir, the great wolf who will catch and swallow the sun at the day of doom, Ragnarok. At that time it is foretold that the gods of Asgard will perish, and earth will be consumed by fire, finally to be cleansed by the rising waters of the sea before being born anew.

Aether
Primordial god of light. Greco-Roman. A remote cosmic deity, the son of Erebos (darkness) and Nyx (night) who overthrew these archetypal deities of chaos. In Hesiod's *Epic Cycle* he is also described as the father of Ouranos.

Agathos Daimon *(good demon)*
God of fortune. Greco-Roman. Known locally from Alexandria and depicted in the form of a snake. May have originated as an androgynous fertility spirit, but later becomes identified as the consort of Agathe Tyche (see Tyche). Libations were made regularly to this deity after meals and he was regarded as a friendly household guardian.

Age
God of animals. Fon [Benin, West Africa]. Revered by hunters in the savannah regions.

Aglibol
Moon god. Pre-Islamic northern Arabian. Known from Palmyra and linked with the sun god Yarhibol. The cult continued into Hellenic times and was later extended to Rome. Attributes include a sickle moon.

AGNI *(fire)*
Origin Hindu [India]. God of fire.

Known period of worship circa 1500 BC onward and still recognized.

Synonyms none.

Center(s) of cult known throughout areas of Hindu influence.

Art references sculptures and reliefs in metal and stone.

Literary sources *Rg Veda* and other texts.

God of the sacrificial fire and the intercessor between gods and mankind, Agni is the son of Kasyapa and Aditi or, alternatively, of Dyaus and Prthivi. His consort is Svaha and, according to some texts, he is the father of the god Skanda. In a destructive capacity he is seen as an aspect of the god Siva. He is also a guardian or *dikpala* of the southeastern quarter. In ancient hymns he is said to have been born in wood as the embryo life force of all trees and plants and he emerges when wood is rubbed together. Vehicles: a she-goat, or a chariot drawn by red horses or parrots. Color: red. Attributes: seven arms and sometimes the head of a goat, carrying a wide variety of objects.

Agnikumara
God. Jain [India]. One of the groups under the general title of *bhvanavasi* (dwelling in places). They have a youthful appearance and are associated with rain and thunder.

Agnostos Theos
The unknown god(s) usually addressed in the plural form. Greco-Roman. They were the subject of altar inscriptions, particularly in Athens, probably out of concern lest certain less popular deities be neglected or forgotten.

Agu'gux
Creator god. Aleut [Aleutian Islands]. The name given to the Christian god under Russian Orthodox influence.

Ah Bolon Dz'acab *(many generations)*
Chthonic fertility god. Mayan (classical Mesoamerican) [Mexico]. A god identified with rain and thunder. Also strongly linked with agriculture and young crops. Possibly a vegetation *avatara* of the iguana god Itzam Na. Attributes include a leaflike ornament worn in the nose. Also God K.

Ah Cancum
Hunting god. Mayan (classical Mesoamerican) [Mexico]. One of a number of deities in Mayan religion identified with the hunt and the protection of animals. Also Acanum.

Ah Chun Caan
(he of the base of the sky)
Local god. Mayan (Yucatec, classical Mesoamerican) [Mexico]. The tutelary deity of the city of Merida. Mentioned in the Vienna Dictionary.

Ah Ciliz
God of solar eclipses. Mayan (classical Mesoamerican) [Mexico]. He is said to eat the sun during an eclipse, but at other times attends upon the sun god, serving him meals.

Ah Cuxtal   *(come to life)*
God of birth. Mayan (Lacandon, classical Mesoamerican) [Mexico]. Responsible for the safe delivery of women.

Ah Hulneb   *(he of the spear thrower)*
God of war. Mayan (classical Mesoamerican) [Mexico]. The local guardian deity of the city of Cozumel.

Ah Kin   *(he of the sun)*
Sun god. Mayan (classical Mesoamerican) [Mexico]. A deity of ambivalent personality, the young suitor of the moon goddess Acna, also the aged sun god in the sky. He is feared as the bringer of drought, but also protects mankind from the powers of evil associated with darkness. Said to be carried through the underworld at night on the shoulders of the god Sucunyum. Ah Kin is prayed to at sunrise and rituals include the burning of incense. He is invoked to cure illness and to bring wives to bachelors. Attributes include a square third eye subtended by a loop, a strong Roman nose, a squint and incisor teeth filed to a T-shape. Also Acan Chob (Lacandon); Chi Chac Chob; Kinich Ahau; God G.

Ah Kin Xoc
God of poetry. Mayan (classical Mesoamerican) [Mexico]. Regarded as a great singer and musician since most Mayan poetry is sung or chanted. He may appear as a hummingbird and is considered by some authorities to be an *avatara* of the sun god. Also Ah Kin Xocbiltun; P'izlimtec.

Ah Kumix Uinicob
Attendant water gods. Mayan (Yucatec, classical Mesoamerican) [Mexico]. The four diminutive deities that take over from the giant Ah Patnar Uinicob deities during the dry season.

Ah Mun
Corn god. Mayan (Yucatec, classical Mesoamerican) [Mexico]. The deity responsible for protecting the unripe corn.

Ah Muzencab
Bee gods. Mayan (Yucatec, classical Mesoamerican) [Mexico]. The patron deities of apiarists still invoked in parts of the Yucatan. They are thought to be represented iconographically on the tops and bottoms of stone columns at the site of Chichen Itza as aged men with long beards and upraised arms. They wear loin cloths with distinctive cross-hatching.

Ah Patnar Uinicob   *(owners of the jars men)*
Attendant water gods. Mayan (Yucatec, classical Mesoamerican) [Mexico]. Four huge deities who pour water on to the earth from jars. The end of the dry season is marked on May 3, completing an eight-day rain ceremony.

Ah Peku
Thunder god. Mayan (Lacandon, classical Mesoamerican) [Mexico]. He lives on the tops of hills and climbs into the clouds before it rains.

Ah Tabai
Hunting god. Mayan (classical Mesoamerican) [Mexico]. One of a number of deities in Mayan religion identified with the hunt and the protection of animals.

Ah Uincir Dz'acab
God of healing. Mayan (Chorti, classical Mesoamerican) [eastern Guatemala]. The patron of herbalists and concerned with the preparation of remedies, he is depicted as having male and fe-

male identities, each concerned with the healing of their respective sexes. Also Ah Uincir Kopot.

Ah Uuc Ticab

Chthonic god. Mayan (classical Mesoamerican) [Mexico]. Minor fertility and vegetation deity.

Aha   *(grandmother)*

River spirit. Yakut [central Siberia]. The guardian and apotheosis of rivers.

Ahriman

Chthonic god of darkness. Zoroastrian (Farsi-Persian). The antagonist of Ahura Mazda, god of light, and his attendant, Mithra. The name is a modern derivation of the original Avestan title Angru Mainyu. Ahriman is said to have tried to persuade his attendant animals, including the scorpion, ant and snake, to drink the blood of the bull slain by Mithra in the primeval legend of dualistic conflict (see Mithra); if he had succeeded he would have prevented life from forming on earth. In another legend he tried to thwart Ahura Mazda by sending a flood to destroy the world. Also recognized in Roman Mithraism. Rituals included animal sacrifice. Also Arimanius (Roman).

AHURA MAZDA

Origin   Persian [Iran]. God of light.

Known period of worship   circa 1500 BC to end of Roman Empire period, circa 400 AD.

Synonyms   none.

Center(s) of cult   throughout ancient Near East during Persian and Roman Empire periods.

Art references   various sculptures and reliefs.

Literary sources   Avestia.

Ahura Mazda probably originates as the Hindu Vedic god Varuna. In Persian religion he becomes the god of light and truth in the Zoroastrian concept of dualism. His chief attendant god is Mithra(s) and his adversary is Ahriman, the god of darkness. According to tradition his first creation, a wild bull, was confined to a cave by Mithras. When it escaped, Mithras was charged with finding and slaying it. The bull's blood fell to earth and from the drops life formed. Ahura Mazda is not mentioned in Roman Mithraic inscriptions but he is, by implication, the central figure in Mithraism. In the Mithraeum in Rome (*S. Prisca*), Ahura Mazda is considered to be a reclining figure on whom Mithras attends.

Although never popular among the civilian population, Mithraism spread under Flavius and was widespread among the Roman military, though it always enjoyed a greater following in the east than in the west. It was one symptom of the more general Roman return to sun worship. In 307 AD a sanctuary on the Danube was dedicated to Mithras (and Ahura Mazda) in an effort to sustain military power in the empire.

Ahurani   *(mistress of Ahura)*

Fertility goddess. Zoroastrian (Persian). Invoked by ordinary people to bring prosperity and children. Water libations were a key part of the ritual.

Ai Apaec

Supreme god. Mochica Indian (pre-Columbian South America) [northern coast of Peru]. Probably originated as a jaguar god but came to rule the destinies of the world. He was thought to live like ordinary people and could reveal himself as man or god at will. He is depicted in anthropomorphic form, but with huge fangs and a catlike wrinkled face with whiskers coming from his nose. He received sacrificial victims hurled from the top of a high cliff.

Aides

See Hades.

A.ne

Obscure sky or sun goddess. Celtic (Irish). May have an association with horses.

Ajalamo

God of unborn children. Yoruba [Nigeria, West Africa]. According to legend, in some vague mythological realm there exist rows of shelves with spirits of the unborn. These are the responsibility of Ajalamo.

Ajaya   *(invincible)*

Minor goddess. Buddhist (Mahayana). An attendant of Buddhakapala.

Aje

Goddess of wealth. Yoruba [Nigeria, West Africa]. She is thought to appear as a fowl scratching the earth and, in creation mythology, was sent down with Oduduwa, the earth goddess.

Aji-Shiki-Taka-Hiko-Ne

Rain god. Shinto [Japan]. One of the Raijin deities whose name is often linked with that of Kamo-Waka-Ikazuchi.

Ajysyt

Maternal spirit. Yakut [central Siberia]. The deity who oversees the lying-in of an expectant mother and who brings the child's soul to the childbed. The term *ajysyt* can also apply to a male spirit, thus the *ajysyt* that oversees the birth of horses is male, while that of horned cattle is female.

Akasagarbha   *(essence of the sky)*

Astral god. Buddhist (Mahayana) and Lamaist [Tibet]. One of the *bodhisattvas* or spiritual meditation *buddhas.* He lives in the "womb of the sky." Color: green. Attributes: book, jewel, lotus and sun disc. Also Khagarbha. In Japanese Buddhism this deity becomes the god Kokuzo.

Akelos

River god. Greek. The son of Okeanos and Tethys. According to mythology he was a rival suitor for Deianeira who became the wife of Herakles. He was the consort of Melpomene and his daughters were allegedly the *sirenes.* A river of the same name runs into the Ionian Sea. Attributes include bull horns. Also Achlae (Etrurian).

Aken

Chthonic underworld god. Egyptian. The keeper of the underworld ferry boat.

Aker

Chthonic earth god of passage. Egyptian. Known from the Old Kingdom (circa 2700 BC onward). Controls the interface between eastern and western horizons of the underworld, and is the guardian of the gate through which the king passes into the underworld. Aker provides a safe course for the craft of the sun god during its passage through the underworld at night. He may be seen as the socket holding the boat's mast. He is also considered benevolent against snake bites. Represented by opposite facing pairs of human or lion heads.

Akeru

Pluralistic chthonic earth gods. Egyptian. Probably stemming from the pre-Dynastic period. Malevolent deities who can seize and imprison the souls of the deceased.

Akonadi

Oracular goddess. Ghanaian [West Africa]. Known in the region around Accra where she has had a celebrated oracular shrine. She is regarded as a goddess of justice and a guardian deity of women.

Akongo

Creat god. Ngombe [Zaire, central Africa]. The supreme deity considered to have given the world, and all that is in it, form and substance.

Aksayajnana-Karmanda
(undecaying knowledge of Karma)

Deification of literature. Buddhist. One of a group of twelve *dharanis.* Color: red. Attributes: basket with jewels, and staff.

AKSOBHYA   *(imperturbable)*

Origin Buddhist [India]. The second *dhyanibuddha* or meditation *buddha.*

Known period of worship circa 500 BC to present.

Synonyms   Vajrasana; Vajraheruka.

Center(s) of cult   pan-Asiatic.

Art references   metal and stone sculptures, paintings.

Literary sources   *Sadhanamala* and Tantric ritual texts.

One of five mystic spiritual counterparts of a human *buddha* in Vajrayana Buddhism. A product of the Adibuddha who represents the branch of the cosmos concerned with consciousness. He originates from the blue mantra HUM and lives in the eastern paradise Abhirati. His *Sakti* is Locana and he is normally accompanied by two elephants. Color: blue. Attributes include bell, three monkish robes and staff, also jewel, lotus, prayer wheel and sword. Aksobhya may also be a tutelary deity in Lamaism [Tibet] in which case his attributes are similar. Emanations include Heruka, Manjusri, Vajrapani and a large number of minor names. See also Amitabha, Amoghasiddhi, Ratnasambhava and Vairocana.

Ala

Chthonic fertility goddess. Ibo [eastern Nigeria, West Africa]. A popular deity who is also goddess of the underworld linked with a cult of the dead (which rest in her womb). Her temple is the Mbari, which contains a cult statue depicting the goddess seated with a child in her arms and adorned with the crescent moon. She is flanked by attendant deities. She enjoys a profusion of local shrines which are well supplied with votive offerings. Serious crimes including murder are considered to be offenses against her. An annual yam festival is celebrated in her honor. Also Ale, Ana, Ani.

Alad Udug Lama

Collective name of guardian deities. Mesopotamian (Sumerian and Babylonian-Akkadian). Vague spirits who accompany major deities and dispense good fortune.

Alaisiagae

Minor goddesses. Romano-Celtic (British). They are identified at Housteads (Northumberland) in a shrine to Mars Thincsus.

Alalu

Primordial god. Hittite and Hurrian. The archetypal deity who precedes An(u) in the formation of the cosmos. He was identified by the Greeks as Hypsistos (the highest).

Alatangana

Creator god. Kono [eastern Guinea, West Africa]. One of two creator deities; the other is Sa. Alatangana created land from swamp and placed vegetation on earth. According to legend he eloped with the daughter of Sa and fathered seven boys and seven girls.

Alaunus

Local god. Romano-Celtic (Continental European). Known from areas around Mannheim and Salzburg. The Romans syncretized him with Mercurius.

Alcis

Unknown status. Germanic and possibly Icelandic (Nordic). The Alcis are twin deities (brothers) known only as sons of the sky gods. From Germanic times we have a La Tene urn with pictures of paired men on horseback and linked by a wooden beam. Tacitus describes the worship of twin gods by the Naharvali tribe, their priests dressed in effeminate costume (see also the Phrygian deity Attis). They may have been worshiped in forest sanctuaries along the northern coast of Europe.

Alemona

Goddess of passage. Roman. Concerned with the health of the unborn child.

Alisanos

Local chthonic earth god. Romano-Celtic (Gallic). Known only from inscription in the region of the Côte d'Or and associated with the land. Also Alisonus, Alisanus.

Alk'unta'm

Sun god. Bella Coola Indian [British Columbia, Canada]. Linked closely with Senx, both are of equal significance. His mother is a cannibal woman,

Nunuso' mikeeqone'im, who can turn into a mosquito.

ALLAH

Origin Nabataean and Arabic. Derived from the western Semitic god Il.

Known period of worship circa 300 BC until present.

Synonyms none (but see below).

Center(s) of cult Mecca [Saudi Arabia].

Art references none.

Literary sources Qur'an.

The creator god of Islam. Perceived in pre-Islamic times as the creator of the earth and water though not, at that time, cosidered monotheistically.

Through the teachings of the prophet Muhammad (born Mecca circa 570 AD), which achieved their first major spread in the seventh century, the faith of Islam (submission to God) proclaimed Allah as a unique and sole deity. He is perceived as the creator of the cosmos and of all existence who will judge mankind at the final apocalypse. It is considered that the revelations delivered through the agency of Muhammad represent the only true message of God and that comparable revelations described in the teachings of Yhwhism and Christianity are defective.

Adherents to the faith are known as Muslims and the sacred book of Islam is the Qur'an (Koran). Devotion to Allah is all-embracing and there is no effective distinction into secular and non-secular life. He is accorded one hundred sacred names or epithets of which ninety-nine are known and are accounted on rosary beads. The final name remains a mystery. No representation of Allah is made in art.

Present estimates put the number of practicing Muslims at about 700 million, rather less than the global estimated total of Catholics. It is anticipated, however, that Islam will have become the major religion of the world, in numerical terms, by the millennium.

Allat *(goddess)*

Astral and tutelary goddess. Pre-Islamic northern and central Arabian. One of the three daughters of Allah. At Palmyra she was regularly invoked as a domestic guardian either as Allat or Astarte with whom she is closely linked. At Ta'if she was symbolized in the form of a white granite stone. In Hellenic times she became syncretized with Athene or, according to Herodotus who called her Alilat, with Aphrodite. See also Ataršamain.

Allatu(m)

Chthonic underworld goddess. Western Semitic. Modeled on the Mesopotamian goddess Ereškigal and possibly also equating with Arsay in Canaanite mythology. Recognized by the Carthaginians as Allatu.

Almaqah

Tutelary astral god. Pre-Islamic southern Arabian. Worshipped by the Saba tribe, his sacred animal is the bull. Attributes include lightning bolts and a sinuate weapon.

Alpanu

Chthonic underworld goddess. Etruscan. Depicted wearing jewels, a loose cloak and sandals but otherwise naked. Also arguably a goddess of sexual love.

Ama-arhus

Fertility goddess. Mesopotamian (Babylonian-Akkadian). Mentioned in texts as being among the pantheon at Uruk in Hellenistic times but also found as an earlier manifestation of the god Gula. Also Arad-Ama-arhus, Amat-Ama-arhus.

Amaethon

God of agriculture. Celtic (Welsh). A son of Don and brother of Gwydion, he is known from a limited number of Welsh texts and was engaged in a mythical battle against the Arawn. Associated with ploughing and husbandry. The modern Welsh name for a farmer is *amaethwr*.

Amašagnul
Fertility goddess. Mesopotamian (Babylonian-Akkadian). Mentioned in prebend documents from the Hellenistic period at Uruk and thought to be the consort of the god Papsukkal.

AMATERASU-O-MI-KAMI
Origin Shinto [Japan]. Sun goddess.

Known period of worship circa 600 AD or earlier until present.

Synonyms Shinmei; O-Hiru-Me-No-Muchi; Tensho-Ko-Daijin.

Center(s) of cult Ise Naiku shrine; many others throughout Japan.

Art references sculptures and paintings, etc.

Literary sources Nihongi; Kojiki (Japanese sacred texts).

The central figure of Shintoism and the ancestral deity of the imperial house. One of the daughters of the primordial god Izanagi and said to be his favorite offspring, she was born from his left eye. She is the sibling of Susano-Wo, the storm god.

According to mythology she and Susano-Wo are obliged to join each other in order to survive. Susano-Wo ascends with her to heaven but is thrown out after trying to enter her house and committing various excesses. Amaterasu refuses to be sullied and obstinately hides herself away in a cave. It requires the combined diplomacy and craft of many other deities to persuade her to come out. The lure is the "perfect divine mirror" in which she sees her reflection. The birth of the two deities is considered to mark the transition between cosmic and material genesis.

The Ise Naiku sanctuary is visited by about five million devotees each year and Amaterasu takes pride of place in every family shrine. Sometimes her shrines are placed adjacent to those of Susano-Wo. She is also the tutelary goddess of the emperor. Hers tends to be a monotheistic cult in which all other deities take a subservient place. Though powerful she does not always succeed and is often subject to attack. She has been arguably identified with the god Vairocana in Buddhist religion.

Ama-Tsu-Mara
God of smiths. Shinto [Japan]. Depicted as a one-eyed ithyphallic god comparable to the Greek Cyclopes. He is strongly instrumental in fashioning the "perfect divine mirror" with which the sun goddess, Amaterasu, is lured from her cave. Also Ma-Hiko-Tsu-No-Kami.

Amaunet *(the hidden one)*
Fertility goddess. Egyptian (Upper). Amaunet seems to have a taken a role as an early consort of Amun, one of the eight deities of the Ogdoad and representing hidden power. In that context she is depicted anthropomorphically but with the head of a snake. She is shown in reliefs and as the subject of a notable statue from the Record Hall of Tuthmosis III at the Karnak complex of Thebes, where she was recognized as a benign protective deity especially called on at times of royal accession. As a fertility goddess she was largely eclipsed by the goddess Mut. She is sometimes equated with Neith, the creator goddess of Sais, and her attributes may include the red crown of the Delta.

Ame-No-Kagase-Wo
Astral deity. Shinto [Japan]. The most important of the star *kami* said to have been executed by the god Futsunushi because he would not be pacified during the process of cosmic genesis.

Ame-No-Mi-Kumari-No-Kami
Water goddess. Shinto [Japan]. One of the daughters of Minato-No-Kami, the god of river mouths and estuaries, she is known as the "heavenly water divider" and her cult is linked with that of Kuni-No-Mi-Kumari-No-Kami.

AME-NO-MINAKA-NUSHI-NO-KAMI *(the deity master of the august center of heaven)*
Origin Shinto [Japan]. Supreme god.

Known period of worship   circa 600 AD until present.

Synonyms   none significant.

Center(s) of cult   none.

Art references   none.

Literary sources   Kojiki (Japanese sacred text).

The highest deity of the Shinto pantheon and the first to emerge in *Takama-No-Hara* (the plain of high heaven) when heaven and earth were fashioned. He was born alone, resides in the ninth heaven and has always hidden himself from mortal eyes. A remote and vague figure of whom no images are ever made and toward whom no cult is directed, his name only appears once in the *Kojiki* and never in the *Nihongi*. Originally his identity may have been strongly influenced by Chinese religion. His name is linked closely with those of two other lesser primordial beings, Taka-Mi-Misubi-No-Kami and Kami-Misubi-No-Kami.

Ame-No-Tanabata-Hime-No-Mikoto

Astral goddess of weavers. Shinto [Japan]. One of two star apotheoses who are, according to tradition, deeply in love with each other. Her partner is Hikoboshi. Her name is generally abbreviated to Tanabata, the title of a festival in honor of the goddess that became a national event in Japan in 755 AD. The festival later became merged with the Tibetan Bon *Ullumbana* festival of the dead. Also Shokujo.

Ame-No-Toko-Tachi-No-Kami
(deity standing eternally in heaven)
Primordial being. Shinto [Japan]. The fifth of the deities to emerge in the heavens, named in both the sacred texts of Shintoism, the *Kojoki* and *Nihongi*, but probably strongly influenced by Chinese religion. Born from a reed floating in the primeval waters. See also Umashi-Ashi-Kabi-Hiko-Ji-No-Kami.

Ame-No-Uzume

Goddess of dancers. Shinto [Japan]. She plays a part in enticing the sun goddess, Amaterasu, from her cave using the perfect divine mirror.

Ame-Waka-Hiko
(heavenly young prince)
God. Shinto [Japan]. According to tradition he was sent to earth on a vital mission but became preoccupied with a number of mortal women, forgot his purpose and did not report back to heaven. His punishment was to be slain by an arrow fired from the "heavenly true deer bow."

Am-Heh
Chthonic underworld god. Egyptian. A minor deity said to inhabit a lake of fire. The so-called "devourer of the millions." Depicted with the head of a hound.

Amida
Primordial deity. Buddhist (Japanese). The Japanese equivalent of Amitabha recognized from the eleventh and twelfth centuries AD.

Amimitl
Minor god of lakes and fish hunters. Aztec (classical Mesoamerican) [Mexico]. One of the deities collectively classed as the Mixcoatlcamaxtli complex.

AMITABHA   *(of unmeasured splendor)*
Origin   Buddhist [India]. The fourth *dhyanibuddha* or meditation *buddha*.

Known period of worship   circa 500 BC to present.

Synonyms   Vajradharma and possibly Amitayaus.

Center(s) of cult   pan-Asiatic.

Art references   metal and stone sculptures, paintings.

Literary sources   Sadhanamala and Tantric ritual texts.

One of five mystic spiritual counterparts of a human *buddha* in Vajrayana Buddhism. A product of the Adibuddha who represents the branch of the cosmos concerned with consciousness, he originates from the red mantra HRIH and lives in the western paradise Sukhavati. The cult may have been influenced by Iranian light religions.

His *Sakti* is Pandara and he is normally accompanied by two peacocks. Color: red. Attributes: lock of hair, lotus, monk's robe and water jar. Amitabha is also taken as a tutelary god in Lamaism [Tibet] in which case his attributes include bell, jewel and three monkish robes. Emanations include Padmapani, Manjusri and many other minor names. See also Aksobhya, Amoghasiddhi, Ratnasambhava and Vairocana.

Amm

Moon god. Pre-Islamic southern Arabian. The tutelary deity of the Qataban tribe. Also revered as a weather god. Attributes include lightning bolts.

Amma (1)

Local tutelary god. Dravidian (Tamil). Known from southern India.

Amma (2)

Creator god. Dogon [Mali, West Africa]. He first created the sun by baking a clay pot until it was white hot and coiling a band of copper around it eight times. He created the moon in similar fashion but used brass. Black people were created from sunlight and white from moonlight. Later, having circumcised the earth goddess, whose clitoris was an anthill, he impregnated her and produced the first creature, a jackal. Next he fertilized her with rain to engender plant life and finally became the father of mankind.

Ammavaru

Primordial mother goddess. Hindu-Dravidian. Known locally from east central India and worshiped by the Dravidian tribe of Telugu. She is said to have generated the cosmic egg in the sea of milk from which the major gods Brahma, Visnu and Siva were born.

Ammut (devouress of the dead)

Chthonic underworld goddess. Egyptian. A significant deity who allegedly consumes the dead if their hearts are found weighed down with guilt in the Judgement Hall of the Two Truths during the Weighing of the Heart ceremony. Ammut has a fearsome aspect and sits alongside forty-two juror gods named in the *Book of the Dead*. Depicted with the head of a crocodile, the trunk and forelimbs of a lion and the hind part of a hippopotamus. See also Thoth and Maat.

Amoghapasa

God. Buddhist. A variety of Avalokitesvara, depicted with one head and six, eight or twenty hands. Attributes: arrow, bell, lotus, noose, prayer wheel, rosary, staff and tiger skin.

AMOGHASIDDHI (unfailing power)

Origin Buddhist [India]. The fifth *dhyanibuddha* or meditation *buddha*.

Known period of worship circa 500 BC to present.

Synonyms Kharmaheruka.

Center(s) of cult pan-Asiatic.

Art references metal and stone sculptures, paintings.

Literary sources Sadhanamala and Tantric ritual texts.
   One of five mystic spiritual counterparts of a human *buddha* in Vajrayana Buddhism. A product of the Adibuddha who represents the branch of the cosmos concerned with consciousness. He originates from the green mantra HUM and lives in the northern paradise. His *Sakti* is Arya-Tara and he is normally accompanied by two Garudas or dwarfs. Color: green. Attributes: staff and sometimes seven-headed snake. Amoghasiddhi is also taken as a tutelary deity in Lamaism [Tibet] in which case his attributes include bell, three monkish robes and prayer wheel. Emanations include Visvapani and many other minor names. See also Aksobhya, Amitabha, Ratnasambhava and Vairocana.

Amor

God of love. Roman. Developed from the Greek god Eros. Depicted as a winged youth. According to tradition he awoke the goddess Psyche with a kiss. Attributes include arrows, bow and torch.

The popular epithet Cupid was only applied by poets.

Amphion
God. Greek. Theban variant on the god Polydeukes.

Amphitrite
Sea goddess. Greek. According to *Theogony* (Hesiod), one of the fifty daughters of Nereus and Doris. Considered to calm stormy seas, traveling in a boat made of mussels. She was among those present at the birth of Apollo.

AMUN   *(the hidden one)*
Origin   Egypt. Supreme creator god.

Known period of worship   probably pre-Dynastic but historically circa 2400 BC to end of Egyptian period (circa 400 AD).

Synonyms   Amun kem-atef (snake god); Amun kamutef (fertility god).

Center(s) of cult   Thebes (Luxor)—Great Temple of Amun at Karnak; Luxor Temple south of Karnak dedicated to the ithyphallic form of Amun kamutef.

Art references   many portraits on temple walls, etc; reliefs; statues; obelisks including notably that of Queen Hatshepsut; stelae.

Literary sources   Pyramid Texts from the end of Dynasty V (2494–2345 BC); temple hymns; the *Book of the Dead*; the Great Harris Papyrus; many other textual references.

Amun is a sun god, lord of the sky and king of the Egyptian world. He is perceived as a primeval deity present in chaos at the creation of the cosmos and is therefore also one of the eight deities of the Ogdoad coupled with the goddess Amaunet and representing hidden power. He is portrayed as a pharaoh, with blue skin and wearing a *modius* (turban) surmounted by two tall plumes of feathers symbolic of dominance over both Upper and Lower Egypt. In addition to the major temples at Luxor, other sanctuaries were built beyond the first Nile cataract at Amada, Soleb, Gebel Barkal and Abu Simbel.

Amun is symbolized chiefly by a ram with curved horns. The Nile goose is also sacred to him. He is a god regarded as hidden but spreading throughout the cosmos, unseen but everywhere. Though depicted anthropomorphically, in temple hymns other deities describe him as "hidden of aspect, mysterious of form." In the New Kingdom, from the middle of the sixteenth century BC onward, Amun was drawn as a manifestation of the ancient sun god of Heliopolis, which effectively raised his prestige still further and earned him the title "king of the gods." He was also regarded as being the father of each pharaoh. At Thebes he was revered as a snake deity with attendant connotations of immortality and endless renewal. As a member of the Ogdoad he has the head of a snake.

Amun's ithyphallic form probably came from the notion that because he was "first formed" of the gods, he could not have a father and therefore had to impregnate his own mother. He is generally regarded as a god with great sexual attributes. The Temple of Queen Hatsepsut at Deir el-Bahari bears a relief of her mother impregnated by Amun. A similar scene exists in the Temple of Amenhotep III at Luxor. The Great Hall of Hypostyle is filled with wall paintings of Amun and the pharaoh, and contains several processions honoring Amun. By the twelfth century BC the Amun priesthood was a powerful force in Egypt, leading to the eventual contest between Amun and Aten, the god "created" by Amenhotep IV. Amun's eclipse was short-lived and he returned to prominence until the end of Egyptian history.

Amurru
Mountain god. Western Semitic. A minor consort of Athirat whose attributes include a shepherd's crook and who was probably worshiped by herders. Known mainly from inscriptions. Also Martu.

AN   *(1) (sky)*
Origin   Mesopotamian (Sumerian) [Iraq]. Supreme creator god.

Known period of worship circa 3500 BC to 2000 BC but continuing as Babylonian creator god (see Anu) until 100 BC or later.

Synonyms Anu (Akkadian).

Center(s) of cult Unug [modern Warka].

Art references none known but probably represented symbolically on seals and seal impressions from third millennium onward.

Literary sources cuneiform texts including Sumerian creation accounts, and the Babylonian epic *Enuma Eliš.*

In Sumerian creation mythology An is the supreme being and, with his chthonic female principle, Ki, is the founder of the cosmos. Also, in some texts, identified as the son of Anšar and Kišar. The head of the older generation of gods. He is believed to have formed the basis for the calendar and is arguably first represented in bovine form having been derived from the old herders' pantheon. He is identified in some texts as the "bull of heaven." According to legends, heaven and earth were once inseparable until An and Ki bore a son, Enlil, god of the air, who cleaved heaven and earth in two. An carried away heaven. Ki, in company with Enlil, took the earth. An is also paired with the goddess Nammu by whom he fathered Enki. Patron god of Unug (Erech in the *Vetus Testamentum*), An is always a remote shadowy figure who occasionally lends a hand to tilt the balance of fate but otherwise tends to be out of touch with the day-to-day affairs of heaven and earth.

His main sanctuary is the Eanna temple. After the Semitic takeover of Sumer by Sargon the Great circa 2500 BC, Enlil supersedes him as supreme national god of the Sumerian city states.

An (2)

Possibly a female principle of the creator god An. Mesopotamian (Sumerian). Early iconography suggests a celestial sky goddess in the form of a cow whose udders produce rain and who becomes Antu(m) in the Akkadian pantheon.

Anaitis

Fertility goddess. Persian [Iran]. Her influence extended through eastern Europe. In pre-Christian Armenia, the center of her cult was at Acilisena, where noble families regularly surrendered their daughters to serve as cultic prostitutes.

Anala *(fire)*

Attendant god. Hindu (Puranic). One of a group of eight *vasu* deities answering to the god Indra.

Ananke

Goddess of destiny. Greek. Considered to be a universal presence. Depicted holding a spindle.

Ananta

Snake god. Hindu (Puranic). One of a group of seven snake deities or *mahanagas.*

Anantamukhi *(with the face of Ananta)*

Deification of literature. Buddhist. One of a group of twelve *dharanis.* Color: green. Attributes: staff and water jar with treasure.

Anantesa

Minor deity. Hindu (Puranic). One of a group of eight emancipated "lords of knowledge" or *vidyesvaras* considered to be aspects of Siva.

ANAT

Origin Canaanite and Phoenician [northern Israel, Lebanon and Syria]. Fertility and war goddess.

Known period of worship From prehistoric times (circa 2500 BC) until 200 AD or later.

Synonyms Anath; Lady of the Mountain; Antit (Egyptian).

Center(s) of cult Ugarit [Ras Šamra] and generally in places down the grain-growing coastal regions of the eastern Mediterranean.

Art references named specifically in Egyptian hieroglyphic on a stele from Bethsan; described on various other votive inscriptions, clay plaques, etc.

Literary sources Ugaritic texts from Ras Šamra; various offering lists.

The sister of Baal, Anat is primarily a fertility goddess. In art she is usually depicted naked, with breasts and vaginal area prominent. Often she wears a coiffure similar to that of the Egyptian goddess Hathor, with whom at times she has been closely linked. Anat is described variously as "mother of the gods" and "mistress of the sky." In addition to her fertility role, she is a youthful and aggressive goddess of war, a capacity in which she was adopted by Egypt from the end of the Middle Kingdom (early eighteenth century BC) and particularly through the Hyksos Dynasty when she was prominent in Lower Egypt. A sanctuary was dedicated to her at Tanis and she was identified as a daughter of the sun god Re with warlike attributes of lance, battleax and shield. She impressed Rameses II whose daughter was called Bin-Anat (daughter of Anat). Rameses III adopted her as his "shield" in battle.

The Ras Šamra stele describes her as "Antit, queen of heaven and mistress of all the gods." Known as the "virgin Anat," she indulged in orgies of violence "wading up to her thighs in blood and gore." She may be one of a triad of goddesses with Athirat and Ašera. In the classic Canaanite confrontation legend, after the primordial battle between good and evil in the guise of Baal and Mot, Anat searched out the body of Baal. She buried it and caught up with his slayer, Mot, to make appropriate retribution. She cleaved and winnowed, burned and ground Mot in a curious variation of a common theme associated elsewhere with gods of vegetation (see Osiris). She also features in the *Legend of Aqhat*, in which she sends an eagle to slay the youth when he refuses to give her his magical bow.

Anaulikutsai'x
River goddess. Bella Coola Indian [British Columbia, Canada]. Said to oversee the arrival and departure of the salmon in the rivers. She lives in a cave called Nuskesiu'tsta.

Anbay
Local tutelary god. Pre-Islamic southern Arabian. Regarded as a god of justice and an oracular source attending the moon god Amm.

Ancamna
Water goddess. Romano-Celtic (Continental European). Known only from inscriptions at Trier.

Andarta
Fertility goddess (probable). Celtic (Gallic). Patron goddess of the Vocontii tribe. Her name seems to have derived either from *artos* (bear) or *ar* (ploughed land). See also Andrasta.

Andjety
Chthonic underworld god. Egyptian (Lower). Minor deity in anthropomorphic form known from the Pyramid Texts. Identified with the ninth nome (district). Responsible for rebirth in the afterlife and regarded as a consort of several fertility goddesses. He was revered at Busiris where he clearly heralded the cult of Osiris. Attributes: high conical crown (similar to the *atef* crown of Osiris) decorated with two tall plumes, crook and flail. In early Pyramid Texts, the feathers are replaced by a bicornuate uterus. See also Osiris.

Andrasta
Goddess of war. Romano-Celtic (British). The patron goddess of the Iceni tribe. The warrior queen Boudicca is reported to have prayed to her before battle and she was the recipient of human sacrifice. Andrasta does not appear in Celtic Gaul, though a deity called Andraste is mentioned by the Roman writer Dio Cassius. The name may also be linked to the goddess Andarta. Also Adraste.

Anextiomarus
Local tribal deity. Romano-Celtic (British). God of uncertain affinities but linked with Apollo.

Angru Mainyu   *(evil spirit)*
Chthonic underworld god of darkness. Persian [Iran]. The original Zoroastrian name of the chief antagonist of Ahura Mazda. See Ahriman.

Anhouri
Minor god. Egyptian. A deity whose mummy was allegedly kept at Tanis.

Ani
Sky god. Etruscan. Identified as residing in the highest heaven and sometimes depicted with two faces, equating possibly with the Roman god Janus.

Anila *(wind)*
Attendant god. Hindu (Puranic). One of a group of eight *vasu* deities answering to the god Indra.

Anjea
Animistic fertility spirit. Australasia. Known to tribesmen on the Pennefather River, Queensland, Australia and believed to place mud babies in the wombs of pregnant women. The grandmother of a newly born infant buried the afterbirth, which was collected by Anjea and kept in a hollow tree or some such sanctuary until the time came to instill it into another child in the womb.

Ankalamman
Guardian goddess. Hindu-Dravidian (Tamil). Known particularly in southern India, where she wards off demons. Alternatively she is an aspect of Kali.

Anna Kuari
Local vegetation goddess. Indian. Worshipped by the Oraon tribe of Chota Nagpur. The recipient of human sacrifice in the spring months, she was believed to endow riches on the sacrificer and to ensure plentiful harvest while living in his house in the form of a child.

Anna Perenna
Protective goddess. Roman. Allegedly she saved the plebeians from famine in their conflict with the patricians in ancient Roman mythology. An open-air festival dedicated to her was held on March 15 each year in a grove north of Rome.

Annamurti
Form of the god Visnu. Hindu (Puranic). The patron deity of kitchens and food. A shrine at Srirangam in southern India contains two-armed bronze images of the god. Attributes: a ball of rice in one hand, and in the other a container of *payasa* (sweetened milk and rice).

Ansa
Minor sun god. Hindu (Puranic). One of six *Aditya* descendants of Aditi.

Anšar
Primordial deity. Mesopotamian (Babylonian-Akkadian). Mentioned in the Babylonian creation epic *Enuma Eliš* as one of a pair of offspring (with Kišar) of Lahmu and Lahamu, and who in turn created Anu. Anšar is linked with heaven while Kišar is identified with earth.

Anti
Guardian deity. Egyptian (Upper). Seems to have become assimilated with Horus and was one of the protectors of the eastern sky in which the sun rises. According to some texts he is also responsible for the decapitation of the goddess Hathor in a conflict for the throne of Egypt. Anti is known from Middle Kingdom coffin texts (circa 2000 BC). Depicted as a falcon, or a human with a falcon's head, standing on a crescent-shaped boat.

ANTU
Origin Mesopotamian (Babylonian-Akkadian) [Iraq]. Creator goddess.

Known period of worship circa 2000 BC, but evolving from prehistory, to circa 200 BC.

Synonyms Antum; Anunitu.

Center(s) of cult Uruk and Babylon.

Art references glyptics, stone carvings, etc.

Literary sources Babylonian creation epic *Enuma Eliš* and documents relating to the *akitu* festival.

Antu is a Babylonian goddess derived from the older Sumerian Ki, though the cosmogony has been altered to suit a separate tradition. The consort of the god of heaven, Anu, she was a dominant feature of the Babylonian *akitu* festival until as recently as 200 BC, her later preeminence possibly attributable to identification with the Greek goddess Hera.

Anu   (1)

Creator god. Mesopotamian (Babylonian-Akkadian). Consort of Antu(m). Derived from the older Sumerian god An. Anu features strongly in the *akitu* festival in Babylon, Uruk and other cities until the Hellenic period and possibly as late as 200 BC. Some of his later preeminence may be attributable to identification with the Greek god of heaven, Zeus, and with Ouranos.

Anu   (2)

Chthonic mother goddess. Celtic (Irish). Closely associated with fertility and the primordial mother of the *Tuatha de Danann*. Twin hills near Killarney in Munster are called "The Paps of Anu." Also Ana.

ANUBIS   [*Greek*]

Origin   Egyptian. Mortuary god.

Known period of worship   circa 2700 BC (but extending from pre-Dynastic times) until end of Egyptian history circa 400 AD.

Synonyms   Imy-ut (he who is in the mortuary); Khenty-imentiu (chief of the westerners); Khenty-seh-netjer (chief of the gods' pavilion); Neb-ta-d-jeser (lord of the sacred land); Tepy-dju-ef (he who is upon the mountain).

Center(s) of cult   the necropolis at Memphis and elsewhere.

Art references   tomb effigies, wall paintings, statuettes, etc.

Literary sources   Pyramid Texts; funerary texts and hymns.

The parentage of Anubis is confused but the most popular notion seems to place him as a son of Re and of Nephthys or Isis. The god of mortuaries, Anubis takes the form of a black dog or jackal usually in a lying down or crouching position, ears pricked and long tail hanging. He wears a collar with magical connotations. Less often he appears in human form with a canine head. The imagery of a dog probably originated from observation of bodies being scavenged from shallow graves and the desire to protect them from such a fate by manifesting Anubis as a dog himself. The *Book of the Dead* has him standing by the scales in which the heart is weighed in the Hall of the Two Truths, and he is sometimes known as the "claimer of hearts." Anubis was perceived to superintend the embalming of kings and courtiers in the mortuary and the subsequent binding with linen bandages. His coat color is thought to be black because of the color of the corpse after the embalming process, which darkened it, and the use of black tar to seal the bindings. His symbol in the context of mortuary god is an animal skin, headless, dripping blood and tied to a pole. At the subsequent funeral ceremony of the Opening of the Mouth the priest wore a jackal headdress. The main cemetery sites are on the west bank of the Nile where the sun sets, hence one epithet for Anubis—"chief of the westernersy"; another, "he who is upon the mountain," conjures an image of Anubis watching over the cemeteries from the high escarpments.

In the Greco-Roman period he became a cosmic deity of earth and sky somewhat removed from his older function.

Anukis   [*Greek*]

Birth goddess. Egyptian (Upper). Minor deity with cult centers in lower Nubia and at Elephantine. She is variously the daughter of Re, and of Khnum and Satis. Anukis lives in the cataracts of the Lower Nile. Her portrait appears in the Temple of Rameses II at Beit-el-Wali where she suckles the pharaoh, suggesting that she is connected with birth and midwifery, but she also demonstrates a malignant aspect as a strangler (see Hathor). Her sacred animal is the gazelle. Depicted anthropomorphically wearing a turban (modius) with ostrich feathers. Also Anuket (Egyptian).

Anunitu

Mother goddess. Mesopotamian (Babylonian-Akkadian). See Antu.

Anunnaki

Children and courtiers of the god of heaven. Mesopotamian (Sumerian and Babylonian-Akkadian). Known from at least 2500 BC until circa 200 BC (in Babylon). The Anunnaki originate as chthonic fertility deities but later feature as the seven fearsome judges of the underworld who answer to Kur and Ereškigal and who are responsible for passing sentence of death including that placed on the goddess Inana. They are often closely identified with the Igigi.

Anuradha

Minor goddess of fortune. Hindu (Puranic). A benevolent *naksatra* or astral deity, daughter of Daksa and wife of Candra (Soma).

Aondo

Creator god. Tiv [central Nigeria, West Africa]. An abstract principle who lives in the sky. He sends the sun each morning, roars with the thunder that heralds his storms and is the creator of the earth.

Apa

Attendant god. Hindu (Puranic). One of a group of eight *vasu* deities answering to the god Indra. Attributes: hook and plough.

Apacita

Guardian spirit. Inca (pre-Columbian South America) [Peru, etc.]. The apotheosis of a pile of stones marking the top of a pass or some other critical point on a route invoked by travelers with small offerings to strengthen them on their journey.

Apam Napat *(grandchild of the water)*

1. God of fresh water. Persian [Iran]. He provides water in arid regions and suppresses rebellions.
2. God of fresh water. Hindu (Vedic). Mentioned in the *Rg Veda*, he is described as "golden in appearance."

Apap

Creator god. Teso [Uganda, East Africa]. Regarded as a benevolent sky god who brings the rain to parched land. Also Akuj.

Aparajita *(unconquered)*

1. God. Hindu (Puranic). One of the eleven *ekadasarudras* or forms of Rudra. Attributes: bell, bowl, club, drum, hook, lance, lotus, prayer wheel, rod, rosary, shield, sword and trident.
2. Minor god. Buddhist (Mahayana).
3. Goddess. Hindu (Puranic). Form of Durga. Her attendant animal is a lion. Attributes: arrow, shield, snake and sword.
4. Goddess. Buddhist (Mahayana). She stands or treads on the god Ganesa. Color: yellow. Attributes: bell, hook, image of Ratnasambhava, noose and staff.

Apedemak

War god. Sudanese (Meroe). An Egyptianized deity, his main sanctuary was contained in a vast religious complex and center of pilgrimage at Musawwarat-es-Sufra, north of the sixth Nile cataract. Sacred animals include cattle and the African elephant. Depicted with the head of a lion and a human body, holding a scepter embellished with a seated lion at the tip.

Aphrodisias

Fertility goddess. Carian [southwestern Turkey]. Equating with the Greek goddess Aphrodite.

APHRODITE *(foamborn)*

Origin Greek and Cypriot. Goddess of sexual love.

Known period of worship identified from circa 1300 BC (evolving from an earlier prehistoric Asiatic model), until Christianization (circa 400 AD) and later.

Synonyms equating with Ištar (Akkadian); Astarte (Syrian); Aštoreth (Phoenician); Dione, Cytherea, Venus (Roman).

Center(s) of cult Paphos, Amathus and Kition (Cyprus), Corinth and elsewhere on Greek mainland.

Art references Bronze Age statuettes (Cyprus); votive stelae; the Parthenon frieze and other contemporary sculpture.

Literary sources *Iliad* and *Odyssey* (Homer); *Theogony* and *Hymn to Aphrodite* (Hesiod); temple hymns, particularly *Hymn of Sappho.*

Aphrodite is one of the major goddesses of the Greek Homeric pantheon, according to legend born as a cosmic deity from the foam of the ocean after her father Ouranos was castrated by Kronos and his genitals were hurled into the sea. In other accounts she is of a "younger" generation, a daughter of Zeus. She is the consort of Hephaistos and occasional mistress of other deities, including Ares. Through a liaison with the herdsman Anchises she bore Aeneas, who is said to have carried his father to safety on his back during the sack of Troy. Her sacred animal is the goat. Aphrodite seems clearly to have evolved from the Phoenician or Mesopotamian model of a goddess of love and one of her strongest early cults was on the island of Cyprus. Her name derives from the Greek word for the sexual act. She is perceived, in some contexts, as being androgynous and even bearded (see also Artemis). As with her Mesopotamian predecessors she is a goddess of war and victory. Immediate predecessors to the Hellenic model seem to be present in the Mycenaean period particularly at the Kition sanctuary. The Paphos sanctuary definitely suggests Phoenician inspiration. In the *Iliad,* Aphrodite rescues Paris from his fight with Menelaus and returns him to the arms of Helen in Troy.

In Hellenic art Aphrodite is particularly drawn wearing fine clothes and jewelry. She possesses a girdle with magical properties. The famed statue of the goddess from Cnidos (circa 340 BC), depicting her naked, is the first of many such erotic interpretations. The temple at Paphos once dispensed model phalli and lumps of salt to cultic pilgrims, and the Corinthian sanctuary enjoyed, according to Strabo, more than a thousand cultic prostitutes.

Apis

Bull god. Egyptian. The living personification of the creator god Ptah in Memphis, he acts as an intermediary between the supreme god and mankind. His mother is Isis, who engendered him in a lightning flash. The bull is depicted as wholly black apart from a small white triangle on the forehead, and it bears vulture wings. Between its horns are surmounted the sun disc (or, in later times, the moon) and the uraeus.

The cult of the bull is very ancient and is attested in Egypt from at least 3000 BC. According to the Greek writer Herodotus, huge statues of Apis supported the temple of Ptah in Memphis. In a ritual of virility, the king paced alongside the charging bull to renew his strength. The average life of an Apis bull was fourteen years, at the end of which each was mummified and interred in huge sarcophagi, which were placed in catacombs at the necropolis at Seqqara. The bull also has strong underworld connections. See also Sarapis.

Aplu

Weather god. Etruscan. No cult is identifiably addressed to this deity. He is depicted partly cloaked and wearing a laurel leaf, but otherwise naked. Attributes include a staff and laurel twig.

Apo *(lord)*

Mountain god. Inca (pre-Columbian South America) [Peru, etc.]. The apotheosis of an Andean mountain, all mountains being sacred to the South American Indians.

APOLLO

Origin Greek and possibly cultures in Asia Minor. God of hunting and healing.

Known period of worship circa 1300 BC and earlier until Christianization (circa 400 AD) and probably later.

Synonyms Apellon (pre-Homeric); Atepomarus (Celtic).

Center(s) of cult Delos, Pylo-Delphi and many other sanctuaries throughout the Greek world.

Art references the Parthenon frieze; the Belvedere Apollo triumphing over the Python; Apollo and Daphne; a famed but lost statue from Delos; Apollo holding the three Graces in his right hand; other contemporary sculpture and painting.

Literary sources *Iliad* and *Odyssey* (Homer); *Theogony* and *Hymn to Apollo* (Hesiod); various other temple hymns.

One of the major Greek deities always perceived as a god who epitomizes youthful masculinity, possibly with early links to Lycia in Asia Minor (Hittite) and to Minoan Crete. Generally a distant rather than an intimate and approachable god. His mother is Leto, who wandered the world in great suffering until she chanced on the island of Delos where she found refuge, and Apollo is often portrayed as part of a triad with Leto and Artemis. He epitomizes the transition between adolescence and manhood in Greek male society. At Delphi his sanctuary is central to the complex. At Delos it appears secondary to that of Artemis. The paean dance of healing that is particularly known from the *Hyakinthia* festival at Amyklai (Sparta) is closely identified with the Apollo cult. Not only is he a god of healing but also of pestilence. He is the father of Asklepios, the god of healing, and he is continually associated with purification rites and oracles.

Generally Apollo is drawn as a god of hunters carrying a bow and arrow and associated with a stag or roe. He is also pictured with lions. He became, improbably, the patron god of poets and leader of the Muses (daughters of Zeus). Literature often presents Apollo in a dual aspect of fearsome hunter and gracious player of the lyre. In the former capacity he was at times merciless,

killing the many children of Niobe, who had boasted of them to the chagrin of Leto. He fought and slew the Delphic python and the Olympic Cyclopes, but in both cases himself became subject to general laws of morality and suffered temporary banishment. Apollo is strongly associated with the mystical number seven (almost certainly a Mesopotamian concept). In Ugaritic inscriptions he is referred to as Rešep of the Arrow (see Rešep). Apollo was widely revered under various local synonyms by the Celts.

Apsaras

Water spirits. Hindu (Vedic). Identified as musicians and protective deities of gamblers bringing good fortune. They may also bring insanity.

Apsu

God of underground primeval waters. Mesopotamian (Babylonian-Akkadian). Derived from the Sumerian Abzu. In the Babylonian creation epic *Enuma Eliš*, Apsu is killed while sleeping by Enki, who establishes his own abode above the deeps. Apsu's death triggered the cosmic challenge between the forces of Marduk and Tiamat.

Aquilo

Weather god. Roman. God of the west winds.

A'ra

Local tutelary god. Pre-Islamic northern Arabian. Known from inscriptions at Bostra [near Damascus]. The name implies an altar or holy place, but its Arabic root also means to dye, suggesting that the altars were stained with the blood of sacrifices, probably children.

Arachne

Minor goddess. Roman. Concerned with the craft of weaving.

Aralo

Local god of agriculture. Pre-Christian Georgian. Probably derived from the Armenian god Aray.

Aranyani

Minor goddess of woodlands. Hindu (Vedic). Possibly having evolved from a primitive animistic guardian spirit of animals, Aranyani is an elusive, rarely seen, deity who is recognized in the sounds of the trees, particularly at dusk. She is a benign figure, sweet-scented and unwilling to destroy unless severely provoked.

Arapacana

God. Buddhist. A *bodhisattva* or spiritual meditation *buddha*. Originally a *dharani* of Manjusri who became deified. Accompanied by four minor deities. Also a collective name for the five *buddhas*. Color: yellow or red. Attributes: standing wearing a monkish garment and carrying book and sword.

Arawa

Moon goddess. Suk and Pokot [Kenya and Uganda, East Africa]. The two tribes share the same pantheon of deities. Arawa is the daughter of the creator god Tororut and his consort Seta.

Arawn

Chthonic underworld god. Celtic (Welsh). The leader of the phantom hunt seen chasing a white stag with a pack of red-eared hounds. He equates with Gwynn ap Nudd, a similar deity known in South Wales. His chief underworld opponent is Hafgan and he bribes Pwyll, prince of Dyfed, to challenge Hafgan in exchange for a gift of pigs.

Aray

War god. Pre-Christian Armenian. Probably derived locally from the Greek Ares. Some traditions suggests that he was also a dying-and-rising god.

ARCHON(S) *(rulers)*

Origin Gnostic Christian [eastern Mediterranean]. Primordial creator gods.

Known period of worship circa 100 AD to 400 AD and probably persisting later.

Synonyms eksousiai (authorities, Greek).

Center(s) of cult undefined cells within the area of early Christian influence.

Art references none.

Literary sources *Nag Hammadi* codices.

The Archons are the primordial celestial rulers of the cosmos. The Gnostic cosmogony argues that the God of Israel was not the original or sole creator but was a product of other older tyrannical forces who were eventually defeated in the conflict of light and dark. The Archons are the original creators of mortal man, though in the form in which they contrived him, he did not possess a soul. The main literary texts include the *Hypostasis of the Archons*, and the treatise on *The Origin of the World*, both forming part of the *Nag Hammadi* collection written down during the third or fourth century AD and probably owing much to Greek philosophy. The material was banned under the censorship of the early Christian fathers.

Arcismati *(brilliant)*

Minor goddess. Buddhist (Vajrayana). One of several deified *bhumis* recognized as different spiritual spheres through which a disciple passes. Color: green. Attributes: blue lotus and staff.

Ardhanari(svara)

(the lord being half woman)

God. Hindu (Puranic). The god Siva combined with his *Sakti* as a single being. His attendant animal is the bull. In iconography the left side of the image is female and the right male. A tutelary deity of eunuchs in India. Attributes: (right side) blue lotus, cup, hatchet, lute, moon disc, pestle, skin, sword and trident; (left side) ax, mirror, noose, pitcher, rosary, sacred rope and trident. May appear as three-headed. Also Ammaiappan (Tamil); Naranari.

Ardra

Minor goddess of misfortune. Hindu (Puranic). A malevolent *naksatra* or astral deity; daughter of Daksa and wife of Candra (Soma).

Arduinna

Goddess of forests and hunting. Romano-Celtic (Continental European). Known only from inscriptions and figurines in the Ardennes region. Depicted riding on the back of a wild boar and presumed to be a guardian deity of boars. Identified by the Romans with the goddess Diana.

Arebati

Creator god. Bambuti [Congo, West Africa]. Worshipped by a pigmy tribe living along the banks of the river Ituri. He is considered to have created mankind from clay and blood, covered with skin.

Areimanios

Chthonic underworld god. Greek. Probably derived from the Persian deity Ahriman. Plutarch identifies him as the embodiment of Hades.

Arensnuphis [*Greek*]

Local god of uncertain affinities. Egyptian (Nubian). Probably significant circa 700 BC to 400 AD as an attendant of Isis. He appeared in Egyptian sanctuaries during the Greco-Roman period and seems to have been of benevolent nature. There is also a sanctuary known from Philae in Greece where he is linked with Isis. Depicted in anthropomorphic form wearing a plumed crown or in the form of a lion. Also Ari-hes-nefer (Egyptian).

ARES (*throng of war*)

Origin Greek. God of War.

Known period of worship circa 800 BC, but probably from earlier times, until Christianization (circa 400 AD).

Synonyms none.

Center(s) of cult no sanctuaries known until Roman times, when a temple was dedicated in the Agora in Athens.

Art references the Parthenon frieze; a celebrated statue by Alkamenes; other contemporary sculpture.

Literary sources chiefly *Iliad* (Homer) and *Theogony* (Hesiod).

Ares is a lesser known member of the Olympic pantheon of great gods, the son of Zeus and Hera, who allegedly lived in Thrace. As a warrior god he is contrasted with the more prominent and successful goddess Athena who fought and vanquished him in a war between the gods. Whilst Athena stands for victory in battle through glory and honor, Ares epitomizes the evil and more brutal aspects of warfare. In the eyes of Zeus he is "the most hateful of gods." His war chariot is pulled by Phobos (fear) and Deimos (terror).

Ares' sons were even more barbaric than he. Kyknos was a ferocious killer who, until slain by Herakles, was proposing a temple constructed of human skulls. Another notorious son of Ares was the dragon slain by Kadmos as he sought to found the city of Thebes. Its teeth, which he sowed in the earth, germinated and sprang up as warriors, the grandsons of Ares, who promptly turned on each other in mortal combat. Ares entered into a brief liaison with Aphrodite, the goddess consort of Hephaistos, and through her fathered a daughter, Harmonia, whom Kadmos later married, thus paving the way to establish Thebes in an atmosphere of peace and harmony.

Ariadne

Goddess of vegetation. Greek. Possibly derived from an unnamed Minoan goddess identified on Crete. According to Homer and Hesiod she is a daughter of Minos and a consort of Dionysos. Her crown, given by Zeus, is the Corona Borealis. Tradition has it that she was wooed and then deserted by the hero Theseus.

Arianrhod

Chthonic earth goddess. Celtic (Welsh). Responsible for initiation of souls in the otherworld in the tower of Caer Sidi. Mentioned in the *Mabinogion* texts as the possible daughter of Beli, consort of Don and mother of Llew Llaw Gyffes and Dylan.

Arimanius

Chthonic underworld god. Roman. See Areimanios.

Arinna (sun goddess of)

Solar deity. Hittite and Hurrian. May have taken androgynous form, but also identified as the consort of the weather god Tešub. Probably the head of the Hittite state pantheon. There is little detail because the religious center of Arinna is known only from texts. The sun goddess was also perceived to be a paramount chthonic or earth goddess. She becomes largely syncretized with the Hurrian goddess Hebat.

Aristaios

God of herdsmen. Greek. The consort of Autonoe. Of ancient origin, worshiped by peasants as a guardian of herds and beekeepers. The cult continued for many centuries at Kyrene [Libya].

Arjuna *(silvery)*

Heroic god. Hindu (Vedic, Epic and Puranic). Arjuna appears in the *Mahabharata* epic. One of the princely sons of the mythical Pandu family, his father is Indra. He generally appears with the warrior god Bhima. Allegedly responsible for requesting Visnu to take his Visvarupa form but also identified as a minor incarnation or *avatara* of Visnu. Attributes: usually depicted bearing a bow received from Agni the fire god, but may also appear carrying a sword and shield. Also Nara.

Arma

Minor moon god. Hittite and Hurrian. Depicted winged and wearing a sickle moon surmounted on a horned helmet.

Armaz

Supreme god. Pre-Christian Georgian. Depicted as a warrior deity clad in golden armor, wearing jewels and wielding a sword.

Arnakua'gsak

Animistic spirit. Eskimo (North American). The ''Old Woman of the Sea'' who supplies all the physical needs of the Eskimo from the ocean.

Arnemetia

Water goddess. Romano-Celtic (British). A deity known only from inscriptions.

Arom

Minor god of contractual agreements. Kafir [Afghanistan]. Arom appears to have been significant only to a tribe known as the Kam in the southern Hindukush. He was honored by sacrifice of a male goat on the occasion of a peace treaty, and had seven brothers.

ARSAN DUOLAI

(terrible dweller of the underground world)
Origin Yakut [eastern Siberia]. Chief spirit of the underworld.

Known period of worship prehistoric times until circa 1900 AD.

Synonyms none.

Center(s) of cult none.

Art references none positively identified though possibly the subject of wooden icons.

Literary sources *The Yakut* (Jochelson).

Little is known of this animistic god, though he was considered to live in the lower world and rule over a nebulous group of spirits, the *Abasy*. To these subterranean deities, horned cattle were sacrificed. Abasy also lived in the upper world, in which capacity they were recipients of horse sacrifice.

Arsay

Chthonic underworld goddess. Western Semitic (Canaanite). According to epic creation texts, she is the third daughter of Baal at Ugarit [Ras Šamra], possibly also equating with Allatum.

Arsu

Astral tutelary god. Pre-Islamic northern Arabian. Locally worshiped at Palmyra where he personifies the evening star, in company with his brother Azizos who is the morning star. He equates with

Ruda elsewhere in northern Arabia. Associated in Palmyra with horses or camels.

ARTEMIS
Origin Greek, but known extensively through western Asia. Principally goddess of animals and hunting, but in Greek-speaking Asia, a mother goddess.

Known period of worship circa 800 BC and earlier until Christianization (circa 400 AD) and probably later.

Synonyms Potnia Theron (mistress of the animals).

Center(s) of cult Antioch-near-Pisidia; Delos; Magnesia-on-the-Maeander; Pamphylia; Perge; Ephesus [Turkey].

Art references cultic statues, etc., most notably the multibreasted figures at Ephesus.

Literary sources cuneiform texts (earlier Asian models); *Iliad* (Homer), *Theogony* (Hesiod).

Artemis is a deity of very ancient origins who survived and attracted great popularity in both Asia Minor and Greece into Christian times, when arguably much of her ethos was transferred to the Virgin Mary. Both figures enjoyed major sanctuaries at Ephesus. As an Asiatic goddess Artemis was often drawn winged and standing between wild animals. In this context she generally appears equipped with boots, a torch and a pointed cap. She is also a strongly androgynous figure, a feature depicted dramatically in the statue of Artemis of Ephesus. Her temple at Ephesus dates from the fourth century BC and is ranked among the seven wonders of the world. The cult statues were carried in procession on May 25 among a congregation of up to 30,000.

To the Greeks she was the daughter of Zeus and Leto. She was honored in the sanctuary on Delos with its celebrated Horn Altar from circa 700 BC. In Greek mythology the androgynous aspect was firmly discounted. In her earliest pre-Homeric form the Mistress of Animals "suckles the young of every wild creature that roams the fields." As a huntress she uses a bow and arrows.

By Homeric times the ferocity of this prehistoric element has waned in favor of a more timid image of a young girl dominated robustly by her stepmother Hera. A contrary character study in the *Odyssey* pictures her more positively as a virgin goddess chasing and killing boars and hinds over the hills and fields, fleet of foot and in company with a band of nymphs. She presides over nature and over the initiation rituals of young girls. She is also a goddess of blood sacrifice. A cruel element emerged in a different sense as she threatened any maiden who turned to the role of wife. Paradoxically, and more in keeping with the old Semitic personality, she is also the goddess of birth.

Arthapratisamvit
Goddess of logical analysis. Buddhist (Vajrayana). One of a group of four. Color: green. Attributes: jewel and noose.

Artio of Muri
Fertility goddess and guardian spirit of bears. Romano-Celtic (Continental European). Known only from inscriptions and sculptures in the Berne region of Switzerland, she is linked with bears. A bronze depicts her offering fruit to a bear. She seems also to be a goddess of prosperity and harvest. She became syncretized with the Roman god Mercury as Mercury Artaios. Also Artemis Brauronia.

Arundhati *(faithfulness)*
Astral goddess. Hindu (Puranic). Personification of the morning star and the wife of all risis or inspired sons of Brahma though particularly associated with Vasistha. Attributes: begging bowls.

Aruru
Mother goddess. Mesopotamian (Sumerian and Babylonian-Akkadian) See Ninhursağa.

Arvernus
Local tribal deity. Celtic (Gallic). God of the Arverni.

Aryaman *(companion)*

Minor sun god. Hindu (Vedic and Puranic). In Vedic times, the god of formal hospitality. One of six *Aditya* sons of the goddess Aditi. Attributes: club, two lotuses and prayer wheel.

Arya-Tara *(the honorable Tara)*

Goddess. Buddhist. The *Sakti* of Amoghasiddhi. Her name is often abbreviated to Tara and she originates from the TAM bija or seed. Color: green. Attributes: green lotus and staff. Also Vasya-Tara.

Aš

Local fertility god. Egyptian (western Sahara). Known from the Early Dynastic Period. By inference a benign god of oases and other fertile areas of the desert. Epithets include "lord of Libya." Depicted anthropomorphically, occasionally hawk-headed.

Asalluha

Minor god. Mesopotamian (Sumerian and Babylonian-Akkadian). A son of Enki who apparently acts as a messenger and reporter to his father. Linked with rituals of exorcism. Cult center Ku'ara. In Babylonian times he became largely syncretized with Marduk.

Asar

Equestrian god. Pre-Islamic northern Arabian. Known only from inscriptions at Palmyra.

Asase Yaa

Chthonic fertility goddess. Ashanti [Ghana, West Africa]. A major deity revered over a wide area of Akan- and Fante-speaking Ghana. She has no temples or priests but days (Thursdays) are set aside in her honor and no ploughing is permitted. By tradition a farmer sacrifices a cockerel to her each year to ensure a good harvest, sprinkling the blood on the ground. As the womb of the earth, she represents the goddess of the dead and she is also goddess of truth. Also Asase Efua (Fante).

AŠERAH

Origin Amorite, then Canaanite and possibly Phoenician [Lebanon from Tyre northwards, Syria]. Mother goddess.

Known period of worship from prehistoric times circa third millennium BC until Christianization (circa 400 AD).

Synonyms Athirat.

Center(s) of cult Ugarit [Ras Šamra] and hill shrines throughout the grain-growing coastal region of the eastern Mediterranean.

Art references none surviving, but once extensively represented.

Literary sources Ugaritic texts from Ras Šamra, particularly *The Legend of Baal and Anat; Vetus Testamentum.*

Ašerah is the great mother goddess of Canaan. Known as "Lady Ašerah of the sea," she seems to have lived close by the place of Il, the Canaanite creator god, and is said to have had many sons. She is described as the "creatress of the gods" and the matron of a number of other goddesses who oversee the natural world. She is also ambiguous in her attitude to Baal. She intercedes with Il when Baal wishes to build a palace of his own yet, when he is vanquished, she attempts to place one of her own offspring on the throne. It is Ašerah who gave her name to the hill shrines under the trees that were vilified by the writers of the biblical prophetic books such as Ezekiel. Translated as "grove" in the King James English version, the *ašerah* seems to have been a carved wooden pillar that formed the focal point of worship in conjunction with a stone *massebah*. The *ašerah* represented the presence of the mother goddess. Its popularity with large numbers of Israelites is beyond dispute, but because of its pagan connotations and particularly its representation of the mother goddess linked with rituals of fertility, the *ašerah* became one of the major irritations of the prophets and other religious leaders of the tribes during the period of the Israelite kingship. It may have stimulated large numbers of rank and file to abandon or take a strongly ambivalent attitude toward Yhwhism.

Ašertu

Fertility goddess. Western Semitic (Canaanite) and Hittite. Identified in Ugaritic (Ras Šamra) texts as an unfaithful consort of Elkunirsa. Also Ašerdus (Hittite).

Ashiakle

Goddess of wealth. Gan [district around Accra, Ghana, West Africa]. The daughter of Nai, god of the sea, she was born in the ocean and came to land in a canoe. Her colors are red and white.

Asira

Local god. Pre-Islamic northern Arabian. Mentioned only in name by the Babylonian king Nabonidus, worshiped at Taima and influenced strongly by Egyptian culture. See also Salm.

Asis

Sun god. Suk and Pokot [Kenya and Uganda, East Africa]. These two tribes share the same pantheon. The younger brother of the supreme god of heaven Tororut. In Nandi [Kenya] religion, Asis becomes the supreme creator god.

ASKLEPIOS

Origin Greek. God of physicians and healing.

Known period of worship circa 800 BC or earlier to Christianization (circa 400 AD).

Synonyms Asklapios, Aisklapios.

Center(s) of cult Epidauros; Kos; the Asklepeion in Pergamon.

Art references various sculptures.

Literary sources Iliad (Homer); Catalogues (Hesiod).

The son of Apollo and a mortal consort, Coronis, Asklepios lived effectively as a mortal and died as such. He was nonetheless regarded as a deity. He was reared by the centaur Charon and fathered two sons, Podaleirios and Machaon, who were also physicians. More familiar from modern usage is his daughter, the goddess Hygieia (health). Asklepios is symbolized by a rod with twin snakes coiled around it. He is also represented in his sanctuaries by a captive snake. According to legend he met his death at the hand of Zeus for presuming to bring a mortal being back from death. Physicians on Kos formed into a guild, the Asklepiadai (sons of Asklepios). The Epidauros sanctuary became an influential place of pilgrimage by the sick and infirm in classical times.

Aslesa(s)   *(adherence)*

Minor goddess of misfortune. Hindu (Epic and Puranic). A malevolent *naksatra* or astral deity; daughter of Daksa and wife of Candra (Soma).

Ašnan

Vegetation goddess. Mesopotamian (Sumerian and Babylonian-Akkadian). Minor deity probably known to the Sumerians from circa 3500 BC or earlier. She is concerned with the abundance of grain in the fields, sent as its protectress by the gods Enlil and Enki. According to creation accounts, she and the cattle god Lahar were first intended to serve the needs of the Annunaki, the celestial children of An, but when the heavenly creatures were found unable to make use of their products, humankind was created to provide an outlet for their services. Attributes: ears of grain sprouting from her shoulders.

Asokottamasri

(the great beauty of Asoka)

Physician god. Buddhist-Lamaist [Tibet]. Accounted among one of a series of medicine *buddhas* or *sMan-bla* in Lamaism. Typically depicted with stretched earlobes. Color: red.

Asopos

Local river god. Greek (Beotian). Known only from regions of central Greece as one of the sons of Poseidon.

Ašpalis

Hunting goddess. Western Semitic. There is scant mention of Ašpalis from Melite in Phthia and she is probably a local version of Artemis. As in certain Artemis mythology, she hanged herself and her body disappeared.

Ašratum

Fertility goddess. Western Semitic (Canaanite). Probably a corruption of the Semitic Athirat or Ašerah. Also mentioned in Babylonian texts from the Hellenistic period. Also Ašrat (Akkadian).

Assur

Tutelary god. Mesopotamian (Babylonian-Akkadian). The national deity of Assyria. In the Assyrian copies of the creation epic *Enuma Eliš*, he replaces Marduk as the hero.

Astabi

Deity. Hittite and Hurrian. Known only from inscriptions.

Astamatara

Generic term for a group of mother goddesses. Hindu (Puranic). Eight deities who are varieties of the goddess Camunda, often malevolent.

Astaphaios

Primordial deity. Gnostic Christian. One of the androgynous principles born to Yaldabaoth, the prime parent, ruling the seven heavens of chaos in gnostic mythology.

Astar

Astral god. Ethiopian. Identified in Axum Empire inscriptions from circa 200–400 AD.

Aštaroth

Fertility goddess. Western Semitic. Goddess of sheep herders equating with the Phoenician goddess Astarte. Also a plural form of the name Aštoreth and used as a collective name for goddesses (cf. Baal).

ASTARTE   *(star)*

Origin   western Semitic, predominantly Phoenician [Lebanon and Syria]. Fertility goddess.

Known period of worship   from circa 1500 BC or earlier until circa 200 BC.

Synonyms   Aštarat; Attart (Ugarit).

Center(s) of cult   predominantly Tyre; also Sidon, Byblos, Ascalon, Carthage, Kition [Cyprus], Eryx [Sicily] and Malta.

Art references   sculptures, plaques, votive stelae, glyptics, etc.

Literary sources   mainly inscriptions.

The goddess of the evening star, of war and of sexual love. Inscriptions from the fifth century BC in her major temple at Sidon suggest she was perceived as an emanation of Baal Šamin, personifying his divine power. She is also his consort. Her animal is the sphinx, which typically appears on either side of her throne. She is often represented by *baetyls* or stone stelae. In Hellenic times she became largely syncretized with the Greek goddess Aphrodite. A first century BC inscription in a sanctuary dedicated to Aphrodite at Delos identifies the "holy Syrian goddess." Astarte is typically depicted naked and, in the Egyptian style, wears a crown of cows' horns enclosing a sun disc. The latter may have rays emanating. See also Aštoreth, Ištar and Ašerah.

Astlik

Astral goddess. Pre-Christian Armenian. Derived from the Mesopotamian model of Ištar. Survived in Christian times as the mother of fairies.

AŠTORETH

Origin   Palestinian and Philistine [Israel, Lebanon]. Fertility goddess.

Known period of worship   circa 1200 BC or earlier until circa 200 BC.

Synonyms   Aštaroth.

Center(s) of cult Palestine coastal region including Jerusalem.

Art references various sculptures.

Literary sources inscriptions; *Vetus Testamentum*.

Aštoreth equates with the Syrian goddess Astarte, both being modeled on the Mesopotamian Ištar. She was adopted, typically, as goddess of both love and war. She is usually depicted wearing a horned headdress. Biblical references include I Kings 11:5 and II Kings 23:13. Solomon is said to have built a temple in her honor near Jerusalem. The name is said, by some authors, to be synonymous with Aštaroth.

Asuha-No-Kami
God of courtyards. Shinto [Japan]. A guardian deity, one of many in Shintoism, concerned with the protection of houses and their environs.

Asurakumara
God. Jain [India]. One of the groups under the general title of *bhvanavasi* (dwelling in places). They have a youthful appearance and are associated with rain and thunder.

Asuras
Sky gods. Hindu (Vedic). Identified in the opening of the *Rg Veda*, they become demonic in later Hinduism, the antagonists of the *deva* gods.

Asvins
Physician gods. Hindu (Vedic). Twin gods owning horses, the sons of Vivasvan and Saranyu. Depicted in a chariot drawn by horses or birds. Attributes: book, vessel with herbs and water jar.

Asvayujau   *(harnessing horses)*
Minor goddess of fortune. Hindu (Epic and Puranic). A benevolent *naksatra* or astral deity; daughter of Daksa and wife of Candra (Soma). Also Asvini and Asvinyau.

Ataa Naa Nyongmo
Creator god. Gan [district around Accra, Ghana, West Africa]. He engendered the earth and also controls the sun and the rain. He causes disasters such as epidemics and earthquakes if his laws and rites are disobeyed.

Ataecina
Local chthonic underworld goddess. Romano-Iberian. Known from inscriptions in the Tagus region, where the Romans identified her with the goddess Proserpina.

Atargatis
Mother goddess. Northern Syrian. She enjoyed major cults at Khirbet Tannur, where she is depicted as the vegetation goddess in nine separate variations, and at Khirbet Brak, where she is associated with dolphins. She often carries a cornucopia linking her with the goddess Tyche (fortune) and may commonly be flanked by lions. She sometimes carries a rudder or wears the mural crown of a city guardian. There are hints of sky affinities in some depictions, with a sign of the zodiac or a nimbus-like veil.

Her earliest consort is Dušara, but in later times she is linked with the Syrian storm god Hadad. At Dura and Hierapolis (Hera-Atargatis), she tended to overshadow Hadad. Atargatis is also a fish goddess depicted like a mermaid and in most of her cult centers she enjoyed a sacred lake stocked with fish. Statues of Hadad and Hera-Atargatis were carried in twice-yearly processions to the sea from Hierapolis, and by the third century BC her cult had reached Egypt. Greek writers of the Hellenic period describe her as a "radiate" goddess, which suggests some links with sun symbolism. Also Allat.

Ataršamain   *(morning star of heaven)*
Astral deity of uncertain gender. Pre-Islamic northern and central Arabian. Worshipped particularly by the Išamme tribe, but revered widely among other Arabs. Known from circa 800 BC and identified in letters of the Assyrian kings Ešarhaddon and Assurbanipal. May be synonymous with

the Arab goddess Allat whose cult was centered on Palmyra.

Ate

Minor goddess of misfortune. Greek. A daughter of Zeus, she personifies blind folly leading to disaster.

Atea

Supreme god. Polynesian. The father of the gods depicted as a hybrid, his body divided vertically, the left half being fishy and the right half of human form. In the tradition of the Hervey Islands, he is the firstborn son of the primordial mother Vari-Ma-Te-Takere. After a short existence low down in the world coconut living immediately above his mother, he moved to the opening of the upper world. He is largely comparable to Tane, the god of light. Also Avatea, Vatea, Wakea.

ATEN *(the sun disc)*

Origin Egyptian. Creator sun god.

Known period of worship circa 2000 BC until late in Egyptian history, but of little influence after 1362 BC.

Synonyms Aton.

Center(s) of cult chiefly at Thebes but also at Heliopolis, Memphis, el-Amarna and other sanctuaries in the Nile valley.

Art references monument at Giza, wall paintings at Karnak and el-Amarna.

Literary sources various papyri, inscriptions and coffin texts.

Aten, the sun as a disc, was revered as a numen in his own right, distinct from Atum or Re, from circa 2000 BC and possibly earlier. His influence had been growing under several pharaohs including Amenhotep II, Tuthmosis IV and Amenhotep III, who initiated a cult of Aten at Heliopolis. Aten rose to ultimate supremacy for a brief period during the reign of Amenhotep IV who renamed himself Akhenaten in honor of the god. During Akhenaten's reign from 1379 BC Aten became the supreme god of Egypt, eclipsing all others.

The iconography of Aten is very distinctive. It began as a winged sun disc with outstretched arms, but this was refined into a sun disc embellished with the *uraeus* (see Wadjet) and subtended by thin arms, like the rays of the sun, each of which ends in a human hand. Where the latter point toward a royal personage they hold the *ankh* symbol of life. The god is never drawn in human or animal form.

Akhenaten first built a sanctuary to Aten adjacent to that of Amun in the Karnak complex at Thebes. The main cult center was to the north of Thebes on the east bank of the Nile at el-Amarna, where a huge sanctuary was constructed. It was open to the sky (and the rays of Aten) and the main ceremonials took place at dawn. It acted as a contentious rival to the cult of Amun-Re at Karnak, which Akhenaten suppressed. All the temples to Aten were later destroyed, as was most of his iconography. Akhenaten ruled from el-Amarna for the remainder of his reign. One of his queens, Nefertiti, was also a staunch Aten worshiper.

The elevation of Aten was influenced by politics (the strength of the Amun-Re priesthood was becoming excessive), and it is notable that Akhenaten alone had access to, or knowledge of, the god. Aten worship was also undeniably the result of a growing interest in the concept of a single creator god and was the first arguable demonstration of monotheism. Very little detail of the cult survives.

Atete

Fertility goddess. Kafa [Ethiopia, northeastern Africa]. She was assimilated into the Christian cult of the Virgin Mary, but is probably the subject of an ancient fertility rite performed by women who collect various sacred plants and throw them into the river. The festival is known as Astar yo Mariam (Epiphany of Mary).

ATHENA

Origin Greek. Goddess of war and patron defender of many Greek cities.

Known period of worship circa 800 BC and earlier until Christianization (circa 400 AD) and later.

Synonyms Athene; Pallas Athenae (maiden goddess of Athens); Minerva (Roman).

Center(s) of cult Athens but also Argos, Sparta, Gortyn, Larisa (Thessaly); Lindos and Ilion (Homer's Troy).

Art references the Parthenon frieze and other sculptures and iconography throughout the Greek world, including notably the Athena of Phidias (Varvakeion) and the *metope* of Olympia in which she assists Herakles to support the sky.

Literary sources *Iliad* and *Odyssey* (Homer); *Theogony* and *Hymn to Pallas Athene* (Hesiod).

Athena is a principal goddess of the Greek pantheon and, according to Hesiod, the daughter of Metis (wisdom) born fully armed from the head of Zeus. A goddess of battle and allegedly a snake goddess, she is a deity who also stands for discipline against the more unruly conduct of such as Hermes and Poseidon. Her most famed sanctuary is the Parthenon. The olive tree is sacred to her, particularly that grown by tradition on the Acropolis, whose oil was given to the victors in the *Panathenaia* festival. According to legend she offered the olive to mankind. Her symbol is the *aigis*—the skin of a sacrificial goat. She is also associated with shipbuilding and with domestic crafts including wool work and spinning—Athenian women have traditionally woven the *peplos* at the *Panathenaia* festival. In legend she is the destroyer of Ajax and lures Hector to his death, while supporting such heroes as Perseus against the Gorgon monster, and Diomedes against Ares. She also acts as a moderating influence in Achilles' conflict with Agamemnon, the most notable instance of her characteristic ability for self-control.

Athirat

Fertility goddess. Western Semitic (Canaanite). In Old Babylonian texts of Hammurabi she is identified as the daughter-in-law of the king of heaven.

She is also known from pre-Islamic southern Arabia as a consort of the moon god Amm. See Ašerah.

Aticandika *(exceedingly great)*

Distinct form of the goddess Durga. Hindu (Puranic). One of a group of nine deities, known as the "nine durgas."

Atl

Creator god. Aztec (classical Mesoamerican) [Mexico]. The sun deity representing the fourth of the five world ages each of which lasted for 2,028 heavenly years, each heavenly year being fifty-two terrestrial years. Assigned to water and presided over by Chalchiuhtlicue. According to tradition, the age ended in a cataclysmic destruction caused by a deluge during which all the human population were turned into fish. Illustrated by the "Stone of the Four Suns" [Yale Peabody Museum]. Also 4(Atl), Atonatiuh and Chalchiutonatiuh.

Atlahua

Minor god of lakes and fish hunters. Aztec (classical Mesoamerican) [Mexico]. One of the group classed as the Mixcoatlcamaxtli complex.

Atropos

Goddess of fate. Pre-Homeric Greek. According to Hesiod, one of the daughters of Zeus and Themis. One of an ancient trio of *Moirai* with Lachesis and Klotho. She is responsible for the final part of a mortal life, the unturning inevitability of death, and she is depicted holding a pair of scales. The name of the plant *Atropa belladonna* (deadly nightshade) derives from her.

Attar

God of the morning star. Western Semitic. In Canaanite legend, he attempts to usurp the dead Baal but proves inadequate to fill the god's throne. In semiarid regions of western Asia where irrigation is essential, he was sometimes worshiped as a rain god. His female counterpart is the Phoenician Astarte. Also probably identified as Dhu-Šamani in more southerly regions.

ATTIS

Origin Phrygia [northwestern Turkey]. Vegetation god.

Known period of worship circa 500 BC and probably earlier until circa 400 AD.

Synonyms none specific.

Center(s) of cult Anatolian region and later throughout Greek and Roman areas of culture.

Art references sculptures and reliefs.

Literary sources Roman writers, especially Virgil.

Attis is a "dying-and-rising" fertility god modeled on the Mesopotamian Dumuzi. He is considered to have originated as a shepherd. In alternative traditions, Kybele, the "great mother," is either his mother or purely his consort. Another legend suggests he was conceived immaculately by the demigoddess Nana when she placed a ripe almond in her bosom. According to one legend he met his death gored by a wild boar. In a more popular alternative, he castrated himself under a pine tree to offer his vitality to Kybele.

The latter legend became enshrined in spring rites during which Greek, and later Roman, priests (Galli) wearing effeminate costumes castrated themselves or gashed themselves with knives and offered blood sacrifices to the goddess by burying them in the earth. The main center of cult was at Pessinus (Phrygia). The cult was brought to Rome in 204 BC when the stone symbolizing the presence of Cybele (the Roman version of her name) was carried from Pessinus and installed in the Temple of Victory on the Palatine Hill. The day sacred to Attis was March 22 when a pine tree was carried into the Temple of Cybele and decorated with flowers and models of Attis. In Christian times the Easter festival took over the date of the Attis rites.

Atua Fafine

Creator being. Polynesian [Tikopia]. One of a pair with Atua I Raropuka when the land of Tikopia was pulled up from the bottom of the ocean. They may have been there from the outset, or arrived on the back of a turtle from foreign parts. They engendered five sons, all gods.

Atua I Kafika

Supreme god. Polynesian [Tikopia]. Regarded as an intercessor rather than as ultimate creator or controller.

Atua I Raropuka

Creator being. Polynesian [Tikopia]. One of a pair with Atua Fafine when the land of Tikopia was pulled up from the bottom of the ocean. They may have been there from the outset, or arrived on the back of a turtle from foreign parts. They engendered five sons, all gods.

ATUM

Origin Egyptian. Sun god and creator god.

Known period of worship Old Kingdom (circa 2700 BC) to end of Egyptian history (circa 400 AD).

Synonyms Atum-Re.

Center(s) of cult Heliopolis.

Art references wall paintings particularly in New Kingdom tombs in the Valley of the Kings (Thebes), votive inscriptions, contemporary sculpture.

Literary sources Pyramid Texts; coffin texts; *Book of the Dead*, etc.

Atum is one of several interpretations of the major creator god of Egypt whose company is the product of a fragmented pre-Dynastic tribal history. Atum shared Heliopolis with another sun god, Re and eventually became joined with him as Atum-Re or Re-Atum. The god was self-created from the primeval ocean and by masturbation he produced the next two great deities of the Egyptian cosmos, Šu and Tefnut, who also constitute the beginnings of the pantheon of nine Heliopolis deities, the Ennead. Atum is generally represented in human form and often wears a crown that combines those of Upper and Lower Egypt.

He is represented as various animals including the bull, lion, snake and lizard. Atum was regarded as the progenitor of the Egyptian pharaohs.

Both Atum and Re are represented by a divine black bull, Mnevis or Mer-wer, wearing the sun disc and *uraeus* or snake between its horns. It acts as an intercessor between the sun god and his priests in Heliopolis.

Atunis
God. Etruscan. Known from circa 350 BC onward in local inscriptions. See Adonis.

Aufaniae
Collective name for a group of mother goddesses. Celtic (Continental European). Known only from votive inscriptions and largely restricted to the Rhineland.

Aurora
Goddess of the dawn. Roman. Derived from the Greek deity Eos.

Auseklis *(morning star)*
Minor astral god. Pre-Christian Latvian. An attendant of the sun god, linked with fertility and involved in the activity of the heavenly bath house.

AVALOKITESVARA *(merciful lord)*
Origin Buddhist [India]. *Bodhisattva* or *buddha-*designate.

Known period of worship circa 500 BC to present.

Synonyms nineteen other forms listed.

Center(s) of cult pan-Asiatic.

Art references metal and stone sculptures, paintings.

Literary sources *Sadhanamala* and Tantric ritual texts.

One of the most important deities of the Mahayana sect of Buddhism. In Lamaism he is the tutelary god of Tibet. He equates with Visnu in Hinduism and bears links with Padmapani. In cosmic mythology he is a creator deity. His *Sakti* is Pandara and his attendant animal is a lion. Many forms of Avalokitesvara exist, which may include varieties with up to eleven heads, sometimes arranged in a pyramid. Color: white or red. Attributes: blue lotus, image of Amitabha (topmost pyramidal head), lotus, rosary, sword and water jar.

NOTE: in Chinese Buddhism he is represented by the goddess Kuan-Yin, and in Japanese by Kwannon.

Avatea
Moon god. Polynesian [Hervey Islands]. The firstborn of the great mother Vari-Ma-Te-Takere and the elder sibling of Tinirau. According to tradition, Vari-Ma-Te-Takere plucked a piece from her right side to engender Avatea, who is half man, half fish. He is divided vertically with his left side fishy and his right side human. He is the father of gods and humankind, and is said to live in the coconut of the world. After a temporary period existing low down in the shell, he was assigned to the opening of the upper world, immediately above the home of Tinirau. Also Vatea; Wakea (Hawaiian).

Aveta
Goddess of birth and midwifery. Romano-Celtic (Gallic). Known mainly from clay figurines found at Toulon-sur-Allier, France. The models show the goddess with infants at the breast and apparently she is concerned especially with nursing mothers. The figure is often accompanied by a small lapdog.

Avrikiti
God of fishermen. Fon [Benin, West Africa]. Statues of this deity, in a sitting position, were placed on the beaches and fishermen and local elders sacrificed to them annually to ensure a good season.

Awonawilona
Creator god. Pueblo Indian (Zuni) [Mesoamerica]. The androgynous creator of heaven and earth and of all life, which he engendered by tossing pieces of his skin into the primeval ocean.

Axo-Mama

Goddess of potato crops. South American Indian [Peru]. A model of this minor deity was made out of parts of the plant as a harvest fetish and kept for a year before being burned in a ritual to ensure a good potato harvest.

Aya

Mother goddess. Mesopotamian (Babylonian-Akkadian). Derived from the Sumerian model of Šerida. Consort of the sun god Šamaš whose marriage was celebrated at New Year in Babylon.

Ayaba

Hearth goddess. Fon [Benin, West Africa]. The sister of Loko, god of the trees, whose wood is burned in the home to cook food.

Ayi'-Uru'n Toyo'n   *(lord bright creator)*

Creator spirit. Yakut [central Siberia]. See Uru'n Ajy Toyo'n.

Ayiyanayaka

Plague god. Singhalese [Sri Lanka]. A deity of fields and woodlands who is still revered as a guardian of crops and a protector against plague.

Ayurvasita   *(control of life)*

Minor goddess. Buddhist. One of a group of twelve *vasitas* or goddesses personifying the disciplines of spiritual regeneration. Color: whitish red. Attributes: image of Amidabuddha and jewel.

Ayyappan

Local god of growth. Hindu. Particularly recognized in the Kerala region.

Azizos

Astral tutelary god. Pre-Islamic northern Arabian. Locally worshiped at Palmyra, where he personifies the morning star, in company with his brother Arsu, who is the evening star. Associated with horses or camels. He was also venerated separately in Syria as god of the morning star, in company with the astral god Monimos.

B

Ba *(1)*
Goddess of drought. Chinese. She is identified in some texts as the daughter of the god Huang Ti.

Ba *(2)*
Ram god. Egyptian (Lower). A fertility deity from early in Egyptian religion invoked particularly at Mendes. In a later cult, the name *ba* comes to represent the spirituality of a deity, often represented in an animal, e.g. the bull, or the mortal manifestation of a god as pharaoh.

Ba Xian
Collective name for gods. Taoist (Chinese). A group of eight divine beings, once mortal, who achieved immortality through their exemplary lives. There are many such groups in Chinese religious belief. The Ba Xian are probably the most widely revered. Many people carry amulets and other charms in the form of the symbols of these deities. The eight gods are Kao Kuo-Zhu; Han Xiang-Zhi; He Xian-Ku; Lan Kai-He; Li Thieh-Kuai; Lu Tong-Pin; Zhang Kuo-Lao; and Zhong-Li Kuan.

BAAL *(lord)*
Origin Western Semitic (Canaanite) [northern Israel, Lebanon and later Egyptian]. Vegetation deity and national god.

Known period of worship circa 2000 BC or earlier to 200 BC.

Synonyms Aliyn Baal; Hadad.

Center(s) of cult Ugarit [Ras Šamra and Jebel el Aqra]; Ašdod during Philistine period. Otherwise generally down the grain-bearing coastal plain of the eastern Mediterranean, including Baal-Hazor, Baal-Sidon and Baal-Tyre [Lebanon]. Memphis [Egypt].

Art references a stele from Ras Šamra has a seated god with bull horns that is thought to be either Baal or Il; a model calf recently discovered there may also symbolize Baal.

Literary sources Ugaritic creation texts from Ras Šamra, particularly the legends of *Baal and Anat* and *Baal and Mot*; *Vetus Testamentum*.

Baal may have originated in pre-agricultural times as god of storms and rain. He is the son of Dagan and in turn is the father of seven storm gods, the Baalim of the *Vetus Testamentum*, and seven midwife goddesses, the Sasuratum. He is considered to have been worshiped from at least the nineteenth century BC Later he became a vegetation god concerned with fertility of the land. Baal is said to have gained his kingship in primeval times wrested, with the help of weapons made by divine craftsmen (see also Othin), from the powers of chaos in the form of the sea and the river tyrannies, or more specifically the god Yamm.

Baal lives in a vast and opulent palace on a mountain called Šapan. Old connotations of a weather god remain in texts that describe the voice of Baal as being like thunder, and a hole in the floor of his palace through which he waters the earth. According to one text his servants are in the form of seven pages and eight boars, all of which, like his daughters, Pidray daughter of mist and Tallay daughter of showers, probably have a fertility function. Brother of the goddess Anat, he reflects the confrontation theme, first established in ancient Near Eastern religions, of a god constantly and energetically engaged with the forces of disorder. It is a combat that causes his temporary ill-fortune but from which, annually, he emerges triumphant. Baal is said to have sired a bull calf, the guarantee of his power in absence, before descending to the underworld to challenge the forces of chaos in the form of the god Mot (see also Inana/Ištar); he dies, is restored through the efforts of Anat and in the seventh year kills Mot (*VT* Exodus 23:10–11 describes six years of harvest followed by a seventh year in which the land must lie fallow). Victory was celebrated at the autumn festival of New Year in the month of Tišri pending the arrival of the rains. Baal-zebul (*VT*) derives from Baal and *zbl* meaning prince.

From the mid-sixteenth century BC in the Egyptian New Kingdom, Baal enjoyed a significant cult following, but the legend of his demise and restoration was never equated with that of Osiris.

In the Greco-Roman period, Baal became assimilated in the Palestine region with Zeus and Jupiter, but as a Punic deity [Carthage] he was allied with Saturnus, the god of seed sowing.

Baal Malage

Local tutelary god. Western Semitic (Phoenician). Probably of Canaanite origin, closely equating with Baal Šamin and known only from inscriptions.

Baal Šamin   (lord of heaven)

Head of the pantheon. Western Semitic (Phoenician). Probably originated in Canaanite culture as a god of rain and vegetation, but became extensively revered in places as far apart as Cyprus and Carthage. Epithets include "bearer of thunder." Baal Šamin is first mentioned in a fourteenth century BC treaty between the Hittite king Suppiluliuma and Nigmadu II of Ugarit. He had a major sanctuary at Byblos, according to inscription, "built by Yehemilk." Josephus confirms that his cult existed at the time of Solomon. At Karatepe his name appears at the head of a list of national deities and on Seleucid coinage he is depicted wearing a half-moon crown and carrying a radiate sun disc. Other epithets include "lord of eternity" and he may also have been god of storms at sea, a patron deity of mariners. By Hellenic times he equated with Zeus in the Greek pantheon and the Romans identified him as Caelus (sky). Also Baal-Šamem.

Baal Sapon

Local tutelary god. Western Semitic (Phoenician). Probably of Canaanite origin and closely equating with Baal Šamin. According to Ugaritic texts he lives on a mountain in the north of Phoenicia known as Saphan, which may have served as a beacon for mariners. Other local variations of mountain deities include Baal Hermon and Baal Brathy.

Baba

Fertility goddess. Mesopotamian (Sumerian and Babylonian-Akkadian). Locally worshiped in Lagaš, where Gudea built her a temple. Also Bau.

Babi

Malevolent god. Egyptian. Known from as early as the Old Kingdom (circa 2700 BC). Babi is seen as a violent and hostile deity whose presence can be highly dangerous during the ceremony of the Weighing of the Heart in the Hall of the Two Truths (see also Ammut). Conversely he can also act in a protective capacity. Closely associated with sexual virility in the underworld, Babi is ithyphallic. A god active in the darkness, his penis serves variously as the mast on the underworld ferry boat, and the bolt on heaven's doors. Depicted as an ithyphallic male baboon.

Baca' -

Attendant gods. Mayan (classical Mesoamerican) [Mexico]. Four deities identified with points of the compass and colors, thus Hobnil (red) resides in the east, Can Tzicnal (white) in the north, Zac Cimi (black) in the west and Hozanek (yellow) in the south. They are also identified as the Toliloch (opossum actors) in the Codex Dresden, where each carries the image of the ruling god for the incoming year on his back. Hobnil is also a patron deity of beekeepers.

Bacax

Local god. Roman-North African. A rare example of a named deity from this region, thought to have been worshiped as a cave god. Known from inscription at Cirta [Constantine].

BACCHUS

Origin Roman. God of wine and intoxication.

Known period of worship circa 400 BC to 400 AD.

Synonyms Liber; Dionysos (Greek).

Center(s) of cult throughout Roman world.

Art references sculptures and reliefs.

Literary sources *Aeneid* (Virgil) etc.

Bacchus is modeled closely on the Greek god Dionysos. In Roman mythology his parents are Jupiter and Semele, the daughter of Kadmos, who became deified only after her death by fire on Olympus. Bacchus grew up through childhood with a wet nurse Ino (Leukothea). As a youth he was entrusted to the satyr Silenus. He is depicted as a youthful figure wearing an ivy or grape crown and carrying a wand or *thyrsus*. He is also frequently drawn riding in a chariot pulled by leopards.

As god of wine and intoxication, his court includes the female Bacchantes, nymphs, fauns and satyrs. Bacchus was worshiped extensively and commanded a number of festivals including the *Liberalia* and *Bacchanalia*. These possess strongly phallic connotations and on occasions the god was represented by a model phallus.

Badb

War goddess. Celtic (Irish). One of the aspects of the Morrigan. Capable of changing shape at will. She confronts the Irish hero Cu Chulainn before a battle and terrifies him by turning into Badb Catha, the crow and harbinger of death.

Badi Mata

Mother goddess. Hindu [northern Indian]. A *Sakti* and one of the seven *saptamataras* (mothers) who in later Hinduism became regarded as of evil intent, attacking children during puberty. Particularly recognized in Bengal.

Bagala *(power of cruelty)*

Goddess. Hindu. One of a group of ten *mahavidyas* personifying the *Sakti* of Siva. Aspects include Viraratri.

Bagba

Animistic spirit. West African. Fetish who allegedly controls the wind and rain and whose shaman keeps the winds locked in a huge pot.

Bagisht

God of flood waters and prosperity. Kafir [Afghanistan]. The son of the supreme goddess Disani, conceived when she was raped from behind by an obscure demonic entity in the shape of a ram who violated her while she was milking cows by a lakeside. Bagisht is said to have been born in the current of the Prasun river whereupon the turbulent waters became smooth flowing and parted to allow the infant to reach the bank. There seem to have been no elaborate sanctuaries but rather an abundance of simple shrines always placed close to water. The god was celebrated at the main festivals of the Kafir agricultural year and received sacrificial portions of meat. Also Opkulu.

Bagvarti

Tutelary goddess. Urartian [Armenia]. The consort of the creator god Haldi.

Bala *(girl)*

1. Mother goddess. Hindu (Epic and Puranic). Of vague affinity but generally of youthful appearance. Seated upon a lotus throne. Attributes: book and rosary.
2. Messenger goddess. Jain [India]. One of the twenty-four *sasanadevatas*.

Balakrsna

God. Hindu (Epic and Puranic). Krsna in child form (see Krsna).

Balam *(jaguar)*

Guardian deities. Mayan (Yucatec, classical Mesoamerican) [Mexico]. Poorly defined spirits who protect individuals in daily life. Four *balam* stand at the cardinal points around a village to guard against dangerous animals. They also protect the four sides of a *milpa* (smallholding) against thieves.

Balaparamita *(perfection of strength)*
Philosophical deity. Buddhist. One of a group of twelve *paramitas*. Spiritual offspring of Ratnasambhava. Color: red. Attributes: book and banner with jewel.

Balarama *(strength of Rama)*
Incarnation of the god Visnu. Hindu (Epic and Puranic). May have originated in Vedic times as an agricultural fertility deity. He is the son of Vasudeva and Devaki, though born from the womb of Rohini. Jointly with Krsna (his brother), he is identified as the eighth *avatara* (incarnation) of Visnu, or, with Rama, as the seventh. Legend describes how Visnu impregnated the belly of the goddess Devaki with two hairs, one black, one white. To ensure their safety against a demon king, they were transferred before birth to Rohini. Krsna grew to be dark skinned, and Balarama light. The latter enjoys similar characteristics to Krsna but fails to attract the same popularity. He is usually depicted on the right side of Krsna, rarely standing alone. The consort of Balarama is Revati and his sons are Nisatha and Ulmuka. Epithets included Ananda (joy). In Jainism he is known as Baladeva. Attributes: arrow, club, drinking cup, fan palm, honey pot, lotus, pestle, pitcher, plough, prayer wheel, shield and sword.

Bala-Sakti
Goddess. Dravidian (Tamil) [southern India]. Youthful deity who presides over six *cakras* or prayer wheels. Often accompanied by a geometric magical diagram or *yantra*. Attributes: book, hook, noose and rosary.

BALDER *(lord)*
Origin Icelandic (Nordic). The dying god.

Known period of worship 700 AD (possibly earlier) through to Christianization (circa 1100 AD).

Synonyms Baldr; Baldaeg (Anglo-Saxon).

Center(s) of cult unknown.

Art references stone carvings.

Literary sources Icelandic codices; *Prose Edda* (Snorri); *Historia Danica* (Saxo), runic inscriptions.

Balder is the spotless "good" god, the "shining one," Othin's favored second son. He lives in a hall named Breidablik. He is the father of the god Forseti. According to Snorri's account, Balder was made invulnerable to injury or death by his mother Frigg who had extracted a promise from "all things" not to harm him. She had omitted the mistletoe as being too small and insignificant and so, using the blind god Hoder as his instrument, Loki caused Balder's death by guiding Hoder's hand and turning a sprig of mistletoe into a lethal dart.

Saxo, in contrast, defines Balder as a warrior slain by a magic sword in a battle of jealous rivalry between him and Hoder for the hand of the goddess Nanna. There are separate suggestions that Balder traveled the road to the underworld ruled by Hel in company with many other slain warriors, implying that he met his death in a wider combat.

There is no evidence of a Germanic precedent for Balder and he is probably of purely Norse extraction. Attempts have been made to cast him as a copy of Christ but these seem wholly unfounded. It is also impossible to relate Balder to the dying-and-rising gods found in other religions (Dumuzi, Telepinu, Osiris, etc.), since there is no suggestion of his return from Hel's kingdom of the dead, though there is an implication that he will be released by Hel at Ragnarok.

Bali
Demonic god. Hindu (Epic and Puranic). The son of Virocana, his power was removed by Visnu in his *avatara* of Vamana.

Baltis
Local goddess. Pre-Islamic Arabian. Known from Carrhae in western Mesopotamia and identified as the apotheosis of the planet Venus.

Banba

Fertility goddess. Celtic (Irish). One of the aspects of the Morrigan. A name of the "Sovereignty of Ireland" to whom the king was married in symbolic ceremony. Also a goddess of war capable of changing shape from girl to hag, and into birds and animals. See also Badb, Eriu, and Maeve.

Banebdjedet

Ram god. Egyptian (Lower). Possibly concerned with arbitration, his consort is the fish goddess Hatmehyt. He is the father of Harpokrates. According to tradition (Chester Beatty I papyrus) he was called upon to intercede in the contest for the Egyptian kingdoms between Horus and Seth. He is placed in some accounts in Upper Egypt on the island of Seheil at the first Nile cataract, but his cult is centered on Mendes in the Delta region of Lower Egypt [Tell el-Ruba] and is closely linked with the mother of Rameses III. He is generally depicted in anthropomorphic form, but with the head of a ram.

Banga

God of clear waters. Ngbandi [northern Zaire and Central African Republic]. One of seven gods invoked at daybreak, the creator deity of white-skinned people.

Bangputys

Sea god. Pre-Christian Lithuanian. Known as the "god who blows the waves."

Ba-Pef

Chthonic underworld god. Egyptian. An obscure malevolent deity known from the Old Kingdom (circa 2700 BC) in which he may have enjoyed a priesthood. According to limited references among the Pyramid Texts, he had a cult following and was associated in some way with pain or spiritual anguish affecting the king.

Barastar

Chthonic underworld god. Ossetian [Caucasus region]. The judge of souls, directing them either to paradise or to oblivion.

Baršamin

Weather or sky god. Pre-Christian Armenian. Probably derived from the Semitic god Baal Šamin.

Basamum

God of healing. Pre-Islamic southern Arabian. The name probably derives from the remedial plant balsam.

BASTET

Origin Egyptian. Feline goddess associated with the vengeance of the sun god.

Known period of worship circa 2700 BC to the end of Egyptian history (circa 400 AD).

Synonyms none.

Center(s) of cult Bubastis in the Delta region of Lower Egypt and probably at the Karnak temple complex in Upper Egypt.

Art references sculptures, wall paintings, papyrus illustrations.

Literary sources Middle Kingdom coffin texts etc.

Bastet is the daughter of the sun god Re and is regarded as his instrument of vengeance, the "rage in his eye." Alternatively she is the eldest daughter of Amun. She has a son, the lion-headed god Mihos.

Texts recounting battles may describe the pharaoh's enemies being slaughtered like the victims of Bastet. Thus she is first depicted as a lioness, and then in the guise of a cat from circa 1000 BC onward when she becomes more peaceable in character. The cat was considered sacred to her and cat cemeteries, containing mummified animals, have been found at various sites. Her name involves the hieroglyph for a sealed alabaster jar containing perfume. In the sanctuary of Khafre at Giza, her name is engraved on the facade with that of the goddess Hathor, symbolizing the protectresses of north and south respectively. In Hellenic times she is partly syncretized with Artemis.

Bat

Cow goddess of fertility. Egyptian (Upper). She was probably well known in the Old Kingdom (circa 2700 BC onward). Associated principally with Upper Egypt, for a while she may have rivaled Hathor in Lower Egypt but by the time of the New Kingdom (sixteenth century BC) her influence had waned. She may be represented on the Narmer Palette (Cairo Museum), which commemorates the unification of the two kingdoms. Bat is only rarely found in large sculptures and paintings, but is often the subject of Egyptian period jewelry, including amulets and ritual sistrum rattles. Depicted as a cow or anthropomorphically with bovine ears and horns. Also Bata.

Baubo

Mother goddess. Western Semitic (Syrian). Known locally from Priene and largely became syncretized with Atargatis, Kybele, etc.

Beg-Tse *(concealed coat of mail)*

God of war. Buddhist and Lamaist [Tibet]. One of a group of eight *dharmapala* with terrible appearance and royal attire. Stands with one foot on a horse and one on a man. Color: red. Attributes: banner, fire, skin and sword. May appear with three eyes. Also Cam-srin.

Behanzin

Fish god. Fon [Benin, West Africa]. Invoked by fishermen to ensure plentiful catches.

Bel

Generic title meaning "lord." Mesopotamian (Babylonian-Akkadian). The Babylonian god Marduk was often addressed as Bel, and the name occurs in the *Vetus Testamentum*. The New Year festival of *akitu* in Babylon included a ceremony of "leading Bel by the hand." The name also appears at Palmyra as the tutelary creator god whose attributes include lightning and an eagle.

Belatucadros

War god. Celtic (British). According to some authors he is the horned god of the north equating to Cernunnos. The Romans syncretized him with the god Mars.

BELENUS

Origin Celtic (Continental European and probably Irish). Pastoral deity concerned with light, solar worship and healing.

Known period of worship prehistoric times until Christianization (circa 400 AD) and in some circumstances much later.

Synonyms Apollo Belenus; Bile (Irish).

Center(s) of cult mainly sanctuaries in northern Italy (Aquileia) and southwestern Gaul (Aquitaine).

Art references horse statuettes; stone carvings and reliefs.

Literary sources *Books of Invasions*; *Cycles of Kings*; Roman writers—Tertullian, Herodian, Ausonius; votive inscriptions.

Considered to be one of the oldest of the Celtic gods thus far recognized. Celebrated long into the Christian era in the festival of *Beltine* or *Cetshamain*, set on May 1, the start of the "warm season." The rites involved lighting huge bonfires and driving cattle between them as a protection against disease. It marked the season when cattle were liberated after winter to graze the open pastures.

Belenus bears many similarities with the Greek deity Apollo as a god of light, sun and healing. Though appearing more often as a purely Celtic god, he was sometimes worshiped as Apollo Belenus, for example at the thermal spring sanctuary at St Sabine [Côte d'Or], and in this guise became associated with horses, which are well-attested as sun symbols in the Celtic Bronze Age. Model horses were found at the Gaul site. Ausonius, a fourth century poet from the Bordeaux region, mentions Belenus sanctuaries in Aquitaine. Tertullian refers to them in Austria, Herodian places others in northern Italy.

Belet-Ili *(lady of the gods)*

Mother goddess. Mesopotamian (Babylonian-Akkadian). Known in Babylon and probably modeled on Ninhursağa.

Belet-Seri

Chthonic underworld goddess. Mesopotamian (Babylonian-Akkadian). The recorder of the dead entering the otherworld. Known as the "Scribe of the Earth."

Belili

Goddess. Mesopotamian (Babylonian-Akkadian). See Geštinanna.

Bella Pennu

Sun god. Indian (Khond). A local deity in the Orissa province synonymous with Boora Pennu.

Bellona

Mother goddess and goddess of war. Roman. She becomes syncretized with the Cappadocian mother goddess Ma. The first known temple dedicated to Ma-Bellona by the Romans is dated to 296 BC. Bellona was attended by Asiatic priests who performed frenzied dances and gashed themselves with swords, offering the blood on the goddess's altars. Because of its violent nature, Rome refused officially to recognize the cult until the third century AD.

Beltiya *(my lady)*

Generic title of goddess. Mesopotamian (Babylonian-Akkadian). Zarpanitum (Sarpanitum), the consort of the Babylonian god Marduk, is often addressed as Beltiya.

Bendis

Mother goddess. Thracian. Hellenized and linked stylistically with Artemis as a huntress. Appeared in Athens during the Peloponnesian War. Attributes: boots, torch and pointed cap.

Benten-San

Goddess of luck. Shinto [Japan]. One of seven deities classed as gods of fortune and the only goddess in the group. A popular deity with many sanctuaries dedicated to her, she is a patron of music and holds a *biwa* instrument in her hand. Snakes, believed to stand for jealousy, are often coiled around her statues. Because of this, married couples are reluctant to visit her shrines together. Her priesthood is both Shinto and Buddhist and she is closely linked with the goddess Sarasvati.

Benu

Transmuted bird-like form of a sun god. Egyptian (Upper). A deity mentioned in Pyramid Texts (circa twenty-fifth century BC) and linked with the sun god of Heliopolis, Atum. He is also said to have been self-created from the primeval ocean and is sometimes a symbol of rebirth in the afterlife. Benu may have augmented the Greek classical tradition of the Phoenix. He appears in the Old Kingdom as a yellow wagtail but later becomes a heron, wearing the conical white crown of Upper Egypt with two slender feathers pointing backwards from its crest.

Bera Pennu

Vegetation goddess. Northern Indian. Worshipped by the Khonds in Bengal. She was the recipient of human sacrifice to ensure good harvest, particularly of the spice turmeric, and as a protection against disease and infirmity. The sacrificial victim or *meriah* was youthful, often kept for years as a holy person before death and was always either the offspring of a previous sacrificial victim, or purchased from impoverished families for the purpose. He or she was generally strangled, sometimes in the fork of a tree, after days of festivities. In other instances the victim was cut up alive.

BES

Origin Egyptian. Guardian deity of women in labor.

Known period of worship appearing in art from circa 1500 BC and probably earlier, until the end of Egyptian history circa 400 AD.

Synonyms none.

Center(s) of cult no specific sanctuaries, but a household god and generally associated with birthplaces, including those of royalty.

Art references walls of temples at Thebes; curved ivory batons from Middle Period; Walls of birth houses.

Literary sources none significant.

A dwarfish and hideous, but essentially benign deity whose ugliness wards off evil. He is generally present at births exerting a protective influence. Bes appears with a large-bearded and barely human face, a thick body, short arms and short bandy legs. He wears a plumed crown and often wields a short sword. He possesses a lion's mane, ears, tail and usually has his mouth open and tongue protruding. As a god of birth, Bes often carries the SA symbol of protection. He is also sometimes drawn as a musician with a tambourine.

Bes was adopted by Greco-Roman culture. The Greeks depicted him in strongly ithyphallic guise with a disproportionately large and erect penis and, from the time of the Roman occupation, he appears in the mode of a soldier wearing a short military tunic.

Bethel

Local tutelary god. Western Semitic (Phoenician). Probably of Aramaean or Syrian origin. First mentioned in a fourteenth century treaty between the Hittite king Suppiluliuma and Nigmadu II of Ugarit [Ras Šamra]. He appears more regularly on inscriptions from the end of the seventh century BC and enjoyed considerable popularity during the Neo-Babylonian period. Bethel is mentioned in the biblical text of Jeremiah 48:13, implying that some Israelites acknowledged this deity. There is no evidence of links with the historical place names, including that mentioned in Genesis 38:13.

Bhadra *(auspicious)*

Minor goddess. Hindu (Epic and Puranic). Attendant of Siva. Generally seated. Attributes: blue lotus, fruit, rosary and trident.

Bhaga *(the dispenser of fortune)*

Minor sun god. Hindu (Vedic and Puranic). In Vedic times, the incarnation of women's good fortune in marriage. One of six *Adityas,* sons of the goddess Aditi. Consort: Siddhi. Attributes: two lotuses, prayer wheel and trident.

Bhagavan *(the lord)*

Tutelary god. Northern and central Indian. Worshipped by the Bhils and other tribes as the original creator spirit and a judge of the dead soul. Also an epithet of Visnu and Krsna. Also Bhagwan.

Bhairava *(terrible)*

Minor frightful form of the god Siva. Hindu (Puranic and later). Guardian deity of doorways. A so-called *ugra* aspect, generally depicted in similar style to Siva but with up to five heads and ten arms and said to have been born from Siva's blood. Attributes: hook and noose. Aspects and epithets include Kalaratri, Ksetrapala and Mahakala. Also Bhairon, linked with the cult of dogs and Bhairava, one of a group of *mahavidyas* personifying the *Sakti* of Siva.

Bhaisajyaguru *(supreme physician)*

Physician god. Buddhist-Lamaist [Tibet]. Accounted among one of a series of medicine *buddhas* known as a *sMan-bla* in Tibet. In Lamaism he is the fifth in a series of *manusibuddhas.* Typically depicted with stretched earlobes and a row of small curls fringing the forehead. Color: blue or gold. Attributes: fruit, sometimes with a bowl.

Bharani *(bearing)*

Minor goddess of misfortune. Hindu (Epic and Puranic). A malevolent *naksatra,* daughter of Daksa and wife of Candra (Soma). Also Apabharanis.

Bharat Mata *(Mother India)*

Mother goddess. Modern Hindu. Evolved from the writings of the nineteenth century Bengali, Bankim Chandra Chatterjee. Shrines are designed in the form of a map of India.

Bharati

Minor goddess of sacrifices. Hindu (Vedic, Epic and Puranic). She is invoked to appear on the sacrifical field before a ritual. Usually associated with the goddess Sarasvati. Also regarded as a consort of Ganesa.

Bhavanavasi

Gods. Jain [India]. A generic name given to deities of youthful appearance who are arranged in ten groups all with the suffix -*kumara*. Thus Agni-; Asura-; Dik-; Dvipa-; Naga-; Stanita-; Suparna-; Udadhi-; Vayu-; Vidyut-.

Bhima   *(terrible)*

1. Warrior god. Hindu (Epic and Puranic). A prince of the mythical Pandu family and one of the heroes of the *Mahabharata* epic, Bhima is usually depicted wielding a sword and a club. He is a son of the god of the winds Vayu. He is perceived as a god of immense strength and great cruelty, which separates him from the heroic figure of Arjuna, his brother, with whom he is linked in the epic. Attribute: a club. Also Bhimasena.
2. Minor goddess. Buddhist (Mahayana). An attendant of Buddakepala.

Bhrkuti-Tara   *(she who frowns)*

Mother goddess. Buddhist-Lamaist [Tibet]. In Lamaism particularly, a cruel form of Tara, the mother of the Buddha. The so-called "yellow Tara." An emanation of Amitabha. Also identified as a female *bodhisattva* or *buddha*-designate. Color: yellow. Attribute: image of Amitabha, lotus, rosary, staff, trident and water jar. Three-eyed. Also Janguli and Vajratara.

Bhumi

(the earth on which all things are formed)
Collective name for a group of deities. Buddhist (Varyana). Twelve personifications of the spiritual spheres through which a *bohhisattva* or *buddha*-designate passes in his quest for perfection of knowledge. Common attribute: a staff.

Bhumi Devata

Vegetation goddess. Indian. Worshipped by many primitive tribes.

Bhumidevi   *(the earth goddess)*

Fertility goddess. Hindu (Epic and Puranic) [southern India]. The second wife of Visnu (or Krsna). Her son is Naraka. Bhumidevi is often depicted standing on the left (occasionally right) hand of the Varaha *avatara* of Visnu. In the north she is known as Pusti. She is often depicted sitting on a lotus throne with bared breasts. Attributes: blue lotus, lotus, lute, pomegranate, pot with herbs, pot with vegetables and water jar. Also Bhu, Bhudevi, Bhumi, Mahi, Prthivi, Vasudhara and Zami-Mata.

Bhumiya   *(guardian of fields)*

Fertility god. Hindu (Vedic and Puranic) [northern India]. Guardian deity of fields, worshiped as a rough stone icon. In later times a form of Visnu.

Bhutadamara   *(tumult of demons)*

God. Buddhist (Mahayana). May be depicted reclining on the Hindu goddess Aparajita. Attributes: snakes in the hair, and staff. Three-eyed.

Bhutamata   *(mother of goblins)*

Terrible goddess. Hindu. A frightful form of Parvati. Accompanied by a lion. Attribute: phallus (on the head), shield and sword.

Bhuvanesvari   *(lady of the spheres)*

Goddess. Hindu (Epic and Puranic). One of a group of ten *mahavidyas* personifying the *Sakti* of Siva. Also an epithet applied to several goddesses. Aspects include Siddharatri. Attributes: hook and noose.

Bia

Goddess of force. Greek. The daughter of the underworld goddess Styx and the sister of Kratos, god of strength.

Bi-har

Guardian deity. Buddhist-Lamaist [Tibet]. One of the guardian *maharajas* protecting against demons. Attended by a lion. Color: white. Attributes: arrow, bow, knife, staff, sword and trident. Three-eyed.

Birdu

Minor chthonic underworld god. Mesopotamian (Babylonian-Akkadian). Consort of Manungal and syncretized with Nergal.

Bishamon

God of luck. Shinto [Japan]. One of seven deities concerned with fortune, he appears as a warrior in full armor holding a spear in one hand and a toy pagoda, identified as a "tower of treasure" in the other. He has been linked with the Buddhist god Vaisravana (Kubera).

Bo Hsian

God. Taoist (Chinese). The Taoist counterpart of the Buddhist deity Samantabhadra. Usually depicted upon a white elephant. He is considered to be a god of wisdom.

Boann   *(she of the white cows)*

River goddess. Celtic (Irish). The local goddess of the river Boyne. She is one of the consorts of the Dagda, alternatively of a minor local deity Elcmar, cuckolded by the Dagda who sent him away on an errand for nine months. The mother of Angus mac Og.

Bodhisattva

(one whose essence is perfect knowledge)
Generic title for a *buddha*-designate. Buddhist [northern India, Tibet, China and Japan]. Any one of the earlier stages of a future *buddha*. Depicted wearing regal dress and trappings, including a crown. The most significant include Avalokitesvara, Maitreya and Manjusri.

Boldogasszony

Tutelary goddess. Pre-Christian Hungarian. The guardian deity of women and children, she became syncretized with the Virgin Mary after Christianization.

Bolon Ti Ku

Chthonic underworld gods. Mayan (classical Mesoamerican) [Mexico]. A collective term for a group of nine deities not otherwise clearly defined. They are probably still invoked by modern Mexican Indians.

Bombay Kamayan

Local disease goddess. Hindu [northern India]. Particularly worshiped at Gaya.

Bonchor

Tutelary god. Pre-Islamic Berber [Tunisia]. Probably recognized as a creator deity.

Boora Pennu

God of light. Indian (Khond). A local deity in the Orissa province who created the earth goddess Tari Pennu as his consort and through her engendered the other great gods. Until recently this deity was the subject of sacrifice in notorious *meriah* rituals, which involved violent human sacrifice.

Bor

Archetypal god. Nordic (Icelandic). In the creation account, according to Snorri, a living creature called Ymir was formed in the misty void of Ginnungagap. Ymir was nourished by the milk of the cow Audhumla, who licked salty ice blocks and released a second individual called Buri. He had a son called Bor. Bor, in turn, engendered the Aesir gods Othin, Vili and Ve. Also Borr. See also Othin.

Boreas

God of the north wind. Greek and also Roman. He controlled the storm that destroyed the Persian fleet sailing against Athens. Identified with winter frosts. According to the *Theogony* (Hesiod), he is the son of Eos and Astraeos and is of Thracian origin: " . . . when Thracian Boreas huddles the thick clouds."

Borvo

God of healing. Romano-Celtic (Gallic). Identified with several therapeutic springs and mineral baths.

BRAGI *(poet; leader)*

Origin Nordic (Icelandic). God of poetry.

Known period of worship Viking period (circa 700 AD) and earlier, until Christianization (circa 1100 AD).

Synonyms described as "the long bearded one."

Center(s) of cult none known.

Art references none known but probably the subject of anonymous carvings.

Literary sources Icelandic codices; *Prose Edda* (Snorri).

A Viking deity, said by Snorri to be a son of Othin and consort of Idunn, the goddess who keeps the apples of immortality for the gods of Asgard. Bragi is possibly also a pseudonym for Othin himself. Often found in company with Aegir. The cup over which oaths were sworn was known as the "cup of Bragi" and he was seen as a poet and orator in the hall of the slain, Valhalla.

BRAHMA *(the creator)*

Origin Hindu [India]. Creator god.

Known period of worship circa 500 BC or earlier until present day.

Synonyms many epithets including Abjaja, Abjayoni, Astakarna, Kamalasana.

Center(s) of cult restricted since circa 700 AD to two sanctuaries—at Lake Puskana in Rajputana, and at Idar near Mount Abu.

Art references sculptures generally in bronze but also in stone. Reliefs.

Literary sources mentioned in *Rg Veda*, but properly from *Ramayana* epic and from Puranic texts.

With Visnu and Siva, Brahma is one of a trinity of supreme creator deities in the Hindu pantheon. His consort is generally the goddess of wisdom, Sarasvati, but some sources identify the goddess of speech, Vac. He also has a second consort, the milkmaid Gayatri. Originally the title referred to the power of occult utterances that became associated with the priests or Brahmans.

Brahma is depicted with four heads, often bearded, facing in four directions, and with four hands, sometimes with one of them raised in blessing or promise. As a god of knowledge he often carries the Vedas (earliest Sanskrit mythology said to have sprung from his head) in one of his hands. Other attributes include a water pot indicating prosperity, a spoon or a string of pearls. He may also carry a staff and an alms dish. He may be depicted with red or pink skin, wearing a white robe or a loin cloth with a sacred cord across the shoulder. His sacred animal is the goose. According to one legendary source he was created from the right side of the primordial creator force. His life is anticipated as a hundred heavenly years, each of 360 days and nights. Each day, or *kalpa*, is equal to 4,320,000 earthly years. Brahma's current age is said to be fifty-one and after each of his years, the universe is destroyed and rebuilt.

Brahma is generally less popular than Visnu or Siva, probably because he is identified solely with the primordial account of creation. Legend describes how he created himself from the primeval waters using the power of his own desire. He thought a seed into existence, which grew into a golden egg and from which he emerged after a year. The two halves of the shell became heaven and earth, within which he fashioned the sky. The *Ramayana* also describes him in the form of a boar that raises the earth on its tusks. By contrast the *Mahabharata* accounts him born from a lotus in the navel of Visnu. Elsewhere he emerges as a fish, or as a tortoise. Negative aspects of Brahma include drunkenness and duplicity.

One source describes how the beautiful goddess Satarupa was formed from half of Brahma's own self but that, in an attempt to prevent him looking on his daughter with incestuous desire, she circled around him. His four heads resulted. There was once a fifth, which Siva decapitated with the thumb of his left hand. It is said that incest with his daughter is also partly responsible for Brahma's limited worship. Alternative legend credits him with a daughter, Vach, by whom he fathered the living world.

2. In Buddhist tradition he is also one of a group of *dharmapala* with terrible appearance and royal attire.

Brahmani
Mother goddess. Hindu (Epic and Puranic). A *Sakti* who in later Hinduism became one of the group of eight *astamataras* or mothers. In another grouping one of nine *navasaktis* or mothers. She is attended by a goose and wears a yellow robe. Attributes: book, label, rosary, trident and water jar. Also Brahmi.

Bres Macelatha
Vegetation god. Celtic (Irish). The son of Eriu and of the Fomorian king Elatha. He is therefore part Tuatha de Danaan by parentage but, having become Lord of Ireland, he sides with the Fomorians in the Battle of Moytura and is defeated. Concerned with the supply of food from the land.

Brhaspati *(lord of prayer)*
Astral god. Hindu (Vedic, Epic and Puranic). The personification of the planet Jupiter. In Vedic texts he appears as a priest. The son of Angiras and the *guru* of the later Hindu pantheon. Considered to be almost identical with Brahma. His consort is the goddess Tara and his son is Kaca. He rides in a chariot drawn by eight horses. Color: golden yellow. Attributes: arrow, ax (golden), book, bow, rosary, staff and water jar.

Brigantia
Tutelary goddess. Romano-Celtic (British). The goddess of the Brigantes in the West Riding of Yorkshire. She became identified with Caelestis. At Corbridge, Northumberland, there is an altar inscribed to various deities, including Caelestis Brigantia. In a carved stone relief at Birrens, on the Antonine Wall in Scotland, she is depicted with the attributes of Minerva. She may also bear

links with the goddess Brigit. She is frequently associated with water and herding.

BRIGIT *(exalted one)*
Origin Celtic (Continental European and Irish). Fertility goddess.

Known period of worship prehistoric times until Christianization (circa 1100 AD) and after.

Synonyms Brigid; Bride; Banfile (poetess).

Center(s) of cult various sanctuaries throughout area of Celtic influence.

Art references stone carvings.

Literary sources *Books of Invasions; Cycles of Kings;* various inscriptions.

A major Celtic pastoral deity, described as a "wise woman, the daughter of the Dagda," Brigit became "Christianized" as St. Brigit of Kildare, who lived from 450–523 AD and founded the first female Christian community in Ireland. She was originally celebrated on February 1 in the festival of *Imbolc*, which coincided with the beginning of lactation in ewes and was regarded in Scotland as the date on which Brigit deposed the blue-faced hag of winter (see Cailleach Bheur). The Christian calendar adopted the same date for the Feast of St. Brigit. There is no record that a Christian saint ever actually existed, but in Irish mythology she became the midwife to the Virgin Mary. The name can be traced into many Irish and European place names. It is also akin to *Brhati* which means "exalted one" in Sanskrit.

Britannia
Tutelary goddess. Romano-Celtic (British). The *genia loci* of Britain who first appears on the coinage of Antoninus Pius in the second century AD. She became the symbol of the British Empire after being partly syncretized with the Roman war goddess Minerva.

Buadza
God of the wind. Gan [district around Accra, Ghana, West Africa]. Also regarded as a storm god. Also Olila.

BUDDHA *(enlightened)*
Origin Buddhist [India]. The founder of Buddhism.

Known period of worship circa 500 BC to present day.

Synonyms Gautama, Siddharta.

Center(s) of cult pan-Asiatic.

Art references metal and stone sculptures, paintings etc.

Literary sources Sadhanamala and Tantric ritual texts.

The deity is regarded as having been a historical figure, born at Kapilavastu near Gorakhpur. He died at Kusinagara circa 486 BC. His father was Suddhodana of the Sakya clan, his mother was Maya and his wife Yasodhara.

Buddha is, in certain respects, the equal of the Hindu god Visnu. He is generally depicted with shaven or cropped head and may be crowned. The hair may be tightly curled. His color attribute is gold.

By tradition, he preached his first sermon at Mrgadava in Sarnath near Varanasi where, after a visit in 1956 by the Dalai Lama, an enclosure of gazelles was erected.

Buddhabodhiprabhavasita *(control of the light of the knowledge of the Buddha)*
Minor goddess. Buddhist. One of a group of twelve *vasitas* personifying the disciplines of spiritual regeneration. Color: yellow. Attributes: prayer wheel on a jeweled banner.

Buddhakapala *(Buddha's skullcap)*
God. Buddhist (Mahayana). A significant emanation of Aksobhya. Alternatively a form of Heruka. His *Sakti* is Citrasena. Color: blue-black. Attributes: club, cup, drum, image of Aksobhya and knife.

Buddhalocana *(Buddha's eye)*
Goddess. Buddhist (Shingon). A female *buddha* (see Locana).

Buddhi *(perception)*
1. Minor goddess. Hindu (Puranic). Sometimes identified as consort of the Maha-Ganapati form of the elephant god Ganesa, depicted seated on his knee.
2. Minor goddess. Jain.

Budha *(awakening)*
1. Astral god. Hindu (Vedic, Epic and Puranic). The personification of the planet Mercury. The son of Soma (Candra) and Tara or Rohini. Depicted in a chariot drawn by eight horses or lions (sometimes a single lion). Color: yellow. Attributes: bow, club, rosary, shield and sword. Also Candraja and Candrasuta.
2. Astral god. Buddhist. The personification of the planet Mercury. Stands on a lotus. Attributes: bow and arrow.

Bugid Y Aiba
God of war. Puerto Rico and Haiti. Classed as one of the *zemis*. The local Indians have believed that the deity can give them strength. When they smoke in a ritual ceremony in honor of the god, their arms increase in size. He will also restore failed eyesight.

Buk
River goddess. Nuer [Sudan]. A guardian against attack by crocodiles, she is invoked by the sacrifice of a goat. Known as the "daughter of the fireflies."

Buluc Chabtan
God of war. Mayan (classical Meso-american) [Mexico]. Associated with human sacrifice and depicted with a characteristic black line encircling the eye and extending down the cheek. Also God F.

Bumba
Creator god. Boshongo (Bantu) [southern Africa]. The progenitor of the world out of chaos. When he experienced a stomach-ache he vomited the

earth, sun, moon and, finally, all living things, including mankind.

Buri

Archetypal god. Nordic (Icelandic). According to Snorri, one of two primordial beings. Ymir was formed from the misty void of Ginnungagap, and Buri emerged from the blocks of salty ice that the cosmic cow Audhumla licked. He had a son, Bor, who engendered the Aesir gods Othin, Vili and Ve. Also Bori. See also Othin.

Buriyas

Tutelary war god. Kassite [Iran]. He was invoked by the Kassite armies that overthrew Babylonia in the sixteenth century BC.

C

Cacoch
Creator god. Mayan (classical Mesoamerican) [Mexico]. According to tradition he engendered the water lily from which sprang all the other deities of the Mayan pantheon. He is also portrayed as a messenger of the creator god Hachacyum. Also Kacoch.

Caelestis
Moon goddess. Carthaginian [North Africa]. The Romanized form of the Punic goddess Tanit. Elsewhere she became syncretized into the cult of Aphrodite-Venus. Annual games were held in her honor. She was brought to Rome in the form of an abstract block of stone (like that of Kybele from Pessinus) and became popular there during the early part of the third century AD; in this guise she was known as the "mighty protectress of the Tarpeian hill."

Cagn
Creator god. Kalahari bushmen [southern Africa]. The progenitor of all life on earth.

Cailleach Bheur
Goddess of winter. Celtic (Scottish). Depicted as a blue-faced hag who is reborn on October 31 (*Samhain*). She brings the snow until the goddess Brigit deposes her and she eventually turns to stone on April 30 (*Beltine*). In later times the mythical, witch-like figure of "Black Annis" probably derived from her.

Cakra   (wheel)
Embodiment of the creator's mind. Hindu. Emerging in the form of a six-spoked wheel (less frequently eight) that also epitomizes the passage of time and is a symbol of wholeness and protection. Particularly associated with Visnu and Krsna, the *cakra* is a common attribute held by many deities. It is probably of great antiquity since it is known from the time of the Indus Valley civilization (prior to 1700 BC). In Jainism and Buddhism it is the "wheel of the law" that leads to perfection.

Cakresvari   (lady of the cakra)
Goddess of learning. Jain [India]. One of sixteen *vidyadevi* headed by the goddess Sarasvati. Also one of the twenty-four *sasanadevata* or messenger goddesses.

Camaxtli
God. Aztec (classical Mesoamerican) [Mexico]. See Mixcoatl-Camaxtli.

Camulos
War god. Celtic (British). Probably the deity from which the name of Camulodunum [Colchester, England] derives. Known from inscriptions and coinage bearing the symbol of a boar.

Camunda
1. Goddess. Hindu (Epic and Puranic). A distinct form of Durga. The name is said to be a contraction of the names of the demonic beings Camda and Munda killed by her. She is also recognized among the *saptamatara* and *astamatara* mothers as well as sometimes being regarded as a *navasakti*. She stands variously on a lion, an owl and a corpse. Attributes: a large and varied assortment of objects are held. Three-eyed. Also Yami.
2. Goddess. Buddhist. She stands upon a corpse. Color: red. Attributes: cup and knife.

Canda *(violent)*
Terrible goddess. Hindu (Epic and Puranic). A distinct form of Durga and one of a group of nine *navadurgas* ("nine durgas"). Canda, with Munda, was also one of the demons killed by a form of Durga known as Camunda (contraction of the two demonic names). She is depicted with a large number of attributes. Also a form of Mahisasuramardini.

Candali *(outcast woman)*
Goddess of terrifying appearance. Buddhist-Lamaist [Tibet]. One of a group of eight *gauri* goddesses. Color: red or blue. Attributes: flames.

Candamius
Astral god. Romano-Iberian. Known from inscriptions and place-names in northern Spain and syncretized with Jupiter.

Candanayika *(mistress of the fierce)*
Goddess. Hindu (Epic and Puranic). A distinct form of Durga and one of a group of nine *navadurgas* ("nine durgas").

Candarosana
God. Buddhist (Mahayana). A form of the god Aksobhya. Color: yellow. Attributes: noose, skin and sword.

Candarupa
Goddess. Hindu (Epic and Puranic). A distinct form of Durga and one of a group of nine *navadurgas* ("nine durgas").

Candavati
Goddess. Hindu (Epic and Puranic). A distinct form of Durga and one of a group of nine *navadurgas* ("nine durgas").

Candelifera
Minor goddess of birth. Roman. Responsible for bringing the newborn child into the light. Usually associated with Lucina and Carmentes.

Candesvara *(the lord of Canda)*
Minor god. Hindu (Epic and Puranic). A benevolent aspect of Siva. Also an attendant on Siva, said to have been a youthful cowherd. He sits on a lotus throne. Attributes: arrow, ax, bow, club, crown, hatchet, noose, rosary, snake, trident and water jar.

Candesvari *(fierce lady)*
Minor goddess. Buddhist (Mahayana). She stands upon a corpse. Color: yellow. Attributes: grass and an antelope.

Candika *(fierce)*
Goddess of desire. Hindu (Epic and Puranic). May be included among the *saptamataras* or *astamataras* (mothers).

Candogra *(fierce and terrible)*
Goddess. Hindu (Epic and Puranic). A distinct form of Durga and one of a group of nine *navadurgas* ("nine durgas").

Candra
1. Planet god. Hindu (Epic and Puranic). Personified by the moon and also seen as a *dikpala* or guardian of the northern direction. Consorts include Kaumundi, Tara and the *naksatras* or astral goddesses. His son is Budha. He drives in a chariot drawn by ten white horses. Color: white. Attributes: club, lotus, sacred rope and prayer wheel. The term *candra* usually refers to the cup containing the sacrificial yellow beverage *soma*, often a synonym for the deity. *Candra* is also the apotheosis of the pale yellow moon disc.
2. Planet god. Buddhist. Attended by a goose. Color: white. Attributes: moon disc on a lotus.

Candrasekhara *(Moon crested)*
Form of the god Siva. Hindu (Puranic). Portrayed standing stiffly upright and wearing snake jewelry with the moon on the left side of his headdress. Attributes: ax and an antelope.

Cankilikkaruppan
(the black man of the chain)
Local god. Hindu-Dravidian (Tamil). Worshipped in southern India.

Carcika *(repetitive chant)*
Goddess. Buddhist (Mahayana). Color: red. Attributes: cup and knife.

Cariociecus
War god. Romano-Iberian. Syncretized with the god Mars.

Carmentes
Minor goddess of birth. Roman. Responsible for bringing the newborn child into the light. Usually associated with Lucina and Candelifera.

Cathubodua
War goddess. Celtic (Continental European). Known only from inscriptions and probably comparable with the Irish Celtic Badb Catha.

Caturmurti
God. Hindu (Epic and Puranic). The specific form of Visnu with four faces. Also the syncretization of Brahma, Visnu, Siva and Surya.

Cauri
Goddess of terrifying appearance. Buddhist and Lamaist [Tibet]. One of a group of eight *gauri* goddesses. Color: yellow. Attribute: noose.

Cautha
Sun god. Etruscan. Attributes include a sun disc crown and fire in each hand. He is depicted rising from the sea.

Ce Acatl
Minor creator god. Aztec (classical Mesoamerican) [Mexico]. One of the deities collectively classed as the Quetzalcoatl complex. Also (1)Acatl.

Cenkalaniyammal
(lady of the red paddyfield)
Local goddess. Hindu-Dravidian (Tamil). Guardian of paddyfields in southern India.

Centeocihuatl
Corn goddess. Aztec (classical Mesoamerican) [Mexico]. Represented at various sites including Tula [Hidalgo]. According to the codices *Borgia*, *Cospi* and *Fejervery-Mayer* she is also one of four temple deities. Also Centeotl.

CERES
Origin Roman. Mother goddess.

Known period of worship circa 400 BC to 400 AD.

Synonyms Demeter (Greek).

Center(s) of cult throughout Roman world.

Art references sculptures and reliefs.

Literary sources Aeneid (Virgil), etc.

Ceres is arguably the most recent model of the "great mother" whose predecessors include Inana, Ištar, Artemis, Kybele and Demeter on whom she is directly modeled. She is the daughter of Kronos (Cronus) and Rhea and one of the more important consorts of Jupiter. Her daughter in the upper world, Kore, is the goddess of the underworld Proserpina who was abducted by Pluto. She became foster mother to Triptolemus, an ill-fated king in the mold of the Mesopotamian Dumuzi, depicted in the classical Greek *Eleusinian Mysteries*. As the embodiment of vegetation, Ceres neglects the natural world during the period that her daughter remains below ground with Pluto (winter), but restores nature annually when Proserpina is returned to her.

Ceres was worshiped at the festivals of *Thesmophoria* and *Cerealia* in sanctuaries throughout the Greco-Roman empires.

Ceridwen
Goddess of inspiration. Celtic (Welsh). Depicted as the hag-aspect of the mother goddess, she is the consort of Tegid Foel. Her children are Creirwy

(daughter) and Afagddu (son). She allegedly prepares the caldron of knowledge.

CERNUNNOS

Origin Celtic (mainly Gallic). Fertility and chthonic god.

Known period of worship prehistoric times until circa 1000 AD.

Synonyms none.

Center(s) of cult none.

Art references Gundestrup Bowl; monumental stone work and relief carvings.

Literary sources votive inscriptions.

Cernunnos appears to have been recognized in the region of Gaul that is now central France. He is typically drawn as a man bearing the antlers of a stag, not necessarily representing an animal spirit but a deity closely involved with animals and one that can transform instantly into animal shape. In the Celtic world, horns and antlers were generally regarded as symbols of virility and fertility. On the Celtic Gundestrup Bowl from Denmark, Cernunnos is attended by a boar—an animal revered by the Celts for its speed, pugnacity and magical connotations—and on the same vessel he seems to be associated with a bull. This latter link reappears on a stone relief from Reims. Cernunnos is also depicted in association with snakes, sometimes bearing rams' horns, as on a stone relief found at Cirencester in England. His legs may be replaced by snakes, and at Sommerecourt [Haute Marne] a relief was found depicting the god in company with an unnamed goddess holding a basket and feeding a snake. The snake symbolism is generally associated with rejuvenation. Other reliefs show him holding purses of money.

Cghene

Creator god. Isoko [southern Nigeria, West Africa]. An abstract being who is embodied by a mediator in the form of a sacred wooden totem, the *Oyise*. The god has no temples or priests.

Chac

Rain god(s). Mayan (Yucatec, classical Mesoamerican) [Mexico]. Not part of the hierarchy of Mayan gods, but worshiped with great devotion at local level. Originally there was a god, Chaac, who was of huge size and who taught mankind agriculture. He was regarded as the god of thunder, lightning, rain and bread, and of *milpas* (smallholdings) and their produce. Also God B.

Later, four leading Chacs become recognized, each with different colors and directions. They are known popularly as the Ah Hoyaob (sprinklers or urinators), since the rain falls from between their legs. They are regarded as musicians and their sacred animals are frogs and tortoises. Attributes include a long pendulous nose, a scroll beneath the eye and a thin, ribbon-like object projecting from a corner of the mouth, which may be toothless. They may also hold burning torches, symbolizing their power to withhold as well as dispense rain. See also Tlaloc.

Chac Uayab Xoc

Fish god. Mayan (Yucatec, classical Mesoamerican) [Mexico]. Known as the "great demon shark," he feeds on the bodies of drowned fishermen, but also provides catches.

Chaitanya

Mendicant god. Hindu (Puranic). A deified mortal who became one of the many incarnations of the god Visnu. Born at Nadiya in 1484 AD, he died at Puri in 1527. Chaitanya was a sickly child who, according to legend, was left to his fate, hanging in a tree to die, but was revived by the gods and thus became deified. He was married twice before adopting a strict ascetic existence at the age of twenty-four, from which time he traveled extensively, eventually settling in the holy city of Benares. He is remembered as a great social reformer. His main sanctuary at Nadiya includes a small statue of Krsna to whom he devoted himself.

Chalchiuhtlatonal   *(jade glowing)*

God of water. Aztec (classical Mesoamerican) [Mexico]. One of the deities collectively classed as the Tlaloc complex, generally concerned with rain, agriculture and fertility.

CHALCHIUHTLICUE
(her skirt is of jade)
Origin Aztec (classical Mesoamerican) [Mexico]. Water goddess.

Known period of worship circa 750 AD to 1500 AD but probably much earlier.

Synonyms none.

Center(s) of cult worshiped widely but chiefly at Teotihuacan.

Art references stone sculptures, murals, codex illustrations.

Literary sources pre-Columbian codices.

Featuring strongly in creation mythology, Chalchiuhtlicue presided over the fourth of the world ages that terminated in a great deluge. She is the tutelary deity of the fourth of the thirteen heavens identified at the time of the Spanish conquest, Ilhuicatl Citlalicue (the heaven of the star-skirted goddess). She takes the role of a vegetation goddess responsible for the flowering and fruiting of the green world, particularly corn; she also takes responsibility for such natural phenomena as whirlpools. The consort of the rain god Tlaloc and one of the group classed as the Tlaloc complex, she is particularly invoked as a guardian goddess of young women and is responsible for unpredictable events. A huge statue, three meters high, was discovered at Teotihuacan, and a larger, unfinished statue, allegedly of the goddess and weighing approximately 200 tons (now in Mexico City), was found on the slopes of the Tlaloc mountain. Attributes include a rattle on a baton, and her dress is adorned with water lilies.

Chalchiutonatiuh
Aztec. See Atl.

Chalchiutotolin *(jade turkey)*
God of penitence. Aztec (classical Mesoamerican) [Mexico]. One of the deities collectively classed as the Tezcatlipoca complex.

Chalmecacihuitl *(chalman lady)*
Minor chthonic underworld goddess. Aztec (classical Mesoamerican) [Mexico]. One of the deities collectively classed as the Mictlantecuhtli complex.

Chalmecatl
Minor chthonic underworld god. Aztec (classical Mesoamerican) [Mexico]. One of the deities collectively classed as the Mictlantecuhtli complex.

Chamer
God of death. Mayan (Chorti, classical Mesoamerican) [eastern Guatemala]. Appears as a skeleton dressed in white. His consort is Xtabai. Attributes include a scythe with a bone blade, probably copied from the traditions of Christian immigrants.

Chang Fei
God of war. Chinese. The counterpart of the god Kuan Ti and often linked iconographically with him and the god Liu Pei, Chang Fei rules over the dark half of the year—autumn and winter. Like the seasons he represents, he is characterized by drunkenness and wildness. According to tradition he was wounded by his subordinates while in a drunken stupor. He is depicted with a black face, a bushy beard and wild staring eyes giving him a ferocious appearance.

Chang Hs'ien
Guardian god of children. Chinese. According to tradition he was the mortal king of Szechuan killed by the founder of the Sung dynasty. His wife was captured and forced to become a concubine in the imperial palace. She was discovered by the emperor kneeling before a picture of her deceased husband, which she identified as a local deity, "the immortal Chang who gives children." This triggered the cult that began locally in Szechuan circa 100 AD. Chang Hs'ien is depicted holding a bow made of mulberry wood and either aiming an arrow at the star Tien Kou, the so-called celestial dog that threatens the earth, or aiming the empty bow at a rat (see Erh Lang).

Chang Tao Ling

God of the afterlife. Taoist (Chinese). The head of the heavenly Ministry of Exorcism, and allegedly the first head of the Taoist church. By tradition he vanquished the five poisonous animals—the centipede, scorpion, snake, spider and toad—placing their venom in a flask in which he concocted the elixir of life. Having drunk the contents at the age of 123, he ascended to heaven. He is depicted riding upon a tiger and brandishing a sword. Before the communist takeover of China, the gods of exorcism lived in a sanctuary on the Dragon Tiger mountain in Kiangsi province. Exorcised spirits were trapped in jars that were stored in the cellars.

Chantico (in the house)

Hearth goddess. Aztec (classical Mesoamerican) [Mexico]. A household guardian deity personified by hearth fires. One of the deities collectively classed as the Xiuhtecuhtli complex.

Chaob (carrying off)

Wind god(s). Mayan (Lacandon, classical Mesoamerican) [Mexico]. They live in the four cardinal directions and, according to tradition, will bring about the end of the current world with earthquakes and tempests when the last of the Lacandon people dies. They will blow so hard that they blast the monkeys out of the trees. The names of two are identified, Hunaunic in the east and Chikinkuh in the west.

Chaos

Primordial deity. Greco-Roman. The amorphous male power who, with the female presence, Nyx, personifies the empty space that existed before the formation of the cosmos.

Charis

Minor goddess. Greek. The consort of Hephaistos. Later the name becomes more familiar as the Gratiae or Graces (Aglaia, Euphrosine and Thalea) who then become the Charites in the Roman pantheon.

Chattrosnisa (with an umbrella)

God. Buddhist. One of eight usnisa deities apparently connected with the guardian sky deities or dikpalas. Color: white. Attribute: parasol.

Chaya (shadow)

Goddess. Hindu (Epic and Puranic). The reflection of the goddess Sanjna, consort of Surya and mother of the astral deity Sani.

Chemosh

See Kemos.

Chi Sung Tzu

Rain god. Chinese.

Chibirias

Chthonic earth goddess. Mayan (classical Mesoamerican) [Mexico]. The consort of the creator god Itzam Na and the mother of the Bacabs. She sends the rain for Itzam Na and, as an iguana, is said to have flooded the world in a previous cycle. She also paints the earth, the leaves of certain plants and the crest of the woodpecker red with her paintbrush. She invented the art of weaving and is the patroness of weavers. Attributes include a hank of cotton or cloth. Also Ix Chebel Yax; Ix Hun Tah Dz'ib (lady unique owner of the paintbrush); Ix Hun Tah Nok (lady unique owner of the cloth); Ix Zacal Nok (lady cloth weaver).

Chiccan

Rain gods. Mayan (Chorti, classical Mesoamerican) [eastern Guatemala]. Giant reptilian deities whose blood is cold and who evolved from snakes. They form a quartet, each living at the bottom of a deep lake situated in the four cardinal directions. They are believed to churn the waters that rise as clouds. The Ah Patnar Uinicob gods then beat the rain from the clouds with stone axes.

Chicomecohuatl

Corn goddess. Aztec and postclassical Mesoamerican. [Mexico]. Her festival was held in September when a young girl was sacrificed having taken on the role of the deity for a period of time during the celebrations. She was decapitated on a heap of corn fruits and her blood was collected in a large bowl before being poured over a wooden figurine of the goddess. Finally the victim's skin was flayed off and worn by a dancing priest. See also Xilonen.

Chicomexochitl

God of painters. Aztec (classical Mesoamerican) [Mexico]. Also described as a god of solar pleasure.

Chiconahui

Hearth goddess. Aztec (classical Mesoamerican) [Mexico]. A household guardian deity personified by hearth fires. One of the deities collectively classed as the Xiuhtecuhtli complex.

Chiconahuiehecatl

Minor creator god. Aztec (classical Mesoamerican) [Mexico]. One of the deities collectively classed as the Quetzalcoatl complex.

Chiconahui Itzcuintli-Chantico

God of lapidaries. Aztec (classical Mesoamerican) [Mexico].

Chikara

Sky god. Korekore (Shona-speaking) [northern Zimbabwe, southern Africa]. He has a son, Nosenga.

Chinnamastaka (decapitated)

Goddess. Hindu (Epic and Puranic). A headless form of Durga. Also one of a group of ten *mahavidyas*, goddesses of great knowledge personifying the *Sakti* of Siva. She may be depicted holding her head in her hands. Aspects include Viraratri. Attributes: scimitar, skull. Also Chinnamasta.

Chiuke

Sky god. Ibo [Nigeria, West Africa]. Regarded as a creator god.

Chors

Sun god. Pre-Christian Slav [Balkans]. Identified from the *Nestor Chronicle*. Attributes include horns and a canine head.

Chos-Skyon (protector)

Tutelary guardian deity. Buddhist-Lamaist [Tibet]. One of a group of gods of fearsome appearance who wear royal apparel. Rides a white elephant. Color: blue. Attributes: knife and noose.

Chu Jung

God of fire. Chinese. Also the heavenly executioner.

Chul Tatic Chites Vaneg
(holy father, creator of man)

Creator god. Mayan (classical Mesoamerican) [Mexico]. Thought to be the Mayan name of the Christian god.

Chung K'uei

God of the afterlife. Taoist (Chinese). He belongs to the heavenly "ministry of exorcism" and, though not the most senior (he is subservient to Chang Tao Ling), is probably the most popular within the category. He was originally a mortal working as a physician in the eighth century AD. He is depicted with a fearsome face, said to be so terrible that it can drive away any demonic spirit who dares to oppose him. He is engaged in combat using a sword and a fan on which is written a magical formula to ward off evil. Symbolic peaches are suspended from his hat and a bat circles his head representing happiness.

Cihuacoatl-Quilaztli

Creator goddess. Aztec (classical Mesoamerican) [Mexico]. Using a magical vessel, she grinds bone fragments obtained from previous generations of mankind in earlier world ages into a powder. The gods then commit self-sacrifice, allowing their blood to drip into the vessel. From the resulting mix, the human race of the fifth sun is formed.

Cinxia
Minor goddess of marriage. Roman. Concerned with the proper dress of the bride.

CIPACTLI *(great earth mother)*
Origin Aztec (classical Mesoamerican) [Mexico]. Primordial goddess.

Known period of worship circa 750 AD until 1500 AD, but probably much earlier.

Synonyms none.

Center(s) of cult none specific.

Art references codex illustrations, stone carvings.

Literary sources pre-Columbian codices.

Not strictly a goddess, but significant enough in Aztec cosmogony to be included here. According to tradition she was created in the form of a huge alligator-like monster by the underworld deities Mictlantecuhlti and Mictecacihuatl. She may equate with Tlaltecuhtli, the toad-like earth monster torn apart to form heaven and earth. According to one tradition she emerged from the primordial waters and engaged in a fierce struggle with the sun god Tezcatlipoca during which he tore off her lower jaw to prevent her sinking back into the depths and she bit off his right foot. The mountains are said to be the scaly ridges of her skin.

Cipactonal
Creator god. Aztec (classical Mesoamerican) [Mexico]. One of the deities collectively classed as the Ometeotl complex.

Cit Chac Coh
God of war. Mayan (classical Mesoamerican) [Mexico]. Identified as a red puma.

Citlalatonac *(glowing star)*
Creator god. Aztec (classical Mesoamerican) [Mexico]. One of the deities collectively classed as the Ometeotl complex. His consort is Citlalicue. Between them they created the stars of the night sky.

Citlalicue *(her skirt is a star)*
Creator goddess. Aztec (classical Mesoamerican) [Mexico]. One of the deities collectively classed as the Ometeotl complex. Her consort is Citlalatonac. Between them they created the stars of the night sky.

Citra *(bright)*
Minor goddess of misfortune. Hindu (epic and Puranic). A malevolent *naksatra* or astral deity; daughter of Daksa and wife of Candra (Soma).

Citrasena *(having a bright spear)*
Goddess. Buddhist (Mahayana). The *Sakti* of Buddhakapala.

Cittavasita *(control of thinking)*
Minor goddess. Buddhist. One of a group of twelve *vasitas* personifying the disciplines of spiritual regeneration. Color: white. Attribute: staff.

Cizin *(stench)*
God of death. Mayan (Yucatec and other tribes, classical Mesoamerican) [Mexico]. The most important death god in the Mayan cultural area. Said to live in Metnal, the Yucatec place of death, and to burn the souls of the dead. He first burns the mouth and anus and, when the soul complains, douses it with water. When the soul complains of this treatment, he burns it again until there is nothing left. It then goes to the god Sucunyum who spits on his hands and cleanses it, after which it is free to go where it chooses. Attributes of Cizin include a fleshless nose and lower jaw, or the entire head may be depicted as a skull. Spine and ribs are often showing. He wears a collar with death eyes between lines of hair and a long bone hangs from one earlobe. His body is painted with black and particularly yellow spots (the Mayan color of death).

Clementia
Minor goddess. Roman. Generally invoked to protect the common man against the emperor's absolute use of power. Under Hadrian the term

clementia temporum (mildness of the times) came into common usage.

COATLICUE
(the serpent-skirted goddess)
Origin Aztec (classical Mesoamerican) [Mexico]. Mother goddess.

Known period of worship circa 750 AD to 1500 AD and probably much earlier.

Synonyms Coatlicue-Chimalman (Valley of Mexico).

Center(s) of cult Tenochtitlan.

Art references stone sculptures, murals, codex illustrations.

Literary sources pre-Columbian codices.

The creator goddess of the earth and mankind and the female aspect of Ometeotl. One of the group classed as the Teteoinnan complex. She has 400 sons, the stars of the southern sky, and is the mother of the goddess Coyolxauhqui. Later, as a widow, she was impregnated by a ball of feathers as she was sweeping the "serpent mountain" of Coatepec near Tula. Her other children decapitated her as punishment for her dishonor, but she gave birth to the sun god Huitzilopochtli who subsequently slew Coyolxauhqui and her brothers, thus banishing night for day. The Great Temple at Tenochtitlan commemorates this primordial battle.

Coatlicue is known iconographically from a colossal headless statue dated to the late Aztec period, circa 1300 AD, which stands in Mexico City. The hands and feet are clawed and the figure bears a necklace of human hands and hearts with a skull pendant. A skirt is formed from snakes and two snakes arising from the neck meet to form a face. Down her back hang thirteen leather cords festooned with snails. According to tradition Coatlicue feeds off human corpses. She is also recognized as the patron deity of florists.

Coca-Mama
Goddess of the coca plant. South American Indian [Peru]. Minor goddess who oversees the harvest of the coca crop. Models of the deity were made from the leaves of the plant and kept for a year before being burned in a ritual to ensure a good coca harvest.

Cocidius
Hunting goddess. Celtic (British). Northern British deity depicted in stone relief at Risingham (Yorkshire).

Cocijo
Rain god. Zapotec (classical Mesoamerican) [Mexico]. Known to have been worshiped by the Monte Alban culture of Zapotec-speaking peoples in the Valley of Oaxaca.

Co(co)chimetl *(soporific)*
Minor god of merchants and commerce. Aztec (classical Mesoamerican) [Mexico]. One of the deities collectively classed as the Yacatecuhtli complex.

Col *(black one)*
Rain god. Nuer [Sudan]. He brings rain and thunderstorms. Souls of people killed by lightning have been described as *colwic*. Also Chol.

Colel Cab *(mistress of the earth)*
Chthonic earth goddess. Mayan (classical Mesoamerican) [Mexico]. This may be another title for the Ix Zacal Nok aspect of the goddess Chibirias.

Colop U Uichkin
(tears out the eye of the sun)
Sky god. Mayan (classical Mesoamerican) [Mexico]. Said to live in the midst of the sky, but with a night *avatara* of the same name who lives in the underworld land of the dead, Metnal, and who is the bringer of disease.

Condatis
River god. Celtic (British). Northern British deity with stone votive inscriptions located in County Durham.

Contrebis
Local god. Romano-Celtic (British). Identified from an inscription at Lancaster in conjunction with another deity, Ialonus.

Corus
God of wind. Roman. Specifically the deity responsible for the northwest winds.

COVENTINA
Origin Romano-Celtic (British). Tutelary and water goddess of uncertain affinities.

Known period of worship circa 200 BC until 500 AD or later.

Synonyms none known.

Center(s) of cult sacred spring near the Roman fort of Brocolitia [Carrawburgh] on Hadrian's Wall.

Art references monumental carvings and bas reliefs.

Literary sources monumental inscriptions.

Little is known of Coventina other than that she was a purely local British goddess of some importance. She is best observed from the period of the Roman occupation, at which time she shows a classical influence but is clearly Celtic in origin. On one bas relief found at Carrawburgh her name is associated with three nymphs holding vessels with issuing streams of water; on another she is pictured as a water nymph on a leaf, pouring water from a vessel. Her Carrawburgh sanctuary, which followed a simple, unroofed design similar to that of a small Romano-Celtic temple, was sited beside a well fed by a sacred spring and was associated with the Roman fort of Brocolitia. The well attests to a cult involving a ritual shaft and water, into which more than 13,000 Roman coins had been thrown dating to the reign of Gratian (407 AD), indicating Coventina's long-standing popularity. From the late period have been discovered incense burners to "Coventina Augusta."

In addition to money, pearls and pins were thrown into the well as votive offerings, the pins possibly implying a role in childbirth. Models of a dog (linked to the Greco-Roman physician Aesculapius) and a horse (a distinct fertility symbol) had also been deposited. Less significant and probably dumped when the temple was desecrated by Christians were a skull, altars and other carved stones. There is no evidence of connection with a severed head cult.

Coyolxauhqui *(golden bells)*
Astral goddess. Aztec (classical Mesoamerican) [Mexico]. A deification and incarnation *(avatara)* of the moon. According to tradition she is the half sister of the sun god Huitzilopochtli. The god sprang, fully armed, from his decapitated mother, Coatlicue, and engaged all his enemies who, by inference, are the 400 astral gods, his half brothers. He slew his sister and hurled her from the top of a mountain. Alternative tradition suggests his sister was an ally whom he was unable to save, so he decapitated her and threw her head into the sky, where she became the moon. She was represented in the Great Temple at Tenochtitlan, where she was depicted in front of successive Huitzilopochtli pyramids. She is also a hearth deity within the group classed as the Xiuhtecuhtli complex.

Cratos
God of strength. Greek. See Kratos.

Cum Hau
Chthonic god of death. Mayan (classical Mesoamerican) [Mexico]. One of several names for a death god listed in the codices.

Cunda
Goddess. Buddhist [eastern Bengal and Tibet]. An emanation of Vajrasattva or Vairocana. A female *bodhisattva* or *buddha*-designate. Also seen separately as a deification of literature, one of a group of twelve *dharanis*. She may stand upon a man. Color: white or green. Very large variety of attributes. Also Aryacunda.

Cunina
Minor goddess of infants. Roman. Responsible for guarding the cradle.

Cupid
See Amor.

Cybele
Mother goddess. Romanized name. See Kybele.

D

Dabog

Sun god. Slav [Balkans and southern Russia]. References found in inscriptions from Kiev. After Christianization he was reduced to a diabolic personality.

Dadimunda

Tutelary god. Singhalese Buddhist [Sri Lanka]. An attendant on the god Upulvan to whom he acted as treasurer. The guardian of Buddhism in Sri Lanka. His sacred animal is an elephant. Also Devata bandara.

Dagan (1)

Grain and fertility god. Mesopotamian (Babylonian-Akkadian). Generally linked with Anu in giving status to cities, e.g., the dedications by the ninth-century BC Assyrian king Assur-nasir-apli at Kalakh. Cult centers existed at Tuttul and Terqa.

Dagan (2)

Grain and fertility god. Western Semitic (Canaanite and Phoenician). The father of Baal in Ugaritic creation epics. A major sanctuary was built in his honor at Mari [Syria] and he was recognized in parts of Mesopotamia where he acquired the consort Šalaš. Worshipped mainly at Gaza and Ašdod, but also the supreme god of the Philistines. Known in biblical references as Dagon (Judges 16:23). Mentioned in the apocryphal Book of Maccabees. The cult is thought to have continued until circa 150 BC. Israelite misinterpretation of the Ugaritic root Dagan led to the assumption that he was a fish god, therefore attributes include a fish tail.

Dagan (3)

Local supreme god. Kafir [Afghanistan]. This god bears no relation to the Semitic god Dagan, but is known by several synonyms including Dagon, Doghan and Deogan. He has been identified in several villages in the south of the Kafir region [southern Nuristan]. "Dagan" may be less a proper name than a title of respect.

DAGDA (the good god)

Origin Celtic (Irish). Father of the tribe.

Known period of worship from prehistoric times until after Christianization circa 400 AD.

Synonyms Ruad ro-fhessa (lord of perfect knowledge); Eochaid Ollathair (all-father).

Center(s) of cult Tara, etc.

Art references possibly various stone carvings, Romano-Celtic and earlier.

Literary sources Books of Invasions; Cycles of Kings.

The Dagda is a strictly Irish tribal god not found among the Continental Celts. He is regarded in a general sense as the protector and benefactor of the people, not "good" in a moral sense but in a practical fashion—"good at anything." A father figure who led the deities of Ireland against the Fir Bolg in the First Battle of Moytura (see Tuatha de Danann). He has no exclusive roles, but in mythology enters a ritualized union with fertility goddesses including Morrigan and Boann. He is the father of Brigit and of Aengus Mac Oc (young god). Dagda is represented in literature as possessing immense strength and a prodigious appetite (see also Thor). Drawn by Christian writers as a boorish and grotesque character, which may be inaccurate, his weapon is a huge club that can slay nine men at a stroke and that was once drawn on a ceremonial cart. He owns a bronze "caldron of abundance" with magical properties of wisdom and rejuvenation, symbol of Irish prosperity. The Dagda may be the subject of a vast naked figure armed with a club cut in chalk at Cerne Abbas in Dorset, England, and probably created during the Romano-Celtic period.

Dagon
See Dagan (2).

Daikoku
God of luck. Shinto [Japan]. One of seven gods of fortune in Shintoism and often linked with the god Ebisu. Originally a god of kitchens, he became a deity concerned with happiness. He is depicted as a fat, well-to-do figure seated on two rice bales and carrying a sack on his back. He also holds a hammer in his right hand. In depictions there is often a mouse nibbling at one of the rice bales. Small gold icons of the god may be carried as talismans of wealth. According to tradition, when Daikoku's hammer is shaken, money falls out in great profusion. In western Japan he is also syncretized with the god of rice paddies, Ta-No-Kami, and thus becomes the god of agriculture and farmers. He may have developed from the Buddhist god Mahakala.

Daksa   *(skilled and able)*
Sun god. Hindu (Vedic and Puranic). The son of Brahma and Aditi, he is an *aditya* and demiurge. His consort is Prasuti, and he is said to have had up to sixty daughters. He appears in conflict with his son-in-law Siva as the main offender against Siva's consort Sati (accounted as one of his daughters), who was so insulted by Daksa that she committed suicide by jumping into a ritual fire. Siva took revenge by decapitating Daksa but later, after intercession from other gods, Brahma brought him back to life, giving him the substitute head of a sacrificial goat. Attribute: head of a goat. Also Prajapati.

Damgalnuna
Mother goddess. Mesopotamian (Sumerian and Babylonian-Akkadian). She first appears as a con-

sort of Enlil and, as Mesopotamian traditions progress, becomes associated with Ea and the mother of the Babylonian god Marduk. Also Damkina (Akkadian).

Damkina
Goddess. Mesopotamian (Babylonian-Akkadian). Consort of Ea. See Damgalnuna.

Danaparamita
Philosophical deity. Buddhist. One of twelve *paramita* deities and a spiritual offspring of Ratnasambhava. Color: reddish white. Attributes: an ear of rice and a banner with pearl.

DANU   *(1)*
Origin   Celtic (Irish). Founding goddess.

Known period of worship   prehistoric times until after Christianization circa 400 AD.

Synonyms   Anu; Don (Welsh).

Center(s) of cult   various sanctuaries.

Art references   none known.

Literary sources   *Books of Invasions; Cycles of Kings; History of Races* etc; *Mabinogion* (Welsh).

Danu is the leader and progenitress of the Irish pantheon, the Tuatha de Danann. Otherwise she is a remote and barely defined figure. She equates closely with the Welsh goddess Don and may have been perceived originally as a fertility and vegetation spirit.

Danu   *(2)*
Primordial goddess. Hindu (Vedic). The word Danu is used to describe the primeval waters and this deity is probably their embodiment. She is known as the mother of the demonic personality Vrtra, who engages in combat with, and is defeated by, the rain god Indra. In later Hinduism she is perceived as a daughter of Daksa and the consort of Kasyapa.

Daphne

Oracular goddess. Greek. A number of oracular shrines were dedicated to her in various places in Asia Minor, including Antiocheia, Mopsuestia (Cilicia), Sura and Patara (Lycia), Telmessos (Caria). Represented by the laurel *Daphne* she is linked with the *Daphnephoria* festivals honoring Apollo. Tradition has it that she was changed into the laurel to avoid sexual submission to the god.

Datin

God. Pre-Islamic northern Arabian. Frequently mentioned in inscriptions, but of uncertain function.

Daya *(compassion)*

Goddess. Hindu (Puranic) A *Sakti* of Acyuta (never falling), a minor aspect of the god Visnu.

Decima

Goddess of birth. Roman. Generally linked with the goddess Nona, she is responsible for watching over the criticial months of gestation. In later times the two were joined by the goddess of death, Morta, to form of trio of fate goddesses, the Parcae.

Dedwen

God of riches and incense. Nubian. Virtually unknown Egyptianized deity to whom sanctuaries were dedicated by Tuthmosis III and who may have brought gifts from southern regions. Usually found in anthropomorphic form but occasionally depicted as a lion. Also Dedun.

DEMETER *(mother)*

Origin Greek. Vegetation and mother goddess.

Known period of worship from circa 800 BC but probably earlier until Christianization (circa 400 AD).

Synonyms Damater (Dorian).

Center(s) of cult throughout Greek world including Agrigentum, Cnidos, Priene, Gela, Siris and Lokroi. Particularly at Eleusis.

Art references various sculptures; terra-cottas showing votary priestesses holding piglets.

Literary sources Hymn to Demeter and *Theogony* (Hesiod).

Demeter displays a complex personality that may be the result of syncretization in prehistoric times between a goddess of the grain and one of the underworld. By Homeric times Demeter was a goddess of vegetation and death. In ancient Athens the dead were titled *demetreioi* and grain was traditionally scattered on new graves. Demeter undergoes a yearly conflict with Hades and a search for her lost daughter, or arguably her alter ego, since the personality of the missing maiden goddess Persephone or Kore (girl) is virtually inextricable from that of Demeter.

The legends of Demeter and Persephone account for seasons of dearth and growth in the fields. Persephone, daughter of Demeter and Zeus, gathers flowers in a meadow surrounded by attendant Okeanides. As she picks one particular bloom the earth opens and the underworld god, Hades, abducts her. Demeter searches the world for her daughter and neglects its prosperity in so doing. The gods, seeing that catastrophe beckons, intervene and Hermes is sent to fetch the girl. There are conditions attached to her release, however, because she has tasted the pomegranate of Hades and is thus bound to the underworld. She may only enter the air above for nine months of the year. For the remaining three she must return and live as mistress of Hades.

One of the most reasonable interpretations of the legend is that the three months when Persephone or Kore is in absence represent the three dry summer months when vegetation in the Mediterranean region shrivels away and when traditionally the grain was stored in underground silos. When the rains come in autumn the youthful aspect of Demeter returns. There are strong parallels with Mesopotamian and Hittite-Hurrian legend (see Inana and Dumuzi; Hebat and Telepinu).

The Demeter cult was practiced in many places, often with a high degree of secrecy and with initiation rituals. Arguably the most famous cult center is Eleusis, where the legends provided a stimulus for the *Eleusinian Mysteries*. There also took place a women's festival of *Thesmophoria*, when pigs were buried alive in pits or *megara*. The sacrifice of young virgins to Demeter is reported but unsubstantiated.

Dena
Goddess. Persian [Iran]. The daughter of the god of light Ahura Mazda.

Deng
Sky god. Nuer and Dinka [Sudan]. Considered to be a foreign deity in the Nuer pantheon and a bringer of disease. His daughter is the moon goddess. In Dinka religion he is a storm and fertility god bringing lightning and rain.

Dercetius
Mountain god. Romano-Iberian.

Derceto
Mother goddess. Western Semitic (Phoenician). Derived from the Syrian model of Atargatis and worshiped locally.

Deva *(the god)*
Generic name of a god. Hindu (Vedic and Puranic). Originally, in the *Rg Veda*, thirty or thirty-three *devas* are indicated, divided into three groups of eleven. In later Hinduism, the term *deva* is generally applied to deities not included in the chief triad of Brahma, Visnu and Siva.

Devaki *(divine)*
Mother goddess. Hindu (Epic and Puranic). Daughter of Devaka and consort of the mythical king Vasudeva, Devaki bore eight sons, including Krsna and Balarama. Her brother Kamsa believed that the eighth child would kill him and he slaughtered the first six sons. In order to save the remaining two, Visnu implanted the "seed" of his *avataras* in Devaki's womb (in the form of hairs from his head), before transferring Balarama to the womb of the goddess Rohini and Krsna to Yasoda, the wife of a cowherd, Nanda.

Devananda *(delight of the gods)*
Goddess. Jain [India]. The mother of Mahavira.

Devapurohita
Astral god. Hindu (Puranic). An epithet for the planet god Jupiter.

Devasena *(heavenly host)*
Goddess. Hindu (Puranic). One of the consorts of Skanda who normally stands to his left. Attribute: lotus in the left hand.

Deverra
Minor goddess of birth. Roman. A guardian of newborn children. Symbolized by a broom used to sweep away evil influences.

Devi *(the goddess)*
Goddess epitomizing the active female principle. Hindu (Epic and Puranic). Devi evolved as a major goddess out of the older notion of mother and vegetation goddesses. She is seen more as an abstract principle who will nevertheless respond directly to worshipers' prayers. By the fifth century AD she appears in many forms as the active (feminine) aspect or power of male deities. General attributes: conch, hook, noose, prayer wheel and trident. Devi is also the generic name given to a female deity, in her capacity as the consort of a god or *deva*. See also Sri-Devi, Bhumidevi.

Dhanada
Goddess. Buddhist (Mahayana). One of the emanations of the *dhyanibuddha* Amoghasiddhi, also a form of the goddess Tara. She sits upon a moon throne with an unnamed animal in attendance. Color: green. Attributes: book, blue lotus, image of Amoghasiddhi, noose and rosary.

Dhanistha *(very rich)*
Minor goddess of misfortune. Hindu (Puranic). A malevolent *naksatra* or astral deity; daughter of Daksa and wife of Candra (Soma). Also Sravistha.

Dhanvantari *(traveling through an arc)*
Sun god. Hindu (Vedic, Epic and Puranic). In later tradition a minor incarnation or *avatara* of the god Visnu, also closely associated with medicine. In Vedic mythology Dhanvantari carried the ambrosia created from the primeval ocean of milk. He brought medical science to mankind. Only as the religion evolved did he become identified as an *avatara*. As Kantatman (Pradyumna), he is thought to be Kama reincarnated after his death at the hands of Siva. Various other epithets and existences are attributed to this deity. Offerings are due to him at dusk in the northeastern quarter. He is the guardian deity of hospitals, which are usually in the vicinity of a sanctuary of Visnu. Attributes: two bowls containing ambrosia. Also Kantatman.

Dhara *(supporting)*
Attendant god. Hindu (Puranic). One of a group of eight *vasu* deities answering to the god Indra. Attributes: lotus, plough, rosary and spear.

Dharani *(earth)*
1. Goddess. Hindu (Epic and Puranic). Consort of Parasurama and an *avatara* of the goddess Laksmi.
2. Collective name for a group of deities. Buddhist. Twelve personifications of a particular kind of short mystical religious text used as a charm. Also *dharini*.

DHARMA *(justice)*
Origin Hindu [India].

Known period of worship circa 300 AD until present.

Synonyms Dharme.

Center(s) of cult none specific.

Art references stone and metal sculptures.

Literary sources epic texts including *Ramayana* and *Mahabharata*; Puranic texts, but also see the *Rg Veda*.

The god of law who originates as a creator god and one of the sons of Brahma, but almost certainly derives from the *dharmas* or archetypal patterns of society identified in the *Rg Veda*. According to tradition he is the consort of thirteen daughters of Daksa and the father of Yudhisthra. Also regarded as a minor *avatara* of Visnu, appearing as a bull standing for the redemption of souls.

In Bengali tradition Dharme (probably of the same derivation) has been annually engaged in a sacred marriage to the earth at the time of year when a tree known as the *sal* is blossoming. Birds are sacrificed in a sacred grove after which the tribe repairs to the hut of the village *shaman* and the marriage is enacted between the priest and his wife, followed by a sexual free-for-all.

Dharmadhatuvagisvara
God of the law. Buddhist. A variety of Manjusri and therefore an emanation of Amitabha. Color: reddish-white. Attributes: arrow, bell, book, bow, hook, image of Amitabha on crown, staff, sword and water jar. Depicted with four heads and setting the law wheel in motion.

Dharmakirtisagaraghosa *(sound of the ocean of the glory of the law)*
Physician god. Buddhist-Lamaist [Tibet]. Accounted among one of a series of medicine *buddhas* known as a *sMan-bla* in Lamaism. Typically depicted with stretched earlobes. Color: red.

Dharmamegha *(cloud of the law)*
Minor goddess. Buddhist (Vajrayana). One of twelve deified *bhumis* recognized as different spiritual spheres through which a disciple passes. Color: blue. Attributes: book and staff.

Dharmapala
Collective name for a group of eight tutelary deities. Buddhist and particularly Lamaist [Tibet]. They wear royal apparel but are of terrible appearance and are considered to be the guardians of the law. General attributes: ax, cup, knife and snake.

Dharmapratisamvit *(analysis of nature)*
Goddess of nature analysis. Buddhist (Vajrayana). One of a group of four *pratisamvits*. Color: whitish-red. Attributes: noose and staff with crook.

Dharmavasita *(control of law)*
Minor goddess. Buddhist. One of a group of twelve *vasitas* personifying the disciplines of spiritual regeneration. Color: white. Attributes: water jar on a red lotus.

Dharti Mata
Mother goddess. Hindu (Puranic). A deity who appears late in Hinduism and equates with Prthivi or Bhumidevi. According to some authors she is the consort of Thakur Deo. Also Dhartri Mai, Darti Awwal.

Dhatar *(creator)*
Sun god. Hindu (Puranic). An original Vedic list of six descendants of the goddess Aditi or *adityas*, all of whom take the role of sun gods was, in later times, enlarged to twelve, including Dhatar. Color: golden. Attributes: two lotuses, lotus rosary and water jar. Also Dhatr.

Dhisana
Minor goddess of prosperity. Hindu (Vedic). Associated with the acquisition of wealth. Also the name given to a bowl of fermented drink or *soma*.

Dhrtarastra *(his empire is firm)*
Minor god. Buddhist. One of the *dikpalas* or guardians of the easterly direction. Color: white. Attribute: lute.

Dhrti *(firmness)*
Goddess. Jain [India]. A minor deity with no significant role or attributes.

Dhruva *(immovable)*
Astral god. Hindu (Epic and Puranic). The son of Uttanapada, a star in the constellation of Ursa Minor, which was the pole star in the last millennium BC. An *avatara* of Visnu. Also one of a group of *vasu* deities answering to the god Indra. In different context, the description of a kind of fixed icon. Attributes: prayer wheel, rosary, spear and water jar.

Dhumavati *(smoky)*
Goddess. Hindu (Epic and Puranic). One of a group of ten *mahavidyas* personifying the *Sakti* of Siva. Aspects include Darunaratri (night of frustration), who is also regarded as one of the personifications of the goddess Sakti.

Dhumorna *(smoke)*
Goddess. Hindu (Epic and Puranic). The consort of Yama. Attribute: a pomegranate.

Dhumravati
Terrible goddess. Hindu (Puranic). Attributes: skull in the hand and garland of skulls, sword and tusks.

Dhupa *(incense)*
Mother goddess. Buddhist-Lamaist [Tibet]. One of the *astamatara* mothers. Color: yellow. Attribute: a censer.

Dhupatara *(incense-Tara)*
Minor goddess. Buddhist (Mahayana). Color: black. Attribute: a censer.

Dhurjati *(with matted hair)*
God. Hindu (Epic and Puranic). A manifestation of Siva in which his body is smeared with ash.

Dhvajagrakeyura *(ring on a banner)*
Goddess. Buddhist (Mahayana). An emanation of Aksobhya. She sits on a sun throne. Color: dark blue, black or yellow. Attributes: club, image of Aksobhya, noose, pestle, prayer wheel, staff, sword, tiger skin and trident. Three-headed and three-eyed.

Dhvajosnisa
God. Buddhist. An *usnisa* deity apparently connected with the guardian deities or *dikpalas* in the southwestern quarter. Color: reddish-blue. Attributes: banner with jewel.

Dhyanaparamita   *(perfection in meditation)*

Philosophical deity. Buddhist. A *paramita* and spiritual offspring of Ratnasambhava. Color: darkish sky blue. Attributes: banner with jewel and white lotus.

Dhyanibuddha

General name of a spiritual or meditation *buddha*. Buddhist (Vajrayana). An emanation of the Adibuddha and generally regarded as one of a group of five representing the cosmic elements. The mystic counterpart of a human *buddha*. When the five are represented as a group, their common attribute is a staff on a lotus.

Dhyanibuddhasakti

Collective name for a group of goddesses. Buddhist. The five *Saktis* of the *dhyanibuddhas*. Common attributes include a cup and knife.

Diana

Moon goddess. Roman. Living in the forests, she is a huntress and protector of animals, also the guardian of virginity. Generally modeled on the Greek goddess Artemis, she had a sanctuary on the Aventine Hill in Rome and, under Roman rule, took over the Temple of Artemis at Ephesus.

DIANCECHT

Origin   Celtic (Irish). Physician god.

Known period of worship   prehistoric times until Christianization circa 400 AD.

Synonyms   none known.

Center(s) of cult   none specifically known.

Art references   monumental carvings and reliefs.

Literary sources   *Books of Invasions*; *Cycles of Kings*.

A god of whom limited description is given but who was clearly one of the more important members of the Tuatha De Danann band of Celtic deities in Ireland. Said to be the grandfather of Lug. He possesses the skills to make every warrior whole again and is referred to as having made a silver arm for the god Nuadu who was injured in the legendary Battle of Moytura and who subsequently took the epithet Nuadu *argatlam* (Nuada of the silver arm). Mortally wounded Tuatha were bathed and revived in Diancecht's sacred well, Slane.

Diang

Cow goddess. Shilluk [Sudan]. Living along the west bank of the Nile, the Shilluk perceive Diang as the consort of the first human, Omara, sent by the creator god. Her son is Okwa, who married the crocodile goddess Nyakaya. Thus the three main elements of Shilluk life are contained in their religious beginnings—men (sky), cows (earth) and crocodiles (water).

Dictynna

Mother goddess. Cretan. She became syncretized with the Greek goddess Rhea.

Didi Thakrun

Plague goddess. Hindu [northern India]. Associated with cholera. Worshipped locally at Bardvan.

Dievs

Sky god. Pre-Christian Latvian. He is depicted in the guise of a gentleman farmer wearing cap and sword and mounted on a horse or driving a cart. Tradition has it that he first set free the sun.

Digambara   *(naked)*

Goddess. Buddhist-Lamaist [Tibet]. The *Sakti* of Yogambara. Attribute: a bowl.

NOTE: Digambara is also an epithet of the goddess Kali in Hindu religion.

Dike

Goddess of justice. Greek. The daughter of Zeus. Depicted as a maiden whom men violently abuse in the streets but who is honored by the gods and who reports to her father on the misdeeds of mankind, causing divine retribution. She is depicted on the Kypselos chest as an attractive woman strangling an ugly goddess of injustice, Adikia.

Dikkumara
God. Jain [India]. One of the groups under the general title of *bhavanavasi* (dwelling in places). They have youthful appearance and are associated with rain and thunder.

Diksa   *(initiation)*
Goddess. Hindu (Epic and Puranic). The consort of Ugra and mother of Santana. Also the name of the Buddhist Tantric initiation ceremony.

DIONYSOS
Origin   Greek. God of wine and intoxication.

Known period of worship   from circa 1500 BC and probably earlier through to Christianization circa 400 AD.

Synonyms   Deunysos; Zonnysos; Liber, Bacchus (Roman).

Center(s) of cult   Pylos; Ayia Irini (Keos).

Art references   chiefly Attic wine amphorae circa sixth century BC.

Literary sources   *Hymn to Dionysos* (fragmentary—Homer); *Catalogues* (Hesiod).

Dionysos is a deity associated with a curious form of mass, intoxicated frenzy encouraged by festivals of wine drinking. He has a retinue of male, phallic satyrs wearing animal masks and joined by female maenads. Although a gigantic phallus was carried in rituals honoring Dionysos, he is not a fertility god and the phallic symbolism is purely that of sexual arousal and carousing. Dionysos is the son of Semele and there is some argument that the cult originated in Phrygia or Lydia linked to that of Kybele and traveled via Mycenaean culture with sanctuaries in such places as Pylos and Keos. Greek women traditionally searched for Dionysos and it is possible that the Roman name Bacchus is of Semitic origin, meaning wailing (see Tammuz). Other authors have suggested that the personality of Dionysos emerged from Thrace and extended to Homeric Greece but this argument is now out of favor. Other than in the opening of the Homeric epic material, Dionysos scarcely appears in literature.

There was a major wine-drinking festival (Ionic-Attic) known as the *Anthesteria*, Greater and Lesser *Dionysia* festivals with strongly phallic connotations and the sacrifice of goats, an *Agrionia* festival (Dorian-Aeolic) and most recently the Athenian celebration of *Katagogia*, which marked the legend of Dionysos emerging from the sea and during which a ship was carried or drawn on wheels.

Dioskouroi
Twin gods. Greek (see Kastor and Polydeukes).

Dipa   *(personification of the oil lamp)*
Goddess of light. Buddhist-Lamaist [Tibet]. Considered to be among the group of *astamataras* (mothers). Color: blue or red. Attribute: a lamp.

Dipa Tara   *(lamp Tara)*
Minor goddess. Buddhist (Mahayana). Color: yellow. Attribute: a torch.

Dipankara   *(light causer)*
Deity. Buddhist-Lamaist [Tibet]. One of a minor group of *buddhas*. Color: yellow. Attributes: none in particular.

Dipti   *(brightness)*
Minor goddess. Hindu (Puranic). No details available.

Dirghadevi   *(long goddess)*
Goddess. Hindu (Epic and Puranic). Consort of the god Nirrti.

Dis Pater
Chthonic underworld god. Roman. Modeled on the Greek god Hades.

Disa   *(the ten directions of space)*
Goddess. Hindu (Epic and Puranic). Consort of Siva in his terrible aspect of Bhima and mother of the minor god Sarga (creation).

DISANI

Origin Kafir [Afghanistan—southern Hindukush]. Supreme fertility and mother goddess.

Known period of worship origins uncertain and still persisting in parts today.

Synonyms Disni (Prasun region); Dizeile.

Center(s) of cult throughout the Kafir region, particularly at the village of Shtiwe (Prasun).

Art references large wooden sculptures.

Literary sources Robertson G.S. *The Kafirs of the Hindukush* (1896); Morgenstierne G. *Some Kati Myths and Hymns* (1951).

Disani is the most important goddess of the Hindukush, particularly revered by the Prasun people. Legend has it that she emerged from the right breast of the creator god Imra. Alternatively she emerged as a golden tree from a sacred lake into which a sun disc had fallen. Other legends place her as the daughter of the god Sudrem, or of Indr and the goddess Nangi-Wutr. She is the consort of Imra and other major deities in the pantheon and therefore bears strong fertility and maternal connotations. She has a son, Baghist, conceived when she was raped by a demon. She also plays the role of huntress. Her home is said to be Sudrem.

Disani is also a benign and comforting goddess of death who carries the deceased into the House of the Great Mother. She is perceived in human form, armed with a bow and quiver, with streams of milk pouring from her breasts. She can appear as a wild goat from whose footprints spring the shoots of wheat, and symbolically as a tree (see Inana) whose roots embody the underworld goddess Nirmali. Her cult centers seem to have been connected with the villages of Shtiwe, Bagramatal and Kamdesh.

As goddess of death, Disani receives the prayers of women whose menfolk are about to go into combat. Legend has it that she lives in a golden fortress with seven doors and seven roads radiating from it. As a fertility goddess she is a guardian of cattle. In her role as vegetation deity, she tills the land. She also sows, threshes and winnows grain.

Sacrifice is in the form of a goat, or more usually milk, butter and cheese.

Disani is the protectress of the bonds of kinship and family loyalty. In conflict with this role she also inadvertently slaughtered her own son by decapitation, which gave rise to an annual spring rite of the dying god, witnessed in the religions of many other agricultural and pastoral societies.

Disciplina

Minor goddess. Roman. Significant in the legions, known particularly from the second century BC.

Discordia

Minor goddess of dissent. Roman. Modeled on the Greek deity Eris.

Disir

Collective name for guardian goddesses. Nordic (Icelandic) and Germanic. They were the subject of a sacrificial ritual in autumn and have strong fertility connotations as vegetation and fertility deities. They are identified in the *Sigrdrifumal* (Poetic Edda) and include the Valkyries and Norns of Germanic mythology.

Diti

Goddess. Hindu (Vedic, Epic and Puranic). The daughter of Daksa, a consort of Aditi (in the *Rg Veda*) or Kasyapa and the mother of a race of demons. Attributes: blue lotus, child and fruit. See also Aditi.

Divona

Fertility goddess. Celtic (Gallic). Associated with water and known only from inscriptions.

Djila'qons

Sea goddess. Haida Indian [Queen Charlotte Island, Canada]. An old woman who lives at the head of a major inlet in Haida territory and controls all the creatures of the sea.

Dogumrik

Local guardian and warrior god. Kafir [Afghanistan]. Known from the village of Shtiwe in the southeastern Hindukush, Dogumrik is the herdsman to the daughters of the god Imra and possibly a localized equivalent of the god Mon.

Dolichenus

Weather god. Western Semitic (Syrian). Depicted bearded and standing upon a bull. Attributes include a double ax and lightning. He became syncretized with the Roman god Jupiter.

Dombi

Goddess of terrifying appearance. Buddhist. One of a group of *gauri*. Color: red or blue. Attribute: a banner.

Don

Mother goddess. Celtic (Welsh). Described in the *Mabinogion* as the progenitress of the Welsh pantheon. Equates with the Irish goddess Danu.

Donar

Storm god. Germanic. The god of thunder whose symbol is either a hammer or an ax. The day name Donnerstag in modern German equates with Thursday, a corruption of Thor's day. See also Thor.

Dongo

Storm god. Songhai [Niger valley, West Africa]. The creator of thunderbolts, which are perceived as stone ax heads. As the celestial smith he forges lightning and strikes a huge bell with his ax to generate thunder.

Donn

Chthonic underworld god. Celtic (Irish). According to legend, he lives on an island southwest of Munster and is responsible for the passage of the dead toward the otherworld.

Doris

Sea goddess. Greek. Daughter of Okeanos and Tethys and consort of Nereus. In Hesiod's *Theog-* *ony* her children include Amphitrite and Thetis among many minor figures.

Doudoun

God of Nile cataracts. Nubian. Depicted as an antelope with twisted horns. His consorts are Sati and Anuket. Modeled on the Egyptian ram god Khnum. Also Dodonu.

Dsahadoldza *(fringe mouth)*

Chthonic god of earth and water. Navaho [USA]. A number of deities are known under this title. The priest impersonating the god has one side of his body painted red and the other side black. He wears a buckskin mask painted with a horizontal yellow band to represent the evening sky and eight vertical black stripes to represent rain.

Duillae

Fertility and vegetation goddesses. Romano-Iberian. Comparable with the *matres* in Gaul.

Dulha Deo

Minor god of the bridegroom. Hindu. Attribute: an ax hanging from a tree.

DUMUZI

Origin Mesopotamian (Sumerian and Babylonian-Akkadian) [Iraq]. Shepherd and vegetation god; underworld god.

Known period of worship circa 3500 BC or earlier to circa ₁00 BC.

Synonyms Damu; Ama-usum-gal-ana; Tammuz (Hebrew).

Center(s) of cult none.

Art references plaques; votive stelae; glyptics, etc.

Literary sources cuneiform texts including the *Inana's Descent and the Death of Dumuzi*.

Dumuzi, as popularly understood, is a male deity who in mythical times was the tutelary god of the city of Bad-tibira between Lagaš and Uruk in southern Mesopotamia. It is believed that there was also a goddess Dumuzi from Kinunir near Lagaš. The two became syncretized as the single male personality who occupies a special place in the Sumerian pantheon as the consort of the goddess Inana. He is the first "dying-and-rising" god to be historically recorded by name.

Dumuzi is particularly associated with the date palm. He is commanded by Inana (who is herself under a pledge to the goddess Ereškigal) to enter the underworld for a period of each year, which accounts for the seasonal demise of the green world to drought.

His worshipers were chiefly women but his cult was very widespread and as late as biblical times there are references to women "weeping for Tammuz." It may be argued that Dumuzi is the model on which later gods including Adonis are modeled. In Syriac tradition he is the son of the mortal father Kautar (Aramaic: Košar).

Dur

Chthonic underworld god. Kassite [Iran]. Equates with the Babylonian-Akkadian god Nergal.

Durangama *(going far away)*

Minor goddess. Buddhist (Vajrayana). One of several deified *bhumis* recognized as different spiritual spheres through which a disciple passes. Color: green. Attributes: staff on a great lotus.

DURGA

Origin Hindu (Puranic) [India]. Vengeful warrior goddess.

Known period of worship circa 400 AD (but probably known from earlier times) until present.

Synonyms Kumari; Shakti; Agni-Durga (eight-armed); Aparajita (unconquered).

Center(s) of cult none.

Art references sculptures generally bronze but also stone. Reliefs.

Literary sources chiefly *Ramayana* and *Mahabharata* epics and Puranic texts, but mentioned by name in Vedic literature.

Durga is one of the angry and aggressive aspects of the goddess Sakti, whose earliest role in Hindu mythology is to fight and conquer demons but who also personifies the *Sakti* or female aspect of any male deity. Iconographically, Durga is depicted as a beautiful golden-skinned woman who rides upon a lion or a tiger. She has eight or ten arms, each bearing a weapon presented to her by different gods and including the conch shell of Visnu, the trident of Siva, the bow of Rama and the *sudarshan* (spoked disc) of Krsna. These gifts extend to her the power of the eight or ten gods. She may wear a necklace of skulls. She is associated with the Himalaya and Vindhya mountains and is often depicted slaughtering the buffalo-demon Mahisa by thrusting her trident into his body.

In a contrasting aspect in later Hindu traditions, Durga takes the role of a mother goddess and consort of Siva and becomes partly syncretized with Parvati. She is also linked with the fertility of crops. In this capacity her most important festival is the *Durga Puja*, celebrated at harvest time, during which devotees persistently make obscene gestures and comments to stimulate her fecundity. She is depicted flanked by four other deities, Laksmi, Sarasvati, Ganesa and Karttikeya, who are said to be her children.

In general Durga is perceived in northern India as the gentle bride epitomizing family unity, while in southern India she is revered more in her warlike and murderous aspect.

Durjaya *(unconquerable)*

Minor goddess. Buddhist (Mahayana). An attendant of the god Buddhakapala.

Dušara *("the one" of šara)*

Local tutelary god. Western Semitic (Nabataean). Associated with vegetation and fertility in the Hauran region from about 312 BC until circa 500 AD. Regarded as a supreme deity, comparable to Baal Šamin, who never achieved Dušara's popularity among the nomadic Nabataeans, for whom farming was precarious. He was represented by a black obelisk at Petra. Sacred animals are the eagle and panther. Attributes include a vine stem. In Hellenic times he was the subject of inscriptions at Delos and Miletus and he was equated with Dionysos. Also Dušares; Dus-Šara.

Duzhi
Local god of uncertain affinities. Kafir [Afghanistan]. Known only from an altar stone that was generally erected beside that of the water god Bagisht. Sacrifice was in the form of a male goat.

Dvipakumara
God. Jain [India]. One of the groups under the general title of *bhavanavasi* (dwelling in places). They are of youthful appearance and associated with rain and thunder.

DYAUS PITAR   *(heaven father)*
Origin   Hindu (Vedic) [India]. Creator god.

Known period of worship   circa 1500 BC or earlier until present.

Synonyms   the Sanskrit *dyaus* is derived from the Indo-European root that also gives Deus (Roman); Zeus (Greek); Tyr (German), etc.

Center(s) of cult   none specific.

Art references   none.

Literary sources   *Rg-Veda* and other Vedic texts.

Dyaus Pitar is a creator god associated with the goddess Prthivi; the primordial couple are normally addressed as Dyavaprthivi. Between them they created the rest of the Vedic pantheon, placed heaven and earth in conjunction with one another and generally preserved the cosmic order. Dyaus is overshadowed and superseded by the rain god Indra in later Hindu tradition, possibly because he was brought into India by the Aryan settlers from the north who had been used to a cold, bleak climate and who needed a supreme deity more relevant to a hot, dry environment.

Dzivaguru
Chthonic mother goddess. Korekore (Shona) [northern Zimbabwe, southern Africa]. Originally said to have ruled both heaven and earth and lived in a palace by a sacred lake near Dande. She is depicted wearing goatskins and bearing a cornucopia holding magical substances. Her sacred creatures are mythical golden sunbirds, probably modeled on swallows, a pair of which were actually discovered in Zimbabwe.

E

E Alom   *(conceiver of children)*
Primeval creator goddess. Mayan (Quiche, classical Mesoamerican) [Guatemalan highlands]. The consort of E Quaholom, identified in the sacred Maya book, the *Popol Vuh*. Her son is Gukumatz, the counterpart of the Aztec god Quetzalcoatl. Also Bitol.

E Quaholom   *(begetter of children)*
Primeval creator god. Mayan (Quiche, classical Mesoamerican) [Guatemalan highlands]. Identified in the sacred Maya book the *Popol Vuh*. The consort of the goddess E Alom and the father of Gukumatz who equates with the Aztec Quetzalcoatl. Also Tzacol.

EA
Origin Mesopotamian   (Babylonian-Akkadian) [Iraq]. God of primordial waters.

Known period of worship circa 1900 BC to circa 200 BC.

Synonyms Ea-šarru; Enki (Sumerian).

Center(s) of cult Eridu, Babylon.

Art references glyptics and other carvings.

Literary sources cuneiform texts including *Enuma Eliš, Epic Of Gilgameš, Nergal and Ereškigal* etc.

One of the major deities in the old Babylonian-Akkadian pantheon who evolved from the model of Enki. God of sweet water and of wisdom. His consort is Damkina and his temple is the Apsu house or *E-engurra* in Eridu (lost). By the neo-Babylonian period his popularity as a major deity had waned and he was relegated to the role of father of the god Marduk.

Eacus
Weather god. Romano-Iberian. Known from the area of Castille and syncretized with the local Roman deity Jupiter Solutorius.

Ebisu
God of luck. Shinto [Japan]. The most popular of seven gods of fortune recognized in Shintoism and frequently linked with the god Daikoku. He is also the most controversial deity in the pantheon. He is depicted as a fat, smiling and bearded fisherman holding a fishing rod in one hand and a sea bream in the other. The name does not appear in the classical sacred texts *Nihongi* and *Kojiki*, but Ebisu is known to have been worshiped in ancient times among fishermen. From about the sixteenth century his character changed and he became a deity associated with profit. Thus he is a patron of commerce and his picture hangs in most establishments. He is perhaps syncretized with the gods Hiru-Ko and Koto-Shiro-Nushi. He may also be identified with Fudo, the god of knowledge. By tradition he does not join the rest of the Shinto pantheon in the great October festival at Izumo (a southern coastal town on Honshu) because he is deaf. His festival is celebrated concurrently in his own temple.

Edeke
God of disasters. Teso [Uganda, East Africa]. The antagonist of the creator god Apap, Edeke is propitiated during times of famine and plague.

Edusa
Minor god of infants. Roman. Responsible for the proper nourishment of the child.

Eee-A-O *(Yao)*
Primordial being. Gnostic Christian. The first of the androgynous principles born to Yaldabaoth, the prime parent, ruling the seven heavens of chaos in gnostic mythology.

Egeria
Fertility goddess. Roman. Deity of oak trees whose priestess enacted an annual sacred marriage with the king of Rome, who took the part of Jupiter. The festival is a variation of that celebrating the marriage of Zeus and Hera that took place in Athens. A number of springs and lakes were sacred to her.

Egres
Fertility god. Karelian [Finland]. The deity responsible for the turnip crop. Also Akras.

Ehecatl
Creator god. Aztec (classical Mesoamerican) [Mexico]. The sun deity representing the second of the five world ages, each of which lasted for 2028 heavenly years, each heavenly year being fifty-two terrestrial years. Assigned to the air or wind and presided over by Quetzalcoatl, to whose complex of deities he belongs. According to tradition, the age ended in a cataclysmic destruction caused by hurricanes. All humanity turned into monkeys. Illustrated by the "Stone of the Four Suns" [Yale Peabody Museum]. Also (4)Ehecatl; Ehecatonatiuh.

Ehecatl-Quetzalcoatl
Primordial god. Aztec (classical Mesoamerican) [Mexico]. A syncretization of Ehecatl and Quetzalcoatl, one of four gods who support the lowest heaven at each cardinal point. He is perceived as residing in the west (codices *Borgia* and *Vaticanus B*). He is the deity who rules over the ninth of the thirteen heavens, Itztapal Nanatzcayan (where the stone slabs crash together). In a separate tradition, Ehecatl-Quetzalcoatl executed the monstrous god Xolotl when he declined to offer his blood in self-sacrifice for the creation of mankind.

EILEITHYIA *(the coming)*
Origin Greek and previously Mycenaean. Goddess of birth.

Known period of worship circa 1500 BC until Christianization (circa 400 AD).

Synonyms Eleuthyia (possibly original Minoan); Ilithyia (Roman).

Center(s) of cult chiefly in Crete where there exists an early (Mycenaean) cave sanctuary at Amnisos, and in the region of Lakonia.

Art references sculptures and reliefs.

Literary sources *Theogony* and *Hymn to Apollo* (Hesiod).

Primarily worshiped by women, Eileithyia is called upon specifically to ease the pain and danger of childbirth. It was said that the cries of labor summoned her presence. The daughter of Zeus and Hera and the sibling of Hebe and Ares, she assisted at the birth of Apollo. Her role is later largely superseded by Artemis. The name is also used in a plural collective sense (reflecting the practice of women in a neighborhood coming together to assist at childbirth). A tablet from Knossos records: "Amnisos, for Eleuthia, one amphora of honey." The cave at Amnisos, near Knossos, has a sacred stalagmite surrounded by a wall and involving an altar. In Sparta there was allegedly a running track at the end of which was a temple to Eileithyia.

Eirene
Goddess of peace. Greek. The daughter of Zeus and Themis and the sister of Horae, Dike and Eunomia.

Eji Ogbe
Tutelary god. Yoruba [Nigeria, West Africa]. The so-called "king" of the pantheon and mentioned in a legend of the dove, which is a symbol of prosperity.

Ek Chuah

God of merchants. Mayan (classical Mesoamerican) [Mexico]. Also the deity responsible for the cacao crop. (The cacao bean was traditionally the standard currency throughout Mesoamerica.) Probably of Putun origin, he is typically depicted painted black, except for a red area around the lips and chin. He has a distinctive downwardly projecting lower lip, horseshoe shapes around each eye and a highly elongated nose. He may also bear a scorpion's tail. Other attributes include a carrying strap in his headdress and sometimes a pack on his back. Also God M.

Ekadasarudra

Collective name for a group of gods. Hindu. The eleven forms of the god Rudra, each typically represented with sixteen arms. Common attributes include ax, moon disc and tiger skin.

Ekajata   *(she who has but one chignon)*

Goddess of good fortune. Buddhist (Varjayana). She offers happinesss and removes personal obstacles. Occasionally found attending the goddess Khadirayani-Tara. She is an emanation of Aksobhya and a form of Tara. She may have one or twelve heads. Color: blue. Attributes: arrow, ax, bell, blue lotus, book, bow, conch, cup, hook, image of Amitabha on the crown, knife, noose, skull, staff, sword and tiger skin. Three-eyed.

Ekanetra   *(one-eyed)*

Minor deity. Hindu (Epic and Puranic). One of a group of emancipated *vidyesvaras* (lords of knowledge) considered to be aspects of Siva. Virtually identical with Ekarudra, but with a single eye.

Ekarudra

Minor deity. Hindu (Epic and Puranic). One of a group of emancipated *vidyesvaras* (lords of knowledge) considered to be aspects of Siva. Virtually identical with Ekanetra, but with normal eyes.

EL

Origin   Western Semitic regions and Israel (northern Hebrew tribes) [Syria, Lebanon and Israel]. Creator god.

Known period of worship   circa 2500 BC to 700 BC.

Synonyms   *el elyon* (most high god); *el sadday* (god of the mountain); *el olam* (everlasting god); *el betel* (god of storms), Il [southern Arabian].

Center(s) of cult   Tirzah, Šamaria, Bethel, Dan and many local hill shrines.

Art references   none extant other than from later artists.

Literary sources   *Vetus Testamentum*; Qum' Ran texts.

Modeled on the creator god of the Canaanites, Il, represented by the bull and revered by the Hebrew tribes who settled northern Palestine. According to some Ugaritic (Ras Šamra) texts, not the original creator but the offspring of an older principal, El'eb (god of the father). In biblical texts the word *el* comes to be used in a descriptive sense as a qualifying epithet meaning "lord." Possibly El came to represent the sum of all the creator spirits of the northern tribes. Israel was unwilling to part with the name against pressure from the southern state of Judah (see Yhwh), but the name fell into disuse after suppression of Israel by Tiglathpileser II (Assyria). The Hebrew term *elohim* may denote an "upper tier" of great gods while *elim* applies to a lower order of deities.

NOTE Biblical traditions were carried by the southern state of Judah. The impression is given that El is a distant, vaguely defined figure perceived in human form—"he" is able to see, hear, walk and touch—though no images in human form seem to have been created. El was apparently symbolized in Israel from circa 922 BC again by the bull calf (I Kings 12), probably emulating the Canaanite precedent. As with the attributes of the Canaanite god Baal, the voice of El is said to be like thunder, the clouds are his chariot and he waters the mountains from heaven.

Elagabal   *(lord of the mountain)*

Local tutelary god. Syrian. Probably originating as a mountain deity with strong solar links. His sacred animal is the eagle. His cult was based on the town of Emesa [Homs], where he was worshiped in the form of a dome-shaped, black stone obelisk. His name became Hellenized as Heliogabalos.

El'eb

Primordial god. Western Semitic (Canaanite). In some texts the god El (Il) is not the original being but is preceded by a father figure. El'Eb translates as "god the father." See also Yaldabaoth.

Elim

Collective term for gods. Judaic. Found in the *Vetus Testamentum* and distinguishing the lower order of gods from the great deities, *elohim*.

Elkunirsa

Creator god. Western Semitic (Canaanite) and Hittite. Allegedly borrowed and modified from the Canaanite god Il. His consort is Ašerdus (Canaanite: Ašertu).

Ellaman   *(lady of the boundary)*

Goddess of passage. Hindu-Dravidian (Tamil) [southern India]. A goddess guarding boundaries of villages and fields. One of the *navasakti* or astral deities. Also Ellaiyamman.

Ellel

Creator god. Hittite and Hurrian. Derived from the Babylonian-Akkadian god Ellil.

Ellil

Creator god. Mesopotamian (Babylonian-Akkadian). See Enlil.

Eloai

Primordial being. Gnostic Christian. The second of the androgynous principles born to Yaldabaoth, the prime parent, ruling the seven heavens of chaos in Gnostic mythology.

Elohim

Collective term for gods. Judaic. Found in the *Vetus Testamentum* and distinguishing the higher order of great gods from the minor deities, *elim*. Also applied to the Israelite god Yhwh.

Emeli Hin

Creator god. Tuareg [central Sudan]. A generic title meaning "my lord."

Eme'mqut

Animistic spirit. Siberian Koryak. See Quikinn.a'qu.

Emeš

Vegetation god. Mesopotamian (Sumerian). Emeš was created at the wish of Enlil to take responsibility on earth for woods, fields, sheepfolds and stables. He is identified with the abundance of the earth and with summer. An unidentified deity who is depicted iconographically with a plough may well be Emeš.

Enbilulu

River god. Mesopotamian (Sumerian and Babylonian-Akkadian). In creation mythology he is placed in charge of the sacred rivers Tigris and Euphrates by the god Enki. He is also god of canals, irrigation and farming. In Babylonian times he becomes the son of Ea and is syncretized with Adad.

Endouellicus

Chthonic oracular and healing god. Romano-Iberian. Known from the Portuguese region. Probably the recipient of pig sacrifice.

Endursaga   *(lofty mace)*

Herald god. Mesopotamian (Sumerian). He leads the Sumerian pantheon particularly in times of conflict. Also Išum (Akkadian).

ENKI   *(lord of the soul)*

Origin Mesopotamian (Sumerian) [Iraq]. Creator god; god of wisdom; god of sweet water.

Known period of worship circa 3500 BC to circa 1750 BC.

Synonyms Ea (god of the deep, Akkadian); Lugal-id(ak) (owner of the river); Lugal-abzu(ak) (owner of the deeps); Nudimmud (image fashioner).

Center(s) of worship probably at Eridu (Abu Šahrain), but known only from literature.

Art references plaques, votive stelae, glyptics.

Literary sources creation epics including *Atrahasis*, *Enki and the World Order*, temple hymns etc.

As god of water in its capacity to nourish the earth, Enki is one of the major Sumerian deities. The son of An and Nammu, he is considered by some to be a late entry to the pantheon. His consort is Damkina and his sanctuary at Eridu is *E-engurra*. He is usually represented as a figure in typical horned headdress and tiered skirt with two streams of water (Tigris and Euphrates) springing from his shoulders or from a vase and including leaping fish. He may also hold the eagle-like Imdugud (thunder) bird, thus signifying clouds rising from the waters. His foot may rest on an ibex. Amongst his offspring are Ašalluha, Nin-sar (by Ninhursaĝa), Nin-imma (by Ninkurra) and Uttu (by Ninmah).

Enki is a complex and, at times, Machiavellian character. The running of day-to-day affairs is left to him and in the creation mythology he organized the earth and established law and order. He is also seen in a heroic light, having been one of three principal deities engaged in the primordial battle between good and evil, the latter personified in the dragon Kur. In the Sumerian creation epic Enki set out in a boat to avenge the abduction by Kur of the goddess Ereškigal. Kur fought back with huge stones.

Enki is perceived to fill the Tigris and Euphrates with sacred sweet water. He also appoints various other minor deities to their duties in connection with the well-being of the natural world. Additionally he is god of artists and craftsmen.

According to one legend, Enki generated the plants from his semen and inside his body until it made him ill, whereupon Ninhursaĝa placed him in her own vagina and gave birth to his progeny. Inana, Ninhursaĝa and Enlil are variously drawn, at times, as serious adversaries.

Enkimdu

God of canals and ditches. Mesopotamian (Sumerian). In creation mythology he is given his task by the god Enki. See also Enbilulu.

ENLIL *(lord wind?)*

Origin Mesopotamian (Sumerian) [Iraq]. God of the air.

Known period of worship circa 3500 BC or earlier to circa 1750 BC.

Synonyms Ellil; Illil; Ilu; Nunamnir.

Center(s) of cult Nippur, Dur Kurigalzu, but also at Eridu and Ur.

Art references plaques, votive stelae and glyptics.

Literary sources creation texts, particularly the *Lament of Ur* and *Creation of the Hoe*; temple hymns including the *Hymn to Enlil*, etc.

Enlil is the son of the primordial An and Ki. The tutelary deity of Nippur where, in his honor, the *Ekur* sanctuary was built (not rediscovered), he was the most important god of southern Mesopotamia during the third millennium BC. His consort is Ninlil who was impregnated by the "waters of Enlil" to create the moon god Nanna. (In the Akkadian pantheon his consort becomes Mulliltu.) He is depicted in horned headdress and tiered skirt, or by a horned crown on a pedestal. According to the "Hymn to Enlil" he works alone and unaided. He is said to have made the pickax, "caused the good day to come forth" and "brought forth seed from the earth." He was invoked to bless his cities and ensure prosperity and abundance. His importance was such that the tutelary gods of other cities "traveled" to Nippur with offerings to Enlil. Enlil created several deities concerned with overseeing the natural world. In his more destructive aspect he allowed the birth goddess to kill at birth and was responsible for miscarriage in cows and ewes. He was seen as manifesting himself in both benevolence and destructive violence. Because of his peculiarly national status he became downgraded in the Babylonian and Assyrian pantheons, being superseded respectively by Marduk and Assur.

Enmesarra

Chthonic god of the law. Mesopotamian (Sumerian and Babylonian-Akkadian). According to texts he controls the *me's* or divine rules.

Ennead

The Heliopolis pantheon. Egyptian (Lower). The nine major deities enumerated and given their genealogy by the priesthood of Heliopolis, the center of the sun-worshiping cult in Lower Egypt. Comprising the sun god Atum (or Atum-Re) and his offspring, Šu, Tefnut, Geb, Nut, Osiris, Isis, Seth and Nephthys. Other Egyptian cult centers possessed similar pantheons though not necessarily including the same list of deities. Thus, for example, the god Ptah presided at Thebes.

Ennugi

God. Mesopotamian (Sumerian and Babylonian-Akkadian). The attendant and throne bearer of Enlil (Ellil).

Enten

Fertility god. Mesopotamian (Sumerian). Created by Enlil as a guardian deity of farmers alongside the minor god Emeš, Enten was given specific responsibility for the fertility of ewes, goats, cows, donkeys, birds and other animals. He is identified with the abundance of the earth and with the winter period.

Enundu

Plague god. Gishu [Uganda, East Africa]. A god identified with smallpox and propitiated with the sacrifice of a goat.

Enzu

God. Mesopotamian (Babylonian-Akkadian). The name is a corruption, apparently a misreading of Suen, the archaic form of Sin.

Eos

Sky goddess. Hellenized Indo-European. The spirit of the dawn. She is the daughter of Hyperion and Thea, and the sister of Helios (sun) and Selene (moon). The consort of Aeolos, the storm god son of Poseidon, she bore six children who represent the various winds. Hesiod accounts her as the consort of Astraeos. In separate tradition she is the mother of Memnon who was slain at Troy, and her tears are the morning dew. See also Aurora.

Eostre

Fertility goddess of spring. Anglo-Saxon. The derivation of "Easter." Probably a number of the obscure folk customs surrounding Easter and still practiced in England trace back to her worship.

Epimetheus

Minor creator god. Greek and Roman. One of the four sons of Iapetos and Klymene (Titan), and the brother of Prometheus. Jointly responsible for the creation of mankind. Epimetheus' strongest claim to fame lies in his liaison with the first mortal woman, Pandora, whom the gods had cautioned him to avoid. Her curiosity caused her to open the box belonging to Jupiter in which he had placed all the vices, diseases and sufferings of humanity but that also included the benevolent spirit of hope.

EPONA *(mare)*

Origin Celtic (Gallic). Horse goddess with fertility connotations.

Known period of worship circa 400 BC and probably earlier until Christianization (circa 400 AD).

Synonyms none.

Center(s) of cult probably originating from Alesia in Gaul but spreading extensively, including Rome.

Art references stone and bronze statuettes (mainly Luxembourg and Côte d'Or); various monumental carvings.

Literary sources inscriptions.

A popular equestrian goddess closely allied with the Celtic trade in, and domestic use of, horses. Concerned with healing and with the fertility of domestic animals. The cult probably originated from Alesia in the heartland of Gallic resistance and location of Vercingetorix's final stand against Julius Caesar. She is arguably the only Celtic goddess to have been worshiped in Rome itself and her popularity was spread throughout the regions of Roman occupation (see also Morrigan). Her festival was celebrated on December 18.

Epona is typically depicted with mares and foals, usually riding sidesaddle or merely in association with horses. She also holds cornucopiae, sheaves of grain and other fruits suggesting an ancillary role as a vegetation goddess. Epona is also, on occasion, linked with dogs and birds.

Votive inscriptions have been found at Allerey, Armançon and Essay (Côte d'Or), Jabreilles, Luxeuil, Santanay and others where sometimes she is alone with horse(s) and sometimes is depicted with the "mothers" (see Matres). She was particularly worshiped by Roman cavalry regiments. At Armançon she rides in a cart reminiscent of the "tour" of other northern fertility goddesses (see Nerthus). In other circumstances Epona figurines are found associated with burial grounds such as La Horgue au Sablon illustrating the common link, well attested in ancient and modern cults, between fertility and death. Epona may also be enshrined close to thermal springs under which circumstance she often appears naked like a water nymph, e.g., Allerey and Saulon-la-Chapelle.

Erebos

Primordial deity. Greco-Roman. Engendered by Chaos and Nyx, he formed an incestuous liaison with his mother to create the first elements of the cosmos, Aether (light) and Hemera (day), in pre-Homeric mythology.

EREŠKIGAL   (the great below)

Origin Mesopotamian (Sumerian and Babylonian-Akkadian) [Iraq]. Chthonic underworld goddess.

Known period of worship   circa 3500 BC or earlier to 200 BC or later.

Synonyms   Allatu(m).

Center(s) of cult   none.

Art references   plaques, votive stelae, glyptics, etc.

Literary sources   creation epics and other texts including *Inana's Descent and the Death of Dumuzi*.

Ereškigal is the consort of Nergal and queen of the underworld. She is also the mother of Ninazu. According to some texts she was once a sky goddess who was abducted by the monstrous deity Kur. She lives in the palace of Ganzir and equates with the Greek Persephone. Arguably, Ereškigal may be seen as a dark alter ego of the goddess Inana and is identified in some texts as her elder sibling. Her consort is also identified as Gugulana. In legend Ereškigal is challenged by Inana but after judgment by the seven Anunnaki, the underworld goddess renders her a corpse for three days until she is revived through the intervention of Enki, the god of wisdom. In western Semitic pantheons Ereškigal becomes Allatu.

Erh Lang   (master)

Tutelary deity. Chinese. Associated with a celestial dog, Erh Lang was once honored with a sanctuary in Beijing (Peking). According to tradition he and the dog saved the city from flooding. His attributes include a bow that he is depicted drawing, and arrows. The dog may be replaced by a rat, in which case the arrows are not included. The rat is a sign of impending wealth and therefore the drawing of an empty bow at the rat is a sign that invokes wealth of children.

Erinys

Chthonic goddess of wrath. Greek. According to legend she was a consort of Poseidon by whom she bore the fabulous horse Areon. By implication she may also have been a grim maternal figure who engendered all horses. She may be equated with a wrathful Demeter who is sometimes given the epithet Erinys. Erinys appears in the collective form of three Erinyes, their heads covered with snake-locks and bearing torches from the underworld. In the *Iliad* they are described as those "who beneath the earth punish dead men, whoever has sworn a false oath." In Roman mythology they are the Furies.

Eris

Goddess of dissent or strife. Greek. The consort of Ares, the god of war, and the mother of Horkos (oath). She is depicted throwing the apple of discord among guests at a wedding, offering it "to the fairest" to provoke argument. In Roman mythology she becomes Discordia.

Eriu

Fertility goddess. Celtic (Irish). An aspect of the Morrigan. One of the deities who were known as the "Sovereignty of Ireland" and wedded symbolically to a mortal king. Also a warrior goddess, capable of changing shape from girl to hag, and into birds and animals. She is patroness of the royal seat of Uisnech in County Meath. Eire and Erin are corruptions of her name. See also Badb, Banba and Fodla.

Erkilek

Hunting god. Eskimo. A malevolent deity with the head and nose of a dog and the body of a man. He carries a bow, with arrows contained in a quiver, and is an expert archer.

Eros

Primordial deity. Greco-Roman. One of the children of Aether and Hemera in the pre-Homeric cosmos. Listed in Hesiod's *Theogony* as one of three archetypal beings with Chaos and Gaia. Also Amor (Roman).

Erra

God of war. Mesopotamian (Babylonian-Akkadian). Known chiefly from the *Erra Epic*, circa 1000 BC, he is also the god of raids, riots and scorched earth. Closely identified with the god Nergal, his cult center is Emeslam in the city of Kutha (lost).

In Babylonian times he is identified as a plague god.

Erua

See Zarpanitu.

Es

Creator god. Ket [Siberian]. Described as an old man with a long black beard, he fashioned the first humans from clay. Those tossed from his right hand became men, and those from his left became women.

Eshu

Itinerant god. Yoruba [Nigeria, West Africa]. An ancient deity regarded as the attendant and messenger of the creator god Olodumare. He passes among mortal people assessing character and meting out punishment. Devotees are identified by necklaces of black or brown beads.

Ešmun

God of healing. Western Semitic (Phoenician). Known first from the Iron Age levels at Sidon, his cult spread as far as Carthage, Cyprus and Sardinia. Possibly became syncretized with the god Melqart and, in Hellenic times, with the physician god Asklepios. His name further became linked with the mother goddess Caelestis.

Estsanatlehi   *(woman that changes)*

Fertility goddess. Navaho [USA]. Probably regarded as the most powerful deity in the Navaho pantheon, she has powers of endless self-rejuvenation. According to tradition, she was created from a small turquoise image into which life was infused through a ritual of the great gods and she is the sister of the goddess Yolkaiestan. She is also the consort of the sun god Tsohanoai and the mother of the war god Nayenezgani. She is said to live in the west and is benevolent in nature, sending the gentle rains of summer and the warm thawing winds of spring.

Esu

God of passage. Edo [Benin and Nigeria, West Africa]. A fearsome deity who stands at the gates of the home of the gods holding a set of keys. He is known for his trickery.

Esus

God of war. Celtic (Continental European). Mentioned by the Roman writer Lucan but otherwise virtually unknown. He may have originated as a tree god. One carving [Trier] identifies Esus felling a tree with birds in the branches (see also Inana). Elsewhere he is asssociated with three cranes and a bull.

Eunomia

Goddess of order. Greek. One of the children of Zeus and Themis, her siblings include the Horae, Dike and Eirene.

Euros

God of the east winds. Greco-Roman. One of the sons of Eos. Particularly known from Sparta and later Romanized as Eurus.

Eurynome

Sea goddess. Greek. The daughter of Nisos and mother of the Graces. Also the mother of Bellepheron, fathered by Poseidon, though she is accounted as the consort of Glaukos. Little else is known, but her cult center was apparently at Phigaleia (Arcadia).

F

Fabulinus
Minor god of infants. Roman. Responsible for the first words of the child.

Faivarongo
God of mariners. Polynesian [Tikopia]. The eldest son of a being known as Ariki Kafika Tuisifo, he is a patron and guardian of seafarers and is also regarded as the origin of the royal Tikopian lineage. Also known as the "grandsire of the ocean." He is closely linked with the chthonic god Tifenua and the sky god Atua I Kafika.

Faraguvol
Votive god. Puerto Rico and Haiti. The deified trunk of a tree that carried to a tribal chief and presented. The being represented, classed as a *zemi*, is considered to wander about and can escape from a closed bag or sack. See also Zemi.

Faro
River god. Bambara [Mali, West Africa]. Regarded as the deity who brought order to the world at the time of creation. He impregnated himself and gave birth to twins who were the first human beings. He is also the progenitor of fish stocks in the river Niger. His chief adversary is the god of the desert wind, Teliko. Faro is propitiated annually by a *Komo* society of men in a ritual of dancing. They use a special mask that is created anew each year. According to legend Faro came to earth after a long period of drought during which most of the living things died. He also gave mankind the gift of speech.

Fauna
Minor vegetation goddess. Roman. Consort of Faunus with guardianship of woods and plants.

Faunus
Minor vegetation god. Roman. Consort of Fauna with guardianship of woods and plants. He was given many of the attributes of the Greek god Pan including horns and legs of a goat.

Fe
Tutelary god. Gai [Ivory Coast, West Africa]. By tradition he arbitrated a dispute between two tribes, the Chuilo and the Nyaio. The Nyaio were eventually defeated and Fe became specifically the god of the Chuilo people. He is propitiated by means of a dance in which a terrifying mask is worn.

Fe'e
God of the dead. Polynesian. Perceived as a giant cuttlefish who was once subdued by the god of deep underground rocks. Part of the principle of Polynesian religion is that every deity has a superior and inferior who have either bested, or been bested by, the other at some mythical time.

Fei Lian
See Feng Po.

Felicitas
Minor god. Roman. Linked with agricultural prosperity. Known particularly from the second century BC.

Feng Po
Sky god. Chinese. Described as the "Count of the Wind," which he releases from a sack, he has strong links with the sea. He was originally regarded as malevolent and the antagonist of the god Shen Yi. Feng Po may be depicted in human form as an old man with a white beard, or in the

guise of a dragon with the head of a bird or a deer. Also Fei Lian; Fei Lien; Feng Bo.

Fides

Minor god. Roman. Identified with faith and loyalty. A sanctuary was dedicated to him in Rome circa 254 BC. Symbolized by a pair of covered hands.

Fidi Mukullu

Creator god. Bena Lulua [Zaire, central Africa]. He provides mankind with food, tools and weapons. The sun and moon were engendered from his cheeks.

FJORGYN

Origin Nordic (Icelandic) region. Early fertility goddess.

Known period of worship Viking period (circa 700 AD) or earlier to Christianization (circa 1100 AD).

Synonyms possibly Iord.

Center(s) of cult none known.

Art references none known, but probably the subject of anonymous carvings.

Literary sources scant mention in various Icelandic codices. Fjorgyn is referred to by Snorri in *Skaldskaparmal*.

Practically nothing is known about Fjorgyn, though it is suggested that she is the mother of Thor. She may therefore be Iord by a different name. May also have been married to, or had a brother by the same name (Fjorgyn). She is mentioned in the *Voluspa* of the *Poetic Edda* and is probably the model for the Wagnerian character Erda.

Snorri Sturluson suggests that a god Fjorgvin (Fjorgynn) may have been the father of the goddess Frigg.

Flaitheas

Tutelary goddess. Celtic (Irish). A name applied to the "Sovereignty of Ireland." By tradition Irish rulers-designate were offered a cup called the *dergflaith* to drink from, denoting their acceptance as consort of the goddess.

Flora

Goddess of flowers. Roman. Consort of Zephyrus and chiefly worshiped by young girls with offerings of fruit and flowers. Her major festivals, with strongly sexual overtones but also identified with the dead, were celebrated in the spring months from April 28 to early May and known as *Floralia*.

Forseti

God of unknown status. Nordic (Icelandic). A god of Asgard said by Snorri to be the son of Balder and Nanna. According to an Icelandic list of dwellings of the gods, Forseti owned a gold and silver hall, Glitnir, and was a good law maker and arbiter of disputes. Also Fosite (Friesian).

Fortuna

Goddess of good fortune. Roman. A deity who particularly appealed to women, partly in an oracular context. She is depicted carrying a globe, rudder and cornucopiae. She probably evolved from the model of the Greek goddess Tyche. Her main symbol is the wheel of fate, which she may stand upon, and Renaissance artists tended to depict her thus. Among her more celebrated sanctuaries in Rome, the temple of Fortuna Redux was built by Domitian to celebrate his victories in Germany. She is depicted in a well-known stone carving in Gloucester Museum, England, holding her three main attributes.

FREYJA *(lady)*

Origin Nordic (Icelandic) or Germanic. Fertility and vegetation goddess.

Known period of worship Viking period (circa 700 AD) and earlier, until after Christianization (circa 1100 AD).

Synonyms Gefn (giver); Mardoll; Syr (sow); Horn; Skialf; possibly Thorgerda in some parts of the north.

Center(s) of cult principally in Sweden and Norway, but spread throughout the Nordic region.

Art references stone carvings.

Literary sources Icelandic codices; *Prose Edda* (Snorri); *Historia Danica* (Saxo); inscriptions; various place names.

Freyja is one of the most popular of the deities in Asgard. A Vanir goddess, twin sister and/or wife of Freyr, and daughter of Njord. A goddess of love concerned with affairs of the heart, marriage and prosperity. Much sought after by giants, and reputed to have enjoyed sexual liaisons with many suitors, including gods and elves. She drives a chariot pulled by two cats and is said to roam at night in the form of a she-goat. She also rides upon a boar with golden bristles, the Hildeswin. Closely associated with death, according to some legends she received half of those slain in battle (see Othin). A weeping goddess with tears of gold, symbolized by the boar (see Frigg), she wears a necklace with ritual significance, the *Brisingamen*. Said to be able to take the shape of a falcon and fly great distances. Associated with a form of witchcraft, *seior*, involving a seeress and divination. Frigg and Freyja are possibly separate aspects of a single divine principle.

FREYR *(lord)*

Origin Possibly Swedish or Germanic but extending throughout the Nordic region with lowest popularity in Iceland. Fertility god.

Known period of worship Viking period (circa 700 AD) and earlier, until Christianization (circa 1100 AD).

Synonyms none confirmed, but possibly including Frodi (Denmark); Yng or Ing; Lytir (Sweden).

Center(s) of cult Uppsala (Sweden), Thrandheim (Norway) and various temples and shrines throughout the Nordic countries (none surviving).

Art references stone carvings.

Literary sources Icelandic codices; *Prose Edda* (Snorri); *Historia Danica* (Saxo); Adam of Bremen; inscriptions; place names.

One of the Vanir gods inhabiting Asgard, and concerned with the fertility, prosperity and peace of the world. The twin of Freyja and one of the children of Njord. Married to the giantess Gerd, a liaison interpreted by some as representing the marriage of a sky god with the earth resulting in the harvest. He was, according to the writer Adam of Bremen, represented in the cult temple at Uppsala by a dramatically ithyphallic statue. The Freyr cult was possibly accompanied by a sacred marriage and he was regarded as the progenitor of the royal Swedish Ynglinge dynasty. According to the *Flateyjarbok* (Icelandic), the statue of Freyr was carried around the countryside in a covered wagon with an attendant priestess to bless the seasons. Other festivals may have included a ritual drama in which male attendants dressed in effeminate costumes.

Freyr enjoys very ancient links with the boar, considered to possess protective powers, and he had a sacred animal with golden bristles called Gullinborsti. A sacred stable is described at Thrandheim, one of the centers of a horse cult with which he was also strongly identified. Freyr is also associated with a ship cult based on the notion of a phantom vessel, Skidbladnir or Skioblaonir, large enough to hold all the gods but small enough to fold into a man's pocket.

FRIGG

Origin Nordic (Icelandic) or Germanic. Mother goddess.

Known period of worship Viking period (circa 700 AD) and earlier, until Christianization (circa 1100 AD).

Synonyms Frija (Germanic).

Center(s) of cult various around Nordic region.

Art references stone carvings.

Literary sources Icelandic codices; *Prose Edda* (Snorri); *Historia Danica* (Saxo); inscriptions; place names.

The senior Aesir goddess living in Asgard; consort of Othin and mother of Balder. Saxo implies that she had been the unfaithful spouse but generally she was revered as a regal consort and "queen of heaven." The Germanic version of her name, Frija, is the origin of Friday. She is thought to have been closely concerned with childbirth and midwifery. She may also have headed a group of shadowy female deities to whom carved stones were often erected in pre-Christian Europe (Roman *matrones*) associated with fertility and protection of the household. Such stones are generally found in the Rhineland. A weeping goddess occasionally described as taking the shape of a falcon (see Freyja).

Fu Shen
God of luck. Chinese. He is often linked in iconography with Tsai Shen, god of wealth, and Shou Lao, god of longevity. Usually depicted with his son, and wearing blue robes, which signify his offical position.

Fujin
God of winds. Shinto [Japan]. Depicted carrying a sack that contains the four winds on his shoulder.

Fukurokuju
God of luck. Shinto [Japan]. One of seven deities in Shintoism concerned with fortune. He is allegedly a Chinese hermit who lived during the Sung dynasty and whose name means happiness, wealth and longevity. He is depicted as a little old man, bald and with a prominent high forehead. He carries a book of sacred teachings tied to his staff. Other occasional attributes include a crane, deer or tortoise.

Fulla
Minor goddess. Germanic. Identified in the second *Merseburg Charm* as an attendant of the goddess Frigg and possibly her sister.

Futo-Tama
Ancestral god. Shinto [Japan]. A significant deity in mythology because he took part in the divination and ritual necessary before the process of drawing the sun goddess Amaterasu out of her cave could begin. He collected together various magical objects, pushed forward the perfect divine mirror, recited the sacred liturgy and begged Amaterasu never again to hide her face. The guardian of Prince Ninigi, ancestor of the imperial dynasty, Futo-Tama is more specifically the ancestor of the Imba clan in Japan.

Futsu-Nushi-No-Kami
God of war. Shinto [Japan]. One of two deities who made the way clear for Prince Ninigi to descend to earth and begin the imperial dynasty. A tutelary deity of swordsmen and judoka artists. Linked with the god Take-Mika-Dzuchi-No-Kami.

G

Gabija
Fire goddess. Pre-Christian Lithuanian. She was invoked by tossing salt on a sacred flame.

Gabjauja
Grain goddess. Pre-Christian Lithuanian. She was degraded to an evil demonic presence after Christianization.

Gad
God of uncertain status. Western Semitic and Punic (Carthaginian). Probably concerned with chance or fortune and known from Palmyrene inscriptions, and from the *Vetus Testamentum* in place names such as Baal-Gad and Midal-Gad. Popular across a wide area of Syrio-Palestine and Anatolia in pre-biblical times. Thought to have been syncretized ultimately with the Greek goddess Tyche.

Gaganaganja *(treasury of ether)*
God. Buddhist. One of a group of *bodhisattvas* (*buddha*-designates). Color: yellow, red or gold. Attributes: blue lotus, book, jewel, lotus and wishing tree in a vase.

GAIA *(earth)*
Origin Greek. Archetypal earth mother.

Known period of worship circa 1500 BC until Christianization (circa 400 AD).

Synonyms Gaea; Ge; Terra.

Center(s) of cult oracle at Delphi.

Art references sculptures and reliefs.

Literary sources *Theogony, Hymn to Gaia* in the so-called Homeric hymns (Hesiod); Aristophanes.

Gaia is an ancient pre-Hellenic goddess who was mainly revered in Attica. She is the primordial essence of the earth, one of the creations of Aether and Hedera, the primordial beings of the cosmos. Through the encouragement of Eros she became the mother of Pontos (sea) and Ouranos (heaven). According to tradition, through liaison with Ouranos, she also engendered the race of Titans. By consorting with the underworld she created the monstrous Typhon.

Perceived as a placid and resilient goddess generally somewhat apathetic to the goings-on around her in the tale of beginnings, she had an oracle at Delphi that predated that of Apollo. In Hellenic times she became Da-meter or Demeter, the grain mother whose daughter is Kore, the grain spirit. Her attributes include fruit and cornucopiae.

Gajavahana
God. Hindu-Dravidian (Tamil). A form of Skanda who has an elephant as a vehicle. Mainly from southern India. Attributes: cockerel and spear.

Gal Bapsi *("hook" god)*
Local god. Hindu-Dravidian (Tamil) [southern India]. Worshipped particularly by the Bhils. To expiate sins, the penitent thrusts a hook into his back and is suspended from it on the day when the sun enters Aries.

Galla
Minor underworld gods. Mesopotamian (Sumerian and Babylonian-Akkadian). Attendants of the goddess Ereškigal. Also Gallu.

Ganapati *(lord of hosts)*
1. God. Hindu (Puranic). The more commonly recognized name of the elephant god Ganesa, particularly favored in western India.

85

2. God. Buddhist (Mahayana). The name of a deity influenced by the Hindu god Ganesa. Depicted riding upon a rat or mouse and carrying an assortment of attributes.

Ganapatihrdaya *(the heart of Ganapati)*
Minor goddess. Buddhist (Mahayana). The *Sakti* of Ganapati.

Ganaskidi *(humpback)*
God of harvests, plenty and of mists. Navaho [USA]. He is said to live at Depehahatil, a canyon with many ruined cliff dwellings north of San Juan. According to tradition he is the apotheosis of a bighorn sheep. His priest wears a blue mask with no hair fringe but with a spruce crown and collar. He has a black bag on his back, filled out with a twig frame, that appears as a deformity, and he carries a staff.

Gandha *(odor)*
Goddess. Buddhist-Lamaist [Tibet]. In Lamaism one of the group of *mataras* (mothers). Color: green. Attribute: conch with sandalwood resin.

Gandhari *(of Ghandhara)*
Goddess of learning. Jain [India]. One of sixteen *sasanadevatas* headed by the goddess Sarasvati. May also be a *vidyadevi*.

Gandha Tara *(fragrance-Tara)*
Minor goddess. Buddhist (Mahayana). Color: red. Attribute: conch with sandalwood resin.

GANESA *(lord of hosts)*
Origin Hindu (Epic and Puranic) [India]. God of wisdom and prudence.

Known period of worship circa 400 AD onward until present.

Synonyms Ganapati.

Center(s) of cult none specific.

Art references sculptures generally bronze but also stone. Reliefs.

Literary sources late *Mahabharata* recensions and *Brihaddharma-Purana* etc.

Ganesa is god of wisdom and art, a benign deity generally assumed to offer help when invoked to overcome difficulties. He may have originated as a fertility god and as a *yaksa* (local forest deity). His father is Siva. His mother, Parvati, is said to have created him from flakes of her skin. He is depicted in human form with an elephant's head (or, less frequently, up to five heads) and a trunk (which removes obstacles), sometimes bearing one tusk, on a stout or obese body (which contains the universe). He has four arms that can carry a large number of attributes but particularly a shell, a discus, a mace and a water-lily. His sacred animal is the bandicoot. He is called upon before going on a journey, moving house or opening a new business.

According to one legend his elephant head was gained after his mother had put him outside the house to guard the doorstep while she took a bath. He barred the way to his father whereupon Siva inadvertently decapitated him. His mother vowed to secure a head for him from the first passing creature, which happened to be an elephant. Another account suggests that Parvati took Ganesa to show him off to the gods but that Sani (Saturn) burned his head to ashes and the elephant's head was provided to save his life by a compassionate Visnu.

Ganesa's great popularity results in his frequent appearance in temples devoted to other Hindu deities. Sculptures are sometimes painted red. He is also a common household guardian made popular by his gentle nature.

Ganga
River goddess. Hindu (Puranic). Guardian deity of the Ganges. The elder daughter of Himavan and Mena, she is the sister of Parvati and the consort of Visnu and Agni. She is also the second consort of Siva. Ganga is regarded as a symbol of purity and is frequently depicted with Brahma washing the raised foot of Visnu Trivikrama. According to tradition she was a heavenly river

brought to earth and caught by Siva in his hair to soften the shock of her fall. She rides on a fish or water monster. Color: white. Attributes: fly whisk, lotus and water jar.

Gangir
Goddess. Mesopotamian (Sumerian). One of the seven daughters of the goddess Baba, known chiefly at Lagaš. Also, and more properly, Hegir-Nuna.

Garmangabis
Tutelary goddess. South Germanic. Invoked by the Suebi tribe to bring prosperity. She may be linked with the north German goddess Gefjon.

Garuda *(the devourer)*
1. Archaic sun god and divine vehicle. Hindu (Vedic). Originally depicted as a solar deity, Garuda evolved into a bird-like human hybrid who became the deified mount of Visnu. Also a chief adversary of *nagas* (snake-like demons), which he devours. In early depictions Garuda has a parrot's beak. Said to have been born from an egg, the son of Vinata and Kasyapa. Epithets include Amrtaharana, Garutman, Tarksya. Attributes: conch, club, lotus and nectar, but may also bear the attributes of Visnu.
2. Mount or *vahana* of Vajrapani. Buddhist. Attributes: flower, horse head, noose, skin and staff. Three-eyed and three-headed.

Gatumdug
Fertility goddess. Mesopotamian (Sumerian and Babylonian-Akkadian). The daughter of the sky god An, she is the tutelary mother goddess of Lagaš.

Gaunab
Malevolent god of darkness. Khoi (Hottentot) [Namibia, southern Africa]. The chief adversary of the creator god Tsunigoab. He was engaged in a primordial struggle for supremacy during which Tsunigoab was wounded but eventually triumphed, consigning Gaunab to the so-called "black heaven."

Gauri *(whitish brilliant)*
1. Goddess. Hindu (Vedic and Puranic). Consort of the god Varuna, said to have been created at the churning of the ocean of milk. An epithet of Parvati as a goddess of the grain. Also a *Sakti* of Mahesvara, a minor aspect of Siva. Her attendant animal is a lion or a wolf. Attributes: fish, forest garland, image of Ganesa, lotus, mirror, rosary, trident and water jar. Three-eyed. Also Varuni.
2. Goddess. Buddhist. One of eight *gauris* of terrible appearance. Attributes: head and noose.
3. Messenger goddess. Jain [India]. A *sasanadevata*. Also one of sixteen *vidyadevis* or goddesses of learning headed by Sarasvati. Color: white. Attribute: a hook.
   NOTE: Gauri-Tara is a distinct minor Buddhist Mahayana goddess.

Gautama Buddha
See Buddha.

Gayatri
Personification of a hymn. Hindu. The name of a popular hymn in the *Rg Veda*, dedicated to the sun. Also the name of one, possibly the second, of the consorts of Brahma. See Sarasvati.

GEB *(earth)*
Origin Egyptian. Chthonic or earth god.

Known period of worship Old Kingdom (circa 2600 BC) to end of Egyptian history (circa 400 AD).

Synonyms Seb (erroneous).

Center(s) of cult none specific but often associated with tombs.

Art references paintings in Valley of the Kings, etc.

Literary sources Pyramid and coffin texts; New Kingdom religious papyri including the Papyrus of Tentamun.

Geb, the offspring of Šu and Tefnut, is a "third generation" deity of the Ennead in Heliopolis and, as the brother and consort of Nut, becomes the father of Isis and Osiris in the Heliopolis genealogy. Geb appears on papyri from the New Kingdom typically wearing the crown of Lower Egypt, lying on the ground with his arms stretched in opposite directions: "one to the sky, one to the earth." When drawn with Nut, who is a sky goddess, his penis is often erect and extended toward her. He may also be accompanied by a goose (his sign in hieroglyphic).

Geb is a vegetation god, frequently colored green and with greenery sprouting from him. He is also seen as a god of healing, particularly called upon for protection against scorpion stings. In a less benign context, Geb reputedly snatches the souls of the dead and may imprison them against passing into the afterlife. He is also a god concerned with judgment in the dispute between Horus and Seth. As Horus's father, he presided over his crowning, and therefore continued to protect each rightful heir to the crown of Egypt.

Gefjon

Goddess of agriculture. Germanic and Nordic (Icelandic). One of the Aesir deities and an attendant of the goddess Frigg according to tradition mentioned by Snorri in the *Edda*. She bore four giant sons whom she turned into oxen and used them to plough a tract of land that was then towed out to sea to become Zeeland (Sjaeland). She is also said to have founded a royal Danish dynasty. Also Gefiun.

Genius

God of men. Roman. The personification of creativity and strength in mortal males, the counterpart of Juno. Roman religion also dictated that every place had its guardian spirit, the *genius loci*.

Gerra

God of fire. Mesopotamian (Babylonian-Akkadian). Derived from the Sumerian Gibil, he is the son of Anu and Anunitu and becomes largely syncretized with both Erra and Nergal.

Geštin-Ana

Chthonic goddess. Mesopotamian (Sumerian). The sister of Dumuzi and consort of Ningisida. The so-called "heavenly grapevine," this minor goddess is involved in the account of Dumuzi trying to escape from his fate at the hands of Inana and Ereškigal. In her house he is changed into a gazelle before being caught and finally transported to the underworld.

Geštu

Minor god of intellect. Mesopotamian (Sumerian and Babylonian-Akkadian). According to legend he was sacrificed by the great gods and his blood was used in the creation of mankind.

Geus Tasan

Cattle god. Persian [Iran]. The creator of cattle. Sometimes considered to be an aspect of Ahura Mazda.

Geus Urvan

Cattle god. Persian [Iran]. The guardian of cattle who appears in the guise of a cow.

Ghantakarna   *(ears like bells)*

God of healing. Hindu (Epic and Puranic). An attendant of Siva, worshiped as a guardian against diseases of the skin. Attributes: bell with noose, and hammer.

NOTE: there is also a poorly defined goddess Ghantakarni.

Ghantapani   *(bell in hand)*

God. Buddhist (Mahayana). One of the group of *dhyanibodhisattva* (meditation *buddhas*). An emanation of Vajrasattva. Color: white. Attribute: a bell.

Ghasmari   *(voracious)*

Goddess of terrifying appearance. Buddhist. One of a group of eight *gauris*. Color: green. Attributes: staff with bell.

Ghentu

Minor god. Hindu. Known in northern India as the god who "sends the itch."

Gibil

Fire god. Mesopotamian (Sumerian). The son of An and Ki. By the Akkadian period he becomes known as Gerra.

Gibini

Plague god. Gishu [Uganda, East Africa]. Associated with the smallpox god Enundu, he is propitiated with offerings of vegetables and is symbolized by special trees planted near the house.

Giltine

Goddess of death. Pre-Christian Lithuanian. She is said to enter the house of a dying person, dressed in a white gown, and suffocate them.

Gish

God of war. Kafir [Afghanistan]. Known chiefly among the Kati people in the southern Hindukush. Gish seems partly modeled on the Aryan (Vedic) god Indra (see also Indr). One of the offspring of the creator god Imra, his mother is named as Utr; she carried him for eighteen months before he wrenched himself from her belly, stitching her up with a needle. His consort is the goddess Sanju. He slaughters with great efficiency but is considered lacking in graces and intellect, emerging in a generally boorish light (see also Thor). His home is a fortress of steel atop a mythical walnut tree, propped up by his mother, that provides nourishment and strength for his warriors. The rainbow is a sling with which he carries his quiver.

Gish is associated chiefly with the villages of Kamdesh and Shtiwe but has been worshiped throughout the Kafir region with the sacrifice of hornless oxen, particularly prior to combat. A feast was given in his honor if the outcome was successful. Also Giwish.

Giszida

God. Mesopotamian (Sumerian and Babylonian-Akkadian). See Ningis Zi Da.

Gita

Mother goddess. Buddhist-Lamaist [Tibet]. One of a group of *astamataras* (mothers). Color: red. Attributes: Indian gong and lute.

Glaucus

Sea god. Roman. See Glaukos.

Glaukos

Sea god. Greek. Allegedly an impoverished fisherman who ate a sea-grass with magical properties, dived into the ocean and remained there as a guardian deity of fishermen and their nets. See Proteus.

Gleti

Moon goddess. Fon [Benin, West Africa]. The consort of the sun god Lisa and the mother of a large number of minor astral deities, the *gletivi*, who became the stars of heaven.

GOBNIU *(smith)*

Origin Celtic (Irish). God of skills including ale-brewing.

Known period of worship early times until Christianization, circa 400 AD.

Synonyms Goibniu; Govannon (Welsh).

Center(s) of cult none specifically known.

Art references various monumental sculptures and inscriptions.

Literary sources Books of Invasions; Cycles of Kings.

Gobniu is known chiefly for his skills as a metal smith and in brewing the immortal beer of the gods. He fashions invincible magic weapons for the Tuatha De Danann. In his brewing activities he uses a vast bronze caldron, a copy of which was housed in various sanctuaries and was apparently at times associated with the ritual slaughter of kings of Ireland. Gobniu forms part of a triad of deities, the *Na tri dee dana* (three gods of skill), with Credne, a deity skillful in soldering, and Luchta.

GOD

Origin Christian (Anglo-Saxon) derived from the western Semitic creator god Il (biblical El) and from the Israelite deity Yhwh. Creator god.

Known period of worship circa 325 AD in the Christian Movement (but an adoption from much earlier times) until present day.

Synonyms   Deus (Latin), Gott (Germanic).

Centers of cult   throughout the Christian world but chiefly Rome and the Vatican (Roman Catholic) and Canterbury (Church of England).

Art references   various, usually as a function of the Trinity, and generally in paintings rather than sculptures.

Literary sources   New Testament; apocryphal Christian texts.

A term employed throughout the English-speaking world as a generic term for a deity but also in a specific sense as the creator god of the orthodox Christian Church as well as that of Judaism and Islam. Derived from, and modeled on, the creator god of Israel known variously as El or Yhwh (Yahweh), God is identified in the New Testatment of the Bible as the heavenly father of Jesus Christ.

Considered by many modern Christian theologians to be asexual, the nature and precise identity of God was in considerable dispute among Christian factions until the Council of Nicea in 325 AD ratified the principle of *homoousios* (of the same substance as the Son and Holy Ghost) with the statement that begins: "We believe in one God, the Father almighty, maker of all things both visible and invisible . . ."

God is perceived to be monotheistic, alone in the heavens and of universal presence, represented in earthly form by his son, Jesus Christ, and spiritually by the Holy Ghost. The wholly monotheistic nature is unusual in historically recorded religious beliefs, the cult of Aten (Egypt) representing one of the few precedents.

God (as Deus) became the official deity of the Roman Empire during the reign of the emperor Constantine, crowned in 311 AD. Constantine's successor, Theodosius, effectively outlawed all non-Christian religious cults. Under various names God was introduced to western Europe from the fifth century AD by Christian missionaries. He is currently worshiped by a Roman Catholic congregation in excess of 900 million and by a smaller number of Anglicans and other Christian denominations.

Gonaqade't
Sea god. Chilkat [American north Pacific coast]. By tradition he brings power and good fortune to all who see him. He appears in several guises, rising from the water as a gaily painted house inlaid with blue and green *Haliotis* shell, or as the head of a huge fish, or as a painted war canoe. Generally depicted in art as a large head with arms, paws and fins.

Gon-Po Nag-Po
God. Lamaist [Tibet]. See Mahakala. Also Bram-zei gzugs-can; mGon-dkar; Gur-gyi mGon-po.

Goraknath
Guardian god. Hindu. An *avatara* of Siva, worshiped among cow-herders and the founder of the *gorakhnathi* sect in Nepal.

Govannon
God of skills. Celtic (Welsh). Son of the goddess Don. See also Gobniu.

Grahamatrka   *(demon mother)*
Goddess. Buddhist (Mahayana). One of the forms of Vairocana. Attributes: arrow, bow, lotus and staff. Three-headed.

Gramadevata
Generic term for a local tutelary deity. India. Such deities are identified as "not being served by Brahman priests." Most are goddesses, e.g., Camunda, Durga, and Kali. Generally they are invoked in small villages where they guard boundaries and fields and are represented by a painted stone, but they are also to be found in larger towns and cities.

Grannus
God of healing. Romano-Celtic (Continental Europe). The name appears across a wide area generally associated with medicinal springs and hot mineral waters, including sites at Aix-la-Chapelle,

Grand (Vosges), Trier, Brittany, and as far distant as the Danube basin. Grannus became syncretized with the Roman god Apollo as Apollo Grannus, and baths were sometimes called *Aquae Granni*.

Gratiae
Goddesses. Roman. The counterparts of the Greek Graces. Identified with the arts and generally depicted with long flowing tresses, but otherwise naked.

Grdhrasya *(face of a vulture)*
Minor goddess. Buddhist.

Grismadevi *(goddess of summer)*
Seasonal goddess. Buddhist-Lamaist [Tibet]. Also an attendant of Sridevi. Usually accompanied by a yak. Color: red. Attributes: ax and cup.

Gugulanna
Minor underworld deity. Mesopotamian (Sumerian). The consort of the goddess Ereškigal, mentioned as the pretext on which the fertility goddess Inana descends to the netherworld.

Gujo
Tutelary guardian deity. Kafir [Afghanistan]. A god of whom there is nothing other than a passing reference from among the extinct southern Hindukush tribe of Pachags. He may have been a local consort of the messenger goddess Zhiwud.

Gukumatz
Sky god. Mayan (Quiche, classical Mesoamerican) [Guatemalan highlands]. The son of the creator gods E Quaholom and E Alom, and equating to the feathered serpent god of Aztec religion, Quetzalcoatl.

Gula *(great one)*
Goddess of healing. Mesopotamian (Sumerian and Babylonian-Akkadian). Consort of Ninurta. Her animal is the dog. She may be synonymous with Nin'insinna. Also mentioned in Hellenistic Baby-

lonian times. A Gula temple is described at Uruk. Also Nintinugga.

Gul-Šeš
Collective name for goddesses of fate. Hittite. They dispense good or evil, life or death. Also Hutena (Hurrian).

Gulsilia Mata
Mother goddess. Hindu (Epic and Puranic). A *Sakti* who in later Hinduism became regarded as of evil intent, inflicting sickness. Particularly known from Bengal.

Gunura
Deity of uncertain status. Mesopotamian (Sumerian and Babylonian-Akkadian). Described variously as the husband of the goddess Nin'insinna and the father of Damu (Dumuzi), but also as the sister of Damu.

Gur-Gyi Mgon-Po
God of tents. Buddhist-Lamaist [Tibet]. A form of Mahakala usually attended by a man. Color: blue. Attributes: club, cup and knife.

Gusilim *(loud voice)*
God. Mesopotamian (Sumerian). See Ištaran.

Gwydion
God of war. Celtic (Welsh). His mother is Don the Welsh mother goddess. He allegedly caused a war between Gwynedd and Dyfed. He visited the court of Pryderi, son of Rhiannon, in Dyfed, and stole his pigs. In the ensuing combat Gwydion used magic powers and slew Pryderi. He seems to have underworld links, hence the route taken by the dead, the Milky Way, was named Caer Gwydion.

Gwynn Ap Nudd
Chthonic underworld god. Celtic (Welsh). Known locally from South Wales. The leader of the phantom hunt that chases a white stag. He equates with Herne in England and Arawn in more northern parts of Wales.

H

Ha

Guardian god. Egyptian. Early deity of the western Sahara referred to as warding off enemies (possibly Libyan) from the west. Depicted in anthropomorphic form crowned by the symbol of desert dunes.

Hachacyum *(our very lord)*

Creator god. Mayan (Lacandon, classical Mesoamerican) [Mexico]. The creator of the world assisted by three other deities, his consort and two brothers, one of whom is Sucunyum, his counterpart (or alter ego) in the underworld. Also Nohochacyum (our great lord).

Hachiman

God of war and peace. Shinto [Japan]. A deity whose origins are confused. The name does not appear in either of the sacred texts of Shintoism, but such a deity was probably worshiped in the distant past with the alternative title of Hime-Gami or Hime-O-Kami. The cult center was on the southern island of Kyushu at Usa. In modern Shintoism, Hachiman originates as a member of the imperial dynasty. Named Ojin-Tenno and born in 200 AD to the empress Jingu-Kogo, he greatly improved the living standards and culture of Japan during his remarkable reign. The place of his birth was marked by a sanctuary and several centuries after his death, a vision of a child *kami* appeared there to a priest. The *kami* identified himself by the Chinese ideogram representing the name Hachiman, and thus the link developed. The site is, today, the location of a magnificent shrine, the Umi-Hachiman-Gu, where Hachiman has been perceived as a god of war. Soldiers departing for battle once took with them relics from the shrine.

Hachiman is also a deity of peace and a guardian of human life and, when pacifism dominated Japan during the post-war era, he became more strongly identified in the latter context.

Hadad

Weather god. Western Semitic (Syrian and Phoenician). Derived from the Akkadian deity Adad. During Hellenic times he was predominantly worshiped at Ptolemais and Hierapolis. His Syrian consort is Atargatis, who overshadowed him in local popularity at Hierapolis. Statues of the two deities were carried in procession to the sea twice yearly. According to the Jewish writer Josephus, Hadad also enjoyed a major cult following at Damascus in the eighth and ninth centuries BC. By the third century BC the Hadad-Atargatis cult had extended to Egypt. In the Greek tradition his consort becomes Hera. See also Adad.

HADES *(the invisible one)*

Origin Greek. God of death.

Known period of worship circa 1500 BC until Christianization (circa 400 AD).

Synonyms Aidoneus (Roman); Dis; Pluto; Orcus (Roman).

Center(s) of cult restricted to Pylos.

Art references none specific.

Literary sources Odyssey, Iliad (Homer); Theogony (Hesiod).

Hades is the son of Kronos and Rhea and may be perceived as the chthonic form of Zeus; he is also the consort of Persephone (Kore). Since all precious metals and stones lie buried in the earth, he is also the god of riches. He rides in a black chariot drawn by four black horses. His home in the underworld is the House of Ais. The closely guarded gates of his kingdom, also called Hades, are identified in the *Odyssey* as lying beyond the ocean at the edge of the world and in the *Iliad* as lying directly beneath the earth. Through Hades run the rivers Styx, beside which the gods made their hallowed oaths, and Lethe, with its waters of forgetfulness. In the *Odyssey* the rivers are identified as the Pyriphlegethon and Kokytos (a tributary of the Styx), which flow into the Acheron. Hades abducts Persephone (Kore), the daughter of Demeter, and brings her to the underworld to reign as his queen for four months in every year. He is depicted as a dark-bearded god carrying a two-pronged harpoon or a scepter, and a key. He may be called Plutos, although the latter is generally regarded as a distinct deity.

Hahana Ku   (much rains house god)

Messenger god. Mayan (classical Mesoamerica) [Mexico]. According to tradition, when the god Hachacyum decides to send rain he directs Hahana Ku to visit the black powder maker Menzabac. Hahana Ku buys only a small quantity, against the wishes of the vendor.

Hahanu

God of uncertain function. Mesopotamian (Sumerian and Babylonian-Akkadian). Known from passing reference in texts and from inscriptions.

Haili'laj

Plague god. Haida Indian [Queen Charlotte Island, Canada]. Particularly associated with smallpox. Believed to be so terrible that he is not even propitiated with food. He sails in a canoe of pestilence with huge sails like those of the white man's ships that brought plague to the Indians.

Hala

Goddess of healing. Kassite [Iraq]. Probably later syncretized with the Akkadian goddess Gula.

Halahala   (lord of poison)

God of poison. Buddhist (Mahayana). A form of Avalokitesvara. Typically seated on a red lotus with the *Sakti* on the left knee. Color: white. Attributes: arrow, bow, cup, grass, image of Amitabha on crown, lotus, tiger skin and trident. Three-headed and three-eyed.

Haldi

Tutelary god. Urartian [Armenia]. Known from circa 1000 BC until circa 800 BC.

Halki   (barley)

Grain god. Hittite and Hurrian. He may also have been invoked by beer makers.

Hamadryades

Animistic tree spirits. Greco-Roman. Vaguely defined female beings whose existence is restricted to the individual trees of which they are guardians.

Hamavehae

Mother goddesses. Romano-Celtic (Rhineland). A trio of *matres* known from inscriptions.

Hammon

God of the evening sun. Libyan. An ancient deity depicted with ram's horns.

Hammu Mata

Mother goddess. Hindu. Locally worshiped by the Bhils.

Han Xiang-Zhi

Immortal being. Taoist (Chinese). One of the "eight immortals" of Taoist mythology. Once mortal beings, they achieved immortality through their exemplary lives. Attributes include a basket of flowers and a flute. See Ba Xian.

Hani(s)

Minor god. Mesopotamian (Babylonian-Akkadian). The attendant of Adad and linked with Sullat.

Hani-Yasu-Hiko
God of potters. Shinto [Japan]. The consort of Hani-Yasu-Hime, he is one of the clay deities made from the feces of the primordial goddess Izanami.

Hani-Yasu-Hime
Goddess of potters. Shinto [Japan]. The consort of Hani-Yasu-Hiko, she is one of the clay deities made from the faeces of the primordial goddess Izanami.

Hannahannas
Mother goddess. Hittite and Hurrian. Described as the "great mother." In the legend of Telepinu, the missing god, she sends a bee to locate him. When the bee stings Telepinu to awaken him, the god vents his rage on the natural world.

NOTE: the priestesses of the Phrygian mother goddess Kybele were, according to the Roman writer Lactantius, *melissai* or bees.

Hansa *(goose)*
Minor *avatara* of Visnu. Hindu (Puranic). Depicted in the form of a goose.

Hanuman *(with large jaws)*
Monkey god. Hindu (Epic and Puranic). Hanuman attends Rama, one of the incarnations of Visnu, and personifies the ideal and faithful servant. He is the son of Pavana, the god of winds, and is noted for his speed and agility in which context he is often worshiped by young men and athletes. He leads a mythical forest army of monkeys, and is depicted as a monkey with a long tail. He takes a major role in the *Ramayana* epic searching for, and rescuing, the goddess Sita who has been captured by the demon Ravana. He may appear trampling on the goddess of Lanka [Sri Lanka]. Worshiped particularly in southern India but more generally in villages. Color: red. Attributes: bow, club, mane, rock and staff. May appear five-headed.

Hao
Creator god. Janjero [Ethiopia]. Personified by the crocodile and considered to reside in the river Gibe. He was propitiated with human sacrifice.

Hapy
Fertility god of the Nile flood. Egyptian. Inhabits caverns adjacent to the Nile cataracts and oversees the annual inundation of the Nile valley. His court includes crocodile gods and frog goddesses. There are no known sanctuaries to Hapy. He is depicted in anthropomorphic form but androgynous, with prominent belly, pendulous breasts and crowned with water plants. He may hold a tray of produce. At Abydos he is depicted as a two-headed goose with human body. See also Khnum.

Hara *(destroyer)*
Epithet of Siva. Hindu (Puranic). Also one of the *ekadasarudras* (eleven rudras).

Hara Ke
Goddess of sweet water. Songhai [Niger, West Africa]. Considered to live beneath the waters in tributaries of the river Niger, attended by two dragons, Godi and Goru. The spirits of the dead are believed to live in a paradise city in the depths of the Niger.

Harakhti
A form of the god Horus. Egyptian. The aspect of the god who rises at dawn in the eastern sky. According to Pyramid Texts, the king is born on the eastern horizon as Harakhti, which contradicts the more commonly held belief that the king is the son of Re, the sun god.

Hara-Yama-Tsu-Mi
Mountain god. Shinto [Japan]. Particularly the deity of wooded mountain slopes.

Hardaul
Plague god. Hindu. A locally worshiped deity known particularly in Bundelkhand, northern India, as a protector against cholera and considered

to have been a historical figure who died in 1627 AD. Also a wedding god.

Harendotes   [*Greek*]
Form of the god Horus. Egyptian. Under this name, Horus specifically guards and protects his father Osiris in death. He thus becomes associated with sarcophagi and appears frequently in coffin texts. Also Har-nedj-itef (Egyptian).

Hari   (*yellowish brown*)
Minor incarnation of the god Visnu. Hindu (Epic and Puranic). Popularized by modern religious movements, Hari is one of the sons of the god Dharma who sprang from the heart of Brahma. He is most closely linked with Krsna, but he and Krsna also parallel Dharma's other sons, Nara and Narayana. Hari can be a more generic epithet applied to several Hindu gods.

Hariti   (*green or stealing*)
1. Mother goddess. Hindu (Epic and Puranic). One of the group of *mataras* (mothers) who are the patrons of children. Considered by some to be identical with the goddess Vriddhi. Her consort is Pancika, alternatively Kubera. In her destructive aspect she steals and eats children. Particularly known from the north and northwest of India. Attribute: a child may be held at her hip, sometimes being eaten.
2. Plague goddess. Buddhist. Associated with smallpox. Also regarded in some texts as the goddess of fertility.

Harmachis   [*Greek*]
Form of the god Horus. Egyptian. Harmachis is Horus as the sun god. Inscriptions from the New Kingdom (circa 1550–1000 BC) identify the sphinx at Giza as Harmachis looking toward the eastern horizon. Also Har-em-akhet (Egyptian).

Harmonia
Goddess of joining. Greco-Roman. Daughter of Ares (Mars) and Aphrodite (Venus) or Cytherea. The consort of Cadmus and mother of Ino, Semele, Agave, Autonoe and Polydorus. She is the apotheosis of harmony in life, which is also displayed in musical euphony. Also Hermione.

Haroeris   [*Greek*]
Form of the god Horus as a man. Egyptian. The name distinguishes the mature deity from Harpokrates, the child Horus. In this form he avenges his father, Osiris, and regains his kingdom from Seth, his uncle. He is depicted as the falcon god. Also Harueris; Har-wer (both Egyptian); Harendotes.

Harpokrates   [*Greek*]
Form of the god Horus as a child. Egyptian. Generally depicted sitting on the knee of his mother, the goddess Isis, often suckling at the left breast and wearing the juvenile sidelock of hair. He may also be invoked to ward off dangerous creatures and is associated with crocodiles, snakes and scorpions. He is generally representative of the notion of a god-child, completing the union of two deities. Also Har-pa-khered (Egyptian).

Harsa   (*desire*)
Goddess. Hindu. The *Sakti* of the god Hrsikesa.

Harsiese
Form of the god Horus. Egyptian. Specifically when personifying the child of Isis and Osiris. According to the Pyramid Texts, Harsiese performs the "opening of the mouth" rite for the dead king.

Harsomtus   [*Greek*]
Form of the god Horus. Egyptian. In this form Horus unites the northern and southern kingdoms of Egypt. He is depicted as a child comparable with Harpokrates. At the Edfu temple, he is identified thus as the offspring of Horus the elder and Hathor. Also Har-mau (Egyptian).

Hasameli
God of metalworkers. Hittite and Hurrian. Invoked by blacksmiths.

Hasta *(hand)*
Minor goddess of fortune. Hindu (Epic and Puranic). A benevolent *naksatra* or astral goddess; daughter of Daksa and wife of Candra (Soma).

Hastehogan
Chief house god. Navaho [USA]. Also a god of farming identified with the west and the sky at sunset. Regarded as a benevolent deity who aids mankind and cures disease. Believed to live in a cave system near San Juan. He also has a malevolent aspect in which he can cast evil spells. His priest wears a blue mask, at the bottom of which is a horizontal yellow band representing evening light, with eight vertical black strokes representing rain. It is decorated with eagle and owl feathers.

Hastsbaka
Male elder of the gods. Navaho [USA]. Otherwise of uncertain status. His priest wears a blue buckskin mask with a fringe of hair, a spruce collar and a scarlet loin cloth with a leather belt decorated with silver and with a fox pelt dangling from the back. He is otherwise naked and painted white. He holds a whitened gourd rattle, which may be decorated with spruce twigs, in his right hand, and a wand of spruce in his left hand. Also Yebaka.

Hastsebaad
Chief of goddesses. Navaho [USA]. She is involved in rites of exorcism and wields considerable influence. The six goddesses of the tribe all wear identical masks, and in ritual the part of the deity is played by a boy or small man wearing a mask that covers the entire head and neck, and who is almost naked but for an ornate scarf on the hips and a leather belt decorated with silver and with a fox pelt dangling behind. The skin is painted white.

Hastseltsi
God of racing. Navaho [USA]. He organizes and oversees athletic races. The priest who impersonates him has to be a good runner and challenges others, using high-pitched squeaking calls. If the priest wins, the contender is whipped with a yucca scourge. If the contender wins, there is no penalty! A fastidious deity who avoids contact with any unclean objects. His ceremonial mask is a domino shape covering mouth and throat with white shells over the eyes and mouth.

Hastseoltoi
Goddess of hunting. Navaho [USA]. She may be seen as the consort of the war god Nayenezgani. She carries two arrows, one in each hand, and wears a quiver and bow case. Navaho tradition dictates that no pictures are drawn of this deity. See also Artemis.

Hastseyalti *(talking elder)*
Chief of gods. Navaho [USA]. Not regarded as a creator deity, but god of the dawn and the eastern sky. Also guardian of animals in the hunt and, possibly, of grain. Regarded as a benevolent deity who aids mankind and cures disease, he also has a malevolent aspect in which he can cast evil spells. His priest invokes him in a ceremonial dance wearing a white mask with a symbol consisting of a corn stalk with two ears. At the bottom is a horizontal yellow band representing evening light, with eight vertical black strokes representing rain. Also Yebitsai.

Hastsezini
God of fire. Navaho [USA]. A "black" god who is reclusive and generally apart from other deities. He is the inventor of fire and of the fire drill and board. His priest dresses in black and wears a black mask with white-bordered eye and mouth holes. The ceremonial fire drill is made from cedarwood.

Hatdastsisi
God. Navaho [USA]. A benevolent deity, he cures disease through the medium of his priest, who flagellates the affected parts. His home is believed to be near Tsegihi in New Mexico. Sacrifices to Hatdastsisi are made up from reeds decorated with a design representing the blue yucca plant, which is buried in the earth to the east of the

tribal lodge. His priest wears a buckskin mask decorated with owl feathers, and a spruce collar, but otherwise ordinary Navaho dress with white buckskin leggings.

HATHOR
Origin Egyptian. Mother goddess and goddess of love.

Known period of worship from Old Kingdom (circa 2700 BC), but possibly earlier, until the end of Egyptian history (circa 400 AD).

Synonyms none significant.

Center(s) of cult Dendara, Giza, Thebes.

Art references wall paintings from the major sanctuary at Dendara; sculptures including an outstanding composition from the temple of King Menkaure at Giza; reliefs in the temple of Queen Hatsheput at Thebes; other contemporary sculpture and painting; sistrum rattles, etc.

Literary sources Book of the Dead, Harris Papyrus etc.

Hathor is a major Egyptian deity, with a benign motherly nature and invariably depicted, in one form or another, as a cow goddess with strong sky associations. Her father is the sun god Re and she is often described as the mother of all Egyptian pharaohs. In early times evidence suggests that she was regarded as the mother of Horus, but once the Osiris legend gained widespread popularity, she came to bear a complex protective rather than maternal relationship with Horus. In a conflicting tradition stemming from the cult center of Horus at Edfu in Upper Egypt, Hathor is also drawn as Horus' consort. In the legend of the "eye of Re," she shows a potentially destructive nature, but this is an isolated instance.

In art she may be depicted as a cow, as in the sculpture of her browsing among papyrus plants and suckling the pharaoh Amenhotep II from the Hathor sanctuary of Tuthmosis III, or in human form wearing a hairstyle that mimics the Mesopotamian "omega" symbol (see Ninhursaĝa). In the latter depiction she wears a crown that consists of a sun disc surrounded by the curved horns of a cow. She is prominent thus in many of the royal tombs in the Valley of the Kings at Thebes where she is seen as a funerary deity strongly linked with Re when he descends below the western horizon. Hathor is also represented, not infrequently, in the capitals of architectural columns. Like Ninhursaĝa she is associated with lions. Other symbols include the papyrus reed and the snake.

Hathor is also a goddess of love and sexuality, and is associated with the erotic aspects of music and dancing. Her priestesses carried *sistrum* rattles and *menat* "necklaces," both of which are percussion instruments used in cultic rites. The pharaoh was the "son of Hathor" and every Egyptian princess automatically became a priestess of the goddess. Many pharaonic tombs and magical papyri include description of "seven Hathors" who predict the fate of a child at birth and these deities were often called upon in spells.

Hathor enjoyed great popularity in Greco-Roman culture and many elements in the makeup of the goddess Aphrodite are modeled on her Egyptian style.

Hatmehyt *(she who leads the fishes)*
Fertility and guardian goddess of fish and fishermen. Egyptian. Local deity whose cult center was at Mendes [Tell el-Ruba] in the Nile delta. She is the consort of the ram god Banebdjedet. Depicted anthropomorphically, or as a fish.

Hatthi
Plague goddess. Hindu. Particularly associated with cholera in northwestern India.

Haubas
Local god. Pre-Islamic southern Arabian. Known from inscriptions.

Hauhet
Primordial goddess. Egyptian. One of the eight deities of the Ogdoad, representing chaos, she is coupled with the god Heh and appears in anthropomorphic form but with the head of a snake.

The pair epitomize the concept of infinity. She is also depicted greeting the rising sun in the guise of a baboon.

Haukim
Local god. Pre-Islamic southern Arabian. Possibly a deity concerned with arbitration and the law.

Haumiatiketike
Vegetation god. Polynesian (including Maori). The deity concerned with wild plants gathered as food, and particularly with the rhizome of the bracken, which has been traditionally relied on by the Maori in times of famine or need.

Haurun
Chthonic or earth god. Western Semitic (Canaanite). Haurun was introduced to Egyptian religion probably by émigré workers who related him to the sculpture of the Sphinx at Giza. Haurun was known locally as a god of healing.

Hayagriva *(horse neck)*
1. The most significant minor incarnation of the god Visnu. Hindu (Epic and Puranic). He probably originated as a horse god and later became an *avatara* associated with wisdom and knowledge. At the behest of Brahma, Hayagriva rescued the Vedas, stolen by two demons, from the bottom of the primeval ocean. Depicted in human form with the head of a horse and, according to the texts, eight hands. Attributes: book (Veda), horse's mane and rosary. Also the attributes of Visnu. Also Hayasirsa, Vadavavaktra.
2. Patron god of horses. Buddhist-Lamaist [Tibet]. One of a group of *dharmapala* with terrible appearance and royal attire, he is considered to be an emanation of Aksobhya or Amitabha. His *Sakti* is Marici. Color: red. Attributes: horse heads, staff and trident, but also arrow, ax, banner, bow, club, flames, flower, image of Aksobhya or Amitabha on the crown, lotus, noose, prayer wheel, skin, snakes, sword and trident. Three-eyed.

Haya-Ji
God of winds. Shinto [Japan]. Particularly the fierce god of whirlwinds and typhoons. In mythology he carried back to heaven the body of Ame-Waka-Hiko (the heavenly young prince) after he had been slain by an arrow from the "heavenly true deer bow."

Hayasum
Minor god. Mesopotamian (Sumerian and Babylonian-Akkadian). Known from texts, but of uncertain function.

Hayasya
1. Horse god. Hindu. Probably identical with Hayagriva.
2. Horse goddess. Buddhist. Attribute: the head of a horse.

Hazzi
Mountain god. Hittite and Hurrian. Invoked in Hittite treaties as a deity responsible for oaths. A deity of the same name was worshiped by the Hurrians, but not necessarily in the same context.

He Xian-Ku
Immortal being. Taoist (Chinese). One of the "eight immortals" of Taoist mythology, she was once a mortal being who achieved immortality through her exemplary life. The tutelary goddess of housewives and the only female deity among the group. Attributes include a ladle, lotus and peach fruit.

He Zur *(the great white one)*
Baboon god. Egyptian. Known from the Old Kingdom and regarded as a manifestation of Thot.

HEBAT
Origin Hittite and Hurrian [Anatolia]. Patron goddess and mother goddess.

Known period of worship 2000 BC or earlier until 1300 BC or later.

Synonyms possibly Hepatu; Hannahannas; Kubaba.

Center(s) of cult Hattusas [Boghazköy and Yazilikaya]; Arinna; other sanctuaries within the Hittite

Empire extending down into the north Syrian plain.

Art references   seals and seal impressions; sculptures; monumental rock carvings.

Literary sources   cuneiform and hieroglyphic texts from Boghazköy, etc.

Hebat was adopted from the Hurrian pantheon as the principal goddess of state religion in the Hittite Empire, though because of name changes her precise role is not always clear. She is described as the "great goddess." In some texts she is also the "sun goddess of Arinna" (a religious center near Boghazköy thus far lost to archaeology) but her relationship to the sun god, in one fragmentary text called Kumarbi and described as the king of the gods, god of right and justice, is unclear. She is more intimately linked with the weather god Tešub, "king of heaven, lord of the land of Hatti" and god of battle who, according to the same legend, displaced Kumarbi as king of the gods.

Hebat is often drawn as a matronly figure, without weapons, but generally in company with a lion. In a famous procession of gods carved on rock faces at Yazilikaya, the leading goddess is called Hepatu.

NOTE: these sanctuaries were often created where vertical rock facades suitable for carving relief sculptures existed near water.

Hebe

Goddess of youth. Greek. The daughter of Zeus and Hera and the consort of Herakles. The cup bearer of the gods of Olympus. In the Roman pantheon she becomes Juventas.

Heh

Primordial god. Egyptian. One of the eight deities of the Ogdoad, representing chaos, he is coupled with the goddess Hauhet and appears in anthropomorphic form but with the head of a frog. The pair epitomize the concept of infinity. He is also depicted greeting the rising sun in the guise of a baboon. In another context he is depicted kneeling, frequently on a basket that represents the hieroglyph for universality. He may carry the *ankh* symbol and hold palm rubs in each hand.

HEIMDALL   *(earth watcher)*

Origin   Nordic (Icelandic). Of uncertain status but probably a guardian deity.

Known period of worship   Viking period (circa 700 AD) and earlier, through to Christianization (circa 1100 AD).

Synonyms   Mardall; possibly Rig; "the white god."

Center(s) of cult   none known.

Art references   none known but probably the subject of anonymous carvings.

Literary sources   Icelandic codices; *Prose Edda* (Snorri); place names.

Heimdall is an enigmatic deity to whom there is considerable reference in the codices. He is drawn as the sentry or guardian, a tireless watcher over Asgard, needing no sleep and able to see in the darkest of nights. According to mythology, he lives beside the rainbow bridge connecting Asgard with the other realms. His symbol is the Gjallarhorn, which is used to alert the gods to the onset of Ragnarok (doom). He came also to be associated with guardianship of the world tree (Yggdrasil). Said to be born of nine giantesses, the waves of the sea (see Aegir) and in some legends he is the father of mankind. The *Voluspa* (Codex Regius) begins with the words: "Hear me, all ye hallowed beings, both high and low of Heimdall's children." Heimdall has close links with Freyja and his synonym Mardall parallels Mardoll (see Freyja). He may even have been a Vanir god. Said to have fought a sea battle with Loki.

HEKATE

Origin   Greek. Goddess of the moon and of pathways.

Known period of worship   circa 800 BC until Christianization (circa 400 AD).

Synonyms   Hecate.

Center(s) of cult   Lagina.

Art references   sculptures and reliefs.

Literary sources   *Theogony* (Hesiod) etc.

Hekate is the daughter of Perses and Asteria and is honored by Zeus as a goddess. She is the mother of Scylla and is specifically a goddess of pathways and crossroads traveled by night. Artistic representations show her carrying torches. Where paths met, a triple figure of Hecate rose from masks placed at the junction. Offerings were left in roadside shrines and at junctions. In later times she tended to become syncretized with the goddess Artemis. Hekate is also the patron of Medea and other witches, and in some parts of Thessaly she was worshiped by occult bands of female moon worshipers. In variations of the Demeter legends Hekate plays a part in the return of Persephone from Hades. She is also invoked as a bestower of wealth and favor.

Heket
Frog goddess concerned with birth. Egyptian. Minor deity who by some traditions is the consort of Haroeris (see Horus). Texts refer to a major sanctuary at Tuna el-Gebel, which has been totally obliterated. The remains of another sanctuary survive at Qus in Upper Egypt. In the Pyramid Texts she is referred to as a deity who eases the final stages of labor. Depicted as wholly frog-like or as a frog-headed human figure, often found on amulets or other magical devices associated with childbirth.

Hel(l)
Chthonic underworld goddess. Germanic and Nordic (Icelandic). The daughter of Loki and the giantess Angrboda, and the sibling of both the Midgard worm who will cause the sea to flood the world with the lashings of his tail, and of Fenrir, the phantom wolf who will swallow the sun at Ragnarok. She is queen of the otherworld, also known as Hel, and she takes command of all

who die, except for heroes slain in battle, who ascend to Valhalla. In some mythologies she is depicted as half black and half white. She was adopted into British mythology.

HELIOS
Origin   Greek. Sun god.

Known period of worship   circa 800 BC in Greece (but an adoption from much earlier times), until Christianization (circa 400 AD).

Synonyms   none.

Center(s) of cult   Rhodes.

Art references   Colossus of Rhodes (lost); other sculptures.

Literary sources   *Odyssey* (Homer); *Theogony* (Hesiod).

Helios is not specifically a Greek deity, since the concept of a sun god was more or less universal in the ancient world, but in the *Theogony* he is identified as the son of Hyperion and his sister Euryphaessa. He drives the chariot of the sun by day and descends beneath the ocean at night. On Rhodes, allegedly the site of the largest Greek statue of a deity, the so-called Rhodes "Colossus" cast in bronze, there was a celebrated festival of Helios during which a chariot with four horses was driven off a cliff, symbolizing the setting of the sun into the sea.

Hemantadevi
Goddess of winter. Buddhist-Lamaist [Tibet]. One of several seasonal deities. Also an attendant of Sridevi. Usually acompanied by a camel. Color: blue. Attributes: cup and hammer.

Hendursaǧa
God of the law. Mesopotamian (Sumerian and Babylonian-Akkadian). He was titled by Gudea of Lagaš "herald of the land of Sumer."

HEPHAISTOS
Origin   Greco-Roman, perhaps preceded by Etruscan. God of fire and smithies.

Known period of worship circa 1500 BC until Christianization (circa 400 AD).

Synonyms Hephaestus (Roman).

Center(s) of cult sanctuaries on Lemnos and, from circa 450 BC, in Athens opposite the Acropolis on the hill above the Agora. Also a significant shrine at Ephesus.

Art references sculptures and reliefs.

Literary sources Iliad, Odyssey (Homer); Theogony (Hesiod).

One of the twelve major deities of Olympus, Hephaistos is one of the sons of Hera who, in disappointment at having borne a child with deformed legs, threw him to earth where he was taken in and cared for by the people of Lemnos. In spite of physical disabilities, which set him apart from the other, physically perfect, deities of Olympus, Hephaistos draws on peculiar powers in the making of metal objects, which often possess magical qualities. He fathered the race of arcane *kabeiroi* blacksmith gods. The Hephaistos cult may have originated on the island of Lemnos with a tribal group the Greeks knew as Tyrsenoi. Hephaistos consorted briefly with Athena, who subsequently gave birth to Erichthonos, the first king of Athens. In the *Odyssey* he is said to be the consort of Aphrodite. In the *Iliad* he is married to Charis (Grace). He made a famous shield for Achilles that was said to reflect the world and all that was in it.

HERA
Origin Greek. The wife of Zeus.

Known period of worship circa 800 BC, but probably earlier, until Christianization (circa 400 AD).

Synonyms none.

Center(s) of cult Plataea (Boeotia) and others.

Art references sculptures and carvings.

Literary sources Iliad (Homer); Theogony (Hesiod).

As the long-suffering, but also jealous and quarrelsome wife of the philandering and all-powerful god Zeus, Hera adopts a position in the Greek pantheon that is at times ambiguous. The relationship with Zeus is incestuous since she is also the eldest daughter of Kronos and therefore Zeus's full sister. Mythology views her both as an independent and willful senior goddess, and as a tragicomic figure. Her marriage involves a degree of subterfuge, persuading Zeus by means of a magic girdle momentarily to forget his preoccupations with the Trojan War. In another piece of legend Zeus turns himself into a cuckoo so that he may fly into Hera's bosom. Who seduced whom thus remains ambiguous. Curiously, neither in literature nor in art is Hera perceived as a mother goddess. She seems to have borne only a limited number of Zeus's named children. The most prominent is Ares, yet he is also the least favored by the god. Other minor offspring included Hebe and Eileithyia. Hera relates to Zeus in three distinct "phases"—consummation in which she is *pais* the girl; wedding and fulfillment as *teleia*; and separation when she becomes *chera*.

As stepmother to Zeus's illegitimate children, Hera displays a jealous and malicious character, directing her anger at Herakles and Dionysos in particular. In a fire festival practiced in Boeotia to the "great Daedala," wooden images were burned to enact a legend whereby Plataea, one of Zeus's concubines, was stripped naked, humiliated and immolated by a jealous Hera.

During a New Year festival, the *Heraia*, to honor Hera, her priestesses were carried to the sanctuary on a cart drawn by oxen, which also presumably contained a statue of the goddess. Traditionally a women's games festival dedicated to Hera was also held on Olympus every four years.

HERAKLES *(the fame of Hera?)*
Origin Greek. Hero. Heroic god.

Known period of worship circa 800 BC, but probably originating from a prehistoric model, until Christianization (circa 400 AD).

Synonyms Heracles (Roman).

Center(s) of cult   none specific.

Art references   sculptures and carvings; pillars of Herakles.

Literary sources   *Herakles* (Euripedes); *Iliad* and *Odyssey* (Homer); *Catalogues* (Hesiod); *Dodekathlos* (Peisandros); votive inscriptions.

Herakles probably originates, out of a diffusion of heroic myths about hunting spirits, as a *shaman* who protected the tribe against wild animals and who possessed the necessary supernatural skills to ensure a safe outcome to the chase. This foundation may then have drawn on role models such as Ninurta, found in ancient Near Eastern culture. Herakles is a son of Zeus and Hera and the consort of Deianeira (destroyer of man). He is a heroic god of massive stature and prodigious appetite (see also Thor) who performs many feats of strength and courage, including the liberation of Prometheus. He is a slayer of lions and engages in combat with mythical creatures comparable to those found on Mesopotamian seals. He thus destroyed the seven-headed serpent and hunted many others. He is frequently depicted wearing a lion skin. His exploits include the cleansing of the Augean stables so as to earn a tenth part of the cattle of the sun, the catching of the Stymphalos birds, the temporary capture of Cerberus, the hound of Hades, and the picking of the golden apples of immortality.

Herakles became the god-ancestor of the Dorian kings. Alexander the Great had an image of him incorporated into his coinage. According to one legend, Deianeira contrived Herakles's death in a fit of jealous pique with a robe tainted with the poisoned blood of a centaur, ironically from one of Herakles's own arrows, which inflicted such torture upon him that he committed suicide by self-immolation on Mount Oita (near Trachis). In a conflicting myth Herakles slew his wife and children at Thebes. Herakles enjoyed cult centers in many places, with the notable exception of Crete. There were major sanctuaries on Thasos and on Mount Oita, where every four years the death of the god was marked by a sacrificial fire

festival. A similar rite is known from Tarsos in Cilicia for the god Sandon. The festivities were often marked by huge feasts. In Roman culture he becomes Hercules.

Hercules
God. Roman. See Herakles.

Heret-Kau
Underworld goddess. Egyptian (Lower). Very little is known of Heret-Kau. She was recognized chiefly in the Old Kingdom (27th to 22nd centuries BC), apparently concerned with guardianship of the deceased in the afterlife and sometimes appearing as a figurine in attendance on Isis in building foundations.

Hermaphroditos
God(dess) of uncertain status. Greek. The offspring of Hermes and Aphrodite and the lover of the water nymph Salmakis. Tradition has it that their passion for one another was so great that they merged into a single androgynous being.

HERMES
Origin   Greek. Messenger of the gods.

Known period of worship   circa 800 BC but probably earlier until Christianization (circa 400 AD).

Synonyms   none.

Center(s) of cult   Pheneos (Arcadia); otherwise few specific places, but strongly associated with wayside shrines and cairns.

Art references   probably certain prehistoric phallic figures marking boundaries; Parthenon frieze; Hermes of Praxiteles in Olympia.

Literary sources   *Iliad*, *Odyssey* (Homer); *Theogony* (Hesiod).

Hermes is the son of a nymph, Maia, who consorted with Zeus. He was born in the Arcadian mountains, a complex, Machiavellian character full of trickery and sexual vigor. His most significant consort is Aphrodite. He is a god of boundaries, guardian of graves and patron deity of shepherds. Perversely, he patronizes both heralds and thieves and is a bringer of good fortune. According to legend Hermes as a day-old infant stole the cattle of his elder brother Apollo while playing a lyre. Legend accords to him the invention of fire, also generated on his first day. Hermes's skills at theft were put to use by the other gods of Olympus, who sent him to liberate Ares from a barrel and to bring King Priam of Troy into conciliatory meeting with the Greek war hero Achilles after the death of Hector.

Classical art depicts Hermes wearing winged golden sandals and holding a magical herald's staff consisting of intertwined serpents, the *kerykeion*. He is reputedly the only being able to find his way to the underworld ferry of Charon and back again. Hence he was sent to bring both Persephone and Eurydice back from Hades. In company with other Greek gods, Hermes is endowed with not-inconsiderable sexual prowess which he directs toward countryside nymphs and with which he also maintains a healthy and thriving population of sheep and goats! He was often represented in wayside shrines in the form of a phallic pillar or post that was regarded as a funerary monument, hence the role of grave guardian.

Hermod

Messenger god. Nordic (Icelandic). One of the sons of the Viking god Othin, he was sent to Hel on a mission to obtain the release of the god Balder, who had been slain by the blind god Hod. The mission failed because only one creature in the world, a hag (probably Loki in disguise), failed to weep at Balder's loss and Hermod returned empty-handed. It may be argued that Hermod is less a deity than a demigod hero modeled on the Danish king in *Beowulf.* Also Heremod; Hermoth.

Hermus

River god. Roman. A sanctuary has been identified at Sardis.

Herne

Chthonic underworld god. Celtic (British) or Anglo-Saxon. Known locally from Windsor Great Park, Berkshire, England, he equates with the Welsh deities Gwynn ap Nudd and Arawn and is, according to legend, the leader of the phantom hunt. Depicted with stag-like antlers.

Heros

Chthonic underworld god. Thracian. Depicted as a horseman. His image regularly appears on funerary stelae.

Heruka

God. Buddhist (Mahayana). One of the most popular deities in the pantheon, though probably owing much to the influence of the Hindu god Siva. Originally an epithet for another Hindu god, Ganesa, but in Buddhism seen as a emanation of Aksobbhya. His *Sakti* is Nairatma and the product of their liaison is *nirvana* (eternal bliss). Typically he stands upon a corpse. In northeastern India, Heruka is worshiped as a compassionate god. Attributes: club, flayed human skin, image of Aksobhya, jewel, knife, fifty skulls, sword, staff and teeth.

HERYŠAF   *(he who is upon his lake)*

Origin   Egyptian. Primeval deity associated both with Osiris and Re.

Known period of worship   from circa 2700 BC, and probably earlier, until the end of Egyptian history (circa 400 AD).

Synonyms   Arsaphes (Plutarch).

Center(s) of cult   Hnes (Ihnasya el-Medina) near Beni Suef.

Art references   reliefs and sculptures including a gold figurine held by the Boston Museum of Fine Arts.

Literary sources   stela from Hnes later moved to Pompeii (Naples Museum).

Heryšaf is a ram god said to have emerged from the primeval ocean, possibly recreated in the form of a sacred lake at Hnes, the capital of Lower Egypt for a time at the beginning of the third millennium (during the First Intermediate Period). The god is depicted with a human torso and the head of a ram wearing the *atef* crown of Lower Egypt.

Heryšaf began as a local deity but took on national importance as the soul (*ba*) of Re, and of Osiris. Heryšaf's sanctuary was enlarged by Rameses II and the god is said to have protected the life of the last Egyptian pharaoh when the Persian and later the Macedonian dominations began. He eventually became syncretized with Herakles in Greco-Roman culture and Hnes became known as Herakleopolis.

Hesat

Goddess of birth. Egyptian. Minor guardian of pregnant and nursing mothers whose milk, the "beer of Hesat," nourishes humanity. Identified in some texts as the mother of Anubis. Depicted as a cow.

HESTIA

Origin Greek. Goddess of hearth and home.

Known period of worship circa 800 BC but probably earlier and through until Christianization (circa 400 AD).

Synonyms Histie.

Center(s) of cult local household shrines.

Art references none.

Literary sources Hymn to Aphrodite (Homer); *Phaedra* (Plato).

Hestia is a minor goddess in the Greek pantheon, but one who enjoyed importance in individual households. One of the daughters of Kronos and Rhea, her adherence to the fireside prevented her from joining the procession of gods described in Plato's *Phaedra*. On oath she remained virginal following the notion that fire is phallic and that she was wedded faithfully to the sacred hearth fire. By tradition maiden Greek daughters tended the household hearth. Hestia was conventionally offered small gifts of food and drink.

Hetepes-Sekhus

Chthonic underworld goddess. Egyptian. A minor deity accompanied by a retinue of crocodiles. As one of the manifestations of the vengeful "eye of Re," she destroys the souls of the adversaries of the underworld ruler Osiris. Depicted as a cobra or anthropomorphically with a cobra's head.

Hevajira

God. Buddhist (Mahayana). A *bodhisattva* (*buddha-designate*) and an emanation of Aksobhya. The Tantric form of Heruka and the Buddhist equivalent of the Hindu god Siva Nataraja. His *Sakti* is Nairatma or Vajravarahi and he may appear dominating the four *maras* (the Hindu gods Brahma, Visnu, Siva and Indra). Color: blue. Attributes: bell, bow, hook, image of Aksobhya on crown, jewel, lotus, prayer wheel, wine glass. He holds a skull in each hand and an assortment of other weapons. Three- or eight-headed, from two to sixteen arms and two or four legs; three-eyed.

Hexchuchan

God of war. Mayan (Itza, classical Mesoamerican) [Mexico]. One of several to whom the resin copal was burned before starting a battle. He may have been a tribal ancestor.

Hi-Hiya-Hi

Sun god. Shinto [Japan]. One of a number of minor sun deities engendered from the blood of the god Kagu-Tsuchi and worshiped in the mountain sanctuary of the fire *kamis*, Kono-Jinja. In Japan certain older people still worship the sun. They go outside at sunrise, face east and bow, clapping their hands.

Hiisi

Tree god. Pre-Christian Karelian [Finland]. Said to reside in pine forests. After Christianization he was degraded to a troll.

Hikoboshi

Astral god. Shinto [Japan]. The consort of the star goddess Ame-No-Tanabata-Hine-No-Mikoto. The two are, according to mythology, deeply in love. Their festival was merged with the Tibetan Bon festival of the dead, the *Ullumbana*. Also Kengyu-Sei.

Hiko-Sashiri-No-Kami

God of carpenters. Shinto [Japan]. One of several minor deities involved in the building of a sacred hall of great beauty, used to entice the sun goddess Amaterasu from her cave. Linked with the god Taoki-Ho-Oi-No-Kami.

Hilal

Moon god. Pre-Islamic Arabian. Specifically the deity of the new moon.

Hi'lina

Tribal god. Haida Indian [Queen Charlotte Island, Canada]. The personification of the thunderbird known to many Indian tribes. The noise of the thunder is caused by the beating of its wings, and when it opens its eyes there is lightning. The thunder clouds are its cloak.

Himavan *(snowy)*

Mountain god. Hindu. The personification of the Himalaya and considered to be the father of Parvati and Ganga. His consort is Mena. Also Himavat.

Himerus

God of desire. Greco-Roman. Member of the Olympian pantheon and attendant on Aphrodite (Venus).

Hina

Moon goddess. Polynesian [Tahiti]. In local traditions the daughter of the god Tangaroa and creator of the moon, which she governs. She lives in one of its dark spots representing groves of trees that she brought from earth in a canoe and planted. She is also represented as the consort of Tangaroa. Hina probably evolved in Tahiti from the Polynesian underworld goddess Hine-Nui-Te-Po. Also Sina (Samoa); Ina (Hervey Islands).

Hine-Ahu-One *(maiden formed of the earth)*

Chthonic goddess. Polynesian (including Maori). Engendered by the god Tane when he needed a consort because, with the exception of the primordial earth mother Papatuanuku, all the existing gods of creation were male. Tane created her out of the red earth and breathed life into her. She became the mother of Hine-Ata-Uira.

Hine-Ata-Uira *(daughter of the sparkling dawn)*

Goddess of light. Polynesian (including Maori). The daughter of the creator god Tane and Hine-Ahu-One. She did not remain a sky goddess but descended into the underworld, where she became the personification of death, Hine-Nui-Te-Po.

Hine-Nui-Te-Po *(great woman of the night)*

Chthonic underworld goddess. Polynesian (including Maori). Originally she was Hine-Ata-Uira, the daughter of Tane and Hine-Ahu-One, but she descended to rule over the underworld. She is depicted in human form but with eyes of jade, hair of seaweed and teeth like those of a predatory fish.

Hinglaj(-Mata)

Mother goddess. Hindu. Locally worshiped in northern India and particularly in Baluchistan.

Hinkon

Hunting god. Tungus (Siberian). Revered as the lord of all animals and controller of the chase.

Hi-No-Kagu-Tsuchi

Fire god. Shinto [Japan]. The deity whose birth caused the death by burning of the primordial goddess Izanami after which the eight thunders sprang from her corpse.

Hiranyagarbha   *(golden egg)*
Creator god. Hindu (Vedic). Identified in the opening of the *Rg Veda*, as the god of the golden seed emerging from the cosmic egg. The halves of the shell become sky and earth, and the yolk becomes the sun. The embryo impregnates the primordial waters.

Hittavainen
Hunting god. Pre-Christian Karelian (Finnish). Guardian deity of hare hunters.

Hlothyn
Goddess. Nordic (Icelandic). A less common name for the goddess Fjorgyn, noted in the *Trymskvoia* from the *Poetic Edda*. The mother of Thor.

HODER
Origin   Nordic (Icelandic). The blind god.

Known period of worship   Viking period (circa 700 AD) and earlier through to Christianization (circa 1100 AD).

Synonyms   Hod, Hodur.

Center(s) of cult   none known.

Art references   none known, but probably the subject of anonymous carvings.

Literary sources   Icelandic codices; *Prose Edda* (Snorri); *Historia Danica* (Saxo); runic inscriptions.

Hoder is one of the less well-defined of the Norse Aesir gods whose chief claim to notoriety lies in that he is responsible, in two separate narratives (Snorri's and Saxo's), for the death of the god Balder. In Snorri's Icelandic version Hoder is persuaded by Loki to hurl a piece of mistletoe at Balder (the only thing from which he is not protected): it turns into a lethal spear. According to Snorri, Hoder may even represent an agent of Hel. Saxo's Danish account has Hoder and Balder contesting the hand of the goddess Nanna. She eventually weds Hoder, who then slays Balder with a magic sword. Hoder himself is slain by his archenemy, the god Vali.

Hoenir
God. Nordic (Icelandic) Identified in the *Voluspa (Poetic Edda)* as the priest of the Viking gods who handles the "blood wands," i.e., divines future events. Some authors believe Hoenir to be a hypostasis of the god Othin, particularly concerned with giving the human race senses and feelings. Also known in north Germanic culture. He is said to have fled to Vanaheim after the great battle between the Aesir and Vanir gods.

Hokushin-O-Kami
Astral deity. Shinto [Japan]. The apotheosis of the "little bear," Ursa Minor.

Ho-Musubi-No-Kami
Fire god. Shinto [Japan]. One of a number of fire *kamis* who are honored in special *Hi-Matsuri* festivals. The sacred fire can only be generated by a board and stick and is regarded as a powerful purifier in Shintoism. The most celebrated temple of the fire *kamis* is on Mount Atago near Kyoto; worshipers come from all over Japan to obtain charms as protection against fire.

Ho-No-Kagu-Tsuchi-No-Kami
Fire god. Shinto [Japan]. One of a number of fire kamis who are honored in special *Hi-Matsuri* festivals. The sacred fire can only be generated by a board and stick and is regarded as a powerful purifier in Shintoism. The most celebrated temple of the fire *kamis* is on Mount Atago near Kyoto to which worshipers come from all over Japan to obtain charms as protection against fire.

Honus
God of military honors. Roman. Depicted as a youthful warrior carrying a lance and cornucopia.

Ho-Po
River god. Taoist (Chinese). The so-called "Count of the River," the deity who controls all rivers but particularly the Yellow River, and who is the subject of an official cult and sacrifice. According to tradition he achieved immortality by weighing himself down with stones and drowning himself.

He received an annual sacrifice of a young girl until the end of the Shou Dynasty circa 250 BC. Also Hebo; Ping-Yi.

Horagalles

Weather god. Lappish. The local embodiment of the Nordic (Icelandic) god Thor. Depicted as a bearded figure carrying a pair of hammers.

Horkos

God of oaths. Greek. The son of Eris (strife).

HORUS [*Greek*] *(the high one)*
Origin Egyptian. Sky god.

Known period of worship circa 3000 BC until end of Egyptian history (circa 400 AD).

Synonyms Har (Egyptian); Haroeris; Har-pa-khered or Harpokrates (Greek); Harsiese. Also Har-nedjitef or Harendotes (Greek); Har-mau or Harsomtus (Greek); Harakhti; Har-em-akhet or Harmachis (Greek).

Center(s) of cult universal throughout areas of Egyptian influence but particularly Mesen [Edfu] in Upper Egypt; Behdet in the delta; Nekhen or Hierakonpolis (Greek) [Kom el-Ahmar]; Khem or Letopolis (Greek) [Ausim]; also at Buhen close to the second Nile cataract; Aniba in lower Nubia.

Art references pre-dynastic monuments; sculptures throughout Egyptian period.

Literary sources Pyramid Texts; coffin texts, etc.

Horus is one of the most universally important gods in the Egyptian pantheon attested from the earliest recorded period. By tradition born at Khemmis in the Nile delta region, Horus's father was the dead Osiris, his mother was Isis, but a complex genealogy recognized him distinctly as Horus, Horus the child (Harpokrates) and Horus the elder. In legend he was the first ruler of all Egypt after an eighty-year struggle for supremacy with his brother and rival Seth.

Horus's symbol is the falcon and he is generally depicted either wholly as a hawk or in human form with a falcon's head. In some places the tradition by which his mother hid him in the papyrus marshes of the delta is recognized by depicting a falcon standing atop a column of papyrus reeds. He is also recognized as the "eye of Horus'—a human eye embellished with a typical Egyptian cosmetic extension and subtended by the markings of a falcon's cheek. As Horus the child, he is typically drawn naked and with fingers in mouth.

Horus is a form of the sun god. The alternative name Harakhti translates "Horus of the horizon" and he is sometimes depicted as a sun disc mounted between falcon's wings. He is also the symbol of the god kings of Egypt. In early dynastic times the ruler was a "follower of Horus" but by 3000 BC he *became* Horus in life and Osiris in death.

As Harpokrates, Horus is depicted naked and being suckled on Isis's knee and he often appears on amulets extending protection against lions, crocodiles, snakes and other dangerous animals. As the adult son of Isis, Haroeris, he performed the "opening of the mouth" ceremony on his dead father, Osiris, and avenged his death, regaining the throne of Egypt from Seth. Horus can also be the son of Horus the elder and Hathor.

The "eye of Horus" arises from the legendary incident in which Seth tore out Horus's eye, which was later restored by his mother. The symbol can represent security of kingship, perfection and protection against the evil influence of Seth.

Hotei

God of luck. Shinto [Japan]. One of seven gods of fortune known in Shintoism. He is depicted with a large belly and dressed in the robes of a Buddhist priest. Attributes include a fan and a large sack on his shoulder that "never stops to give, despite continuous demand."

Hotr(a) *(invoker)*

Minor goddess of sacrifices. Hindu (Vedic). She is invoked to appear on the sacrificial field before a ritual and is particularly identified with the act of prayer. Usually associated with the goddess Sarasvati.

Hours

Underworld goddesses. Egyptian. The twelve daughters of the sun god Re. They act in concert against the adversaries of Re and control the destiny of human beings in terms of each person's life span, reflecting the supremacy of order and time over chaos. The Hours are sometimes represented on the walls of royal tombs in anthropomorphic form with a five-pointed star above the head. Also Horae (Greek).

Hrsikesa *(lord of the senses)*

God. Hindu. Minor *avatara* of Visnu. His *Sakti* is Harsa.

HSI WANG MU

(queen of the western heaven)

Origin Taoist (Chinese). Goddess of longevity.

Known period of worship from prehistoric times until present.

Synonyms Xi Wang Mu.

Center(s) of cult throughout Chinese culture.

Art references paintings and sculptures.

Literary sources various philosophical and religious texts, mostly inadequately researched and untranslated.

One of the oldest deities known in China, she may have originated as a plague goddess depicted with feline fangs and tail. Under Taoism she became more benign in nature, identified as both governing the length of mortal life and granting the boon of longevity and, in some instances, immortality. Her home is in the western Chinese K'un Lun mountains or, alternatively, in the Hindukush, where she is accompanied by five jade ladies. According to tradition she visited the earth on two occasions, once in 985 BC to the emperor Mu, and again in the second century BC to the emperor Wu Ti.

She is the ruler of the west and is associated with the autumn, the season of old age. She is also identified in some texts as the golden mother of the tortoise, the animal that embodies the universe but that is also the dark warrior symbolizing winter and death. Her sacred animal is the crane, which is the Chinese symbol of longevity (it is often incorporated into funeral rituals). She is also said to be represented by the mythical phoenix.

Hu

God personifying royal authority. Egyptian. One of several minor deities born from drops of blood emitting from the penis of the sun god Re (see also Sia). Hu epitomizes the power and command of the ruler.

Huaca

Spirit being. Inca (pre-Columbian South America) [Peru, etc.]. The apotheosis of a natural object such as a rock or a place of local importance such as a spring. It is uncertain whether the principle is one of animism (when a deity takes on different natural shapes at will) or animatism (when an object *is* a supernatural being in its own right).

Huanacauri

Guardian spirit. Inca (pre-Columbian South America) [Peru, etc.]. The apotheosis of a special spindle-shaped stone sited near Cuzco that protected the Inca royal family and also featured strongly in the maturation rites of male Inca adolescents. Also Wanakawri.

Huang Ti

Astral god. Chinese. Allegedly a deified emperor, the so-called "yellow emperor," who rules the *moving* as distinct from *dark* heavens, the latter being presided over by the god Pak Tai. He is attributed with giving mankind the wheel.

Hubal

Local tutelary and oracular god. Pre-Islamic Arabian. An anthropomorphic figure of the deity in red carnelian still stands in the holy city of Mecca.

Huban

Tutelary god. Elamite [Iran]. Equating with the Sumerian Enlil.

Huehuecoyotl   *(old coyote)*

Minor god of sexual lust. Aztec (classical Mesoamerican) [Mexico]. One of the group classed as the Xiuhtecuhtli complex.

Huehuecoyotl-Coyotlinahual
(coyote his disguise)

Minor god of feather workers. Aztec (classical Mesoamerican) [Mexico]. One of the group classed as the Xiuhtecuhtli complex.

Huehuetotl   *(old god)*

God of fire. Aztec (classical Mesoamerican) [Mexico]. Associated with paternalism and one of the group classed as the Xiuhtecuhtli complex.

Huiracocha

See Vairacocha.

HUITZILPOCHTLI
(blue hummingbird on left foot)

Origin   Aztec (classical Mesoamerican) [Mexico]. Sun god, patron god of the Aztec nation.

Known period of worship   circa 750 AD, but probably much earlier, to circa 1500 AD.

Synonyms   Blue Tezcatlipoca.

Center(s) of cult   Tenochtitlan [Mexico City].

Art references   stone sculptures, murals, codex illustrations.

Literary sources   pre-Columbian codices.

The tutelary god of the Aztecs who also regarded him as a war god. He is the southern (blue) aspect or emanation of the sun god Tezcatlipoca, the so-called high-flying sun, and the head of the group classed as the Huitzilpochtli complex. He is regarded, in alternative tradition, as one of the four sons of Tezcatlipoca. His mother is the decapitated earth goddess Coatlicue, from whose womb he sprang fully armed. He slaughtered his sister (moon) and his 400 brothers (stars) in revenge for the death of his mother, signifying the triumph of sunlight over darkness. By tradition he led the people from their ancestral home in Aztlan (perhaps in the state of Nayarit) with the promise of securing a great empire. He appeared to them in the form of an eagle clutching a serpent in its talons and standing atop a cactus growing on a rocky island. This was Tenochtitlan, on the site of which Mexico City now stands.

The Great Temple of Coatepec was dedicated to the cosmic battle. In ritual Huitzilopochti was fed on human hearts taken from captives, the blood of which was said to cool his heat; several wars were instigated to gain sacrificial material. For the origin of the name "blue hummingbird on left foot," see Tezcatlipoca.

Huixtocihuatl   *(lady of Huixtotin)*

Goddess of salt makers. Aztec (classical Mesoamerican) [Mexico]. One of the group classed as the Tlaloc complex, generally involved with rain, agriculture and fertility.

Hun Hunapu

Creator god. Mayan (Yucatec and Quiche, classical Mesoamerican) [Mexico]. The father of Hunapu and Ix Balan Ku. According to the sacred Mayan text *Popol Vuh*, he was decapitated during a football game and his head became lodged in the calabash tree, which bore fruit from that day.

Hunab Ku

Creator god. Mayan (Yucatec, classical Mesoamerican) [Mexico]. The greatest deity in the pantheon, no image is created of Hunab Ku since he is considered to be without form. His son is the iguana god, Itzam Na, and he may have become the Mayan counterpart of the Christian god.

Hunapu

Creator god. Mayan (Yucatec and Quiche, classical Mesoamerican) [Mexico]. According to the sacred text *Popol Vuh*, the son of Hun Hunapu and the twin brother of Ix Balan Ku. Tradition has it that, like his father, he was decapitated in a historic struggle with the underworld gods and subsequently became the sun god, while his sibling is the apotheosis of the moon.

Hunaunic
See Chaob.

Hung Sheng *(holy one)*
Guardian god. Chinese. A deity who protects fishing boats and their crews against danger at sea in the Southern Ocean. His role is similar to that of the goddess Kuan Yin. Little is known of the origin of Hung Sheng, but he was allegedly a mortal who died on the thirteenth day of the second moon, which falls two days before the spring equinox when the sea dragon king, Lung Wang, is believed to leave the ocean and ascend into the heavens. The god is propitiated with cakes made from the first grain of the year, on the fifth day of the fifth month and in some traditions he is seen as an aspect of the sea dragon king.

Hunhau
God of death. Mayan (Yucatec and Quiche, classical Mesoamerican) [Mexico]. One of several "lords of death" listed in the codices who rule the underworld, Mictlan. He is generally depicted with canine attributes, or with the head of an owl. See also Yum Cimil. Also God A.

Hurabtil
God of uncertain status. Elamite [Iran]. Known only from passing mention in Akkadian texts. Also Lahurabtil.

Huracan
Creator god. Mayan (Quiche, classical Mesoamerican) [Guatemalan highlands]. Having created the world, he fashioned the first humans from pieces of corn dough. The counterpart of the Yucatec Hunab Ku.

Huvi
God of hunting. Ovimbundu [central Angola, West Africa]. All meat is kept in front of his shrines, which are decorated with poles capped by skulls. He is propitiated by dance and offerings, and presided over by a priesthood.

Hyakinthos
God of vegetation. Greek. An ancient pre-Homeric deity known particularly from Amyklai (pre-Dorian seat of kingship at Sparta). He is beloved by Apollo who perversely kills him with a discus and changes him into a flower. At Amyklai the bronze of Apollo stands upon an altar-like pedestal said to be the grave of Hyakinthos and, prior to sacrifice being made to Apollo, offerings to Hyakinthos were passed through a bronze door in the pedestal.

Hygieia
Goddess of health. Greek. The daughter of Asklepios, the physician god of healing. *Hygieia* was also a remedial drink made from wheat, oil and honey. She is depicted as Hygieia-Salus in a marble group sculpture in the Vatican, with Asclepius (the Roman god of healing) and the snake, which she is touching.

Hymenaios
God of marriage. Greco-Roman. Member of the Olympian pantheon and attendant on Aphrodite (Venus). Depicted with wings and carrying a torch, and invoked at the wedding ceremony.

Hyperion
God of primordial light. Greek. A pre-Homeric deity, one of the race of Titans whose consort is, according to some texts, Thea and who is the father of Helios and Selene.

Hypnos
God of sleep. Greek. One of the sons of the goddess of the night Nyx and the brother of Thanatos.

Hypsistos
Local tutelary god. Greco-Roman. Known from the region of the Bosphorus circa 150 BC until 250 AD. As late as the fourth century AD there are mentions in texts of *hypsistarii* in Cappadocia, who seem to have been unorthodox, Greek-speaking, Jewish fringe sectarians. The word *hypsistos* occurs in the Septuagint version of the *Vetus Testamentum* and means "almighty."

I

Ialonus
God of meadows. Romano-Celtic (British and Continental European). Known from inscriptions at Lancaster (Ialonus Contrebis) and Nimes.

Iapetos
God. Greek. One of the sons of Ouranos (heaven) and a member of the Titan race who clashed with the Olympian gods. He is the father of the heroes Atlas and Prometheus.

Icauna
River goddess. Romano-Celtic (Gallic). Guardian deity of the river Yonne [Brittany].

Icci
Animistic spirits. Siberian. See Urun Ajy Toyon.

Iccovellauna
Water goddess. Celtic (Continental European). Known only from inscriptions.

IDUNN
Origin Nordic (Icelandic) and possibly Germanic. Keeper of the apples of immortality.

Known period of worship Viking period (circa 700 AD) and earlier until Christianization (circa 1100 AD).

Synonyms Idun (German); Iduna.

Center(s) of cult none known.

Art references none known, though possibly the subject of anonymous carvings.

Literary sources Icelandic codices; *Prose Edda* (Snorri).

Little is recorded in mythology. Idunn is the consort of Bragi, the poet god, and she guards the golden apples of eternal youth for the gods of Asgard. She was abducted by Loki and handed over to the giant Thiassi as payment for the building of Valhalla. When the gods began to age, Loki assisted in recovering Idunn with her vital fruit. She reflects a northern version of the ancient symbolism of a deity who guards the life-sustaining fruit of heaven.

Ifa
God of wisdom. Yoruba [western Nigeria, West Africa]. An oracular deity who, according to tradition, lives in a sanctuary in the holy city of Ile Ife but who is called on by the tutelary god, Oldumare, for advice. He is the father of eight children, all of whom became paramount chiefs. At one time he is said to have left the earth whereupon famine and plague descended. His wisdom is gained through the implements of divination, namely palm nuts.

Ifru
God. Roman-North African. A rare example in this region of a named deity. Known from an inscription at Cirta [Constantine, Algeria].

Igalilik
Hunting spirit. Eskimo. He travels the icy wastes with a kitchen strapped to his back that includes a pot big enough to carry a whole seal. It boils as he carries it.

Igigi
Collective name of a class of gods. Mesopotamian (Sumerian and Babylonian-Akkadian). The group

of younger sky gods in the pantheon headed by Enlil (Ellil). They are often described in the texts in conjunction with the Anunnaki.

Ignerssuak   (great fire)
Sea god. Eskimo. One of a group of generally benevolent deities. Numbers of Ignerssuak are thought to surround mariners and the entrance to their home is on the seashore.

Ih P'en
Chthonic fertility god. Mayan (classical Mesoamerican) [Mexico]. The deity concerned with the growth of plants, and consort of the bean goddess Ix Kanan. He is also god of family life, property and other wealth. The couple are invoked as a single personality with the sacrifice of turkeys and chickens at sowing time. Ih P'en may be represented sowing corn.

Ihoiho
Creator god. Polynesian [Society Islands]. Before Ihoiho there was nothing. He created the primeval waters on which floated Tino Taata, the creator of mankind.

Ihy
God of music. Egyptian (Upper). Minor deity personifying the jubilant noise of the cultic sistrum rattle generally associated with the goddess Hathor. The son of Hathor and Horus. Particularly known from the Hathor sanctuary at Dendara. Depicted anthropomorphically as a nude child with a side lock of hair and with finger in mouth. May carry a sistrum and necklace.

Ikal Ahau
Chthonic god of death. Mayan (Tzotzil, classical Mesoamerican) [Mexico]. Perceived as a diminutive figure who lives in a cave by day but wanders at night attacking people and eating raw human flesh. He is also considered to inhabit Christian church towers in Mexico and is probably personified by vampire bats.

Ikenga   (right forearm)
God of fortune. Ibo [Nigeria, West Africa]. A benevolent deity who guides the hands of mankind. He is depicted wearing a horned headdress, and carrying a sword and a severed head. He is invoked as a household guardian.

Iksvaku
Creator god. Hindu (Vedic). One of the ancestral dynasty of sun gods or *Aditi*.

Iku-Ikasuchi-No-Kami
God of thunder. Shinto [Japan]. The most significant of the eight thunder deities that emerged from the corpse of Izanami after she was burned to death.

IL
Origin Canaanite [northern Israel, Lebanon and Syrian coastal regions]. Creator god.

Known period of worship circa 2000 BC, and probably earlier, until circa 200 BC or later.

Synonyms El (Hebrew); Latipan; Tor-'Il.

Center(s) of cult Ugarit (Ras Šamra), but also generally throughout areas of Canaanite influence.

Art references possibly a limited number of seals and stone reliefs.

Literary sources Ugaritic texts from Ras Šamra.

Il is the model on which the northern Israelite god, El, may have been based. The supreme authority, morally and creatively, overseeing the assembly of gods. The god to whom Baal is ultimately answerable. According to legend he lives in royal surroundings in a remote place lying at the confluence of two rivers. A stele found at Ras Šamra has a seated god with bull horns that may depict Il or Baal.

Ila
Minor goddess of sacrifices. Hindu (Vedic). She is invoked to appear on the sacrificial field before a

ritual. Usually associated with the goddess Sar-asvati, Ila is linked with the sacred cow and her epithets include "butter-handed" and "butter-footed."

Ilaalge
Local god. Western Semitic (Nabataean). Worshipped at Al-Ge [el-Gi in Wadi Musa, in the Arabian (esert].

Ilabrat
Minor god. Mesopotamian (Babylonian-Akkadian). The attendant and minister of state of the chief sky god Anu.

Ilat
Rain god. Pokot and Suk [Uganda and western Kenya, East Africa]. The son of the creator god Tororut. According to legend, when his father calls on him to fetch water Ilat always spills some, which descends to earth as rain.

I'lena   (rain woman)
Animistic spirit. Koryak [Siberia]. The consort of the creator spirit "universe" or Tenanto'mwan.

Ilmarinen
Sky god. Pre-Christian Finnish. A weather god who places the stars in the sky. Also a guardian deity of travelers and a smith-god who educated man in the use of iron and forging.

Ilyapa
Weather god. Inca (pre-Columbian South America) [Peru, etc.]. Also perceived as a thunder god, he became syncretized with Santiago, the patron saint of Spain. The Indians called Spanish firearms Ilyapa. Also Inti-Ilyapa; Coqi-Ilya; Illapa; Katoylla.

Im
Storm god. Mesopotamian. The cuneiform generally taken to refer to a storm god and therefore probably meaning either Iškur (Sumerian) or Adad (Akkadian).

Imana
Creator god. Burundi [East Africa]. He engendered the first man, Kihanga, who descended from heaven on a rope. Symbolized by a lamb or a young ram, he is also thought to speak through the roar of the bull.

Imiut
Minor chthonic god. Egyptian. One of the attendant deities of the necropolis, he is linked with Anubis, and in pre-dynastic times was represented by a skin hung on a pole.

Immap Ukua
Sea goddess. Eskimo [eastern Greenland]. The mother of all sea creatures and invoked by fishermen and seal hunters. See also Sedna.

Immat
Demonic god. Kafir [Afghanistan]. A deity to whom sacrifices were addressed in the Ashkun villages of southwestern Kafiristan. Legend has it that Immat carries off twenty virgin daughters every year. A festival includes blood sacrifice and dances by twenty carefully selected young priestesses.

Imporcitor
Minor god of agriculture. Roman. The deity concerned with harrowing the fields.

IMRA
Origin   Kafir [Afghanistan-southern Hindukush]. Creator god.

Known period of worship   unknown origins and continuing locally today.

Synonyms   Mara (Prasun region).

Center(s) of cult   chiefly at Kushteki.

Art references   large wooden sculptures.

Literary sources   Robertson G.S. *The Kafirs of the Hindukush* (1896); Morgenstierne G. *Some Kati Myths and Hymns* (1951).

Supreme Kafir creator god who generated all other deities by churning his breath to life inside a golden goatskin. Other legendary sources have him taking his paramount position through guile from among an existing pantheon and possibly superseding an earlier creator god, Munjem Malik. His mother was said to be a giantess with four tusks. Imra is a sky god who lives among cloud and mist and who is responsible, at least in part, for cosmic creation. He positioned the sun and moon in the heavens. He is the ancestor of all Prasun tribal chiefs. His sacred animal is the ram, which was sacrificed regularly, as was the cow and, less frequently, the horse. Figures of the god are crudely anthropomorphic. The main sanctuary to Imra, at a small town called Kushteki, was destroyed in the early 1900s, but was an imposing and ornately carved wooden structure. Other smaller shrines survive, scattered throughout the region.

Imra is generally perceived as a beneficent teacher who has endowed mankind with various gifts including cattle, dogs, wheat, the wheel and the element iron. He also has a destructive side to his nature, causing floods and other havoc.

Ina'hitelan

Guardian spirit. Koryak [southeastern Siberia]. The father of cloud man Ya'halan, he is perceived as a supervisor of the skies and reindeer are sacrificed to him.

INANA   *(queen of heaven)*

Origin Mesopotamian (Sumerian) [Iraq]. Goddess of fertility and war.

Known period of worship circa 3500 BC to 1750 BC.

Synonyms Inninna; Ištar [Akkadian]; Nin-me-sarra (lady of a myriad offices).

Center(s) of cult Unug [Warka]; also Erbil and Nineveh.

Art references plaques, reliefs, votive stelae, glyptics, etc.

Literary sources cuneiform texts, particularly the *Gilgameš Epic* and *Inana's Descent and the Death of Dumuzi*; temple hymns, etc.

The paramount goddess of the Sumerian pantheon. Though not technically a "mother goddess," she constitutes the first in a long line of historically recorded female deities concerned with the fertility of the natural world. Inana is also a warrior goddess. She is the daughter of the moon god Nanna and sister of Utu and Iškur. In alternative tradition, she is the daughter of An. Her attendant is the minor goddess Ninšubur, and her champion is the mythical hero Gilgameš. Of her many consorts, the most significant is the vegetation god Dumuzi. She becomes the handmaiden of An, the god of heaven. She is also identified as the younger sister of the underworld goddess Ereškigal. She is the tutelary deity of the southern Mesopotamian city of Unug (Uruk), where her sanctuary is the Eanna temple.

Inana is usually depicted wearing a horned headdress and tiered skirt, with wings and with weapon cases at her shoulders. Her earliest symbol is a bundle of reeds tied in three places and with streamers. Later, in the Sargonic period, her symbol changes to a star or a rose. She may be associated with a lion or lion cub and is often depicted standing atop a mountain. She may be embodied in the sacred tree of Mesopotamia, which evolved into a stylized totem made of wood and decorated with precious stones and bands of metal.

Originally Inana may have been goddess of the date palm, as Dumuzi was god of the date harvest. Her role then extended to wool, meat and grain and ultimately to the whole of the natural world. She was also perceived as a rain goddess and as the goddess of the morning and evening stars. She was worshiped at dawn with offerings, and in the evening she became the patron of temple prostitutes when the evening star was seen as a harlot soliciting in the night skies. In less commonly encountered roles she is goddess of lighting and extinguishing fires, of tears and rejoicing, of enmity and fair dealing and many other, usually conflicting, principles.

According to legend, Enki, who lives in the watery abyss or Abzu beneath the city of Eridu, was persuaded while drunk, and through Inana's subterfuge, to endow her with more than a hundred divine decrees, which she took back to Unug in her reed boat and which formed the basis of the Sumerian cultural constitution.

Inana is one of three deities involved in the primordial battle between good and evil, the latter personified by the dragon Kur. She is further engaged in a yearly conflict, also involving her consort Dumuzi, with Ereškigal. She descends to the underworld to challenge Ereškigal and finds herself stripped naked and tried before the seven underworld judges, the Anunnaki. She is sentenced and left for dead for three days and nights before being restored at the behest of Enki, the god of wisdom, who creates two beings, Kur-gar-ra and Gala-tur-ra, to secure her release and to revive her by sprinkling her with the food and water of life.

Inara

Minor goddess. Hittite and Hurrian. Daughter of the weather god Tešub. In the legendary battle with the dragon Illuyankas she assists her father to triumph over evil.

Inari   (rice grower)

God(dess) of foodstuffs. Shinto [Japan]. The popular name of a god(dess) worshiped under the generic title Miketsu-No-Kami in the Shi-Den sanctuary of the imperial palace, but rarely elsewhere. The deity displays gender changes, develops many personalities and is revered extensively in Japan. Inari is often depicted as a bearded man riding a white fox but, in pictures sold at temple offices, (s)he is generally shown as a woman with long flowing hair, carrying sheaves of rice and sometimes, again, riding the white fox. Inari sanctuaries are painted bright red, unlike most other Shinto temples. They are further characterized by rows of wooden portals that form tunnels leading to the sanctuary. Sculptures of foxes are prolific (an animal endowed, in Japanese tradition, with supernatural powers) and the shrines are deco-

rated with a special device, the Hoju-No-Tama, in the shape of a pear surrounded by small flames. Often identified with the food goddess Toyo-Uke-Bime.

Inazuma

Goddess of lightning. Shinto [Japan]. The so-called consort of the rice. In certain regions when lightning hits a rice field bamboos are erected around the spot to signify that it has been sanctified by the fire of heaven. Also Ina-Bikari (light of rice) and Ina-Tsurubi (fertility of rice).

Indr

Tutelary and weather god. Kafir [Afghanistan]. The brother of Gish and father of Disani and Pano. Probably derived from the more widely recognized Aryan god Indra, Indr is known chiefly from the Waigal and Prasun areas of the southern Hindukush. It is generally assumed that he was ousted from major importance by the god Imra. Indr is also a god of wine who owns substantial vineyards and is associated in south Nuristan with wine rituals (the annals of Alexander the Great suggest that he met with wine-drinking "worshipers of Dionysos" in the Hindukush).

In the Ashkun region of southwestern Kafiristan, a famous vineyard near the village of Wamais, is sacred to Indr. Also Inder.

INDRA   (possibly meaning "mighty")
Origin   Hindu [India]. Weather god.

Known period of worship   circa 1500 BC and possibly earlier until present day.

Synonyms   none.

Center(s) of cult   none.

Art references   sculptures in metal and stone; reliefs.

Literary sources   *Rg Veda* and other texts.

One of the most important of the Vedic deities. It is uncertain if he originated as a weather god or as a solar deity. The *Rg Veda* identifies him with the bull and he is considered to be related to the Hittite weather god Tešub. He is thus also god of fertility and war. In the later Vedas he is described as the son of Dyaus Pita and Prthivi. His consort is Indrani and his sons are Jayanta, Midhusa, Nilambara, Rbhus and Rsabha.

In later Hinduism he is a *dikpala* (guardian) of the eastern direction.

2. In Buddhism Indra is a *dikpala* with the color yellow, but of lesser importance than the Hindu god.

3. In Jainism Indra is a head of various heavens but, again, of lesser importance.

Indrani
Goddess of wrath. Hindu (Vedic and Puranic). Daughter of Puloman, a demonic figure killed by the god Indra, and the *Sakti* and consort of Indra. One of seven *mataras* (mothers) who in later Hinduism became regarded as of evil intent. Also one of a group of eight *astamataras* personifying jealousy (also named Aindri in this capacity). In another grouping one of nine *navasaktis* or astral deities who, in southern India, rank higher than the *saptamataras*. Her attendant animal is either an elephant or a lion. Attributes: hook, rosary, Santana flower, staff and water jar. One thousand-eyed. Also Aindri; Mahendri; Paulomi; Saci; Sujata.

Indukari
Goddess. Hindu (Epic and Puranic). Consort of the god Samba. Attribute: a shield.

Ing
Ancestral god. Anglo-Saxon. According to a runic poem he is the father of the Saxons and appeared from across the sea and then disappeared, never to return. He may also be classed as one of the Nordic Aesir gods.

Inkanyamba
Storm god. Zulu [southern Africa]. The deity specifically responsible for tornados and perceived as a huge snake coiling down from heaven to earth.

According to some Zulu authorities, Inkanyamba is a goddess of storms and water.

Inmar
Sky goddess. Votyak (Finno-Ugric). The name became incorporated into Christian tradition and interpreted as "the mother of God."

Inmutef   *(pillar of his mother)*
Minor god. Egyptian. The "bearer of the heavens," his cult is linked with that of the goddess Hathor.

Insitor
Minor god of agriculture. Roman. The deity concerned with sowing of crops.

Inta   *(gods their father)*
God of fire. Aztec (classical Mesoamerican) [Mexico]. Associated with paternalism and one of the group classed as the Xiuhtecuhtli complex.

Intercidona
Minor goddess of birth. Roman. A guardian deity invoked to keep evil spirits away from the newborn child. Symbolized by a cleaver.

Inti   *(sun)*
Sun god. Inca (pre-Columbian South America) [Peru, etc.]. His consort is the moon goddess Mama-Kilya. Inti was depicted as a trinity in the sanctuaries in Cuzco, possibly in deference to the Christian Trinity. The Temple of the Sun is reported to have housed images, in gold, of all the sky gods in the Inca pantheon on more or less equal terms, since the sun is regarded as one of many great celestial powers. Inti may also have been depicted as a face on a gold disc. The so-called "fields of the sun" supported the Inca priesthood. The three sun deities are Apo-Inti (lord sun), Cori-Inti (son sun) and Inti-Wawqi (sun brother). The sun god(s) is perceived as the progenitor of the Inca rulers at Cuzco through two children—a son Manco Capac and his sister/consort Mama Ocllo Huaco. The Quechua Indians of the central Andes call the same deity Inti Huayna

Capac and perceive him as part of a trinity with the Christian god and Christ.

Io
See Kiho.

Iord
Earth goddess. Nordic (Icelandic). In Viking tradition Iord embodies the abstract sacredness of the earth. Said to be the mother of Thor and in some legends, the wife of Othin. See also Fjorgynn.

Ipalnemoani *(he who through one lives)*
Creator god. Aztec (classical Mesoamerican) [Mexico]. One of the group classed as the Ometeotl complex.

Ipy
Mother goddess. Egyptian. In the Pyramid Texts Ipy appears occasionally as a benevolent guardian and wet nurse to the king. She is also perceived to exert a benign influence on amulets. Depicted as a hippopotamus or anthropomorphically with a hippo's head. Also Ipet.

Iris *(rainbow)*
Messenger goddess. Greek and Roman. The special attendant of the goddess Hera, Iris is a virgin goddess who forms the rainbow bridge between heaven and earth. Depicted with wings and carrying a staff.

Irmin
War god. Germanic. Probably equating with Tiwaz, the name implies one of great strength. In Saxony, there is the so-called Irmin pillar that may be a reference to the deity.

Iruva
Sun god. African. A number of tribes worship the sun by this generic name, particularly in Cameroon, Congo and Tanzania.

Isa *(1)*
a. An aspect of Siva. Hindu (Puranic). Also a *dikpala* or guardian of the northeastern quarter, and an *ekadasarudra* (one of the eleven rudras). Rides upon a goat or a bull. Color: white. Attributes: five arrows, ax, drum, fruit, hatchet, hook, lute, noose, rosary, staff. Three-eyed.
b. Guardian deity. Buddhist. A minor *dikpala* attended by a bull. Color: white. Attributes: cup, moon disc and trident.

Isa *(2)*
River goddess. Songhai [Niger, West Africa]. The mother goddess of the river Niger.

Išara
Goddess of marriage and childbirth. Mesopotamian (Babylonian-Akkadian) and western Semitic. Also a deity concerned with the enforcing of oaths. Known chiefly from early inscriptions and some Akkadian texts. Her Mesopotamian cult center was the Babylonian town of Kisurra, but she is also thought to have been worshiped across a wide area among Syrians, Canaanites and Hittites. Her symbol is the scorpion. Also Ešara.

Isdes
Chthonic god of death. Egyptian. Known from the Middle Kingdom onward, he is one of the minor deities concerned with the judgment of thse dead. He became syncretized with Anubis.

Ishi-Kori-Dome
God(dess) of stone cutters. Shinto [Japan]. Of ambiguous gender, this deity created the stone mold into which the bronze was cast to make the perfect divine mirror. It was used so that Amaterasu, the sun goddess, could see her glorious reflection and so be enticed from the dark cave where she had hidden herself to escape the excesses of the god Susano-wo. Ishi-Kori-Dome is also the tutelary deity of mirror makers and was one of the escorts for Prince Ninigi when he descended from heaven to earth. Generally invoked beside fire and smith *kamis*.

Isimud

Messenger god. Mesopotamian (Sumerian). Readily identified by possessing two faces looking in opposite directions, Isimud is the messenger of the god Enki. Also Isinu; Usumu (Akkadian).

ISIS

Origin   Egyptian. Mother goddess.

Known period of worship   Early dynastic period (circa 2700 BC) and probably earlier until the end of Egyptian history (circa 400 AD).

Synonyms   none.

Center(s) of cult   universal throughout area of Egyptian influence, but particularly at Giza and at Behbeit el-Hagar in the Nile delta. Also at Thebes on the west bank, at Dendara and in the temple of Seti I at Abydos. A Greco-Roman sanctuary existed on Philae (now moved to Agilqiya).

Art references   monumental carving; contemporary sculptures; wall paintings and reliefs.

Literary sources   Pyramid Texts; the *Great Hymn to Isis* from the stele of Amenemose (Louvre); etc.

Isis is one of the great deities of the Egyptian pantheon and, with Osiris, probably maintained the most universal appeal outside Egypt. Greco-Roman culture was particularly enamored of her and called her the *Stella Maris* (star of the sea), represented in the heavens by the north star. An offspring of Geb and Nut in the Heliopolis genealogy, Isis is the mother of the god kings of Egypt and both elder sister and consort of Osiris. The other siblings include Seth and Nephthys. Isis is depicted in human form, but usually wearing a crown in the form of a throne or cow horns encircling a sun disc (see Hathor). She may also be depicted, wholly or in part, as a hawk. From the New Kingdom (circa 1500 BC) onward she is also associated with a device not dissimilar to the *ankh* symbol and known as the "Isis knot." The symbol was incorporated into a bloodstone amulet known as the *tyet*.

In legend she is responsible twice for restoring Osiris, once after Seth has thrown his body into the Nile and again after Seth has dismembered it. She impregnates herself from his corpse as he is entering the underworld as its ruler, and from Osiris's semen conceives Horus, to whom she gives birth in the papyrus swamps at Khemmis in the Nile delta. Thus, since Horus instilled himself into the king of Egypt during life, and Osiris took over on death (see also Horus and Osiris), the ruler was perceived to suckle at the breast of Isis (as Harpokrates). As Isis guarded Horus against injury, so she also protected the earthly king of Egypt as a child. In the courts of the gods, Isis put up a strong challenge in support of Horus's claim to the throne against that of her brother Seth, and she showed Seth to be guilty of sodomy against Horus.

In the Greco-Roman period, Isis sanctuaries were built on the island of Delos and at Pompeii. There is much argument that the Isis cult influenced the portrayal of the Christian Virgin Mary, who was also known as *Stella Maris* and whose portraits with the Christ often bear a striking similarity to those of Isis with Horus.

IŠKUR

Origin   Mesopotamian (Sumerian) [Iraq]. Storm god.

Known period of worship   circa 3500 BC and probably earlier, until circa 1750 BC.

Synonyms   Adad (Akkadian).

Center(s) of cult   Karkara.

Art references   plaques: votive stelae; glyptics, etc.

Literary sources   cuneiform texts.

The chief rain and thunder god of herdsmen, Iškur is described as the brother of the sun god Utu. In creation mythology Iškur is given charge over the winds, the so-called "silver lock of the heart of heaven," by the god Enki. According to some authors, in prehistoric times he was perceived as a bull or as a lion whose roar is the thunder. He may be depicted as a warrior riding across the skies in a chariot, dispensing raindrops and hailstones. In one text he is identified as the son of An and twin brother of Enki. He is to be compared with Ninurta who was primarily a god of farmers. He was also adopted by the Hittites as a storm god.

Issaki
Goddess. Hindu (Epic and Puranic). Depicted carrying a headless child. Also Kerala.

Istadevata
1. Generic title of a personal god. Hindu. The name given to a deity chosen by an individual for special worship in return for protection and spiritual guidance. Also the name given to a household icon.
2. Tutelary god. Buddhist, particularly in Tibet. The personal deity of one preparing for Tantric initiation.

Ištanu
Sun god. Hittite. A god of judgment, depicted bearing a winged sun on his crown or headdress, and a crooked staff.

IŠTAR *(star of heaven)*
Origin Mesopotamian (Babylonian-Akkadian) [Iraq]. Goddess of fertility and war.

Known period of worship circa 2500 BC until circa 200 AD.

Synonyms Inana [Sumerian].

Center(s) of cult throughout Mesopotamia particularly at Babylon and Nineveh, with smaller sanctuaries across a more extensive area of the ancient world including Mari.

Art references votive inscriptions; cylinder seals and seal impressions; limestone reliefs, etc.

Literary sources cuneiform texts including *The Descent of Ištar, Gilgameš and Etana*; temple hymns.

Ištar is probably the most significant and influentual of all ancient Near Eastern goddesses. She is the counterpart of, and largely takes over from, the Sumerian Inana. She is the daughter, in separate traditions, of the moon god Sin and of the god of heaven Anu. She is generally depicted with wings and with weapon cases at her shoulders. She may carry a ceremonial double-headed mace-scimitar embellished with lion heads and is frequently accompanied by a lion. She is symbolized by an eight-pointed star.

In Egypt she was revered as a goddess of healing. There is evidence from the el-Amarna letters that Amenhotep III, who apparently suffered from severe tooth abscesses, was loaned a statue of Ištar from Nineveh in the hopes that its curative powers might help his suffering.

Ištaran
Local god. Mesopotamian (Sumerian). The tutelary god of the city of Der, east of the river Tigris in northern Babylonia. Also Gusilim.

Isten
Creator god. Pre-Christian Hungarian. According to tradition, his sacred animal, the eagle, guided the Hungarian people to their homeland. Other attributes include arrow, horse phallus and tree.

Išum
Minor god. Mesopotamian (Babylonian-Akkadian). The brother of Šamaš, the sun god, and an attendant of the plague god Erra. He may have been a god of fire and, according to texts, led the gods in war as a herald but was nonetheless generally regarded as benevolent. Known particularly from the Babylonian legend of *Erra and Išum*. Also Endursaga.

Isvara
Epithet of the god Siva. Hindu (Puranic). In Sanskrit designated the "supreme god who rules the universe." The generic title of a Hindu's personal high god. In Buddhism the name of a *yaksa* attending the eleventh *tirthankara*.

Itonde
God of death. Mongo and Nkundo [central Zaire, Africa]. He consumes rats as food and is also the

god of hunters in the dark jungle forests. Described in the *Epic of Lianja* as the first man to die whose spirit reincarnated at the instant of death, into his son Lianja. He possesses a bell with magical properties, the *elefo*, by which he predicts where death will strike.

Itzam Cab

Chthonic earth god. Mayan (classical Mesoamerican) [Mexico]. The earth aspect of the creator god Itzam Na. He is also a god of fire, and hearthstones are called "head of Itzam Cab." Sticks of firewood are his thighs, flames his tongue and the pot resting on the fire his liver. In his vegetation aspect he is depicted with leaves of corn sprouting from his head.

ITZAM NA   *(iguana house)*

Origin   Mayan (classical Mesoamerican) [Mexico]. Creator god.

Known period of worship   circa 300 AD until circa 900 AD.

Synonyms   Hun Itzamna; Yaxcocahmut; God K.

Center(s) of cult   Chichen Itza and other sites, mainly in the Yucatan peninsula.

Art references   stone carvings, codex illustrations.

Literary sources   mainly the *Vienna* Codex.

The principal god in the Mayan pantheon according to the *Vienna* codex. He lives in the sky and sends the rain. Also a god of medicine and a fire god. By tradition the Maya believed that the world was set within a vast house, the walls and roof of which were formed by four huge iguanas standing upright but with their heads bent downwards. Each reptile has its own direction and color.

Itzam Na is not invoked in the rites of modern Yucatan peasants but, at one time, was the subject of a ritual that involved daubing the lowest step of a sanctuary with mud and the other steps with blue pigment (the color peculiar to rain gods). At Chichen Itza sacrifice was regularly made to a huge crocodile believed to be the personification of the god.

Itzam Na is probably the same deity as Hunab Ku, who is identified in some texts as his father, but in the guise of a reptile. He may also be depicted anthropomorphically. In his aspect as a vegetation god, Itzam Na may be the same as the so-called God K of the codices, recognized by a long branching nose in the form of a pair of infolded leaves. His earthly aspect is called Itzam Cab, in which guise corn leaves sprout from the top of his head.

Itzcuintli

Goddess of hearths. Aztec (classical Mesoamerican) [Mexico]. A guardian deity of the home personified by fire. One of the group classed as the Xiuhtecuhtli complex.

Itzpapalotl   *(obsidian butterfly)*

Minor mother goddess. Aztec (classical Mesoamerican) [Mexico]. One of the group classed as the Teteoinnan complex. Also recognized as a fire goddess.

Itzpapalotl-Itzcueye   *(possessor of obsidian skirt)*

Minor mother goddess. Aztec (classical Mesoamerican) [Mexico]. One of the group classed as the Teteoinnan complex. Limited to the Valley of Mexico.

Itztapal Totec   *(our lord the stone slab)*

Fertility god. Aztec (classical Mesoamerican) [Mexico]. A god of agriculture but also a patron of precious metallurgists. One of the group classed as the Xipe Totec complex.

Itztli   *(obsidian blade)*

God of justice. Aztec (classical Mesoamerican) [Mexico]. One of the group classed as the Tezcatlipoca complex.

Iunones

Goddesses of femininity. Greco-Roman. Generally depicted as a trio of *matres*. A shrine at Saintes

Maries on the Rhone delta was originally dedicated to the Iunones Augustae.

Iusaas

Creator goddess. Egyptian (Lower). Locally known from Heliopolis and perceived as being a feminine principle in the cosmos equating to the sun god Atum. Depicted anthropomorphically with a scarab on her head.

Iuturna

Goddess of springs and wells. Roman. Invoked particularly in times of drought.

Ix Chebel Yax

Mother goddess. Mayan (classical Mesoamerican) [Mexico]. Goddess of weaving and patroness of weavers, whose tutelage is shared with Ix Chel. See also Chibirias.

Ix Chel

Moon goddess. Mayan (Yucatec and Quiche, classical Mesoamerican) [Mexico]. Also the goddess of childbirth and medicine and of rainbows. A consort of the sun god. She has a major shrine as Cozumel and small figurines of the goddess have been conventionally placed beneath the beds of women in labor. Such women are considered to be in great danger at times of lunar eclipse when the unborn child may develop deformities. Ix Chel is a guardian against disease and the Quiche Indians regard her as a goddess of fertility and sexual intercourse.

A goddess of weaving, believed to be the first being on earth to weave cloth, she was employed in this craft when she first attracted the attention of the sun god. She carries her loom sticks across the sky to protect her from jaguars. Under Christian influence she has been largely syncretized with the Virgin Mary. Also Goddess I. See also Ix Chebel Yax.

Ix Kanan

Vegetation goddess. Mayan (classical Mesoamerican) [Mexico]. The guardian of the bean plant. Her consort is the corn god Ih P'en. The couple are invoked at sowing time when turkeys and chickens are sacrificed.

Ix Zacal Nok   (lady cloth weaver)

Creator goddess. Mayan (classical Mesoamerican) [Mexico]. The consort of the sun god Kinich Ahau and also the inventor of weaving. She may represent another aspect of the mother goddess Colel Cab. Also Ix Azal Uoh; Ix Chel.

Ixcozauhqui   (yellow face in the house)

God of fire. Aztec (classical Mesoamerican) [Mexico]. Associated with paternalism and one of the group classed as the Xuihtecuhtli complex.

Ixnextli   (eyelashes)

Goddess of weavers. Aztec (classical Mesoamerican) [Mexico]. One of the group classed as the Teteoinnan complex.

Ixpuztec   (broken face)

Minor underworld god. Aztec (classical Mesoamerican) [Mexico]. One of the group classed as the Mictlantecuhtli complex.

Ixquimilli-Itzlacoliuhqui   (eye-bundle curved obsidian blade)

God of justice. Aztec (classical Mesoamerican) [Mexico]. One of the group classed as the Tezcatlipoca complex.

Ixtab

Goddess. Mayan (classical Mesoamerican) [Mexico]. Tutelary goddess of suicides.

Ixtlilton   (little black face)

Minor god of sexual lust. Aztec (classical Mesoamerican) [Mexico]. One of the group classed as the Xuihtecuhtli complex.

Izanagi-No-Kami   (his augustness the one who invites)

Creator god. Shinto [Japan]. One of seventeen beings involved in creation. His consort is Izanami-No-Kami. They are strictly of Japanese origin with no Chinese or Buddhist influence. Jointly they are responsible to the other fifteen primordial deities to "make, consolidate and give birth to this drifting land." The reference, in the *Kojiki* sacred text, is to the reed beds that were considered to float on the primal waters. The pair were granted a heavenly jeweled spear and they stood upon the floating bridge of heaven, stirring the waters with the spear. When the spear was pulled up, the brine that dripped from it created the island of Onogoro, the first dry land, believed to be the island of Nu-Shima on the southern coast of Awagi. According to mythology, the pair created two beings, a son Hiru-Ko and an island Ahaji. They generated the remaining fourteen islands that make up Japan and then set about creating the rest of the *kami* pantheon. Izanagi's most significant offspring include Amaterasu, the sun goddess, born from his nose and Susano-Wo, the storm god,

born from his left eye, who are the joint rulers of the universe. Also Izanagi-No-Mikoto.

Izanami-No-Kami
(her augustness the one who invites)
Creator goddess. Shinto [Japan]. See Izanagi for full details. Izanami was burned to death by the birth of the fire god Hi-No-Kagu-Tsuchi, after which the eight thunders sprang from her corpse. Also Izanami-No-Mikoto.

Izquitecatl
Fertility god. Aztec (classical Mesoamerican) [Mexico]. One of the group classed as the Ometochtli complex personifying the maguey or agave plant from which a potent drink called pulque is brewed.

J

Jabru
Sky god. Elamite [Iran]. Local deity largely eclipsed by An.

JAGANNATH *(lord of the world)*
Origin Hindu (Puranic) [India]. Transmutation of the essence of the god Visnu.

Known period of worship circa 400 AD and probably earlier until present day.

Synonyms Juggernaut.

Center(s) of cult Bengal and Puri (Orissa).

Art references bronze sculptures. Well-known wooden image at Puri.

Literary sources *Ramayana* epic; Puranic texts.

Jagannath occupies an obscure position. His sister is Subhadra and his brother Balabhadra. He is depicted in hideous fashion as a monster with an enormous head and bulging eyes, but with no legs and only the stumps of arms. According to legend, when Visnu was accidently slain by a hunter, his bones were placed in a box and Visvakarman, the Hindu god of artisans, was commissioned to create a new body to cover the bones. His agreement was conditional on no one seeing the work until it was finished. Krsna's curiosity got the better of him and the resultant half-finished freak was Jagannath.

In an unusual departure from normal ritual practice, the image of Jagannath is removed from his sanctuary at Puri for a week each year and aired in public view. Two festivals, the *Rathayatra* and *Snanayatra*, are dedicated to Jagannath and his siblings.

Jagaubis
Fire god. Pre-Christian Lithuanian. Largely eclipsed by Gabija.

Jahwe
See Yhwh.

Jakomba
God of morality. Bangala [Zaire, central Africa]. Also known as the god of hearts, he controls human thought. Also Nzakomba.

Jalinprabha *(light of the sun)*
God. Buddhist. A *bodhisattva* or *buddha*-designate. Color: red. Attributes: staff, sun disc and sword. Also Suryaprabha.

Jambhala *(devouring)*
God. Buddhist (Mahayana). An emanation of Aksobhya, Ratnasambhava or Vajrasattva, or a collective emanation of the five *dhyanibuddhas*, he is the equal of the Hindu god Kubera. His *Sakti* is Vasudhara and he may stand upon a man or a conch. Color: blue or white. Attributes: arrow, bow, cup, hook, Ichneumon fly, image of Aksobhya in the hair, jewel, noose, other jewels, staff, sword and trident. Three-headed, each head representing one of the three named *dhyanibuddhas*.

Janguli *(knowledge of poisons)*
Snake goddess. Buddhist (Mahayana). Prevents and cures snake bite. An emanation of Aksobhya. Also one of a group of *dharanis* (deification of Buddhist texts). Accompanied by a snake or other unidentified creature. Color: green, white or yellow. Attributes: arrow, blue lotus, bow, image of

Aksobhya on crown, lute, peacock feather, snake, staff, sword and trident. One- or three-headed.

JANUS
Origin Roman. God of passage.

Known period of worship circa 400 BC to circa 400 AD.

Synonyms Ianus.

Center(s) of cult many sanctuaries throughout Italy, including the celebrated Janus Quadrifons temple (not extant).

Art references sculptures and relief carvings.

Literary sources Aeneid (Virgil).

Janus is generally known as the "god with two faces" and is the deity responsible for gates, doorways and of all beginnings. He is also specifically a benign intercessor in times of war. He has no Greek counterpart but is the god of past, present and future. According to legend the son of Apollo, born in Thessaly, he founded the city of Janiculum on the Tiber.

Janus is depicted with two faces turned in opposite directions, symbolizing his dominance over past and future. He holds a key in his right hand and a staff in his left when invoked as guardian of a gate or roadway; alternatively he holds the numbers 300 and 65 when presiding over the start of a new year. He is also equated with the rising and setting of the sun. Each new season, and the dawn of each day was sacred to Janus. He was particularly celebrated at New Year and the month name January is derivative. The Janus Quadrifons temple was reputedly a perfectly symmetrical square, each side possessing one door representing each of the four seaons, and three windows collectively comprising the twelve months of the year.

Jarri
Plague god. Hittite and Hurrian. Also war god known as the "lord of the bow" who protected the king in battle.

Jayakara *(victorious)*
God. Buddhist. Probably of Hindu derivation, he rides in a carriage drawn by cockatoos. Color: white. Attributes: arrow, bow, garland and wine glass.

Jayanta *(victorious)*
God. Hindu (Vedic and Puranic). One of the sons of Indra, and one of the eleven *ekadasarudras* or forms of the god Rudra. Attributes: arrow, ax, bow, club, cup, drum, hammer, hook, prayer wheel, rosary, spear, trident and water jar.

Jayatara *(victorious Tara)*
Minor goddess. Buddhist (Mahayana).

Jaya-Vijaya *(victorious)*
Twin goddesses. Hindu (Epic and Puranic). Possibly forms of Durga accompanied by a lion.

Jehovah
Creator god. Christian. The name came into usage from circa 1200 AD and is an adulteration that has largely replaced the title Yhwh in the English-speaking churches. See Yhwh.

Jnanadakini *(knowledge)*
Goddess. Buddhist (Mahayana). An emanation of Aksobhya and the *Sakti* of yogambara. Color: blue. Attributes: ax, bell, club, cup, staff and sword.

Jnanaparamita *(perfection of knowledge)*
Philosophical deity. Buddhist. Spiritual offspring of Ratnasambhava. Color: white. Attributes: the tree of wisdom and a jeweled banner.

Jnanavasita *(control of knowledge)*
Minor goddess. Buddhist. One of a group of *vasitas* personifying the disciplines of spiritual regeneration. Color: whitish blue. Attributes: sword on a blue lotus.

Jok
Creator god. African. A generic term employed by a large number of tribes. Generally the *jok* is represented by a totem and also has an animal

name. The Acholi in Uganda perceive *jok* to live in caves to which they deliver food and drink offerings. For the Shilluk in Sudan, Jwok created mankind from river clay.

Jokinam
Lake god. Lake Albert [East Africa]. The owner of the "lake cows" that graze at the bottom of Lake Albert and that are herded by drowned fishermen.

Jumis
Fertility god. Pre-Christian Latvian. Symbolized by grain stalks joined at the heads, or bent over and buried in the ground.

JUNO
Origin Roman. Queen of heaven.

Known period of worship circa 400 BC to circa 400 AD.

Synonyms Hera (Greek).

Center(s) of cult Sparta, Rome and Heraeum.

Art references large numbers of sculptures.

Literary sources *Aeneid* (Virgil) etc.

Juno is modeled on the Greek goddess Hera. In the Roman pantheon she is the daughter of Cronos and Rhea and the sister and incestuous consort of Jupiter, who seduced her in the guise of a cuckoo. Following their wedding on Mount Olympus, Juno was accorded the title of goddess of marriage, though subsequently she was obliged to endure Jupiter's philandering with numerous concubines. Juno is the mother of Mars, Vulcan and Hebe. Her sacred animals are the peacock and the cuckoo and she is invariably depicted in majestic apparel. Her chief festival in Rome was the *Matronalia*.

Junrojin
God of luck. Shinto [Japan]. One of seven deities in Shintoism concerned with fortune. He is depicted as a Chinese hermit and is sometimes confused with the god Fukurokuju. A small figure with a large head, he carries a staff to which is attached a little book. By tradition the book contains information about the lifespan of each mortal person. He is accompanied by a black deer, said to have been made thus by old age.

JUPITER
Origin Roman. Head of the Roman pantheon.

Known period of worship circa 400 BC to circa 400 AD.

Synonyms Iuppiter; Jove; Juppiter.

Center(s) of cult throughout Roman world.

Art references sculptures, reliefs, etc.

Literary sources *Aeneid* (Virgil).

Jupiter parallels the Greek supreme deity Zeus, as the father of the gods. His origins lie in the Indo-European sky god Dyaus Pitar. His consort is Juno. His main sanctuary is located on the Capitoline Hill in Rome and epithets include Tonans (thunderer) and Fulgurator (sender of lightning) although he is, above all, the giver of the bright light of day. He is, like Zeus, believed to hurl thunderbolts from the sky and he was represented in the sanctuary of Jupiter Feretrius by a crude lump of stone. He is particularly responsible for the honoring of oaths, which led to the practice of swearing in his name.

In Rome he formed part of an early trinity with Mars, god of war and farming, and Quirinus. This was later revised to include Jupiter, Juno and Minerva, all three of whom shared the Capitoline Temple.

Jupiter became known under a variety of assimilated names. Thus he was Jupiter Victor leading the legions to victory, or Jupiter Stator when they were in a defensive role, or Jupiter Protector. Away from Rome he was allied with the Syrian/Hittite god Dolichenus and in this form became popular with the Roman military with shrines as far away as Britain.

Juventas
Goddess of youth. Roman. Modeled on the Greek goddess Hebe.

Jvaraharisvara   *(lord of fever)*
Plague god. Hindu. Associated with malaria, particularly in Bengal.

Jyestha
Goddess of misfortune. Hindu (Puranic and earlier). The elder sister of the goddess Laksmi, Jyestha personifies poverty and is depicted with a large belly and long nose. In earlier Hinduism she was worshiped particularly in southern India. Also a *naksatra* of evil influence; daughter of Daksa and wife of Candra (Soma). Her animal is an ass. Attributes: arrow, banner with crow, cup, blue lotus, hair ornament and staff.

K

Ka Tyeleo

Creator god. Senufo [Ivory Coast, West Africa]. Significantly in such an environment, according to tradition, he fashioned the fruit-bearing trees on the seventh day of creation.

Kabeiroi

Blacksmith gods. Greek. According to tradition the sons or grandsons of the blacksmith god Hephaistos. The cult was centered particularly on Lemnos, where there was an Etruscan tradition until circa 500 BC, and at Thebes. The Kabeiroi are thought to derive from pre-Greek Asian fertility deities in Anatolia [Turkey].

Kabta

God of artisans. Mesopotamian (Sumerian). In creation mythology he is given charge over brick molds and pickaxes.

Kabrakan

Earthquake god. Mayan (classical Mesoamerican) [Mexico]. The so-called "destroyer of mountains" usually coupled with the god Zipakna who builds mountains.

Ka'cak

Sea spirit. Asiatic Eskimo [eastern Siberia]. A fierce old woman who lives in the ocean depths and owns all the creatures of the sea. She is said to feed off the bodies of drowned fishermen and is the subject of sacrifice. See also Arnakuagsak.

Kadeš

Fertility goddess. Canaanite. Depicted naked carrying a snake and usually standing upon a lion. Taken over by the Egyptians (see Quodeš).

Kadru   *(russet)*

Goddess. Hindu (Epic and Puranic). One of the daughters of Daksa, consort of Kasyapa and mother of the *nagas* (snake demons).

Kagu-Tsuchi-No-Kami

Fire god. Shinto [Japan]. One of a number of fire *kamis* who are honored in special *Hi-Matsuri* festivals. He is worshiped in the mountain shrine of Kono-Jinja. The sacred fire can only be generated by a board and stick and this is regarded as a powerful purifier in Shintoism. The most celebrated temple of the fire *kamis* is on Mount Atago near Kyoto to which worshipers are drawn from all over Japan to obtain charms as protection against fire.

Kahilan

Tutelary god. Pre-Islamic Arabian. Known only from inscriptions.

Kai Yum   *(singing lord)*

God of music. Mayan (Lacandon) (classical Mesoamerican) [Mexico]. He lives in the sky and is attendant on Cacoch, one of the aspects the Mayan creator god. Depicted as a brazier shaped like a pottery drum.

Kaikara

Harvest goddess. Bunyoro [Uganda, East Africa]. Propitiated before harvest with offerings of millet.

Kakaku

River god. Shinto [Japan]. His name is often inscribed on the edge tiles of a house to protect against fire.

Kakasya *(crow-faced)*
Minor goddess. Buddhist. No further information available.

Kakka
Minor god. Mesopotamian (Babylonian-Akkadian). The attendant and minister of state to both Anu and Anšar. Known particularly from the text of *Nergal and Ereškigal.*

Kakupacat *(fiery glance)*
War god. Mayan (classical Mesoamerican] [Mexico]. Said to bear a shield of fire with which he protects himself in battle.

Kala
God of death. Hindu (Vedic and Puranic). An epithet of Yama and occasionally of Siva. Also the personification of time in the *Atharvaveda.*

Kalacakra *(time wheel)*
Tutelary god. Buddhist (Mahayana) and Lamaist [Tibet]. One of a group of *yi-dam* tutelary deities chosen on a basis of personal selection. Perceived as time in the form of a *cakra* (rotating wheel) and one who dominates the Hindu gods Kama and Rudra. *Sakti* with two to four heads. Color: blue. Attributes: a large variety held in up to twenty-four hands. Typically four-headed.

Kaladuti *(messenger of death)*
Goddess. Buddhist (Mahayana). May be accompanied by a horse. Color: red. Attributes: cow head, cup, hammer and trident.

Kalavikarnika
Fever goddess. Hindu (Puranic). Attributes include a cup or skull.

KALI *(1)*
Origin Hindu (Puranic) [India]. Goddess of destruction.

Known period of worship circa 400 AD, but known from much earlier times, until present.

Synonyms many epithets, also linked with Durga.

Center(s) of cult chiefly in Bengal.

Art references sculptures in stone and bronze.

Literary sources *Ramayana* epic and various Puranic texts.

Kali is the most terrible and malignant aspect of the goddess Sakti (see also Durga) though the name Kali is an epithet applied to several goddesses. She is the central figure of the *sakta* cult in Bengal. Her consort is generally perceived as Siva, whom she aids and abets in his more malignant aspects. Also one of the *mahavidya* personifications of the *Sakti* of Siva. In her earliest form she may have been the personification of the spirit of evil.

She is depicted variously with long ragged locks, fang-like teeth or even tusks, lips smeared or dripping with blood and claw-like hands with long nails. Her tongue often protrudes. She has no special vehicle but may be seen dancing on a prostrate Siva. She possesses ten (sometimes as many as eighteen) arms and may wear a necklace of skulls, a belt of severed arms, earrings of children's corpses, and snakes as bracelets. Often she is half-naked with black skin. Kali is depicted wading through gore on the battlefield and drinking the blood of her victims. Frequently she holds a severed head in one of her hands and a large sword in another. At cremation sites she sits upon the body of the deceased surrounded by attendant jackals.

There are also more benign aspects of Kali. She slaughters demons and sometimes her hands are raised in blessing. The conflict of her personality follows the widely held notion that out of destruction comes rebirth.

Kali is worshiped in Bengal during the *Dipavali* festival. In southern India she is worshiped as a distinct plague goddess associated with cholera.

Kali *(2)*
Goddess of learning. Jain. One of sixteen headed by the goddess Sarasvati.

Kalika   *(black)*

1. Goddess. Buddhist (Mahayana). Often depicted standing upon a corpse. Color: dark blue. Attributes: cup and knife.
2. Goddess. Hindu (Puranic). A *Sakti* of Nirrti, and an epithet of Durga.

Kalisia

Creator god. Pigmy [Zaire and Congo, central Africa]. The guardian of hunters and the jungle forests. Pigmy hunters invoke the god with special rituals and he delivers dream messages identifying the location of game.

Kaliya

Minor serpent god. Hindu (Epic and Puranic). One of the *nagas* in the endless conflict between good and evil, he poisoned the fresh water with his venom. The young Krsna revived all the life that had drunk from it and then almost destroyed Kaliya before taking the snake as one of his followers. By tradition he lives in depths of the river Yamuna.

Kalki(n)   *(with white horse)*

Horse god. Hindu (Vedic, Epic and Puranic). Possibly the tenth *avatara* of Visnu. He rewards the good and punishes evil. The counterpart of the Buddhist deity Maitreya. Horses became associated with divine kingship in ancient India because of their speed of movement. Solar deities were perceived to ride horses across the sky and horse sacrifice became highly significant. Kalki is depicted either anthropomorphically or with the head of a horse and has four arms. He is attended by a white horse. Attributes: arrow, conch, prayer wheel, shield and sword. Also Visnuyasas.

Kalligeneia

Obscure birth goddess. Greek. Known only from ritual texts in Athens.

Kaltesh

Fertility goddess. Ugric (western Siberian). A goddess concerned with childbirth and the future destiny of the infant. Consort of the sky god Num.

Her sacred animals include the hare and the goose and she may be symbolized by a birch tree.

Kalunga

Creator god. Ndonga [northern Namibia, southern Africa]. Said to take the form of a giant man who is always partially hidden by clouds and generally seen only by women intermediaries known as *nelagos* who go to converse with him in sacred places. He is the father of Musisi. The god is invoked at times of warfare and illness, but also as a fertility deity and before making a journey.

KAMA(DEVA)   *(desire)*

Origin   Hindu (Puranic) [India]. God of carnal love.

Known period of worship   circa 1000 BC, and probably earlier, until present.

Synonyms   Kama; Manmatha; Ananga.

Center(s) of cult   various.

Art references   stone and metal sculptures; reliefs.

Literary sources   *Ramayana* epic and various Puranic texts.

As god of love Kamadeva stimulates physical desire. The son of Visnu and Laksmi, or of their reincarnations Krsna and Rukmini, in which instance he is titled Kama. An alternative legendary beginning accounts that he rose from the heart of the creator god Brahma. His chief ally is the god of spring, Vasanta, his principal consort the goddess of affection, Rati, and he is attended by a band of nymphs, the *Apsaras*. Kamadeva is depicted as a youthful god with green or red skin, decked with ornaments and flowers, armed with a bow of sugarcane, strung with a line of honey bees, and arrows tipped with a flower. He may be three-eyed and three-headed and frequently rides on a parrot.

The consorts of Kamadeva are the goddesses Rati and Priti. Legend accounts that Kamadeva met his death at the hands of Siva, who incinerated him with flames from his middle eye. Kamadeva had inadvertently wounded the meditating god with one of his shafts of desire and had caused him to fall in love with Parvati. The epithet Ananga (bodiless) is applied to Kamadeva in this context. Kamadeva is reincarnated as Kama, who in turn is reincarnated as Pradyumna, the son of Krsna. The god is invoked particularly when a bride-to-be departs from her family home.

Kamado-No-Kami

Household god. Shinto [Japan]. Specifically the *kami* responsible for the cooking stove.

Kama-Gami

God of potters. Shinto [Japan]. Each kiln has a small stone statue of the deity standing upon it to which the potters offer sake and salt before lighting the fire. Also Kamadokami.

Kamaksi   (of amorous appearance)

Goddess. Dravidian (Tamil) [southern India and Sri Lanka]. A *Sakti* of Siva recognized locally at Kanchipuram, but also in her own right at several places in southern India. Also Kamatchi (Tamil).

Kamala   (lotus born)

Goddess. Hindu (Epic and Puranic). Particularly worshiped in southern India. One of a group of *mahavidyas* or personifications of the *Sakti* of Siva, representing Maharatri.

Kami

Generic name for a deity. Shinto [Japan]. The title applied to the gods and goddesses of Shintoism.

Kami-Musubi-No-Kami

(divine producing wondrous deity)
Creator being. Shinto [Japan]. The third in the list of primordial deities appearing in the *Kojiki* and *Nihongi* sacred texts. A remote and vaguely defined deity who was born alone in the cosmos and whose presence remains hidden from mankind. Probably influenced by Chinese religion.

Kamini   (loving woman)

Minor goddess. Buddhist (Mahayana). An attendant of Buddhakapala.

Kamo-Wake-Ikazuchi

Rain god. Shinto [Japan]. One of many rain *kamis* invoked in Shintoism and included in a generic grouping of Raijin, deities of thunder, storm and rain.

Kamrusepa

Goddess of healing. Hittite and Hurrian. Mother of Aruna. Involved in the legend of Telepinu, the "missing" vegetation fertility god.

Kana-Yama-Biko-No-Kami

God of miners. Shinto [Japan]. Born from the vomit of Izanami and worshiped in the Nangu-Jinja and other shrines. His consort is Kana-Yama-Hime-No-Kami. One of the *kamis* of the so-called "metal mountain."

Kana-Yama-Hime-No-Kami

Goddess of miners. Shinto [Japan]. Born from the vomit of Izanami and worshiped in the Nangu-Jinja and other shrines. Her consort is Kana-Yama-Biko-No-Kami. One of the *kamis* of the so-called "metal mountain."

Kane

God of light. Polynesian [Hawaii]. A sky god comparable with the more widely known Polynesian deity Atea. Considered to be part of a primordial trinity with Ku (stability) and Lono (sound). See also Tane.

Kangalogba

Primordial spirit. Pokot and Suk [Uganda and western Kenya, East Africa]. The female spirit personified in the dragonfly and also the apotheosis of the sacred river Oubangui. The mother of the creator god Toro.

Kankar Mata

Mother goddess. Hindu (Epic and Puranic). A *Sakti* who in later Hinduism became regarded as a *saptamatara* (mother) of evil intent. Known particularly from Bengal as a goddess who spreads disease.

Kantatman

Obscure god of medicine. Hindu (Epic and Puranic). The twentieth of the thirty-nine minor *avataras* of the god Visnu and possibly the same as Dhanvantari, as he is said to be a "carrier of nectar." By different genealogy he has been equated with Pradyumna, the god of love.

Kanti *(desire)*

Goddess. Hindu (Epic and Puranic). The *Sakti* of Narayana.

Kao Kuo-Jiu

Immortal being. Taoist (Chinese). One of the "eight immortals" of Taoist mythology, he was once a mortal being who achieved immortality through his exemplary life. The tutelary god of actors. Attributes include musical rattles or castanets. See also Ba Xian.

Kapali *(wearing skulls)*

God. Hindu (Epic and Puranic). One of the group of eleven *ekadasarudras* or forms of Rudra.

Kapalini *(carrying a cup)*

Minor goddess. Buddhist (Mahayana). An attendant of Buddhakapala.

Karaikkal Ammaiyar

Local mother goddess. Hindu [southern India]. Known from the town of Karikal as a deified ascetic who is depicted with an emaciated form. Attribute: playing cymbals.

Karai-Shin

God of lightning. Buddhist [Japan]. One of the deities grouped in Shintoism as the Raijin gods of thunder, storm and rain.

Karini

Inferior goddess. Buddhist (Mahayana). An attendant of Buddhakapala.

Karkota

Snake god. Hindu. One of a group of seven *mahanagas*. Color: black. Attributes: rosary and water jar. Three-eyed.

Karmavasita *(control of karman)*

Minor goddess. Buddhist. One of a group of twelve *vasitas* or goddesses personifying the disciplines of spiritual regeneration—*karma(n)* is an act, rite or deed originating in the hope of future recompense. Color: green. Attribute: a staff.

Karta

Goddess of destiny. Pre-Christian Latvian. Known only from folk traditions.

Karttikeya

1. God. Hindu (Epic and Puranic). A form of Skanda who was reared by the Pleiades stars and is generally represented therefore with six heads. (In Hindu mythology there are only six Pleiades, not the seven recognized in modern astronomy.) His *Sakti* is Karttiki and his attendant animal is a peacock. Attributes: conch, hook, noose, prayer wheel, shield, spear, staff, sword and wood apple. 2. God. Buddhist. Equating with the Hindu god Skanda. Color: red. Rides upon a peacock. Attributes: cock, *Sakti* and staff.

Karttiki

Mother goddess. Hindu (Epic and Puranic). One of a group of nine *navasaktis* who, in southern India, rank higher than the *saptamataras*.

Kašku

Moon god. Pre-Hittite and Hittite. Known from inscriptions. Also Kušuh (Hurrian).

Kasyapa

(deriving from the Sanskrit for "tortoise")
Primordial god. Hindu (Vedic and Puranic). In Vedic literature a divine demiurge and father of mankind, snake demons, *devas* etc. His name stems, arguably, from the notion of the cosmos as a giant tortoise. He has had thirteen consorts. In other texts he is the father of the god Narada who

consorted with one of the daughters of Daksa. Also Prajapati.

Kataragama
Tutelary god. Tamil [Sri Lanka]. One of four great national deities and equating to the Hindu god Skanda. Also Seyon.

Katavul
Supreme god. Tamil [southern India and Sri Lanka]. The ultimate creator of all that exists in the world and the judge of humanity able to reward or punish at will.

Katyayani
Form of the goddess Durga or Parvati. Hindu (Puranic). Parvati, as the ascetic Kali, possessed a black skin. When Siva ridiculed her she cast it off, and it was subsequently filled "with the combined brilliance of the gods" to create Katyayani. Her attendant animal is a lion or tiger.

Kauket
Primordial goddess. Egyptian. One of the eight deities of the Ogdoad representing chaos, she is coupled with the god Kek and appears in anthropomorphic form but with the head of a snake. The pair epitomize the primordial darkness. She is also depicted greeting the rising sun in the guise of a baboon.

Kaumari
Mother goddess. Hindu (Epic and Puranic). The *Sakti* of Skanda (Kaumara) who in later Hinduism became regarded as one of a group of seven *mataras* (mothers) of evil intent. Also one of a group of eight *astamataras*. She embodies lack of envy or, alternatively, delusion. Her animal is a peacock. Attributes: arrow, ax, bell, book, bow, cockerel, lotus, spear, staff and water jar.

Kaumudi *(moonlight)*
Goddess of the light of the moon. Hindu. The consort of Candra.

Kavra'nna *(walking around woman)*
Sun spirit. Chukchee [eastern Siberia]. The consort of the sun in Chukchee mythology. Also Ko'rgina (rejoicing woman).

Kazyoba
Sun god. Nyamwezi [Tanzania, East Africa]. Regarded as the tutelary deity and creator of the tribe.

Kebechet
Chthonic snake goddess. Egyptian. The daughter of Anubis who was involved in the cult of the dead as the deity responsible for libations. She is depicted as a serpent.

Kek
Primordial god. Egyptian. One of the eight deities of the Ogdoad representing chaos, he is coupled with the goddess Kauket and appears in anthropomorphic form but with the head of a frog. The pair epitomize the primordial darkness. He is also depicted greeting the rising sun in the guise of a baboon.

Kemoš
Tutelary god. Moabite [Jordan]. Mentioned under the name of Chemosh in the *Vetus Testamentum*: 1 Kings 11:7 as being one of the gods worshiped by the Israelite king Solomon. Eventually adopted by the Greeks and absorbed into the cult of Ares.

Kere'tkun
Sea spirit. Chukchee [eastern Siberia]. The chief being in the ocean depths, known to the maritime Chukchee. His consort is Cinei'nen. He owns all the creatures of the sea and is said to wear a cloak of walrus gut and to be extremely fierce. He feeds on the bodies of drowned fishermen and is the subject of sacrifice. Also Peruten.

Kesava *(long haired)*
Minor *avatara* of Visnu. Hindu (Epic and Puranic). His *Sakti* is Kirti.

Kesini *(hairy)*
Goddess. Buddhist. An attendant of Arapacana.

Ketua
God of fortune. Ngbandi [Zaire, central Africa]. One of seven deities invoked at daybreak. He controls both good luck and ill fortune. According to tradition he has seven children: morning, noon, evening, night, sun, moon and water. He accords to water the privileges of a first-born son.

Khadir
Vegetation god. Pre-Islamic north African. He wanders the earth returning to the same spot once in every 500 years and is said to have gained his immortality by drinking from the well of life. Similar in some respects to the Syrian god Adonis and revered by Alexander the Great. Normally referred to as *Al-Khidr* (the green one).

Khandoba
Form of the god Siva. Hindu (late). Khandoba is believed to have emerged as a deity with a distinct cultic following no earlier than the thirteenth or fourteenth century, mainly in western India and centered on Jejuri, near Poona. The god is generally regarded as one of several martial forms that Siva took to combat demons. His consort is the goddess Mhalsa, considered to be a form of Parvati. He is depicted bearing four arms and is usually mounted on a horse, but may also be accompanied by a dog. Attributes: bowl, drum, sword and trident. Also Makhari; Mallari; Martland.

Khasa *(itch)*
Minor goddess. Hindu (Vedic). Daughter of Daksa, consort of Kasyapa and a deity controlling spirits of forests.

Khasaparna *(gliding through the air)*
God. Buddhist. A variety of Avalokitesvara. Color: white. Attributes: image of Amitabha on the crown, and lotus.

Khen-Ma
Goddess. Buddhist [Tibet]. The female controller of the earth's demons, attended by a ram. Attribute: a golden noose.

Khen-Pa
God. Buddhist [Tibet]. The male counterpart of Khen-Ma, he controls the demons of heaven, attended by a white dog. Attribute: a crystal staff.

Kherty *(lower one)*
Chthonic or earth god. Egyptian. Known from at least 2500 BC, Kherty acts as a guardian of royal tombs but displays a more ominous aspect threatening the soul of the ruler. Pyramid Texts warn that the king must be protected from Kherty by the sun god Re. Depicted anthropomorphically or with the head of a ram.

Khipa
Tutelary deity. Hittite and Hurrian. This may be an archaic name for the goddess Ma. Also Khebe.

Khnum
Chthonic or earth god. Egyptian (Upper). Said to create human life on a potter's wheel but strictly at the behest of creator deities. He is usually seated before a potter's wheel on which stands a naked figure in the process of molding. The Khnum cult was principally directed from sanctuaries at Esna, north of the first Nile cataract, and at Elephantine where mummified rams covered with gold leaf and buried in stone sarcophagi have been discovered. Khnum supervises the annual Nile flood, which is physically generated by the god Hapy. His consort at Esna is the goddess Menhyt. Khnum is also described at other sites as the *ba* or soul of various deities including Geb and Osiris. Depicted anthropomorphically or with the head of a ram.

Khons(u) *(wanderer)*
Moon god. Egyptian (Upper). Recognized from at least 2500 BC but best known during the New Kingdom (mid-sixteenth century BC). A significant deity at Thebes, where he is described as an off-

spring of Amun and Mut. His sacred animal is the baboon. There is a Khonsu precinct as part of the Temple of Amun in the Karnak complex. From the Greco-Roman period there exists a sanctuary of Kom-ombo where Khonsu is seen as the off-spring of the crocodile god Sobek and the mother goddess Hathor. Depicted anthropomorphically or with a falcon's head, but in either case envel-oped in a close-fitting robe. He wears a crown consisting of a crescent moon subtending a full moon orb.

Khyung-Gai mGo-Can
Local god. Buddhist [Tibet]. Equating to the Hindu god Garuda.

Ki *(the great one)*
Archetypal chthonic principle. Mesopotamian (Sumerian). According to some traditions, Ki is the daughter of Anšar and Kišar and consort of An. As the cosmos came into being, An took the role of god of heaven and Ki became the person-ification of the earth and underworld. She is the mother of the god of the air, Enlil, with whom she descended from the heavens. Some authori-ties argue that she was never regarded as a deity. There is no evidence of a cult and the name appears in a limited number of Sumerian creation texts. The name Uraš (tilth) may relate. See also Antu(m).

Kianda
God of the sea. Kimbundu [Angola, southern Af-rica]. Guardian of the Atlantic Ocean and its crea-tures. Invoked by fishermen who place offering on the shore. His presence may be symbolized by a skull.

Kibuka
God of war. Buganda [Uganda, East Africa]. The brother of the creator god Mukasa, said to reside on the island of Sese. According to tradition, he secured victory in war for the Buganda by taking the form of a cloud that hovered above their enemies and rained spears and arrows. He appar-ently enjoyed a succession of temples in the past

that housed the hidden statue of the god and his sacred shield.

Kini'je
Sky spirit. Yukaghir (eastern Siberia). The being in charge of keeping account of time. Also Ki'njen.

Kinnar *(divine lyre)*
Musician god. Western Semitic. Mentioned in Ugaritic texts and known from Phoenicia. Proba-bly equating with the Syrian Adonis. Also Kinnur.

Kinyras
Local god of metalwork. Greek. Known from Cy-prus as a magician and smith. Derived from an older western Asiatic model. See Kotar.

Kirti *(glory)*
Goddess. Hindu (Epic and Puranic). The *Sakti* of Kesava. Attribute: water jar.

Kišar
Primordial god(dess). Mesopotamian (Sumerian and Babylonian-Akkadian). The consort or equal of Anšar and mother or creator of An and Ki in the creation cosmos.

Kitanitowit *(good creator)*
Creator god. Algonquin Indian [eastern Canada]. The first being who is present everywhere in the universe. He is invisible and is represented dia-grammatically by a point surrounded by a circle on which are marked the four quarters.

Kiya'rnarak *(I exist)*
Supreme being. Eskimo. An indistinct and remote character, out of touch with ordinary mortals, who created the world.

Klehanoai *(night bearer)*
Moon god. Navaho [USA]. According to tradition, he was created at the same primordial time as the dawn, from a crystal bordered with white shells. His face is said to be covered with sheet lightning and the sacred primeval waters. The moon disc is actually a shield behind which the god moves

invisibly across the night sky. He is never impersonated or depicted. Also Tlehanoai.

Klotho
Goddess of spinning. Pre-Homeric Greek. According to Hesiod, one of the daughters of Zeus and Themis. An ancient deity linked with Lachesis and Atropos as one of a trio of *Moirai* or Fates. She is depicted with a spindle.

Kollapura-Mahalaksmi
Goddess. Hindu (Puranic). Six-armed. Attributes: club, shield and wine glass.

Kondos
God of cereal crops. Pre-Christian Finnish. Particularly identified with the sowing of wheat. After Christianization, he was absorbed by the figure of St. Urban.

Kono-Hana-Sakuya-Hime-No-Kami
Mountain goddess. Shinto [Japan]. The deity who guards the sacred Mount Fuji. A daughter of O-Yama-Tsu-Mi and the consort of Prince Ninigi, her shrine is located on the summit of the mountain. She is also closely associated with Mount Asama about 80 kilometers to the north.

Kore   *(the girl)*
Youthful goddess of grain. Greek. The more generic name for the goddess Persephone. Identified as the daughter of Demeter. She is the *spirit* of grain as distinct from her mother who is the *giver* of grain. Depicted on coinage as a woman's head adorned with ears of grain. She is integral to the *Eleusinian Mysteries* in which she is abducted to Hades, resulting in the distress of her mother and the blighting of nature. At Samaria-Sebaste in Syrio-Palestine, Kore was the only deity worshiped, apart from the emperor.

Korravai
War goddess. Dravidian (Tamil) [southern India and Sri Lanka]. Worshipped in desert regions in southern India, thought to live in trees and equating to Durga. She has a son, Murukan. Also Katukilal; Korrawi.

Kotar
Blacksmith god. Western Semitic (Syrian). Identified in the Ugaritic (Ras Šamra) texts as building a palace for the god Baal and forging his weapons for the conflict against the sea god Yamm. Known also from Phoenician inscriptions. Also Košar, Chusor.

Kotisri
Mother goddess. Buddhist. The so-called "mother of 7,000 *buddhas*."

Koto-Shiro-Nushi
God of luck. Shinto [Japan]. Probably syncretized early in Shintoism with the god Ebisu.

Kouretes
Forest deities. Greek. Known from Ephesus and other sites as the spirits of trees and streams, they are also perceived as nymphs who dance in attendance on the baby Zeus. The term is also applied to a bride or young woman.

Kourotrophos
Obscure wet-nurse goddess. Greek. Known only from ritual texts.

Koyote
Tutelary god. North American Indian. Recognized by several tribes, including the Navaho and Apache. He acts as a cult hero who intercedes with more remote creator spirits and teaches the Indian.

Kratos
God of strength. Greek. One of the sons of the goddess Styx and brother of Bia (force).

Kronos
Archetypal fertility god. Pre-Greek. He is of unknown origin but is the son of the earth mother Gaia and the sky god Ouranos, whom he usurped after castrating him. His consort is Rhea. So as not to suffer a fate similar to his father he swal-

lowed all his children except Zeus who was kept from him by a ruse. Zeus eventually hurled Kronos into Tartaros, the abyss in which all the Titans were confined. He was celebrated in the Greek harvest festival of *kronia*, which equalled the Roman *saturnalia*. During Hellenic times he was the supreme god at Byblos [Syria]. He is depicted on coinage of Antiochus IV (175–164 BC) nude, leaning on a scepter, with three pairs of wings, two spread and one folded.

KRSNA *(the dark one)*

Origin Hindu (Epic and Puranic) [India]. Incarnation of Visnu.

Known period of worship circa 300 BC or earlier until present.

Synonyms Kannan (Tamil). Many epithets.

Center(s) of cult generally throughout India, but particularly Mathura.

Art references sculptures generally bronze but also stone. Reliefs.

Literary sources *Mahabharata* epic, *Bhagavad-Gita* and *Bhagavata-Purana*.

Krsna is the eighth and arguably the most important incarnation or *avatara* of the god Visnu. He appears inauspiciously in the Vedic texts, but grows in stature and popularity. Allegedly born at Mathura on the bank of the river Yamuna, he is the son of Vasudeva and Devaki, fostered by Nanda and Yasoda. He is a deity who epitomizes human aspirations and shortcomings together. Thus he is both a Hindu divine hero, and a drinker and womanizer. He has no legal consort but his chief mistress, a married woman, is Radha. He is reputed to have enjoyed as many as 16,000 such liaisons.

Almost certainly, Krsna originated as a fertility god of herdsmen and vegetation who became syncretized with the hero of the *Mahabarata* epic. In the *Bhagavata-Purana*, Krsna is also perceived as the embodiment of the cosmos—the vault of heaven is his navel, the stars his chest, the sky his eyes.

Krsna's incarnation was, by tradition, designed to save the world from the demonic king Kansa. He is particularly worshiped as a baby (Balakrsna) and as a youthful shepherd accompanied by Radha. He is seen as a skilled musician often depicted playing the flute at the sound of which nature pauses to listen, storms are calmed, rivers flow serenely and maidens are roused. The legends of Krsna's childhood depict him as a somewhat precocious child who plays tricks and ransacks kitchen jars of butter and curds. The incident with butter has been a popular theme for sculptures. As an adult he champions the struggle with the adversaries of mankind, the *nagas*, subduing the serpent Kaliya (see also Garuda). He may be seen standing on Garuda. Color: black or dark blue. Attributes: flute, the hill of Govardhana on one finger, an ornament, prayer wheel and shepherd's staff. He may, on occasion, carry other objects.

Krsodari *(thin waisted)*

Goddess. Hindu. An emaciated form of Camunda, a personification of famine. She stands upon a corpse. Attributes: club, iron rod, skull and trident.

Krttika(s)

Minor goddess(es) of fortune. Hindu (Epic and Puranic). Strongly malevolent *naksatra(s)* consisting of the six stars in the Pleiades cluster who become nurses of the god Skanda. (In Hindu mythology there are only six Pleiades, not the seven recognized in modern astronomy.)

Ksama *(patience)*

Minor goddess. Hindu (Epic and Puranic). One of the daughters of Daksa. Attribute: trident.

Ksantiparamita

Philosophical deity. Buddhist. One of the *paramitas*. Spiritual offspring of Ratnasambhava. Color: yellow. Attributes: jeweled banner and white lotus.

Ksetrapala

God of passage. Hindu (Puranic). Form of the god Bhairava specifically designated as a guardian deity of doorways. Also regarded as a tutelary deity in Saivite temples. Stands upon a lotus and possesses a number of attributes.

Kshumai

Fertility goddess. Kafir [Afghanistan]. A beneficent goddess appearing in the guise of a goat. Legend has it that either she or her eldest daughter is the mother of the god Mon. She is said to have given mankind the boon of goats, grapes, other fruit and vegetation in general. She was called upon in times of sickness. She is depicted in wooden statues with prominent long breasts and vulva. Also Kime.

Ksitigarbha *(womb of the earth)*

Goddess. Buddhist (Mahayana). Known extensively from northern India to China and Japan. One of the group of female *boddhisattvas* or *buddha-designates*. Color: yellow or green. Attributes: book, bowl, jewel, staff and water jar. In China she is recognized as an underworld deity, Di-zang. In Japan she becomes a guardian deity of passage, Jizo.

Ku

Primordial being. Polynesian [Hawaii]. An aspect of a tripartite deity that also includes Kane, the light, and Lono, sound. They existed in chaos and darkness, which they broke into pieces to allow the light to come in.

KUAN TI

Origin   Taoist (Chinese). God of war.

Known period of worship   circa 300 AD until present.

Synonyms   Guan Di; Kuan Kung.

Center(s) of cult   throughout China.

Art references   paintings and sculpture.

Literary sources   various philosophical and religious texts, mostly inadequately researched and untranslated.

The most powerful figure in the pantheon, the god is based on a historical figure who lived 162–220 AD. He was a general in the imperial army and came to prominence after a successful battle with the warlord Tung Cho. He was subsequently deified.

The epitome of austerity, loyalty and integrity, he is worshiped as the personification of the sacred principles of the *hsieh* or knightly warrior. He was the tutelary deity of the Chung emperors and is the god of the military, but also of restaurants, pawn shops, curio dealers and literature. He is a guardian of secret societies, including Triads, and brotherhoods, particularly in Hong Kong, but also of the police, thus many CID offices possess an altar to Kuan Ti, as Kuan Kung.

He is depicted seated on a tiger skin, sometimes with the face of a tiger on the breast of his robe. His magical sword is the "black dragon" and his horse is the "red hare." His festivals are celebrated on the fifteenth day of the second moon and on the thirteenth day of the fifth moon. He thus presides over the light half of the year—spring and summer.

Images of Kuan Ti are kept by most households in China, facing the entrance of the building, to frighten away evil influences.

KUAN YIN   *(hearer of cries)*

Orgin   Taoist (Chinese). Benign guardian goddess.

Known period of worship   circa 100 AD, though in various forms, until present.

Synonyms   Guan Yin; Kwannon (Japanese).

Center(s) of cult   throughout Chinese culture.

Art references   paintings and sculptures.

Literary sources   Various philosophical and religious texts, mostly inadequately researched and untranslated.

An essentially foreign deity, derived from the Buddhist god Avalokitesvara, and therefore probably of Indian origin. Introduced into China as a male deity until circa 600 AD when the transition to a goddess began; it was completed by circa

1100 AD. Although accepted into Taoism, in contrast to all other Chinese deities, she is not provided with the normal offerings of food and wine.

An alternative tradition places her in a mortal existence as the Princess Miao Shan who committed suicide by strangling herself and was subsequently taken by the Buddha to an island, P'u T'o, where she spent nine years perfecting herself.

Kuan Yin enjoys a major popularity as a pure and benevolent spirit whose influence has eclipsed that of the historical Buddha incarnation, Sakyamuni, in China. Her name is invoked if danger threatens and she has strong fertility connotations—newly married couples pray to her for children.

Several other Chinese goddesses are considered by some authors to be manifestations of Kuan Yin. She frequently shares sanctuaries with the queen of heaven, Tin Hau, and has taken over part of her area of influence. She is thus titled Goddess of the Southern Sea, which is technically an accolade due to Tin Hau.

Kuan Yin is depicted seated upon a lotus with attributes including a vase filled with the dew of compassion and a willow branch. Her attendant Lung Nu may stand behind her with other objects, including a peacock-like bird, pearls and a rosary.

Kubaba

Mother goddess. Anatolian and northern Syrian. She was worshiped particularly at Carchemish and seems to equate with the Hittite goddess Šauška. Attributes include pomegranate and mirror. Also Gubaba, Kupapa.

Kubera *(misshapen)*

1. God of riches. Hindu (Vedic, Epic and Puranic). He was originally the head of the *yaksas* spirits of the forests, but by Puranic times was associated with wealth and productivity. He is also a *dikpala*, guardian of the northern quarter. The son of Pulastya and Idavida, his consorts include Yaksi, Vasudhara and Vriddhi. Identified with the city of Alaka. He is depicted as a dwarfish figure riding upon a Brahman or a chariot. Color: white. Attributes: generally carrying a purse, but occasionally with various other items. Also Kuvera, Kauveri.

2. God of riches. Buddhist-Lamaist [Tibet]. One of a group of *dharmapala* with terrible appearance and royal attire. Also a *dikpala* or guardian of the northern quarter. Color: yellow. Attributes: ax, banner, club, cup, hook, Ichneumon disgorging jewels, noose, reliquary and occasionally a trident.

Kubjika *(humpback)*

Goddess of writing. Hindu. Personification of the thirty-two Tantric syllables.

Kubuddhi *(stupid)*

Minor goddess. Hindu. One of the consorts of Ganesa.

Kucumatz

Supreme god. Mayan (Quiche Indian, classical Mesoamerican) [Mexico]. An androgynous being who created all things out of itself. Comparable with Kukulcan.

Kuei Shing

God of literature. Chinese. Believed to reside in the star constellation of Ursa Major. Also Zhong-Kui.

Kuju

Sky spirit. Yukaghir [eastern Siberia]. A benevolent being who supplies mankind with food. When fish appear in great numbers in the lakes, they are thought to have fallen from the sky.

Kuku-Ki-Waka-Muro-Tsuna-Ne-No-Kami

Guardian deity. Shinto [Japan]. The god who guards the house and its environs as a whole.

Kukulcan

Creator god. Mayan (classical Mesoamerican) [Mexico]. Kukulcan is, in origin, a Toltec god who was adopted by the Mayan culture and who corresponds closely with the Aztec deity Quetzalcoatl. He is chiefly concerned with reincarnation, but is also responsible for the elements of fire, earth and water. He is depicted with various attributes, including a torch or a lizard representing fire, corn for earth, and a fish for water. Also God B.

Kuku-Toshi-No-Kami
God of grain. Shinto [Japan]. The deity responsible for the harvest of full-grown rice. His shrines are often serviced by Buddhist priests.

Kuladevata *(family god)*
Generic name of a household god. Hindu. The god is chosen by a family to be their guardian deity and they all assemble at his temple, as and when necessary, for worship. Also Kulanayaka.

Kuladevi
Goddess. Hindu. The female equivalent of a Kuladevata.

Kulika *(of good family)*
Snake god. Hindu. One of a group of seven *mahanagas*. Attributes: rosary and water jar. Three-eyed.

Kulisankusa *(having an ax and a goad)*
Goddess of learning. Jain [India]. One of sixteen *vidyadevi* headed by the goddess Sarasvati.

Kulisesvari *(lady of the ax)*
Goddess. Buddhist (Mahayana). Often depicted with a corpse. Color: white. Attribute: a staff.

Kulla
God of builders. Mesopotamian (Sumerian and Babylonian-Akkadian). The god responsible for the creation of bricks.

Kumari *(virgin)*
Goddess. Hindu. Generally recognized to be an epithet of Durga. Worshipped at a famous temple on the southernmost tip of India at Cape Comorin. Also known in Nepal, where a small girl provides an earthly incarnation of the goddess.

Kumarbi
Creator god. Hittite and Hurrian. An antique deity who was usurped by more "modern" gods. He is the father of Ullikummi in Hittite legend.

Kumokums
Creator god. Modoc Indian [Oregon, USA]. He sat beside Tule Lake, which was all that existed, and created the world by scooping out mud to form the earth. He added animals and plants, but finally became tired and went to sleep in a hole at the bottom of the lake, which he dug using a hill as a shovel.

Kunado-No-Kami
Guardian deity. Shinto [Japan]. One of three *kamis* particularly concerned with the protection of roads and crossroads. They also guard the boundaries of the house and the ways leading to it. They may be known as Yakushin deities who protect against plague. Generally identified as Michi-No-Kami or Chiburi-No-Kami.

Kundalini
Mother goddess. Aztec (classical Mesoamerican) [Mexico]. The spirit of the earth perceived in human form and responsible for the provision of all food from the soil. The earth is considered to be sacred and should not be owned by any one person, but can be utilized for the benefit of the community as a whole. Kundalini is believed to have been the mother of all other vegetation deities.

Ku'nkunxuliga
Tribal god. Ma'malelegale Indian [British Columbia, Canada]. The personification of the thunderbird, known to many Indian tribes, who lives in a palace in the upper world. The noise of the thunder is the beating of its wings.

Kun-Rig *(knowing all)*
God. Buddhist [Tibet]. Four-headed form of Vairocana. Attribute: prayer wheel.

Kuntu bXan Po

Head of pantheon. Bon (pre-Lamaist) [Tibet]. The chief god in the Bon pantheon, he engendered the world from a handful of mud scraped from the primeval waters and created all living things from an egg.

Kura-Okami-No-Kami

(great producer of rain on the heights)
Rain god. Shinto [Japan]. Known alternatively as the "dark rain god," he may also generate snowfalls.

Kurdaligon

God of smiths. Ossetian [Caucasus]. He assists the passage of dead souls by attending to their horses' shoes.

Kurma(vatara)

Incarnation of the god Visnu. Hindu (Epic and Puranic). The second *avatara* of Visnu, Kurma appears in the form of a tortoise that acts as a pivot for the mountainous churning rod the gods employ to make ambrosia from the primal sea of milk after the flood. Kurma is depicted with a human torso surmounting a tortoise shell. Visnu is said to have appeared in this form in order to recover some of the possessions lost during the deluge. Attributes: club, conch, lotus and prayer wheel. Also the name for a vehicle of various deities.

Kurukulla

1. Goddess of boats. Hindu. A Tantric deity generally depicted in a boat made of jewels. Also goddess of wine.
2. Goddess. Buddhist (Mahayana). The *Sakti* of Amitabha. Usually of terrifying appearance. Attributes: arrow, bow, flower, hook, noose, rosary and trident.

Kus

God of herdsmen. Mesopotamian (Sumerian and Babylonian-Akkadian). Identified in the *Theogony of Dunnu*.

Kushi-Dama-Nigi-Haya-Hi

(soft fast sun)
Sun god. Shinto [Japan]. The apotheosis of the morning sun sent down by the sun goddess Amaterasu before Prince Ninigi appeared on earth.

Kushi-Iwa-Mado-No-Mikoto

Guardian deity. Shinto [Japan]. The god who protects entrance gates.

Kušuh

Moon god. Hittite and Hurrian [Anatolia]. Also Kašku.

Kutkhu

Guardian spirit. Kamchadal [southeastern Siberia]. The counterpart of the Koryak Quikinn.a'qu, he fashioned the created world into its present form and is the majordomo of the creator god. His consort is Ilkxum and his sister is Xutlizic. His children include Si'mskalin, Ti'zil-Kutkhu and Si-'duku. In mythology he is depicted as a salacious character. Also Kutq; Kutkinnaqu.

Ku'urkil

The founder of the world. Chukchee [eastern Siberia]. Not only a deity, but a powerful *shaman* and the first human. He equates with the Koryak deity Quikinn.a'qu.

Kvasir

Minor god of wisdom. Nordic (Icelandic). By tradition he was created from the saliva of the Aesir and Vanir deities, who thus combined their knowledge into a single being. He was slain by dwarfs who concocted a fermented drink from his blood, mixed with honey, and this mead became the inspiration of poets. He is also identified in Welsh mythology.

Kwannon

Form of Avalokitesvara. Buddhist [Japan]. See also Kuan-Yin.

Kwoth

Creator god. Nuer [Sudan]. The Nuer people have been affected by the expansion of Islam, and probably by Christianity, and recognize a supreme deity, or spiritual being, responsible for all creation. One of his epithets is Tutgar, meaning "strong and without limit."

KYBELE

Origin Phrygian [northwestern Turkey]. Mother goddess.

Known period of worship circa 1500 BC and probably much earlier in prehistory, until Christianization (circa 400 AD).

Synonyms Cybele (Roman); Kybebe.

Center(s) of cult Pessinus (Asia Minor) and Rome, but also extensively elsewhere.

Art references black obelisk (lost); many classical sculptures; a dish from Parabiago (in Milan); possibly the subject of a well-known seal from Knossos.

Literary sources votive inscriptions, etc.

One of the most important of the Asian mother goddesses. She probably originates as a mountain goddess who became closely equated with the Greek mother goddesses Rhea and Demeter. According to legend, the Greek god Zeus raped her and she bore a monstrous son Agdistis. Her consort is Attis, whom she discovered to be unfaithful. In remorse, he castrated himself under a pine tree and bled to death.

In circa 204 BC the black stone by which she was personified in Pessinus (Phrygia) was carried to Rome and installed in the Temple of Victories on the Palatine as Cybele Magna Mater. This fulfilled a prophecy that if the "great mother" was brought to Rome, the war with the invader Hannibal would be won. She is often depicted riding in a chariot drawn by panthers or lions and is accompanied by frenzied dancers or Korybantes. She was invoked in the three-day festival commencing with mourning (*tristia*) followed by joy (*hilaria*) in the spring during which her emasculated priests, the *galloi*, gashed themselves with knives. Attributes include key, mirror and pomegranate.

Kyumbe

Creator god. Zaramo [Tanzania, East Africa]. Tradition has it that the earth and sky may have been present before this being emerged. He is, however, perceived as having engendered all living things on earth. He first created animals' bodies without tails. When they had their legs fitted, Kyumbe added tails as an afterthought.

L

Lachesis
Goddess of lot casting. Pre-Homeric Greek. According to Hesiod one of the daughters of Zeus and Themis. One of an ancient trio of *Moirai* with Klotho and Atropos, she sustains the thread of life and is depicted carrying a scroll.

Lactanus
Minor god of agriculture. Roman. Said to make the crops "yield milk" or thrive.

Laghusyamala *(lightly dark colored)*
Minor goddess. Hindu (Puranic). Attributes: lute and wine glass.

Lahamu
Primordial deity. Mesopotamian (Babylonian-Akkadian). Known from the Babylonian creation epic *Enuma Elis* as one of a pair who were created by Tiamat from the primeval ocean and who, it is suggested, were represented by the silt of the seabed. Lahamu and Lahmu in turn created Anšar and Kišar, who created Anu.

Lahar
God of cattle. Mesopotamian (Sumerian). According to legend, he was sent to earth by the gods Enlil and Enki to work in conjunction with the grain goddess Ašnan. In iconography he usually has ears of grain sprouting from his shoulders. He may also carry a bow and club and is often depicted with a ram at his feet.

Lahmu
Primordial deity. Mesopotamian (Babylonian-Akkadian). Known from the Babylonian creation epic *Enuma Eliš* as one of a pair who were created by Tiamat from the primeval ocean and who, it is suggested, were represented by the silt of the seabed. Lahmu and Lahamu in turn created Anšar and Kišar, who created Anu.

Laima
Goddess of fate. Pre-Christian Latvian. Particularly concerned with guarding women at childbirth, and with the newborn. Regarded as a household goddess of prosperity and good fortune.

Laka
Goddess of dancing. Polynesian [Hawaii]. A minor deity who is nonetheless greatly revered by islanders in a hedonistic cult of song, dance and sexual liberality.

Laksmana *(with auspicious marks)*
God. Hindu (Epic and Puranic). A half- or younger brother of the god Rama. The son of Dasaratha and Sumitra, his consort is Urmita. He often stands to the left of Rama and may be depicted holding a bow (see also Satrughna). Color: golden. Attributes: bow and ornaments.

LAKSMI
Orgin Hindu (Epic and Puranic) [India]. Consort of Visnu.

Known period of worship circa 300 BC and earlier, through to present times.

Synonyms Sri-Laksmi; Sri-Devi; Dharani (earth); see also Sita.

Center(s) of cult no temples, but revered generally throughout India.

Art references   sculptures generally bronze but also stone. Reliefs.

Literary sources   *Ramayana* and *Mahabharata* epics; Puranic literature.

A major Hindu goddess who originated perhaps as a mother goddess but who now represents wealth and prosperity and epitomizes the later Hindu (Brahmanical) notion of the active female principle or *Sakti* in a male deity. According to the *Ramayana,* she arose from the primal Hindu sea of milk. Identified as the consort of Visnu from circa 400 AD onward, she is generally depicted as a beautiful golden-skinned woman possessing four or, more commonly, two arms. She stands or rests on a lotus that may be watered by two attendant elephants. Another favored portrait finds her washing Visnu's feet as he reclines on the thousand-headed serpent Sesha, an action that is said to bring Visnu dreams. She emerges in many guises, changing form as Visnu changes his own incarnations. She is perceived also to emerge as the black-skinned and destructive Kali. Many attributes, but most commonly a lotus.

Laksmi embodies the model Hindu wife, faithful and subservient. She may be depicted on the knee of Visnu's *avatara* Narayana as Laksmi-Narayana. She is reincarnated with each of his other avatars—thus beside Rama she becomes Sita, said to have been born from a furrow, and with Krsna she is first Radha, then Rukmini. She is worshiped particularly at the start of the business year in India. In the *Divali* (Feast of Lamps) on the last day of the dark lunar period toward the end of October or early in November, every household lights a lamp in honor of Laksmi. She is also propitiated by gambling.

Lalaia'il

God of *shaman*s. Bella Coola Indian [British Columbia, Canada]. The deity who initiates into the shamanistic circle. He lives in the forest and carries a wooden wand bound with cedar bark that he waves, creating a singing noise. He also frequents woodland lakes and ponds. When a woman meets him she is said to menstruate, while a man develops a nosebleed. Also Kle-klati-e'il.

Lamaria

Tutelary goddess. Svan [Caucasus]. Particularly invoked by women as a hearth goddess and protector of cows. Her name may have been derived under Christian influence.

Lan Kai-He

Immortal being. Taoist (Chinese). One of the "eight immortals" of Taoist mythology, the deity is of ambiguous sex, sometimes depicted as a girl. Once a mortal being who achieved immortality through a perfect life. Attributes include flowers and a flute. See also Ba Xian.

Lao-Tsze

God. Taoist (Chinese). Also known as the Most High Prince Lao, he is one of the three holy San Ch'ing whose images stand in a Taoist sanctuary. The tutelary god of alchemists. He is the founder of Taoism who, according to tradition, was born with full command of speech, and with white hair, under a plum tree. His sacred animal is the water buffalo.

Lar Familiaris

Ancestral spirit. Roman. A personal and vaguely defined deity brought into the house from the land around about.

Lara

See Larunda.

Laran

God of war. Etruscan. Depicted as a youth armed with a lance and helmet and dressed in a cape.

Lares

Hearth deities. Roman. The *lares* are a peculiarly Roman innovation. Two children, born of a liaison between the god Mercury and a mute naiad, Lara, whose tongue had been cut out by Jupiter, became widely revered by Romans as house guardians. Iconographically they are depicted in the guise of monkeys covered with dog skins with a barking dog at their feet.

Larunda

Chthonic goddess. Sabine. An early Italic earth mother who, in Roman times, according to some traditions, became the mother of the Lares. Also Lara (Roman).

Lasya   *(dancing girl)*

Mother goddess. Buddhist-Lamaist [Tibet]. One of the group of *astamataras* (mothers). She is generally depicted dancing the *lasya* dance. Color: white. Attribute: a mirror. Also the generic name of a group of four goddesses, including Gita, Mala, Nrtya and headed by Lasya.

Latipan

Creator god. Canaanite. See Il.

Lau

Spirit beings. Andaman Islands [Sea of Bengal]. Generally invisible but perceived in human form and living in the jungles and the sea. When an Andaman islander dies he or she becomes a *lau*.

Lauka Mate

Goddess of agriculture. Pre-Christian Latvian. Worshipped in the fields at ploughing time.

Laukika-Devatas

Generic name for a group of deities. Hindu. Gods known from local folklore as distinct from those of the Vedic texts.

Laverna

Chthonic underworld goddess. Italic. Propitiated by libations poured with the left hand.

LEBIEN-POGIL   *(owner of the earth)*

Origin   Yukaghir [southeastern Siberia]. Animistic "owner" spirit.

Known period of worship   prehistoric times until early twentieth century.

Synonyms   none known.

Center(s) of cult   no fixed sanctuaries known.

Art references   none known, but possibly the subject of anonymous wood carvings.

Literary sources   *The Yukaghir* (Jochelson).

The chief protector of the earth. His subordinates are Yobin-Pogil, the owner of the forest; the owner of fire Lo'cin-po'gil; the various protectors and keepers of animals (mo'yepul) and individual or group protectors (peju'lpe). The Yukaghir, as a hunting people, maintained a delicate and sensitive relationship with these owners.

Legba

God of fate. Fon [Benin, West Africa]. The youngest son of the supreme god Lisa and his consort, the moon goddess Mawu. He is also regarded as a messenger god, moving between Lisa and mankind on earth.

Lei Kung

God of thunder. Taoist (Chinese). He heads the deities of the pantheon who are responsible for storm, wind and rain and is usually accompanied by Yu Shih, the god of rain. He appears in anthropomorphic form from about the beginning of the Christian era, depicted as a strong, youthful figure holding hammer and chisel. In drama his movements are punctuated by rumblings on strings and drums. Circa 1000 AD he becomes depicted as a bird-like being with a monkey face. The transition was probably influenced by the popularity of the Hindu god Garuda.

Lelwani

Chthonic underworld goddess. Hittite and Hurrian. Associated with charnel houses and probably modeled on the Sumerian Ereškigal.

Lendix-Tcux

Tutelary god. Chilcotin Indian [British Columbia, Canada]. The so-called transformer known by different names among many Indian tribes. He is a wanderer who can change shape from human to animal and who educates the human race. He often appears in the guise of a raven, or as a dog, and has three sons.

LENUS
Orgin Celtic (Continental European). God of healing.

Known period of worship prehistoric times until Christianization circa 400 AD.

Synonyms Iovantucarus; Lenus Mars (Romano-Celtic).

Center(s) of cult left bank of the Moselle opposite Trier; also at Chedworth (England) and Caerwent (Wales).

Art references sculptures, stone reliefs, votive plaques.

Literary sources Romano-Celtic inscriptions.

A god of healing worshiped by the Celtic tribe of Treveri but later adopted by the Romans. The Trier sanctuary was a place of pilgrimage where large numbers of offerings were deposited, and carvings suggest that child patients were often present. Lenus's sanctuaries were usually associated with springs and some, if not all, had an *abaton* or room for recuperation.

Lesa
Creator god. Southeastern African. The name by which the supreme deity is known across a wide area of Zambia and Zimbabwe. Equating to Lisa in regions of West Africa. Also regarded as a rain god. Probably strongly influenced by Islam and, to a lesser extent, by Christianity. Also Leza.

LETO
Origin Greek. Mother goddess.

Known period of worship circa 800 BC but probably earlier through to Christianization (circa 400 AD).

Synonyms Lato (Dorian); Latona (Roman).

Center(s) of cult Lycia and Phaistos, Crete.

Art references sculptures and carvings.

Literary sources *Iliad* (Homer); *Theogony* (Hesiod).

The word "Leto" is a local term for *lady*. The Greek goddess probably derives from an earlier western Asiatic model. She is the daughter of the Titans Koeos and Phoebe. Leto's main claim to celebrity in Greek religion is that she was impregnated by Zeus to become the mother of the deities Artemis and Apollo. She often tries to protect Artemis from the wrath of her stepmother, Hera. Also a guardian goddess of graves. A very early bronze image of her was discovered, with those of Apollo and Artemis, at Dreros on Crete. In Lycia she was the principal goddess; at Phaistos she was the center of an initiation myth.

Leukothea
Sea goddess. Greco-Roman. Popular around the coasts of the Mediterranean with fishing communities. A mermaid who was originally Ino, a mortal daughter of Kadmos. She was wet nurse to Dionysos (Bacchus), but became mad and threw herself in the sea with her son Melikertes. In another version of the story she was escaping the wrath of Athamas, King of Thebes. The gods elevated her to the status of goddess and her son became the god Palaemon.

Lha
Generic term for a deity. Buddhist Lamaist [Tibet]. Also the title for a deity in the old Bon pantheon, equating to the Sanskrit term *deva*.

Lha-Mo *(the goddess)*
Goddess. Buddhist-Lamaist [Tibet]. Coming from the old Bon pantheon and equating with the Hindu goddess Sridevi.

Li Thieh-Kuai
Immortal being. Taoist (Chinese). One of the "eight immortals" of Taoist mythology, he was once a mortal being who achieved immortality through his exemplary life. Attributes include a bat, a gourd and an iron crutch. See also Ba Xian.

Lianja

God. Nkundo [Zaire, central Africa]. He became the subject of an epic known as *Nsongo and Lianja* and is regarded today less as a god than a heroic figure, probably under the influence of Christianity.

Libanza

Creator god. Bangala [Zaire, central Africa]. One of a pair of supreme deities with his sister/consort Nsongo. He lives at the bottom of the river Congo, traveling the waterways and bringing floods as punishment as well as to generate prosperity. He is regarded as being generally benevolent. Also Ibanza.

Liber

Chthonic fertility god. Italic. Originally associated with husbandry and crops but then assimilated with Dionysos. The consort of Ceres and father of the goddess Libera. His festival, the *Liberalia*, was on March 17 when young men celebrated the arrival of manhood.

Libera

Chthonic goddess. Italic. The daughter of Liber and Ceres.

Liberalitas

Minor god. Roman. Spirit of generosity, employed as a propaganda vehicle by the emperors. Worshipped particularly from the second century BC.

Libertas

Minor god(dess). Roman. Deity of constitutional government and the notion of freedom, known particularly from the second century BC. Attributes include the scepter, lance and a special hat, the *pileus*, which emancipated slaves were permitted to wear as a sign of their liberation.

Libitina

Chthonic goddess of death. Roman. Associated with funerals and interment.

Lietna'irgin *(genuine dawn)*

Spirit of the dawn. Chukchee [eastern Siberia]. One of four beings concerned with the dawn in different directions. See also Tne'sqan, Mratna'irgin and Na'chitna'irgin.

Lilith

Goddess of desolation. Mesopotamian (Sumerian). She is perceived as a demonic figure who, in the epic legend of *Gilgameš and the Huluppu Tree* takes up residence in Inana's holy tree growing on the banks of the Euphrates in Unug. When the hero Gilgameš attacks Lilith she escapes into the desert wastes.

Liluri

Mountain goddess. Western Semitic (Syrian). The consort of the weather god Manuzi, her sacred animal is the bull.

Linga

Symbol representing a god. Hindu. The phallic form of Siva.

Lir

God. Celtic (Irish). The father of the sea god Manannan, the consort of Aobh and later of her sister Aoife. He had four children by Aobh: Aed, Conn, Fiachra and Fionnuala. Out of jealousy Aoife turned the four into swans and set father and children against one another.

Lisa

Creator god. Fon and others [Benin, West Africa]. Probably the equivalent of Lesa in parts of East Africa. The supreme deity, whose more or less monotheistic role may have been influenced by the spread of Islam and Christianity.

Liu Pei

God. Taoist (Chinese). The third member of a trio of deities with Kuan Ti and Chang Fei. He is the embodiment of the imperial ideal and carries the seal of heaven's authority. He is considered to be humane and moderate. In art he usually takes a central position between Chang Fei on his left and Kuan Ti on his right.

Llew Llaw Gyffes
God. Celtic (Welsh). The counterpart of the Irish god Lugh. The son of Arianrhod, he was raised by Gwydion. The heroic figure of Lancelot may be derived from him.

Loa
Spirit beings. Puerto Rico and Haiti. The gods of the voodoo cult who were originally imported by slaves from West Africa. An amount of Christian influence is present in their makeup.

Loba
Sun god. Duala [Cameroon, West Africa]. Local people pray to this deity after sunset to ensure that he will appear again the following morning.

Locana   *(the eye)*
Goddess. Buddhist (Mahayana). The *Sakti* of a *dhyanibuddha* (spiritual meditation *buddha*), generally Aksobhya or Vairocana. Color: blue or white. Attributes: cup, prayer wheel and lotus with one or more staves. Also Buddhalocana.

Lo'cin-coro'mo
Hearth spirit. Yukaghir [southeastern Siberia]. The guardian of the household who migrates with the family. Also Lo'cil, Yegi'le.

Lo'cin-po'gil
Fire spirit. Yukaghir [southeastern Siberia]. One of the "owners," the apotheosis of fire.

Lodur
Creator god. Germanic. Mentioned in passing in the creation mythology as being one of a trio of deities, with Odin and Hoenir, who engendered mankind.

Logos
Primordial spirit of reason. Greek. A concept promoted by the Stoics, who perceived Logos as the mind of Jupiter, but more generally recognized as the divine essence from which all deities arise. Philo of Alexandria apportioned human characteristics to Logos. The Gnostic Christian, Valentinus, identified Logos as the word coming from the mind of the father. The Christian father Clement of Alexandria claimed it to be the first principle of the universe, while Origen perceived it as the principle embodied in the flesh by Jesus Christ.

Lokapala
Gods. Hindu. See Dikpala.

Lokesvara   *(lord of the world)*
Generic name for a group of deities. Buddhist. These are thought to be a syncretization of Hindu and Buddhist deities and include such gods as Siva, Visnu and others that have come to be defined as forms of a primeval *buddha* or *dhyanibuddha*. The *lokesvara* are usually represented by a small figure, identified as Adibuddha or Amitabha, which rests on the head of the main statue. Also a group name for the many forms of the Buddhist deity Avalokitesvara.

LOKI
Origin Nordic (Icelandic). Ambivalent character well represented in mythology.

Known period of worship Viking period (circa 700 AD) until Christianization (circa 1100 AD).

Synonyms Lopt.

Center(s) of cult none evidenced and probably Loki was not worshiped as were the other Asgard deities.

Art references probably the subject of anonymous carvings.

Literary sources Icelandic codices; *Prose Edda* (Snorri); *Historia Danica* (Saxo).

Loki is a mischievous, Machiavellian, humorous, sometimes sinister character. Snorri describes him as being "pleasing and handsome in appearance, evil in character, very capricious in behavior." He is the "poor relation" among the gods who has strong affinities with the giants, particularly at Ragnarok (doom) when he steers their ship, and whose loyalties are always suspect. Said to be the son of the giant Farbauti. He is also a scandalmonger. He was indirectly responsible for the death of Balder (directly so according to Snorri) and fought with Heimdall. Sometimes he appears as a hero rescuing gods from various predicaments through cunning. He also stands for evil, though less often, and was compared strongly by Christian times with the Devil. Able to change shape at will—said at various times to have impersonated a mare, flea, fly, falcon, seal and an old crone. As a mare he gave birth to Othin's horse Sleipnir and he also allegedly sired the world serpent, the mistress of the netherworld, Hel, and the wolf Fenrir, which will devour the sun at Ragnarok.

One of his prominent attributes, said to come from antiquity, is that of accomplished thief, stealing at various times Freyja's necklace, Thor's belt and iron gloves, and the apples of youth. There is little to support the notion of Loki (Wagnerian: Loge) as a fire god other than similarity of name—*logi*, meaning fire.

Loko

God of trees. Fon [Benin, West Africa]. The brother of the hearth goddess Ayaba. Invoked particularly by herbalists before obtaining medicines from the bark and leaves of forest trees.

Lomo

Goddess of peace. Ngbandi [Zaire, central Africa]. One of seven deities invoked at sunrise each day.

Lono *(sound)*

Primordial being. Polynesian [Hawaii]. An aspect of a tripartite god that also includes Kane, the light, and Ku, stability. They first existed in chaos and night, which they broke into pieces, allowing light to come in. Also Ono (Marquesas Islands).

Lothur

God of physical senses. Nordic (Icelandic). According to a brief mention in the *Voluspa* (Poetic Edda) the god concerned with physical being, i.e.,

sight, hearing and speech. According to some authors he may be a hypostasis of the god Othin. Lothur is also known in northern Germanic tradition. Also Lodur.

Lu Pan

God of artisans. Chinese. The deity concerned with builders, bricklayers, housepainters and carpenters. He is particularly revered in Hong Kong. According to tradition he was born in 606 BC in the kingdom of Lu, where he became a skilled carpenter. He turned into a recluse on the Li Shan mountain, where he perfected his skills. He is said to have constructed the palace of the queen of the western heaven. Because of his powers he was murdered. He is also an invoker of harmonious relationships. His festival takes place on the thirteenth day of the sixth month, when the rains are due. Attributes include a set square and carpenter's plane. He is also depicted with an ax, the symbol of a marriage go-between.

Lu Tong-Pin

Immortal being. Taoist (Chinese). One of the "eight immortals" of Taoist mythology, he was once a mortal being who achieved immortality through his exemplary life. The tutelary god of barbers. Attributes include a sword with which he conquers demons. See also Ba Xian.

Lubanga

God of health. Bunyoro [Uganda, East Africa]. He is invoked by offerings of beer and his sanctuaries are surrounded by rows of trees.

Lubangala

Rainbow god. Bakongo [Zaire, central Africa]. The chief adversary of the storm god. He stills the thunder and makes his appearance in the sky. Considered to be the guardian of the earth and sea, including the village and its community.

Lucina

Minor goddess of birth. Roman. Concerned with bringing the child into the light. Usually associated with Candelifera and Carmentes.

LUG *(possibly lynx)*
Origin Celtic (Irish). Lord of skills.

Known period of worship early times until Christianization circa 400 AD or later.

Synonyms none specific.

Center(s) of cult Lugudunum (modern Lyons) and elsewhere in Continental Europe; possibly brought to Ireland in the first century BC by settlers from Gaul.

Art references various stone carvings.

Literary sources *Books of Invasions*; *Cycles of Kings*.

The texts imply that Lug was a latecomer to the Irish pantheon, a tribal god who was particularly skilled in the use of a massive spear and a sling both of which possessed invincible magic properties. One of his epithets is *lamfhada*—"of the long arm." A young and apparently more attractive deity than the Dagda. The main festival in his honor seems to have been *Lugnasad* on August 1, a particularly agrarian celebration in a country that otherwise tended to observe pastoral calendar dates, suggesting again that Lug was a later arrival who possibly superseded an arcane tribal god Trograin. An alternative name for the August festival was *Bron Trograin* (Rage of Trograin). It is implied that, like many Celtic deities, Lug was capable of changing shape, hence the possible translation of the name as lynx. There appear to be strong Romano-Celtic associations in Continental Europe and Britain with place names such as Lugudunum [Lyons] and Luguvalium [Carlisle].

Lugal-Irra
Chthonic underworld god. Mesopotamian (Sumerian and Babylonian-Akkadian). Probably a minor variation of Erra, the Babylonian plague god. The prefix Lugal means "lord." Often coupled with Mes lam taea, god of war.

Lulal
God of uncertain status. Mesopotamian (Sumerian and Babylonian-Akkadian). Mentioned as living in Badtibira in the Sumerian text *Descent of Inana*. Also linked with a god Latarak.

Luna
Moon goddess. Roman. She derives from the Greek model of Selene, but is also comparable with Hekate. She enjoyed a major temple on the Aventine Hill in Rome.

Lunang
River goddess. Kafir [Afghanistan-Hindukush]. The patron goddess of the Prasun river, Lunang is perceived as a young and capricious girl, reflecting the turbulent moods of the river. She rules over watermills.

Lupercus
God of wolves. Roman. Celebrated in the festival of *Lupercalia* on February 15.

M

Ma

Fertility and vegetation goddess. Cappadocian (Anatolia) [Turkey]. The tutelary goddess of Pontic Comana, she was served by votary priestesses acting as sacred prostitutes, and biennial festivals were celebrated in her honor. Gradually she took on an added role as a warrior goddess with solar connotations and ultimately became syncretized with the Roman goddess Bellona. On coins of the Comana region she is depicted with the radiate head of a solar deity carrying weapons and a shield.

Ma Kiela

Female spirit being. Bakongo [Zaire, central Africa]. The deified head of a band of mortal women who died specifically from knife wounds.

Maat

Minor goddess of cosmic order. Egyptian. Epitomizing the harmonious laws of the cosmic order. She is recognized from the middle of the third millennium, and probably earlier, closely associated with the creator deities and particularly the sun god. In later times she was described as the "daughter of Re." Her only known sanctuary is in the complex of Karnak at Thebes. Maat is depicted either in human form wearing an ostrich plume on her head or by an ostrich feather alone. The rulers of Egypt believed that they governed under her aegis and frequently had themselves described as "beloved of Maat." Maat was also integral to the success of a soul passing through the Hall of the Two Truths, where the heart was weighed, to reach paradise.

Mabon *(son)*

God of youth. Celtic (Welsh). The son of an earthly mother, Modron. According to legend he was abducted when three days old. Also a god of hunters and fishermen. He is known particularly from northwestern Britain and his cult extends along the region of Hadrian's Wall. Known from many Romano-Celtic inscriptions and syncretized with the Romano-Greek god Apollo.

Macha

Fertility goddess. Celtic (Irish). One of the aspects of the Morrigan (a trio of warrior goddesses with strong sexual connotations), she appears as the consort of Nemed and of Crunnchu. She is also a warrior goddess who influences the outcome of battle by magical devices. She can change shape from girl to hag and is generally dressed in red. She is depicted with red hair. She appears thus to the Irish hero, Cu Chulainn, before the Battle of Moytura when she suddenly changes herself into a crow, the harbinger of death. Heads of slaughtered soldiers were fixed on the so-called Pole of Macha, and the ancient religious center of Emain Macha in Ulster is named after her. See also Banbha, Eriu and Fodla.

Madhukara *(honey maker)*

God. Buddhist. Derived from a Hindu deity and equating with Kama. He rides in a chariot drawn by parrots. Color: white. Attributes: arrow, banner, bow and wine glass.

Maeve

Mother goddess. Celtic (Irish). The mythical Queen of Connaught. According to tradition her consort is Ailill and she represents the "Sovereignty of Ireland" at Connaught. She is thus the apotheosis of the land, which is sacred.

Mafdet

Minor goddess. Egyptian. She acts as a guardian against snakes and scorpions. She is depicted in the form of a panther, often with the instrument of an executioner.

Magha

Minor goddess of fortune. Hindu (Epic and Puranic). A benevolent *naksatra*; daughter of Daksa and wife of Candra (Soma).

Mah

Moon god. Persian [Iran]. The progenitor of the cow, typically depicted with the tips of a crescent moon projecting from his shoulders.

Mahabala *(very strong)*

God. Buddhist (Mahayana). A fearsome emanation of Amitabha and a *dikpala* (guardian) of the northwestern quarter. Color: red. Attributes: jewel, snakes, sword, tiger skin, trident and white fly whisk. Three-headed.

Mahabja

Snake god. Hindu (Puranic). One of a group of seven *mahanagas*.

Mahacinatara *(Tara of Tibet)*

Goddess. Buddhist (Mahayana) and Lamaist [Tibet]. An emanation of Aksobhya and, in Lamaism, a fearsome form of the Vajrayana goddess, Ekajata, who may be depicted with up to twelve heads and twenty-four hands. She stands upon a corpse. Attributes: arrow, ax, blue lotus, bow, cup, image of Aksobhya on crown, knife, skull, snake, staff, sword, tiger skin and trident. Three-eyed.

Mahadeva *(mighty god)*

God. Hindu (Puranic). An important epithet of Siva with three heads (two male, one female) signifying the three aspects— Aghora (right), Saumya (center) and Sakti (left). Attributes: ax, bell, hook, mirror, noose, staff, sword, tree and trident. Also identified as a manifestation of Siva and one of the *Ekadasarudras* (eleven forms of Rudra). In northern India among tribes including the Gonds,

the expression Mahadeo (great god) is directed toward Siva as the supreme deity.

Maha-Ganapati

Elephant god. Hindu (Puranic). This form of the god Ganesa possesses ten arms instead of the more normal four and may have a goddess, Buddhi or Siddi, seated on his knee.

Mahakala *(the great death)*

1. God. Hindu (Puranic). A violent aspect of Siva. His *Sakti* is Mahakali. Rides upon a lion. Color: black. Attributes: five arrows, ax, Brahma-egg, club, cup, rosary of skulls, staff and trident. Three-eyed. Also considered to be a form of the god Bhairava in which context he is a guardian of the faith.

2. Guardian god of tents and science. Buddhist-Lamaist [Tibet]. Derived from the Hindu god Siva and an emanation of the five *dhyanibuddhas*. Also one of a group of *dharmapalas* with terrible appearance and royal attire. A deity of riches. He treads on the god Vinayaka, or on a man, a corpse, or on two elephant-headed men. Color: black, blue or white. Attributes: mainly elephant skin, prayer wheel and trident, but may hold various other objects.

Mahakali

1. Goddess of learning. Jain [India]. One of sixteen *vidyadevi* headed by the goddess Sarasvati.

2. Form of the goddess Kali. Hindu. Also a *Sakti* of Mahakala. Attributes: conch, cup, headdress, hook, knife, noose, rosary of skulls, staff, sword, water jar and wheel.

Mahakapi *(great ape)*

God. Buddhist. Epithet of the Buddha in a previous incarnation, appearing as an ape.

Mahamanasika *(great minded)*

Goddess of learning. Jain [India]. One of sixteen *vidyadevi* headed by the goddess Sarasvati.

Mahamantranusarini
(following the great sacred text)
Guardian goddess. Buddhist. One of a group of five *maharaksas* (protectors) who are thought to be personifications of amulets or *mantras*. Also an emanation of the *dhyanibuddha* Ratnasambhava, alternatively of Aksobhya. She is a guardian of the west, south and eastern quarters according to separate traditions. Color: blue, black, green, white or red. Attributes: most commonly noose and staff. From four to twelve arms; may be three-headed.

Mahamataras
Group of goddesses. Hindu. Personifications of the *Sakti* of the god Siva.

Mahamayuri *(great daughter of the peacock)*
Goddess. Buddhist (Mahayana). An extremely popular deity and an emanation of Amoghasiddhi. A female *bodhisattva* or *buddha*-designate. Also one of a group of five *maharaksas* (protectors) who are thought to be personifications of amulets or *mantras*. Color: green, red or yellow. Attributes: alms bowl, arrow, banner, bow, fly whisk, image of Amoghasiddhi on crown, jewel, mendicant, peacock feather, prayer wheel, sword and water jar. Three-eyed and may occasionally appear three- or four-headed.

Mahanaga
Snake god. Hindu. A group of seven deities identical with a group of seven *nagadevas*.

Mahapadma *(great lotus)*
Snake god. Hindu. Attributes: rosary and water jar. Three-eyed.

Mahaparinirvanamurti
God. Buddhist. The depiction of the Buddha lying in *nirvana* (paradise).

Mahaprabhu
Tutelary god. Orissa [India]. The local supreme deity of the Bondo tribe.

Mahapratisara *(great protectress)*
Guardian goddess. Buddhist. One of a group of five *maharaksas* (protectors) who are thought to be personifications of amulets or *mantras*. A guardian of the central or southern direction. Also an emanation of the *dhyanibuddha* Ratnasambhava. Color: yellow. Attributes: arrow, ax, banner, bow, conch, image of Ratnasambhava on crown, jewel, noose, parasol, prayer wheel, reliquary, sword, staff and trident. Three-headed and three-eyed.

Mahapratyangira *(great goddess whose speech is directed westwards)*
Goddess. Buddhist (Mahayana). An emanation of the *dhyanibuddha* Aksobhya. Color: blue. Attributes: hook, image of Aksobhya on crown, noose, red lotus, sword and trident.

Maharaksa *(great protectress)*
Group of guardian goddesses. Buddhist. Personifications of amulets or *mantras*. Common attribute: a parasol.

Maharatri *(the great night)*
Goddess. Hindu (Epic and Puranic). Associated with Kali and Kamala.

Mahasahaspramardani
(the thousand-fold destroyer)
Goddess. Buddhist. An emanation of Vairocana, and one of the *maharaksas*. Color: white. Attributes: particularly noose, prayer wheel and sword, but also depicted with other objects including image of Vairocana on crown. May be four-headed.

Maha-Sarasvati
1. Goddess. Hindu (Puranic). An emanation of Laksmi. Attributes: book, hook, lute and rosary.
2. Goddess. Buddhist. A variety of Sarasvati. Depicted upon a lotus. Color: white. Attributes: garland of pearls and white lotus.

Mahasitavati *(great cold one)*
Guardian goddess. Buddhist. One of a group of five *maharaksas* (protectors) who are thought to be personifications of amulets or *mantras*. Also an

emanation of the *dhyanibuddha* Amitabha (or sometimes Ratnasambhava). A guardian of the north or west quarter. Color: red, yellow or green. Attributes: arrow, ax, banner, book, bow, bowl, image of Amitabha on the crown, lotus, noose, peacock feather, staff, sword and trident. Three-eyed and may be three-headed.

Mahasri-Tara   *(of great beauty)*
Goddess. Buddhist (Mahayana). An emanation of Amogasiddhi. Depicted seated upon a moon. Color: green. Attributes: image of Amogasiddhi and lotuses.

Mahasthama(prapta)
(he who has attained great power)
God. Buddhist (Mahayana). A *dhyanibodhisattva* who personifies great wisdom. Color: white or yellow. Attributes: lotus, six lotuses and sword. (May have no attributes present.)

Mahavidya
Collective name of a group of goddesses. Buddhist (Mahayana). Ten personifications of *Sakti* as the femaleness of Siva, associated with the possession of knowledge.

Mahayasa   *(most glorious)*
Minor goddess. Buddhist (Mahayana). An attendant of Buddhakapala.

Maheo   *(all-spirit)*
Creator god. Cheyenne Indian [USA]. He first lived in the void and then created the great primordial water of life. He made the earth from a ball of mud and engendered mankind from one of his ribs, which he implanted in earth woman (Christian influence has probably been exerted here).

Mahes
Sun god. Egyptian. An ancient deity worshiped chiefly in the region of the Nile delta and representing the destructive power of the sun's heat. Depicted in the form of a lion. Also Miysis (Greek).

Mahesvari
Mother goddess. Hindu (Epic and Puranic). A *Sakti* who in later Hinduism became one of a group of seven *mataras* regarded as of evil intent. Also one of eight *astamataras*. In another grouping one of a group of nine *navasaktis* who, in southern India, rank higher than the *saptamataras*. Attributes: antelope, arrow, ax, bow, club, drum, prayer wheel, staff and trident.

Mahi   *(earth)*
Minor goddess of sacrifice. Hindu (Vedic). She is invoked to appear on the sacrificial field before a ritual, and is identified with the act of prayer. Usually associated with the goddess Sarasvati.

Mahisa   *(buffalo)*
Demonic god. Hindu (Epic and Puranic). Depicted most frequently in the form of a buffalo, but he also confounds the gods by changing himself into many other animal guises. He is eventually slain by the goddess Devi in the form of Mahisasuramardini.

Mahisasuramardini
(slayer of the buffalo demon)
Form of the goddess Devi. Hindu (Puranic). Appearing from the fourth century AD onward, this goddess is a *durga* form of Devi. She possesses up to twelve arms holding an assortment of weapons and may be seated on a lion. According to legend, the form arose in response to the threat from the demonic Mahisa who was eventually slain by the goddess Devi with his own sword. Attributes: ax, banner, bell, bow, club, conch, drum, hook, lizard, mirror, noose, prayer wheel, shield, sword, staff and trident. Three-eyed.

Mahodadhi   *(the great ocean)*
Minor goddess. Buddhist (Mahayana). An attendant of Buddhakapala.

Mahrem
Head of pantheon. Axumite (ancient Ethiopic kingdom). A warrior deity after whom the Axumite kings titled themselves "sons of Mahrem."

Mahuikez

Fire god. Polynesian. Identified with earthquakes and possibly paralleling Touia Fatuna (iron stone goddess) in Tongan belief.

Maia

Chthonic or earth goddess. Greco-Roman. Originally, in pre-Homeric times, a mountain spirit who subsequently became a minor consort of Zeus. The Romans worshiped her as an obscure goddess of the plains who became briefly a consort of Jupiter, and they perceived her as the mother of the messenger god Mercury. Her cult was associated with that of Vulcanus. Possibly the origin of the name of the month of May.

MAITREYA   (the loving one)

Origin Buddhist [India]. *Bodhisattva or buddha-designate.*

Known period of worship circa 500 BC to present.

Synonyms none.

Center(s) of cult pan-Asiatic.

Art references metal and stone sculptures, paintings.

Literary sources Sadhanamala and Tantric ritual texts.

One of the most popular deities of the Mahayana and Hinayana sects of Buddhism. He originates from the yellow mantra syllable MAIM in the Tusita heaven. He is also regarded as a *manusibuddha* or future human *buddha*. He equates with Kalkin in Hinduism and is perceived as a happy, rubicund figure of benevolent character. He has no *Sakti* and his attendant animal is a lion. Color: gold or yellow. Attributes: five *dhyanibuddhas*, flower, prayer wheel, shrine (in the hair) and water jar. May be three-eyed or three-headed. He may also be identified symbolically by white blossoms. Also Mi-lo Fo (Chinese).

Majas Gars

Household god. Pre-Christian Latvian. Invoked until very recent times in country districts as a deity who would bring prosperity to the family home.

Maju

God. Basque [Pyrenean region]. The consort of the mother goddess Mari, he appears in the guise of a serpent. See also Mari.

Make Make

Sea god. Polynesian [Easter Island]. The tutelary deity of the Easter Islanders, he created mankind and animals. His sacred animal is the sea swallow and the huge anthropomorphic stone figures that characterize the island's archaeology form part of his cult.

Mal

Creator god. Early Dravidian (Tamil). Probably equating with a syncretization of Visnu and Krsna. The name implies a deity of great stature. In Sangam texts, his face is like the moon, his eyes are lotuses and his *cakra* is the beams of the sun. Also Tirumal.

Mala   (garland)

Mother goddess. Buddhist-Lamaist [Tibet]. One of a group of *astamatara* deities. Color: red or yellow. Attributes: garland of forest flowers or of jewels.

Malakbel

Vegetation god. Pre-Islamic northern Arabian. Mentioned as the brother of Aglibol on an inscription at Palmyra dated to 132 AD.

Malamanganga'e   (light eastward)

Creator being. Polynesian. One of the two personifications of light who, with Malamangangaifo, engendered Lupe, the dove, whose consort is rock. From these primordial principles came several generations of supernatural beings whose descendents engendered mankind.

Malamangangaifo   (light westward)

Creator being. Polynesian. See Malamanganga'e.

Malhal Mata
Mother goddess. Hindu (Epic and Puranic). One of seven *Saktis* who in later Hinduism became regarded as *saptamataras* (mothers) of evil intent. Particularly known in Bengal as a bringer of disease.

Malik *(king)*
Tutelary god. Pre-Islamic northern Arabian. Known from inscriptions.

Mam
God of evil. Mayan (Yucatec, classical Mesoamerican) [Mexico]. A much-feared deity who lives beneath the earth and only emerges in times of crisis. Depicted in the form of a flat, life-sized piece of wood dressed as a scarecrow and set upon a stool. He is offered food and drink during Uayeb, the period of five unlucky days at the end of the year, after which the figure is undressed and unceremoniously thrown away. During Uayeb devotees fast and refer to the god as "grandfather."

Mama
See Mami.

Mama Qoca *(mother sea)*
Goddess of the ocean. Inca (pre-Columbian South America) [Peru, etc.]. Originally a pre-Inca goddess of coastal regions who retained her influence under Inca rule. Invoked by all Indians who gain their livelihood from the sea. Today probably syncretized largely with the Christian Virgin Mary. Also Mama Cocha.

Mamaki *(greedy)*
Goddess. Buddhist. The *Sakti* of Ratnasambhava or Aksobhya. Also a *bodhisattva* or future *buddha*, originating from the blue *mantra* MAM. Color: yellow or blue. Attributes: cup, flowers, jewel, knife and staff.

Mama-Kilya *(mother moon)*
Moon goddess. Inca (pre-Columbian South America) [Peru, etc.]. The consort of the sun god Inti, she is important in the calculation of time and regulating the Inca festival calendar. The Indians consider that an eclipse of the moon is a time of great danger, caused by a mountain lion or snake eating the moon, and perform a ritual making as much noise as possible to frighten the predator off.

Mami
Mother goddess. Mesopotamian (Sumerian and Babylonian-Akkadian). Identified in the *Atrahasis* texts and other creation legends and probably synonymous with Ninhursaǧa. She was involved in the creation of mankind from clay and blood. The name almost certainly came into use because it is the first word that a child formulates. Also Mama; Mammitum.

Mamitu
Goddess of oaths and treaties. Mesopotamian (Babylonian-Akkadian). One of the consorts of Nergal and subsequently identified as a chthonic underworld deity. Also Mammetu.

Mamlambo
River goddess. Zulu [Natal, South Africa]. Considered to control all the rivers running through Natal. Also a patron of beer makers, who are usually women.

Manannan (Mac Lir)
Sea god. Celtic (Irish and British). Extensively worshiped. From the name is derived the "Isle of Man" where, according to tradition, the god is buried. He rules the "Isle of the Blessed" and determines the weather at sea. Father of the Irish hero Mongan. Also Mahawyddan (Welsh).

Manasa
Snake goddess. Hindu. The daughter of Kasyapa and Kadru and the sister of the lord of serpents, Vasuki. She is also a gracious aspect of Parvati. Known particularly from Bihar, Bengal and Assam. She stands upon, or is shaded by, a seven-headed snake. Attributes: snake and water jar.

Manasi *(spiritual)*
Goddess of learning. Jain [India]. One of sixteen *vidyadevi* headed by the goddess Sarasvati.

Manat *(fate)*
Goddess. Pre-Islamic Arabian. One of the so-called Daughters of Allah, she is primarily identified with a shrine (lost) between Mecca and Medina.

Manavi *(descended from Manu)*
Goddess of learning. Jain [India]. One of sixteen *vidyadevi* headed by the goddess Sarasvati.

Manawat
Goddess of destiny. Western Semitic (Nabataean). Mentioned in a large number of inscriptions.

Manawyddan
Sea god. Celtic (Welsh). The counterpart of the Irish god Manannan. He is the consort of Rhiannon and is regarded as a skilled craftsman.

sMan-Bla *(physician)*
God. Buddhist-Lamaist [Tibet]. One of the more popular medicine-*buddha*s and possibly derived from Persian light religion. Attributes: fruit and water jar.

Mandah
Collective name of gods. Pre-Islamic Arabian. Guardian deities, whose chief responsibility is irrigation.

Mandanu
God of divine judgment. Mesopotamian (Babylonian-Akkadian). Known from the neo-Babylonian period.

Mandhata *(thoughtful)*
God. Hindu (Epic and Puranic). Minor *avatara* of Visnu. One of the "lords of the universe."

Mandulis *[Greek]*
Sun god. Nubian. Mandulis was chiefly revered in a Greco-Roman cult. His most important sanctuary was at Kalabsha, close to the Aswan High Dam, and now relocated. A sanctuary was also constructed on the Greek island of Philae where he seems to have enjoyed an association with the goddess Isis. Also Merwel (Egyptian).

Manes
Hearth deities. Roman. Technically souls separated from the body, these objects of ancestor worship became classed as guardian divinities in Roman households. Celebrated in the feast of *Parentalia*. Origin of the title on graves: *Dis Manibus*.

Mangala *(auspicious)*
1. Astral god. Hindu. Personification of the planet Mars. Depicted by a chariot drawn by eight red fire-horses. According to some authors Mangala is a form of the god Siva in his cruel aspect. Attributes: club and lotus. Three-eyed.
2. Goddess. A form of Parvati. She rides upon a lion and may bear up to ten arms, carrying arrow, mirror, moon disc, rosary, shield and sword. Three-eyed.

Mani
Moon god. Germanic and Nordic (Icelandic). He guides the chariot of the moon through the night sky and is involved in the downfall of the world at Ragnarok.

Manidhara *(holding a gem)*
Minor god. Buddhist (Mahayana). An attendant of Sadaksari. Attributes: jewel and lotus.

Manito
Creator being. Eskimo (Ojibwa). One of a number of very powerful beings all identified by the same title. These deities include the four winds, the thunderbirds, the underwater manitos and the heroic god Nanabozho. They are the ultimate source of existence and are essential to the continuance of life. It is necessary for mankind to maintain close communication with them.

Manitu
Creator god. Algonquin Indian [USA]. A vaguely defined being who controls all things and imparts

knowledge to the tribe. He may be identified as the great spirit in the sky. Probably similar to Manito.

Manjughosa   *(sweet sounding)*
God. Buddhist. Form of the god Manjusri and an emanation of Aksobhya. Attended by a lion. Color: white or gold. Attributes: arrow, bell, blue lotus, book, bow, image of Aksobhya, staff and sword.

MANJUSRI   *(pleasing splendor)*
Origin Buddhist [India]. *Bodhisattva* or *buddha-*designate, also god of wisdom.

Known period of worship circa 500 BC until present.

Synonyms large number of forms.

Center(s) of cult pan-Asiatic.

Art references metal and stone sculptures, paintings.

Literary sources *Sadhanamala* and Tantric ritual texts.

An important and popular deity throughout all sects of Buddhism. He is the son of either Amitabha or Aksobhya and is closely linked with the goddess Prajnaparamita who is seen as the personification of a holy text that Manjusri habitually carries, the *pustaka*. His attendant animal is the tiger or the lion. Color: black, white, red or yellow. Attributes: chiefly book and sword, but also arrow, blue lotus and bow. May be three-headed.

Manmatha
Form of the god of carnal love. Dravidian (Tamil). A local southern Indian form of Kama with similar attributes and genealogy, named in Sangam literature.

Manohel-Tohel
Creator god. Mayan (classical Mesoamerican) [Mexico]. The deity concerned specifically with the creation of mankind, giving mortals body and soul and leading them from the caves into the light.

Manu
Primordial creator god. Hindu (Vedic). The son(s) of Surya. The name given to the fourteen original progenitors of mankind during the mythical or heroic ages. According to tradition, the consort of Manu is Ida, who was engendered from milk and butter offered to Siva as a propitiation.

Manungal
Chthonic underworld god. Mesopotamian (Sumerian and Babylonian-Akkadian). A minor deity, the consort of Birdu.

Maponos
Tribal deity. Celtic (British and Continental European). A youthful god worshiped by the Brigantes tribe in Britain and probably assimilated with Apollo in the Romano-Celtic period.

Mara   *(the destroyer)*
1. God. Buddhist. An evil deity who puts obstacles in the way of the Buddha. The equal of the Hindu god Kama. In Buddhist tradition, the Hindu gods Indra, Brahma, Visnu and Siva are *maras* who become vanquished by various Buddhist deities. Attributes: fish standard.
2. God. Hindu. An epithet of Kama(deva).

Marama
Moon goddess. Polynesian (Maori). She equates with the Tahitian goddess Hina, daughter of Tangaroa. Tradition has it that her body wastes away with each lunar cycle but is restored when she bathes in the sea from which all life springs.

Maramalik
Chthonic underworld god. Kafir [Afghanistan]. No details known.

MARDUK
Origin Mesopotamian (Babylonian) [Iraq]. Creator and national god.

Known period of worship circa 2000 BC, or earlier, to circa 200 BC.

Synonyms Lugal-dimmer-an-ki-a (divine king of heaven and earth); Ašalluhe; Merodach (Hebrew). At least fifty other divine names, according to the Babylonian creation epic.

Center(s) of cult Babylon.

Art references plaques, votive stelae, glyptics, etc.

Literary sources cuneiform texts, particularly the Babylonian creation epic *Enuma Eliš.*

Marduk is the chief deity of Babylonia and tutelary god of the city of Babylon though perhaps derived, in part, from a Sumerian model. His parents are Enki and Damgalnuna or Ea and Damkina. His consort is the goddess Zarpanitu(m) with whom his marriage was reenacted in an annual New Year festival. In the Old Babylonian period he was comparatively insignificant, but in subsequent times he rose to prominence, taking over the role of An and replacing Enlil. At the time of the Assyrian takeover, Assyrian scribes replaced Marduk with Assur.

In the mythology of the creation epic, Marduk is engaged in a primordial cosmic battle with Tiamat, the power of the ocean. He kills her, splitting her in half and using parts of her corpse to make heaven and earth. Tiamat fought him in revenge for the death of Apsu, the deep, and is said to have created an exact replica of Apsu, the Ešarra.

The symbol of Marduk is the triangular device used in Mesopotamia as an agricultural tool and called a *mar.*

The main Marduk festival was the *akitu,* also performed at New Year, which continued up to as late as 200 BC. It was performed by the Persian ruler Cambyses circa 538 BC. Marduk's sanctuary in Babylon is the Esagila and the E-temen-anki ziggurat.

Mari *(killing) (1)*
1. Deification of literature. Buddhist. One of a group of *dharanis.* Color: reddish white. Attributes: needle, thread and staff.
2. Mother goddess. Dravidian (Tamil) [southern India]. See Mari Mai.

Mari *(queen) (2)*
Supreme mother goddess. Basque [Pyrenean region]. She is both a sky and chthonic goddess and her consort is Maju. She is depicted dressed in rich clothing and jewels. Her home is within the earth but she also rides through the air in a chariot pulled by four horses or carried by a ram. She may breathe fire and is symbolized by the rainbow. When she and her consort meet, a thunderstorm forms. Her symbol is a sickle, which is still employed as a device to ward off evil.

Mari Mai *(mother death)*
Plague goddess. Hindu. The sister of Sitala, associated with cholera. Her Tamil counterpart is Mariyamman.

Marici *(shining)*
1. Astral goddess. Buddhist (Mahayana). An emanation of Vairocana and also his female aspect or *Sakti.* She is further identified as a *buddha*-designate or *bodhisattva.* She may also be the mother of Sakyamuni (a form of the Buddha). Considered by some to be the equal of the Hindu Surya. She may be depicted in a three-headed form (as the *Sakti* of Hayagriva), in which case her left head is that of a pig. She rides in a chariot drawn by seven boars. Color: red, yellow or white. Attributes: arrow, bow, fly whisk, horse's head image in the hair, needle, prayer wheel, staff, sword, thread and trident. Three-eyed.
2. Demiurge. Hindu. A product of the creator god Brahma.

Mariyamman *(mother of smallpox)*
Plague goddess. Dravidian (Tamil) [southern India]. A terrible goddess, one of the *navasaktis* and linked with the goddess Kali. She is honored in a ritual during which victims (in penance) are suspended from a rope and an iron hook through the flesh of the back and whirled around a pole. Also Mariyattal.

Marnas
Local tutelary god. Pre-Islamic northern Arabian. Probably regarded as a fertility deity, his cult was

centered at Gaza at the Marneion sanctuary and probably succeeded that of Dagon. He may have been the subject of a colossal statue attributed to Zeus found near Gaza.

MARS

Origin Roman. God of war.

Known period of worship circa 400 BC to circa 400 AD.

Synonyms Ares (Greek).

Center(s) of cult the Mars Ultor sanctuary (Augustine) in Rome.

Art references large number of sculptures and carvings.

Literary sources *Aeneid* (Virgil), etc.

Mars may have originated as a god of vegetation, but becomes closely modeled on the Greek war god Ares. The son of Jupiter and Juno, he is one of the major deities on the Roman pantheon and the patron of all soldiers. He was particularly popular in Roman Britain.

He is depicted wearing a suit of armor with a plumed helmet. He bears a shield and spear. His retinue includes Metus (Fear), Demios (Dread), Phobos (Alarm), Eris (Discord) and Pallor (Terror). Mars is frequently linked with Bellona, the minor Roman war goddess who drives his chariot. He took an active part in the primordial war between gods and giants. His consort is Venus and he is the father of Harmonia, Cupid and Anteros. He is also romantically linked with the *vestal* Ilia, who was buried alive for contravening the laws of her sisterhood. Through Ilia Mars fathered Romulus, the alleged founder of the city of Rome, and Remus, who was slain by Romulus. It was the convention that a Roman general, before setting out for combat, would invoke Mars in his sanctuary. The name of the month of March, noted for its violent weather, is derivative and the month was dedicated to the god.

The training ground for would-be Roman legionaries was known as the Campus Martius (field of Mars). Mars's sacred animals include the bull, wolf and woodpecker.

Martu

Tutelary god. Mesopotamian (Sumerian). The patron god of the city of Ninab mentioned in the texts but never rediscovered. Probably not a true Sumerian deity but adopted from an unknown western Semitic culture. He is sometimes identified as a storm god.

Marutgana

Storm gods. Hindu (Vedic). The sons of Rudra and attendants of Indra. Also Maruts.

Mata (great mother)

Primeval mother goddess. Hindu. The archetypal progenitor of all living things. She becomes the tutelary goddess of every village in northern India, but is also seen as a plague goddess associated with smallpox, in which case her epithet becomes Maha Mai. Her Tamil counterpart is Amman.

Matara

Mother goddess. Hindu. Applied collectively to groups of deities, the divine mothers, also more specifically to the consort of the god Kasyapa. As divine mothers they are also regarded as *Saktis*. The numbers vary according to separate traditions and they are therefore identified as the *saptamataras* (seven), *astamataras* (eight) and *navasaktis* (nine). Less commonly there may be up to fifty *mataras* in a group. Their images are normally carved in stone (very few exist in metal) and they are depicted seated, often upon a corpse, and may be of terrifying appearance.

Matarisvan

Minor messenger god. Hindu (Vedic). The attendant of Agni.

Mater Matuta

Sky goddess. Italic. The personification of the dawn light who evolved into a fertility deity concerned with childbirth. She is also a tutelary goddess of mariners. See also Isis.

Matlalcueye *(her skirt is blue)*
Minor fertility goddess. Aztec (classical Meso-american) [Mexico]. One of the group classed as the Tlaloc complex, closely associated with water.

MATRES *(mothers)*
Origin Romano-Celtic (across Europe but particularly Rhineland). Triads of mother goddesses.

Known period of worship circa 400 BC, but probably much earlier, until Christianization (circa 400 AD).

Synonyms Deae Matres; Matronae.

Center(s) of cult various shrines.

Art references various Romano-Celtic sculptures, reliefs and votive plaques. An excellent example comes from Cirencester, England.

Literary sources inscriptions.

Triads of benevolent mother goddesses were probably worshiped, in the main, as household deities guarding against disease or famine. An important sculpture of Matres was found embedded in the walls of London on a section of fourth century rebuilding adjacent to the Thames. Another, the *Matres Aufaniae*, was dedicated by Quettius Severus, the quaestor of the colony of Cologne. Several unnamed Matres are held in the Corinium museum at Cirencester. The sculptures are often associated with cornucopiae, baskets of fruit, loaves, sheaves of grain, fish or other symbols of prosperity and fertility. They may also carry or suckle children. Many of the triads were specific to regions, hence the Treverae among the Treveri tribe around modern Trier, or the Nemausicae at Nimes.

Many of the dedications to such mothers were made by soldiers. There is a slight suggestion that they might also have been linked to victory in battle. The plaque found in London seems to have the mothers holding palm fronds. They are also not infrequently depicted with dogs, which were generally included as symbols of healing. Some, particularly from the Rhineland, show young and older figures, suggesting the different ages of womanhood.

Matsuo
God of sake brewers. Shinto [Japan]. Celebrated annually in a festival in Kyoto, when the presence of the god is carried on a palanquin. It is rowed down the river prior to a general celebration, during which sake is drunk liberally.

Matsya
Incarnation of the god Visnu. Hindu (Epic and Puranic). In this first *avatara* Visnu appears as a fish that, according to one legend, tows a ship carrying the lawgiver Manu to safety after the primal flood. Matsya engages in an epic battle with the demon Hayagriva who stole the *Vedas* from a sleeping Brahma. Usually depicted with a human torso carrying symbols, e.g. wheel and conch, on a fish's body.

Maturaiviran
Locally worshiped god. Hindu. Of fearsome character, he is the deification of a seventeenth century policeman who eloped with a princess and was slain. Known from southern India, where he is also a god of wine. Attributes: shield and sword.

Maui
Tutelary god. Polynesian (Maori) [New Zealand]. Not a creator god but one who assists mankind in various supernatural ways. According to tradition he was apparently stillborn and cast into the sea by his mother, who thought he was dead. He was rescued entangled in seaweed. He is the deity who drew the islands of New Zealand from the floor of the ocean in a net. Maui caught the sun and beat it into submission, making it travel more slowly across the sky so that the days became longer. He also brought fire from the underworld for mankind and tried, unsuccessfully, to harness immortality for him by entering the vulva of the underworld goddess Hine-Nui-Te-Po while she was asleep. She awoke and crushed him to death. Though a deity, he had been made vulnerable to death by a mistake during his rites of birth (see also Balder). Also Mawi.

Mawu

1. Moon goddess. Fon [Benin, West Africa]. The sister of the sun god Lisa. She is also considered to bestow fertility and motherhood and is generally benevolent in nature.
2. Sky god. Ewe [Togo, West Africa]. Among the tribe neighboring the Fon, Mawu is perceived as male and a creator deity. He favors the color white and is also benevolent and generous in nature.

Maya(devi)

Mother goddess. Buddhist. The mother of the Buddha perceived as the world lotus or *padma* from which the Buddha was born. She equates with the Hindu goddess Laksmi. The term is also applied to the personification of the visible universe and, in Hinduism, as an epithet of the goddess Durga.

Mayahuel

Minor fertility goddess. Aztec (classical Mesoamerican) [Mexico]. One of the group classed as the Ometochtli complex associated with the maguey plant from which pulque is brewed. She may be depicted seated upon a tortoise beside an agave plant in bloom. According to legend she was abducted by Quetzalcoatl and subsequently dismembered by wild animals. From the fragments grew the first agave plants.

Mayajalakrama-Kurukulla

(one who proceeds in the net of illusion)
Goddess. Buddhist (Mahayana). The personification of all *dhyanibuddhas*. Color: red. Attributes: arrow, bow, hook, images of the five *dhyanibuddhas*, lotus (red), pitcher, rosary and water jar.

Mayin

Supreme god. Tungus [eastern and central Siberia]. A benevolent but remote deity who breathes life into newborn children and receives the spirits of the dead.

Mayon   *(the black one)*

Creator god. Early Dravidian (Tamil) [southern India and Sri Lanka]. Animistic high god of the pastoral regions, found in Sangam literature and thought to reside in trees. Perhaps equating with Visnu or Krsna.

Ma-zu

Sea goddess. Chinese. Known from the coastal regions of southeastern China as a benevolent guardian of fishermen, and closely linked with the goddess Kuan-Yin.

Mbomba

Creator god. Mongo and Nkundo [Zaire, central Africa]. He operates through intermediaries known as *bilima* and through the spirits of the dead, *bakali*. Also known as Ianda, Komba, Mbombo, Njakomba and Wai. Among the Ngbandi people there is recognized a vast water monster or river god by the same name.

Mbombe

Mother goddess. Nkundo [Zaire, central Africa]. The consort of Itonde and mother of the hero Lianja.

Mbongo

River god. Ngbandi [Zaire, central Africa]. One of seven deities invoked at sunrise each morning. The creator god of all black people, said to reside in black waters.

Mbotumbo

Creator god. Baule [Ivory Coast, West Africa]. A generally benevolent guardian deity with the head of an ape.

Medeine   *(of the trees)*

Woodland goddess. Pre-Christian Latvian. Known from medieval manuscripts.

Medha   *(wisdom)*

Minor goddess. Buddist (Mahayana). The *Sakti* of Sridhara.

Meditrina

Goddess of healing. Roman. Syncretized into the cult of Aesculapius.

Meghanada *(cloud roar)*
Minor god. Hindu. A son of Ravana who once briefly bested Indra and became known as the "Indra-conqueror."

Mehen
Minor chthonic underworld god. Egyptian. The guardian of the boat of the sun god Re during its passage through the underworld at night. Depicted in the form of a coiled snake.

Meher
Sun god. Pre-Christian Armenian. Closely linked with the Persian model of Mithra, he is the son of Aramazd who appears in the form of fire. In contrast to this imagery, his home is said to be in a cave and he takes the animal guise of a raven.

Mehet-Weret *(great flood)*
Minor goddess associated with creation accounts. Egyptian. In some versions of the story she epitomizes the primeval ocean, while in others she is the waterway on which the boat of the sun god Re travels. She is depicted as a cow bearing a sun disc between its horns and lying on papyrus reeds.

Mellonia
Goddess of bees. Roman.

MELQART
Origin Phoenician [Turkey]. Heroic tutelary god.

Known period of worship circa 1200 BC to 200 BC.

Synonyms Milk-quart.

Center(s) of cult Tyre.

Art references possibly sculptures in stone.

Literary sources Herodotus and local inscriptions; *Vetus Testamentum.*

A god of youthful appearance often associated with the sea. Known mainly from Tyre, where he was regarded as the consort of Astarte and probably consitituted part of a trio of major deities with Baal Šamin and Astarte. He may be depicted on coinage riding a sea horse. The cult of Melqart spread extensively through Egypt, Carthage, Cyprus, etc. Melqart equates with Ešmun, the tutelary god of Sidon. Known in Hebrew tradition as the ruler of the underworld and probably based on the Sumerian/Akkadian Nergal. In Hellenic times he becomes defined more as a sun god, but is largely syncretized with Herakles. The pillars in the sanctuary at Gadeira/Cadiz were renamed the Pillars of Hercules by the Romans.

Me'mdeye-Eci'e
Fire spirit. Yukaghir [eastern Siberia]. A benevolent being residing in the sky and known as "father fire."

Men
Moon god. Phrygian [Turkey]. Ruler of both upper and lower worlds. Probably also a god of healing, he was subsequently adopted by the Greeks and Romans. The cult was popular during the imperial period, but its inscriptions were written in Greek.

Men Ascaenus
Local tutelary god. Antioch-near-Pisidia. Possibly originating as a Persian moon god and known chiefly from a description by Strabo. He enjoyed a substantial cult including a temple some 1,200 meters above sea level. His symbol is the head of a bull above a crescent moon and wreath; it appears on local coinage circa 200 AD. The popularity of the cult earned antagonism from the Roman occupation. See also Men.

Men Shen
God of passage. Chinese. One of a pair of deities, armed with bow and arrows, who guard doorways and gates. Paper images are pinned to entrances of homes during the New Year celebrations to ward off evil spirits.

Mena
Mountain goddess. Hindu. The consort of Himavan and the mother of Ganga and Parvati.

Menechen   *(master of men)*
Supreme god. Araucania Indian [southern Andes]. Also known as Pillan (heaven) and, west of the Andes, Guenu-Pillan (spirit of heaven).

Meness
Moon god. Pre-Christian Latvian. Consort of the sun goddess Saule. He is a guardian deity of travelers and military expeditions.

Menulis
Moon god. Pre-Christian Lithuanian. Consort of the sun goddess.

Menzabac   *(black powder maker)*
Weather god. Mayan (classical Mesoamerican) [Mexico]. He sprinkles black dye on the clouds, which causes them to generate rain. Believed to live on the edge of a lake. Also a fever god and, by contrast, a keeper of good souls. Also Metzabac.

MERCURIUS

Origin   Roman. Messenger god.

Known period of worship   circa 400 BC to circa 400 AD.

Synonyms   Psychopompus; Oneicopompus; Hermes (Greek); Mercury.

Center(s) of cult   Circus Maximus (Rome).

Art references   sculptures and carvings.

Literary sources   *Aeneid* (Virgil), etc.

One of the twelve major deities of Olympus, Mercury is modeled closely on the Greek god Hermes. In Roman mythology he is the son of Jupiter and the plains goddess Maia, born in a cave on Mount Cyllene in Arcadia. He is attributed with the invention of the lyre made from a tortoise shell, and with various misdemeanors, including the theft of cattle from Apollo, an allegory on the blowing away of the clouds (Apollo's herds). Mercury also personifies the wind. Apollo presented Mercury with the gift of his winged baton, the *caduceus*, which had the power of resolving conflict and dispute. The gods also presented Mercury with the winged sandals or *talaria* and cap or *petasus*.

Originally he was a god of riches but became a patron of travelers and thieves. The French for Wednesday, *mercredi*, derives from his name. His main annual festival, the *Mercuralia*, took place in Rome in May and his statues were frequently placed as boundary markers.

As Psychopompus he leads the souls of the dead into Hades, and as Oneicopompus he oversees the world of dreams.

Meretseger
Localized chthonic goddess associated with the underworld. Egyptian. At Thebes she acted in either benign or destructive fashion against workers building tombs in the Valley of the Kings. She is generally depicted as a coiled cobra that may possess a human head and arm. One of the best representations is on the sarcophagus of Rameses III. She lost her popularity when the use of Thebes as a royal cemetery was discontinued early in the first millennium BC.

Mes An Du
God. Mesopotamian (Sumerian and Babylonian-Akkadian). Probably an alternative title for the sun god (see Šamaš).

Mes Lam Taea
God of war. Mesopotamian (Sumerian and Babylonian-Akkadian). An aggressive aspect of the chthonic underworld god Nergal. Often linked with the god Lugal-irra.

Messor
Minor god of agriculture. Roman. Concerned with the growth and harvesting of crops.

Meter
Mother goddess. Greek. The essence of the great mother of all gods, equating most closely to Gaia. Known throughout the Greek Empire and generally the object of devotion by individuals rather

than large cult followings. Also known as *Meter oriae* (mother of the mountain). Her popularity is thought to have spread from northern Ionia. Herodotus mentions a festival of Meter in Kyzikos. Probably derived originally from the western Asiatic great mother (see Kybele).

Metis

Goddess of wisdom. Greek. The daughter of Okeanos and Tethys. The original consort of Zeus and mother of Athena. According to legend, Zeus swallowed her because he feared she would engender a child more powerful than he.

Metsaka

Moon goddess. Huichol Indian (Mesoamerican) [Mexico]. Known as "grandmother moon," she is the consort of the fire god Tatevali. She guards the Huichol against the god of death, Tokakami.

Metztli

Minor moon god. Aztec (classical Mesoamerican) [Mexico]. One of the group of deities belonging to the Texcatlipoca complex.

Mexitli   *(maguey hare)*

Minor god of war. Aztec (classical Mesoamerican) [Mexico]. One of the group of deities belonging to the Huitzilpochtli complex.

Mhalsa

Minor goddess. Hindu (late). The consort of Khandoba and considered to be a form of the goddess Parvati. Locally worshiped at Jejuri, near Poona in western India.

Micapetlacoli   *(dead mat chest)*

Minor chthonic underworld goddess. Aztec (classical Mesoamerican) [Mexico]. One of the group of deities belonging to the Mictlantecuhtli complex.

Michi-No-Kami

Gods of passage. Shinto [Japan]. The generic name for three *kamis* associated with roads and crossroads. They also protect the boundaries of house

and environs and may be known as Yakushin gods, guardians against plague. See Yachi-Mata and Kunado. Also Chiburi-No-Kami.

Mictecacihuatl

Chthonic underworld god. Aztec (classical Mesoamerican) [Mexico]. One of a pair of deities with Mictlantecuhtli. In the primeval waters of the cosmos, they generated the monstrous goddess Cipactli, from whom the earth was formed.

Mictlantecuhtli

Chthonic underworld god. Aztec (classical Mesoamerican) [Mexico]. The creator of the underworld, Mictlan. Depicted with a skull-like appearance and protruding teeth. Also one of a pair of deities with Mictecacihuatl. In the primeval waters of the cosmos, they generated the monstrous goddess Cipactli, from whom the earth was formed. In alternative traditions he is the god of the sixth of the thirteen heavens, Ilhuicatl Mamalhuazocan (the heaven of the fire drill), or he is one of the gods who support the lowest heaven at the four cardinal points. Mictlantecuhtli is perceived to reside in the south (codices *Borgia* and *Vaticanus B*). He is also one of the four great temple deities (codices *Borgia, Cospi* and *Fejervery-Mayer*).

Midir

Chthonic god. Celtic (Irish). Appears in polymorphic form. According to legend the consort of Etain and ruler of the land of Mag Mor. He lost an eye when hit by a hazel wand; the eye was subsequently replaced by Diancecht, the physician god. In Roman times he became more of an underworld deity. Also Mider.

Mihos

Lion god. Egyptian. The son of the goddess Bastet. Depicted in leonine form and originating from a cult center at Leontopolis [Tell el'Muqdam] in Lower Egypt. A sanctuary in his honor was built at Bubastis. Also Miysis (Greek).

Mika-Hiya-Hi   *(terrible swift sun)*
Sun god. Shinto [Japan]. A deity subservient to the sun goddess Amaterasu and engendered from the blood of the fire *kami* Kagu-Tsuchi. Certain Japanese still worship the sun, going outside in the morning, facing east, bowing and clapping their hands in a daily ritual. See also Hi-Hiya-Hi.

Mikal
Local god. Western Semitic (Phoenician). The cult was followed strongly on Cyprus. Some authorities believe he was invoked as a plague god.

Mi-Kura-Tana-No-Kami
(august storehouse chief kami)
House god. Shinto [Japan]. One of a number of domestic guardian *kamis,* he is particularly concerned with the protection of storehouses.

Milkastart
Local tutelary god. Western Semitic. Known only from Umm el-Ammed where his cult apparently coexisted with that of Baal Sapon. One of two major temples built at Umm el-Ammed in the third century BC was probably dedicated to Milkastart, and the name is regarded as a syncretization of Melqart and Astarte.

Milkom
Tutelary god. Western Semitic (Ammonite). One of the deities mentioned in the *Vetus Testamentum* (1 Kings 11:5) as being worshiped by the Israelite king Solomon. Also Milcom.

Mi-Lo Fo
God. Chinese Buddhist. The local name given to the *bodhisattva* Maitreya. Like the Indian model he is represented as a rubicund figure. Attributes include roses and a purse.

MIMIR
Origin   Nordic (Icelandic). God of wisdom and inspiration.

Known period of worship   Viking period (circa 700 AD) and possibly earlier until Christianization (circa 1100 AD).

Synonyms   Mimr; Mimi; Mim.

Center(s) of cult   none known.

Art references   none known, but possibly the subject of anonymous carvings.

Literary sources   Icelandic codices; *Prose Edda* (Snorri).

An Aesir god who lives in the world of the Frost Giants. He guards the well of knowledge, filled by a spring that flows beneath the World Tree, Yggdrasil, and that is supplied from the primeval waters. The god Othin drank from the spring to acquire knowledge, having forfeited one of his eyes to Mimir. Said to be the wisest among the gods. According to some sources he was sent as hostage to the Vanir in their war with the Aesir and was killed by them (see Othin). Some authors argue that he is more properly a giant than a god. Said to be accompanied often by the silent god Hoenir. Mimir warns Othin of the final onslaught at Ragnarok (doom).

MIN
Origin   Egyptian. Fertility god.

Known period of worship   circa 3000 BC until the end of Egyptian history (circa 400 AD).

Synonyms   Menu (Egyptian).

Center(s) of cult   Qift at the western end of the Wadi Hammamat, lying between Luxor and Qena; Akhmim, north of Qena.

Art references   sculpture including fragmented limestone colossi from Qift dating from 3000 BC or earlier; stone reliefs, wall paintings, etc.

Literary sources   Pyramid Texts, coffin texts, etc.

Min is the most significant deity in the Egyptian pantheon in respect to sexual virility. In some genealogies he is the son of Isis, in others he represents Isis's consort with Horus as their child. Min is depicted in anthropomorphic form wearing a modius bearing two plumes and a hanging ribbon. He is generally drawn in profile, legs together and with his left arm raised into the angle made by his royal flail. The most obvious feature of the iconography is a strongly erect penis. Min is represented in older art by two serrated cones projecting horizontally from a disc. His sacred animal is probably a white bull and he is also associated with the tall lettuce species *(Lactuca sativa)*, the shape of which may be reminiscent of an erect phallus.

By the end of the second millennium, Min had become partly syncretized with Horus as a god Min-Horus. Min is also a guardian deity of mines, hence his cult centers at Qift and Akhim, which were bases for gold-mining expeditions. Temple buildings at both sites are only known from the Greco-Roman period. Min was celebrated as part of the coronation rites of a ruler in Egypt, thus ensuring the sexual vigor and fertility of the new pharaoh. The festival is found depicted at Thebes in association with Rameses II and III. At the time Min was frequently presented with offerings of flowers and sacred lettuces.

Minaksi   *(fish eyed)*

Local fish goddess. Hindu. Regarded as a *Sakti* of Siva (i.e., Parvati) and the daughter of Kubera. She is the mother of Ugra. Minaksi is known mainly from southern India where one of her main temples is at Madurai.

Minato-No-Kami

God of river mouths and estuaries. Shinto [Japan]. The son of Izanagi and Izanami and father of the heavenly and earthly water dividers.

MINERVA

Origin   Roman. Goddess of war.

Known period of worship   circa 400 BC until 400 AD.

Synonyms   Pallas, Athena (Greek).

Center(s) of cult   main Capitoline temple shared with Jupiter and Juno, also an important sanctuary on the Esquiline (see Athena).

Art references   depicted with Juno and Jupiter on the Great Arch of Trajan at Beneventum erected in 115 AD; frequently appearing on sarcophagi offering new life beyond the grave. See also Athena.

Literary sources   Aeneid (Virgil), etc.

Minerva is probably derived from an Etruscan goddess Menrva but later becomes modeled on the Greek goddess Athena. Like the latter, she sprang fully armed from the head of Jupiter (Zeus), whose head had been cleaved with Vulcan's ax. As Minerva Medica she is the tutelary goddess of Rome. She is perceived variously as goddess of war and peace, but also of wisdom and the arts and crafts including needlework. Annual festivals in her honor included the *Minervalia* and *Quinquatria* (March 19–23) at which the Palladium statue that had allegedly fallen from Olympus was carried in procession.

Minos

Minor underworld god. Greco-Roman. A son of Zeus and Europa. The mythical king of Crete. One of three judges of the dead souls entering Hades. His cult is linked with the worship of bulls.

Mirsa

God of light. Pre-Christian Caucasus region. Probably derived from the Persian god Mithra. Also the deity responsible for fire.

MITHRA   *(friend)*

Origin   Persian [Iran]. God of the upper air.

Known period of worship   circa 400 BC to 200 AD.

Synonyms   Mitra (Hindu); Mithras (Roman).

Center(s) of cult   throughout area of Persian influence.

Art references   various sculptures and reliefs.

Literary sources   Avesta.

Originating in India, Mithra is a god of light who was translated into the attendant of the god Ahura Mazda in the light religion of Persia; from this he was adopted as the Roman deity Mithras. He is not generally regarded as a sky god but a personification of the fertilizing power of warm, light air. According to the *Avesta*, he possesses 10,000 eyes and ears and rides in a chariot drawn by white horses.

In dualistic Zoroastrianism, which effectively demoted him, Mithra is concerned with the endless battle between light and dark forces; he represents truth. He is responsible for the keeping of oaths and contracts. He was born from a rock and, according to legend, engaged in a primeval struggle with Ahura Mazda's first creation, a wild bull, which he subdued and confined to a cave. The bull escaped, but was recaptured by Mithra, who slit its throat. From the blood sprang plant life on earth. His chief adversary is Ahriman, the power of darkness.

Mithra is not generally worshiped on his own, but as an integral part of the Mithraic worship of Ahura Mazda, where he acts as an intercessor between gods and men. In the Hellenic period he was transformed more closely to the role of a sun god. See also Ahura Mazda.

Mithras

God of soldiers. Greco-Roman. Derived from the Indian-Persian model. He became particularly prominent among the military throughout the Roman Empire during the first and second centuries AD, as a god symbolizing loyalty and truth. Rituals were performed in an underground temple, the *mithraeum*, and involved the sacrifice of a bull. Mithraism, under Roman influence, was an exclusively male cult.

Miti

Maternal spirit. Koryak [southeastern Siberia]. The consort of Quikinna'qu. According to tradition her father is twilight man, Gi'thililan, who deserted her when she was very young. She is regarded as the mother of the Koryak people, whose imme-diate sons and daughters are Eme'mqut, Na'nqa-Ka'le, Yine'ane'ut and Cana'ina'ut.

Mi-Toshi-No-Kami
(the august harvest kami)
Agricultural god. Shinto [Japan]. The offspring of O-Toshi-No-Kami, the harvest god of rice, and Kagayo-Hime (refulgent princess), he is in charge of crops other than rice.

Mitra   *(friend)*
Minor sun god. Hindu (Vedic and Puranic). An *aditya*, one of six descendants of Aditi, he was originally associated with Varuna (Vedic), ruling the day while Varuna ruled the night. It is from this model that first Mithra (Persian) and then Mithras (Roman) were derived. He is also the god of intimate friendship. Attributes: two lotus, trident and a sacrificial drink or *soma*.

Mi-Wi-No-Kami
God of wells. Shinto [Japan]. One of three deities responsible for wells, worshiped jointly in the Mi-Wi-Jinja shrine. He is particularly the god of domestic wells. See also Saku-Wi-No-Kami and Tsunaga-Wi-No-Kami.

Mixcoatl-Camaxtli   *(cloud serpent)*
God of war. Aztec (classical Mesoamerican) [Mexico]. Also a deity of hunting and fire who received human sacrifice of captured prisoners. According to tradition, the sun god Tezcatlipoca transformed himself into Mixcoatl-Camaxtli to make fire by twirling the sacred fire sticks.

Mizu-Ha-No-Me
Water goddess. Shinto [Japan]. The senior water deity who was engendered from the urine of the primordial creator goddess Izanami during her fatal illness, having been burned producing the fire god Hi-No-Kagu-Tsuchi.

Mkulumncandi
Creator god. Swazi [Swaziland, South Africa]. There is no worship of this deity, though he is known as the "great first one."

Mlentengamunye *(one leg)*
Messenger god. Swazi [Swaziland, South Africa].
The intermediary between mankind and the creator god Mkulumncandi.

Mlk-Amuklos
Heroic god. Western Semitic [Syrio-Palestine] and
Cyprus. Known from inscriptions circa 1100 BC
and possibly one of the original pre-Hellenic models
from which Apollo was derived.

Mnemosyne
Goddess of memory. Greek. A consort of Zeus
and mother of the legendary nine Muses of Helicon.

Moccus
Local swine god. Romano-Celtic (Continental European). Assimilated with Mercury.

Modimo
Universal god. Tswana [Botswana, South Africa].
A monotheistic deity possibly, though not with
certainty, influenced by Christianity. Not specifically a creator god, since the universe and Modimo
have "always been." Perceived as the river of
existence that flows endlessly through space and
time. He rules the light and dark opposites in the
universe, as well as the proper order of life on
earth.

Modron *(another)*
Mother goddess. Celtic (Welsh). The mother of
Mabon, whom she subsequently loses. Her cult is
closely linked with that of Mabon and she may
originally have been one of the aspects of the
goddess(es) Morrigan. In Christian times some
authors believe that she became St. Madrun.

Mogounos
Local tribal deity. Romano-Celtic (Gallic). Assimilated with Apollo.

Mohini *(illusion)*
Minor incarnation of Visnu. Hindu (Epic and Puranic). Mohini is an *avatara* who appears in the
form of an enchantress whose form Visnu adopted
briefly to deceive demons attempting to remove
the ambrosia created by churning the primeval
ocean of milk (see also Garuda). Visnu used the
same guise to dupe and seduce the god Siva.

Moirai
Collective name for a group of goddesses. Greek.
The Fates of human life: Klotho, the spinner,
Lachesis, the caster of lots, and Atropos, the unturnable inevitability of death. The daughters of
Zeus and Themis, depicted with spindle, scroll
and scales respectively. Also Moires.

Mokos
Goddess of fertility. Pre-Christian Slavonic European. Identified in the *Nestor Chronicle* as a goddess of midwifery. Her cult was taken over by
that of the Virgin Mary.

Molek
God. Western Semitic (Ammonite). Synonymous
with the god Moloch (Hebrew) of the *Vetus Testamentum* to whom Israelite children were sacrificed by burning (1 Kings 11:7 and 2 Kings 23:10).

Moloch
See Molek.

Moma
Creator god. Uitoto Indian [South America]. Originally the creator of mankind. When he was slain
he entered and ruled the underworld. Also the
apotheosis of the moon.

Mombo Wa Ndhlopfu *(elephant face)*
Tutelary god. Ronga [Mozambique, southern Africa]. An ancestral deity who lives in and controls
the forests, also appearing in the guise of a huge
snake. He is propitiated by the sacrifice of a cockerel.

MON *(great god)*
Origin Kafir [Afghanistan-Hindukush]. Warrior
god and hero.

Known period of worship   from prehistoric origins and persisting in certain localized parts today.

Synonyms   Mandi.

Center(s) of cult   chiefly at the village of Pashki and at Dewa (Prasun region), but also at numerous smaller sanctuaries throughout Kafir region.

Art references   wooden sculptures.

Literary sources   Robertson G.S. *The Kafirs of the Hindukush* (1896), Morgenstierne G. *Some Kati Myths and Hymns* (1951).

Mon is a senior deity in the Kafir pantheon who challenges and defends mankind against demons and giants. He is the first offspring of the creator god Imra. He is also a weather god who controls clouds and mist. Mon is perceived as a deity of vast size and vigor who creates glaciers with his footprints. He is also a god of flowing water. Some legends place him as a creator of mankind and lawgiver, but only mirroring the actions of the supreme creator Imra. He appears as a mediator between heaven and earth.

Mon is depicted, in wood, either in human form carrying a golden bow and quiver made by his brother Kshibere, or as a humped bull. Alternatively he is represented by a standing stone slab with two attendant smaller stones.

According to legend, when the giants locked up the sun and moon in a gold house, Mon turned himself into a child and in this guise was protected by a giantess mother. After many attempts to break into the house, he succeeded, restored the sun and moon to their place in the heavens and assisted Imra in the creation of mankind.

Moneta

Minor goddess of prosperity. Roman. The spirit of the mint, known particularly from the second century BC.

Montu

Local god of war. Egyptian. Worshipped in and around the district of Thebes in Upper Egypt. He is known from circa 2000 BC and possibly earlier, but came to special prominence overseeing the aggressive posture of Theban kings from the XI to XVIII Dynasty (2133–1320 BC). Montu is depicted in human form but with a falcon's head surmounted by twin plumes, a sun disc and the *uraeus* (cobra). At some stage, probably as Month (Greek), he became identified with a sacred bull, Buchis.

Mor

Sun goddess. Celtic (Irish). The progenitor of the royal lineage of the kings of Munster.

Morpheus

Minor god of dreams. Greek. The son of Hypnos, there is no record of worship of this deity.

MORRIGAN   *(queen of demons)*

Origin   Celtic (Irish). War, fertility and vegetation goddess.

Known period of worship   from prehistoric origins until Christianization (circa 400 AD).

Synonyms   Macha (Ulster); Medb or Maeve (Connaught); Etain Echraide (Tara); also probably Badb Catha; Eriu; Fodla; Nemain; Rhiannon.

Center(s) of cult   various sanctuaries throughout Ireland.

Art references   inscriptions and carvings on Romano-Celtic altars, stone pillars, etc.

Literary sources   *Books of Invasions; Cycles of Kings.*

A complex goddess displaying various characteristics that are both generative and destructive (see also Anat, Inana, Ištar, Athene). At the festival of *Samain*, she mates with the Dagda to ensure the future prosperity of the land and as Queen Maeve (Medb) of Connaught she was ritually wedded to the mortal king whose antecedent was Ailill. As Nemain (panic) and Badb Catha (raven of battle), she takes on a more warlike and destructive aspect. Rather than engaging directly in conflict, she uses her supernatural powers to spread fear and disarray. The Irish hero Cu Chulainn was thus visited on the battle field by Badb driving a chariot and dressed in a red cloak and with red eyebrows presenting an all-intimidating appearance. She is capable of changing her shape into various animal forms and in the guise of a raven or a crow is able to foretell the outcome of battle.

Morrigan is also closely associated with horse symbolism, befitting a horse-oriented culture with strong links east toward Asia. Mare forms the basis of the names Macha and Medb. She may also at times have been syncretized with the horse goddess Epona. As with other Celtic goddesses Morrigan is an intrinsic part of the land rather than a tribal deity, the "Sovereignty of Ireland."

The Celtic goddess is frequently described as a triad of separate aspects. Hence Morrigan, Nemain and Badb are linked and become collectively the *Morrigna* (see also Matres). In association with the vitality of Irish kings, Morrigan assumed the appearance both of a young girl and of a hag, the latter signaling the banishment or slaughter of a ruler who had become infirm or otherwise scarred with signs of mortality.

Mors

Minor god of death. Roman. Mors replaces the Greek Thanatos and, according to legend, is one of the twin sons of Nyx, goddess of the night. He lives in part of the remote cave occupied by Somnus, god of sleep, beside the river Lethe. Ovid depicts him as a hideous and cadaverous figure dressed in a winding sheet and holding a scythe and hour glass. Known particularly through Lacedaemonian culture where twin statues of Mors and Somnus were placed side by side.

Morta

Goddess of death. Roman. In later Roman times she becomes linked with the birth goddesses Decima and Nona, as a trio of goddesses of fate, the *Parcae.*

Morva

Sky spirits. Andaman Islands [Sea of Bengal]. Invisible but thought to be of human form.

Morvran   *(sea crow)*

Local god of war. Celtic (Welsh). The son of Ceridwen and Tegid Foel. Legend has it that he was extremely ugly and that his mother tried to imbue him with wisdom by preparing a special brew of inspiration. It was drunk by Gwion. Morvran was invincible in battle because his enemies thought him a demon.

MOT   *(death)*

Origin Canaanite and Phoenician [northern Israel, Lebanon and Syrian coastal regions]. God of natural adversity.

Known period of worship from prehistoric times until circa 200 BC.

Synonyms Muth (Phoenician).

Center(s) of cult possibly Byblos.

Art references none known.

Literary sources Ugaritic texts from Ras Šamra; Philon of Byblos; inscriptions.

Mot is the Canaanite representation of adversity in the natural world. He lives in a pit within the earth and is responsible for its annual death from drought and heat: "he has scorched the olive, the produce of the earth and the fruit of the trees." He engages in the classic confrontation with the Canaanite hero and national god, Baal. Though the duel results in Baal's demise, his death is avenged by his twin sister Anat, who slays Mot, then cleaves, winnows, burns and grinds him with a millstone, in what appears to be a ritual allied to the sowing of seed and harvesting (see Osiris). Baal is later restored. The conflict probably formed the basis of an annual ritual drama at the Canaanite New Year, which was held in the autumn. In the texts Mot is the son of Il and his mother is Ašerah (Athirat).

Moyocoyani   *(maker of himself)*

Minor god of universal power. Aztec (classical Mesoamerican) [Mexico]. One of the group of deities known as the Tezcatlipoca complex.

Mratna'irgin *(right hand dawn)*
Spirit of the dawn. Chukchee [eastern Siberia]. One of four beings responsible for the dawn in different directions. See also Tne'sqan, Lietna'irgin and Na'chitna'irgin.

Mrgasiras *(head of a gazelle)*
Minor goddess of fortune. Hindu (Epic and Puranic). A benevolent *naksatra*; daughter of Daksa and wife of Candra (Soma).

Mu Gong
God of immortality. Taoist (Chinese). The personification of the principle of Yang and the consort of Xi-Wang-Mu. He lives in the east, she in the west.

Muati
Obscure local god. Mesopotamian (Sumerian). Associated in some texts with the mythical island paradise of Dilmun, he becomes syncretized with Nabu.

dMu-bDud Kam-Po Sa-Zan
Sky god. Bon [Tibet]. The head of the ancient pantheon in the Bon religion.

Mucalinda
Tutelary god. Buddhist. The guardian of a lake near Bodh Gaya. He is identified as a king of the *nagas* or snake gods and is said to have protected the Buddha from a storm by coiling around him.

Mugasa
Sky god. Pigmy [central Africa]. Originally he headed a paradise land in which the first human beings lived. They disobeyed him, however, by entering his hut where he resided unseen, after which he left them and made them mortal. He is not worshiped in any conventional sense. Also Mugu.

Mugizi
Lake god. Bunyoro [Uganda, East Africa]. The guardian deity of Lake Albert, invoked with offerings by those wishing to cross the lake in boats.

Muhingo
God of war. Bunyoro [Uganda, East Africa]. Invoked specifically by warriors before entering battle.

Mujaji
Rain goddess. Lovedu [South Africa]. She is said to reside in the northern Drakensberg Mountains and sends both destructive tempests and gentle generative rain. In past times she was propitiated with sacrifices of cattle and occasionally young girls. She is represented by a lineage of mortal queens on whose fabulous reputation the author Rider Haggard based the novel *She*. Also Modjadji.

Mukasa
Supreme god. Buganda [Uganda, East Africa]. A benevolent deity whose main oracular sanctuary was on the island of Bubembe, Lake Victoria. His first high priest was Semagunga and, by convention, only the tribal leader was permitted to consult with the oracle there. Mukasa provides rain, food and cattle.

Mula
Minor goddess of fortune. Hindu (Epic and Puranic). A malevolent *naksatra*; daughter of Daksa and wife of Candra (Soma).

Mulindwa
Guardian goddess. Bunyoro [Uganda, East Africa]. The tutelary protector of the tribal chiefs and their families constituting the royal clan.

Mulliltu
Goddess. Mesopotamian (Babylonian-Akkadian). The consort of Ellil (Enlil) and of Assur. She derives from the Sumerian goddess Ninlil.

Mullo
Mule god. Romano-Celtic. Known from inscriptions and apparently associated with the the god Mars.

Munakata-No-Kami

Sea gods. Shinto [Japan]. A group of three *kamis*, generally identified as the Sumiyoshi-No-Kami, who protect seafarers, including fishermen. They are the subject of special worship by the Jingu-Kogo sect, whom they escorted to Korea in distant times. They are also tutelary deities of poets and may have a purifying function. Their main sanctuaries are the Sumiyoshi Taisha in Osaka and the Munakata-Taisha. See also Uni-No-Kami.

Mungu

Creator god. Swahili [East Africa]. The name applied to the notion of a single god in the heavens, influenced by the spread of Christianity. Also Mulungu.

Munisvara

Deified saint. Hindu. Technically a demigod but worshiped as a deity by Dravidians in southern India. Also Municami (Tamil).

Munjem Malik

Chthonic or earth god. Kafir [Afghanistan]. He appears as a rival and possible predecessor of the god Imra, but one whose realm is in the earth rather than the sky. Imra controls mountains and high pastures. Munjem Malik rules the earth of the valleys. He presides over the council of gods. His main sanctuary was at Arte in the Parun valley where a large boulder represented his head.

Munume

God of weather. Bunyoro [Uganda, East Africa]. Invoked during times of drought or deluge and propitiated by means of sacrifice, usually an ox from the tribal chief and sheep or fowl from the villagers. The blood is sprinkled on the floor of the sanctuary and the flesh is eaten at the door.

Muraja

Goddess of music. Buddhist. Deification of a kind of large drum or tambourine. Color: smoky. Attribute: tambourine.

Murukan

Hunting and war god. Dravidian and Tamil [southern India]. Identified with the Hindu god Skanda. His vehicle is an elephant or a peacock. Color: red. Attributes: spear and staff with garland.

Musdamma

God of buildings. Mesopotamian (Sumerian). Described as the "great builder of Enlil," Musdamma is a minor deity appointed by the god Enki to take responsibility for building projects and for houses.

Musisi

Messenger god. Ndonga [Namibia, southwest Africa]. The intercessor between the creator god Kalunga and mankind. His father is Kalunga.

Muso Koroni *(the pure woman with the primeval soul)*

Chthonic fertility goddess. Bambara [Mali, West Africa]. The mother of all living things, she introduced mankind to the principles of farming. She has a terrifying appearance, depicted either in human form, sometimes with many breasts (cf. Artemis at Ephesus), or as a panther. In the latter guise she uses her claws to bring on menstruation in women and to circumcise both sexes. Prior to circumcision a youth is said to possess *wanzo*, an untamed wildness. Muso Koroni is pursued by the sun god, Pemba, who impregnates her in the form of a tree (*Acacia albida*). Also Mousso Coronie.

Mut

The patron goddess of Thebes. Egyptian. In Upper Egypt she is the counterpart of Sakhmet, the Lower Egyptian goddess from Memphis. After superseding the goddess Amaunet, she became locally the consort of the sun god Amun, in which capacity she is the mother of the moon god Khonsu. She was also regarded as the divine mother of the Theban kings. Mut is depicted in human form wearing a vulture headdress surmounted by the twin crowns of Upper and Lower Egypt. She is typically dressed in a bright red or blue patterned gown. Less frequently she is drawn with a lion's head. She enjoyed a cult center at Thebes where her sanctuary was known as the Iseru.

Mutinus
Minor fertility god. Roman. Depicted as strongly ithyphallic and invoked by women seeking to bear children.

Muttalamman   *(pearl mother)*
Plague goddess. Dravidian (Tamil) [southern India]. Specifically identified with smallpox. Also Mutyalamma.

Mylitta
Goddess. Greek. The Hellenized version of the Akkadian goddess Mulliltu, consort of Ellil and of Assur.

Myoken-Bodhisattva
Astral god. Buddhist Chinese. The apotheosis of the Pole Star, equating with Ame-No-Kagase-Wo in Japanese Shintoism.

Myrrha
Fertility goddess. Western Semitic (Phoenician). Known from inscriptions as the mother of the god Kinnur. Also Syyrna.

N

NA CHA   *(here is a loud cry)*
Origin   Taoist (Chinese). Guardian god.

Known period of worship   circa 300 AD until present.

Synonyms   Li No Cha.

Center(s) of cult   throughout Chinese culture.

Art references   paintings and sculptures.

Literary sources   various philosophical and religious texts, mostly inadequately researched and untranslated.

A somewhat ambiguous god who is generally regarded as benevolent, but whose traditions hint at a more destructive aspect. He was *born* a god of human parents, the reincarnation of an older deity, Ling Chu-Tzu, the "intelligent pearl." According to tradition, his father was Li Ching, who threatened to kill his mother because she claimed she was made pregnant by the mystical actions of a Taoist priest who told her she was to bear the child of a unicorn. Na Cha is said to have fought in the Shang-Chou war on the side of the Chou dynasty circa 1027 BC. His chief adversary was the sea dragon king. Ultimately he became involved with the goddess Shih-Chi Niang Niang, accidentally killed her attendant and, in remorse, committed suicide.

Na Cha is the tutelary god of Yung Lo, the third emperor of the Ming Dynasty, and is credited with the mission of ridding the world of evil, but he himself attacks the guardians of both Taoist and Buddhist temples and can only be defended against by Li Ch'ing, the first minister of heaven. He is also titled "grand marshal of the skies" and "guardian of the gates of heaven."

He is depicted surrounded by a red aura, with a white face and wearing red silk trousers that emanate a dazzling golden radiance. His attributes include a bracelet on the right wrist. Originally he also carried a thunderbolt, but when his name changed to Li No Cha, circa 1420 AD, this attribute changed to a pagoda.

Na Ngutu
God of the dead. West and central Africa. Essentially the guardian deity of warriors slain in battle.

Nabu
God of writing and wisdom. Mesopotamian (Babylonian-Akkadian). The son of Marduk and Zarpanitu(m), his consort is Tasmetu(m). He is symbolized by the inscribing stylus. A major deity in neo-Babylonian times from the eighth century BC onward, with an important sanctuary at Borsippa, near Babylon, known as the Ezida. He is considered a god of mountain regions, described as the "firstborn son of Marduk" and his image is closely involved in the New Year *akitu* festival. Also Nebo (*Vetus Testamentum*).

Na'chitna'irgin   *(genuine dawn)*
Spirit of the dawn. Chukchee [eastern Siberia]. One of four beings responsible for the different directions of the dawn. The brother of Wu'squus, spirit of darkness. See also Tne'sqan, Mratna'irgin and Lietna'irgin.

Nachunde
Sun god. Elamite [Iran].

Nagakumara
God. Jain [India]. One of the groups under the general title of *bhvanavasi* (dwelling in places).

They have a youthful appearance and are associated with rain and thunder.

Nagaraja
Snake god. Hindu. The generic title of a deity equating with the terms *mahoraga* (great serpent) or *nagadeva*. Such deities were worshiped in India as early as the Indus Valley civilization (prior to 1700 BC).

Nagini
Goddess. Jain [India]. The counterpart of the Hindu goddess Manasa.

Nagual
Tutelary deity. Aztec (classical Mesoamerican) [Mexico]. A generic name for a personal god. A *nagual* generally takes the form of an animal and it may be adopted either by a mortal being or by another deity.

Nahi
Guardian god. Pre-Islamic northern Arabian. Generally of benevolent nature.

Nahui Ehecatl
Minor water god. Aztec (classical Mesoamerican) [Mexico]. One of the group of deities belonging to the Tlaloc complex. Also (4)Ehecatl.

Nahui Ollin *(earthquake sun)*
Creator god. Aztec (classical Mesoamerican) [Mexico]. According to most of the codices, at the time of the Spanish conquest there had been four previous world ages, each represented by a sun and terminated by a cataclysm. Ollin, the fifth sun, was created at Teotihuacan and at the conquest was just under 2,000 years old. It is presided over by the god Tonatiuh. Each creation is considered to last 2028 x 52 terrestrial years and the present one is destined to be destroyed by a great earthquake. Tradition has it that Ollin was originally a sickly or humble deity named Nanahuatl (the diseased one). Also (4)Ollin; Ollintonatiuh.

Nai
God of the ocean. Gan [Accra, Ghana, West Africa]. The second-in-command to the supreme god Ataa Naa Nyongmo. His eldest daughter is the goddess Ashiakle.

Naiades
Animistic water spirits. Greco-Roman. Female personalities assigned the guardianship of fresh waters by the great gods, and invoked locally at sacred pools and springs. They were also regarded as minor patrons of music and poetry.

Naigameya
God. Hindu. Either the son or the brother of the god Skanda. Generally depicted with the head of a goat.

Na'ininen
Creator being. Koryak [southeastern Siberia]. Known as "outer one," or "world," he is perceived as a remote but benevolent spirit comparable to the Supreme Being, Ta'yan. Also Na'rninen (Chukchee).

Nai-No-Kami
Earthquake god. Shinto [Japan]. One of the Raijin deities responsible for thunder, storms and rain. His worship began in 599 AD.

Nainuema
Creator god. Uitoto Indian [South America]. He created the earth from his own imagination and stamped upon it until it was flat. He then engendered the forests and other living things from his saliva.

Nairamata *(no soul)*
Goddess. Buddhist (Mahayana). An emanation of Aksobhya. A *Sakti* of Heruka and a personification of knowledge. She bears five or six arms in different gestures and often stands upon a corpse. Color: blue or black. Attributes: arrows, club, cup and knife. Three-eyed.

Naksatra(s)

Generic title for a group of astral goddesses. Hindu. Stars or constellations that became personified as deities, accounted as twenty-seven daughters of Daksa and consorts of Candra or Soma. They can exert benign or evil influence.

Namasangiti *(the chanting of the name)*

God. Buddhist. A form of Avalokitesvara, but also a distinct emanation of Vairocana. The personification of a sacred text. He stands upon a lotus. Color: white. Attributes: club, lotus, sword, half-staff and water jar.

NAMMU

Origin Mesopotamian (Sumerian and Babylonian-Akkadian) [Iraq]. Chthonic creator and birth goddess.

Known period of worship circa 4000 BC until circa 1750 BC.

Synonyms none.

Center(s) of worship mainly identified with Ur.

Art references stele of Ur-Nammu (circa 2050–1950 BC), etc.

Literary sources creation epics, including *Enki and the World Order*; Sumerian and Akkadian temple hymns and poems.

Nammu is identified in various texts as the goddess of the watery deeps. As a consort of An she is the mother of Enki and the power of the riverbed to produce water. Alternatively Nammu is the progenitrix of An and Ki, the archetypal deities of heaven and earth. She also engendered other early gods and in one poem is the mother of all mortal life. She molded clay collected by creatures called *sig-en-sig-du* and brought it to life, thus creating mankind. She is attended by seven minor goddesses and may ultimately have become syncretized with Ninhursağa.

Namtar *(fate)*

Messenger god(dess). Mesopotamian (Sumerian). A go-between and either minister or maidservant of the underworld goddess Ereškigal, who brings death to mankind at the appropriate time.

Nana

Mother goddess. Pre-Christian Armenian. Her cult became widespread and she may be equated with the Phrygian goddess Kybele.

Nanabozho

Heroic god. Eskimo (Ojibwa). A god of hunters who directly influences the success or failure that determines whether individuals survive or perish. His brothers are the four winds, which exert changes in the seasons and weather. Nanabozho gained control over them to ensure good hunting and fishing for the Ojibwa tribe.

Nanahuatl *(tumor)*

Creator god. Aztec (classical Mesoamerican) [Mexico]. In cosmogony, when on the fifth day of creation the gods sat in judgment to elect the new sun god, Nanahuatl and Tecciztecatl cremated themselves in the sacred fire. The heart of Nanahuatl ascended to become the new sun and that of Tecciztecatl became the moon. Tradition suggests that Nanahuatl is diseased and impoverished but of great courage, while Tecciztecatl is wealthy and a coward. In an alternative tradition, in which Nanahuatl is the son of Quetzalcoatl and Tecciztecatl is the son of Tlaloc, both deities are hurled into the fire by their fathers.

NOTE: eventually all the gods sacrificed themselves so that mankind might be engendered from their remains. Also Nanahuatzin.

Nanaja

Fertility goddess. Mesopotamian (Babylonian-Akkadian). She is also a war goddess who became syncretized with the Babylonian Tašmetu.

Nandi(n) *(rejoicing)*

Bull god. Hindu (Epic and Puranic). Generally associated with Siva as a bull-vehicle and an embodiment of fertility. Color: white. The image usually stands in an anteroom of the temple guarding the place where the statue of Siva is located. A Siva devotee touches the image's testicles on entry to a shrine. In anthropomorphic form he may be known as Nandisa.

Nang Lha
House god. Tibetan. A personal family guardian depicted with the head of a pig. He is propitiated with libations.

NANNA (1) (full moon)
Origin Mesopotamian (Sumerian) [Iraq]. Moon god.

Known period of worship circa 3500 BC until circa 1750 BC.

Synonyms As-im-babbar (new light), Suen or Sin (crescent moon) (Akkadian).

Center(s) of cult Ur.

Art references glyptics, etc.

Literary sources creation epics including *Enki and the World Order* and other texts.

A major astral deity in the Sumerian pantheon, probably originating in very early preagricultural times, Nanna is the tutelary god of Ur. He is the firstborn son of Enlil. His wife is Ningal and he is the father of the gods Utu and Iškur and of the goddess Inana. During the Third Dynasty of Ur, the New Year *akitu* festival was performed in his honor. He was considered to light up the night, to measure time and to provide fertility. He is depicted as traveling in a carriage across the sky bringing light to the darkness.

Nanna (2)
Vegetation goddess. Nordic (Icelandic). The consort of Balder. According to some legends she died of a broken heart after Balder was slain by Hoder and went with him to Hel. See also Hoder.

Na'nqa-ka'le
Guardian spirit. Koryak [southeastern Siberia]. He is one of the sons of Quikinna'qu and, according to tradition, sits in one place all the time painting his belly. He is, nonetheless, perceived as a strong and heroic figure.

Nanše
Goddess of justice. Mesopotamian (Sumerian). A daughter of Enki (or Ea), she is linked with the interpretation of dreams. Mentioned sporadically in texts and most closely identified with the city of Lagaš with a cult center at Sirara, but also the subject of a highly ethical hymn from Nippur. Also Naš, Nina.

Nan-Sgrub (the black one)
God. Buddhist [Tibet]. Possibly a counterpart of the Hindu god Kala. In Lamaism he is a form of Yama. He stands upon a man. Color: dark blue. Attributes: cup and knife.

Nantosuelta (winding river)
Goddess of water. Celtic (Gallic). Identified as a possible consort of the god Sucellos. She frequently holds a pole surmounted by a dovecote. In addition she carries the cornucopia of a fertility or mother goddess, but is also a domestic guardian deity and is often depicted with ravens, which may suggest further links with the underworld.

Napaeae
Animistic spirits of valleys. Greco-Roman. Female personalities assigned the guardianship of fertile green valleys by the great gods and invoked locally in small country shrines.

Napir
Moon god. Elamite [Iran]. Known from inscriptions.

Nappatecuhtli (four-times lord)
Minor god of mat makers. Aztec (classical Mesoamerican) [Mexico]. One of the group of deities belonging to the Tlaloc complex generally associated with rain, agriculture and fertility.

Nappinnai

Local goddess. Hindu-Dravidian (Tamil). Consort of Krsna. Mentioned in the Vaisnavite and Saivite literature, the Krsna-Nappinnai cult was prominent in Tamil-speaking areas of southern India in the seventh to ninth centuries. According to tradition Krsna wed Nappinnai after a bull-baiting contest during which he took on and defeated seven bulls. Nappinnai may be a localized form of Sri-Laksmi. Also Pinnai.

Nara *(man)*

Minor incarnation(s) of the god Visnu. Hindu (Epic and Puranic). Some authorities place these as separate *avataras*, but they are usually linked. Two of the sons of Dharma, who was born from the heart of Brahma, they spent a thousand years as severe ascetics in the Himalaya, where they were subject to various temptations by Indra. They are described as sages. The texts depict Nara colored green and bearing two hands, while Narayana has four hands and is colored blue. They may also be paralleled by Hari and Krsna. Also Narayana.

Narada *(giver of advice)*

Minor but popular deity. Hindu (Vedic, Epic and Puranic). Narada is depicted as a sage who is also a messenger and teacher. Born from the head, or throat, of Brahma, and alternatively a minor incarnation of Visnu. In various roles he is a guardian deity of women, a musician and a wanderer. Narada, often bearded, is generally depicted standing with the musical instrument that is his invention, the *vina* (lute). By contrast to his benign nature he is also described as a "maker of strife" and as "vile." Also Kali-karaka; Pisuna.

Naradatta *(daughter of Nara)*

Goddess of learning. Jain [India]. One of sixteen *vidyadevi* headed by the goddess Sarasvati.

Narasinha *(man-lion)*

Incarnation of the god Visnu. Hindu (Epic and Puranic). The fourth *avatara* of the god is depicted as a man-lion hybrid. According to legend, the demonic king Hiranyakasipu had taken on a dangerous invulnerability. To thwart this, Visnu took the form of Narasinha and hid inside a pillar of the king's palace whence he sprang, capturing Hiranyakasipu and tearing out his entrails. Iconographically, the scene is portrayed with the victim thrown across Narasinha's lap and the god's claws plunged into his body. Narasinha may also appear seated in a yoga position with the goddess Laksmi on his knee.

Narasinhi

Mother goddess. Hindu (Epic and Puranic). A *Sakti* of Narasinha who is one of a group of *astamatara* mothers. In another grouping, one of nine *navasaktis* who, in southern India, rank higher than the *saptamataras*. Also Candika.

Narayana

Creator god. Hindu (Epic and Puranic). More or less synonymous with Visnu, but specifically describing the embodiment of the "abode of man." He is said to have sucked his toe while sailing the primeval ocean on a banana leaf, until his own inspiration created the world. Often depicted supported by the bird god Garuda. See also Nara.

Nareu

Creator god. Melanesia [Vanuatu]. As in many comparable legends, he created the world inside the shell of a mussel. He engendered a son from sand and water who, in turn, created the sun and moon from his father's eyes, rocks from his flesh and bones and mankind from his spine.

Narisah

Goddess of light. Manichaean. The so-called "virgin of the light," she may also be androgynous as the father of the virgins of light who equate with the twelve zodiac signs.

Narkissos

Minor god. Greek. The son of the river god Kephissos, he wasted away after falling in love with his own image reflected in water. The gods took pity on him and changed him into the flower of the same name. In Roman religion he becomes Narcissus.

Nataraja *(lord of the dance)*
Form of the god Siva. Hindu (Puranic). Emerging from 1200 AD onward, this form depicts Siva as "lord of the dance" ringed by fire and with one foot on a demon in the form of a black dwarf. Nataraja arguably epitomizes the moving power in the cosmos. Largely seen in southern Indian bronzes that display the dance-form *anandatandava*.

Natha
Tutelary god. Buddhist [Sri Lanka]. One of four local emanations of the *bodhisattva* Avalokitesvara.

Naunet
Primordial goddess. Egyptian. One of the eight deities of the Ogdoad representing chaos, she is coupled with the god Nun and appears in anthropomorphic form but with the head of a snake. The pair epitomize the primordial abyss. She is also depicted greeting the rising sun in the guise of a baboon.

Navadurga(s)
Generic title of a group of deities. Hindu. The nine forms of the god Durga. The common vehicle is a chariot shaped like a lotus. Each carries a wide assortment of attributes.

Navasakti(s)
Generic title of a group of goddesses. Hindu. The nine *mataras* or mothers. In southern India they are considered virgin goddesses and are held in higher esteem than the comparable group of *saptamataras*.

Nayenezgani *(slayer of alien gods)*
God of war. Navaho [USA]. The most powerful of the Navaho war gods. The son of the sun god Tsohanoai and the fertility goddess Estsanatlehi. According to tradition, he vanquished a race of giants who had nearly destroyed the human race. He is a benevolent god, ready to help mankind in times of trouble. He also cures diseases brought about through witchcraft. Said to live at the junction of two rivers in the San Juan valley, he is invoked by warriors preparing for battle. His priest wears a buckskin bag mask, painted black and adorned with five zigzag lightning streaks, the eye and mouth holes covered with white sea shells. He also wears a fox skin collar, a crimson cloth around the hips and a leather belt with silver ornamentation, but is otherwise naked. No depictions are made of this deity.

Ndaula
Plague god. Bunyoro [Uganda, East Africa]. Particularly associated with smallpox. His shrines are usually situated on the edge of a community and on the frontiers of the tribal land so that he may be invoked to keep the disease in neighboring territory.

Ndjambi
Sky god. Herero [Namibia, southwest Africa]. A benevolent deity who protects and lifts up all who die natural deaths. The utterance of his name is generally forbidden.

Nebethetpet
Local primordial goddess. Egyptian. She was worshiped in Heliopolis and is a female counterpart to the sun god Atum in creation mythology. Specifically she is the hand with which he grasped his penis to self-create the cosmos.

Nebo
God of writing and wisdom. Western Semitic. Known from Syrio-Palestinian inscriptions and equating to the Akkadian Nabu. Mentioned in the *Vetus Testamentum*.

Nediyon
Creator god. Early Dravidian (Tamil) [southern India]. Equates with a syncretization of Visnu and Krsna. The name implies a deity of tall stature. Sangam texts describe him wearing a golden robe. Attributes: conch, prayer wheel and lotus. Also Neduvel.

Nefertum

Minor god of primordial creation. Egyptian (Lower). Specifically he is the blue lotus blossom of Re. Nefertum was worshiped in the Nile delta as the son of the cobra goddess Wadjet. At Memphis he is the son of the goddess Sakhmet, while elsewhere in Lower Egypt his mother is considered to be the goddess Bastet. Also Nephthemis (Greek).

Negun

Minor goddess. Mesopotamian (Sumerian). Known from limited references and of uncertain function. Possibly associated with the goddess Sirara. Her brother is Ašai and they are linked with the cities of Adab and Keš. Also Lisin.

Nehalennia

Goddess of seafarers. Romano-Celtic. Worshipped extensively between the second and thirteenth centuries AD, particularly in the Netherlands with sanctuaries at Domberg at the mouth of the Rhine and Colijnsplaat on the Scheldt. Probably began as a tribal deity of the Morini tribe. She is generally depicted with the attributes of fertility—a basket of fruit or cornucopia. She may also often have a small lap-dog. Alternatively, she stands with one foot on the prow of a boat and grasps an oar or the rope.

Nehebu-Kau

Minor snake god. Egyptian. Known from circa 1500 BC. Essentially a chthonic deity he is, according to tradition, the son of the god Geb. Allegedly having eaten seven cobras, Nehebu-Kau offers protection against snake bite and scorpion sting. He is also one of the guardians of the Egyptian king in the afterlife.

Neit

God of war. Celtic (Irish). A minor deity identified as the consort of the goddess Morrigan in her aspect as Nemain. Also the grandfather of Balor, he was killed at the second legendary Battle of Moytura.

NEITH

Origin Egyptian. Creator goddess.

Known period of worship circa 3000 BC until the end of Egyptian history circa 400 AD.

Synonyms none.

Center(s) of cult Sais [Sa el-Hagar] in the Nile delta.

Art references various sculptures, reliefs and wall paintings.

Literary sources Pyramid Texts; a papyrus from Dynasty XX; etc.

Neith is a goddess of Lower Egypt specifically associated with Sais but soon becoming part of the national pantheon with a sanctuary at Memphis. According to legend, when Neith emerged from the primeval ocean to create the world, she followed the course of the Nile down toward the sea and, on reaching the delta, founded the city of Sais. She is also a birth goddess both of the cosmos and of other deities when she is depicted as the great celestial cow. She is the mother of Egyptian rulers.

Neith is depicted in human form wearing the red crown of Lower Egypt and in ancient times her preanthropomorphic symbol was a shield bearing crossed arrows. She was sometimes called upon for advice and judgment, as in the case of the eighty-year battle of the gods between Seth and Horus, when she advised the sun god Re in favor of Horus. In other legends she becomes the consort of Seth and the mother of the crocodile god Sobek.

Nekhbet

Local mother goddess. Egyptian (Upper). Known from Nekhab (el-Kab), she is generally depicted in the form of a vulture with one or both wings spread and holding the symbols of eternity in her talons. Nekhbet is known from at least 3000 BC and is mentioned in the Pyramid Texts as the "great white cow"—a familiar epithet in respect of Egyptian mother or creator goddesses.

Nekmet Awai

Goddess of justice. Egyptian. Locally known from Hermopolis, she later became syncretized with the goddess Hathor.

Nemausius

God of water. Romano-Celtic (Gallic). Associated locally with a sacred spring at Nimes in France.

Nemesis

Goddess of justice and revenge. Greco-Roman. The dreaded deity who, with the Furies, is responsible for transporting the souls of the guilty to Tartarus. She is also described as the deification of indignation. Her presence may be symbolized by the fabulous winged griffon. Her cult was predominantly at Rhamnus (Attica), where a magnificent temple was built in her honor in the fifth century BC, and in Smyrna. She also had a temple at Iconium in Asia Minor. According to legend, Zeus raped her and she bore Helen in consequence. In certain respects she provides a parallel with the goddess Erinys. Her cult became one of morality.

Nemetona

Goddess of sacred groves. Romano-Celtic. Consort to the Roman deity Mars. Evidenced at places such as Bath (England) and Mainz (Germany); but also in place names that include the etymological base *nemeton* (a shrine).

Ne'nenkicex

Creator god. Kamchadal [southeastern Siberia]. The name given to the Christian god by the Kamchadals under influence of the Russian Orthodox church.

Neper

God of grain crops. Egyptian. The son of the snake spirit Renenutet, he is subservient to Hapy, the god of the Nile flood, and has links with Osiris as a vegetation deity who dies and is reborn to the afterlife. In female form the deity becomes Nepit.

Nephthys [*Greek*]

Funerary goddess. Egyptian. Nephthys is the younger sister of Isis, Osiris and Seth, who are the offspring of the chthonic god Geb and the sky goddess Nut in the *Ennead* genealogy of Egyptian deities defined by the priests of Heliopolis. Nephthys is depicted in human form wearing a crown in the style of the hieroglyphic for a mansion, the translation of her Egyptian name. She can also take the form of a hawk watching over the funeral bier of Osiris. According to legend Nephthys had a brief liaison with Osiris and bore the mortuary god Anubis. She is said to guide the dead Egyptian ruler through the dark underworld and to weep for him. Also Neb-hut (Egyptian).

Neptunus

God of irrigation. Italic and Roman. Identified with the planet Neptune, but thought to have originated as an agricultural deity concerned with watering. He was celebrated in the festival of *Neptunalia* on July 23. Also the patron deity of horse racing. He became syncretized with the Greek god Poseidon, but Neptune's modern association with the sea is a misrepresentation.

Nereides

Animistic spirits of the sea. Greco-Roman. Female personalities, the best known of whom is Amphitrite, assigned the guardianship of the oceans by the great gods and invoked by seafarers. Also attendants of the god Poseidon.

Nereus

Minor sea god. Greek. The son of Pontos and Gaia, and the father of the Nereides. See Proteus.

NERGAL

Origin Mesopotamian (Sumerian and Babylonian-Akkadian) [Iraq]. Chthonic underworld god.

Known period of worship circa 3500 BC to circa 200 BC.

Synonyms Erakal, Lugal-Irra, Mes Lam Taea.

Center(s) of cult Kuthu and Tarbisu.

Art references plaques, votive stelae and glyptics.

Literary sources cuneiform texts particularly *Nergal and Ereškigal.*

The son of Enlil and Ninlil and the consort of the underworld goddess Ereškigal. He is depicted as a god of war and sudden death as well as being ruler of the underworld. He may be also seen as a plague god. His sanctuary is known as the *Emešlam.* He is usually depicted as a bearded figure emerging from the ground and carrying a double-edged mace-scimitar typically embellished with lion heads. By the Hellenic period he is identified with the god Herakles.

Nerrivik
Sea goddess. Eskimo. The mother of all sea creatures, invoked by fishermen and seal hunters. See also Sedna.

NERTHUS *(north)*
Origin probably Danish [Sjaeland, Denmark]. Fertility goddess associated with peace.

Known period of worship circa 100 AD, though probably much earlier, until 400 AD or later (difficult to determine).

Synonyms none known.

Center(s) of worship a sacred grove "in an island of the ocean" identified only by the writer Tacitus.

Art references none.

Literary sources *Germania* 40 (Tacitus).

Some authors argue that Nerthus is a female counterpart, possibly the sister, of the Viking god Njord. Tacitus alludes to her as *Terra Mater* and describes how her cult statue was carried around in a covered sacred wagon drawn by oxen (see also Freyr). The vehicle was taboo to all but the priest of the goddess and, after each tour, was returned to the grove where it was washed and stored. All ministering attendants were immediately slaughtered. A pair of elaborate ceremonial wagons, dated to about 200 AD, were excavated from a peat bog at Dejbjerg (Denmark) and are thought to be of a type that carried such a deity.

Nesu
Tutelary god of royalty. Fon [Benin, West Africa]. The guardian of the tribal chiefs, his shrine, the Nese-we, is located close by royal palaces.

Nethuns
God of fresh water. Etruscan. Identified with wells and springs and depicted as a naked bearded figure. He is probably to be equated with the Roman god Neptunus.

Neti
Chthonic underworld god. Mesopotamian (Sumerian and Babylonian-Akkadian). Chief gatekeeper of the netherworld. The servant of the goddess Ereškigal. Neti features prominently in the epic legend of *Inana's Descent into the Underworld* when he opens the seven gates of the realm and admits the goddess, removing one emblem of her power at the threshold of each gate.

Nextepehua *(ash scatterer)*
Minor chthonic underworld god. Aztec (classical Mesoamerican) [Mexico]. One of the group of deities belonging to the Mictlantecuhtli complex.

Ngai
Creator god. Kikuyu and Masai [East Africa]. The name given to a single god in the heavens, influenced by the spread of Christianity. He is also perceived as, and may have evolved from, a weather god whose presence is symbolised by lightning.

Ngunuwo
Generic title of guardian deities. Ewe [Togo, West Africa]. The name means, approximately, the fates.

Ni
Sea god. Chimu Indian (pre-Columbian South America) [coastal areas of Peru]. A significant deity in the pantheon, revered by fishermen. Often linked with Si, the moon god.

Niamye

Creator god. Baule [Ivory Coast, West Africa]. He engendered a consort for himself and proceeded to create all other living things on earth. His anger is evidenced by lightning and thunderbolts.

Niha-Tsu-Hi-No-Kami

Fire god. Shinto [Japan]. Specifically the fire *kami* responsible for household fires in the yard.

Nike

Goddess of victory. Greco-Roman. Depicted as a winged messenger bringing the laurel wreath to the victor of battle. Though of Greek origin, appearing in the *Theogony* of Hesiod, she was adopted by the Romans and worshiped extensively throughout Asia Minor, including Sardis. In some depictions the goddess Athena carries Nike as a small winged figure. Also Victoria (Roman).

Nikkal

Moon goddess. Western Semitic (Syrian). The consort of the moon god Jarih and probably evolved from the Mesopotamian pantheon.

Niladanda

God. Buddhist. A *dikpala* or guardian deity of the southwestern quarter. Color: blue. Attributes: jewel, lotus, staff, sword and trident.

Niladevi   *(black goddess)*

Consort of the god Visnu. Hindu (Puranic). Mentioned only in the *Vaikhanasagama* text as the third wife of Visnu, no art representation of this goddess has been discovered. She may be identical with the goddess Pinnai known in Tamil-speaking regions.

Nilalohita

God. Hindu. One of the *ekadasarudras* or eleven forms of the god Rudra.

Nin Ezen (La)

Goddess. Sumerian. An alternative name for the goddess of healing, Gula.

Nin Mar Ki

Goddess. Mesopotamian (Sumerian). See Ninmah.

Nin Me En

Goddess. Mesopotamian (Sumerian). Probably equating to Ninmena.

Nin Ur

God. Mesopotamian (Sumerian). Probably synonymous with Ninurta.

Ninazu

Chthonic god. Mesopotamian (Sumerian). Less frequently encountered in the texts than Nergal. Son of Enlil and Ninlil or, in alternative traditions, of Ereškigal and the father of Ning-is-zida. The patron deity of Ešnunna until superseded by Tispak. His sanctuaries are the E-sikil and E-kurma. Also identified as a god of healing, he is (unlike Nergal) generally benevolent.

Nindara

God. Mesopotamian (Sumerian). The consort of the goddess Nanše.

Nindub

God. Mesopotamian (Sumerian). Locally known and identified with the city state of Lagaš.

Ninegal   *(strong-armed lord)*

God of smiths. Mesopotamian (Babylonian-Akkadian). A minor patron deity.

Ningal   *(great queen)*

Reed goddess. Mesopotamian (Sumerian and Babylonian-Akkadian). Ningal is the daughter of Enki and Ningikugal and the consort of the moon god Nanna by whom she bore Utu the sun god. She was probably first worshiped by cowherds in the marsh lands of southern Mesopotamia. Chiefly recognized at Ur.

Ningikuga   *(lady of the pure reed)*

Goddess of reeds and marshes. Mesopotamian (Sumerian and Babylonian-Akkadian). One of the consorts of Enki and the daughter of An and Nammu.

Ningilin
Obscure deity. Mesopotamian (Sumerian and Babylonian-Akkadian). His symbol is probably the mongoose. Also Ninkilim.

Ningirama
God of magic. Mesopotamian (Sumerian and Babylonian-Akkadian). A minor deity invoked particularly as a protection against snakes.

Ningirsu
Tutelary god. Mesopotamian (Sumerian and Babylonian-Akkadian). His mother is Ninhursaĝa. Known from the city of Lagas (Girsu) where Gudea built a major temple in his honor, the *Eninnu*. His symbol is a lion-headed eagle and his weapon the mace Šarur. Texts describe Ningirsu making a journey to Eridu to notify the god Enki of Gudea's achievement.

Ningis Zi Da
The god of light coming from the horizon. Mesopotamian (Sumerian and Babylonian-Akkadian). Tutelary god of Gudea of Lagaš, the son of Ninazu. Identified in Akkadian texts and on a seal of Gudea. Also Giszida.

NINHURSAĜA
(queen of the mountain)
Origin Mesopotamian (Sumerian and Babylonian-Akkadian) [Iraq]. Mother goddess.

Known period of worship circa 3500 BC until circa 1750 BC.

Synonyms Ninmah (great queen); Nintu (lady of birth); Mama or Mami (mother); Aruru (sister of Enlil); Belet-ili (lady of the gods—Akkadian). Minor synonyms include Nin-ziznak (lady of the embryo); Nin-dim (lady fashioner); Nagar-sagak (carpenter of insides); Nin-bahar (lady potter); Nin-mag (lady vulva); Nin-sig-sig (lady of silence); Mud-kesda (blood stauncher); Ama-dug-bad (mother spreading the knees); Ama-ududa (mother

who has given birth); Sag-zu-dingirenak (midwife of the gods); Ninmenna (lady of the diadem).

Center(s) of worship Tell el 'Ubaid [Ur]. Mari. Other temples, according to literature, were located at Keš, Adab (modern Bismaya) and Hiza, none of which have been found. Smaller temples and shrines scattered around southern Mesopotamia and beyond.

Art references plaques, votive stelae, glyptics.

Literary sources cuneiform texts-epics including *Enki and World Order* and *Creator of the Hoe,* temple hymns, etc.

Ninhursaĝa is one of seven great deities of Sumer. Assuming her symbol to be the "omega," it has been depicted in art from circa 3000 BC, though more generally from early second millennium. It appears on some *kudurru* boundary stones—on the upper tier, which indicates her importance. She is principally a fertility goddess though technically any female deity could take on the role. Temple hymn sources identify her as the "true and great lady of heaven" and kings of Sumer were "nourished by Ninhursaĝa's milk." Distinct from the goddess Inana, she enjoys closer links with fecundity and birth and is sometimes portrayed as a midwife, or with bosom bare and carrying a baby on her left arm. She is typically depicted wearing horned headdress and tiered skirt; often with bow cases at her shoulders; not infrequently carrying a mace or baton surmounted by the *omega* motif or a derivation; sometimes accompanied by a lion cub on a leash. The tutelary deity to several Sumerian rulers, in *Creator of the Hoe* she completed the birth of mankind after the heads had been uncovered by Enki's hoe.

Most Mesopotamian gods lived in mountains and the name Ninhursaĝa bears significance because, according to legend, it was changed from Ninmah by her son Ninurta to commemorate his creation of the mountains. Her name "lady of silence" derives from the notion that the child in the womb is susceptible to both good and bad influence. Thus the wrong incantations may jeopardize the child's well-being. As "lady of the diadem," according to a Babylonian investiture ritual, she placed the golden crown on the king in the *Eanna* temple.

Ninigi (Prince)
Ancestral god. Shinto [Japan]. The deity who, according to tradition, is the heir apparent of the sun goddess Amaterasu. He was sent to earth from heaven to rule at the behest of the gods. His parents are Taka-Mi-Musubi and Ame-No-Oshi-Ho-Mimi and he takes the title of "divine grandchild." He is the ancestral deity of the imperial dynasties.

Nin-Ildu
God of carpenters. Mesopotamian (Babylonian-Akkadian). Minor tutelary deity.

Nin-Imma
Fertility goddess. Mesopotamian (Sumerian and Babylonian-Akkadian). Deification of the female sex organs, fathered by Enki with Ninkurra.

Nin'insinna
Fertility goddess. Mesopotamian (Sumerian and Babylonian-Akkadian). A daughter of An and Uraš and probably an alternative name for Ištar. She is the consort of the god Pabilsag and is mentioned in respect of a sanctuary built by Warad Sin during the Isin dynasty. Texts describe her going to present Enlil with gifts in Nippur. Other inscriptions suggest she was the mother of the god Damu (Dumuzi).

Ninkarnunna
Barber god. Mesopotamian (Sumerian and Babylonian-Akkadian). An attendant of the god Ninurta.

Ninkigal
Chthonic god. Mesopotamian (Babylonian-Akkadian). Worshipped at Ur and Umma during the period of the third dynasty of Ur. Celebrations included the *eses* monthly lunar festivals.

Ninkurra
Minor mother goddess. Mesopotamian (Sumerian and Babylonian-Akkadian). Ninkurra is linked briefly as consort to Enlil (her grandfather), by whom after nine days of gestation she gave birth to the goddess Uttu. In alternative mythology she was the mother of Nin-imma, the deification of female sex organs.

Ninlil
Goddess of the air and of grain. Mesopotamian (Sumerian). She is the daughter of the god of stores, Haia, and the barley goddess, Ninsebargunnu. The consort of the air god Enlil, who impregnated her with water to create the moon god Nana, she also conceived the underworld god Nergal when Enlil impregnated her disguised as the gateman of Nippur. In a similar manner she conceived the underworld god Ninazu when Enlil impregnated her disguised as the "man of the river of the nether world, the man-devouring river." According to some texts she is also the mother of Ninurta, the god of the plough and thunderstorms.

Ninmah
Mother goddess. Mesopotamian (Sumerian and Babylonian-Akkadian). Probably an early syncretization with Ninhursaǧa. Identified in creation texts acting as midwife while the mother goddess Nammu makes different kinds of human individuals from lumps of clay at a feast given by Enki to celebrate the creation of humankind. Also regarded as the mother of the goddess Uttu by Enki. See also Ninhursaǧa.

Ninmena *(lady of the crown)*
Mother goddess. Mesopotamian (Sumerian). Probably became syncretized with Ninhursaǧa.

Ninni
Goddess. Mesopotamian (Sumerian). A modern misreading of Innin, which is itself an outmoded version of the name Inana.

Nin-šar *(lady plant)*

Minor mother goddess. Mesopotamian (Sumerian). Nin-šar is linked briefly as consort to either Enlil (her father) or Enki by whom, after nine days of gestation, she gave birth to the goddess Ninkurra who, in turn, became the mother of the goddess Uttu.

Ninsikil

The goddess of Dilmun. Mesopotamian (Sumerian). The patron deity of the mythical paradise land of Dilmun, which seems to have been perceived as somewhere off the coast of the Persian Gulf but firmly beyond the frontiers of Sumer. It is Ninsikil who pleads with Enki to provide the earth with the boon of fresh water in the sacred rivers Tigris and Euphrates.

Ninšubur

Messenger god(dess). Mesopotamian (Sumerian and Babylonian-Akkadian). The servant of the goddess Inana, she is particularly prominent in the legend of *Inana's Descent and the Death of Dumuzi*. In Akkadian texts the sex changes to a male personality, the minister of Anu.

Ninsun(a) *(lady wild cow)*

Cow goddess. Mesopotamian (Sumerian and Babylonian-Akkadian). Tutelary goddess of Gudea of Lagaš. Consort of the Sumerian heroic king Lugalbanda and also identified as the mother of the hero Gilgameš.

Ninšušinak

National god. Elamite [Iran]. Derived from a Sumerian model.

Nintinugga

Goddess. Mesopotamian (Sumerian). See Gula.

Nintu

Mother goddess. Mesopotamian (Sumerian and Babylonian-Akkadian). According to legend she pinched off fourteen pieces of primordial clay that she formed into womb deities, seven on the left and seven on the right with a brick between them, who produced the first seven pairs of human embryos. She is closely identified with the goddess Ninhursaǧa and may have become Belet Ili (mistress of the gods) when, at Enki's suggestion, the gods slew one of themselves and used his blood and flesh, mixed with clay, to create mankind.

NINURTA *(lord plough)*

Orgin Mesopotamian (Sumerian and Babylonian-Akkadian) [Iraq]. God of thunderstorms and the plough.

Known period of worship circa 3500 BC to 200 BC.

Synonyms probably Ningirsu.

Center(s) of cult Nippur and, as Ningirsu, at Girsu.

Art references plaques, votive stelae, glyptics, etc.

Literary sources creation epics including *Atrahasis* and *Anzu*; temple hymns, etc.

Ninurta is the Sumerian god of farmers and is identified with the plough. He is also the god of thunder and the hero of the Sumerian pantheon, closely linked with the confrontation battles between forces of good and evil that characterize much of Mesopotamian literature. He is one of several challengers of the malignant dragon or serpent Kur said to inhabit the empty space between the earth's crust and the primeval sea beneath. Ninurta is the son of Enlil and Ninhursaǧa, alternatively Ninlil, and is the consort of Gula, goddess of healing. He is attributed with the creation of the mountains, which he is said to have built from the giant stones with which he had fought against the demon Asag.

He wears the horned helmet and tiered skirt and carries a weapon Šarur that becomes personified in the texts, having its own intelligence and being the chief adversary, in the hands of Ninurta, of Kur. He carries the double-edged scimitar-mace embellished with lions' heads and, according to some authors, is depicted in nonhuman form as the thunderbird Imdugud (sling stone), which bears the head of a lion and may represent the hailstones of the god. His sanctuary is the *E-paduntila*.

Ninurta is perceived as a youthful warrior and probably equates with the Babylonian heroic god Marduk. His cult involved a journey to Eridu from both Nippur and Girsu. He may be compared with Iškur, who was worshiped primarily by herdsmen as a storm god.

Nirmali

Birth goddess. Kafir [Afghanistan]. Goddess of the childbirth hut usually separated from the rest of the village. She is invoked by women during labor or menstruation. Her sacred animal is the ram. There is an argument that she is, in fact, a manifestation of the goddess Disani rather than a distinct deity. Also Shuwe.

Nirrti *(destruction)*

1. Destructive goddess of darkness. Hindu (Vedic and Puranic). Known chiefly from the *Rg-Veda*, Nirrti has a generally malignant aspect and is associated with pain, misfortune and death. She is believed to live in the south (the land of the dead). She is dark-skinned, wears dark dress and receives the "dark husks" of sacrifice. She is feared by many Hindus, whose offerings are frequent and repeated. In later Hinduism, Nirrti changes sex and becomes a *dikpala* god of terrifying appearance, guarding the southwestern quarter; he has various consorts including Davi, Kalika and Krsnangi. He stands upon a lion, a man or a corpse. Attributes: javelin, shield, staff, sword and teeth.
2. God. Buddhist. A *dikpala* or guardian. Color: blue. Stands upon a corpse. Attributes: shield and sword.

Niruktipratisamvit

Goddess of etymological analysis. Buddhist (Vajrayana). One of a group of four. Color: red. Attributes: chain and lotus.

Nissaba

Goddess of writing and wisdom. Mesopotamian (Sumerian). A daughter of An and probably originally a vegetation deity. Her symbol is the inscribing stylus. She is a patron deity of Unug [Warka].

Nispannatara

Minor goddess. Buddhist (Mahayana).

NJORD *(north)*

Origin Nordic (Icelandic). God of the sea and winds.

Known period of worship Viking period circa 700 AD and earlier, until Christianization (circa 1100 AD).

Synonyms possibly Nerthus, though with change of sex from female to male.

Center(s) of cult none known, but many place names along the Norwegian coast and inland by lakes and fjords suggest a widespread devotion.

Art references none known, but probably the subject of anonymous carvings.

Literary sources Icelandic codices; *Prose Edda* (Snorri); *Historia Danica* (Saxo); runic inscriptions.

Njord originates as a Vanir deity, but during the war between Vanir and Aesir he is handed over as a hostage and becomes the pledge of truce between the two races. He is a god of seafarers and fishermen, and brings the wealth of the sea to mankind. He also controls the winds and storms. Consort of Skadi, the daughter of the giant Thiassi, he is the father of Freyr and Freyja. According to one poem, he lives among an enclosure of ships, Noatun. The use of ships as burial chambers was probably closely associated with Njord, and further links between ships and fertility seem well established, strengthening the connection with this Vanir deity.

Nodotus

Minor god of cereal crops. Romano-Celtic. Specifically the deity responsible for the well-being of grain stalks.

Nomi-No-Sukune

God of Sumo wrestlers. Shinto [Japan]. According to tradition in the *Nihongi* text he came to prominence during the reign of the emperor Suinin-Tenno when he matched and worsted a strong man, Kuyahaya, in a wrestling contest. He killed the latter by aiming a kick at his ribs.

Nommo

Generic title of a group of gods. Dogon [West Africa]. The primordial spirits at the head of whom is the creator god Amma. They are associated with rain and fertility and have imparted certain skills to mankind.

Nona

Minor goddess of birth. Roman. Responsible for the ninth month of gestation, she is often linked with the goddess Decima. In later Roman times she becomes one of a trio of goddesses of fate, with Decima and Morta, the goddess of death, collectively known as the *Parcae*.

Nong

God of winter and cold weather. Kafir [Afghanistan]. Nong lives in a glacier. He cracks the ice and is seen in the melt water. He is perceived as a misogynist and depicted in a wooden effigy, though whether in human form is unclear. His cult center seems to have been the village of Zumu in the southern Hindukush. Also Zuzum.

Nortia

Goddess of fate. Etruscan. She enjoyed an important sanctuary at Volsini, where her presence was symbolized by a large nail. In a New Year rite, the nail was hammered into a block of wood, probably derived from an old fertility ritual symbolizing the impregnation of life into the new year. She has been identified with the Greek goddess Tyche.

Nosenga

Tribal god. Korekore (Shona) [Zimbabwe, southern Africa]. He is accessible to mankind through a mortal medium or oracle known as *Hore*, who lives in the town of the tribal chief and is consulted only with the chief's permission. Nosenga has several human priestess consorts who are wedded to him in chastity in the fashion of Christian nuns.

Notus

God of the southwest winds. Roman. Derived from a Greek model. Also Auster.

Nrtya   *(dance)*

Mother goddess. Buddhist-Lamaist [Tibet]. One of the *astamataras*. Color: green or various. Attribute: staff.

Nsongo

Moon goddess. Bangala [Zaire, central Africa]. The sister and consort of the supreme sun god Libanza. In the epic legend of *Nsongo and Lianja* she is the twin sister and consort of a deified folk hero.

Nu Kua

Creator goddess. Chinese. A primordial deity who may be androgynous and who engendered mankind out of lumps of yellow clay. The invention of the flute is also attributed to her. Also Nu-Gua.

Nu Mus Da

Tutelary god. Mesopotamian (Sumerian). The patron deity of the lost city of Kazallu, mentioned in texts.

NUADU   *(wealth)*

Origin Celtic (Irish). Tribal war god associated with healing.

Known period of worship prehistoric times until Christianization circa 400 AD.

Synonyms Nuada argatlam; Nodens (Romano-Celtic); Nudd (Welsh).

Center(s) of cult   the best known is the sanctuary of Nodens at Lydney, Gloucestershire, England.

Art references   none specific, though possibly the subject of anonymous carvings.

Literary sources   *Books of Invasions*; *Cycles of Kings*; votive inscriptions.

One of the Tuatha de Danann who lost an arm at the Battle of Moytura against the Fir Bolg. The arm was replaced by the physician god Diancecht who made a prosthesis out of silver, hence Nuada *argatlam* (Nuadu of the silver hand). The original sanctuary at Lydney in Gloucestershire was taken over and enlarged by the Romans who renamed the god Nodens. Also considered to be the father of the Irish royal dynasty.

Nudimmud

Creator god. Mesopotamian (Sumerian). Rapidly syncretized with the Akkadian god Ea.

Nuli'rahak   *(big woman)*

Sea spirit. Asiatic Eskimo [eastern Siberia]. A fearsome old woman who lives in the ocean depths and owns all the sea creatures. She feeds off the bodies of drowned fishermen. See also Arna'ku-agsak.

Nun

Primordial god. Egyptian. One of the eight deities of the Ogdoad representing chaos, he is coupled with the goddess Naunet and appears in anthropomorphic form but with the head of a frog. No cult is addressed to Nun but he is typically depicted holding aloft the solar boat or the sun disc. He may appear greeting the rising sun in the guise of a baboon. Nun is otherwised symbolized by the presence of a sacred cistern or lake as in the sanctuaries of Karnak and Dendara.

Nunbarsegunu

Obscure mother goddess. Mesopotamian (Sumerian and Babylonian-Akkadian). Mentioned in creation texts as the "old woman of Nippur," she is identified as the mother of Ninlil, the air goddess. Nunbarsegunu allegedly instructs her daughter in the arts of obtaining the attentions of Enlil.

Nušku

God of light. Mesopotamian (Sumerian and Babylonian-Akkadian). The son of Enlil. Also a god

of fire, he is symbolized by a lamp. Sanctuaries have been identified at Harran and Neirab.

NUT

Origin   Egyptian. Creator goddess.

Known period of worship   circa 3000 BC and probably earlier, until the end of Egyptian history circa 400 AD.

Synonyms   none.

Center(s) of cult   Heliopolis, Karnak and many other sanctuaries throughout Egypt.

Art references   wall paintings in the royal tombs at Thebes; sarcophagi, etc.

Literary sources   Pyramid Texts, etc.

Nut is the most important female principle of the creation force in Egyptian cosmogony. According to the *Ennead* genealogy of the Heliopolis priests, she is the daughter of the god Šu and the goddess Tefnut. Generally, however, she is seen as the creator goddess who, with the sun god, gives birth to the other deities of the pantheon. In legend she becomes the consort of her brother, the chthonic god Geb. Their partnership generates Isis, Osiris, Seth and Nephthys. In her earliest appearances Nut is a celestial cow stretching across the sky, often held aloft by the figure of the air god Šu. This depiction continues into later times. In human form she often appears as a slim, arched figure, nude and balanced on her toes and fingertips, which touch the four cardinal points of the compass. In this posture she forms an arch over Geb, whose erect penis points upwards toward her. She is alternatively often supported and separated from Geb by Šu.

Nut is perceived as the barrier of the firmament that separates the ordered cosmos from primordial matter. The thunder is her laughter. The solar boat travels along the arch of her body, entering her mouth as night falls to pass through her and emerge at dawn from her vulva.

In a funerary context, when the ruler dies he is said to be enfolded by the arms of Nut and to pass within her body: "the doors of the sky are opened to him."

Nu'tenut

Earth spirit. Chukchee [eastern Siberia]. The owner of the world who sits in a large house built of iron. He is surrounded by the spirits of sun, moon, sky, sea, dawn, darkness and world who are suitors for his daughter (unnamed).

Nyakaya

Crocodile goddess. Shilluk [Sudan]. A deity residing in the Nile, she is the consort of Okwa and the mother of the first Shilluk king. Shilluks continue to sacrifice to Nyakaya.

Nyame

Creator god. Akan [southern Ghana, West Africa]. An androgynous being symbolized in his male aspect by the sun, and his female aspect by the moon. He gave mankind its soul and is the controller of destiny. He enjoys a dedicated priesthood and is worshiped in the form of a tree trunk. Also Odomankoma; Onyame; Onyankopon; Totrobonsu.

gNyan

Tree spirits. Tibetan. Malevolent forces residing in the mountains that can bring sickness or death.

Nyavirezi

Lion goddess. Rwanda [central Africa]. According to legend she was originally a mortal daughter of the tribal chief. While walking, she was transformed into a lioness. Though returning to human form, she occasionally became leonine again and, in this guise, slew at least one husband who discovered her secret.

Nyx

Primordial goddess. Greek. The essence of the night whose sons were the twin brothers Hypnos, god of sleep, and Thanatos, god of death.

Nzambi

Creator god. Bakongo [Zaire, central Africa]. He created the first mortal pair or, in alternative tradition, an androgynous being in the guise of a palm tree called *Muntu Walunga* (the complete person). He also endowed this being with intelligence. In wooden sculptures the tree bears a woman's head and breast on one side and a bearded face on the other. Eventually the tree divided into two separate sexes. Also Nyambi; Nzambe; Yambe; Zambi.

Nzapa

Creator god. Ngbandi [Zaire, central Africa]. One of seven deities invoked at sunrise each morning. The progenitor of all life on earth, he also gave mankind laws and controls destiny or fate. He has four children who specifically appear in the guise of palm trees.

Nze

Moon god. Ngbandi [Zaire, central Africa]. One of the seven children of Ketua, the god of fortune and Lomo, the goddess of peace. He is closely linked with women and fertility. At menstruation he is said to have "cut the girl" and, during pregnancy, "the moon is dark for her."

O

Obarator

God of agriculture. Roman. Specifically responsible for overseeing the fertilizing of crops.

Obatala

Fertility god. Yoruba [Nigeria, West Africa]. The first deity engendered by the creator god Olodumare. His consort is Yemowo. Among other responsibilities, he makes barren women fertile and shapes the fetus in the womb. He is considered to be the sculptor of mankind. He is depicted wearing white robes and symbolizes cleanliness. Offerings include coconuts and corn. A jar of clean water is carried by a priestess to his sanctuary each morning and the water is drunk by women to make them fertile. Also Orishanla (archaic); Orisha-Popo; Orisha-Ogiyan; Orisha-Ijaye.

Occator

God of agriculture. Roman. Specifically responsible for overseeing growth and harvesting of crops.

Ocelotl

Creator god. Aztec (classical Mesoamerican) [Mexico]. The sun deity representing the first of the five world ages, each of which lasted for 2,028 heavenly years, each heavenly year being fifty-two terrestrial years. Assigned to the earth and presided over by Tezcatlipoca. According to tradition, the age was populated by a race of giants and it ended in a catalclysmic destruction caused by huge and ferocious jaguars that devoured them. Illustrated by the *Stone of the Four Suns* [Yale Peabody Museum]. Also Ocelotonatiuh; Yoaltonatiuh; Tlalchitonatiuh.

Ocelus

God of healing. Romano-Celtic (British). He becomes largely syncretized with the Roman god Mars, thus there is an inscription to Mars Ocelus at Carlisle.

Odin

See Othin.

Oduduwa

Creator goddess. Yoruba [Nigeria, West Africa]. The consort, or alternatively the daughter, of the supreme god Olodumare. She is perceived as the substance, or matrix, of the earth that Olodumare impregnated to generate life. She is also a goddess of war and her sons include the great heroic Yoruba god Ogun. According to some traditions Oduduwa is also perceived as a god.

Ogdoad

Primordial forces. Egyptian. The elements of chaos, eight in number, that existed before the creation of the sun god and that are known from Khemnu in Middle Egypt (Greek Heliopolis). The Ogdoad also had a sanctuary at Medinet Habu. They created, out of themselves rather than by sexual coupling, the mound that emerged from the primeval waters and upon which rested the egg from which the young sun god emerged. They are usually depicted as baboons heralding the sun as it rises. They are grouped in pairs and include Nun and Naunet representing the primordial abyss, Kek and Kauket representing darkness, Heh and Hauhet representing infinity, and Amun and Amaunet representing hidden power.

Ogma

See Ogmius.

Ogmios
See Ogmius.

Ogmius
God of poetry and speech. Celtic (Irish). Very little is known of him, but the Roman writer Lucian mentions a Romano-Celtic god of wisdom. Ogmios apparently assimilated with Hercules and is described as an old man with lion's skin holding a crowd of people chained to his tongue by their ears.

NOTE: a goddess Ogma is also mentioned; she may have been a mother goddess in the original Irish pantheon.

Ogiuwu
God of death. Edo [Benin, West Africa]. Believed to own the blood of all living things, which he smears on the walls of his palace in the otherworld. Until recent times human sacrifice was made regularly to this deity in the capital of the Edo region, Benin City.

Ogun
God of war, hunting and metalwork. Edo [Benin, West Africa]. This rather loosely defined deity was sent by the god Osanobua to cut open the land to allow crops to be planted. He is the strength inherent in metals and piles of metal objects are left beside his sanctuaries. As a god of war he defends the tribe and is depicted wearing armor and with red eyes. As a god of hunters and farmers he is generally benevolent.

Ohoroxtotil *(god almighty)*
Creator god. Mayan (classical Mesoamerican) [Mexico]. The creator of the sun and the deity who made the world inhabitable for mankind by destroying the jaguars that once infested it.

Oi
Sickness god. Suk [western Kenya, East Africa]. A spirit of personal illness rather than plague. The sick person's house is emptied and the priest exorcizes Oi from the dwelling.

O-Iwa-Dai-Myojin
God of stoneworkers. Shinto and Buddhist [Japan]. Probably more a Buddhist deity, but also revered in Shintoism.

Okeanides
Sea deities. Greco-Roman. Minor goddesses assigned the guardianship of oceans by the great gods and invoked by seafarers. In alternative tradition, they are river gods, the sons of Okeanos.

Okeanos
God of the oceans. Greek. A deity who remained at his post when most of the other gods were summoned to Olympus by Zeus. His consort is Tethys and he fathered children who included the Okeanides, mainly river gods, and a large number of daughters headed by Styx, and including Doris, Metis, and Tyche. See also Hesta.

Oki-Tsu-Hiko-No-Kami
God of kitchens. Shinto [Japan]. One of the offspring of O-Toshi-No-Kami, the god of harvests. The consort of Oki-Tsu-Hime-No-Kami and responsible for the caldron in which water is boiled.

Oki-Tsu-Hime-No-Kami
Goddess of kitchens. Shinto [Japan]. One of the offspring of O-Toshi-No-Kami, the god of harvests. The consort of Oki-Tsu-Hiko-No-Kami and responsible for the caldron in which water is boiled.

Oko *(hoe)*
God of agriculture. Yoruba [Nigeria, West Africa]. According to tradition he descended from heaven and lived at a farm near the town of Irao, where he attained a great age. One day he disappeared, leaving only his staff, which was taken as a symbol of his presence. Annually, at the start of the rainy season, a festival with strong fertility emphasis is held in his honor.

O-Kuni-Nushi-No-Mikoto
Creator god. Shinto [Japan]. The great organizer and consolidator of the earth in the creation mythology of Shintoism. He took up his duties after

Izanagi and Izanami had created the land. Tradition has it that he first underwent a series of ordeals and then reigned over the world. He has many consorts and innumerable offspring.

Ola Bibi
Local plague goddess. Hindu. Worshipped in Bengal where she is associated with cholera.

Olodumare
Creator god. Yoruba [Nigeria, West Africa]. He engendered the god Obatale as his deputy. The souls of the dead are expected to make confession to Olodumare. When he created the earth, he filled a snail's shell with dirt, placed inside it a hen and a pigeon and threw it down, whereupon the hen and pigeon began to scatter the earth and create land. Olodumare then sent a chameleon to report on progress. Sand was added, followed by a palm, a coconut and a kola nut tree. When these were established the god placed on earth the first sixteen humans. Also Alaaye; Elemii; Olojo Oni; Olorun; Orishanla.

Olokun
God of fresh waters and oceans. Fon and Yoruba [Benin and Nigeria, West Africa]. The eldest son of the creator god Osanobua. He is symbolized in the sacred river Olokun, which runs almost the length of Benin and from the source of which come the souls of unborn children. A girl baby is given a shrine of the god that includes a pot of river water and that she takes with her to her new home when she marries. The god is particularly popular among women and has a cult of priestesses. Olokun is also a guardian deity of mariners.

Olorun
See Olodumare.

Omacatl
Minor god of feasting and revelry. Aztec (classical Mesoamerican) [Mexico]. One of the group classed as the Tezcatlipoca complex. Also (2)Acatl.

Ome Tochtli
Fertility god. Aztec (classical Mesoamerican) [Mexico]. Slaughtered and then revived by Tezcatlipoca. Head of the group classed as the Ometochtli complex of fertility deities who personified the maguey plant and the intoxicating drink brewed from it, pulque or octli. Also (2) Tochtli.

O'meal
Tribal spirit. Na'kwaxdax Indian [British Columbia, Canada]. The chief of the ancients who lives in "Narrow Entrance at Open Plain" and whose siblings are the "myth people."

OMETECUHTLI (two lord)
Origin Toltec-Aztec (classical Mesoamerican) [Mexico]. Supreme deity.

Known period of worship circa 750 AD to Spanish conquest circa 1500 AD but probably much earlier.

Synonyms Olin-Tonatiuh.

Center(s) of cult None.

Art references codex illustrations; stone carvings.

Literary sources pre-Columbian codices.

The supreme being of Aztec religion, the god represents dual aspects of all living things and of the fecundity of the natural world. One of the group classed as the Ometeotl complex. Probably of Toltec origin, "he" is perceived as androgynous. He has no sanctuaries, but is personified in the moment of birth, or in the conception of life. He is depicted in human form and is often accompanied by the further depiction of a couple engaged in sexual intercourse.

The household hearth is sacred to Ometecuhtli and he is closely linked with the fire god Xiuhtecuhtli. For alternative creation mythology see Tezcatlipoca.

Ometeotl (two god)
Primordial being. Aztec (classical Mesoamerican) [Mexico]. According to some traditions, the dual principle personified in a bisexual force that the

Aztecs believed to be the only reality, all else being illusory. Ometeotl rules in the highest (thirteenth) heaven, Omeyocan (place of duality) that rests above sun, moon, wind and other elements. Ometeotl impregnated itself to engender the four Tezcatlipocas (aspects of the sun). Another female aspect, Coatlicue, gave birth to the national Aztec god Huitzilopochtli. No formal cult existed for Ometeotl, but he was considered to be present in every aspect of ritual. See also Tonacatecuhtli and Tonacacihuatl.

Omichle

Primordial principle. Phoenician (Hellenic). The element of darkness in chaos that fuses, or consorts, with Pothos to engender the spiritual and physical elements of the cosmos.

Onuava

Fertility goddess. Celtic (Gallic). Associated with the earth and known only from inscriptions.

Onuris [*Greek*]

God of hunting and war. Egyptian. Onuris is first known from This, near Abydos in Upper Egypt. In later times his main cult center was at Samannud in the Nile delta. His consort is the lion goddess Mekhit. Onuris is generally depicted in human form as a bearded figure wearing a crown with four plumes and wielding a spear or occasionally holding a rope. He is sometimes accompanied by Mekhit in iconography. Seen as a hunter who caught and slew the enemies of Re, the Egyptian sun god, some legends place him close to the battle between Horus and Seth. In classical times, Onuris became largely syncretized with the Greek war god Ares. Also Anhuret (Egyptian).

Opo

God of the ocean. Akan [Ghana, West Africa]. One of the sons of the creator god Nyame, he is also considered to be the god of the great inland lakes and rivers of Ghana.

Opochtli *(left)*

Minor god of lake fishermen and hunters. Aztec (classical Mesoamerican) [Mexico]. One of the group classed as the Tlaloc complex.

Ops

Goddess of harvests. Greco-Roman. Honored in an annual festival on August 25. She is also concerned with regulating the proper growth of seeds. A sanctuary is dedicated to her in the *Regia* in Rome.

Oraios *(wealth)*

Primordial deity. Gnostic Christian. One of the androgynous elements born to Yaldabaoth, the prime parent, and ruler of the seven heavens of chaos in Gnostic mythology.

Orcus

Chthonic underworld god. Roman. Modeled on the Greek god Hades.

Ordog

Chthonic malevolent god. Pre-Christian Hungarian. After Christianization he became syncretized with the devil.

Oreades

Animistic spirits of the mountains. Greco-Roman. Female personalities assigned the guardianship of mountains by the great gods. Invoked by travelers to ensure their safety.

Ori *(mind)*

God of wisdom. Yoruba [Nigeria, West Africa]. The deity who, in heaven, guides the soul but who also acts as a personal guardian, controlling individual mental ability, so that one person becomes wise and another foolish.

Orisanla

Sky god. Yoruba [Nigeria, West Africa]. Delegated by Olodumare as a creator of earth and living things. See Olodumare.

Oro

God of war. Polynesian [Tahiti]. One of the sons of Tangaroa.

Orotalt

Tutelary god. Pre-Islamic Arabian. Thought to equate with the northern Arabian god Ruda (Ruldaiu). Mentioned by Herodotus in Hellenic times as a supreme god and possibly syncretized with Dionysos.

Orthia

Mother goddess. Sparta. Locally worshiped and probably soon syncretized with the more widely recognized maternal deities of Asia Minor such as Kybele.

Orunmila

God of destiny. Yoruba [Nigeria, West Africa]. He accompanied the creator god Olodumare at the creation of the world and when the destinies of mankind were decided. He is consulted in an oracular capacity at Ifa and makes decisions on such matters as choice of sacrificial animals. He is also a god of healing and in many households enjoys personal shrines that include palm nuts, fragments of ivory and sea shells.

Osande

Guardian deity. Ovimbundu [central Angola, southwest Africa]. A benign elderly god who forms an integral part of ancestor worship. Considered to be the founder of each family lineage.

Osanobua

Creator god. Edo [Benin, West Africa]. The father of the god Olokun, he is regarded as a benevolent deity controlling prosperity, health and happiness.

OSIRIS

Origin Egyptian. Chthonic god of the underworld, also a grain or vegetation god.

Known period of worship circa 3000 BC until the end of Egyptian history circa 400 AD.

Synonyms none, but many epithets are applied, reflecting the universality of his cult.

Center(s) of cult many throughout Egypt but chiefly at Abydos (Ibdju) in Upper Egypt and Busiris (Djedu) in the Nile delta of Lower Egypt. Other important sanctuaries are located at Biga (Senmet) in Upper Egypt south of Aswan, and at the Karnak complex of Thebes. Outside Egypt there is a major sanctuary at Philae in Greece.

Art references innumerable sculptures, stone reliefs, wall paintings and papyrus illustrations.

Literary sources Pyramid Texts; coffin texts including the *Book of the Dead*, etc.

Osiris is among the most significant and widely revered deities of the Egyptian pantheon. According to the genealogy drawn up by the priests at Heliopolis, he was born at Rosetau in the necropolis (gate of the underworld) of Memphis. His parents were Geb and Nut and he was the eldest of four siblings including his sister and consort Isis, his adversary Seth and younger sister Nephthys. Isis bore the god Horus having impregnated herself with the semen of Osiris after his death. Though Osiris is most closely linked with Isis, he is also associated with Anubis, the mortuary god of embalming and the scorpion-like mortuary goddess Serket.

Osiris is depicted in human form but often tightly wrapped in mummy linen with only his arms free, He holds the crook and flail. His crown, the *atef*, is distinctive, consisting of the conical white crown of Lower Egypt framed by tall plumes and rams' horns. Often his skin is colored green. Osiris was perceived as the counterpart in death of the sun god Re.

As a grain god, Osiris was worshiped in the form of a sack filled with seed that sprouted green. He is also depicted by models with articulated members that women paraded through the streets at festivals and manipulated to demonstrate the god's virility. His relationship with the Egyptian kingship was crucial. Each king was the divine embodiment of Horus in life, but became Osiris on his death.

The Osirian legend is known from pure Egyptian textual sources and from an embellished account of the Greek writer Plutarch. The latter describes how Osiris was persuaded by Seth to step into an exactly fitting sarcophagus during a drunken party. The coffin was nailed tight and thrown into the Nile. It was washed ashore at Byblos in the Lebanon where it became encased in the trunk of a growing tree. Eventually, the trunk was cut down and incorporated as a pillar in the palace of the local ruler. After years of searching, Isis found Osiris and brought his body home. She breathed life into it and impregnated herself with Osiris's semen. She bore his son Horus. Meanwhile Seth found the body and once more destroyed it by hacking it into fourteen pieces and scattering them along the Nile valley. With the exception of Osiris's penis, which Seth had thrown to a crocodile, Isis found all the pieces and buried them at the sites of various sanctuaries. She restored the penis with a replica that subsequently became a focus of the Osirian cult. The scattering of the body was allegorized with the winnowing and scattering of grain in the fields.

The purely Egyptian account omits the incident of the sarcophagus and the discovery at Byblos. Isis is sometimes represented in the form of a hawk being impregnated by the erect phallus of the dead god. The reference to the fate of the penis with a crocodile is also omitted. In the Egyptian version, the god's phallus was buried at Memphis.

Ostara

Sun goddess. Germanic. Associated with the coming of spring and one of the derivations of the term Easter, she equates with the Anglo-Saxon deity Eostre.

Ostaraki   *(covering)*

Minor goddess. Buddhist (Mahayana). An attendant of Buddhakapala.

Osun

River goddess. Yoruba [Nigeria, West Africa]. The daughter of Oba Jumu and Oba Do and the consort of the god Shango. The guardian deity of the river Osun, revered particularly in the towns and villages along the banks of the river where sacred weapons are kept in her shrines. Also a goddess of healing. She is worshiped particularly by women and is honored in an annual festival, the *Ibo-Osun*, during which new cultic priestesses are selected.

OTHIN   *(all father)*

Origin   Nordic (Icelandic) and Germanic. Head of the Aesir sky gods and principal god of victory in battle. God of the dead.

Known period of worship   Viking period (circa 700 AD) and earlier through to Christianization (circa 1100 AD) and beyond.

Synonyms   Odin; Sigtyr (god of victory); Val-father (father of the slain); One-eyed; Hanga-god (god of the hanged); Farma-god (god of cargoes); Hapta-god (god of prisoners).

Center(s) of cult   Uppsala (Sweden).

Art references   various stone carvings.

Literary sources   Icelandic codices; *Prose Edda* (Snorri); *Historia Danica* (Saxo); votive inscriptions.

Othin is the chief among the Viking Aesir sky gods, the lord of hosts and god of victory who lives in the Hall of Valhalla in Asgard. He rules over an army of warrior spirits, the Valkyries. Othin peoples Valhalla with chosen heroes, slain in battle on earth, who will defend the realm of the gods against the Frost Giants on the final day of reckoning, Ragnarok, the doom of the gods. Othin passes out magic weapons to his selected earthly heroes including Sigmund the Volsung (see also Baal). In spite of his eminence Othin is considered to be untrustworthy, a breaker of promises. He rides a winged eight-legged horse, Sleipnir, and is able to change shape at will, an indication that he derives from an older, *shamanistic* religion.

His symbol is the raven and his weapon is a spear carved with runes or treaties said, when hurled by the god, to influence the course of combat. He is also symbolized by a knotted device, the *valknut*, probably representing his power to bind or unbind the minds of warriors and thus influence the outcome of battle. Othin is perceived as a *shaman*, his constant desire the pursuit of occult knowledge through communication with the dead. He wanders the earth disguised as a traveler, and once pierced himself with his own spear and hung himself from the World Tree, Yggdrasill, to this end. He gave an eye to the god Mimir as payment for permission to drink from the well of knowledge that rises from a spring beneath the tree.

Othin has links with the goddess Freyja in literature. The goddess Skadi, wife of Njord in some legends, was reputed also to have borne children to Othin, thus linking him with the Vanir gods. Adam of Bremen reports a special festival of the gods in Uppsala when men and animals were slaughtered and hung in trees. Followers of Othin were also burnt on funeral pyres. Othin is thought to have evolved as a syncretization of the Germanic war gods Wodan and Tiwaz. He was the patron god of a fanatical warrior cult, the Berserks.

O-Toshi-No-Kami

God of harvests. Shinto [Japan]. The son of Susano-Wo and Kamu-O-Ichi-Hime, he heads the pantheon of agricultural deities and is generally the guardian of rice fields.

Ouranos

Primordial god of heaven. Greek. The creator and incestuous consort of the earth mother Gaia with whom he engendered six giant sons—Okeanos, Koeos, Kreos, Hyperion, Iapetos and Kronos—and six daughters—Klymene, Rhea, Thea, Thetis, Mnemosyne and Phoebe—the twelve collectively being known as the Titans. Fearing their power, Ouranos hurled them into the abyss of Tartaros and chained them up.

Owiot

Moon god. Luiseno Indian [California, USA]. The ancestral deity of the tribe.

Oxlahun Ti Ku

Sky gods. Mayan (classical Mesoamerican) [Mexico]. The collective name for a group of thirteen celestial deities who are probably still invoked by Mesoamerican Indians today.

Oya

River goddess. Yoruba [Nigeria, West Africa]. The consort of the god Shango, she is the guardian deity of the river Niger. Also a goddess of storms and thunder. Her sacred animal is the buffalo and her presence is symbolized by its horns.

O-Yama-Tsu-Mi

God of mountains. Shinto [Japan]. The most senior apotheosis of mountains in Japan, he is one of the sons of Izanagi and Izanami and is worshiped extensively.

P

Pa-bil-sag
Tutelary god of Isin. Mesopotamian (Sumerian and Babylonian-Akkadian). The consort of the goddess Nininsina. Identified with the city of Larak (lost), texts describe Pabilsag journeying to Nippur and presenting the god Enlil with gifts. He is given the epithet of "the wild bull with multicolored legs."

Paca-Mama *(earth mother)*
Chthonic earth goddess. Inca (pre-Columbian South America) [highlands of Peru]. Worshipped extensively by farmers but now largely syncretized with the Christian Virgin Mary.

Pachacamac *(earth creator)*
Creator god. South American Indian [Lima region of Peru]. Near the town of Pachacamac is the site of a huge pyramidal sanctuary dedicated to the god. In origin he is pre-Inca but the Inca rulers who took over the region allowed his worship to continue; eventually he became syncretized with the god Vairacocha.

Padma *(lotus)*
1. Snake god. Hindu (Epic and Puranic). One of a group of seven *mahanagas*. Attributes: rosary and water jar. Three-eyed.
2. Goddess. An incarnation of Laksmi, the consort of an *avatara* of Visnu. She is depicted as emanating from the *padma* or lotus *(Nelumbium speciosum)* which is the symbol of creation and one of the most important iconographic devices in Hinduism. Also Kamala.

Padmantaka *(destructive to the lotus)*
God. Buddhist. A *dikpala* or guardian of the western direction. Color: red. Attributes: jewel, red lotus, prayer wheel and sword. Three-headed.

Padmapani *(with lotus in hand)*
God. Buddhist. A *bodhisattva* or *buddha*-designate, and a distinct form of Avalokitesvara. Color: white or red. Attributes: book, image of Amitabha on the crown, knot of hair, lotus, rosary, trident and water jar. Three-eyed.

Padmatara *(lotus Tara)*
Minor goddess. Buddhist (Mahayana).

Padmosnisa
God. Buddhist. Apparently connected with the guardian deities or *dikpalas* and associated with the western direction. Color: red.

Paean
See Paiawon.

Pahtecatl *(medicine lord)*
Minor fertility god. Aztec (classical Mesoamerican) [Mexico]. One of the group of deities known as the Ometochtli complex and concerned with the brewing of the alcoholic drink pulque from the maguey plant.

Paiawon
War god. Greek and Cretan. Known from Knossos and mentioned in the *Iliad* (Homer) as Paean.

Painal *(hasty)*
Minor god of war. Aztec (classical Mesoamerican) [Mexico]. One of the group of deities known as the Huitzilpochtli complex to whom sacrifice of captured prisoners was regularly offered.

Pajainen
God. Pre-Christian Finnish. The deity who kills the great bull in Finnish legend.

Pajonn

God of thunder. Pre-Christian Lappish. The name is derived from "the one who dwells in the heaven."

PAK TAI

Origin Taoist (Chinese). Astral god of war.

Known period of worship probably from Shang Dynasty (second millennium BC) until present.

Synonyms Hsuan T'ien Shang Ti; Shang-ti yeh (Taiwanese).

Center(s) of cult Palace of Jade Vacuity on Cheung Chau Island.

Art references paintings and sculptures.

Literary sources various philosophical and religious texts, mostly inadequately researched and untranslated.

As first general of heaven's armies, he is regarded as a guardian of the Chinese state comparable to Kuan Ti, but older in mythology and identified with the north. According to tradition he lived circa 2000 BC and was deified during the war between the Chou and Shang dynasties. During his mortal lifetime he was allegedly responsible for the introduction of flood control and land drainage systems. Alternatively, he spent much of his life seeking a Buddhist-style perfection on the mountain of Wu T'ang Shan. He was taken to heaven to assist the established pantheon in defeating two traditional monsters, the tortoise and the snake. Pak Tai hurled them into a deep chasm and, on his return, was made first lord of heaven.

He is also titled emperor of the north. His full title, Hsuan T'ien Shang Ti, means superior ruler of the *dark* heaven, as distinct from the *moving* and more accessible heaven ruled by the god Huang Ti. Before his deification, the north of China was believed to be ruled by the tortoise, the so-called dark warrior.

Pak Tai is also closely connected with death and fertility. He is a guardian of society who may descend from heaven to restore stability in times of unrest or destruction. On the island of Cheung Chau he is believed to have been responsible for ending a plague that afflicted the islanders at the end of the nineteenth century.

Pakhet

Goddess of hunting. Egyptian. Known locally from the eastern desert regions with a sanctuary at Beni Hasan.

Palaemon

Minor sea god. Greco-Roman. Originally Melikertes, the son of Ino, Palaemon was deified by the gods when his mother hurled herself from a cliff with her son in her arms. According to versions of the legend she was either insane or escaping the wrath of Athanas, King of Thebes.

Palaniyantavan

Local god. Hindu-Dravidian (Tamil). Known only from southern India and considered to be a form of Skanda or of Murukan, who is an old Tamil tribal snake god.

Pales

Pastoral goddess. Roman. A guardian of flocks and herds. Her festival was celebrated annually in Rome on April 21.

Pallas (Athene)

Goddess. Greek. The full name of the deity who is thus Pallas of Athens. The origin and meaning of the word Pallas is unknown. See Athena.

PAN

Origin Greco-Roman. God of shepherds and personification of undisciplined procreation in nature.

Known period of worship circa 800 BC and earlier until Christianization circa 400 AD.

Synonyms Consentes.

Center(s) of cult Arcadia; Marathon (Attica).

Art references stone reliefs and carvings.

Literary sources *Theogony* (Hesiod), etc.

According to tradition, Pan is the son of Hermes (Mercury) and a nymph, Penelope. One of the company of Satyrs, Pan possesses the horns and feet of a goat, is typically shown with phallic connotations and is reputed to live in caves. Well-known as a pipe player, an interest stemming from an infatuation with the nymph Syrinx, whom the earth goddess Gaia changed into a clump of reeds to protect her from Pan's amorous advances. The pipes of Pan are cut from hollow reeds and called the *syrinx*. The name Pan may also be applied in a pluralistic sense. Pan's reputation extended to sudden frightening of travelers, whence derives the term "panic." Pan is depicted wearing a garland of pine boughs and bearing the *syrinx* pipes and a shepherd's crook.

Pancabrahma

Collective name for five aspects of Siva. Hindu. The five aspects are Aghora, Isana, Sadyojata, Tatpurusa and Vamadeva. Also Isanadayas.

Pancamukha-Patradeva

God. Buddhist. A "bowl-god." Attributes: an alms bowl in each of sixteen hands. Five-headed.

Pancanana

Demonic deity. Hindu (Puranic). Regarded as a form of the god Siva possessing five faces, each face having three eyes. Depicted with the naked body of an ascetic, wearing a necklace of snakes. Shrines symbolize the god with a stone, its top painted red and usually placed beneath a tree. Pancanana is worshiped extensively in Hindu villages throughout Bengal where women make invocations and anoint the stones, particularly when sickness strikes. There is a belief that children in the throes of epilepsy have been seized by the god.

Pancaraksa *(five-fold protection)*

Group of goddesses. Buddhist. Five tutelary or guardian deities who personify protective spells or magic formulas. They are thus known as "spell goddesses."

Pandara

Goddess. Buddhist. The *Sakti* of Amitabha and a female *bodhisattva* or *buddha*-designate. She originates from the Tantric syllable PAM. Color: rose. Attributes: blue lotus, cup, knife and prayer wheel.

Panao

Creator god. Kafir [Afghanistan]. Local deity worshiped in Ashkun villages in southwestern Kafiristan. Also a generic title for deities controlling the natural world and said to live in the mountains. These include Lutkari Panao (fertility), Saramun Panao (health), Plossa Panao (rain and good health), Passamun Panao (rain and good health), Indermun Panao (fruit and wine), Malek Panao (nut trees). These gods were generally worshiped in sacred open spaces where their wooden images were regularly drenched with blood sacrifices.

Paneu

A collective term for seven gods. Kafir [Afghanistan]. The divine brothers are cast as the hunters and henchmen of the supreme goddess Disani. Each is equipped with a golden bow and quiver. They generally appear as merciless and malignant forces. Also Paradik, Purron.

Pansahi Mata

Mother goddess. Hindu. A *Sakti* and one of seven *saptamataras* (mothers) who in later Hinduism became regarded as of evil intent, inflicting sickness on children under the age of seven. Particularly known from Bengal.

Pao Kung

God of magistrates. Chinese. Lived as a mortal from 999–1062 AD during the Sung Dynasty. Depicted with a dark face, implying impartiality, and wearing yellow and purple robes. Attributes include a wooden scepter. He is attended by two minor deities, one holding his seal of office and the other holding the rod of punishment.

Papas

Local god. Phrygian [northwestern Turkey]. According to tradition, he inseminated a rock and so engendered the hermaphrodite being Agdistis. Later became syncretized with Zeus.

Papatuanuku

Chthonic mother goddess. Polynesian (including Maori). According to tradition she evolved spontaneously in the cosmic night personified by Te Po and became the apotheosis of *papa*, the earth. In other traditions she was engendered, with the sky god Ranginui, by a primordial androgynous being, Atea. Paptuanuku and Ranginui are regarded as the primal parents of the pantheon who, through a prolonged period of intercourse, produced at least ten major deities as their children. In Maori culture Papatuanuku, like all deities, is represented only by inconspicuous, slightly worked stones or pieces of wood and not by the large totems, which are depictions of ancestors.

Pap-nigin-gara

(lord of the boundary stone)
God of war. Mesopotamian (Babylonian-Akkadian). Syncretized with Ninurta.

Papsukkal

Messenger god. Mesopotamian (Babylonian-Akkadian). Identified in late Akkadian texts and known chiefly from Hellenistic Babylonian times. His consort is Amasagnul and he acts as both messenger and gatekeeper for the rest of the pantheon. A sanctuary, the *E-akkil*, is identified from the Mesopotamian site of Kiš. He becomes syncretized with Ninšubur.

Paramasva *(great horse)*

God. Buddhist (Mahayana). Considered to be a form of Hayagriva depicted with four legs and trampling the four major Hindu deities underfoot. Color: red. Attributes: arrow, bow, head of a horse, great lotus, lotus, staff and sword. Three-eyed.

Paramita

Descriptive name of a philosophical deity. Buddhist. Applied to one of the group of twelve whose spiritual father is Ratnasambhava. Common attributes: banner with a pearl and a lotus.

Parasurama *(Rama-with-the-ax)*

Incarnation of the god Visnu. Hindu (Epic and Puranic). The sixth *avatara* of Visnu (see also Rama) in which form he saved the world from an army of tyrannical warriors. According to legend, Rama, the son of a wise man, became a skilled bowman and in gratitude he went to the Himalaya where he stayed, devoting himself to Siva. His consort is Dharani. Though without his bow, Rama acted as a champion of the gods in a war against the demons and was rewarded with an ax. In another legend, Visnu took the form of Parasurama to rid the world of despotic rulers. This *avatara* appears in human form, with two arms and with an ax in the right hand. Other attributes: arrow, bow, knife, skin and sword. Also Parasuramavatara.

Parcae

Goddesses of fate. Greco-Roman. Originally a pair of birth goddesses, Decima and Nona, later joined by a goddess of death, Morta.

Parendi

Minor goddess of prosperity. Hindu (Vedic). Associated with the acquisition of wealth.

Pariacaca

Weather god. Pre-Inca central Andean [South America]. The deity responsible for rain and thunder, personified by the falcon.

Pariskaravasita *(control of purification)*

Minor goddess. Buddhist. One of a group of *vasitas* personifying the disciplines of spiritual regeneration. Color: yellow. Attribute: jeweled staff.

Parjanya *(rain giver)*

God of rain. Hindu (Vedic). Became replaced by, or syncretized with, Indra in later Hinduism, but in the Vedas he is seen as a god of gentle, fructifying rain. May be regarded as an *aditya*.

Parna-Savari   *(dressed in leaves)*
Goddess. Buddhist (Mahayana). An emanation of
Aksobhya and *bodhisattva* or *buddha*-designate. Also
one of a group of *dharanis* (deifications of literature). She is particularly recognized in the northwest of India. Her vehicle is Ganesa surmounting
obstacles. Color: yellow or green. Attributes: arrow, ax, bow, flower, noose, peacock feather, skin
and staff. Three-eyed and three-headed.

Partula
Minor goddess of birth. Roman. Concerned with
parturition.

PARVATI   *(daughter of the mountain)*
Origin   Hindu (Epic and Puranic) [India]. Mother
goddess.

Known period of worship   circa 400 AD until present
times.

Synonyms   Sakti; Ahladini-Sadini; Sati; Uma. Many
epithets including Amba (mother); Aja (she goat);
Gauri (grain goddess aspect); Bhutamata (mother
of goblins).

Center(s) of cult   none specific.

Art references   sculptures, chiefly in bronze but
also in stone; reliefs.

Literary sources   *Ramayana* epic and various Puranic texts.

Parvati may have originated from the mountain
tribes in the Himalaya. As a goddess of fertility
she is the youngest of the benign aspects of the
goddess Sakti. She also appears as a reincarnation
of Sati. She is the daughter of Himavan (the Himalaya) and Mena, a sister of Visnu and the
younger sister of Ganga. She becomes the consort
of the god Siva and, as such, personifies the
extreme example of the devoted and steadfast
Hindu wife. Her sons include Ganesa and Skanda.

She is presented to Siva, the ascetic, as a beautiful dancing girl. On becoming aware of his lack
of interest, she pursues a life of self-denial until

he finally appears to her as an old Brahman and
takes her as his consort.

Parvati is depicted with two arms when accom-
panying Siva, but four when standing alone; she
may be elephant-headed or carrying Ganesa as a
baby, and appears in many varieties. Attributes:
conch, crown, mirror, ornamented head-band, rosary and occasionally a lotus.

Pasupati   *(lord of animals)*
God of animals. Hindu [India]. His consort is
Svaha and his son is Sanmukha. Thought to have
been derived from an earlier pre-Indo Aryan deity
worshiped by the Indus Valley civilization as a
horned god with three faces, sitting surrounded
by animals. In Hindu culture regarded as an aspect of Siva and depicted standing upon a corpse.

Patadharini   *(bearing a cloth)*
Goddess of passage. Buddhist. She watches over
curtains and doorways. Color: blue. Attribute: a
curtain.

Pattinidevi   *(queen of goddesses)*
Mother goddess. Hindu (Singhalese) [Sri Lanka].
A deification of Kannaki, the consort of Kovolan
who, according to ancient Tamil tradition, jour-
neyed to the town of Madurai to sell a gold anklet.
Through trickery she was convicted of theft and
executed, but was canonized. According to another tradition, she was born from a mango pierced
by a sacred arrow. In southern India and Sri Lanka
a goddess of chastity and fidelity in marriage. Also
a guardian against diseases, including measles
and smallpox. She is associated with fire-walking
rituals. Attributes: cobra hood behind the head
and a lotus.

Pavana   *(purifier)*
God of the winds. Hindu. His consort is Anjana.
Also Vayu.

Pax
Spirit of peace. Roman. Became well-known as
Pax Romana and Pax Augusta from the second
century BC and was accorded a shrine on the Field

of Mars. Depicted as a young woman bearing a cornucopia, an olive branch and a sheaf of grain.

Peitho

Goddess of persuasion. Greek. A minor attendant of the goddess Aphrodite.

Peju'lpe

Guardian spirits. Yukaghir [southeastern Siberia]. Attendant deities who look after the well-being of animals in their care. They are benevolent toward the hunter so long as he observes certain regulations and kills only when necessary.

Pekko

God of cereal crops. Pre-Christian Finnish and Baltic regions. In Finland he is Pellon Pekko and specifically a god of barley used in brewing beer. In Estonia he is a grain god whose image, made of wax, was kept in the grain chest. He was originally honored on a day taken over by a Christian festival for St Peter.

Pele

Volcano goddess. Polynesian [Hawaii]. According to tradition she arrived in Hawaii in a canoe, having sailed from Tahiti. She may derive locally from the more familiar Polynesian moon goddess, Hina, since one of her alternative names is Hina-Ai-Malama (Hina who devours the moon).

Pellon Pekko

Vegetation god. Pre-Christian Finnish. The deity responsible for the germination and harvesting of barley used to make beer. The first brewing is dedicated to Pellon Pekko. He may have largely become syncretized with St. Peter under Christian influence. See also Pekko.

Pemba *(great thing)*

Creator god. Bambara and Mande [Mali, West Africa]. He was created out of the empty or *Fu* and his first task was to form the egg of the world. He descended to earth as an acacia seed (*Acacia albida*), which first grew to a mighty tree and then died. From the wood Pemba generated human

souls and a female being whom he impregnated to engender all human and animal life. His brother is the god Faro, creator of the river Niger.

Pen Annwen

Underworld god. Celtic (Welsh). Virtually synonymous with Pwyll and Pryderi.

Penates

Hearth deities. Roman. These gods are a peculiarly Roman innovation, unknown to the Greeks. The *penates*, chosen individually by the head of the household, oversaw the domestic affairs of most Roman families. They were considered sufficiently important that, if a move was anticipated, they were taken to and established in the new residence *a priori*. They are represented in the form of small statues made of anything from clay to gold according to the wealth of the owner, and were provided with regular offerings of scraps of food.

Perende

Storm god. Pre-Christian Albanian. In the ancient Illyrian culture his presence was announced by thunder and lightning. The name subsequently became adopted to identify God in the Christian sense.

Perkons

God of thunder. Pre-Christian Latvian. Depicted armed with iron weapons, he is also a fertility god who brings beneficial rain. Also Perkunas (Lithuanian).

Perkunas

See Perkons.

Perse

Chthonic underworld goddess. Greek. The consort of the sun god Helios and the mother of Kirke and Pasiphae, she personifies the underworld aspects of the moon. Also Neaira.

PERSEPHONE
Origin Greek. Chthonic goddess of death.

Known period of worship circa 1200 BC to circa 400 AD.

Synonyms Kore; Persephassa; Pherrephatta (Attic); Proserpina (Roman).

Center(s) of cult Eleusis; temple to Demeter and Persephone in Syracuse.

Art references sculptures and reliefs.

Literary sources Hymn to Demeter, Iliad (Homer); Theogony (Hesiod).

The daughter of Zeus and the grain goddess Demeter, Persephone's *persona* is intricately entwined with that of her mother; the two may be seen as aspects of each other, though Persephone's name suggests an earlier, independent identity as a major goddess in prehistory. Persephone is perceived as Kore, the immature daughter, or aspect, of the grain mother, but also specifically as mistress of the dead and ill-fated consort of the underworld god Hades-Aidoneus or Aides.

According to tradition Persephone leaves her mother's house to pick flowers with a group of girls, the Okeanides. As she bends to collect a particularly beautiful bloom, the earth suddenly opens and the god of the underworld rides out in a chariot drawn by black horses to seize her and take her to Hades, where she is to reign as its queen. The flower meadow is traditionally believed to lie on the island of Sicily close to the Lago di Pergus at Enna, though other sites, including one near Syracuse, contest the claim. Subsequently, Demeter wanders the earth in fruitless search for her child. Eventually she locates Persephone and Hermes is allowed to bring her back to the upper world but, because Persephone has tasted the pomegranate of death, she may return only for two thirds of each year. When Persephone returns to her mother as Kore, the girl, nature flourishes, but when she returns to Hades as its queen, Demeter is distraught and angry and the living world shrivels and dies.

According to one legendary source, Zeus in the form of a snake raped Persephone and sired Dionysos, though Dionysos's mother is more generally regarded as Semele.

Perun *(striker)*
God of thunder. Pre-Christian Slavonic (Balkan). His attribute is a club and his sacred animal is the bull. He is known to have been worshiped at Kiev.

Peruwa
Horse god. Hittite. Known only from inscriptions. Also Pirwa.

Phanebal *(face of Baal)*
Minor attendant god. Western Semitic. A youthful warrior deity with right hand raised who appears on coins struck at Ascalon from the time of Augustus.

Phanes
Primordial sun god. Greek. The first god to emerge from the cosmic egg engendered by Kronos, he personifies light emerging from chaos. According to one tradition, his daughter is Nyx, the night.

Phorkys
Minor sea god. Greek. According to Hesiod, he is the son of Pontos and Gaia. The consort of a sea serpent, Keto, and the father of the Gorgons and Graii. Also Phorkos.

Phosphoros
God of the morning star. Greek. His mother is Eos, the dawn, and he is depicted as a naked youth running ahead of her, carrying a torch. In Roman culture he becomes Lucifer.

Phul Mata
Mother goddess. Hindu (Epic and Puranic). A *Sakti* who in later Hinduism became one of the *saptamataras* regarded as of evil intent, inflicting sickness on children under seven years old. Particularly known from Bengal.

Phyi-Sgrub *(the external one)*
God. Buddhist-Lamaist [Tibet]. A form of the god Yama who rides a buffalo or a bull. Color: blue, yellow or white. Attributes: noose, prayer wheel and staff surmounted by a skeleton.

Picullus
Chthonic underworld god. Romano-Celtic (Prussian). He becomes syncretized with the devil in Christian times.

Picvu'cin
God of hunters. Chukchee [eastern Siberia]. A diminutive figure who rides on a sled drawn by mice. He is the guardian of reindeer and other animals and is invoked by sacrifice, usually of camp dogs.

Pidray
Minor fertility goddess. Canaanite and Phoenician. Mentioned in epic creation texts and treaties at Ugarit (Ras Šamra) as the first daughter of Baal. She is the consort of Baal-Sapon, the mother of Tly and may be the goddess Peraia described by the Greek writer Philo.

Pietas
Minor god. Roman. A sanctuary dedicated to him circa 191 BC is still in existence in Rome. He became Pietas Augusta and is associated with family solidarity and patriotism.

Pilumnus *(staker)*
Minor guardian god. Roman. Concerned with the protection of an infant at birth. A ceremony to honor the deity involved driving a stake into the ground.

Pinikirz
Mother goddess. Elamite [Iran]. Known only from inscriptions.

PISTIS *(faith)*
Origin Gnostic Christian. Primordial female force.

Known period of worship probably circa 200 BC to circa 400 AD.

Synonyms Pistis Sophia.

Center(s) of cult undefined cells in areas of early Christian influence.

Art references none.

Literary sources *Nag Hammadi* codices.

The exact origin of Pistis is never made clear and the *Nag Hammadi* narratives are in places confused and contradictory. It is, however, an unmistakably female principle typical of most religions in their concept of the origin of the world. Pistis appears to be a benign female element among the primordial immortals who ruled before even the cosmos was created. She is closely allied with Sophia (wisdom). Pistis appears to have been formed out of infinity before the "shadow" that was to evolve into chaos, and from which the cosmos would take shape, defined itself within limitless light (see also Sophia and Yaldabaoth).

Pitao Cozobi
Corn god. Zapotec (classical Mesoamerican) [Mexico]. Worshipped by the Monte Alban culture of Zapotec-speaking peoples in the Valley of Oaxaca. Sculptures were often adorned with casts of corn ears.

Pitari *(snake catcher)*
One of the consorts of Siva. Hindu (Puranic and later). A benevolent *navasakti*. The cult of Pidari probably evolved in the sixth and seventh centuries AD and is generally restricted to southern India. She is considered an aspect of the goddess Kali and is invoked in many villages to ward off evil and demons. She has most of the attributes of Kali and may also have snakes around her breasts, but may also be represented by a stone. Her cult moved at one time and reached a climax in eastern India between the eighth and twelfth centuries. Attributes: cup, fire, noose and trident. Also Pitali; Kala-Pidari.

Piyusaharana
Obscure physician god. Hindu (Epic and Puranic). Identified in the texts as the eighteenth of the

thirty-nine minor incarnations of the god Visnu; said to be a "carrier of nectar."

Pluto

God of the underworld. Roman. Derived from the Greek model of Hades, he abducted the daughter of Ceres, Proserpina, to reign as his queen. The three-headed dog Cerberus was set to guard the gate of Hades and through the kingdom flowed the two rivers of death, the Cocytus and the Acheron, which could be crossed only by the ferryman Charon. According to Roman tradition, the entrance to the underworld was at Avernus in Rome where the Christian church of St. Maria del Inferno was built. See also Hades.

Plutos

Minor god of riches. Greek. A son of Demeter who was abandoned in childhood and reared by the goddess of peace, Eirene, who is sometimes depicted holding him in her lap. Plutos was blinded by Zeus because of his discrimination in favor of the righteous.

Poeninus

Mountain god. Romano-Celtic (Continental European). Known locally from the alpine regions and generally thought to be assimilated with Jupiter.

Poleramma

Plague goddess. Telegu [India]. Associated with smallpox and offered blood sacrifices.

Pollux

Horse god. Roman. See Polydeukes.

Poluknalai

Goddess of animals. Kafir [Afghanistan]. Locally revered, with the goddess Disani, among Askun villages in the southwest of Kafiristan.

Polydeukes

Horse god. Greek. One of the Dioskouroi twins; the other is Kastor. According to tradition, they are together associated with a Spartan cult whence they originated. The pair probably derive from the Indo-European model of the Asvins in Vedic mythology. Kastor is mortal while Polydeukes is immortal. Thus, during battle, Kastor is mortally wounded but, even in death, the two brothers remain inseparable. They rescue individuals from distress and danger, particularly at sea, and are thought to be embodied in the electrical discharges known as St. Elmo's Fire. Also Castor and Pollux (Roman).

Pomona

Goddess of orchards and gardens. Roman. Consort of Vertumnus generally represented by garden implements and offered fruits and flowers.

PON (something)

Origin Yukaghir [central Siberia]. Supreme creator god.

Known period of worship from prehistoric times until circa 1900 AD.

Synonyms Pon-yu'lec (something got dark); Pon-o'moc (something has become good); Pon-ti'boi (something makes rain); Cu'kun.

Center(s) of cult no fixed sanctuaries.

Art references none known.

Literary sources Jochelson *Memoirs of the American Natural History Society* Vol. 10 (1905).

Pon is a vague and indefinite creator spirit who controls all visible phenomena of nature. As far as can be ascertained, no specific cult was ever addressed to this deity; he seems to be a remote figure, largely out of touch with everyday life. No invocations or prayers are addressed to Pon, nor are sacrifices.

Pontos

God of the sea. Greek. His mother and consort is Gaia and he is the father of the sea gods Nereis and Phorkys.

Pore

Creator god. Guyanan Indian [South America]. Engendered the earth and all living things. Also Pura.

Portunus

God of passage. Roman. The deity responsible for guarding the entrance of the city and the house alike. He was celebrated in the *Portunalia* festival, held annually on August 17, when keys were thrown into a fire to bless them. He is also the guardian of the Tiber estuary, the main access by sea to the city of Rome.

POSEIDON

Origin   Greek. God of the sea and mariners.

Known period of worship   from circa 1600 BC through Minoan Crete (art evidence only) until circa 400 AD.

Synonyms   Poseidaon (Mycenaean); Poteidan (Dorian).

Center(s) of cult   Cape Sunium [southern Greece]; Pylos [Crete]; Mount Mykale [Turkey]; early sanctuary on the island of Kalauria; otherwise widespread through areas of Greco-Roman influence, particularly at Berytus [Syria].

Art references   sculpture, plaques, coins, etc.

Literary sources   *Iliad* (Homer); *Theogony* (Hesiod), etc.

Poseidon is perceived as a sea god, one of the three sons of Kronos and Rhea. His brothers are Zeus and Hades. He is the father of Theseus who became king of Athens, and is also linked with the ancestral king of the city, Erechtheus, whom he supposedly rammed into the ground. Among his other sons are Neleus, king of Pylos, and Pelias of Iolkos in Thessaly. He is also, by tradition, the father of the ancestors of the Aeolian and Boeotian races.

The horse is sacred to him and he is said to have inseminated the ground from which was conceived the first horse. Poseidon's chief consort is Amphitrite, but other consorts emphasize the affinity with horses. They include the infamous Gorgon, Medusa, from whose dead body came the winged horse Pegasus and the warrior Chrysaor. A liaison with the goddess Erinys produced another fabulous winged horse, Areon. In a parallel legend Areon's mother is Demeter while in the guise of a mare.

Poseidon appears never to have been envisaged in youthful form, but always as an elderly, bearded deity who carries the emblem of a trident harpoon. According to tradition, Zeus took the sky, Poseidon the sea, and Hades the underworld, while the earth was shared between all three. Poseidon was a popular oracular deity, suggested in one legend to be the first keeper of Delphi. Another oracle at Cape Tainaron is dedicated to Poseidon.

There exist ruins of a striking Poseidon sanctuary, constructed of white marble, on the cliffs of Cape Sunium at the extreme southern tip of Greece, past which all ships sail when making for Athens. Regattas were held there in honor of the god and he was particularly invoked during the tuna-hunting season, which was conducted using traditional trident harpoons.

On Argos horses were sacrificed to Poseidon, drowned in a whirlpool; on Pylos and elsewhere he received the offering of slaughtered bulls.

Posis Das

Sky god. Greek. In pre-Hellenic times the consort of the earth mother Gaia. One of the primordial partnership identified in *Theogony* (Hesiod). He later becomes syncretized with Zeus.

Pothos

Primordial being. Phoenician (Hellenic). According to the cosmogony, he is desire, and consorts with Omichle, darkness, to engender out of chaos the spiritual force Aer, and its living physical manifestation Aura.

Potina

Minor goddess. Roman. Associated with the safe drinking ability of infants.

Poxlom

God of disease. Mayan (Tzeltal Indian, classical Mesoamerican) [Mexico]. Apparently perceived as a star in the sky or a ball of fire. He may also be depicted as a fertility god shelling corn or as a fisherman, doctor, musician or hunter. An image of the god was discovered in the Christian church in Oxchuc, and the Indians were forced to revoke and spit on the icon before it was publicly burnt.

Prabhakari *(light maker)*

Minor goddess. Buddhist (Vajrayana). One of several deified *bhumis* recognized as different spiritual spheres through which a disciple passes. Color: red. Attributes: sun disc on a great lotus and staff.

Prabhasa *(shining dawn)*

Attendant god. Hindu (Epic and Puranic). One of a group of *vasu* deities answering to the god Indra. Attributes: cup, hook, *Sakti* and staff.

Pracanda *(furious)*

Distinct form of the goddess Durga. Hindu (Epic and Puranic). One of a group of *navadurgas* or "nine durgas."

Pradhana *(most important)*

Mother goddess. Hindu (Epic and Puranic). One of a group of nine *navasaktis* who, in southern India, rank higher than the *saptamataras*.

Pradipatara

Minor goddess of light. Buddhist (Mahayana).

Pradyumna

God of love. Early Dravidian (Tamil) [southern India]. The son of Krsna and Rukmini, and the elder brother of Sama. Equating with Kamadeva, or Kama returned to life after being killed by Siva. In later Hinduism regarded as an *avatara* of Visnu with consorts including Mayadevi and Kakudmati.

Prajapati *(lord of creatures)*

Primordial being. Hindu (Vedic, Epic and Puranic). In the Vedic legends he is described variously as the creator of the world and the creator of heaven and earth. He is an androgynous being who impregnated himself by fusing elements of mind and speech. In later epics he is the guardian deity of the sexual organ. Prajapati is also a name of the god Brahma in later Hinduism.

Prajna *(wisdom)*

Goddess. Buddhist (Mahayana). Regarded as the *Sakti* of a number of Mahayana gods, or specifically as the *Sakti* of Adibuddha.

Prajnantaka

God. Buddhist. One of the *dikpalas*, guardians of the southern direction. Color: white. Attributes: jewel, lotus, sword, trident and white staff.

Prajnaparamita

Goddess. Buddhist. The personification of the religious text *Prajnaparamita* and the *Sakti* of Vajradhara. An emanation of the deity Aksobbhya. Also a philosophical deity, the spiritual offspring of Ratnasambhava. The embodiment of transcendental intuition. She stands upon a lotus. Color: white, reddish white or yellow. Attributes: blue lotus, book, cup, knife, jeweled staff and red lotus.

Prajnapti *(teaching)*

Goddess of learning. Jain [India]. One of sixteen *vidyadevi* headed by the goddess Sarasvati.

Prajnavardhani *(growth of wisdom)*

Deification of literature. Buddhist. One of a group of *dharanis*. Color: white. Attributes: staff and sword on blue lotus.

Prakde *(parade)*

Local deity. Kafir [Afghanistan]. Known from Ashkun villages in southwestern Kafiristan and perhaps one of the seven divine Panao or Paradik brothers.

Pramudita *(delighted)*

Minor goddess. Buddhist (Vajrayana). One of several deified *bhumis* recognized as different spiritual spheres through which a disciple passes. Color: red. Attributes: jewel and staff.

Pranasakti

Goddess. Hindu. A terrifying deity ruling the "centers of physical life." She stands upon a lotus. Attribute: a cup filled with blood.

Pranidhanaparamita

Philosophical deity. Buddhist. Spiritual offspring of Ratnasambhava. Color: blue. Attributes: jewel and sword on blue lotus.

Pranidhanavasita
(control of abstract contemplation)

Minor goddess. Buddhist. One of a group of *vasitas* personifying the disciplines of spiritual regeneration. Color: yellow. Attributes: blue lotus and jeweled staff.

Prasannatara *(the gracious Tara)*

Minor goddess. Buddhist (Mahayana). Regarded as a form of Ratnasambhava who tramples on Hindu gods including Indra, Brahma, Rudra and Upendra. Color: yellow. Carries a large variety of attributes. Three-eyed.

Prasuti

Goddess. Hindu. The daughter of Svayambhuva Manu and one of the consorts of Daksa.

Pratibhanakuta *(excellent intelligence)*

God. Buddhist. A *bodhisattva* or *buddha*-designate. Color: yellow or red. Attribute: sword on lotus.

Pratibhanapratisamvit

Goddess of context analysis. Buddhist (Vajrayana). One of a group of four. Color: green. Attributes: three-pronged staff and bell.

Pratisamvit *(analytical science)*

Generic name for four goddesses. Buddhist (Vajrayana). The personifications of logical analysis.

Pratyangira
(whose speech is directed westward)

Goddess of terrifying aspect. Hindu. She rides upon a lion. Attributes: cup, drum, flaming hair, snake noose and trident.

Pratyusa *(scorching)*

Attendant god. Hindu (Epic and Puranic). One of a group of *vasu* deities answering to the god Indra. Attributes: hook, knife, *Sakti* and sword.

Prende

Goddess of love. Pre-Christian Albanian. The consort of the thunder god Perende who became absorbed into Christianity as a saint.

Priapos

Fertility god. Greco-Roman and Phrygian. The son of Dionysos and Aphrodite, he was also a guardian of mariners. Priapos was not regarded as a significant deity in Greece until very late times—during the Macedonian period, circa fourth to second century BC—and was only locally popular during the Roman Empire period. He is particularly known from Phrygia and is depicted as a satyr-like creature with pronounced genitals.

Priapus

God of the shade. Roman. A rural deity whose worship appears to have been restricted to the shores of the Hellespont and clearly derives from the god Priapos.

Prithivi

See Prthivi.

Priti *(pleasure)*

Goddess. Hindu (Epic and Puranic). A daughter of Daksa and consort of the god of love Kamadeva. One of twelve *Saktis* associated with the god Visnu in his various incarnations.

Priyadarsana *(pleasant to the eye)*

Minor goddess. Buddhist (Mahayana). An attendant of Buddhakapala.

PROMETHEUS *(forethought)*
Origin Greek. Heroic god and creator of man.

Known period of worship circa 800 BC and probably earlier until Christianization circa 400 AD.

Synonyms none.

Center(s) of cult predominently Athens.

Art references sculptures, relief carvings, etc.

Literary sources *Theogony* (Hesiod); Aeschylus drama.

Prometheus, one of four sons of the Titan Iapetos and his consort Klymene, is probably best known as a heroic opponent of Zeus. He stole fire from the latter and gave it to mankind as the boon that separates the human race from all other living creatures. Legend accords to Prometheus, and his brother Epimethius (afterthought), the creation of mankind and the role of its protector, in response to which Zeus created Pandora and her box of problems, set loose to afflict the human race. Zeus also imprisoned Prometheus by fastening him to a great rock in the Caucasus mountains with adamantine chains and sending an eagle to consume his liver. He was rescued by Herakles, who killed the eagle and liberated the god from his torment.

Promitor
Minor god of agriculture. Roman. Responsible for the growth and harvesting of crops.

Pronoia *(forethought)*
Primordial being. Gnostic Christian. The feminine aspect of one of the androgynous principles born to Yaldabaoth, the prime parent, and ruling the seven heavens of chaos in Gnostic cosmogony. Also described in other Gnostic tracts as Protennoia, the voice of the thought, and alternatively the voice of Logos (logic), who descends to earth in human form and plays a part in the primordial salvation of the world.

Proserpina
Goddess of death. Roman but derived from a Greek model. Abducted by the underworld god Pluto to reign as his queen (see Persephone).

Proteus
Minor sea god. Greek. Depicted as an old man who attends Triton and whose principal concern is the creatures of the oceans. He also has oracular powers. The poet Cowper wrote:
"In ages past old Proteus, with his droves Of sea calves sought the mountains and the groves."
Also known as Glaukos, Nereus and Phorkys.

Providentia
Goddess of forethought. Roman. Recognized from the reign of Tiberias in second century BC.

Proxumae
Generic title of a group of goddesses. Romano-Celtic. Personal guardian deities.

Prsni
Primordial earth goddess. Hindu (Vedic). The so-called "dappled cow" of the *Rg Veda*. She is also perceived as the brightly colored *soma* stalk and is linked with a male counterpart, also Prsni, the dappled bull of the sun.

PRTHIVI *(earth mother)*
Origin Hindu (Vedic) [India]. Mother goddess of earth.

Known period of worship circa 1500 BC and probably earlier through to present day.

Synonyms Bhudevi.

Center(s) of cult none specific.

Art references sculptures in bronze and other metals; stone reliefs, etc.

Literary sources *Rg Veda* and other texts including the *Atharva-veda*.

In Vedic literature Prthivi is the female aspect of the creator god Dyaus Pitar. The two formed the once inseparable primordial cosmos until separated by the god Varuna. According to one illogical legend of Prthivi's genealogy, she was the daughter of Prithu who had granted the blessing of life on earth and who, in her turn, had emerged from the arm of the corpse of King Vena.

Prthivi is a chthonic or earth goddess with whom the sky god Dyaus couples when he fertilizes her with rain. She is said to kiss the center of the world and she symbolizes the eternal patience and resilience of the earth, permitting herself to be abused without rancor. She is also a vegetation goddess, the source of all plant life. In some legends Prthivi is perceived as the consort of the rain god Indra, who protects her, and of lesser-known creation deities including Parjanya, Prajapait and Visvakarma. Visnu strides over her body. As the inseparable partner of Dyaus she is rarely addressed alone, though in the *Atharva-veda* Dyaus is not mentioned. Usually the pair are referred to as Dyavaprthivi. Though the goddess was present in early Indian culture, she persists into late Hinduism and may be associated with Visnu as one of the personifications of his *Sakti*.

Many Hindus worship Prthivi at dawn and before ploughing and sowing. In the Punjab, the first milk from a cow is offered to the goddess by allowing it to soak into the earth. With similar sentiment a dying man may be laid on the earth to be received by Prthivi.

Prthu   *(broad)*

Creator god. Hindu (Vedic). The head of the solar pantheon who introduced agriculture to the human race and who, in later Hinduism, is identified as an *avatara* of Visnu.

PTAH

Origin Egyptian. Creator god and god of craftsmen.

Known period of worship circa 3000 BC, possibly earlier, until the end of Egyptian history circa 400 AD.

Synonyms Ptah-Nun; Ptah-Naunet; Khery-bakef.

Center(s) of cult chiefly at Memphis, but with sanctuaries throughout the Nile valley.

Art references sculptures, relief carvings, wall paintings, papyrus illustrations.

Literary sources Pyramid Texts, etc.; the *Shabaka Stone*.

Ptah is the patron deity of Memphis in Lower Egypt at the southerly approach to the Nile delta. With Atum, the sun god of Heliopolis, he is the main rival claimant to seniority as a creator god in the Egyptian pantheon. His consort is the lion-goddess Sakhmet and, by implication only, his son is Nefertum, the god of the primeval lotus flower. Ptah is depicted in human form wearing a closely fitting robe with only his arms free. His most distinctive features are the invariable skull-cap exposing only his face and ears, and the *was* or rod of dominion that he holds, consisting of a staff surmounted by the *ankh* symbol of life. He is otherwise symbolized by his sacred animal, the bull.

According to the genealogy laid down by the Memphis priests, Ptah upstaged Atum as the "father of the gods." He generated not only Atum but the whole Heliopolis pantheon (see Ennead) by thinking and speaking the cosmos into existence. All life and matter was generated by the heart and the tongue of Ptah. In this cosmogony, Nun represents the amorphous primeval matter out of which Ptah generated himself as a bisexual entity, the maleness of which is Ptah-Nun and the femaleness Ptah-Naunet. Ptah is occasionally known by the title Khery-bakef, meaning "he who is under his tree," suggesting that he was syncretized with a older local tree god at Memphis whose symbol is the *moringa* tree.

In addition to his role as creator god, Ptah is also the patron deity of craftsmen and his presence is often denoted in art by dwarfish craftsmen who work at various trades including jewellery. Ptah is envisaged as molding mankind out of base materials. In Greco-Roman times he became identified with the Greek god of smithies, Hephaistos.

Pu Ma

Generic name for deities. Polynesian. The title given to any god of high rank.

Pudicita

Goddess of chastity. Roman. Depicted as a matronly lady, her cult fell from popularity as the Roman Empire veered increasingly toward decadence.

Pu'gu

Sun god. Yukaghir [eastern Siberia]. A spirit associated with justice and honorable living who punishes those who are evil or violent.

Pukkasi

Goddess of terrifying appearance. Buddhist (Vajrayana) and Lamaist [Tibet]. One of a group of *gauri*. Color: yellowish white or blue. Attribute: water jar.

Punarvasu

Minor goddess of fortune. Hindu (Epic and Puranic). A benevolent *naksatra*; daughter of Daksa and wife of Candra (Soma). Concerned with restoring lost or stolen property.

Punitavati   *(purified)*

Local goddess. Hindu. Worshipped at Karaikkal near Ammaiyar. The deification of a Brahman businessman's wife.

Puranai   *(fullness)*

Mother goddess. Dravidian (Tamil) [southern India]. A *navasakti* and one of the consorts of Aiyanar.

Purandhi

Minor goddess of prosperity. Hindu (Vedic). Associated with the acquisition of wealth and sometimes identified with Indra or other male deities.

Purusa

Primeval creator god. Hindu (Vedic). Described as the primordial being from whom the cosmos was formed, possibly the male component of the great mother, Mata. In later Hinduism regarded as an *avatara* of Visnu.

Purvabhadrapada

Minor goddess of fortune. Hindu (Epic and Puranic). A benevolent *naksatra*; daughter of Daksa and wife of Candra (Soma).

Purvaphalguni

Minor goddess of fortune. Hindu (Epic and Puranic). A moderately disposed *naksatra*; daughter of Daksa and wife of Candra (Soma).

Purvasadha

Minor goddess of fortune. Hindu (Epic and Puranic). A moderately disposed *naksatra*; daughter of Daksa and wife of Candra (Soma).

Pusan   *(nourisher)*

Sun god. Hindu (Vedic and Puranic). The original Vedic list of six descendants of the goddess Aditi or *adityas*, all of whom take the role of sun gods, was, in later times, enlarged to twelve, including Pusan. He is the charioteer of the sun and a guardian deity of journeys and pathways. Color: golden. Attributes: four lotuses.

Pusi

Fish god. Polynesian [Tikopia]. The apotheosis of the reef eel who probably accompanied the Tongan ancestors who migrated to Tikopia.

Puspa   *(flower)*

Mother goddess. Buddhist-Lamaist [Tibet]. One of the group of *astamataras* (mothers). Color: white. Attribute: a flower.

Puspatara   *(flower-Tara)*

Minor goddess. Buddhist (Mahayana). Color: white. Attribute: a forest garland.

Pusti   *(growth)*

Fertility goddess. Hindu (Epic and Puranic). In northern India she is the second consort of Visnu, but elsewhere may also be linked with Sarasvati and named as a consort of Ganesa.

Pusya

Minor goddess of fortune. Hindu (Epic and Puranic). A benevolent *naksatra*; daughter of Daksa and wife of Candra (Soma).

Puta

Goddess of agriculture. Roman. Specifically responsible for the proper pruning of trees and shrubs.

Pwyll

Chthonic god. Celtic (Welsh). The so-called "lord of Dyfed" who, according to tradition, brought the pig to Wales having received it as a gift from Arawn, the underworld god. He earned the reward by substituting for Arawn and fighting his enemy Hafgan, in payment for an unintended slight to Arawn, whom he met one day while out hunting. His consort is Rhiannon and his son is Pryderi.

Q

Qaitakalnin

Guardian spirit. Koryak [southeastern Siberia]. The brother of Big Raven, Quikinna'qu, and of the mother spirit Ha'na (A'na).

Qamai'ts

Creator goddess. Bella Coola Indian [British Columbia, Canada]. Said to live in the upper heaven, Atsa'axl, from where she controls the earth. According to tradition the mountains were once malevolent beings who made the world uninhabitable, until she conquered them and reduced them in size. She is never invoked or prayed to. Also Tsi Sisnaaxil (our woman); Ek Yakimtolsil (afraid of nothing).

Qa'wadiliquala

Supreme god. Dza'wadeenox Indian [British Columbia, Canada]. The guardian of the tribe but also a river deity responsible for bringing the salmon each year. Said to live in the river Gwae. His eldest son is Tewi'xilak, the god of goat hunters. His attributes include a headband of red cedar bark.

Qaynan

God of smithies. Pre-Islamic southern Arabian. Known from inscriptions.

Qeskina'qu *(big light)*

Sky spirit. Koryak [southeastern Siberia]. One of the sons of Quikinna'qu, he is the apotheosis of daylight, a precious commodity during the long winter months.

Qos

Local weather god. Pre-Islamic northern Arabian. Apparently known as the deification of an outcrop of black basalt on the north side of the Wadi Hesa [near Kirbet Tannur]. Also a god of rainbows. Depicted seated on a throne flanked by bulls. Attributes include a branched thunderbolt held in the left hand. A worshiper is seen offering him an eagle.

Quadeš *(the holy one)*

Fertility goddess. Western Semitic, probably originating in Syria. She epitomizes female sexuality and eroticism in the mold of Astarte. She was adopted by Egypt with the fertility gods Min and Rešep and became partly associated with the goddess Hathor. She is usually depicted nude standing on the back of a lion (see also Inana and Ninhursaĝa) between Min to whom she offers a lotus blossom, and Rešep for whom she bears snakes. Her cult followed the typically ancient Near Eastern pattern of a sacred marriage carried out by her votary priestesses and their priests or kings.

Quat

Creator god. Polynesian [Banks Islands]. As with many Polynesian deities, the god is depicted as being very inactive, sitting around all day doing nothing.

Qudsu

Personification of holiness. Western Semitic. Known from inscriptions at Tyre where a human figure stands naked on a lion, wearing a spiral headdress and holding lotus blossoms and serpents.

QUETZALCOATL

(the feathered serpent)

Origin Aztec (classical Mesoamerican) [Mexico].

Known period of worship circa 750 AD to 1500 AD and probably much earlier.

Synonyms nine-wind; White Tezcatlipoca; Tlahuizcalpantecuhtli.

Center(s) of cult Teotihuacan, Cholula, Xochicalco, Malinalco and others.

Art references stone sculptures, murals, codex illustrations.

Literary sources pre-Columbian codices.

One of the four suns that are manifestations of the sun god Tezcatlipoca. He presided over the second of the five world ages represented by the sun Ehecatl. The heroic creator god of the Aztecs, he is also identified as the god of the wind. According to one of many traditions he fashioned mankind from his own blood and provided food by turning himself into an ant so as to steal a kernel of corn that the ants had hidden inside a mountain. A titanic struggle between Quetzalcoatl and the black Tezcatlipoca resulted in the creation and destruction of four worlds or suns prior to the current sun. Conversely, Quetzalcoatl and Tezcatlipoca together bore the responsibility for restoring the shattered universe and initiating the fifth sun, Ollin. They are said to have passed through the body of the earth monster Tlaltecuhtli and split it in two to form heaven and earth. Later Quetzalcoatl descended to the underworld Mictlan to obtain from its rulers the bones and ashes of generations of mankind to create the humanity of the fifth sun. He is said to have dropped the bones and broken them, thus accounting for the differing statures of men.

First depicted as a feathered serpent, he was known to the Nahua Indians as Quetzalcoatl; they also revered him for his gift of science and arts. Worshipped at Teotihuacan from circa 750 AD or earlier. Temples of Quetzalcoatl include a six-tiered step-pyramid at Teotihuacan, and the huge pyramid of Cholula on the Puebla plain, the largest ancient structure in the New World. The bearded Spanish conquistador Cortez was believed by the emperor Motecuhzoma to be Quetzalcoatl.

Represented iconographically as a composite feathered hybrid, his aspect or *avatara* Tlahuizcalpantecuhtli was perceived as the Morning Star.

NOTE: Topiltzin Quetzalcoatl was also a historical figure born circa 935 AD.

Quiahuitl

Creator god. Aztec (classical Mesoamerican) [Mexico]. The sun deity representing the third of the five world ages each of which lasted for 2,028 heavenly years, each heavenly year being fifty-two terrestrial years. Assigned to the element fire and presided over by the rain god Tlaloc. According to tradition, the age ended in a cataclysmic destruction caused by a great fiery rain. The human population perished and in doing so were transformed into dogs, turkeys and butterflies. Illustrated by the "Stone of the Four Suns" [Yale Peabody Museum]. Also Quiauhtonatiuh; Tletonatiuh.

QUIKINN.A'QU *(big raven)*

Origin Koryak [Kamchatka peninsula, southeastern Siberia]. Founder of the world.

Known period of worship from early times until circa 1900 AD.

Synonyms none.

Center(s) of cult no fixed sanctuaries.

Art references none specific, though wooden carvings may relate.

Literary sources Jochelson *Memoirs of the American Natural History Society* Vol. 10 (1905).

A spirit of a primitive culture still heavily influenced by animism. Quikinn.a'qu is not only a deity but also the first man and a powerful *shaman*. Everything had existed before, but he was responsible for revealing that which hitherto had been concealed. Married to Miti and said to have twelve children, the most significant of whom are Eme'mqut and Yina-a-naut (see also Aesir) who are in constant conflict with the evil spirits or Kalau. The subject of many heroic adventures in which he undertakes to make safe the activities of mankind. He possesses a raven cloak with which he can indulge in shape-changing and fly to the heavens. Acts as a celestial majordomo and an intercessor with the creator god. According to legend, he died when he swallowed the sun. His daughter took it from his mouth and returned it to the sky.

Quinoa-Mama

Minor goddess of the quinoa crop. Pre-Columbian Indian [Peru]. Models of the deity were made from the leaves of the plant and kept for a year before being burned in a ritual to ensure a good quinine harvest.

Quirinus

God of war. Roman. One of a triad of warrior gods including Jupiter and Mars. He originated as the tutelary god of the Sabines, living on the Quirinal, one of the seven hills of Rome. His warrior status is primarily one of defense and he is depicted bearded and in a combination of military and clerical clothing. The myrtle is sacred to him.

Quzah   *(archer)*

Mountain and weather god. Pre-Islamic northern Arabian. Probably equating to Qoš and worshiped by the Idumaean tribe to the south of Judea as a storm god. Also claimed to have been known near Mecca. Attributes include a bow that shoots arrows of hail.

R

RADHA *(prosperity)*
Origin Hindu (Epic and Puranic) [India]. Goddess of emotional love.

Known period of worship circa 1000 BC and earlier until present day.

Synonyms Bhumidevi [southern India].

Center(s) of cult none.

Art references virtually none.

Literary sources later Puranic literature—the works of Vidyapati (1352–1448), including the *Brahma-vaivarta-purana*.

Radha is a goddess whose role is limited to that of a favored mistress of Krsna. She only emerges fully as a goddess from the twelfth century AD onward and she is one of the central figures in the poetry of Vidyapati, who places her as a cosmic queen. One of the creation accounts describes how Krsna divides himself into two parts, one of which is Radha. They make love for an age and their sweat and heavy breathing become the world's oceans and winds. Radha gives birth to the golden egg of the universe, which floats on the primal waters for a year until the god Visnu emerges. Other mythology accounts that Radha enjoys an illicit relationship with an adolescent Krsna. Their tryst is set in the village of Vraja and in the surrounding forests at a time before Krsna takes as his consort Rukmini and later Satyabhama.

Radha is sometimes considered to be an *avatara* of Laksmi and thus a consort of Krsna and, in southern India, as Bhumidevi, she becomes associated with Sarasvati. She always stands as the personification of emotional love in stark contrast to Sati, the faithful and legitimate consort of Vis-nu's other *avatara*, Rama. In the *bhakti* cult she symbolizes the yearning of the human soul to be drawn to Krsna. Attribute: a lotus.

Rahu *(seizer)*
Primordial cosmic deity. Hindu. The son of Kasyapa or Rudra, according to legend he seizes the sun and moon to generate eclipses. Rahu is depicted with four hands and a tail, or as a head alone, his body having been destroyed by Visnu. He stands upon a lion or in a chariot drawn by eight black horses. Color: dark blue. Attributes: half moon, knife, sword and trident.

Raijin
Weather god(s). Shinto [Japan]. A generic title for a large group of deities controlling thunder, storms and rain. Among the most significant is Ryujin, the dragon god of thunder and rain.

Rajamatangi
Goddess. Hindu. She stands upon a lotus. Attributes: blue lotus, lute, moon and parrot.

Raka *(1)*
Minor goddess of prosperity. Hindu (Vedic). Associated with the acquisition of wealth.

Raka *(trouble)* *(2)*
God of winds. Polynesian [Hervey Islands]. The fifth child of Vari-Ma-Te-Takere, the primordial mother. His home is Moana-Irakau (deep ocean). He received as a gift from his mother a great basket containing the winds, which became his children, each allotted a hole in the edge of the horizon through which to blow. The mother god-

dess also gave him knowledge of many useful things, which he passes on to mankind.

Rakib-El

Moon god. Western Semitic (Syrian). Known chiefly from inscriptions circa eighth century BC.

Rakta-Yamari *(red Yamari)*

God. Buddhist. An emanation of Aksobhya and a variety of Yamari. Color: red.

Raluvimbha

Creator god. Baventa [northern Transvaal, South Africa]. The tribal chief converses with the god, who is responsible for all natural phenomena from thunderstorms to floods and plagues.

Rama *(pleasing)*

Incarnation of the god Visnu. Hindu (Epic and Puranic). The seventh *avatara* (sun aspect) of Visnu. Rama began as a comparatively minor incarnation who became one of the great heroes of the *Ramayana* epic, as well as featuring in the *Mahabharata*. The son of Dasaratha and Kausalya, he was a king of Ayodhya who, in the *Ramayana*, slew the demon Ravana that had captured his consort Sita and was upheld as a deity *par excellence* in respect of manhood and honor, though his subsequent treatment of his wife might be regarded as cavalier (see Sita). Rama rides in a chariot and is depicted in human form with two arms, typically holding a sugar cane bow and with a quiver at his shoulder. Also Ramacandra.

Ran

Storm goddess. Nordic (Icelandic). The consort of the god Aegir. She was presumed to gather mariners in her net having carried them to the bottom of the sea in whirlpools. She was propitiated with money and other offerings thrown overboard.

Rang

God of hunting. Nuer [Sudan]. The rays of the sun are his flaming spears. Also Garang.

Ranginui

Sky god. Polynesian (including Maori). The so-called sky father of the Polynesian culture whose consort is Papatuanuku, the earth mother. During a prolonged period of inseparable intercourse they became the prime parents of the Polynesian pantheon of gods. The children found life between the bodies of the parents too cramped and conspired to force them apart. Though one offspring, Tumatauenga, wanted to slay them, the advice of Tanemahuta, the forest god, prevailed and Ranginui and Papatuanuku were merely forced apart.

Rasnu

God of passage and justice. Persian [Iran]. The guardian of the bridge that leads to the otherworld. He weighs souls in the scales at the final judgment.

Rati

Goddess of sexual desire. Hindu (Epic and Puranic). A daughter of Daksa (in some texts Siva) and the consort of the god Kamadeva. One of twelve *Saktis* associated with the god Visnu in his various incarnations. Attribute: a sword.

Ratnapani *(with a jewel in the hand)*

God. Buddhist. A form of Ratnasambhava and also a *dhyanibodhisattva* or meditation *buddha*. Color: yellow or green. Attributes: a jewel and the moon disc.

Ratnaparamita

Philosophical deity. Buddhist. Spiritual offspring of Ratnasambhava. Color: red. Attributes: jeweled staff and moon on a lotus.

RATNASAMBHAVA *(born of a jewel)*

Origin Buddhist [India]. The third *dhyanibuddha* or meditation *buddha*.

Known period of worship circa 500 BC until present.

Synonyms Ratnaheruka.

Center(s) of cult pan-Asiatic.

Art references metal and stone sculptures; paintings.

Literary sources *Sadhanamala* and Tantric ritual texts.

One of five mystic spiritual counterparts of a human *buddha* in Vajrayana Buddhism. A product of the Adibuddha who represents the branch of the cosmos concerned with sensation. He originates from the yellow mantra symbol TRAM and lives in the southern paradise. The head of a group of deities who carry jewels and are family symbols, his *Sakti* is Mamaki and he is normally accompanied by two lions or horses. Color: yellow. Attributes: jewel and three monkish robes. Ratnasambhava is also taken as a tutelary deity in Lamaism [Tibet] in which case his attributes include a bell and a jewel. Emanations include Aparajita, Jambhala, Mahapratisara, the *paramitas*, Prasannatara, Ratnapari,Vajratara, Vajrayogini and Vasudhara. (See also Aksobhya, Amitabha, Amoghasiddhi and Vairocana.) Color: yellow. Attributes: bell and jewel.

Ratnolka *(jewel meteor)*
Goddess of light and deification of literature. Buddhist. One of a group of *dharanis*. Color: yellow. Attribute: jeweled staff.

Ratnosnisa
God. Buddhist. An *usnisa* deity apparently linked with the guardian sky deities or *dikpalas* in the southern direction. Color: blue.

Ratri
Goddess of the night. Hindu (Vedic). Ratri is the personification of darkness bedecked with stars. Her sister is Usas, the dawn goddess, who, with Agni the fire god, chases her away. She is perceived as the guardian of eternal law and order in the cosmos and of the waves of time. She is generally a benign deity who offers rest and renewed vigor, and who may be invoked to ensure safety through the hours of darkness. She deposits the gift of morning dew. She also offers a bleaker aspect as one who brings gloom and barrenness.

Raudna *(rowan tree)*
Goddess. Pre-Christian Lappish. The consort of the thunder god Horagalles.

Raudri
Mother goddess. Hindu (Epic and Puranic). One of a group of nine *navasaktis* who, in southern India, rank higher than the *saptamataras*. She may also equate with the terrifying aspect of Parvati as Durga or Kali.

Rauni
Storm goddess. Finno-Ugrian. Consort of the thunder god Ukko and responsible for rainbows after storms.

Rbhus *(skillful)*
Sun gods. Hindu (Vedic). Identified in the *Rg Veda* as the craftsmen of the gods and linked with the Maruts. They are led by Indra.

RE
Origin Egyptian. Creator god and sun god.

Known period of worship circa 3000 BC until the end of Egyptian history, circa 400 AD.

Synonyms Ra (Roman and Greek); Re-Atum; Re-Khepri; Amun-Re.

Center(s) of cult Heliopolis and elsewhere through the Nile valley.

Art references sculpture, stone reliefs, carvings, wall paintings, papyrus illustrations.

Literary sources Pyramid Texts, coffin texts, etc; the *Westcar* Papyrus.

Re is one of several manifestations of the sun god and creator god of Egypt, emphasizing a fragmented tribal past in the pre-Dynastic period. According to legend he created himself out of the mound that emerged from the primeval ocean. In other depictions he arose as a child from the primeval lotus blossom. He is generally depicted in the form of a falcon wearing the sun disc on its head, surrounded by the serpentine form of the cobra-goddess Wadjet. Re is also perceived as god of the underworld. He is known in some inscriptions as "Re in Osiris, Osiris in Re," in which case he often rides in his boat as a human figure with a ram's head surmounted by a sun disc and accompanied by the cobra goddess. The notion of the "Eye of Re" is a very complex one, suggesting several things including, in essence, his power and perfection.

The cult of Re took on major importance at Heliopolis from the middle of the third millennium when the V Dynasty rulers entitled themselves as the sons of Re. Closely linked with the underworld god Osiris, the notion took shape that the combined deity was Re by day as the sun climbed above the eastern horizon and became Osiris, lord of the western horizon, at the onset of night.

Re was regarded with a considerable amount of fear. The cobra element suggests his ability to deliver instant retribution. By contrast, he is said to have created mankind from his tears. Several minor deities were also, by repute, generated out of drops of blood falling from Re's penis, which he self-mutilated (see Sia).

Redarator

Minor god of agriculture. Roman. Associated with second ploughing and invoked by sacrifice, generally with Tellus and Ceres.

Renenutet

Snake goddess. Egyptian. Also possessing fertility connotations, she guarded the pharaoh in the form of a cobra. There is some evidence that she enjoyed a cult in the Faiyum, the highly fertile region of the Nile valley. She is depicted either in human form or as a hooded cobra, in which case she bears close association with the goddess Wadjet who is embodied in the *uraeus*. Her gaze has the power to conquer enemies. In her capacity as a fertility goddess she suckles infant rulers and provides good crops and harvests, linked in this capacity to Osiris and the more ancient grain god Neper. She is also a magical power residing in the linen robe of the pharaoh and in the linen bandages

with which he is swathed in death. At Edfu she takes the title "lady of the robes." In the Greco-Roman period, Renenutet became adopted by the Greeks as the goddess Hermouthis and was syncretized with Isis.

Reret

See Taweret.

Rešep (A)Mukal

War and plague god. Western Semitic (Canaanite and Phoenician), originating in Syria. Introduced into Egypt by the XVIII Dynasty during the sixteenth century BC and rapidly achieved some prominence. His wife is Itum and he was also known as Rešep-Amukal and Rešep-Sulman. Rešep is probably modeled on the Mesopotamian Nergal. He is depicted as a youthful, warlike god, often with a gazelle's head springing from his forehead, and with a spear in his right hand. In Egyptian iconography he is depicted wearing the crown of Upper Egypt surmounted in front by the head of a gazelle. He has links with the Theban war god Montu and was thought of as a guardian deity in battle by many Egyptian pharaohs; he is said to have shot firebrands with a bow and arrow. He also exerted a benign influence against disease. The influence of Rešep extended to Cyprus during the pre-Hellenic period and at the time of Hellenization he was allied to and perhaps syncretized with Apollo. Also Rašap, Rešef.

Revanta *(with wealth)*

God of hunters. Hindu. The son of Surya and Sanjna. Known mainly from eastern India and Gujarat, he protects mankind against the dangers of the forest. Infrequently depicted in art.

Revati

Minor goddess of fortune. Hindu (Epic and Puranic). A benevolent *naksatra*; daughter of Daksa and wife of Candra (Soma).

Rhadamanthos

Minor chthonic underworld god. Greco-Roman. One of three judges attending the goddess of justice Themis evaluating the souls of the dead entering Hades.

Rhea

Primordial goddess. Greek. The daughter of Ouranos and Gaia, she is the consort of Kronos and mother of Zeus and other gods of Olympus, known only from the *Theogony* (Hesiod) and *Iliad* (Homer). She is also recognized in Roman literature under the same name. Also Rheie.

Rheie

See Rhea.

Rhiannon

Chthonic horse goddess. Celtic (Irish). The daughter of Hefaidd Hen and consort of Pwyll, she rides upon a white mare and is associated with the underworld and with fertility. May be virtually synonymous with the Romano-Celtic goddess Rigantona whose name means "great queen." Authors suggest she is modeled on the goddess Modron and she partly equates with Epona.

Riddhi   *(prosperity)*

Goddess. Hindu (Epic and Puranic). One of the consorts of Ganesa, but otherwise very close in appearance to Laksmi. She carries Laksmi's attributes when standing alone.

Riddhivasita   *(control of prosperity)*

Minor goddess. Buddhist. One of a group of *vasitas* personifying the disciplines of spiritual regeneration. Color: green. Attribute: moon disc.

Rigisamus

God of war. Romano-Celtic (Gallic). Assimilated with Mars.

Rind

Chthonic goddess. Northern Germanic and Nordic (Icelandic). She is mentioned as a consort of Othin and mother of Vali. Also Rinda; Rindr.

Ritona

Goddess of river fords. Romano-Celtic. Known from inscriptions and associated with the Treveri tribe.

Rohini   *(red)*

1. Minor goddess of fortune. Hindu (Epic and Puranic). A benevolent *naksatra*; daughter of Daksa and wife of Candra (Soma). She is the mother of Budha.
2. Goddess of learning. Jain. One of sixteen *vidyadevi* headed by the goddess Sarasvati.

Roma

Tutelary goddess. Greek and Roman. The deity was actually conceived by the Greeks and shrines were set up at centers including Smyrna and Ephesus.

Rongomatane

God of agriculture. Polynesian (including Maori). He is the father of cultivated food and the special gardener of the *kumara* or sweet potato, which is a vital crop in Polynesia. In New Zealand the first sweet potatoes are offered to Rongomatane. In the traditions of the Hervey Islands, Rongo is one of the five sons of the moon god, Vatea, and the mother goddess, Papa.

Rosmerta   *(great provider)*

Fertility goddess. Romano-Celtic (Gallic and British). Consort to the god Mercury. Probably locally worshiped and often depicted carrying a basket of fruit, purse or cornucopia. She and Mercury frequently appear together. In addition to her purse, she may bear a twin-headed ax or, alternatively, she may carry Mercury's *caduceus* (snake-entwined wand).

Rsabha   *(the bull)*

God. Hindu (Epic and Puranic). An unusual *avatara* of Visnu. Said to be similar to the Jain deity Rsabhanatha and therefore may represent an attempt to meld the two religions by absorbing Jainism locally.

Rubanga

Creator god. Alur [Uganda and Zaire, Africa]. His sacred bird is the ibis.

Ruda

Tutelary god. Pre-Islamic northern Arabian. An androgynous being symbolized by the evening star. Also Arsu (Palmyra).

Rudiobus

Probably a horse god. Romano-Celtic (Gallic). Known from an inscription at Neuvy-en-Sullias that includes a depiction of a stallion.

Rudra   *(howler)*

Weather god. Hindu (Vedic). An early deity, largely superseded by Siva, who controls gales and storms. Often linked with the fire god Agni and the rain god Indra. Generally a malignant god, Rudra lives in the mountains and is deemed to be either tall or dwarf, depending on the severity of the storm. He brings death and disease to man and domestic animals through his "thousand shafts," and is considered to be highly unpredictable.

Rudracandra

Distinct form of the goddess Durga. Hindu. One of a group of nine *navadurgas*, known as the "nine durgas."

Rudracarcika

Mother goddess. Hindu (Puranic). One of the *astamataras*, alternatively a variety of the goddess Durga.

Rudrani

Goddess. Hindu. An epithet of Durga, impersonated by a young prepubescent girl in the Durga festivals.

Rugievit

Local tutelary and war god. Slav. Identified by the historian Saxo Grammaticus as inhabiting the island of Rügen, depicted with seven heads and carrying a sword.

Ruhanga

Creator god. Bunyoro [Uganda, East Africa]. The initiator of the world, he is regarded as a distant figure and seldom invoked.

Rukmini   *(with gold ornaments)*

Goddess. Hindu (Epic and Puranic). The daughter of Bhismaka, she is the first consort of Krsna and typically stands to his right. Her son is Kama. She is also an *avatara* of Laksmi. Attribute: a lotus. Also Rukmabayi.

Rumina

Minor goddess. Roman. Associated with breast-feeding.

Rundas

God of fortune. Hittite and Hurrian. Also associated with hunting, he is symbolized by a double eagle carrying prey in its talons.

Rupini

Minor goddess. Buddhist (Mahayana). An attendant of Buddhakapala.

Ryangombe

Tutelary god. Rwanda [East Africa]. An ancestral deity and king of the spirit world who has an oracular capacity.

Ryujin

Dragon god. Shinto [Japan]. A deity controlling thunder and rain and probably the most significant of the group of weather gods known as the Raijin. He is of Chinese origin and more Buddhist than Shinto. He does not appear in the sacred Shinto texts *Kojiki* or *Nihongi*, but enjoys shrines in many Shinto sanctuaries and is worshiped by farmers, particularly in times of drought. He lives in the sea, lakes and large ponds from which he ascends in mists and winds. He generates dark rain clouds that then burst. His main festival takes place in June.

S

Sa

Chthonic creator god. Kono [eastern Guinea, West Africa]. One of a pair of creator deities, with Alatangana. Sa inhabited the primeval swamps before the sky or the light existed and before there were any living things on earth. He had a daughter who eloped with Alatangana and bore fourteen children, three pairs of black and four pairs of white, all of whom spoke different languages and to whom Sa gave the tools of survival.

SABAOTH

Origin Gnostic Christian [eastern Mediterranean]. Creator god.

Known period of worship uncertain origins until circa 400 AD.

Synonyms none, but see below.

Center(s) of cult undefined cells within the area of early Christian influence.

Art references none.

Literary sources *Nag Hammadi* codices.

Sabaoth, in Gnostic cosmogony, is one of the seven offspring of the "primal parent" Yaldabaoth. The narrative that emerges in such works as *Origin of the World* is confused and in places contradictory. Sabaoth rebelled against his father, who had become arrogant and impious, and backed the primordial female force Sophia who, having been responsible for Yaldabaoth, was horrified at what she had created. She describes Yaldabaoth as "a blind god, Samael." Sabaoth is joined by seven benign archangels and in the first great battle of the cosmos comes to rule over all, including the forces of chaos. Arguably Sabaoth equates to the god of Israel, Yhwh.

Sabazios

God. Phrygian [northwestern Turkey]. Eventually Hellenized, identified with Zeus and Dionysos and linked with Dionysiac mysteries, appearing in Athens from circa 400 BC. His device is a right hand cast in bronze and decorated with symbols representing his benevolence. His influence extended into Roman culture where he reached a height of popularity circa 200 AD. As late as 300 AD there are frescoes of Sabazios in the tomb of Vibia, whose husband was a priest of the god's cult.

Sadaksari (Lokesvara)

Variety of Avalokitesvara. Buddhist-Lamaist [Tibet]. The form of Avalokitesvara that is incarnate in the succession of Dalai Lamas. Color: white. Attributes: book, conch, jewel, lotus and rosary.

Sadbhuja-Sitatara

God. Buddhist. An emanation of Amoghasiddhi and a variety of Sitatara. Color: white. Attributes: arrow, blue lotus, bow, image of Amoghasiddhi on crown, lotus and rosary. Three-headed.

Sadhumati *(good)*

Minor goddess. Buddhist (Vajrayana). One of several deified *bhumis* recognized as different spiritual spheres through which a disciple passes. Color: white. Attributes: staff, and sword on a blue lotus.

Sadrapa

God of healing. Western Semitic (Syrian) and Pontic. He is depicted on reliefs as a youth holding a scorpion or snake. Known originally from Palmyra, his popularity spread to Carthage and, during the Hellenic period, to the Greek coast. Also Satrapis (Greek).

Sagaramati *(mind of the ocean)*
God. Buddhist. A *bodhisattva* or *buddha*-designate. Color: white. Attributes: conch, and sword with staff.

Sahar
Moon god. Western Semitic (Aramaic). Known from inscriptions.

Sai' Al Qaum *(the good and beautiful god who does not drink wine)*
Local guardian deity. Western Semitic (Nabataean). Known from two inscriptions at Palmyra that suggest him to be a protector of caravans. Attributes include a helmet. He may have developed from an Egyptian god Sai (Greek: Psais).

Sajara
Rainbow god. Songhai [eastern Mali, West Africa]. Perceived as a rainbow-colored snake and symbolized by a tree where white rams are sacrificed and hung. The animals' blood is sprinkled on the tree. The ritual is accompanied by a rain dance.

SAKHMET *(the powerful one)*
Origin Egyptian. Goddess of war.

Known period of worship circa 3000 BC until the end of Egyptian history circa 400 AD.

Synonyms Sachmet; possibly Šesmetet.

Center(s) of cult Heliopolis, Memphis and other sanctuaries along the Nile valley.

Art references sculptures, particularly at Karnak from sixteenth century BC onward; wall paintings, royal tombs at Thebes, etc.

Literary sources coffin texts, royal tombs at Thebes, etc.

Sakhmet is a significant deity in the Egyptian New Kingdom at Memphis. Her father is the sun god Re and she is the consort of Ptah. She is, by implication, the mother of the god of the primordial lotus blossom, Nefertum. In iconography Sakhmet is generally depicted in human form, but with the head of a lioness surmounted by a sun disc. Occasionally she is drawn with a rosette pattern over each breast (see Ištar).

Sakhmet is, to an extent, syncretized with the goddess Mut, who is the consort of the sun god of Thebes, Amun. In the Karnak complex large numbers of Sakhmet's statues, typically hewn in black granite and in which she holds the *ankh* symbol of life or a papyrus stem, were raised in the precinct of the Mut sanctuary.

She is said to breathe fire against the enemies of the pharaoh and, like Hathor in her attempt to destroy the human race, she can be the vengeful "eye of Re." She is sometimes linked with Hathor who is described as the "mistress of the house of Sakhmet." In a more benign aspect, Sakhmet is a guardian goddess against disease.

Šakka(n)
God of cattle. Mesopotamian (Babylonian-Akkadian). A patron god of herdsmen, probably deriving from the Sumerian god Lahar. Also Amakandu; Sumuqan.

Sakra *(the mighty one)*
God. Buddhist. The god of the month *asvina* and an epithet of the Vedic god Indra.

Sakti *(energy)*
Personification of a god. Hindu, Jain and Buddhist. The effective power, or creative force, of a deity in a female aspect. In a more specific context, the *Sakti* identifies the creative force of the god Siva, particularly the *ugra* or violent aspects Durga and Kali. The *Sakti* may frequently have the same characteristics and carry the same attributes as the principal god. In Tantrism, the unity of opposites is defined by the *Sakti*, which is the *yoni* or female sexuality that unites with the male *lingam* of Siva.

Sakumo

God of war. Gan [Accra region, Ghana, West Africa]. The guardian deity of the Gan tribe.

Sakyamuni *(the sage of the Sakyas)*

God. Buddhist-Lamaist [Tibet]. The historical *buddha*, known mainly from Tibet. He stands upon a lotus. Color: golden. Attribute: a bowl.

Šala

War goddess. Mesopotamian (Babylonian-Akkadian). A consort of Adad, she carries a double-headed mace-scimitar embellished with lion heads.

Salagrama

Aniconic form of the god Visnu. Hindu (late). A fossil ammonite shell embodying the god and forming a part of daily ritual in many Vaisnava households as well as appearing in monasteries.

Salevao

Primordial god of rocks. Polynesian. He is the brother of Savea Si'uleo, god of the dead, and the consort of Papatuanuka, the earth mother, who became pregnant and gave birth to Moa in the center of the earth. (Moa may have been the ancestor of mankind, roughly equating to Adam.)

Šalim

God of evening. Western Semitic (Syrian). Generally linked with Šar, the god of dawn.

Salm of Mahram *(image of Mahram)*

Local tutelary god. Pre-Islamic northern Arabian. Correspondence of the Babylonian king Nabonidus (559–539 BC) mentions that this deity was worshiped at Taima, an important trade and religious center where he was head of the pantheon. Gods in the region were often named after local places and personified by a stone stele carved with schematic anthropomorphic features and a winged disc showing strong Egyptian influence. Also Salman.

Salus *(salvation)*

Minor god of health. Roman. A sanctuary dated to 302 BC on the Quirinal, one of the seven hills of Rome, is dedicated to the deity. He was also worshiped within the colonies of the empire. There is an altar at Corbridge in Northumberland, England with a votive inscription to Salus. Attributes include a bowl and a snake.

Sama

Obscure heroic god. Dravidian (Tamil) [southern India]. Known circa first to fifth century AD. The younger brother of the god of love Kama and equating to Samba, worshiped in northern India.

Samael

Creator god. Gnostic Christian. The "blind god." See Yaldabaoth.

Samantabhadra *(all-good)*

God. Buddhist. A form of Vairocana and a *dhyanibodhisattva* (spiritual meditation *buddha*). He sits on a throne carried by a white elephant. Color: blue, green or white. Attributes: bell, cup, jewel, lotus with prayer wheel or sword. In Tibet he is also known as Kun-tu-bzan-po. See also Bo Hsian.

Samantaprabha *(possessing universal splendor)*

Minor goddess. Buddhist (Vajrayana). One of several deified *bhumis* recognized as different spiritual spheres through which a disciple passes. Color: red. Attributes: an image of Amitabha carried in the hand, and a staff.

Šamaš

Sun god. Mesopotamian (Babylonian-Akkadian). The patron deity of Sippar and Larsa. His consort is the mother goddess A-a. Šamaš derives from the god Utu in the Sumerian pantheon. He is associated with justice. His symbol is the sun disc and a star surrounded with radiating sunbeams. He may carry a single-headed scimitar embellished with a panther head. His sanctuary is known as the *E-babbar*. Also associated with human-headed bulls. His attendant deities include Mešaru, justice, and Kettu, righteousness. He came to much greater prominence in the pantheon at Babylon from about the eighteenth century BC.

Samba
Heroic god. Hindu [northern India]. The son of Krsna and Rukmini, alternatively the son of Visnu. The younger brother of the god Kama and consort of Indukari. Also one of the minor incarnations of Visnu worshiped in the cult of the *pancaviras* by the Vrisni clans.

Samkarsana
Localized form of Balarama. Dravidian (Tamil) [southern India and Sri Lanka]. Has a complexion "white like milk," wears a blue robe with a red garland and carries a *nanjil* (plough).

Sampsa *(sedge)*
Vegetation god. Pre-Christian Finnish. He is perceived as a giver of life to seed that lies dormant through the winter months. His unnamed consort, to whom he is wed in a form of sacred marriage that takes place at sowing time, is also his stepmother.

Šams
Sun deity. Pre-Islamic Arabian. In the north the being is male, in the south female. Probably derived from Šamaš.

Samvara *(keeping out)*
God. Buddhist (Mahayana). One of the emanations of Aksobhya and also of Hevajra. In Lamaism he is a four-headed tutelary *yi-dam* god. His *Sakti* is Vajravarahi. He stands upon one or more four-armed Hindu deities including Kalaratri and Bhairava. Color: blue or black. Attributes: ax, bell, cup, drum, image of Aksobhya on the crown, image of four-faced Brahma, knife, moon disc, skin, staff and trident.

San Chou Niang Niang
Mother goddess. Chinese. First deified during the Sung Dynasty (960–1279 AD) to combat the popularity of Kuan Yin, no mortal existence is recog-

nized for this deity who is referred to simply as "heavenly mother." By tradition she rules over the "islands of the blessed," the three mythical islands that are the home of the gods. She is depicted wearing a yellow robe signifying imperial rank and carries the attribute of a scepter. Typically she displays an enigmatic smile.

gSan Sgrub
God. Bon and Lamaist [Tibet]. Originally a Bon deity who became syncretized as a variety of the god Yama in Lamaism. His animal is the bull and he may appear bull-headed. Color: red. Attributes: cup, knife and prayer wheel.

Sandhya
Goddess. Hindu (Epic and Puranic). The daughter of Brahma and consort of Siva or other deities.

San-Dui
Tutelary god. Buddhist-Lamaist [Tibet]. One of a group of Lamaist tutelary or *yi-dam* deities chosen on an individual basis as personal guardians. Color: blue. Attributes: bell, jewel, lotus, prayer wheel, regal trappings, staff and sword. Three-eyed and three-headed.

Sangarios
River god. Phrygian [northwestern Turkey]. A Hellenized version of an Asiatic god whose daughter, Nana, is, according to some traditions, the mother of the vegetation god Attis. She impregnated herself with an almond seed.

Sango
God of thunder. Yoruba [Nigeria, West Africa]. His sacred animal is the ram whose bellowing is likened to the noise of thunder. Attributes include an ax that is worn on the head and bears six eyes.

Sani
1. Astral god. Hindu. The son of Surya and Chaya and the personification of the planet Saturn. Stands upon a lotus or rides in an iron chariot drawn by eight spotted horses. Color: black or blue. Attributes: arrow, bow, rosary, staff and trident.

2. Astral god. Buddhist. Stands upon a tortoise. Color: blue-black. Attribute: a staff.

Saning Sari

Rice mother. Javan. Represented by parts of the rice plant known as *indoea padi* (mother of the rice). At planting, the finest grain is picked out and sown in the nursery bed in the form of the goddess, after which the rest of the grain is sown round about. At transplanting, the shoots making up the rice mother are given a similar special place in the paddy field. At harvest, the rice mother plants are "found" and brought home for the following year's planting.

Sanjna   *(conscience)*

Goddess. Hindu. The daughter of Tvastar, a consort of Surya and, in some texts, the mother of Yama.

Sanju

Harvest goddess. Kafir [Afghanistan]. A little-reported deity, the consort of the war god Gish and daughter of Sanu. She controls the harvesting, threshing and winnowing of grain and the safe storage of wheat and butter. She carries a golden winnow and is either depicted in human form or as a goat. Her cult is known chiefly from the village of Pronz in the southern Hindukush where she enjoyed an important sanctuary with stone seats around the icon, part of which reportedly still exists. Wooden statues depict her in human form, nude to the waist. Alternatively, she is perceived as a bird that acts as a messenger. The blood of sacrificial animals was poured over the figure. Also Sulmech.

Sankari

Mother goddess. Hindu (Epic and Puranic). One of the *saptamataras*.

Sankha(pala)

Snake god. Hindu (Epic and Puranic). One of a group of seven *mahanagas* or *nagadevas*. Attributes: cup and rosary. Three-eyed.

Sanmukha   *(six-headed)*

God. Hindu (Epic and Puranic). A form of Skanda and the son of Pasupati and Svaha. God of the month *asadha*. His *Saktis* include Vijaya and Jaya. He holds a large variety of attributes. Also Arumukan.

Santa   *(appeased)*

Mother goddess. Hindu (Epic and Puranic). A *Sakti* who is one of a group of both *saptamatara* and *astamatara* mothers. Also Camunda.

Santana   *(offspring)*

Minor god. Hindu. The son of Ugra and Diksa. Also the personification of one of the five trees of paradise.

Santi   *(peace of mind)*

Goddess. Hindu. The consort of Trivikrama.

Santoshi Mata

Mother goddess. Modern Hindu. She first appeared in northern India in 1960 and has since developed a sizeable cult following. She is invoked to assist in gaining personal advancement and prosperity.

Sanu

God of obscure affinities. Kafir [Afghanistan]. The father of the goddess Sanju and an adversary of the war god Gish. Described as a "Muslim," so perhaps of foreign import. Also Sanru.

Sao Ching Niang Niang

Mother goddess. Chinese. One of the "nine dark ladies" of the pantheon who adopt a protective role. She removes rain clouds when they threaten to flood crops.

Šapaš

Sun god. Western Semitic (Canaanite). Modeled on the Mesopotamian (Babylonian-Akkadian) god Šamaš.

Saptamatara

Generic title of a group of mother goddesses. Hindu (Epic and Puranic). Seven deities of evil influence, who generally inflict disease or other harm on children. Common color: red. Attributes: cup and lotus.

Šar

God of the the dawn. Western Semitic (Syrian). Generally linked with the god of evening, Šalim.

Šara

Minor war god. Mesopotamian (Sumerian and Babylonian-Akkadian). Mainly identified with the city of Umma, north-east of Unug (Uruk), and identified in some texts as the son of Inana (Ištar).

Saraddevi   (goddess of autumn)

Fertility and vegetation goddess. Buddhist-Lamaist [Tibet]. Associated with autumn, and an attendant of the goddess Sridevi. Her sacred animal is an antelope. Attributes: cup, knife and peacock feather.

Sarama   (the nimble one)

Attendant goddess. Hindu (Vedic, Epic and Puranic). She acts as a messenger to the god Indra and guards his herds. In later Hindu texts Sarama is reputedly the mother of all dogs and is given the epithet the "bitch of heaven." The *Rg Veda* accounts her as having punished the minor deity Panis for stealing cows.

Saranyu   (the fleet one)

Primordial goddess of uncertain affinities. Hindu (Vedic). Saranyu is the daughter of the god Tvastar, and the sister of Visvarupa. Her consort is Vivasvat, by whom she is said to be the mother of Yama and Yami, the twin progenitors of the human race. Little else is known of her, but she is accounted as having an impetuous nature.

Sarapis

God. Late Egyptian. Known only from the Greco-Roman period of the early Ptolemys (fourth century BC) but persisting in Europe until second or third century AD. In Egyptian religion Sarapis is a hybridization of certain aspects of Osiris, the underworld god, and Apis, the bull god, who symbolizes the earthly presence of Ptah. Sarapis is perceived to epitomize both the fertility of the land and the life of the sacred bull after death. In Greek mythology he takes on aspects of Zeus, Helios, Asklepios and Dionysos. He was worshiped extensively in the Roman Empire period. A sanctuary at York in England was dedicated by a soldier of the sixth legion, and magnificent statues were discovered in the Walbrook Mithraeum in London, and at Merida in Spain. Also Seraphis (Greek).

SARASVATI   (flowing water)

Origin Hindu (Vedic, Epic, and Puranic) [India]. Mother goddess and goddess of wisdom. Later, patron of the arts.

Known period of worship circa 600 BC, but undoubtedly based on much earlier prehistoric models, until present.

Synonyms Brahmi; Vagdevi (goddess of speech). Other epithets include Bharati.

Center(s) of cult throughout India.

Art references sculptures generally in bronze, but also in stone. Reliefs.

Literary sources *Rg Veda* and other Vedic texts; *Ramayana* epic and Puranic texts.

Sarasvati, as an identifiable personality, may have begun as a Vedic river goddess (the actual river Sarasvati has now disappeared but she may also be linked with the Indus, etc.). In the Vedic capacity her waves are said to smash mountains and her voice is the roar of the torrent. Since her source of strength is the primeval water, she is inexhaustible and she is a bringer of fertility and bountiful harvests. Thus, by inference, she also provides prosperity. Her presence purifies and, in antiquity, she slew Vrtra, the demonic god of chaos. In her capacity as a Vedic goddess she is invoked on the sacrificial field with the lesser goddesses Ila, Bharati, Mahi and Hotra.

In later Puranic literature Sarasvati (Brahmi) becomes the first consort of the creator god Brahma (see also Gayatri). Other texts offer her in contention with Laksmi as consort of Visnu. She also became syncretized with the goddess Vac. She is said to have invented Sanskrit and is identified as goddess of wisdom and of the arts. The Vedas are her inspiration and she may be known as the "mother of the Vedas." A Hindu festival in her honor is celebrated in early January or late February. She is a patron goddess of students, and books, pencils and pens are offered to her by children before they begin classes. Her image often appears on the portals of school gates.

She is generally depicted with either two or four arms. Color: white. She may be seated or ride upon a swan or a peacock or a lotus. Attributes include particularly the lute but also arrow, bell, book, bow, conch, club, hook, prayer wheel, rosary, water jar and other items. She may offer a piece of sugar cane or a flower to Brahma. Infrequently three-headed.

Sarpanitu(m)
See Zarpanitum.

Šarra Itu
Fertility goddess. Mesopotamian (Sumerian and Babylonian-Akkadian). Originally the tutelary deity of the city of Šu-Sin. By Hellenistic times she probably became the more important goddess Sarrahitu who is included in the pantheon at Uruk and mentioned in various cult texts where she is described as "the bride" and was presumably involved in a sacred marriage ceremony.

Šarrahitu
See Šarra Itu.

Sarritor
Minor god of agriculture. Roman. Invoked during growing and harvesting of crops.

Šarruma
God. Hittite and Hurrian. Originally a Hurrian deity adopted by the Hittite state religion. The son of the weather god Tešub and his consort Hebat. His sacred animal is a panther. Attribute: ax.

Sarvabuddhadharma-Kosavati
(with the virtues of all the buddhas)
God of literature. Buddhist. The deification of texts. One of a group of *dharanis*. Color: yellow. Attributes: basket of jewels and staff.

Sarvakarmavaranavisodhani *(washing away the obstruction of all deeds)*
God of literature. Buddhist. The deification of texts. One of a group of *dharanis*. Color: green. Attribute: staff.

Sarvanivaranaviskambhin
(remover of stain)
God. Buddhist (Mahayana). A *dhyanibodhisattva* or spiritual meditation *buddha*. Color: white. Attributes: book, jewel, moon disc, sword and staff.

Sarvapayanjaha *(remover of miseries)*
God. Buddhist (Mahayana). A *dhyaniboddhisattva* or spiritual mediation *buddha*. Color: white. Attribute: hook in two hands.

Sarvasokatamonirghatamati *(destroyer of sorrow)*
God. Buddhist. A *dhyanibodhisattva* or spiritual meditation *buddha*.

Sarvastramahajvala *(the great blaze of all weapons)*
Goddess of learning. Jain [India]. One of sixteen *vidyadevi* headed by the goddess Sarasvati.

Sasanadevata
Messenger goddess. Jain [India]. Generic name for one of a group of twenty-four who minister to the *tirthankaras* or saints of Jainism.

Sasuratum
Midwife goddesses. Western Semitic (Canaanite). A group of seven female deities fathered by Baal. Also Kosharot (Hebrew).

Satabhisa

Minor goddess of fortune. Hindu (Epic and Puranic). A malevolent *naksatra*; daughter of Daksa and wife of Candra (Soma).

Satarupa *(with a hundred forms)*

Minor goddess. Hindu (Puranic). The daughter of Brahma with whom he committed incest and whose beauty caused him to generate four heads so that he might view her from all directions.

SATI *(truth)*

Origin Hindu (Epic and Puranic) [India]. Mother goddess.

Known period of worship circa 400 AD until present.

Synonyms Sakti, Parvati.

Center(s) of cult none specific.

Art references sculptures generally in bronze, but also in stone.

Literary sources *Ramayana* and other texts.

Sati is the older incarnation of the benign aspect of the goddess Sakti. Alternatively she is perceived as an incarnation of Laksmi. According to legend her father was Daksa and her mother Prasuti. She bore sixteen daughters, the youngest of whom was Sati. She is perceived as an ideal Hindu wife and mother who, as a maiden, falls in love with the god Siva. At her choosing-of-a-husband ceremony she is distressed that her father has not invited Siva and throws her bridal wreath into the air, whereupon Siva appears in front of her. She becomes the consort of Siva, but the marital association is generally recognized when he is in his form known as Bhava, an epithet meaning "existence." Eventually she dies at Daksa's feet from the self-immolating heat of her own purity and zeal. She is reincarnated as Parvati.

The mythology is the basis of the practice of self-sacrifice that came to be known as *sati* or *suttee*. She is also connected with fire-walking rituals.

Satis *[Greek]*

Minor goddess. Egyptian. A guardian of the southern (Nubian) border of Upper Egypt. The consort of the ram god Khnum and, by implication, the mother of Anukis, she is depicted wearing the conical white crown of Upper Egypt, bearing tall plumes or antelope horns. Satis is described in Pyramid Texts, particularly the Step Pyramid at Saqqara, and there is reference to a sanctuary built for her at Elephantine. Also Satjit; Satet (both Egyptian).

Satrughna *(destroyer of foes)*

Minor god. Hindu (Epic and Puranic). The brother of Laksmana and a half-brother to the god Rama. His mother is Sumitra. He may be depicted holding a fly whisk in each hand. See also Laksmana.

Saturnus

Astral god. Roman. Identified with the planet Saturn, but thought to have originated as an agricultural deity concerned with sowing of seed. A sanctuary existed on the Roman forum from as early as 450 BC, also functioning as the imperial treasury. Saturnus was celebrated in the *Saturnalia* festival (December 17–19), during which masters and slaves exchanged roles and candles were given as gifts to symbolize the winter darkness.

Satyabhama *(with true luster)*

Goddess. Hindu-Dravidian (Tamil). Known particularly from southern India as the second consort of Krsna, who stands on her left; also as the second consort of Visnu. Attribute: a flower.

Satyr

Woodland god. Greco-Roman. Generic term for an assortment of divine beings with a human torso and the legs, hair and horns of a goat. They include the god Pan and the demigod Silenus who raised the adolescent Bacchus.

Saubhagya-Bhuvanesvari *(buddha of good fortune)*

Goddess of good fortune. Buddhist. A gentle and benevolent deity. Color: red. Attributes: red lotus, and water jar with jewels.

Saule

Sun goddess. Pre-Christian Latvian. Also having agricultural links, she is perceived as living on a heavenly farm atop a mythical mountain and invoked to induce fertility and ripening of crops. Her consorts are the sky god Dievs and the moon god Meness.

Šauška

Fertility goddess. Hittite and Hurrian. Of Hurrian origin, Šauška was adopted by the Hittite state religion. She is also identified with war and is particularly renowned as a goddess of healing. She is depicted in human form with wings, standing with a lion and accompanied by two attendants. Šauška is known in detail only because she became the patron goddess of the Hittite king Hattusilis II (1420–1400 BC).

Savari

Goddess of terrifying appearance. Buddhist-Lamaist [Tibet]. One of a group of *gauris*. Color: white. Attributes: holding the mountain known as Meru.

Savea Si'uleo

God of the dead. Polynesian. The brother of Salevao, god of rocks.

Savitar *(impeller)*

Sun god. Hindu (Puranic). The original Vedic list of six descendants of the goddess Aditi or *adityas*, all of whom take the role of sun gods was, in later times, enlarged to twelve, including Savitar. The god of the rising and setting sun. Color: golden. Attributes: club, prayer wheel and two lotuses.

Saxnot

Tutelary god. Saxon. He is mentioned beside Woden and Thunor as one of the deities to be renounced at Christian baptism. As Saxneat he was allegedly the founder of the Saxon royal dynasty in Essex. The name may derive from the word *sahsginot* meaning "companion of the sword." He may also equate with the German god Tyr.

Šay

Minor god of destiny. Egyptian. Depicted wholly in human form. Šay is mentioned in the *Ani* papyrus as being present at the ritual of the weighing of the heart, in company with funerary goddesses including Meskhenet, Šepset and Renenutet. In Greco-Roman times he was syncretized with the snake god Agathos Daimon.

Sebitti

Group of minor war gods. Mesopotamian (Babylonian-Akkadian). The children of the god Anu who follow the war god Erra into battle. They are, in alternative traditions, of good or evil influence. In Greek tradition they become the Pleiades.

Securita

Guardian goddess. Roman. She was invoked to ensure the continuing stability of the Roman empire.

Šed

Guardian god. Egyptian. Popular as a personal deity and often identified on protective amulets.

Sedna

Sea goddess. Eskimo [Baffin Land]. The mother of all the creatures of the sea and invoked by fishermen.

Sefkhet-Abwy
(she who has seven horns)

Local goddess of libraries and writing. Egyptian. Probably a form of the goddess Sešat. Depicted in human form bearing a seven-pointed star or rosette on her head below a bow-shaped object.

Sekhet-Hor

Cow goddess. Egyptian (Lower). The foster mother of the god Horus and particularly invoked to safeguard cattle.

Selardi

Moon god. Urartian [Armenia]. The counterpart of the Mesopotamian deity Sin.

Selene *(radiant)*
Moon goddess. Greek. The daughter of Hyperion (a Titan) and sister of the sun god Helios. The tutelary deity of magicians, she rides in a chariot drawn by two horses. According to legend she fell in love with the sleeping Endymion. She becomes largely syncretized with Hekate and in Roman culture equates with the goddess Luna.

Semele *(earth)*
Mother goddess. Greco-Roman but probably of Thracian or Phrygian origin. According to legend she was the mortal daughter of Cadmos and became the mother of the god Dionysos (Bacchus) after a brief liaison with Zeus (Jupiter) in mortal guise. Semele was burned to death on Olympus, unable to withstand the presence of Zeus in godly form, but was subsequently deified by him.

Semnocosus
God of war. Romano-Iberian. Popular locally with troops of the Roman legions who occasionally sacrificed prisoners to him.

Senx
Sun god. Bella Coola Indian [British Columbia, Canada]. The ruler of the lower heaven, Sonx, in which is situated the home of the gods, Nusmeta (the house of myths). The only deity to whom the Bella Coola pray and make offerings. Hunters throw small pieces of mountain goat or seal flesh into a sacrificial fire. Also Ta'ata (our father); Smai-'yakila (sacred one).

Šepset
Local funerary goddess. Egyptian. Known chiefly at Memphis, where she appears as an attendant at the ritual of the weighing of the heart.

Sequana
River goddess. Romano-Celtic (Gallic). The tutelary goddess of the Sequanae tribe. A pre-Roman sanctuary northwest of Dijon near the source of the Seine has yielded more than 200 wooden votive statuettes and models of limbs, heads and body organs, attesting to Sequana's importance as a goddess of healing. During the Roman occupation the site of Fontes Sequanae was sacred to her and was again considered to have healing and remedial properties. A bronze statuette of a goddess was found wearing a diadem, with arms spread and standing in a boat. The prow is in the shape of a duck, her sacred animal, with a cake in its mouth. Also found were models of dogs, an animal specifically associated with healing through its affinity with the Greco-Roman physician deity Aesculapius.

Šerida
Mother goddess. Mesopotamian (Sumerian). Became known as Aya in the Akkadian pantheon.

Serket(-hetyt)
Minor mortuary goddess. Egyptian. Known from the middle of the third millennium BC, she protects the throne of the king in the guise of a scorpion. She is depicted in human form wearing a headpiece in the form of a scorpion with its sting raised. In the Pyramid Texts she is the mother of the scorpion god Nehebu-Kau. In her role as a mortuary goddess she is partly responsible for guarding the jars containing the viscera of the deceased. Although she is never identified as warding off the effect of scorpion stings, her influence has been regarded as effective against other venomous attacks. Also Selkis (Greek).

Sesa(naga) *(remainder)*
Snake god or *naga*. Hindu (Vedic, Epic and Puranic). The great serpent lying in the primeval sea and encircling the world. The son of Kasyapa and Kadru. A many headed attendant on Visnu who uses the snake as a couch on which to rest between cycles of the universe. Its many hoods overshadow and protect him. Not technically a deity but important enough in literature to be included here. Also Adisesa; Ananta.

Sešat
Goddess of libraries and the art of writing. Egyptian. Known from 2500 BC, or earlier, until the end

of Egyptian history circa 400 AD. She is depicted anthropomorphically bearing a seven-pointed star or rosette on her head, sometimes atop a wand and below a bow-shaped object. Early in her career she was associated with the ritual of "stretching the cord" during which boundary poles were rammed into the ground by the king before measuring out the foundations of a sanctuary. As a scribe she recorded the lists of foreign captives and their tributes. At Karnak in Upper Egypt and at Dendara she recorded the royal jubilees on a notched palm stem. See also Sefkhet-Abwy.

Sese

Chthonic goddess. Ngbandi [Zaire, central Africa]. One of seven deities invoked at sunrise each day.

Šesmetet

Egyptian goddess. See Sakhmet.

Seta

Fertility goddess. Pokot and Suk [Uganda and western Kenya, East Africa]. The consort of the creator god Tororut who is embodied in the Pleiades. Their children are Ilat, the rain god; Arawa, the moon goddess; and Topoh, the evening star. The appearance of the Pleiades in the night sky marks the start of the planting season.

SETH

Origin Egyptian. God of chaos and adversity.

Known period of worship from 3000 BC or earlier until the end of Egyptian history, circa 400 AD.

Synonyms Set, Setekh, Seteš, Šutekh, Suty.

Center(s) of cult chiefly a sanctuary in Upper Egypt at Ombos-Naqada, but also in Lower Egypt, in the northeast of the Nile delta.

Art references sculptures, stone reliefs, wall paintings, etc.

Literary sources Pyramid Texts, coffin texts, *Book of the Dead*, etc.

Seth is a deity who generally represents hostility and violence, but who has also claimed considerable respect. His parents are Geb and Nut and his fellow siblings include Isis, Osiris and Nephthys, who at times is also seen as his consort. More typically he is linked with Semitic war goddesses including Anat and Astarte. Legend has it that he tore himself violently from his mother's womb. He is depicted in human form with the head of an animal that seems to bear faint similarity to an aardvark with erect ears and a long curving snout. He is also depicted in wholly animal form, in which case the beast bears no real similarity to any living creature, but has a stiffly erect tail. Other animals symbolizing the god include the oryx, pig, boar and the hippopotamus when it is a disruptive element of the river. Seth is also represented by the crocodile (see Geb).

Sometime during the middle of the third millennium, in the II Dynasty, there was a break with the tradition whereby the kings of Egypt were linked with the god Horus. The falcon symbolism of Horus was replaced with that of the creature of Seth. Several Egyptian rulers followed his cult closely. Tuthmosis III in the XVIII Dynasty, for example, titled himself "the beloved of Seth."

In the Osirian legend first recorded in the Pyramid Texts and later popularized and embellished by the Greek writer Plutarch, Seth is the jealous adversary of his brother Osiris (see Osiris for details). Later he fought an eighty-year war of attrition with the son of Osiris, the falcon god Horus (see also Horus). During this time, the implication remains that he was favored by the sun god and only forceful wrangling resulted in victory falling to Horus as rightful overlord of the two Egyptian kingdoms. A separate mythology credits Seth with defense of the sun god Re as he is about to be swallowed by Apophis, the perennially hostile serpent god of the underworld. The so-called *Book of the Dead* accounts Seth as the "lord of the northern sky" who controls the storm clouds and thunder.

Rameses II, in a treaty with the Hittites, implied a fusion of Seth with the Hittite storm god Tešub.

Seyon *(the red one)*
Creator god. Dravidian (Tamil) [southern India and Sri Lanka]. An early deity associated particularly with hilly regions in parts of southern India and thought to live in trees. Also Muruga.

Šezmu
Minor god of wine and oil presses. Egyptian. Known from circa 3000 BC until the end of Egyptian history, circa 400 AD. In later iconography he is depicted as a lion, but more generally is in human form. Šezmu had a definite cult following in the fertile Faiyum region of the Nile valley, but was probably represented in most sanctuaries, particularly where ritual unguents were made and stored. He is recognized in both benign and malevolent roles. In the latter he is reputed to squeeze human heads like grapes, but in beneficent mood he provides aromatic oils and ointments.

Sga'na
Sea god. Haida Indian [Queen Charlotte Island, Canada]. Embodied in the killer whale *(Orca)*. The universe is believed to be inhabited by supernatural beings called Sga'na Qeda's for whom the land was first created. Also Masset San.

Shadanana-Subrahmanya
Form of the god Karttikeya. Hindu (Puranic). The form possesses six heads and twelve arms. According to legend, the six heads arose because the fire god Agni had an adulterous relationship with the six consorts of the *risis* (astral gods) who all needed to suckle the offspring. Like Karttikeya, he is usually depicted riding on a peacock.

Shang Kuo-Lao
Immortal being. Taoist (Chinese). One of the "eight immortals" of Taoist mythology, tradition has it that he was embodied as a bat that achieved immortality in human form. His sacred animal is an ass. Attributes include drum and drumsticks. See also Ba Xian.

Shang Ti
Creator god. Taoist (Chinese). See Yu Huang Shang Ti.

Shango
Chthonic storm god. Yoruba [Nigeria, West Africa]. As an earth deity he was once a mortal man, the king of Oyo, who transformed himself into an immortal. According to tradition, during his life he breathed tongues of fire. He then ascended into the sky by climbing a golden chain and became the god of thunder and lightning. He is also god of justice, punishing thieves and liars. His consorts include Oya, Oshun and Oba. Cult followers of Shango are believed to be able to make lightning strike an adversary. In shrines to Shango, the image of the god is adorned with a ram's head. Also Sango.

Shani
Astral god and bringer of misfortune. Hindu (late). The cult of Shani evolved in about the eighth century AD with the advance of Indian astronomy. He is propitiated frequently to ward off ill luck and may be depicted sitting on a lotus or riding in a chariot. Attribute: a staff.

Shankpana
Plague god. Yoruba [Nigeria, West Africa]. The son of Shango, he is credited with having once been a god of war who invaded the country (as a disease). He is particularly identified with smallpox. His symbol is the sesame plant, which takes the form of a taboo and brings disease to anyone who takes it into their house. A festival is held in September to propitiate Shankpana with sacrifices of animals and fruit.

Sheela Na Gig
Mother goddess. Celtic (Irish). The primal earth mother closely associated with life and death. One of the rare depictions of Irish Celtic deities that have survived into the Christian era. She is shown naked, with large breasts, with her legs apart and holding open her vagina. The image frequently adorns walls of Irish churches. Also Sheila na Cioch.

Shen Nung
God of agriculture. Chinese. Known as the divine farmer. According to tradition, during his lifetime

he invented the plough and taught basic agriculture and the use of herbs. In a more destructive aspect, he is also the god of the hot winds. He is depicted with the head of an ox and is regarded by some authors as a successor to Nu Kua. Also Shen Nong.

gShen-Lha-Odkhar
God of light. Bon (pre-Lamaist) [Tibet]. In the ancient religion he is a creator deity from whom all other gods are engendered. In Lamaism he evolves into a god of wisdom.

gShen-Rab
Supreme god. Bon (pre-Lamaist) [Tibet]. In the ancient religion he is the remote and barely defined creator deity. Attributes include a lotus and swastika.

Shichi-Fuku-Jin
Gods of luck. Shinto [Japan]. The seven principal deities concerned with fortune: Ebisu, Daikoku, Benten-San, Bishamon, Fukurokuju, Hotei and Junrojin. The group is often represented together on their treasure ship Takara-Bune, which carries various magical devices including a hat of invisibility, a roll of brocade, an inexhaustible purse, keys to the divine treasure house and so on.

Shina-Tsu-Hiko
God of winds. Shinto [Japan]. The most senior of his group of wind deities, he disperses the morning mists and brings soft rustling breezes. His consort is Shina-Tsu-Hime and the couple are extensively worshiped by farmers and seafarers. They were allegedly responsible for bringing about a miracle in the thirteenth century AD when they kept at bay, with offshore winds, the army of Gengis Khan. They are honored in the main Ise-Jingu temple of Shintoism but their chief sanctuary is at Tatta, a small town in Yamamoto. Also Shina-Tobe-No-Mikoto.

Shina-Tsu-Hime
See Shina-Tsu-Hiko.

Shomde
Creator god of localized observance. Kafir [Afghanistan]. Known from various villages in the southern Hindukush. Shomde is regarded either as equating or senior to the more generally recognized god Imra. According to observers he provides gold, silver and silk as well as butter, cheese, cream and flour. The main sanctuary was probably at the village of Dewa and in various wooden sculptures Shomde is depicted in human form. Also Wushum; Usum.

Shong Li-Kuan
Immortal being. Taoist (Chinese). One of the "eight immortals" of Taoist mythology, he was once a mortal being who achieved immortality through his exemplary life. Attributes include a fan that he waves over the dead to revive them. See also Ba Xian.

Shong-Kui
God of literature. Taoist (Chinese). According to tradition he committed suicide when he failed in his examinations. Also a guardian deity against demons, his attribute is a sword.

Shou Lao
God of longevity. Chinese. He originates as an astral deity but comes to head the heavenly ministry responsible for setting the span of a person's life. He is also known as Nan-ji Hsian Weng, "the ancient of the South Pole." His sacred animal is the crane, embodiment of long life.

Shurdi
Storm god. Illyrian [Albania]. Believed to send thunder and lightning and revered into more recent times.

Si
Moon god. Chimu Indian (pre-Columbian) [coastal regions of Peru]. The head of the pantheon and guardian of weather and of harvests. He is depicted subtended by a sickle moon, wearing a feathered crown and an armored projection on his back. May also be represented as a goddess.

Sia

God of perception. Egyptian. Minor deity depicted at Re's right hand where he holds the papyrus of intellect. He travels in the sun god's boat. According to legend he was one of several deities formed in drops of blood falling from Re's penis.

Ši'a

Minor attendant goddess. Western Semitic (Phoenician). The personification of the holiness of sanctuaries of Baal Šamin. In Hellenic times she may have become syncretized with Tyche.

Siddhi   *(accomplishment, success)*

Minor goddess of good fortune. Hindu (Epic and Puranic). A deity who grants favors. Sometimes associated with the elephant god Ganesa or Maha-Ganapati, on whose knee she may sit. In earlier times she was described as a consort of Bhaga.

Si'duku

Mother spirit. Kamchadal [southeastern Siberia]. The daughter of Kutkhu, Si'duku is the consort of her brother Ti'zil-Kutkhu and the mother of Amle'i. Amle'i married another unnamed daughter of Si'duku and fathered the Kamchadal race.

Siduri

Minor goddess of brewing. Mesopotamian (Babylonian-Akkadian). Also identified with wisdom.

Sif

Grain goddess. Nordic (Icelandic) and Germanic. The consort of Thor. She is mentioned in the Eddaic *Lay of Lokasenna* and in the *Lay of Harbarth*. According to Snorri Sturluson she was originally a prophet called Sibyl. She possesses great beauty and has long golden hair. Her sons are Ull and Loridi. According to tradition, Loki cut off Sif's hair in mischief, but when confronted and threatened by Thor, he had the dwarves make her a magical hairpiece of pure gold that, when it touched her head, became a living part of her and grew.

Sigyn

Goddess. Nordic (Icelandic). The consort of Loki and listed among the Aesir goddesses. Her son is Nari or Narfi. According to tradition, Skadi, the consort of Niord, set a poisonous snake to drip poison on the captive Loki but Sigyn collected most of the venom in a bowl and threw it away.

Sikhandin   *(with a tuft of hair)*

Minor deity. Hindu (Epic and Puranic). One of a group of emancipated *vidyesvaras* (lords of knowledge) considered to be aspects of Siva. Attributes: knife and sword.

Sikhin

Physician god. Buddhist-Lamaist [Tibet]. Accounted among one of a series of medicine *buddhas* or *sMan-bla*. Typically depicted with stretched earlobes. Color: yellowish red.

NOTE: the term also defines the symbolic use of fire.

Silaparamita   *(perfection of character)*

Philosophical deity. Buddhist. Spiritual offspring of Ratnasambhava. Color: white. Attributes: floral prayer wheel and jeweled staff.

Silma Inua

Supreme god. Eskimo. A remote and vaguely defined figure only rarely invoked or prayed to.

Silvanus

Minor god of woodlands and forests. Roman. Worship of Silvanus seems largely to have been limited to northern Italy. He became incorporated into the Celtic pantheon where his symbolism includes a billhook, pots and hammers. His sacred animal is the stag. The name was extended to embrace groups of woodland deities, the Silvani or Silvanae.

Si'mskalin

Guardian spirit. Kamchadal [southeastern Siberia]. One of two sons of Kutkhu.

Sin

Moon god. Mesopotamian (Babylonian-Akkadian). Derived from the older Sumerian model of Nanna. His consort is Nikkal (Ningal). He is symbolized by the new moon and perceived as a bull whose horns are the crescent of the moon. Cult centers are identified at Ur, Harran and Neirab. Also Suen (archaic).

Sina

Moon goddess. Polynesian (Samoan). See Hina.

Sindhu

River goddess. Hindu (Vedic). Identified only in the *Rg Veda* and of unknown source.

Singala

Local god. Pre-Islamic northern Arabian. Mentioned only in name by the Babylonian king Nabonidus, worshiped at Taima and influenced strongly by Egyptian culture. See also Salm.

Sinhanada   *(lion's roar)*

Physician god. Buddhist-Lamaist [Tibet]. A variety of Avalokitesvara. Typically depicted with stretched earlobes and attended by a lion. Color: white. Attributes: cup, fly whisk, image of the Amitabha on the crown, lotus, moon disc, rosary, skin, snake, sword and trident. Three-eyed. Also accounted among one of a series of medicine *buddhas* or *sMan-bla.*

Sinivali

Minor goddess of prosperity. Hindu (Vedic). Associated specifically with the boon of children. The mistress of the nuclear family. She is depicted as a matronly lady.

Sins Sga'nagwai   *(power of the shining heavens)*

Supreme god. Haida Indian [Queen Charlotte Island, Canada]. The god who gives power to all things.

Siofn

Goddess. Nordic (Icelandic). Listed by Snorri (*Prose Edda*) as one of the Aesir goddesses.

Sipe Gialmo

Mother goddess. Bon (pre-Lamaist) [Tibet]. The so-called "queen of the world." Her animal is a mule. Attributes: banner, bowl, parasol, swastika, sword and trident. Three-eyed.

Sipylene

Mother goddess. Smyrna (Anatolia) [west coast of Turkey]. The localized name of the great mother, worshiped in the Metroon sanctuary.

Sirara

Goddess of the Persian Gulf. Mesopotamian (Sumerian and Babylonian-Akkadian). In creation mythology she is given charge over the waters of the Gulf by the god Enki.

Sirona

Local goddess of healing. Romano-Celtic (Gallic). Known from limited inscriptions in which she is usually associated with the god Grannos or with the Celtic Apollo. A sculpture from Hochscheid in the Moselle basin in Germany describes her with a snake round her wrist reaching toward a bowl of three eggs in her left hand. She may also have a small lapdog. Some authors suggest she has sky associations. See also Divona and Onuava.

Sirsir

God of mariners. Mesopotamian (Babylonian-Akkadian). The guardian of boatmen.

Sirtur

Sheep goddess. Mesopotamian (Sumerian and Babylonian-Akkadian). Known from inscriptions and passing comments in texts. Syncretized with Ninsun.

Sisyphos

Sun god. Corinthian. Specifically the god of the faded sun, probably equating to the Hittite weather god Tešub.

SITA   *(furrow)*

Origin Hindu (Epic and Puranic). [India]. Chthonic or earth goddess.

Known period of worship   circa 300 BC and earlier through to present day.

Synonyms   an *avatara* of Laksmi.

Center(s) of cult   none specific.

Art references   sculptures generally in bronze, but also in stone.

Literary sources   *Ramayana of Valmiki* and later Puranic literature.

In Vedic mythology Sita is strictly an earth deity, born from a furrow and associated with ploughing and ploughed fields. She appears as the consort of the rain gods Indra and Parjanya. She usually stands to the right of Rama. In later times, effectively from 200 AD onward, Sita (see also Radha) is the consort of Rama, one of the major reincarnations of the god Visnu, though she is generally eclipsed by the goddess Laksmi with whom she is seen as a separate aspect.

Legend gives Sita an unhappy life, though she epitomizes the perfect Hindu wife. Early in her marriage to Rama she is abducted by the foreign god Ravana, who carries her off to Lanka [Sri Lanka], where he imprisons her in a garden. Maintaining total fidelity to her husband, she returns to him inviolate, but he is sceptical of her purity and rejects her. Eventually, when she has threatened to immolate herself through the inner fire of her purity, Rama grudgingly has her back, though only briefly. His doubts return and, pregnant, she is banished to exile where she gives birth to twin sons. Rama's rejection finally takes its toll. Sita begs her mother, the earth, for salvation, whereupon a golden throne rises from the ground. She takes her place on it and descends forever while Rama is left eternally to mourn his loss. Attributes: blue lotus and a single braid of hair.

Sitala(mata)   *(possibly meaning "mother cold")*
Mother goddess. Hindu (Epic and Puranic). One of seven *Saktis* who in later Hinduism became regarded as of evil intent, inflicting sickness. Particularly known from Bengal where she may be identified with the goddess Kali. Usually standing naked upon a lotus or riding an ass. Alternatively symbolized by a stone on which a face is painted. Attribute: water jar.

Sitapatra   *(with a white umbrella)*
Goddess. Buddhist (Mahayana). An emanation of Vairocana and a female *bodhisattva* or *buddha*-designate. Color: white. Attributes: arrow, bow, hook, noose, parasol, prayer wheel and white staff. Sometimes three-eyed and three-headed.

Sitatara   *(the "white Tara")*
Goddess. Buddhist-Lamaist [Tibet]. Of mild disposition, she is regarded as one of the forms of the goddess Tara and an emanation of Amoghasiddhi or Vairocana. In later times she became identified as a female variety of Avalokitesvara-Padmapani. By tradition she is the incarnation of a Chinese princess. Color: white. Attributes: arrow, blue or white lotus, bow, image of Amoghasiddhi, jewel, moon disc and rosary. Three- or seven-eyed.

SIVA   *(the destroyer)*
Origin   Hindu [India]. Principal creative and destructive god.

Known period of worship   circa 300 BC, and probably earlier as Rudra, until present.

Synonyms   accredited with more than a thousand epithets in Hindu writings (see also Bhairava, Khandoba).

Center(s) of cult   Benares, etc.

Art references   sculptures generally in bronze, but also in stone; reliefs.

Literary sources   *Ramayana* epic and Puranic texts.

Siva is a deity with the linked roles of both creator and destroyer of life, more generally the latter. He personifies the inexorable passage of time and out of destruction he creates new life. He may have evolved from the Vedic storm god Rudra, though he is now thought to be an older pre-Indo-European deity whose attributes appear on seals from the Indus Valley civilization. His consort, or more precisely his female aspect, is Sakti, but he is also closely linked with the terrible Kali and the goddess Sati.

He is generally depicted in the role of an ascetic with a blue-painted throat, attributed to holding the primal poison *halahala* in his throat before swallowing it to save mankind from its deadly effect. His sacred animal is the bull Nandi. He bears four arms (less commonly two) that hold a variety of attributes including a bow, a club to which is fastened a skull, a drum *(damaru)*, representing the rhythm of creation, and a noose. He has a strong association with fire and may hold a ball of flame—the destructive corollary to creation. His symbol is the *linga* (phallus), often accompanied by the female *yoni* and these objects in stone may form the focus of worship.

The Saivite sect envisages Siva as creator, preserver and destroyer and he is manifest in three aspects of his own divine power. As the ascetic, represented by the *Yogi*, he is in his destructive aspect. His consorts are Kali and Durga. He destroys without emotion. The *Yogi* is naked, smeared with ashes and with matted hair, sitting under a banyan tree holding a beggar's bowl. As the "lord of the dance," Nataraja, Siva's steps follow the rhythm of the universal forces. He dances in a circle of fire, treading upon the dwarfish figure who is the personification of ignorance (see also Vamana). In this aspect he can be drawn as a jolly figure, a drinker of wine and a hunter. As the *linga*, the form of Siva that devotees generally worship, he is the symbol of creative powers. In his cosmic capacity he appears as Nataraja.

Legend has it that Siva lives in Kailas, a place beyond the Himalaya. The Lingayats, a particular Saivite sect founded in the twelfth century AD, may carry a small stone *linga* mounted in a silver box and worn round the neck or arm. Chiefly centered on southern India, sanctuaries to Siva are often home to *devadasis*, troupes of dancing girls who also serve as cultic prostitutes. Siva also enjoys popular worship as a domestic deity. See also Pancanana.

Sivini
Sun god. Urartian [Armenia]. Known from inscriptions.

Sivottama   *(highest Siva)*
Minor god. Hindu (Epic and Puranic). One of a group of emancipated *vidyesvaras* (lords of knowledge) considered to be aspects of Siva.

Skadi
Goddess. Nordic (Icelandic). One of the Aesir goddesses. The daughter of the giant Thiassi and consort of the god Njord. By tradition she lives apart from her husband, he preferring the coast and she the mountains. She is described as "ski lady," a huntress who travels on skis and hunts game with a bow. She is constantly at odds with the god Loki and on one occasion, when he had been captured and held down with stones, she tried to poison him by suspending a poisonous snake over his face. Loki's consort Sigyn saved him by collecting the venom in a bowl.

SKANDA
Origin   Hindu (Epic and Puranic) [India]. God of war.

Known period of worship   circa 300 BC or earlier until present.

Synonyms   Kumara; Karttikeya; Subrahmanya; many other minor epithets.

Center(s) of cult   various.

Art references   sculptures generally in bronze, but also in stone.

Literary sources   *Ramayana* and *Mahabharata* epics; Puranic texts.

Regarded as the leader of the divine army of gods. One of the sons of Siva, his birth is accounted in bizarre fashion. The gods persuaded Siva and Parvati to curb their incessant lovemaking. The vast quantity of unused semen then had to be disposed of. After shuttling it between fire (Agni) and water (Ganges), Brahma placed it on the mountain of the rising sun where, after ten millennia, it became Skanda.

His consorts include Kaumari (Devasena) and Valli, and his sons are Sakha, Visakha and Naigameya. Perceived as virile and youthful, his name may signify the emission of semen. He is also seen as "one who jumps" while fighting and his sacred animals include the peacock and the cockerel, the latter being both aggressive and a jumper. Attributes: banner, cockerel, hatchet, peacock feather and staff. He may also carry a wider assortment of objects and weapons. As Karttikeya he is often depicted bearing six heads and twelve arms.

Smertrios
God of war. Celtic (Gallic). The tutelary deity of the Treveri. Allegedly the subject of a votive monument that depicts a bearded god holding a snake.

Smrti *(tradition)*
Minor god. Buddhist (Mahayana).

Snulk'ulxa'ls
Archetypal god. Bella Coola Indian [British Columbia, Canada]. The old ruler of mankind, who provided a conflict of benign and malevolent treatment. He was superseded by the gods Senx and Alk'unta'm.

So
Weather god. Ewe and Hua [Togo and southeastern Ghana, West Africa]. An emanation of the combined personae of the deities Sogblen and Sodza.

Sobek *(rager)*
God epitomizing the might of the pharaohs. Egyptian. Said to be the son of Neith, the creator goddess of Sais. He is depicted as a crocodile wearing a plumed headdress, or as a part-human hybrid. The crocodile imagery suggests an ability to attack and kill with sudden speed. Sobek's cult was extensive along the Nile valley, but was particularly prominent in the fertile Faiyum region. Near Aswan in Upper Egypt a sanctuary dedicated to Sobek identifies him as the consort of Hathor and the father of Khonsu. Also Suchos (Greek).

Sodasi *(girl of sixteen)*
Minor goddess. Hindu (Epic and Puranic). One of a group of *mahavidyas* personifying the *Sakti* of Siva. Aspects include Divyaratri.

Sodza
Sky god. Ewe [Togo, West Africa]. Propitiated with yams and the sacrifice of a white sheep in an annual festival and his priests pray to him weekly to send rain. The priests wear white robes.

Sogblen
Messenger god. Ewe and Hua [Togo and southeastern Ghana, West Africa]. Considered to relay the prayers of devotees to the great gods and to return with blessings or punishment. Generally benevolent, bringing the boon of fertile crops and children. He is propitiated with the sacrifice of a white sheep in an annual festival.

Sogbo
Storm god. Fon [Benin, West Africa]. The sibling of the gods Lisa and Mawu, he controls thunder and lightning and is a god of fire and rain.

Sohodo-No-Kami
God of scarecrows. Shinto [Japan]. Identified as the apotheosis of the actual scarecrow made by Japanese farmers and known as a *kakashi*. Traditionally it is constructed from reeds and wears a round peasant hat. According to the sacred texts, "though his legs do not walk he knows everything under heaven."

Sokar
Chthonic underworld god. Egyptian. Guardian deity of the necropolis at Memphis with possible fertility connotations and with strong links to Osiris

beside whom he is also perceived as a restored god of the dead. He is also syncretized with the Memphis creator god Ptah in the Old Kingdom (circa 4500 BC), where he may have originated as a god of various crafts associated with the manufacture of funerary trappings. He is depicted either as a hawk on a boat, or in human form with the head of a hawk and an elaborate *atef* crown (see Osiris). Sokar also enjoyed a major cult at Thebes where, in an annual festival celebrating the healthy continuation of the divine kingship, he was conveyed in an elaborate boat. Also Sokaris (Greek).

Soko

Sky god. Nupe [Nigeria, West Africa]. The name refers specifically to the dark sky that stimulates the growth of crops at the beginning of the rainy season.

Sol   *(1)*

Sun god. Roman. Known by the full title of Sol Indiges, meaning "the indigenous Sol," which may suggest a purely Roman cult on the Quirinal Hill, but there are also indications that this deity is of more ancient origin. Coins from southern Italy depicting the god with a radiate image date back to circa 200 BC but he rose to particular prominence during the republican period. His festival was celebrated annually on August 9. Nero had a huge statue of himself, as Sol, erected in Rome and the emperor Aurelian elevated Sol to supreme god in the Roman pantheon when *Jupiter Conservator* gave way to *Sol Invictus* (the unconquered sun). Sol may sometimes be linked with Aurora, the goddess of dawn.

Sol   *(2)*

Sun goddess. Nordic (Icelandic). One of the Aesir goddesses. The daughter of Nubdilfaeri (Mundilferi). She drives the horses that draw the sun chariot across the sky.

Soma   *(essence)*

Minor god. Hindu (Vedic, Epic and Puranic). The deification of the sacred yellow drink *soma*. Also the consort of Surya. Regarded in later Hinduism

as the *dikpala* of the northern direction and as one of a group of *vasu* deities answering to the god Indra. Attributes: hook, lotus and prayer wheel. See also Candra.

Somaskanda

God. Hindu (Epic and Puranic). Aspect of the god Siva. Of uncertain origin, but possibly representing a composite trio of Siva with his consort Uma (Parvati) and his son Skanda (as a boy). Four-armed. Attributes of Siva: ax, corpse and hatchet. Attribute of Uma: lotus. Attributes of Skanda: book, headdress, mango fruit and ornament.

Somnus

Minor god of sleep. Roman. He equates with the Greek god Hypnos. According to legend he is one of the two sons of Nyx, goddess of night, and lives in a remote cave beside the Lethe river. He is depicted by Ovid dressed in black but with his robe scattered with stars, wearing a crown of poppies and holding a goblet of opium juice. His attendant is Morpheus and he oversees the spirits of dreams and nightmares. Particularly noted from the art of the Lacedaemonians who placed statues of Somnus and Mors side by side.

Somtus

See Harsomtus.

Sopedu

Guardian deity. Egyptian. A god who protects the eastern border, usually depicted as a falcon or a Bedouin with a headdress of tall plumes. His cult was followed chiefly at Saft el-Henna in the Nile delta. Sopedu is linked in Pyramid Texts with the hawk god Horus. He also acted as a patron deity of the turquoise mines in the Sinai with inscriptions at Serabit el-Khadim. Also Sopdu.

SOPHIA   *(wisdom)*

Origin Greek principle adopted by Gnostic Christians. Primordial female force in the cosmos.

Known period of worship   unknown origins to circa 400 AD.

Synonyms   Pistis Sophia.

Center(s) of cult   undefined cells within the area of early Christian influence.

Art references   none.

Literary sources   Plato and other Greek philosophers; *Nag Hammadi* codices.

According to the Gnostic Christian writers whose thoughts were a syncretization of Jewish, ancient Near Eastern and Greek philosophical elements, Sophia descended from Pistis (faith) before the formation of the cosmos. She is described as a likeness of Pistis and seems to be the primeval element of light. She acts as a mediator or "veil" between the immortal beings (Archons) and mankind. She is also the challenger to the primordial "shadow" that becomes chaos. In the Nag Hammadi text *On the Origin of the World*, Pistis Sophia generates Yaldabaoth, the father or "prime parent" of the seven androgynous beings who rule the heavens in the likeness of the original authorities so that the likeness may persist forever. See also Pistis and Yaldabaoth.

Sore-Gus
Sky god. Hottentot [Namibia, southern Africa]. The sun god, embodied in the shape of a golden ram with long fluffy wool.

Sors
God of luck. Roman. Derived from the Greek model of Tyche, he is less prominent in the pantheon than the goddess Fortuna.

Sothis   [*Greek*]
Astral goddess. Egyptian. She heralds the Nile inundation as the personification of the star Sirius, which rises coincidentally in the dawn sky in July. She is depicted as a nude figure wearing the conical white crown of Lower Egypt surmounted by a star. Late in Egyptian history she becomes largely syncretized with Isis. Also Sopdet (Egyptian).

Souconna
River goddess. Romano-Celtic (Gallic). Guardian of the river Saône and known chiefly from inscriptions at Chalon.

Soului
Vegetation god. Hua [southeastern Ghana, West Africa]. A benevolent deity who can bestow wealth as well as good harvests. He is also god of medicine and of the sounds of music. His devotees wear white and daub white chalk on their faces. His symbol is the cowrie shell.

Spandaramet
Chthonic goddess. Pre-Christian Armenian. Concerned with the fertility of the earth and with death. Under Christian influence, her name equates with hell.

Spes
Goddess of hope. Roman. Foundations of a sanctuary were commenced by the emperor Tiberius, linked with a similar building dedicated to the god Janus. She is associated with gardens and depicted as a young woman bearing a bunch of flowers.

Spiniensis
Minor god of agriculture. Roman. Mentioned by the writer Fabius Pictor, he is the deity responsible for the uprooting of thorn bushes.

Sravana   (*lame cow*)
Minor goddess of fortune. Hindu (Epic and Puranic). A benevolent *naksatra*; daughter of Daksa and wife of Candra (Soma). Also Srona.

Sravistha
Minor goddess of fortune. Hindu (Epic and Puranic). A benevolent *naksatra*; daughter of Daksa and wife of Candra (Soma).

Sri(devi)   (*prosperity*)
1. Goddess. Hindu (Epic and Puranic). An early name that was syncretized with that of Laksmi to form Sri-Laksmi.

2. Goddess. Buddhist-Lamaist [Tibet]. One of a group of *dharmapala* with terrible appearance and royal attire who protect the Dalai Lama. A manifestation of the goddess Devi sometimes seen in company with Visnu, when conventionally she stands on his right. Her breasts are covered by a narrow band of cloth. She may be invoked to provide wealth (see also Laksmi). Her retinue includes the goddesses of the seasons and her animal is a mule. Color: blue. Attributes: chiefly cup and staff but on occasion several other objects including a pink lotus. Three-eyed and may be three-headed. Also Lha Mo.

3. Goddess. Jain.

Srikantha *(beautiful throat)*

Minor deity. Hindu (Epic and Puranic). One of a group of emancipated *vidyesvaras* (lords of knowledge) considered to be aspects of Siva, in this instance referring to his darkish blue neck. Also one of the *ekadasarudras* or eleven forms of Rudra. Attributes: hatchet and trident.

Srivasumukhi *(excellent faced)*

Minor goddess. Buddhist (Mahayana). An attendant of Vasudhara.

Srivasundhara *(earth)*

Minor goddess. Buddhist (Mahayana). An attendant of Vasudhara.

Srividyadevi *(of excellent knowledge)*

Minor goddess. Hindu. A deity of terrifying appearance. Attributes: necklace of bones, teeth.

Stanitakumara

God. Jain [India]. One of the deities grouped under the general title of *bhvanavasi* (dwelling in places). Of youthful appearance.

Sterculius

Minor god of agriculture. Roman. Concerned with the manuring of the fields.

Stribog

God of winds. Slav. Mentioned in the *Chronicle of Nestor,* and the euphemism "Stribog"'s grandchildren" refers to the winds.

Styx

Chthonic underworld goddess. Greek. A daughter of Okeanos and Tethys, and mother of Nike. The deity of the river Styx beside which the gods swear their oaths.

Šu

Primordial god of the air. Egyptian. According to the genealogy of the priests of Heliopolis, he is the first born of the creator sun god Atum and by his sister Tefnut is the father of the chthonic god Geb and the sky goddess Nut. Šu is typically represented in human form standing over the supine form of Geb and holding Nut aloft with his raised arms. He can also, as one of several manifestations of the "eye of Re," be represented as a lion, as can his sister.

Subhadra *(very splendid)*

Goddess. Hindu (Epic and Puranic). The daughter of Vasudeva and sister of Krsna. She may appear standing beside Jagganath.

Subhaga

Minor goddess. Buddhist (Mahayana). An attendant of Buddhakapala.

Subhamekhala
(with a marvelous girdle)

Minor goddess. Buddhist (Mahayana). An attendant of Buddhakepala.

Subrahmanya

Minor warrior deity. Hindu (Epic and Puranic). A form of Karttikeya that is depicted with six heads and twelve arms. Also Shadanana-Subrahmanya; see also Skanda.

SUCELLOS *(the good striker)*
Origin Romano-Celtic (Gallic).

Known period of worship prehistoric times until Christianization, circa 400 AD.

Synonyms Sucellus.

Center(s) of cult various.

Art references bronze and stone sculpture and reliefs.

Literary sources votive inscriptions.

Sucellos carries a long-handled hammer and a cup or dish that is arguably the equal of the Irish Celtic Dagda's caldron. He is known principally from the valleys of the Rhone and Saône and is often coupled in art and votive inscriptions with the river goddess Nantosuelta. In at least two instances, Unterseebach [Lower Rhine] and Varhely [Romania], Sucellos is accompanied by a raven and a three-headed dog suggesting the Roman guardian of the underworld, Cerberus, and a link with funerary practices. Sucellos also has associations with the woodland god Silvanus, suggesting a fertility connotation and, in France, is associated both with springs and with dogs and snakes, which suggest healing and rejuvenating powers (dogs were more generally linked with the Roman healing god Aesculapius than with death).

Suddhodana *(having pure rice)*
Primordial god. Buddhist. The father of the Buddha. The deified king of the Sakya tribe from which the Buddha descended; his consort is Mayadevi.

Sudrem
Weather god. Kafir [Afghanistan]. Little is known of this deity. He was created from the breath of the supreme god Imra. Alternatively he sprang from a juniper branch. His wife is the goddess Nangi-Wutr and he is the father of the major fertility goddess Disani. He is depicted as a great golden buck with horns reaching to the sky. As a deity specifically concerned with rain, he lives in a sacred lake, Sudrem Sur, at which all wild animals must drink once to survive. Also Sujum; Sudaram; Sataram.

Sudurjaya *(very difficult to conquer)*
Minor goddess. Buddhist (Vajrayana). One of several deified *bhumis* recognized as different spiritual spheres through which a disciple passes. Color: yellow. Attributes: emerald and staff.

Sugriva *(beautiful strong neck)*
Monkey god. Hindu. The son of the sun god and leader of the monkey army which, according to epic tradition, supported Rama.

Suijin
Collective name for water gods. Shinto [Japan]. These deities are worshiped at shrines at the sources of irrigation canals, lakes and ponds. They are depicted as snakes, eels and fish and invoked particularly by women. Chief among them is the goddess Mizu-Ha-No-Me.

Sukarasya *(face of a sow)*
Minor goddess. Buddhist.

Sukla-Tara
Goddess. Buddhist (Mahayana). Considered to be an emanation of all the *dhyanibuddhas* (meditation *buddhas*), but also regarded as being indistinguishable from the "white Tara" (see also Tara). Color: white.

Sukra *(bright)*
Astral god. Hindu (Epic and Puranic). The personification of the planet Venus and the tutor of the demons. He may, on occasion, be represented as female, owing to the fact that he was once made to swallow his attendant Kaca and then restore him to life. Color: white. Rides in a golden or silver chariot drawn by eight or ten horses. Attributes: book, prayer wheel, purse, staff, treasure and water jar.

Suksma *(very small)*
Minor deity. Hindu (Epic and Puranic). One of a group of emancipated *vidyesvaras* (lords of knowl-

edge) considered to be aspects of Siva. Attributes: hatchet and trident.

Suku

Creator god. Ovimbundu [central Angola, West Africa]. He created the sky, the rivers and mountains, and the people on earth.

Sukuna-Hikona

God of healing. Shinto [Japan]. With the god O-Kuni-Nushi-No-Mikoto, he established the various methods of healing diseases and the means for control of, and protection against, wild beasts, snakes, insects, etc. He is also worshiped as a tutelary god of traders, both maritime and on land. He is the *kami* of communications and, during the Japanese Empire period, was often installed by the authorities in the temples and shrines of conquered lands. He is worshiped in Buddhism as Yakushi-Bosatsu-Hyojin.

Suleviae

Goddesses of passage. Romano-Celtic (Gallic). Collective name for female deities associated with crossroads.

Sulini

Minor goddess. Hindu. Of terrible appearance. Animal: lion. Attribute: trident.

Sulis

Chthonic underworld goddess. Romano-Celtic. Also a deity concerned with knowledge and prophecy. The tutelary goddess of the thermal waters at Bath, England, she is closely linked with the Roman goddess Minerva.

Šullat

Minor god. Mesopotamian (Babylonian-Akkadian). An attendant of the sun god Šamaš.

Šulman(u)

Chthonic and fertility deity. Mesopotamian (Babylonian-Akkadian) and western Semitic. Also identified as a war god. Found in Assyria circa 1400 BC to 700 BC and known from Bronze Age inscriptions at Sidon.

Šulmanitu

Fertility goddess. Western Semitic. Concerned with love and war; also has underworld connections. Recognized chiefly at Sidon, but included in the Ugaritic pantheon. Thought by some authors to be the immediate derivation of the biblical "Shulamite woman" (*Vetus Testamentum* Song of Solomon 6:13).

Šul-pa-e   (youthful radiance)

Fertility and astral god. Mesopotamian (Sumerian). Identified as the personification of the planet Jupiter and, in one list, the consort of the mother goddess Ninhursaĝa.

Šulsaga

Astral goddess. Mesopotamian (Sumerian).

Šul-utula

Tutelary god. Mesopotamian (Sumerian). Known only as a personal deity to Entemena, king of the city of Eninnu.

Sumalini   (well-garlanded)

Minor goddess. Buddhist (Mahayana). An attendant of Buddhakapala.

Sumati   (very wise)

Deification of literature. Buddhist. One of a group of *dharanis*. Color: yellow. Attributes: ear of rice and staff.

Sumbha

Goddess. Buddhist. A female *dikpala* or guardian of the downward direction (her male counterpart is Sumbharaja). Color: blue. Attribute: snake noose.

Sumbharaja

God. Buddhist. A *dikpala* or guardian of the downward direction. Color: blue. Attributes: jewel, lotus, staff and sword. Three-headed.

Sumiyoshi-No-Kami

Sea gods. Shinto [Japan]. A general name for guardian deities of seafarers, including fishermen, they include the three Munakata-No-Kami. They are the focus of special worship by the Jingu-Kogo sect, whom they escorted to Korea. They are also patrons of poets and have a purifying role. The main sanctuary is the Sumiyoshi Taisha at Osaka.

Summamus

Storm god. Etruscan. Specifically a deity responsible for lightning and thunderbolts. A sanctuary was dedicated to him in Rome.

Šumugan

God of the river plains. Mesopotamian (Sumerian). In creation mythology he is given charge by the god Enki over the flat alluvial lands of southern Mesopotamia.

Sun Hou-Shi

Monkey god. Chinese. He emerged from a cosmic egg conceived out of emptiness and engendered by the wind; he provides various arts and skills to mankind. According to tradition he discovered the elixir of immortality in a fruit that he consumed. Also Sun Wu-Kong.

Sundara (charming)

1. Goddess. Hindu (Puranic). A prosperous aspect of the god Siva.
2 Minor goddess. Buddhist (Mahayana). An attendant of Buddhakapala.

Suparikirtitanamasri (lord with a celebrated name)

Physician god. Buddhist-Lamaist [Tibet]. Accounted among a series of medicine *buddhas* or *sMan-bla*. Typically depicted with stretched earlobes. Color: yellow.

Suparnakumara

God. Jain [India]. One of the groups under the general title of *bhvanavasi* (dwelling in places). Of youthful appearance.

Sura (wine)

Goddess of wine. Hindu. She is considered to be of terrible appearance and has no consort. Three-eyed.

Suraksini

Minor goddess. Buddhist (Mahayana). An attendant of Buddhakapala.

Surangama (bright colored)

God. Buddhist (Mahayana). A *bodhisattva* or *buddha*-designate. Color: white. Attribute: sword.

Suresvara (lord of the gods)

God. Hindu (Epic and Puranic). One of the eleven *ekadasarudras* or Rudra gods. Attributes: arrow, ax, bell, bow, bowl, club, drum, hook, iron rod, lotus, prayer wheel and trident.

Survarnabhadravimalaratnaprabhasa (the bright, pure jewel splendor)

Physician god. Buddhist-Lamaist [Tibet]. Accounted as one of a series of medicine *buddhas* or *sMan-bla*. Typically depicted with stretched earlobes. Color: yellowish white.

SURYA (1)

Origin Hindu (Vedic, Epic and Puranic) [India]. Sun god.

Known period of worship circa 1700 BC until present.

Synonyms Diakara (day maker); Grahapati (king of planets); Surya Narayana.

Center(s) of cult the "Black Pagoda" shrine at Konorak in Orissa; also throughout India.

Art references sculptures from circa 600 AD, including erotic reliefs at the "Black Pagoda," usually in bronze, less frequently in stone.

Literary sources Rg Veda and other Vedic texts, Epic and Puranic texts.

In the *Vedas* Surya is a prominent figure, not only the personification of the sun in the heavens and of cosmic order, but also a source of infinite knowledge. Considered to have been introduced from Iran, he is head of the *aditya* group of sun deities. He is the son of Dyaus and Aditi and his consorts include Laksmi, Chaya and Sanjna. His children include Manu, Revanta, Yama and Yamuna, and a sun goddess also called Surya.

Surya is depicted either standing or seated, sometimes driving a one-wheeled chariot drawn across the sky by up to seven horses. He bears four arms. In northern India he is usually found wearing knee-length boots. In the south he goes barefoot. Attributes: band, club, conch, knife, two lotuses, prayer wheel, staff with lion, trident and war drum. May be three-eyed.

Surya *(2)*

Sun goddess. Hindu (Vedic, Epic and Puranic). The daughter of the sun god Surya. According to legend she was courted by all the gods, but won finally by the twin Asvin gods with whom she rides in a chariot. Other legends include among her consorts Soma and Pusan. She is the essence of the cosmos. Also Savitr.

SUSANO-WO

Origin Shinto [Japan]. Chthonic and weather god.

Known period of worship circa 600 AD and probably earlier until present.

Synonyms none.

Center(s) of cult throughout Japan.

Art references sculptures and paintings.

Literary sources *Nihongi* and *Kojiki* texts.

The brother of the sun goddess Amaterasu, he was born from the nose of the primordial creator god Izanagi and represents the physical, material world. His consorts include the goddess Inada-Hime, by whom he fathered a son, Ya-Shima-Ji-Nu-Mi, the eight-island ruler, and the goddess Kamu-O-Ichi-Hime. His offspring by her include the great harvest god O-Toshi-No-Kami.

The appearance of Susano-Wo and Amaterasu in the creation account marks the final separation of the ethereal cosmos into a vast multiplicity of material objects. The god and goddess are obliged to join each other in order to survive, but while Susano-Wo recognizes the necessity for this union, Amaterasu finds his excesses repugnant. When he tries to enter her house in the heavens she hides herself away in a cave from which she emerges only after considerable effort and ruse on the part of the other members of the pantheon. Susano-Wo is expelled from heaven and takes up residence on earth where he first has to beg food from the goddess Oki-Tsu-Hime-No-Kami. See also Amaterasu.

Susinak

Local god. Elamite [Iran]. The patron deity of Susa.

Šutekh

Weather god. Hittite and Hurrian. Of Hurrian origin, but incorporated into the Hittite state pantheon. Identified on the seal of a Hittite/Egyptian treaty between Hattusilis II and Rameses II in 1271 BC. Probably another name for the god Tešub.

Svadha *(invoked with offerings)*

Minor goddess. Hindu. The daughter of Daksa and Prasuti. Sometimes identified as a consort of Rudra or Agni.

Svantevit

God of war. Pre-Christian Latvian. Mentioned by the author Saxo Grammaticus as riding upon a white horse and holding a cornucopia, he is known locally from the island of Rügen. Also a guardian deity of crops.

Svaraghosaraja

Physician god. Buddhist-Lamaist [Tibet]. Accounted among a series of medicine *buddhas* or *sMan-bla*. Typically depicted with stretched ear-lobes. Color: yellowish red.

Svarozic
Sun god. Slav. Also the giver of fire and the smith god, and further linked with marriage. Also Svarog.

Svasthavesini *(entering a natural state)*
Goddess. Hindu. One of terrifying appearance. Color: scarlet. Attribute: drum. Three-eyed and three-headed.

Svati
Minor goddess of fortune. Hindu (Epic and Puranic). A benevolent *naksatra*; daughter of Daksa and wife of Candra (Soma). Also Nistya.

Syamatara *(the "black Tara")*
Goddess. Buddhist-Lamaist [Tibet]. A gracious form of the goddess Tara. Also an emanation of Amoghasiddhi and a form of Avalokitesvara. Color: black, possibly green. Attribute: blue lotus.

T

Tabiti

Goddess of fire. Scythian. Also the guardian deity of all animals. The Romans syncretized her with the hearth goddess Vesta.

Ta-Bitjet

Scorpion goddess. Egyptian. In incantations against scorpion bite she is identified as a consort of the god Horus. Her blood, which flowed when Horus ruptured her hymen, is considered to possess magical and remedial properties against the poison.

Taditkara *(lightning)*

Goddess of light. Buddhist. Color: green. Attributes: lightning in the form of a creeper. Also Vidyddhara.

T'ai Shan

God. Chinese. The senior deity in the heavenly ministries, he is the immediate controller of the earth and mankind. Titled the "god of the eastern peak." Also Di Zang.

T'ai Yi

Primordial god. Chinese. The spirit of the universe who was present before the cosmos was created and who is known as the great unity. During the Sung Dynasty (960–1279 AD) he was elevated to the head of the ranks of astral gods and he is embodied in the Pole Star, otherwise identified in Chinese mythology as the Purple Planet.

Tailtiu

Goddess. Celtic (Irish). By tradition the consort of Eochaid of the Tuatha de Danann, she is the foster mother of the god Lugh and associated with the *Lughnasad* festival on August 1.

Tai-Sui-Jing

God of temporal time. Chinese. The apotheosis of the planet Jupiter, which orbits the sun in a twelve-year cycle.

Tajin

Generic title for a group of rain gods. Totonac (Mesoamerican) [Mexico]. Worshipped by a modern tribe and believed to reside in the ruins of El Tajin, a classic Veracruz site whence they control the thunder clouds. See also Tlaloc.

Taka-Mi-Musubi-No-Kami

(high august producing wondrous deity)

Primordial creator being. Shinto [Japan]. The second of the deities listed in the sacred *Kojiki* text. He appeared in the Takama-No-Hara (plain of high heaven) after Ame-No-Minaka-Nushi-No-Kami. A remote and vaguely defined being, he was born alone in the cosmos and hides himself from mankind.

Taka-Okami-No-Kami *(great producer of rain in the mountains)*

Rain god. Shinto [Japan]. Specifically the god of rain generated in mountains. A god of fierce rain, also known as the "god of the dividing of the waters." See also Kura-Okami-No-Kami.

Take-Mika-Dzuchi-No-Kami

God of thunder. Shinto [Japan]. One of the Raijin gods of thunder, storms and rain, he is also one of the warrior deities who guarded Prince Ninigi on his descent from heaven to earth. A tutelary god of swordsmen and judoka artists. See also Futsu-Nushi-No-Kami.

Takkiraja
God. Buddhist. A *dikpala* or guardian of the southeastern quarter. Color: blue. Attributes: blue staff, jewel, lotus staff, sword and trident. Also Vajrajvalanalarka and Vajrayaksa.

Takotsi Nakawe
(our grandmother growth)
Chthonic vegetation goddess. Huichol Indian (Mesoamerican) [Mexico]. The earth and all plant life belong to her and she is regarded as the mother of the gods, particularly of the fire god Tatevali. She is very old and is invoked to give the boon of longevity. Her sacred tree is a form of fig, the *salate*.

Taksaka
Snake god. Hindu (Epic and Puranic). One of a group of seven *mahanagas*. Attributes: rosary, swastika and water jar.

Ta'lab
Moon god. Pre-Islamic southern Arabian. He also has an oracular function.

Tam Kung
Local sea god. Chinese. A deity with control over rain and water and who extinguishes fires. His worship is restricted to a coastal region between Hong Kong and Macau. According to tradition he was an eight-year-old boy emperor, the last of the Sung Dynasty, who committed suicide by jumping over a cliff in the face of Kublai Khan's advance in 1276 AD. His attendant is Ho Wang, who joined him in death. A sanctuary in Coloane Town in Macau, sited at the end of a narrow peninsula, is dedicated to him. Tam Kung is strongly linked with the symbolism of dragons and the shrine contains a sacred whale rib modeled into the shape of a dragon boat. He is normally depicted seated and holding a bell, which may be interpreted as an instrument of warning or as a means of calling attention to the voices of the ancestors.

Tama-No-Ya
God of jewelers. Shinto [Japan]. The deity who made a complete string of curved jewels nearly three meters long, one of the lures that enticed the sun goddess Amaterasu from the cave where she hid herself.

Tamats Palike Tamoyeke *(our eldest brother walking everywhere)*
God of wind and air. Huichol Indian (Mesoamerican) [Mexico]. The messenger of the gods, he also put the world into its present form and shape.

Tanara
Sky spirit. Yakut [central Siberia]. The apotheosis of the sky.

Tana'oa
Weather and sea god. Polynesian [Marquesas Islands]. A local variation on the Polynesian god Tangaroa, known as a god of winds and a tutelary deity of fishermen.

Tane(mahuta)
God of light. Polynesian (including Maori). One of the children of the prime parents Ranginui and Papatuanuku. Also god of trees, forests and boat builders, his consort is the goddess Hine-Ahu-One and he is the father of Hine-Ata-Uira who descended to the underworld to become the goddess of death, Hine-Nui-Te-Po. In other traditions he is the consort of Hine-Nui-Te-Po, whom he joins each evening when he descends to the underworld. It was he who proposed that his parents should be pushed apart rather than slaughtered. In Maori culture Tanemahuta, like all deities, is represented only by inconspicuous, slightly worked stones or pieces of wood and not by the large totems, which are depictions of ancestors. Also Kane (Hawaiian).

Tangaroa
Sea and creator god. Polynesian (including Maori). The deity responsible for the oceans *(moana)* and the fish *(ika)* within them. In Hawaiian belief he was the primordial being who took the form of a

bird and laid an egg on the surface of the primeval waters that, when it broke, formed the earth and sky. He then engendered the god of light, Atea (cf. Tane). According to Tahitian legend, he fashioned the world inside a gigantic mussel shell. In a separate tradition Tangaroa went fishing and hauled the Tongan group of islands from the depths of the ocean on a hook and line. He is the progenitor of mankind (as distinct from Tumatauenga who has *authority* over mankind). His son Pili married Sina, the tropic bird and they produced five children from whom the rest of the Polynesian race was born. In Maori culture Tangaroa, like all deities, is represented only by inconspicuous, slightly worked stones or pieces of wood and not by the large totems, which are depictions of ancestors.

Tango
God. Polynesian [Hervey Islamds] The third child of the primordial mother Vari-Ma-Te-Takere, he was plucked from her right side and lived in Enua-Kura, the land of the red parrot feather immediately below the home of Tinirau in the world coconut.

Ta'ngwanla'na *(greatest one in the sea)*
Supreme sea god. Haida Indian [Queen Charlotte Island, Canada]. His home is said to be in the deeps.

Tanit
Moon goddess. Phoenician and Pontic (Carthaginian). Known largely from inscriptions at various sites along the North African coast and linked with the goddess Astarte. Her symbol is a triangular device with horizontal bars supporting a moon disc. Both deities are described as "ladies of the sanctuary." Tanit was the supreme goddess at Carthage, known as the "face of Baal," until usurped by the Roman goddess Juno; she survived under the name Caelestis. The goddess Ceres was also worshiped in the Tanit temple at Carthage. Also Tenit.

Ta-No-Kami
Agricultural deity. Shinto [Japan]. A generic name for several gods of crops and harvests. May also be identified as a mountain *kami*.

Tanu'ta
Earth spirit. Koryak [southeastern Siberia]. A guardian of the earth and its plants and animals, Tanu'ta is the consort of Yine'ane'ut (in other legends she is married to the son of the supreme being Ta'yan).

T'ao Hua Hsiennui
(peach blossom girl)
Goddess. Chinese. The spirit of the peach blossom and the deity of the second spring month. She is primarily a guardian deity who defends against evil. A figure of the goddess was traditionally brought by a mother for the protection of a bride and she is closely connected with marriage, which involves potential danger for the family with the introduction of an unknown element. The wedding ceremony includes a ritualized kidnapping of the bride. The figure is also placed in a doorway to ward off evil. She is depicted in warlike posture wearing a skirt with four black flags, each representing an army and bearing the character for wealth. She holds a sword by its scabbard end. One of her cult centers, the Temple of Jade Vacuity in Cheung Chan, holds a celebrated statue in which she is depicted holding the scabbard only.

Taoki-Ho-Oi-No-Kami
God of carpenters. Shinto [Japan]. One of the gods who built the beautiful sacred hall designed, in part, to lure the sun goddess Amaterasu from the cave in which she hid herself. See also Hiko-Sashiri-No-Kami.

Tapio
Hunting god. Pre-Christian Finnish. Believed to inhabit forests and invoked before a hunt.

Tar
Chthonic earth god. Tiv [Nigeria, West Africa]. Engendered by the creator god Aondo, Tar is

depicted as a prostrate figure with his head toward the east, comparable with the Egyptian god Geb.

Tara   *(power of hunger)*

1. Goddess. Hindu (Vedic, Epic and Puranic). May originally have had astral connotations, since the word can be interpreted as "star." One of a group of *mahavidyas* personifying the *Sakti* of Siva. She may also be the consort of Candra (Soma). Aspects include Krodharatri. Attributes: knife, skin, skull, snakes and sword. Three-eyed.

2. Goddess. Buddhist (Mahayana and Vajrayana). An epithet of the mother of the Buddha, Maya. Also one of a series of female deities, the *dhyani-buddhasakti* considered to be aspects of the *Sakti* of Avalokitesvara or of Amogashiddhi. She may also be the *Sakti* of Adibiddha and of the various *dhyanibuddhas,* in which case she is characterized by their colors. These Taras thus become "White Tara" and so on. See also Bhrkuti, Ekajata, Kurukulla, Sitatara and Syamatara. In Tibetan Buddhism she is known as sGrol-ma.

Taranis

Thunder god. Romano-Celtic (Gallic). Known only from limited inscriptions, but may emulate the Germanic god Donar and is possibly the same as Taranucos. The Romans equated him with Jupiter and a Jupiter Tanarus inscription at Chester in England may refer to Taranis. His symbol is a spoked wheel and he is presumed to be the object of savage rites. The modern Breton word for thunder is *taran.* Also Taranos.

Tarhunt

Weather god. Hurrian (Anatolian). Known from inscriptions as the father of Telepinu.

Tari Pennu

Chthonic goddess. Indian (Khond). Created by the sky gods Boora Pennu and Bella Pennu so as to conceive the rest of the pantheon. She is identified as a malevolent deity, the subject of regular propitiation human sacrifices in the notorious *meriah* rituals in Orissa province.

Taru

Weather god. Hittite and Hurrian. Known from inscriptions and equating with Iškur. Probably of Hurrian origin. See also Tarhunt; Telepinu.

Tarvos Trigaranos

Bull god. Romano-Celtic (Gallic). Known chiefly from a four-sided monument erected near Paris by boatmen of the Seine during the reign of the emperor Tiberius. It depicts Esus, Vulcanus, Jupiter and Tarvos. As Tarvos Trigaranos, he is drawn as a bull with three cranes on its back and can be seen at such places as Dorchester in England. The bull may alternatively bear three horns.

Tasenetnofret

Goddess. Egyptian. The consort of Horus as Haroeris and regarded as a minor emanation of the goddess Hathor. Known from the sanctuary of Kom-Ombo.

Tašmetu(m)

Goddess. Mesopotamian (Babylonian-Akkadian). The consort of the god Nabu.

Tašmišu

Attendant god. Hittite and Hurrian. The sibling of the weather god Tešub.

Tate

Creator god. Sioux [USA]. He appears in the clouds, his voice is the wind and he controls the changing of the seasons. He is also the guide of the spirits of the dead. He is the deity with whom the Sioux *shamans* intercede.

Tate Hautse Kupuri
(mother north water)

Rain and water goddess. Huichol Indian (Mesoamerican) [Mexico]. Similar to Tate Kyewimoka, but also responsible for mists and fogs.

Tate Kyewimoka   *(mother west water)*

Rain and water goddess. Huichol Indian (Mesoamerican) [Mexico]. Appears in lightning and is said to resemble a red snake. She lives in a deep gorge with caves, in Santa Catarina, and brings the rain from the west. Her animals include deer and ravens and she is also the goddess of grain.

Tate Naaliwahi *(mother east water)*
Rain and water goddess. Huichol Indian (Mesoamerican) [Mexico]. Appears in lightning and brings rain from the east. She lives in a deep gorge with caves, in Santa Catarina.

Tate Oteganaka *(mother grain)*
Grain goddess. Huichol Indian (Mesoamerican) [Mexico]. The mother of the sun god Tayau.

Tate Rapawiyema *(mother south water)*
Rain and water goddess. Huichol Indian (Mesoamerican) [Mexico]. Similar to Tate Kyewimoka, but also the patron goddess of Laguna de Magdalena, where she is believed to take the form of a water lizard.

Tate Velika Vimali
Sun goddess. Huichol Indian (Mesoamerican) [Mexico]. Perceived as a young girl or as a royal eagle who holds the world in her talons and guards it. In human form the night sky with its stars are her dress.

Tatenen *(exalted earth)*
Chthonic god. Egyptian. Originates as a vegetation god from Memphis, the apotheosis of the Nile silt that appears after the inundation has subsided. As a vegetation god, he is depicted anthropomorphically with green face and limbs and wearing a crown with plumes subtended by ram's horns. By the time of the Old Kingdom (twenty-seventh to twenty-second centuries BC) he is recognized as an emanation of the god Ptah, involved in the creation process and mentioned on the Shabaka Stone (Memphis), where he is described as "father of the gods" and is perceived as an androgynous being. He also protects the royal dead.

Tatevali *(our grandfather)*
God of fire. Huichol Indian (Mesoamerican) [Mexico]. Also a deity of life and health, perceived as

a *shaman* who prophesies and cures disease. He is the tutelary god of *shamans* and is said to have built the first Huichol temple with the god Tatosi. His animals include the macaw, royal eagle, cardinal, puma and opossum.

Tathatavasita *(control of the such-ness)*
Minor goddess. Buddhist. One of a group of *vasitas* personifying the disciplines of spiritual regeneration. Color: white. Attribute: white lotus.

Tatosi *(great grandfather deer tail)*
God of fire. Huichol Indian (Mesoamerican) [Mexico]. A deity regarded as the son of Tatevali, having been created from the plumes of his father, but also the chief god of deer. His sacred animal is the white-tailed hawk. Also Mara Kwari.

Tatqa'hicnin *(root man)*
Vegetation spirit. Koryak [southeastern Siberia]. A vaguely defined being who is chthonic and lives under the ground, presumably controlling edible roots and their availability.

Taumata-Atua
Vegetation god. Polynesian (including Maori). He presides over the fields and may be the god Rongomatane under an alternative name. In Maori culture Taumata-Atua, like all deities, is represented only by inconspicuous, slightly worked stones or pieces of wood and not by the large totems, which are depictions of ancestors.

Tawa
Creator god. Pueblo Indian [USA]. The apotheosis of the sun and father of the tribe.

TAWERET *(the great one)*
Origin Egyptian. Goddess of childbirth.

Known period of worship probably circa 2500 BC until the end of Egyptian history circa 400 AD.

Synonyms Thoueris (Greek).

Center(s) of cult no obvious cult centers, but represented in the Karnak complex at Thebes.

Art references a favorite subject for amulets and perforated vases.

Literary sources generally in texts including magical spells.

Taweret is a goddess who enjoyed popularity among rank-and-file Egyptians and whose protection was sought particularly by women in pregnancy. She is depicted either in human form or as a hybrid with the head of a hippopotamus, human breasts and swollen belly, leonine limbs and a crocodile tail. This unusual aspect is intended to frighten off malignant forces before and during childbirth. Taweret often holds the SA symbol of protection clasped over her vulva. Talismanic vases are fashioned in the shape of the goddess, with holes at the nipples through which milk could be poured during rites.

Her benign nature contrasts with that of Seth, often depicted as a male hippopotamus, an animal whose destructive behavior in the river and adjacent fields was well known.

Tawhirimatea
God of winds. Polynesian (including Maori). One of the children of the prime parents Ranginui and Papatuanuku. He was uniquely opposed to the separation of his mother and father, sky and earth, at the time of the creation of the cosmos, and in consequence spends his time harassing and troubling mankind. In Maori culture Papatuanuku, like all deities, is represented only by inconspicuous, slightly worked stones or pieces of wood and not by the large totems, which are depictions of ancestors.

Ta'xet
God of death. Haida Indian [Queen Charlotte Island, Canada]. The deity responsible for those who die violently. See also Tia.

Ta'yan
Supreme being. Koryak [southeastern Siberia]. An indefinite character living somewhere in the zenith and generally out of touch with ordinary mortals. His consort is Supervisor Woman, Lapna'ut and his son is Cloud Man, Ya'halan. He conducts business with the physical earth through his majordomo Big Raven, Quikinna'qu. See also Tenanto'mwan.

Tayau (father sun)
Sun god. Huichol Indian (Mesoamerican) [Mexico]. According to tradition, he was created by the ancient *shamans*, who threw the youthful son of the grain mother Tate Oteganaka into an oven in full ceremonial attire. He traveled underground and emerged in the east as the sun. In late May, the Huichol sacrifice a sheep and a turkey in a ritual fire, after which they sing all night until sunrise. Also Tau; Taverik.

Tayau Sakaimoka
Sun god. Huichol Indian (Mesoamerican) [Mexico]. The deity of the setting sun in the west, regarded as the assistant of Tayau.

Te-Aka-Ia-Roe (root of all existence)
Creator being. Polynesian [Hervey Islands]. Perceived in the form of a giant worm, this being is one of three spirits that govern and ensure the permanence of the universe. He lives in the lowest part of the root of the coconut shell that represents the world.

Te-Manava-Roa (long lived)
Creator being. Polynesian [Hervey Islands]. Perceived in the form of a giant worm, this being is one of three spirits that govern and ensure the permanence of the universe. He lives in the highest part of the root of the coconut shell that represents the world.

Te Kore (the void)
Primordial being. Polynesian (including Maori). The personification of the darkness of chaos before light came into being. Usually coupled with Te Po, the unknown night.

Te Po
Primordial being. Polynesian (including Maori). The personification of the night that existed in

chaos before the creation of light. Usually coupled with Te Kore, the void.

Te-Tanga-Engae   (breathing)
Creator being. Polynesian [Hervey Islands]. Perceived in the form of a giant worm, this being is one of three spirits that govern and ensure the permanence of the universe. He lives in the middle part of the root of the coconut shell that represents the world.

Tecciztecatl   (conch shell lord)
Moon god. Aztec (classical Mesoamerican) [Mexico]. In cosmogony, when on the fifth day of creation the gods sat in judgment to elect the new sun god, Nanahuatl and Tecciztecatl cremated themselves in the sacred fire. The heart of Nanahuatl ascended to become the new sun and that of Tecciztecatl became the moon. Tradition suggests that Nanahuatl is diseased and impoverished but of great courage, while Tecciztecatl is wealthy and a coward. Alternatively, the pair are sons of Quetzalcoatl and of Tlaloc and were hurled into the fire by their fathers. Also one of the group classed as the Tezcatlipoca complex.

NOTE: eventually all the gods sacrificed themselves for mankind.

Tefnut
Primordial goddess of moisture. Egyptian. According to the genealogy laid down by the priests of Heliopolis, Tefnut was created out of the breath or spit of the creator sun god Atum. She is the sister of Šu, god of the air, and the mother of Geb and Nut. Her main cult sanctuary was at Heliopolis. Tefnut, like Šu, can become one of several manifestations of the "eye of Re" in which case she appears as a lion, or in human form but with a leonine head. According to the Pyramid Texts, she creates pure water from her vagina. In a different context she takes the form of a snake encircling a scepter.

Tegid Voel
Water goddess. Celtic (Welsh). One of a pair with Cerridwen, identified by the poet Taliesin.

Teharon(hiawagon)   (he who holds heaven in his hands)
Creator god. Mohawk [USA and Canada]. He engendered the world and all living things and is invoked by shamans to provide good health and prosperity. His adversary is the demonic figure Tawiskaron, symbolizing darkness.

Teicauhtzin   (younger brother)
Minor god of war. Aztec (classical Mesoamerican) [Mexico]. A patron god of Mexico and one of the group classed as the Huitzilpochtli complex.

Teisbas
Tutelary god. Urartian [Armenia]. Known from inscriptions.

Tejosnisa   (sharp)
God. Buddhist. Apparently connected with the guardian deities or dikpalas in the southeastern quarter. Color: whitish red. Attribute: sun disc.

TELEPINU
Origin   Hittite and Hurrian (Anatolia) [Turkey]. Vegetation and fertility god.

Known period of worship   circa 1800 BC or earlier until 1100 BC or later.

Synonyms   Telipuna.

Center(s) of cult   associated with at least four cities in the Turus region, including Nerik, but also known down into the Syrian plain.

Art references   seals and seal impressions; sculptures; monumental rock carvings.

Literary sources   texts from Boghazköy, etc.

Telepinu is a fertility god, the son of Tešub or, in alternative tradition, Taru, who brings thunder, lightning and rain. He may be of Hurrian origin. He disappears and is rediscovered to symbolize the annual demise and restoration of nature.

The story of his disappearance is told in several differing narratives, and his role is sometimes taken by the weather god Tešub. Essentially the legend describes how Telepinu departs from the Hittite kingdom in a rage with boots on the wrong feet. The sun god gives a feast for the thousand gods of Hatti, but is unable to feed all the guests because there is not enough food in the land. First an eagle, then Tešub himself, go out to search. Finally the goddess Hannahannas sends a bee, which finds and stings the sleeping Telepinu, provoking still further rage in nature (the Finnish legend of the hero Lemminkainen tells a comparable story). Telepinu eventually returns home, calmed, and nature returns to prosperity.

The god may have received a form of tree worship in which a hollow trunk was filled with harvest offerings.

Teliko

God of hot winds. Bambara [Mali, West Africa]. According to tradition the water god Faro challenged him in a primordial struggle and smashed him against a mountain.

Teljavelik

Creator god. Pre-Christian Lithuanian. He engendered the sun god Saule and is described as the heavenly smith.

Tellus

Chthonic primordial earth mother. Roman. A grain deity, generally regarded as benevolent, but also a goddess of the dead. Enemy armies were offered to her and cursed in her name. Both she and the grain goddess Ceres were propitiated with human sacrifice. Also Terra Mater.

Telpochtli   (male youth)

Omnipotent god. Aztec (classical Mesoamerican) [Mexico]. A universal and generally malevolent power. One of the group classed as the Tezcatlipoca complex.

Tenanto'mni

Creator spirit. Chukchee [eastern Siberia]. An indefinite and remote character living somewhere in the zenith of the sky. He created the world, which was then transformed into its present state by the raven-like majordomo Ku'urkil.

Tenanto'mwan

Creator spirit. Koryak [southeastern Siberia]. Identified particularly with the reindeer-hunting Koryak on the Taigonos peninsula. An indefinite and remote character living somewhere in the zenith of the sky. He created the world, which was then transformed into its present state by Quikinna'qu. Tenanto'mwan is the name always used when addressing the creator in incantations. See also Ya'qhicnin.

Tepeyollotl   (hill heart)

Minor chthonic or earth god. Aztec (classical Mesoamerican) [Mexico]. One of the group classed as the Tezcatlipoca complex. He was originally an earthquake god, symbolized by the jaguar and later adopted into the Aztec pantheon.

Tepoztecatl

Minor fertility god. Aztec (classical Mesoamerican) [Mexico]. One of the group classed as the Ometochtli complex concerned with the maguey plant and the brewing of the alcoholic drink pulque.

Terminus

God of passage. Roman. Embodied in boundary marker stones. He was celebrated in the *Terminalia* festival on February 23.

Terra Mater

Chthonic primordial earth mother. Roman. Derived from Greek model. See Tellus.

TEŠUB

Origin   Hittite and Hurrian (Anatolia) [Turkey]. Weather god.

Known period of worship   circa 1800 BC or earlier until circa 1100 BC or later.

Synonyms   Tešup and possibly Šutekh.

Center(s) of cult Hattusas (Boghazköy); Arinna; many other sanctuaries in the Taurus region and northern Syrian plain.

Art references seals and seal impressions; sculpture; rock carving.

Literary sources cuneiform and hieroglyphic texts from Boghazkoy and elsewhere.

Tešub is the most important deity in Hittite state religion, although he may be subservient to the Sun God(dess) of Arinna. Principally a weather god, as befits a mountainous region experiencing frequent storms and otherwise changeable climate. Also a god of battle and "king of heaven, lord of the land of Hatti." His consort is generally identified as Hebat. According to legend, Tešub is involved in a typical confrontation battle with the forces of disorder in the form of a dragon, Illuyankas. He defeats the dragon, thus symbolizing the re-invigoration of the earth after winter and the triumph of life over death. The drama seems to have been enacted in a New Year spring festival of Purulliyas.

The king of the Hittite kingdom was Tešub's high priest. A fragmented document describes a ritual in which the statue of the god is taken, in company with temple prostitutes, to a Tarnu (cultic or bath) house in a sacred grove where various rites are performed over it. Tešub sometimes plays the role of the missing vegetation god (see Telepinu). Sculptures at Malatya identify ram sacrifices. Tešub is depicted holding a bow and standing on a horned animal or in a chariot drawn by bulls.

Tešub was imported into Greece during the Mycenaean period (circa 1500–1200 BC). Bronze statuettes of the god have been discovered at Mycenae, Tiryns, Phylakopi and Delos.

Teteo Innan Teteo *(gods their mother)*
Minor god of fire. Aztec (classical Mesoamerican) [Mexico]. A paternalistic deity associated with fire. One of the group classed as the Xiuhtecuhtli complex.

Teteoinnan
Goddess of curers and medical diviners. Aztec (classical Mesoamerican) [Mexico]. The head of the group classed as the Teteoinnan complex.

Teteoinnan-Toci
Goddess of midwives. Aztec (classical Mesoamerican) [Mexico]. Known locally in the Valley of Mexico and invoked by women in childbirth. One of the group classed as the Teteoinnan complex.

Tethys
Sea goddess. Greek. One of the Titans, the daughter of Ouranos and Gaia and both sister and consort of Okeanos.

Tetzahauteotl *(god of fearful omen)*
Minor god of war. Aztec (classical Mesoamerican) [Mexico]. A patron god of Mexico and one of the group classed as the Huitzilpochtli complex.

Tetzahuitl *(fearful omen)*
Minor god of war. Aztec (classical Mesoamerican) [Mexico]. A patron god of Mexico and one of the group classed as the Huitzilpochtli complex.

Teuhcatl *(he of Teutlan)*
Local god of war. Aztec (classical Mesoamerican) [Mexico]. Also a hunting god and one of the group classed as the Mixcoatl complex.

Teutates
Local tribal deity. Romano-Celtic (Gallic). Known only from limited inscriptions. Teutates may be less the name of a deity than an epithet meaning "great." According to the Roman writer Lucan, he is one of three Celtic gods encountered by Caesar's army in Gaul and the object of savage rites in which victims were drowned in sacrificial lakes. He may equate with a British god, Totatis. He becomes assimilated variously with Mercury or Mars. Also Teutatis.

Tewi'xilak
God of goat hunters. Dza'wadeenox Indian [British Columbia, Canada]. The eldest son of the

supreme god Qa'wadiliqala. Said to kill goats with great ease and feed the tribe. Attributes include a headband of red cedar bark.

Tezcacoac Ayopechtli
(mirror serpent tortoise bench)
Birth goddess. Aztec (classical Mesoamerican) [Mexico]. An aspect of Xochiquetzal. One of the group classed as the Teteoinnan complex.

TEZCATLIPOCA   *(smoking mirror)*
Origin   Aztec (classical Mesoamerican) [Mexico]. Sun god.

Known period of worship   circa 750 AD to 1500 AD, but probably much earlier.

Synonyms   Moyocoya.

Center(s) of cult   none.

Art references   stone sculptures; murals; codex illustrations.

Literary sources   pre-Columbian codices.

According to creation mythology, the great mother in the thirteenth heaven became pregnant and the 400 star gods who were jealous of her child plotted to destroy it at birth. They were restrained in a cavern, however, until the moment when Tezcatlipoca emerged, fully armed, from his mother and destroyed his enemies. His only ally was his sister Coyolxauhqui, who was lost in the battle and whose head the god hurled into the heavens to live there as the moon. Alternative tradition describes Tezcatlipoca as the product of the self-created primordial beings Tonacatecuhtli and Tonacacihuatl.

He presides over the first of the five world ages personified by the sun 4 Ocelotl. He is also the ruler of the tenth of the thirteen heavens known at the time of the Spanish conquest, Teotl Iztacan (the place of the white god).

Tezcatlipoca and Quetzalcoatl are, in some contexts, antagonists, but alternatively they work together to restore the shattered universe and initiate the fifth (present) sun. Tezcatlipoca transformed himself into an *avatara* Mixcoatl Camaxtli, the "red Tezcatlipoca" (also said to be his son), to create fire. He is also the great magician who dragged the earth mother from the primordial waters in the form of a huge alligator, Cipactli. In the struggle she bit off his left foot, but to prevent her from sinking back into the waters of creation he tore out her lower jaw.

Tezcatlipoca is the patron deity of young warriors and is capable of excesses of cruelty. A sacrificial victim was chosen annually and killed by having his heart torn out.

The god is perceived in various aspects and colors, according to the position of the sun. In the east he is yellow or white, in the south blue (see also Huitzilpochtli), in the west red and in the north black.

Tezcatlipoca-Itztlacoliuhqui
Temple deity. Aztec (classical Mesoamerican) [Mexico]. One of four described in the codices *Borgia*, *Cospi* and *Fejervary-Mayer*. See also Tonatiuh, Centeocihuatl and Mictlantecuhtli.

Tezcatzoncatl
Minor fertility god. Aztec (classical Mesoamerican) [Mexico]. One of the group classed as the Ometochtli complex concerned with the maguey plant and the brewing of the alcoholic drink pulque.

Thab-Iha
Hearth god. Bon (pre-Lamaist) [Tibet]. Color: red. Attribute: a snake in the form of a noose.

Thakur Deo
Local god. Hindu. Known from various villages in northern India. His consort is Dharti Mata. May appear with a white horse. Also Thakkur.

Thalna
Goddess of childbirth. Etruscan. Depicted as a youthful woman, often associated with the sky god Tin.

Thanatos
Minor god of death. Greek. According to legend, he is one of the two sons of Nyx, the goddess of

night, and lives beside the river Lethe in a remote cave that he shares with his twin brother Hypnos, god of sleep.

Thatmanitu

Local goddess of healing. Western Semitic. Recognized chiefly at Sidon, but also included in the Ugaritic pantheon.

Thea

Goddess. Greek. One of the Titans, consort of Hyperion and mother of the sun god Helios and of the goddesses Eos (dawn) and Selene (moon). Also Theia.

Theandros

God. Pre-Islamic northern Arabian. Known only from Greek and Roman inscriptions.

Themis

Goddess of justice and order. Greco-Roman. A daughter of the sky god Ouranos and earth mother Gaia, though not classed as one of the Titans. A consort of Zeus and the mother of the *Horae* and *Moires*. She is the impartial deity who sits blindfolded in Hades and judges the souls of the dead to determine whether they will pass to the Elysian fields or to the fires of Tartarus. Attended by three lesser judgment deities, Aeacos, Minos and Rhadamanthos. The guilty are handed over to the Furies—the Dirae, Erinyes or Eumenides. At Rhamnus in Attica, Themis was accorded a sanctuary built in the sixth century BC beside which that of Nemesis, goddess of indignation, was built in the fifth century.

Thesan

Goddess of the dawn. Etruscan. Also invoked at childbirth, since she brings new life into the world each day with her light.

Thetis

Goddess of rivers and oceans. Greek. One of the daughters of Nereus, Thetis takes responsibility, with Okeanos, for the oceans and rivers. She is among the lesser known deities; according to my-thology she is a mermaid, but she is particularly significant as the mother of Achilles by an unnamed mortal. According to legend she attempted to render him immortal by immersing him in the waters of the Styx. She failed because the heel by which she held him had remained dry. His education she entrusted to the centaur Chiron. She was surrounded by attendant sea creatures known as Nereids and after Achilles's death she returned to the ocean depths.

THOR   *(thunder god)*

Origin Nordic (Icelandic). Primarily god of war but also a deity of the sky, storms, sea journeys and the administration of justice.

Known period of worship Viking period circa 700 AD and earlier, until well into the Christian era, probably until 1100 AD or later.

Synonyms Horagalles (Lappish); Thunor (Anglo-Saxon).

Center(s) of cult Uppsala (Sweden); Dublin (Ireland); many others throughout the Nordic region.

Art references small sculptures and reliefs; probably the subject of other anonymous carvings.

Literary sources Icelandic codices; *Prose Edda* (Snorri); *Historia Danica* (Saxo); votive inscriptions; place names.

Thor is one of the more important Aesir sky gods in Norse religion, the chief defender of the realms of Asgard. His mother is said to be Iord, the *prima materia* of earth, and he lives in the hall Bilskirnir. He probably achieved greater popularity than Othin. Described as a massive red-bearded champion wearing iron gloves and a girdle of might, and wielding a short-handled hammer, Mjollnir, that creates lightning when struck against stone and becomes a thunderbolt when thrown. He may also carry an ax and both may represent fertility symbols. The swastika, thought to derive from the ax, becomes associated with him and he may be further symbolized by a sacred gold or silver arm ring.

Thor possesses a prodigious appetite for food and drink. He rides the heavens in a chariot drawn by two goats, Tanngniost and Tanngrisnir, whose wheels cause the sound of the thunder. He is strongly linked with trees and sacred groves. The name Thor is the origin of Thursday.

THOTH

Origin Egyptian. God of the moon and of wisdom.

Known period of worship circa 3000 BC until the end of Egyptian history circa 400 AD.

Synonyms Djeheuty (archaic).

Center(s) of cult Khemnu [el-Ashmunein] or Hermopolis (Greek). Also in the Sinai, in Nubia and in the Dakhleh oasis in the western desert.

Art references sculpture; stone reliefs; wall paintings, etc.

Literary sources Pyramid Texts; coffin texts, etc.

Thoth is the patron deity of scribes and of knowledge, including scientific, medical and mathematic writing, and is said to have given mankind the art of hieroglyphic writing. He is important as a mediator and counselor among the gods and is the scribe of the Heliopolis Ennead pantheon. Thoth is described in some inscriptions as a son of Re, but according to mythology he was born from the head of the god Seth. He may be depicted in human form with the head of an ibis, wholly as an ibis, or as a seated baboon sometimes with its torso covered in feathers. His attributes include a crown that consists of a crescent moon surmounted by a moon disc.

Thoth is generally regarded as a benign deity. He is also scrupulously fair and is responsible not only for entering in the record the souls who pass to the afterlife, but of ajudicating in the Hall of the Two Truths.

The Pyramid Texts reveal a violent side of his nature by which he decapitates the adversaries of truth and wrenches out their hearts.

Thuremlin

God of passage. Australasia. Local deity of several tribes in New South Wales. Said to oversee the transition from adolescence to manhood. The initiate was taken away by the god, "killed," restored to life and endured a tooth being knocked out to signify the arrival of adulthood and full incorporation into the society of the tribe. Also Daramulun.

Tia *(death by violence)*

God of death. Haida Indian [Queen Charlotte Island, Canada]. Those who are about to die a violent death are said to hear him groaning about the camp and see him as a headless corpse with blood flowing endlessly from his severed neck. He flies through the air. See also Ta'xet.

TIAMAT

Origin Mesopotamian (Babylonian-Akkadian) [Iraq]. Primordial creator goddess.

Known period of worship circa 2000 BC until circa 200 BC.

Synonyms none.

Center(s) of cult Babylon.

Art references plaques, votive stelae; glyptics, etc.

Literary sources cuneiform texts, particularly the creation epic *Enuma Eliš*.

Tiamat is the power of the ocean waters and is intimately involved with the Babylonian creation story. She combines with the underground fresh waters of Apsu to give birth to eleven monstrous beings and is said to have been enraged by the death of Apsu at the hands of Enki and at the behest of a group of gods headed by Marduk. In revenge she forms other deities in the primordial cosmos into a rival group and chooses, as her second consort, the minor god Kingu to lead her army against Marduk. Marduk ultimately splits her in two, making the vault of heaven out of one half, using her eyes as the sources of the Tigris and Euphrates, and heaping the mountains over her head.

Tiberinus

River god. Roman. The deity of the river Tiber. His consort is one of the Vestal Virgins sacrificed by drowning. His sanctuary was built on an island in the river and, until some time during the Republican period, all bridges across the river were made wholly of wood so as not to offend him. The adverse connotations of iron are unclear, but its use was forbidden by official decree.

Tien Mu

Goddess of lightning. Chinese. She is said to flash her mirror at an intended victim of the god Lei Kung's thunderbolts to ensure his aim.

T'ien Tsun *(heavenly and honored)*

Generic title of gods. Taoist (Chinese). The name given to each of the three holy images in a Taoist temple: the "perfect holy one," the "highest holy one" and the "greatest holy one." Also Tian-zhu.

Tienoltsodi

God of oceans and fresh water. Navaho [USA]. He controls the waters that have fallen on earth, as distinct from those in the heavens, which are ruled by the rain god Tonenili.

Tifenua *(lord of the land)*

Chthonic fertility god. Polynesian [Tikopia]. He is linked with the sea god Faivarongo and with the sky god Atua I Kafika. His father is Pusiuraura, a powerful deity personified by the reef eel, and his mother is one of the Sa-Nguti-Te-Moana. Also Pu-I-Te-Moana.

Ti'hmar

Supreme god. Kolyma Tungus [Siberia]. The name by which the Christian god was still addressed after local culture was influenced by Russian Orthodoxy.

Tiki

Creator god. Polynesian (including Maori). One of the children of Ranginui and Papatuanuku who created mankind. In some Polynesian traditions he is represented as the first man, akin to Adam. The word is also incorporated in *tiki-wananga* or "god stick," which describes the wooden or stone images of deities that are usually minimally worked and stand about fifty centimeters tall. Only thirty or so examples of these are known, most having been destroyed by Christian missionaries. The celebrated large Maori totems are depictions of ancestors who appear as human/bird or reptile hybrids. Also Ki'i (Hawaiian).

Tiksnosnisa *(hot and sharp)*

God. Buddhist. Apparently connected with the guardian deities or *dikpalas* in the northwestern quarter. Color: sky green (possibly meaning "overcast"). Attributes: book and sword.

Tilla

Bull god. Hittite and Hurrian. The attendant and vehicle of the weather god Tešub.

Timaiti-Ngava Ringavari *(soft-bodied)*

Primordial being. Polynesian [Hervey Islands]. The female principle that, with Timatekore, engendered the earth mother Papatuanuku.

Timatekore *(nothing more)*

Primordial being. Polynesian [Hervey Islands]. The male principle that, with Timaiti-Ngava Ringavari, engendered the earth mother Papatuanuku.

Tin

Sky god. Etruscan. His attribute is a bunch of lightning flashes and he may appear in association with Thalna, goddess of birth. In Roman culture he becomes syncretized with Jupiter.

TIN HAU *(queen of heaven)*

Origin Taoist (Chinese). Goddess of waters.

Known period of worship circa 1300 AD until present.

Synonyms Lin Ma-Tzu; Ma-Niang; Ma-Tzu.

Center(s) of cult Hangchow and throughout Chinese culture.

Art references paintings and sculptures.

Literary sources various philosophical and religious texts, mostly inadequately researched and untranslated.

Tin Hau originates as a mortal born on the island of Mei-Chou in the Fukien province of China, the daughter of a minor official. She died at the age of twenty-eight, having perfected herself and having experienced recurrent dreams of saving fishing boats from the waters close to her village. This tradition was inscribed on the walls of a sanctuary in Hangchow in 1228 AD. She was deified in 1278 by the Mongol emperor Kublai Khan, who introduced the title "queen of heaven." The first of the Ch'ing emperors subsequently conferred on her the title "imperial consort." She was thus subordinate only to Yu Huang Shang Ti, the Jade Emperor.

Tin Hau was first worshiped as a guardian goddess of boats and fishermen, but her role was extended so that she became the deity of oceans and fresh waters. She is celebrated in a festival on the twenty-third day of the third month. In art she is frequently depicted with two grotesque attendant figures known as "Thousand League Eyes" and "Favoring Wind Ears."

Tinirau *(innumerable)*
Fish god. Polynesian [Hervey Islands]. The second offspring of the great mother Vari-Ma-Te-Takere and the younger sibling of Avatea. He is said to live in the coconut of the world on a sacred isle called Motu-Tapu immediately below the home of Avatea and to own ponds full of all kinds of fish. He is depicted as half man (right side) and half fish (left side) in the form of a sprat.

Tinnit
Goddess. Pontic (Carthaginian). See Tanit.

Tino Taata
Creator god. Polynesian [Society Islands]. Probably regarded as the tutelary deity who engendered mankind and equating therefore to the more widely recognized Polynesian god Tangaroa.

Tir
God of wisdom. Pre-Christian Armenian. Also concerned with writing and revered as an oracle.

Tirawa
Creator god. Pawnee Indian [USA]. A remote and vaguely defined figure who is present in the elements of wind and storm. Lightning is the flashing of his eye. He provides the tribe with all their needs and is invoked by the Pawnee *shamans*.

Tirumal *(the excellent black one)*
Creator god. Early Dravidian (Tamil). Thought to reside in trees and equating with Visnu. In later Hinduism used as an epithet of Visnu.

Tišpak
God. Mesopotamian (Babylonian-Akkadian). The tutelary deity of the city of Ešnumma.

Titans
A race of gods. Greek. The secondary group of deities in the pre-Hellenic pantheon, headed by the sky god Ouranos and the earth mother Gaia. They have six pairs of children: Okeanos and Tethys, Kronos and Rhea, Hyperion and Thea, Koeos and Phoebe, Iapetos and Klymene, Kreos and Eurybe. According to legend the children usurped their father but were eventually beaten by Zeus, heading the major group of the pantheon, who hurled them into the abyss of Tartaros.

Titlacahuan *(we his slaves)*
Omnipotent god. Aztec (classical Mesoamerican) [Mexico]. A universal and generally malevolent power. One of the group classed as the Tezcatlipoca complex.

TIWAZ   *(derives from Indo-European word for god, dieus)*
Origin Germanic (northwestern Europe). Chief sky god; god of war.

Known period of worship circa 500 BC and probably earlier until Christianization circa 1100 AD.

Synonyms Tyr; Tiw or Tig (Anglo-Saxon); Teiwa (archaic).

Center(s) of cult scattered forest sanctuaries.

Art references reliefs in stone and metal.

Literary sources runic inscriptions (see Wodan).

Germanic war god and probably chief among their sky gods, one of two contenders on which Othin may have been modeled in Nordic (Icelandic) culture. Classical writers identified the Roman war god Mars with Tiwaz, thus for the third day of the week we have *mardi* in French but Tuesday in English. The runic symbol for Tiwaz is sometimes cut on spears, presumably to offer talismanic protection. Tiwaz represents law and order and appears as a more honest judiciary than Othin (see Othin).

According to legend, Tiwaz is a one-armed god, having sacrificed his hand to the jaws of the wolf Fenrir so that it might be bound up. This may have been the origin of a practice by which, according to Tacitus, the Germanic Semnones tribe bound the hands and feet of those entering a woodland sanctuary, probably dedicated to Tiwaz. At Ragnarok (doom) it is believed that Fenrir will break free and swallow the sun. According to Snorri (*Prose Edda*) the wolf Garm, possibly Fenrir by another name, kills Tiwaz in the final battle of the gods. Place names such as Tuesley in Surrey, England, derive from the name of the god.

Ti'ykitiy
Sun spirit. Yakut [southeastern and central Siberia]. Often identified with the supreme being Ayi'urun Toyo'n.

Ti'zil-Kutkhu
Guardian spirit. Kamchadal [southeastern Siberia]. One of the sons of the creator spirit Kutkhu,

his consort is Si'duku and he is considered to be the progenitor of the Kamchadal tribe.

Tlacahuepan   *(human beam)*
Minor god of war. Aztec (classical Mesoamerican) [Mexico]. A patron god of Mexico and one of the group classed as the Huitzilpochtli complex.

Tlahuizcalpantecuhtli
(lord of the dawn)
God of the morning star (Venus). Aztec (classical Mesoamerican) [Mexico]. An incarnation or *avatara* of the god Quetzalcoatl and one of the group classed as the Mixcoatl complex. The ruler of the twelfth of the thirteen heavens known at the time of the Spanish conquest, Teotl Tlatlauhcan (the place of the red god). In other traditions (described in codices *Borgia* and *Vaticanus B*) he is one of the four gods supporting the lowest heaven at each cardinal point; he resides in the east.

Tlalchitonatiuh   *(on the earth sun)*
Chthonic underworld god. Aztec (classical Mesoamerican) [Mexico]. One of the group classed as the Mictlantecuhtli complex.

TLALOC
Origin Aztec (classical Mesoamerican) [Mexico]. Rain god.

Known period of worship mainly circa 750 AD to 1500 AD, but probably much earlier and still continuing among peasants in rural areas.

Synonyms none.

Center(s) of cult Tenochtitlan, Teotihuacan, Tula, etc.

Art references stone sculptures; murals and codex illustrations.

Literary sources pre-Columbian codices.

One of the principal personalities in Aztec creation mythology, Tlaloc was fashioned with the water goddess Chalchiuhtlicue. According to some traditions he is the father of the moon god Tecciztecatl, whom he sacrificed in the great fire to engender the moon. He is also perceived as the ruler of the eighth of the thirteen heavens known at the time of the Spanish conquest, Ilhuicatl Xox-ouhcan (the blue heaven). He is a fertility god who created water and rain and presided over the third of the five world ages, which he ended with a great fiery rain. He has control over lightning. He is perceived in four forms—black, white, blue and red—but typically blue with "goggles" over the eyes and serpent fangs. It has been suggested that he evolved from a jaguar-type animistic deity worshiped by the Olmecs. He was propitiated to bring rain at the end of the dry season by sacrificing large numbers of small children on mountain altars.

At Tenochtitlan, the Great Temple is dedicated jointly to Huitzilopochtli and Tlaloc. One of the best sculptures is from Cuilapan, Oaxaca (early classic period). A tableau among the palace murals of Tepantitla is allegedly dominated by the god from whose hands flow droplets of water with a background of trees, butterflies and human figures. Wall paintings including a mural depiction exist at Zacuala. At Tula, Hidalgo, Pyramid B used by the Toltecs includes human sculptures known as *chacmools,* holding dishes that are believed to have held human hearts for Tlaloc.

Tlaloque-Tepictoton *(the small molded ones)*
Fertility and rain god. Aztec (classical Mesoamerican) [Mexico]. The personification of small, rain-bearing hills. One of the group classed as the Tlaloc complex.

Tlaltecuhtli
Chthonic creator goddess. Aztec (classical Mesoamerican) [Mexico]. In Aztec cosmogony, Tlaltecuhtli is a monstrous, toad-like figure whose body is cleaved in two by the gods Tezcatlipoca and Quetzalcoatl to fashion heaven and earth. The ruler of the second of the thirteen heavens known at the time of the Spanish conquest, Ilhuicatl Tlalocan Ipan Metztli (the heaven of the paradise of the rain god over the moon), she is also one of

the group classed as the Mictlantecuhtli complex. She is said to swallow the sun each evening and disgorge it in the dawn. She also devours the blood and hearts of sacrificial victims and the souls of the dead. See also Cipactli.

Tlazolteotl (Ixcuiname)
Chthonic or earth goddess. Aztec (classical Mesoamerican) [Mexico]. Known locally from the gulf coast region of Huaxteca. A maternal goddess linked with sexual sin and personifying filth. One of the group of fertility deities classed as the Teteoinnan complex.

Tloque Nahauque *(ruler of the near and the adjacent)*
Creator god. Aztec (classical Mesoamerican) [Mexico]. One of the group classed as the Omeotl complex.

Tna'nto *(dawn coming out)*
Spirit of the dawn. Koryak [southeastern Siberia]. The apotheosis of the first light of dawn in the eastern sky.

Tnecei'vune *(dawn walking woman)*
Spirit of the dawn. Chukchee [southeastern Siberia]. The female consort of the dawn. See also Tne'sqan, Mratna'irgin, Lietna'irgin and Na'chit-na'irgin.

Tne'sqan *(top of the dawn)*
Spirit of the dawn. Chukchee [southeastern Siberia]. One of four beings controlling the dawn in different directions. Sacrifice is made and blood is sprinkled in the appropriate direction.

Toa'lalit
God of hunters. Bella Coola Indian [British Columbia, Canada]. Oversees the hunting of mountain goats. He is invisible, but great hunters may catch a glimpse of his hat, moccasins or mountain staff moving about. His animals are the lynx and raven.

Tobadzistsini *(child of the water)*
War god. Navaho [USA]. Considered younger and inferior to Nayenezgani, the chief war god of the Navaho. His mother conceived him through the magical power of a waterfall. His priest wears similar attire to that of Nayenezgani, but the mask is painted with red ochre except for a triangular black area bordered with white. It also has a fringe of yellow or red wool.

Tokakami
God of death. Huichol Indian (Mesoamerican) [Mexico]. His chief antagonist is the moon goddess Metsaka.

Toko'yoto *(crab)*
Guardian spirit. Koryak [southeastern Siberia]. In Koryak tradition, one of the "owners" of the world, the master and creator of the Pacific Ocean. His name is that of a large sea crab. In some legends he is the father of Miti, the mother of the Koryak people.

Tomiyauhtecuhtli *(our male corn efflorescence lord)*
Fertility and rain god. Aztec (classical Mesoamerican) [Mexico]. One of the group classed as the Tlaloc complex.

Tomor
Creator god. Illyrian [Albania]. Also a god of the winds. Depicted in human form attended by eagles and still invoked by rural peasants.

Tomwo'get *(self-created)*
Archetypal creator being. Koryak [southeastern Siberia]. The consort of Ha'na and father of Supreme Being, Tenanto'mwan, and of Big Raven, Quikinna'qu.

Tonacacihuatl *(our flesh lady)*
Primordial deity. Aztec (classical Mesoamerican) [Mexico]. In the most widely accepted Aztec cosmogony, this is the self-created, eternal, female principle who combines with Tonacatecuhtli to create all life, transferring souls from heaven to the mortal womb. It exists in the highest, thirteenth heaven and once engendered the sun god Tezcatlipoca, from whom all other deities in the pantheon stemmed. One of the group classed as the Omeotl complex. Also Omecihuatl.

Tonacatecuhtli *(our flesh lord)*
Primordial deity. Aztec (classical Mesoamerican) [Mexico]. In the most widely accepted Aztec cosmogony, this is the self-created, eternal, male principle who combines with Tonacacihuatl to create all life. It exists in the highest, thirteenth heaven and once engendered the sun god Tezcatlipoca, from whom all other deities in the pantheon stemmed. Also one of the group classed as the Ometeotl complex. According to tradition Tonacatecuhtli drove four roads through the center of the earth after the cataclysm of the fourth world age (Atl) to disperse the flood waters of the deluge. His four sons, aided by four unnamed beings, raised the fallen sky, which they propped up on great trees created by Tezcatlipoca and Quetzalcoatl at the four cardinal points. See also Tlahuizcalpantecuhtli, Ehecatl-Quetzalcoatl and Mictlantecuhtli.

In alternative mythology Tonacatecuhtli is the ruler of the sixth of the thirteen heavens known at the time of the Spanish conquest, Ilhuicatl Yayauhcan (the blackish heaven). Also Ometecuhtli.

Tonaleque
Goddess. Aztec (classical Mesoamerican) [Mexico]. The ruler of the fifth of the thirteen heavens known at the time of the Spanish conquest, Ilhuicatl Huixtotlan (heaven of the salt fertility goddess).

Tonatiuh *(soaring eagle)*
Creator god. Aztec (classical Mesoamerican) [Mexico]. He presides over the fifth (present) world age, personified by the sun Ollin and destined to end in a cataclysmic earthquake. He is the ruler of the fourth of the thirteen heavens known at the time of the Spanish conquest, also called Ilhuicatl Tonatiuh (the heaven of the sun). In other texts,

specifically codices *Borgia, Cospi* and *Fejervary-Mayer*, he is depicted as a temple deity.

Tonenili
Rain god. Navaho [USA]. The so-called "lord of the celestial waters," he controls the rain from the skies as opposed to that of lakes, rivers and seas. He is said to scatter his waters to the four cardinal points and storm clouds begin to gather. He is also the water carrier for the other gods in the pantheon. He wears a blue mask with a fringe of hair and a spruce collar, but is otherwise naked save for a scarlet loincloth and a leather belt with silver ornamentation and a fox skin dangling at the back. His attributes, in mythology only, are two wicker water bottles, one blue and one black, whose strings are rainbows.

Topoh
Astral god. Pokot and Suk [Uganda and western Kenya, East Africa]. The son of the creator god Tororut and his consort Seta, he is god of the evening star.

Tork
Mountain god. Pre-Christian Armenian. Of terrifying appearance, he is the guardian deity of mountains and their inhabitants.

Tornarssuk *(big tornak or shaman)*
Supreme being. Eskimo. The master of the *tornat,* the group of controlling deities. He is essentially benevolent and can be communicated with through the individual *tornak* of a *shaman.* His home is in the underworld in the land of souls. He is described as being of vague appearance, possibly in the guise of a huge bear, though in Greenland Eskimo tradition he lives in the sea, appearing as a large fat seal with long tentacles (i.e., possibly a cuttlefish). He devours the souls of those he can capture. With the introduction of Christianity he was syncretized with the devil.

Toro
Creator god. Ngbandi [Zaire, central Africa]. He is perceived as a great serpent, the son of Kan-

galogba, who is both the spirit of the dragonfly and the symbol of the sacred river Oubangui.

Tororut
Creator god. Pokot and Suk [Uganda and western Kenya, East Africa]. He is invoked in a special annual ceremony, which involves the sacrifice of an ox, to ensure safety of crops and cattle. The same ritual is performed in times of drought, famine or plague. His brother is Asis the sun god. His consort is Seta and their children include the rain god Ilat, Arawa the moon and Topoh the evening star.

Totatis
See Teutates.

Totilma'il *(father-mother)*
Creator being. Mayan (Tzotzil, classical Mesoamerican) [Mexico]. An androgynous personality who represents the ancestral source of creation.

Totoltecatl
Fertility god. Aztec (classical Mesoamerican) [Mexico]. One of the group classed as the Ometochtli complex concerned with the maguey plant and the brewing of the alcoholic drink pulque.

Tou Mou
Goddess of measure. Chinese. Usually depicted with many arms and with a caste mark on her forehead, suggesting that she derives from the goddess of the aurora, Marici, in Indian Buddhism. She is considered to live in the constellation of Ursa Major and may also be an aspect of the astral goddess Tin Hau.

Touia Fatuna *(iron stone)*
Earth goddess. Polynesian [Tonga]. The daughter of Kele (slime) and Limu (seaweed), she is the apotheosis of rock deep in the earth and is periodically in labor, at which time she rumbles and shakes and produces children.

Toumou
God of uncertain function. Egyptian. A deity whose mummy was allegedly kept at Heliopolis.

Toyo-Uke-Bime
Goddess of foodstuffs. Shinto [Japan]. An ambiguous deity often identified with Inari, she is said in the *Kojiki* to be a daughter of Waku-Musubi-No-Kami and a great granddaughter of Izanagi and Izanami. Her main sanctuary is the Geku in Ise, whither she was allegedly removed from Tamba after the emperor had received a dream message from the sun goddess Amaterasu in 478 AD.

Tozi
Goddess of healing. Aztec (classical Mesoamerican) [Mexico]. Also the deity of sweet water remedial baths.

Trailokyavijaya *(lord of three worlds)*
God. Buddhist (Mahayana). Seen standing on the Hindu deities Mahesvara (Siva) and Gauri. Color: blue. Attributes: arrow, bell, bow, club, hook, noose, prayer wheel, staff and sword. Also an alternative name for Acala.

Trayastrinsa *(the thirty-three)*
Collective name for the group of *deva* gods. Hindu (Vedic). One of the many lists of deities in Hinduism, this one is contained in the *Rg Veda* and includes thirty-three names divided into three groups of eleven in each of the three worlds. Subsequently, the *devas* were separated into eight *vasus*, twelve *adityas*, eleven *rudras* and two *asvins*. In later Hinduism the number thirty-three is increased hyperbolically to 330 million and *deva* refers to gods excluding the major triad of Brahma, Visnu and Siva.

Triglav
God of war. Slav (Baltic). The head of the pantheon in Stettin and also mentioned in association with Brandenburg, he is described in chronicles as bearing three heads.

Trikantakidevi *(goddess of three thorns)*
Goddess. Hindu. Of terrible appearance. Color: part red, part black. Attributes: conch, two lamps, prayer wheel and teeth.

Trimurti
Collective title for the major triad. Hindu. A three-headed representation of Brahma, Visnu and Siva as one entity. Contested by some authors, who argue that Brahma, who is almost invariably represented with four heads, would be included here with only one.

Tripura *(lady of the three cities)*
Mother goddess. Hindu and Jain. In Jainism regarded as one of the *astamataras*. In Hinduism the *Sakti* of Tripurantaka, an *ugra* (terrible) representation of the god Siva, alternatively a form of the goddess Parvati. The "three cities" are the cities of gold, silver and iron, one in heaven, one in the air and one on earth, which Siva destroyed in his form as Tripurantaka. Tripura is depicted attended by vultures. Attributes: book, hook, noose and rosary.

Trita
God(dess). Hindu (Vedic). Known from the *Rg Veda*. An obscure form of Indra with strong water attributes. Also Aptya.

Tritons
Minor sea gods. Roman. The children of Poseidon and Amphitrite who are depicted as hybrid fish-men. Generally included in the royal court of the god Neptune. Attributes: conches.

Trivikrama *(taking three steps)*
God. Hindu (Epic and Puranic). It may originally have been the name of a sun god, but is taken as the incarnation of Visnu which strides the world in three steps in his dwarfish manifestation, and is linked with the Hindu perception of the three parts of the world—heaven, air and earth. His *Sakti* is Santi. Normally depicted with the left leg raised. Attributes: arrow, bow, club, conch, knife, lotus, noose, plough, prayer wheel, staff and sword.

Trograin
Minor god. Celtic (Irish). See Lug.

Tsai Shen
God of wealth. Chinese. The deity associated with mandarins. He is depicted wearing a pink robe associated with Yin and the season of spring. His attributes include a ring of coins around the hem of the robe, a lotus motif of fertility on the breast and a golden mushroom, a symbol of longevity, carried in the hand. One of his attendants carries a deer horn, symbol of potency, while the other carries a bowl of money and a sheaf of golden grass. Tsai Shen may appear in company with Fu Shen, god of luck, and Shou Lao, god of longevity.

Tsa'qamae
God of salmon migration. Qwe'gsotenox Indian [British Columbia, Canada]. The so-called "head winter dancer," his attributes include head ring and neck ring of bark to which heads are attached.

Tsohanoai *(day bearer)*
Sun god. Navaho [USA]. Not regarded as a supreme god, Tsohanoai moves across the sky, invisible, behind the disc of the sun, *sa,* which is his shield. His consort is the fertility goddess Estsanatlehi and he is the father of the war god Nayenezgani. He is also attributed with the creation of all the big game animals. He is thought to walk on a rainbow and ride a blue steed. He is never depicted in art nor impersonated.

Tsuki-Yomi
Moon god. Shinto [Japan]. Engendered from the right eye of Izanagi immediately after Amaterasu was engendered from the left. There is very little reference to him in the sacred texts and his is a highly aesthetic form of worship. Allegedly he slew the food *kami* Uke-Mochi. He is depicted riding a horse and a number of sanctuaries are addressed to his cult, including the two Tsuki-Yomi-No-Miya shrines in the Ise Jingu temple. He

also enjoys an ancient sanctuary on the island of Iki. Also Tsuki-Yomi-Otoko.

Tsunigoab *(wounded knee)*
Creator god. Khoi [Namibia, southwestern Africa]. As his name suggests, he walks with a limp. His injury was sustained in a primordial battle with his archrival Gaunab, the god of darkness, who was eventually driven away to live in the black heaven. Tsunigoab used to be invoked at dawn each day.

Tu *(1)*
Chthonic earth goddess. Chinese. A fertility spirit also identified as she who was invoked to bring good harvests by phallic-shaped mounds of earth left in the fields.

Tu *(2)*
Primordial god. Polynesian. One of three elements, with Tane and Lono, who existed in chaos and night, which they broke into pieces, allowing day to come in. Tu represents stability. He is also regarded as a war god. Also Ku (Hawaiian).

TUATHA DE DANANN *(peoples of the goddess Danu)*
Origin Celtic (Irish). Collective name for the pantheon.

Known period of worship prehistoric times until Christianization circa 400 AD.

Synonyms none.

Center(s) of cult various throughout Ireland, but chiefly Tara.

Art references various stone sculptures and reliefs.

Literary sources Books of Invasions; Cycles of Kings; votive inscriptions.

An association of deities probably going back to pretribal times. The deities include the Dagda, Lug, Gobniu, Nuadu Argatlam and others and represent a possibly nontribal hierarchy of the supernatural joined against a common foe, the powers of destruction and misfortune, the *Fomoire*, and the *Fir Bolg* who were allegedly an agricultural tribe from Greece. These were prehistoric invaders of Ireland who were defeated in two battles fought at Moytura.

Tule
Spider god. Zande [Sudan and Zaire, Africa]. He descended from the sky on a rope, carrying all plants and seeds. He also gave mankind water and the tools of cultivation.

Tumatauenga
God of war. Polynesian (including Maori). One of the children of the prime parents Ranginui and Papatuanuku, he proposed the slaughter of his parents when it was decided to separate them as sky and earth. He was subsequently given charge over mankind (*tangata*), which he imbued with his lust for the warfare and violence that was characteristic of Maori culture. Also Kumatauenga (Hawaiian).

Tu-Metua   *(stick-by-parent)*
God. Polynesian [Hervey Islands]. The sixth child of Vari-Ma-Te-Takere, the primordial mother. Torn from her right side, he stays with her in the confined space at the bottom of the world coconut and lives in endless silence.

Tumuteanaoa   *(echo)*
Goddess. Polynesian [Hervey Islands]. The fourth child of Vari-Ma-Te-Takere, the primordial mother. Torn from her right side, Tumuteanaoa lives in Te-Parai-Tea (hollow gray rocks) below the home of the god Tango.

Tunek
God of seal hunters. Eskimo. A fearsome being of huge stature (four meters tall) who lives on the ice fields and is capable of running very fast. He also sits in his kayak in the fog and catches seal in huge traps.

Turan
Goddess of love. Etruscan. The tutelary deity of Vulci, she is depicted bearing wings and with attributes including a swan, a dove and a blossom.

Turms
Chthonic underworld god. Etruscan. Modeled on the Greek messenger god Hermes, with *caduceus* (winged rod), winged shoes and cloak, he leads the souls of the dead toward the underworld.

Tutu
God. Mesopotamian (Babylonian-Akkadian). The tutelary god of Borsippa, near Babylon, during the reign of Hammurabi in the old Babylonian period, but later superseded by Nabu.

Tvastar   *(carpenter)*
Creator god. Hindu (Vedic). The "divine builder" who fashions living creatures on earth. The Hindu equivalent of the Roman god Vulcanus. An *aditya* or sun god and the father of Saranyu. Attributes: *homajakalika* (an uncertain fire device), ladle and two lotuses. Also Tastar; Tvashtri; Visvakarman.

Tyche
Goddess of fortune. Greco-Roman. She appears as a nereid in the *Hymn to Demeter* (Homer). According to Hesiod's *Theogony* she is the daughter of Okeanos. Elsewhere she is identified as the daughter of Zeus and Hera. She is depicted carrying a rudder or, alternatively, cornucopiae. Also mentioned as Agathe Tyche, the consort of Agathos Daemon. She became widely identified with the Asian mother goddess Kybele but was replaced, in Roman times, by the goddess Fortuna and associated symbolically with a wheel device. She retained popularity for a long time. There is a record that the Emperor Julian sacrificed to Tyche at Antioch in 361–62 AD and her temple was still intact during the reign of Theodosius (379–95).

Tyr
See Tiwaz.

Tzontemoc *(head-descending)*
Minor underworld god. Aztec (classical Meso-american) [Mexico]. One of the group classed as the Mictlantecuhtli complex.

Tzu Sun Niangniang

Mother goddess. Chinese. One of the "nine dark ladies" of the pantheon who are regarded as having a protective role. She was the mortal wife of a minor official and, having borne him five sons and two daughters, committed suicide in order to ensure her future chastity. She is invoked at weddings to provide children, especially sons, and special cakes are eaten by the bride and groom. One of her more famous sanctuaries, on the island of Taiwan, is the Yin Yang Stone.

Tzultacah *(mountain valley)*
Chthonic and thunder gods. Mayan (classical Mesoamerican) [Mexico]. A group of deities who combine the features of earth and rain gods. Although there are considered to be an indefinite number of Tzultacahs, only thirteen are invoked in prayers. They live in, and may personify, springs and rivers, but each is the owner of a specific mountain. They are attended by snakes that are dispatched to punish mankind for wrongdoing. Nonpoisonous varieties are sent to discipline against minor offenses, rattlesnakes for more serious depravity.

U

Ua-Ildak

Vegetation goddess. Mesopotamian (Babylonian-Akkadian). The deity responsible for pastures and poplar trees.

Ubertas

Minor god of agriculture. Roman. Known particularly from the reign of Tiberias in the second century BC and associated with prosperity.

Ucchusma

God. Buddhist. An emanation of Aksobhya or Ratnasambhava. Also a form of Jambala. He is depicted as potbellied and stands upon Kubera, the Hindu god of riches, who lies with jewels spewing from his mouth. Attributes: cup, ichneumon fly, image of Aksobhya in the hair, moon disc and snakes. Three-eyed.

Udadhikumara

Generic name of a god. Jain [India]. One of a group of deities under the general title of *bhvana-vasi* (dwelling in places). They have youthful appearance.

Ugar

Vegetation god. Western Semitic (Syrian). Possibly linked with the Canaanite city of Ugarit [Ras Šamra].

Ugracandika *(violent Canda)*

Distinct form of the goddess Durga. Hindu (Epic and Puranic). One of a group of *navadurgas*, the "nine durgas."

Ugratara *(violent Tara)*

Goddess. Hindu (Puranic). A terrible deity who carries a cup and a corpse upon her head.

Ukko

Thunder god. Pre-Christian Finnish. Drives a cart which generates flashes of lightning as the horses' hoofs hit stones along the way; the noise of thunder comes from the wheels or from Ukko grinding grain with a big stone. Attributes: ax, blue robe, hammer and sword.

Ukur

Chthonic underworld god. Mesopotamian (Babylonian-Akkadian). See Kus.

ULL *[Gothic] (glory)*

Origin Nordic (Icelandic) and Germanic. May have originated as an early northern German sky god, but also connected with fertility and with the sea.

Known period of worship prehistoric times until Christianization circa 1100 AD.

Synonyms Ullr.

Center(s) of cult none known, but several place names in Norway and Sweden allude.

Art references possibly the subject of anonymous carvings.

Literary sources Icelandic codices; *Prose Edda* (Snorri); *Historia Danica* (Saxo); place names.

A sky god of Asgard, but with some links to the Vanir gods. The son of Sif and stepson of Thor, he is responsible for justice, and oaths were once sworn over the "ring of Ull." He may also have a role in the fertility of crops. Skaldic verse mentions the "ship of Ull," presumed to be a reference to the use of Ull's shield as a boat. A scabbard excavated in Denmark in the third century AD bears a runic inscription "servant of Ull."

271

According to Snorri he wears a bow and snow shoes. Saxo describes him crossing the sea on a magic bone—a ski? He may have a sister, Ullin.

ULU'TUYAR ULU TOYO'N
(titular horrible lord)
Origin Yakut [central Siberia]. Malevolent creator spirit.

Known period of worship prehistoric times until circa 1900 AD.

Synonyms none.

Center(s) of cult no fixed sanctuaries.

Art references possibly wood carvings.

Literary sources *The Yakut* (Jochelson).

A creative being superintending the *icci* (masters or owners) and generally seen in a destructive capacity. He lives in the upper world, and "in the west." See also Uru'n Ajy Toyo'n.

Uma
A form of the goddess Parvati. Hindu (Puranic). Uma is identified as the consort of Chandrashekhara, a form of Siva that includes the moon among his attributes. The meaning of her name is unclear, but possibly has maternal connotations. As Uma Maheshvara she fought with demons including Mahisha. Attributes: lotus, mirror, rosary and water jar. See also Somaskanda.

Umashi-Ashi-Kabi-Hiko-Ji-No-Kami
(pleasant reed shoot prince elder deity)
Creator being. Shinto [Japan]. The fourth of the deities to be listed in the *Kojiki* sacred text. He was engendered from the reeds floating on the primordial waters and is perceived as a remote and vague figure who hides himself from mankind.

Umvelinkwangi
Creator god. Zulu [South Africa]. He engendered all plants and animals on earth and is the father of the god Unkulunkulu, who was born from a reed and engendered mankind.

Uni
Tutelary goddess. Etruscan. The consort of the sky god Tin and linked with the region of Perugia.

Unkulunkulu
Creator god. Zulu [South Africa]. The androgynous son/daughter of Umvelinkwangi, and the progenitor of mankind, he was born from a reed.

Unumbote
Creator god. Bassari [Togo, West Africa]. Engendered all living things on earth.

Unxia
Goddess of marriage. Roman. Concerned with anointing the bridegroom's door.

Upakesini
Minor god. Buddhist. An attendant of Arapacana.

Upapattivasita   *(control of fitness)*
Minor goddess. Buddhist. One of a group of *vasitas* personifying the disciplines of spiritual regeneration. Color: mixed. Attribute: a creeper.

Upayaparamita
(perfecting success against enemies)
Philosophical deity. Buddhist. Spiritual offspring of Ratnasambhava. Color: green. Attributes: jeweled staff and staff on yellow lotus.

Upulvan   *(like the blue lotus)*
Local god. Singhalese [Sri Lanka]. The most senior of the four great gods of the Singhalese pantheon. Identified with Visnu, according to one tradition this deity had the specific task of protecting the culture of Sri Lanka from Buddhism. Conversely he stood by Gautama Buddha against the Hindu Mara.

Uranos
See Ouranos.

Uraš

Chthonic earth goddess. Mesopotamian (Sumerian). One of the named consorts of the sky god An and the mother of Nin'insinna.

URU'N AJY TOYO'N
(white creator lord)
Origin Yakut [central Siberia]. Creator spirit.

Known period of worship prehistoric times until circa 1900 AD.

Synonyms Ayi'-Uru'n Toyo'n (lord bright creator).

Center(s) of cult no fixed sanctuaries.

Art references possibly sculptures in wood.

Literary sources *The Yakut* (Jochelson).

A creator being said to live in the zenith of the upper world, and also "in the northeast," superintending the *icci* (masters or owners). He may also personify the sun. He tends to act for good and horses were sacrificed to him. Generally addressed by a beneficent or white shaman (*ajy ayuna*). See also Ulu'tuyar Ulu Toyo'n.

Usas

Goddess of the dawn. Hindu (Vedic). The daughter of Dyaus and, according to some texts, the consort of the sun god Surya. An auspicious deity, Usas brings the dawn, heralding Surya, and drives away darkness. She is the all-seeing eye of the gods. In the *Rg Veda* she is depicted as a beautiful young virginal figure who rides in a hundred chariots. She sets all things in motion and can render strength and fame to her devotees. In addition to being perceived as a sky goddess, she is also drawn as a mother goddess in the guise of a cow. Epithets include "mother of the gods" and "mother of cows." She is invoked to give the boon of longevity, but a more malignant aspect reveals her as a huntress who wastes human life. Usas sometimes enjoys domestic worship as a guardian hearth goddess who drives away darkness and evil spirits. She disappears, however, from the later traditions of Hinduism.

Usins

Astral god. Pre-Christian Latvian. Associated with both the morning and evening star and also has links with beekeepers and spring. Under Christian influence he becomes absorbed into the figure of St. George.

Uslo

Spirit of mountains. Yakut [central Siberia]. One of the guardians of the natural world answering to the mountain owner Xaya Iccita.

Usnisa

God. Buddhist. A *dikpala* or guardian of the upward direction. Also a collective term for a group of eight deities, including Usnisa, who are perceived as extensions of the *dhyanibuddhas*.
NOTE: the word describes, additionally, a type of curled hairstyle found in the characteristic iconography of *buddhas*. Color: yellow. Attributes: jewel, lotus, prayer wheel and sword. Three-headed.

Usnisavijaya   *(victorious)*

Primordial goddess. Buddhist (Mahayana). Form of Vairocana, widely worshiped in Tibet. Regarded as a female *bodhisattva* or *buddha*-designate, and a *dikpala* or guardian of the zenith direction. Also a deification of literature. One of a group of *dharanis*. Color: white. Attributes: arrow, bow, image of the Buddha on a lotus leaf, jewel, noose, prayer wheel, staff and water jar. Three-eyed, three-headed and with eight arms.

Uttarabhadrapada

Minor goddess of fortune. Hindu (Epic and Puranic). A moderate *naksatra*; daughter of Daksa and wife of Candra (Soma).

Uttaraphalguni

Minor goddess of fortune. Hindu (Epic and Puranic). A moderate *naksatra*; daughter of Daksa and wife of Candra (Soma).

Uttarasadha

Minor goddess of fortune. Hindu (Epic and Puranic). A benevolent *naksatra*; daughter of Daksa and wife of Candra (Soma).

Uttu

Vegetation goddess and goddess of weaving. Mesopotamian (Sumerian). Not to be confused with Utu the sun god, Uttu is a minor deity whose father is Enki. According to legend, Enki first impregnated the mother goddess Ninhursaǧa, whose nine-day gestation produced the goddess Nin-šar. She in turn was impregnated by Enki and, after a similar nine-day gestation, gave birth to the goddess Ninkurra. Through the same procedure with her grandfather, Ninkurra conceived the goddess Uttu. She is depicted as the goddess of weaving and of spiders.

UTU

Origin   Mesopotamian (Sumerian) [Iraq]. Sun god.

Known period of worship   circa 3500 BC to circa 1750 BC.

Synonyms   Šamaš (Akkadian).

Center(s) of cult   Sippar.

Art references   plaques, votive stelae and glyptics.

Literary sources   various creation epics and other texts.

Utu is the power of sunlight and, in a social context, of justice and the implementation of law. He is the son of the moon god Nanna and the goddess Ninlil. His brother and sister are Iškur and Inana. He rises "in the mountains of the east" and sets "in the mountans of the west." He is usually depicted wearing a horned helmet and carrying a sawedged weapon not unlike a pruning saw, which it is thought he has used to cut through the side of a mountain from which he emerges, symbolizing the dawn. He may also carry a mace and stand with one foot on the mountain.

V

Vac *(speech)*
1. Goddess of the spoken word. Hindu (Vedic). In some texts she is a daughter of Daksa and consort of Kasyapa. Alternatively she is the daughter of Ambhrna. Also known by the epithet "queen of the gods," Vac is the personification of the phenomenon of speech and oral communication. She gives the boon of hearing, speech and sight and she can lead a man to become a Brahman. She also personifies truth and sustains *soma* —the liquid essence of vision and immortality. She is said to have created the four Vedas, the basis of the earliest Hindu mythology. Though she takes a prominent place in the *Rg Veda*, Vac largely disappears from later Hindu traditions. She may have become syncretized with the goddess of wisdom, Sarasvati. She is generally depicted as an elegant womanly figure dressed in gold, but in the secondary capacity of a mother goddess she is also drawn as a cow.
2. God. Buddhist. An emanation of Amitabha and a variety of Manjusri.

Vadali
Minor goddess. Buddhist (Mahayana). An attendant of Marici. Attributes: flower, needle, noose and staff.

Vagisvara *(lord of speech)*
God of speech. Buddhist. The tutelary deity of Nepal. An emanation of all *dhyanibuddhas* (spiritual meditation *buddhas*) and a variety of Manjusri. Accompanied by a lion or seated upon a lion throne. Attribute: blue lotus.

Vagitanus
Minor god of passage. Roman. The guardian of the infant's first cry at birth.

Vahagn
God of victory. Pre-Christian Armenian. Considered to epitomize bravery, he is depicted born from a fire and with flames for hair.

Vahguru
Creator god. Sikh. Worshiped in the Golden Temple of Amritsar, in northern India. He has no icons.

Vaimanika
Generic title for a group of deities. Jain [India]. A class of gods said to be borne by, or living within, a flying palace, the *vimana*.

VAIRACOCHA
Origin Inca [Peru]. Creator god.

Known period of worship circa 400 AD to circa 1500 AD.

Synonyms Huiracocha; Viracocha.

Center(s) of cult Cuzco.

Art references various sculptures in stone and precious metals and carvings (all lost).

Literary sources none.

Vairacocha is the creator of all other supernatural beings and of men and animals, and is perceived to rule the heavens in the fashion of an Inca emperor. He is the source of all divine power, but not immediately concerned with administration of the world and appears only in times of crisis. He is also depicted as a heroic figure who once traveled the world teaching mankind various arts and crafts. He is said to have crossed the Pacific Ocean walking upon the water.

In the chief sanctuary at Cuzco the deities of the pantheon were represented in gold statues, that of Vairacocha being the most important. It is described as having been the size of a small boy, right hand upraised with fist clenched, but with the thumb and forefinger stretched out. His full Inca name, contracted by the Spanish invaders, is Ilya-Tiqsi Wiraqoca Pacayacaciq (ancient foundation, lord, instructor of the world). The title Vairacocha has been used by South American Indians into recent times to address white people.

Va'irgin   (I exist)
Supreme being. Chukchee [eastern Siberia]. A remote and poorly drawn character who lives in the zehith of the sky and who created the world. Comparable with the Koryak deity Tenento'mwan.

VAIROCANA   (coming from the sun)
Origin   Buddhist [India]. The first and oldest *dhyanibuddha* or meditation *buddha*.

Known period of worship   circa 500 BC to present.

Synonyms   Buddhaheruka.

Center(s) of cult   pan-Asiatic.

Art references   metal and stone sculptures, paintings.

Literary sources   *Sadhanamala* and Tantric ritual texts.

One of five mystic spiritual counterparts of a human *buddha* in Vajrayana Buddhism. A product of the Adibuddha who represents the branch of the cosmos concerned with bodily form. He originates from the white mantra syllable OM and lives in the highest paradise. His icon is normally placed in the innermost part of a *stupa* or shrine. His *Sakti* is Vajradhatvisvari and he is normally accompanied by a lion or two dragons. Color: white. Attributes: three monkish robes and prayer wheel. He is also taken as a tutelary deity in Lamaism [Tibet] in which case his attributes include bell and prayer wheel. Emanations include chiefly Samantabhadra but also Cunda, Graha-

matrka, Mahasahasrapramardani, Marici, Namasangiti, Sitatapatra-Aparajita, Usnisavijaya and Vajravahi. See also Aksobhya, Amitabha, Amoghasiddhi and Ratnasambhava.

Vairotya   (having an ax and a goad)
Goddess of learning. Jain [India]. One of sixteen *vidyadevi* headed by the goddess Sarasvati.

Vaisnavi
Mother goddess. Hindu (Epic and Puranic). A *Sakti* of Visnu, also regarded as a form of Laksmi. In later Hinduism she became one of a group of *mataras* regarded as of evil intent. Also one of a group of eight *astamataras*. In another grouping one of nine *navasaktis* who, in southern India, rank higher than the *saptamataras*. Her vehicle is the hybrid beast Garuda. Attributes: child, club, conch, lotus and prayer wheel

Vajracarcika
Goddess. Buddhist (Mahayana). An emanation of Aksobhya, she stands upon a corpse. Color: red. Attributes: cup, image of Aksobhya on the crown, jewel, lotus, skull with noose, staff and sword. Three-eyed.

Vajradaka
God. Buddhist (Mahayana). An emanation of Aksobhya bearing one, three or four heads.

Vajradhara
God. Buddhist. An epithet of the Adibuddha but also an allegory for the highest *buddha*. Known particularly from Nepal and Tibet. His *Sakti* is Prajnaparamita. Attributes: cup, hook, noose, regal ornaments and staff. Three-headed.

Vajradhatvisvari   (lady of the adamantine world)
Goddess. Buddhist. The *Sakti* of Vairocana and also a variety of Marici. Attributes: many, including an image of Vairocana on the crown.

Vajragandhari

Minor goddess. Buddhist (Mahayana). Color: blue or gold. Attributes: arrow, ax, bell, bow, hook, image of Amoghasiddhi, knife, noose, prayer wheel, staff, sword, and trident.

Vajragarbha

(substance of a thunderbolt)

God. Buddhist (Vajrayana). A *bodhisattva* or *buddha*-designate. Color: blue. Attributes: blue lotus, book and staff.

Vajraghanta

Minor goddess. Buddhist (Mahayana). A female *dikpala* or guardian of the northern direction. Color: green or white. Attributes: staff with bell.

Vajramrta   *(immortal of the Vajra sect)*

God. Buddhist (Mahayana). An emanation of Amoghasiddhi. His vehicle is an animal of uncertain identity. Color: green. Attributes: bell, club, hook, prayer wheel, staff and sword.

Vajrapani

God. Buddhist [mainly Tibet]. An emanation of Aksobhya but also sometimes identified with Adibuddha. Generally thought to reflect the second *dhyanibuddha* or spiritual meditation *buddha*. Sometimes depicted with a peacock. Alternatively considered to be a counterpart of the Hindu god Indra. Color: dark blue or white. Attributes: noose, snake and staff. Also Acala-Vajrapani; Acarya-Vajrapani.

Vajrapasi

Minor goddess. Buddhist (Mahayana). A female *dikpala* or guardian of the southern direction. Color: yellow. Attributes: staff with noose.

Vajrasphota

Goddess. Buddhist. A female *dikpala* or guardian of the western direction. Attribute: staff.

Vajrasrnkhala   *(personification)*

1. Minor goddess. Buddhist. One of the Mahayana deities said to be an emanation of Amoghas-

iddhi. Some texts describe her as the *Sakti* of Hevajira. Color: green. Attributes: arrow, bow, cup, image of Amoghasiddhi on the crown, mane, noose, skin, and staff. Three-eyed and three-headed.

2. Goddess of learning. Jain. One of sixteen *vidyadevi* headed by the goddess Sarasvati.

Vajratara

Goddess. Buddhist (Mahayana). Considered to be an emanation of all the *dhyanibuddhas* or spiritual meditation *buddhas*. Also identified as a emanation of Ratnasambhava or a form of Bhrkuti. She stands upon a lotus. Color: golden. Attributes: arrow, blue lotus, bow, conch, hook, images of the five *dhyanibuddhas* on the crown, noose and staff. Three-eyed.

Vajravarahi   *(diamond sow)*

Goddess. Buddhist (Mahayana) and Lamaist [Tibet]. An emanation of Vairocana and sometimes identified as the *Sakti* of Hevajra. In Lamaism she accompanies Vajradaka. She is depicted treading on a man. Color: red. Attributes: principally club, cup, image of Vairocana on the crown and knife, but with an assortment of other attributes from time to time. Three-eyed and three-headed.

Vajravidarani   *(tearing asunder)*

Minor goddess. Buddhist (Mahayana). Attributes: arrows, banner, bow, hook, noose, shield, staff and sword. Five-headed.

Vajrayogini

Minor goddess. Buddhist (Mahayana). She can sometimes be identified carrying her severed head in her hand. Color: yellow. Attributes: club, cup, knife and staff. Three-eyed.

Vajrosnisa

God. Buddhist. Apparently connected with the guardian deities or *dikpalas* in the easterly direction. Color: white. See also Padmantaka.

Vali

God. Nordic (Icelandic). One of the sons of Othin, his mother is Rind. A hardened, bold warrior and an excellent shot. He slew Hoder and thus avenged the death of Balder. One of the survivors of Ragnarok destined to live in the land that replaces Asgard, Idavoll. Also Ali.

Valli

Goddess. Hindu. The second consort of Skanda, usually depicted standing to his right. In its original context the word Valli may mean "earth."

Vamana

Incarnation of the god Visnu. Hindu (Epic and Puranic). The fifth *avatara* of Visnu which appears as a dwarf, symbolizing the puny state of mankind in the cosmos. According to legend, the god took the guise in order to trick Bali, a great-grandson of Hiranyakashipu (see Narasimha), whose prestige had begun to overshadow that of Indra. To restore a proper balance Vamana requested from Bali a plot of land three paces wide on which to meditate. Visnu returned to his proper stature and claimed heaven and earth in two steps. He declined to take the third, which would have also claimed the underworld, but instead gave its rule to Bali. The dwarfish form bears two arms. Attributes: umbrella and water pot.

VANIR

Origin Nordic (Icelandic). A major group of Norse deities concerned primarily with peace and prosperity and with the fertility of the land.

Known period of worship Viking period circa 700 AD and earlier, until Christianization circa 1100 AD and in some instances beyond.

Synonyms none.

Center(s) of cult various throughout areas of Nordic influence, but particularly at Uppsala in Sweden.

Art references stone carving and sculpture; artwork on weapons, etc.

Literary sources Icelandic codices; *Prose Edda* (Snorri); *Historia Danica* (Saxo); various classical authors.

A smaller race of deities than the Aesir gods led by Othin. The most important among them are Freyr and Freyja. The sea god, Njord, had originally been a Vanir but became hostage to the Aesir when the two races were at war. See also Aesir.

Varaha (boar)

Incarnation of the god Visnu. Hindu (Epic and Puranic). The third *avatara* of Visnu, which appears as a boar. According to legend, he descends in this guise to the bottom of the primeval sea to rescue the earth, which has been removed there by a demon. He retrieves it in the shape of a girl. The *avatara* may be depicted in wholly animal form or as a human with a boar's head. Epithets include Adivaraha.

Varahi

Mother goddess. Hindu (Epic and Puranic). A *Sakti* who in later Hinduism becomes one of a group of *mataras* regarded as of evil intent. Also one of a group of eight *astamataras*. In another grouping, one of nine *navasaktis* who, in southern India, rank higher than the *saptamataras*. She sits upon a boar, buffalo or elephant. Attributes: boar's head, bow, club, cup, knife, noose, plough, sword and trident.

Varahmukhi (having a boar's head)

Minor goddess. Buddhist (Mahayana). An attendant of Marici. Attributes: arrow, bow, flower and staff.

Varali

Minor goddess. Buddhist (Mahayana). An attendant on Marici. Color: white. Attributes: flower, needle, noose and staff.

Vari-Ma-Te-Takere
(the very beginning)

Mother goddess. Polynesian [Hervey Islands]. The creator being who lives at the very bottom of the world coconut, sitting in a cramped space with her knees and chin touching. She lives in Te-Enua-Te-Ki (mute land) in eternal silence and is the mother of six children, all deities, three of which she plucked from her right side and three from her left. See Avatea, Tinirau, Tango, Tumutean-aoa, Raka and Tu-Metua.

VARUNA (coverer)
Origin Hindu (Vedic, Puranic and early Tamil) [India]. Major guardian deity.

Known period of worship circa 1700 BC until present.

Synonyms none.

Center(s) of cult throughout India but as a rain god in the south.

Art references sculptures and reliefs in metal and stone.

Literary sources Rg Veda, etc.

Varuna is one of the major Vedic gods, concerned with the secure operation of the world's systems and of water. Lord of the *asura* class of deities, he is thought to equate with the Persian deity Ahura Mazda. In later times, a *dikpala* or guardian of the western direction. He is also regarded as an *aditya* or sun god, the son of Kardama and consort of Gauri.

In southern India he is still worshiped during periods of drought, particularly in coastal regions where he is thought to live in trees.

In Vedic times his sacred animal was the ram. He rides upon a fish or sea monster, or in a chariot drawn by seven horses. Attributes: conch, lotus, parasol, sacred thread, snake noose, trident and water jar with jewels. Potbellied and four-headed.

Vasantadevi
Goddess of spring. Buddhist-Lamaist [Tibet]. Particularly known from Tibet, where she appears in the retinue of Sridevi. Her animal is a mule. Attributes: cup and sword.

Vasita (will power)
Generic title for a group of goddesses. Buddhist. Twelve deities who personify the disciplines that result in spiritual regeneration.

Vasu(s) (excellent)
Generic title for a group of gods. Hindu (Vedic). Eight deities attendant on the Vedic weather god Indra, comprising day, dawn, fire, moon, pole star, sun, water and wind. Generally carrying a rosary and with a *Sakti*.

Vasudeva
God. Hindu. The princely father of Krsna and Balarama. Consorts include Devaki, Rohini, etc.

Vasudhara (treasurer)
1. Fertility goddess. Hindu (Epic and Puranic). The *Sakti* of Kuvera.
2. Goddess. Buddhist. A female *bodhisattva* or *buddha*-designate who is the *Sakti* of Vajrasattva and a form of Aksobhya or Ratnasambhava. Color: yellow. Attributes: book, ear of rice, images of Aksobhya and Ratnasambhava on the crown, parasol, pearl and water jar with jewels.

Vasumatisri (beautiful with an excellent mind)
Minor goddess. Buddhist (Mahayana). An attendant of Vasudhara.

Vasusri (beautiful one)
Minor goddess. Buddhist (Mahayana). An attendant of Vasudhara.

Vasya-Tara (the subjected Tara)
Goddess. Buddhist (Mahayana). A emanation of Amoghasiddhi and considered to be indistinguishable from Arya-Tara. Color: green. Attributes: blue lotus and image of Amoghasiddhi on the crown.

Vata
God of wind. Hindu (Vedic) and Persian [Iran]. The name appears in the *Rg Veda* as a deity of violent personality. According to Asvestan tradition the god of victory, Verethragna, appeared to Zarathustra in the guise of Vata.

VAYU *(1) (the wind)*
Origin Hindu [India]. God of the winds.

Known period of worship circa 1700 BC to present.

Synonyms Pavana.

Center(s) of cult none specific.

Art references sculptures and carvings in metal and stone.

Literary sources the Vedic texts, including *Rg Veda.*

One of the most important deities of the Vedas. In later Hinduism he evolves into a *dikpala* or guardian of the northwestern quarter. He is also depicted in some texts as a chariot driver for the god Agni. Color: dark blue. Attributes: arrow, hook, prayer wheel, staff and water jar.

Vayu *(2)*
God. Buddhist. A *dikpala* or guardian of the northwestern quarter.

Vayukumara
God. Jain [India]. One of the groups under the general title of *bhvanavasi* (dwelling in places). Of youthful appearance.

Ve
God. Nordic (Icelandic). Listed by Snorri in the *Prose Edda* as one of the sons of Bori and, among the gods of Asgard, the brother of Othin and Vili. The three gods are said to have made the land and sea out of the flesh and blood of the primeval giant Ymir.

Ve'ai *(grass woman)*
Vegetation spirit. Koryak [southeastern Siberia]. The personification of the grasslands and their guardian deity. She is perceived as a *shamanka* and is the consort of Eme'mqut.

Veive
Minor god. Etruscan. A youthful deity whose attributes include arrows. His animal is a goat.

Veja Mate
Goddess of winds. Pre-Christian Latvian. Also responsible for birds and woodlands.

Velaute'mtilan *(sedge man)*
Vegetation spirit. Koryak [southeastern Siberia]. The personification of the sedges and therefore guardian of the boggy tundras and their animals.

Veles
Chthonic underworld god. Slav. Also identified as the "cattle god." Also Volos.

Velu Mate
Chthonic underworld goddess. Pre-Christian Latvian. The "queen of the dead." She is depicted wearing white and she greets the dead at the cemetery.

Venda
Creator god. Dravidian (Tamil) [southern India]. An ancient vegetation deity. Worshipped in villages on the plains, thought to live in trees and equated with Indra.

Venkata
Form of the god Visnu. Hindu (Epic and Puranic). According to the *Aditya Purana*, Venkata is a deity of considerable importance in southern India. The name does not occur in the north. He is worshiped extensively by Hindus but particularly in the Tamil shrine of Tirupati where there is argument that the deity depicted is Siva or Karttikeya. The image appears to carry attributes of Visnu on the left and Siva on the right. Also Venkatesa.

VENUS
Origin Roman. Goddess of sexual love and beauty.

Known period of worship circa 400 BC to circa 400 AD.

Synonyms Aphrodite (Greek); Dione; Cytherea.

Center(s) of cult various; Eryx [Sicily] (as Venus Erycina).

Art references various sculptures including the Venus of Milo.

Literary sources *Aeneid* (Virgil), etc.

The name is neuter in form but Venus is modeled on the Greek goddess Aphrodite. In Roman mythology she is a daughter of Jupiter and Dione. Her consorts include Mars and the ill-fated Adonis. She is also linked romantically with Anchises, King of Troy. She is a goddess of gardens. In the second century AD the Emperor Hadrian dedicated a sanctuary to her on the Via Sacra in Rome; it was restored as late as the fourth century. She was celebrated in the *Veneralia* festival on April 1.

Verbti
God of fire. Pre-Christian Albanian. He is associated with the north winds. Under Christian influence he becomes identified with the devil.

Verethragna
God of victories. Persian [Iran]. He is embodied by the wild boar that possesses iron-shod feet to crush opponents and is perceived to be present in the wind.

Vervactor
Minor god of ploughing. Roman. Associated with sacrifices to Tellus and Ceres.

Vertumnus
Minor god of gardens and orchards. Roman. Of Etruscan origin, he is the consort of the goddess Pomona. Usually represented with garden implements and offered fruit and flowers. He was celebrated annually in the *Vertumnalia* festival on August 13.

VESTA
Origin Roman. Goddess of fire and the hearth.

Known period of worship circa 400 BC to 400 AD.

Synonyms Hestia (Greek).

Center(s) of cult many sanctuaries throughout Italy, but centered on the circular temple in Rome where allegedly the Palladium of Troy with the sacred flame of the gods was preserved.

Art references sculptures and reliefs.

Literary sources *Aeneid* (Virgil), etc.

Vesta was worshiped with considerable celebration in the various public *Vestalia* festivals, but she was also popular as a household guardian. She enjoyed a small sanctuary at the foot of the Palatine Hill. She is generally depicted as a woman of great beauty holding a lighted torch and a votive bowl. Her mortal attendants are the Vestal Virgins, selected for office as guardians of the sacred flame from the age of six for a minimum of thirty years, during which they were expected to maintain strict vows of chastity on penalty of burial alive. The Vestals dressed in white gowns edged with purple and were highly respected members of Roman society, enjoying many privileges. During *Vestalia* festivals, donkeys were decked with wreaths. The worship of Vesta was abolished by the Emperor Theodosius in 380 AD.

Vetali
Goddess of terrifying appearance. Buddhist-Lamaist [Tibet]. One of a group of *gauri*. Color: red. Attribute: a chain.

Victoria
Goddess of victory. Roman. Known particularly from the second century BC and closely linked with Jupiter. Became adopted by the Christian church in an angelic capacity.

Vidar
God of war. Nordic (Icelandic). A little known Aesir god, described as the silent one. One of the sons of Othin. An alternative tradition places him as the offspring of a brief liaison between Thor and the giant Gird. A god of great strength and support in times of danger. The prospective avenger of Othin's death by the wolf Fenrir at Ragnarok, he is said to wear a shoe made of material collected throughout time that he will place between Fenrir's jaws before he tears them apart and runs the

beast through with his sword. One of the survivors of the final great fire and flood, destined to live in Asgard's successor, Idavoll.

Vidyadevi

Generic title for a group of goddesses. Jain [India]. Sixteen deities led by Sarasvati who are associated with knowledge or learning.

Vidyesvara

Generic title for a group of deities. Hindu. Eight liberated or emancipated "beings" who are considered to be aspects of Siva.

Vidyraja

Tutelary god. Buddhist (Mahayana). One of several deities who are concerned with the implementation of the law.

Vidyujjvalakarili *(tongues of fire)*

Goddess. Buddhist. A twelve-headed form of Ekajata who is said to have been formed in the Buddha's sweat. She is often depicted trampling the four Hindu deities Brahma, Indra, Siva and Visnu. Color: blue or black. Attributes: many and varied.

Vidyutkumara

God. Jain [India]. Belonging to one of the groups under the general title of *bhvanavasi* (dwelling in places). Of youthful appearance.

Vighnantaka *(remover of obstacles)*

God. Buddhist (Mahayana). An emanation of Aksobhya who may equate with the Hindu god Ganesa. Color: blue. He is also seen as a *dikpala* or guardian of the northerly direction, in which case his color is green. Attributes: cup, drum, hook, knife, noose and staff. Three-headed. Also Analarka.

Vijaya *(victory)*

God. Hindu (Epic and Puranic). An *ekadasarudra* (one of the eleven Rudra deities). Hiranyaksa is considered one of his incarnations. Attributes: club, knife, rosary and staff. Vijaya is also the name of the bow of Indra.

Vikalaratri *(twilight night)*

Minor goddess. Buddhist (Mahayana). An attendant of Buddhakapala.

Vili

God. Nordic (Icelandic). Listed by Snorri in *Prose Edda* as one of the sons of Bori and, among the gods of Asgard, the brother of Othin and Ve. The three gods are said to have made the land and sea out of the flesh and blood of the primeval giant Ymir.

Vimala *(stainless)*

Minor goddess. Buddhist (Vajrayana). One of several deified *bhumis* recognized as different spiritual spheres through which a disciple passes. Color: white. Attributes: lotus and staff.

Vina

Goddess of music. Buddhist. The personification of a lute. Color: yellow. Attribute: a lute.

Vindhya

Mountain god. Hindu. Personification of the hills forming the northern edge of the Deccan area of central India.

Virabhadra *(great hero)*

War god. Hindu (Epic and Puranic). Considered to be a form of Siva, and occasionally of Visnu, Virabhadra acts as a martial aspect of Siva against the god Daksa, who according to some accounts abused Siva's wife Sati and drove her to angry suicide by self-immolation to avenge the slight. He is depicted bearing four arms. Attributes: arrow, bow, shield and sword. He sometimes wears a necklace of skulls. Three-eyed and three-headed.

Viraj

Primordial goddess. Hindu (Vedic). Identified as the active female creative principle in the *Rg Veda*.

Viraratri *(night of courage)*
Hindu. See Chinnamastaka.

Virtus
God of military prowess. Roman. Known particularly from the second century BC.

Virudhaka *(sprouted)*
God. Buddhist. A *dikpala* or guardian of the southerly direction. Color: blue or green. Attributes: skin from the head of an elephant and sword. Also identified as the head of a group of demons, the *kumbhandas*.

Virupaksa *(misinformed eyes)*
1. God. Hindu. Epithet of Siva and one of the *ekadasarudras* or eleven Rudra deities. Attributes: ax, bell, club, cup, drum, hook, knife, lotus, prayer wheel, rosary, *Sakti* and sword. Three-headed.
2. God. Buddhist. A *dikpala* or guardian of the western direction. God of snakes. Color: red. Attributes: jewel, snake and *stupa* or domed shrine.

Viryaparamita
Philosophical deity. Buddhist. Spiritual offspring of Ratnasambhava. Color: green. Attributes: blue lotus and jewelled banner.

VISNU
Origin Hindu (Vedic, Epic and Puranic) [India]. One of a triad of creator gods.

Known period of worship possibly from circa 1700 BC until the present day.

Synonyms appearing as ten major incarnations or *avataras*: Matsya, Kurma, Varaha, Narasinha, Vamana, Parasurama, Rama, Krsna or Balarama, Buddha, and Kalki(n). Other epithets include Abjaja, Abjayoni, Adhoksaja, Anantasayana, Aniruddha.

Center(s) of cult many sanctuaries throughout the subcontinent.

Art references sculptures generally in bronze, but also in stone. Reliefs.

Literary sources Rg Veda; Mahabharata and Ramayana epics Puranic literature.

Visnu began, according to the Vedas, as a minor cosmic deity imagined striding the sky in three giant steps—rising, zenith and setting. He was never a solar god, but became briefly associated with the movements of the sun in the sky.

Visnu's prestige developed with the Epics and of the three deities making up the apex of the modern Hindu pantheon, he is the most widely worshiped and preeminent (see also Brahma and Siva). The keeper of civilized morality and order. In the *Mahabharata*, he is partly identified with Krsna. According to one Puranic legendary source, Visnu was created from the left side of the primordial creator force. The Puranas also provide complex classifications for various aspects of Visnu. His most frequent consort is the goddess of fortune, Laksmi, with whom he is often depicted standing or resting on a lotus. His sacred animal is Garuda.

Visnu is the preserver of the world. He rules real time, or history, and through the concept of *karma* he maintains a moral balance that he corrects occasionally in the guise of one of his incarnations. He is a chief adversary of Yama, the god of the dead, and has the power to repel death. He is also closely identified with sacred water or *nara*, his presence pervading the Ganges. He is believed to sleep for four months each year, resting on the serpent Sesa with a lotus sprouting from his navel, after which he is roused by a special rite.

The followers of Visnu are the Vaisnavas and are mainly in the north of India, though there exists a strong following among the Tamils in the south. The Vaisnava caste mark is a V-shaped sign identified with water that has a property of descending.

Visnu is depicted with many heads or with four heads, generally with four arms, typically holding a wide assortment of attributes including conch and prayer wheel. He may also carry a discus, which reflects a destructive aspect, a mace of authority and a lotus. Around his neck may be the sacred stone, the *kausrabha*, and typically he has an obvious shock of chest hair.

Visnu Trivikrama

Form of the god Visnu. Hindu (Epic and Puranic). Trivikrama is the transformation into a giant from Visnu's dwarf *avatara* Vamana, in order to confirm his dominance over the world by covering it in three huge strides.

Visvakarman (architect of the universe)

Poorly defined creator god. Hindu (Vedic). Similar to Dyaus Pitar, he is described as the artist of the gods who may be linked or identified with Tvastar. He evolved, as the son of Prabhasa and Yogasiddha, into an occasional consort of the mother goddess Sarasvati.

Visvamitra

Minor god. Hindu (Puranic). According to legend, the father of the god Narada.

Visvarupa

Lesser known incarnation of the god Visnu. Hindu. In Vedic literature he is identified as the son of Tvastar. Visnu took the *avatara* at the request of Arjuna. His animal is Garuda. Attributes: many. Also Viratapurusa.

Visvosnisa

God. Buddhist. An *usnisa* apparently connected with the guardian deities or *dikpalas* in the southerly direction. Color: green.

Vitthali

God. Hindu (Epic and Puranic). A lesser known incarnation of the god Visnu (or Krsna). The cult of Vitthali is centered mainly on Panharpur, near Bombay, where he is the object of devotion by the Varkari sect. Generally depicted standing on a brick, wearing a fez-like hat and with hands on hips. Also Vithoba; Panduranga.

Vivasvan (shining)

Sun god. Hindu (Vedic and Puranic). The original Vedic list of six descendants of the goddess Aditi or *adityas*, all of whom take the role of sun gods was, in later times, enlarged to twelve, including Vivasvan. One of his titles is the "embodiment of ancestral law." His consort is Saranyu and he is identified as the father of Yama and Yami, as well as Manu and the Asvins. Color: golden. Attributes: forest garland, two lotuses and trident. Also Vivasvat.

Vodu

Collective name for gods. Fon [Benin, West Africa]. The origin of the term *voodoo* in the Caribbean region.

Voltumna

Tutelary god. Etruscan. Originally a vegetation deity who was elevated to the position of supreme god in the Etruscan pantheon and known in Roman culture as Vertumnus.

Volumna

Nursery goddess. Roman. The guardian deity of the nursery and of infants.

Vor

Goddess. Nordic (Icelandic). Of Germanic origin, one of the Aesir goddesses listed by Snorri in *Prose Edda*. He suggests that Vor may be concerned with the making of oaths and of marriage agreements, punishing those who break them. Possibly also Var(a), though Snorri lists her as a separate Aesir goddess.

Vosegus

Mountain god. Romano-Celtic. A local deity from the Vosges known only from inscriptions.

Vrtra

Demonic god of chaos. Hindu (Vedic). A primordial being who existed before the formation of the cosmos and who was slain by the mother goddess Sarasvati.

VULCANUS

Origin   Roman. God of fire and forges.

Known period of worship   circa 400 BC to circa 400 AD.

Synonyms   Hephaistos (Greek).

Center(s) of cult   tutelary god at the seaport of Ostia.

Art references   various sculptures and relief carvings.

Literary sources   *Aeneid* (Virgil), etc.

The patron god of artisans and blacksmiths, Vulcanus is modeled closely on the Greek Hephaistos. Attached to the smithy and rarely ascending Olympus, in Roman genealogy he is the son of Jupiter and Juno. He is generally depicted as a rather grotesque figure with one leg shorter than the other, a deformity gained as a result of being hurled to earth by Jupiter while trying to protect his mother from the god's wrath. Thereafter he determined to shun the company of other gods and set up home in the heart of Mount Etna, where he fashioned a giant forge. His workers are the one-eyed Cyclopes. He created a golden throne for Juno and he fashioned both Jupiter's magical thunderbolts and Cupid's arrows. He enjoyed short-term relationships with various goddesses, including Venus and Minerva, and with one of the Graces. His offspring seem generally to have been monstrous. He was celebrated in the *Vulcanalia* festival on August 23, which coincides with the period of greatest drought and the highest risk of fire in Italy.

Vyasa

Minor incarnation of the god Visnu. Hindu (Vedic, Epic and Puranic). Vyasa is said to be the author of the Vedas, the *Mahabharata* epic and the Puranas. He ranks with Hyagriva and Sarasvati as a lord of knowledge and wisdom, and is responsible for dividing the Tree of Knowlege into parts. In the texts he is depicted as dark skinned and accompanied by four students, Sumanta, Paila, Vaisampayana and Jaimini. He may be bearded. Also Vedavyasa.

W

Wadd

Moon god. Pre-Islamic southern Arabian. His sacred animal is the snake.

Wadj Wer *(the mighty green one)*

Fertility god. Egyptian. Sometimes depicted in androgynous form, he personifies the Mediterranean Sea or the major lakes of the Nile delta. He is depicted carrying the *ankh* symbol of life, and a loaf. The figure often appears pregnant and is associated with the richness of the Nile delta waters.

Wadjet

Goddess of royal authority. Egyptian. Wadjet takes the form of a fire-breathing cobra and, as the *uraeus* symbol worn on the headdress of the ruler, she epitomizes the power of sovereignty. She is a goddess of Lower Egypt equating to Nekhbet in Upper Egypt, with her main cult center at Buto (Tell el-Farain) in the Nile delta. She forms an integral part of the symbolism of the sun god Re, coiling around the sun disc to symbolize Re's powers of destruction. According to mythology, she created the papyrus swamps of the delta. She is described as a wet nurse to the god Horus and is the mother of the god of the primeval lotus blossom, Nefertum.

Wai

Sun god. Ntomba [Zaire, central Africa]. Probably originating as a god of hunters who protects and controls the animals in the forest. He has a son, Mokele.

Waka

Creator god. Oromo [Ethiopia]. Largely syncretized with the Christian god, but regularly invoked in the morning.

Waka-Hiru-Me

Sun goddess. Shinto [Japan]. Arguably the younger sister of the great Shinto sun goddess Amaterasu, or an early manifestation, she is associated with the morning sunrise. Also involved with weaving the garments of the *kami*.

Wakan Tanka

Creator god. Dakota Indian [USA]. A remote and vaguely defined deity invoked by the *shamans* of the tribe. Also a generic term equating to the spirit that, in an animistic and *shamanistic* religion, all things existing in nature possess.

Waka-Sa-Na-Me-No-Kami

Agricultural goddess. Shinto [Japan]. The deity specifically concerned with the transplanting of young rice. A daughter of Ha-Yama-To-No-Kami and O-Ge-Tsu-Hime. Generally served by Buddhist priests. See also Waka-Toshi-No-Kami and Kuku-Toshi-No-Kami.

Waka-Toshi-No-Kami

Agricultural god. Shinto [Japan]. The deity specifically concerned with the growing of young rice. A son of Ha-Yama-To-No-Kami and O-Ge-Tsu-Hime. Generally served by Buddhist priests. See also Waka-Sa-Na-Me-No-Kami and Kuku-Toshi-No-Kami.

Wakonda

Creator god. Omaha Indian [USA]. A remote and vaguely defined deity invoked by the *shamans* of the tribe. Also a generic term equating to the spirit that, in an animistic and *shamanistic* religion, all things existing in nature possess.

Wamala

God of plenty. Bunyoro [Uganda, East Africa]. A sanctuary has existed near the royal palace and Wamala is propitiated to give the boon of children, domestic animals and crops. He is also seen in an oracular capacity and has an official intermediary.

Wanka

Guardian spirit. Inca (pre-Columbian South America) [Peru, etc.]. The apotheosis of a tall stone or boulder (*huaca*) set upright in the center of a field.

Waralden Olmai

Tutelary god. Lappish [Finland]. Revered as a creator and guardian deity.

Wawki

Guardian spirit. Inca (pre-Columbian South America) [Peru, etc.]. The apotheosis of a stone or *huaca* that each Inca emperor carried with him as a personal tutelary deity. The object was known as a "brother."

Weng Shiang

God of literature. Taoist (Chinese). His name tablet hangs on the wall in many Chinese houses.

Wepwawet

God of passage. Egyptian. Depicted as a jackal, Wepwawet began as a god of Upper Egypt, but his cult spread along the whole of the Nile valley. According to Pyramid Texts, he was born beneath a tamarisk tree in the sanctuary of the goddess Wadjet at Buto. He is also closely linked with the falcon god Horus. He is perceived preceding the ruler either to or from battle, or to the afterlife, when his adze is used to break open the mouth of the dead person. In a similar context he is linked to the sun god Re when he "opens the dawn sky" to the deceased. As a god of passage, he also opens the way to the womb.

Wer

Storm god. Mesopotamian (Babylonian-Akkadian). A minor deity linked with Adad and Amurru.

His attendant is the fierce guardian of the pine forest, Huwawa, the focus of the one of the Gilgameš epic sagas. Cult centers include Afis, south of Aleppo.

Weri Kumbamba

Creator god. Gishu [Uganda, East Africa]. A deity embodied in rocks and specifically invoked before and after circumcision to ensure the speedy recovery of the patient.

Whope

Goddess. Sioux Indian [USA]. The daughter of Wi, the sun god, and consort of the south wind. She is credited with giving the Sioux the pipe of peace through which (narcotic) they commune with the great spirit Wakan Tanka.

Wi

Sun god. Sioux Indian [USA]. The father of the goddess Whope, his sacred animal is the bison.

Windigo

Ice god. Eskimo (Ojibwa). A terrible being formed of ice who symbolizes the starvation of winter. There are said to be many *windigos*, but they are always referred to in the singular. Cannibalistic, the *windigo* appears as an ice skeleton and a human being can be turned into one through possession.

Wiu

God of war. Nuer [Sudan]. The word means spear.

WODAN

Origin Germanic. God of war.

Known period of worship prehistoric times until circa 500 AD.

Synonyms Wotan; Woden (Anglo-Saxon).

Center(s) of cult scattered forest sanctuaries.

Art references stone carvings and engravings on metal.

Literary sources Germania (Tacitus); *Gothic War* (Procopius); *History of the Goths* (Jordanes); *Geography* (Strabo); *History of the World* (Orosius).

Wodan may have possessed similar characteristics to Othin, believed to have been a Norse descendant of Wodan. Germanic tribes including the Heruli, the Celtic Cimbri and the Goths all practiced sacrificial appeasement rites to Wodan, including stabbing and burning. The Cimbri hung their captives over bronze caldrons while priestesses cut their throats. Booty, including mutilated weapons, gold and silver, animals and human sacrifices who had been hanged, strangled or had their throats cut, was also thrown into sacred lakes as sacrifices for Wodan.

The classical writers substituted the name of the Roman god Mercury, thus the same day of the week is called Wednesday in English but *mercredi* in French. Many Anglo-Saxon kings traced their royal lineage back to Wodan as divine ancestor.

Wong Taisin
(the great immortal Wong)
God. Chinese. Probably an incarnation or *avatara* of the god Huang Ti (the yellow emperor), he is considered benevolent. Closely associated with a district in Kowloon that is named after him. His cult arrived in Hong Kong in 1915 from Kwangtung in the form of a painting brought by a man and his son. It was installed in a small temple in Wanchai. In 1921 a larger sanctuary was built, from public funds, facing the sea and backed by Lion Rock.

Wosret
Localized guardian goddess. Egyptian. With a cult center at Thebes, Wosret is, according to some inferences, an early consort of the creator god Amun and was superseded by Mut. She is identified with the protection of the young god Horus. Also Wosyet.

Wu
Sea god. Ewe [Benin, West Africa]. His priest, the Wu-no, invokes the god whenever the weather is too severe for the fishing boats to land. He is propitiated with offerings delivered from the shore and in past times was occasionally appeased with human sacrifice taken out to sea and thrown overboard.

Wu'squus
Spirit of darkness. Chukchee [eastern Siberia]. The personification of the night and the sibling of Na'chitna'irgin, the spirit of the left-hand dawn.

X

Xaya Iccita
Mountain spirit. Yakut [central Siberia]. The owner or master of the mountains.

Xewioso
Thunder god. Ewe. [Benin, West Africa]. Depicted as a ram accompanied by an ax, he is also perceived as a fertility deity whose thunder and lightning are accompanied by rain.

Xil Sga'nagwai
Medicine god. Haida Indian [Queen Charlotte Island, Canada]. Said to appear as a raven.

Xilonen
Minor vegetation goddess. Aztec (classical Mesoamerican) [Mexico]. An aspect of the corn goddess Chicomecoatl, personifying the young corn plant.

XIPE TOTEC   *(our lord the flayed one)*
Origin   Aztec (classical Mesoamerican) [Mexico]. Vegetation god.

Known period of worship   circa 750 AD to 1500 AD, but probably much earlier.

Synonyms   Red Tezcatlipoca.

Center(s) of cult   Teotihuacan, Tenochtitlan.

Art references   stone sculptures, murals and codex illustrations.

Literary sources   pre-Columbian codices.

A major deity of the Mesoamerican pantheons. The red *avatara* of the sun god Tezcatlipoca (see also Mixcoatl-Camaxtli). God of spring and a symbol of the annual renewal of vegetation. Often represented in ritual by a priest wearing the flayed skin of a human sacrifice, seen to be the new vegetation of the earth that emerges after the rains. The skin was worn for twenty-one days. Xipe Totec is also the tutelary god of precious metallurgists, including goldsmiths.

Xiuhtecuhtli
Astral god. Aztec (classical Mesoamerican) [Mexico]. The ruler of the first or lowest of the thirteen heavens known at the time of the Spanish conquest, Tlalticpac (on the earth).

Xochiquetzal
Goddess of fertility and childbirth. Aztec (classical Mesoamerican) [Mexico]. The mother of the demigoddess (unnamed) whose consort was Piltzintecuhtli and who engendered the first mortals Oxomoco and Cipactonal. One of the group classed as the Teteoinnan complex. A popular deity among Aztec women, the goddess is invoked particularly to make a marriage fruitful. The bride plaits her hair and coils it around, leaving two "plumes" representing the feathers of the Quetzal, which is sacred to Xochiquetzal. Pottery figurines are adorned with plumes of feathers. Worshiped at various sites, including Tula (Hidalgo). Also recognized as the patron goddess of weavers.

Xochiquetzal-Ichpuchtli   *(maiden)*
Minor fertility goddess. Aztec (classical Mesoamerican) [Mexico]. One of the group classed as the Teteoinnan complex. Depicted as a youthful deity associated with sexual love, flowers and pleasure.

Xolotl   *(monster)*
Monstrous deity. Aztec (classical Mesoamerican) [Mexico]. He performed the role of executioner

when the gods sacrificed themselves to create mankind. He then sacrificed himself. In alternative tradition he tried to evade his own fate, but was himself executed by Ehecatl-Quetzalcoatl. Also one of a pair of twins in the group classed as the Xiuhtecuhtli complex, regarded as patron of the ball game.

Xolotl Nanahuatl   *(tumor)*
Monstrous deity. Aztec (classical Mesoamerican) [Mexico]. One of the group classed as the Xiuhtecuhtli complex, described as a twin of Xolotl and copatron of ball games.

Y

Yacacoliuhqui *(curved nose)*
Minor god of commerce and merchants. Aztec (classical Mesoamerican) [Mexico]. One of the group classed as the Yacatecuhtli complex.

Yacahuiztli *(nose spine)*
Underworld goddess. Aztec (classical Mesoamerican) [Mexico]. With her consort Yoaltecuhtli she engendered the night in Aztec cosmogony. One of the group classed as the Mictlantecuhtli complex.

Yacapitzahuac *(sheep nose)*
Minor god of commerce and merchants. Aztec (classical Mesoamerican) [Mexico]. One of the group classed as the Yacatecuhtli complex.

Yacatecuhtli *(nose lord)*
God of commerce and merchants. Aztec (classical Mesoamerican) [Mexico]. Head of the group classed as the Yacatecuhtli complex.

Ya'china'ut *(moon woman)*
Moon spirit. Koryak [southeastern Siberia]. The personification of the moon.

Yah
Moon god. Egyptian. Yah may have been an import to Egypt brought by Semitic immigrants who based his profile on the Mesopotamian god Sin. He is mentioned largely from the twentieth century BC onward and is depicted in human form, but can also be represented by the falcon and the ibis.

Ya'halan *(cloud man)*
Guardian spirit. Koryak [southeastern Siberia]. The son of the supreme being Tenanto'mwan, his con-

sort is Yine'ane'ut. In alternative tradition he is the son of the supervisor being, Ina'hitelan. He is a protector of young couples, and youths beat a sacred drum invoking the spirit to turn the heart of a girl.

Ya'halna'ut *(cloud woman)*
Guardian spirit. Koryak [southeastern Siberia].

Yajna *(sacrifice)*
God. Hindu. A minor *avatara* of Visnu and embodiment of the Brahmanic ritual.

Yaksas
Tree spirits. Hindu. Generic title for animistic beings mentioned circa fifth century BC by Panini.

Yaldabaoth
Creator God. Gnostic Christian. The so-called "prime parent" of Gnostic cosmogony, engendered by Pistis Sophia out of the nothingness of chaos, provided with form and given charge over the substance of the cosmos. Yaldabaoth is, at first, unaware of her existence and, by his own powers, engenders seven androgynous beings, placing them in seven heavens. He decrees himself alone and all-powerful, whereupon Pistis Sophia names him Samael (blind god). Of his offspring, the most significant is Sabaoth, who stands against his father and on the side of Pistis Sophia. When she finally reveals herself to Yaldabaoth as pure radiant light, he is humbled.

Yama *(twin; alternatively the restrainer)*
1. God of death. Hindu (Vedic). The son of Vavasvan and Saranju, or of Surya and Sanjna, his consort is Dhumorna or Yami. Yama is also the

judge of the dead and the twin sibling of Yami, goddess of death. When Krsna is perceived as the embodiment of the cosmos, his eyeteeth are Yama. He evolved into a *dikpala* or guardian of the southerly direction. His animal is a black buffalo. Color: black.

2. Guardian deity. Buddhist-Lamaist [Tibet]. One of a group of *dharmapala* with terrible appearance and royal attire who guard the Dalai Lama. He stands upon a man. Color: red, blue, white or yellow. Attributes: most commonly a noose and staff, but also club, net, shield, sword, trident and two tusks.

Yamaduti

Messenger goddess. Buddhist (Mahayana). An attendant of Yama. Her vehicle is a buffalo. Color: blue. Attributes: cup, fly whisk, knife and lotus.

Yama-No-Kami

Mountain god. Shinto [Japan]. Specifically the deity who comes down to the rice paddies in spring and returns in autumn. The festival of *No-Ide-No-Shinji* marks his descent.

Yamantaka   (destroyer of Yama)

Guardian deity. Buddhist-Lamaist [Tibet]. A emanation of Aksobhya and one of a group of *dharmapala* with terrible appearance and royal attire who guard the Dalai Lama. By tradition he stifled the great rage of Yama. His *Sakti* is Vidyadhara. He is also a *dikpala* or guardian of the easterly direction. He tramples a number of creatures including a man, and possesses thirty-two arms and sixteen legs. Color: red, blue, black or white. Attributes: many.

Yamari   (enemy of Yama)

God. Buddhist (Vajrayana). Probably influenced by the Hindu deities Siva and Yama. His vehicle is a buffalo. Color: red. Attributes: club, cup, noose and staff.

Yami

Mother goddess. Hindu (Epic and Puranic). One of seven *Saktis* who in later Hinduism became regarded as of evil intent. Also Camunda.

Yamm

God of the ocean. Semitic. A Syrian deity who is mentioned briefly in an Egyptian papyrus as an extortioner of tribute from other deities.

Yamuna

Minor river goddess. Hindu. A daughter of Surya and Sanjna and the sister of Yama. She is described in Puranic texts and associated with the river Yamuna on which lies the city of Mathura. Color: blue.

Yaotl   (enemy)

Omnipotent god. Aztec (classical Mesoamerican) [Mexico]. A universal and generally malevolent deity. One of the group classed as the Tezcatlipoca complex.

Ya'qhicnin

Creator god. Koryak [southeastern Siberia]. The name given to the Christian god by the Koryaks to distinguish him from their own supreme being, Tenanto'mwan.

Yaro

Creator god. Kafa [Ethiopia]. A sky god to whom sacrifice is still possibly enacted on hill tops and river banks in rural areas. Became largely syncretized with the Christian god. Also Yero.

Yasodhara   (preserving glory)

Goddess. Buddhist. The daughter of Dandapani and the consort of the Buddha before attaining his full status.

Yauhqueme

Fertility and rain god. Aztec (classical Mesoamerican) [Mexico]. One of the group classed as the Tlaloc complex.

Yayu

Sky god. Ngbandi [Zaire, central Africa]. One of seven gods invoked at daybreak.

Yeloje

Sun god. Yukaghir [Siberia]. A benevolent deity who personifies justice and morality. The rainbow is said to be his tongue. Also Pu'gu; Ye'rpeyen.

Yemekonji

Creator god. Mongo and Nkundo [Zaire, central Africa]. According to tradition, he gave the sun god Nkombe three parcels when the people complained the world was too dark; two were brightly colored and one was a dull gray. Realizing that he was about to be tricked, Nkombe opened the gray parcel and the world was flooded with light.

Yemoja

Goddess of water. Yoruba [Nigeria, West Africa]. The creator of all the rivers in the area, particularly the river Ogun. She is chiefly worshiped by women and the sacred river water is considered a remedy for infertility. She is propitiated with animal and vegetable sacrifices. Attributes: cowrie shells.

Yen Kuang Niang Niang

Mother goddess. Chinese. One of a group of "nine dark ladies" who have a protective function. She cures the eye disease ophthalmia.

YHWH *(I am what I am)*

Origin Judaic [Israel]. Creator god.

Known period of worship circa 1200 BC until present day.

Synonyms Yahweh; Jehovah.

Center(s) of cult Hebron, Jerusalem until 587 BC but subsequently throughout the Christian world.

Art references none extant.

Literary sources Vetus Testamentum; Qum' Ran manuscripts.

The creator god of the southern tribes of Israel headed by Levi and Benjamin. Possibly a copy of the Egyptian deity Atum (Aten), introduced by the pharaoh Amenhotep IV in the fifteenth century BC. The object of monolatrous but not necessarily monotheistic worship by the Hebrew settlers in Palestine. Arguably the first surviving concept of a truly universal deity. Yhwh is the god who, according to tradition, was revealed to Moses on Mount Sinai (Mount Horeb) and who provided the Covenant, the ten tablets of law.

Said to sit in judgment between two facing cherubim on the Mercy Seat that rested above the focal point of Israelite worship, the Ark of the Covenant (*VT:* Exodus 25). Yhwh eventually superseded the northern god, El, to become supreme deity of Israel. During Hellenic occupation, the sanctuary of Yhwh on Mount Gerizim in Samaria (northern kingdom) was rededicated to Zeus. The name Yhwh survived into Christian religion though, in English translation, it is now generally replaced by the term "Lord." "Jehovah" is a corruption introduced circa 1200–1300 AD.

Yina'mna'ut *(fog woman)*

Spirit of mists and fogs. Yakut [southeastern Siberia]. Her consort is fog man Yina'mtilan and she is believed to live in a mythical settlement with other spirits.

Yina'mtilan *(fog man)*

Spirit of mists and fogs. Yakut [southeastern Siberia]. His consort is fog woman Yina'mna'ut and he is believed to live in a mythical settlement with other spirits.

Yine'ane'ut

Guardian spirit. Koryak [southeastern Siberia]. One of the daughters of Big Raven, Quik'inna'qu, regarded as a *shamanka* engaged in a constant struggle with the underworld demons, the *kalau*. Her sister is Cana'ina'ut and she is the consort of the earth spirit Tanuta.

Yng

Creator god. Nordic (Icelandic). Progenitor of the earliest Swedish kings. Also, in Germanic tradition, Ing, the father of the Baltic coastal tribe, the Ingwaeones.

Yoalli Ehecatl *(night wind)*

Creator god. Aztec (classical Mesoamerican) [Mexico]. One of the group classed as the Omeotl complex.

Yoaltecuhtli *(lord of night)*

Creator god. Aztec (classical Mesoamerican) [Mexico]. With his consort Yacahuiztli he engendered the night in Aztec cosmogony. The ruler of the sixth of the thirteen heavens known at the time of the Spanish conquest, Teotlcozauhcan (the place of the yellow god). One of the group classed as the Mictlantecuhtli complex.

Yobin-Pogil
Forest spirit. Yukaghir [southeastern Siberia]. The apotheosis of the woodlands and their guardian deity.

Yocahu
Tutelary god. Puerto Rico and Haiti. A benevolent deity, the son of the universal mother, and known as the "great spirit." Believed to live in the sun. Also Marcoti; Jocakuvague-Maorocon.

Yogesvari
Mother goddess. Buddhist (Epic and Puranic). Personifying desire and listed among both the *saptamataras* and the *astmataras*. Attributes: bell, club, drum, shield, sword and trident.

Yolkai Estan
Fertility goddess. Navaho [USA]. The sister of the principal fertility goddess, Estsanatlehi, she was engendered by the gods, who gave life to an image made from white shells.

Yspaddaden Pencawr
God. Celtic (Welsh). Possibly the counterpart of the Irish deity Balor and the Icelandic Balder. In the legend of *Culhwch and Olwen*, Olwen is identified as his daughter. He sets Culhwch several difficult tasks before he can obtain Olwen's hand. Culhwch retaliates by wounding him severely, but he cannot be killed until Olwen marries. This is presumably a distorted fertility legend, the original meaning of which is lost.

Yu Huang Shang Ti
Supreme god. Taoist (Chinese). He achieved paramount prominence during the Sung Dynasty and the Jade Emperor is his earthly, mortal incarnation. As a deity he is remote and out of touch with ordinary people. No iconography is applied to him and he has no physical description. He engendered the universe from chaos and is the unifying principle of the cosmos, which is perceived to be divided into thirty-six heavens above the earth. Also Shang Ti; Shang Di.

Yu Shih
Rain god. Taoist (Chinese). The so-called "master of the rain," he provides rain to ripen the harvest. He is often accompanied by the god of thunder, Lei Kung.

Yu-Chiang
God of ocean winds. Chinese. He is depicted with the body of a bird and a human face.

Yum Cimil
God of death. Mayan (Yucatec, classical Mesoamerican) [Mexico]. Depicted with a skull head, bare ribs and spiny projections from the vertebrae, or with bloated flesh marked by dark rings of decomposition. He wears bell-like ornaments fastened in the hair. Sacrificial victims were offered to the god by drowning in the sacred pool or *cenote*. Also God A.

Yum Kaax
Vegetation god. Mayan (classical Mesoamerican) [Mexico]. The deity concerned with the growing and harvesting of corn, but also of husbandry in general. Depicted as a youthful figure with an ear of corn in his headdress. Also God E.

Yu-ti
Sky god. Taoist (Chinese). The title by which the "Jade Emperor," the most senior deity in the Taoist pantheon, is commonly known. He emerges as a deity circa 1000–1100 AD during the Sung Dynasty. The Chinese emperor is his earthly and more accessible incarnation. See also Yu Huang Shang Ti.

Z

Zababa

God of war. Mesopotamian (Babylonian-Akkadian). The tutelary god of the city of Kiš, whose sanctuary is the *E-meteursag*. Also Zamama.

Zalmoxis

Sky god. Thracian. Known from the writings of Herodotus. According to tradition he lived for some time on earth and then became ruler of the underworld. His makeup may have been influenced by the Osirian cult in Egypt.

Zapotlantenan

Healing goddess. Aztec (classical Mesoamerican) [Mexico]. Deity of medicinal turpentine and ointment dealers. One of the group classed as the Tlaloc complex.

Zara-Mama

Corn goddess. South American Indian [Peru]. A minor deity, models of whom were made from the leaves of the plant and kept for a year before being burned in a ritual to ensure a good corn harvest.

Zarpanitu(m)

Birth goddess. Mesopotamian (Babylonian-Akkadian). The consort of Marduk whose marriage was celebrated annually at New Year in Babylon. Also Erua; Sarpanitum.

Zemepatis

Chthonic god. Pre-Christian Lithuanian. A tutelary deity of farmers and guardian of cattle.

Zemi

One of a pair of primordial beings. Puerto Rico and Haiti. Known as Morobo and Binatel, they are the parents of all other deities, though they did not create the cosmos, which, according to belief, has always been in existence. They are depicted in stone, wood or clay figures and are invoked in prayers. Two wooden *zemis* used to be kept in a sacred cave at Toaboyna in Haiti and were the subject of several annual pilgrimages. The sun and the moon were believed to have emerged from the cave.

Zemyna

Chthonic goddess. Pre-Christian Lithuanian. A deity with responsibility for vegetation and crops. She was invoked at sowing and harvesting times.

Zephyrus

God of the south winds. Roman. Announces the arrival of spring.

Zethos

God. Greek. Theban twin god who had mortal weaknesses. Comparable to Kastor.

ZEUS *(sky father)*

Origin Greek. Head of the Greek pantheon.

Known period of worship circa 800 BC but undoubtedly earlier until Christianization circa 400 AD.

Synonyms Dyaus (Indo-European); Diu-pater, Jupiter (Roman).

Center(s) of cult Athens (sanctuary begun by Pisastratus and completed by Hadrian) and throughout Greek sphere of influence where, in every city, the major temple is that of Zeus.

Art references abundant sculpture and carving; votive inscriptions, etc.

Literary sources Iliad (Homer); Theogony (Hesiod).

Zeus leads the pantheon of twelve great Greek gods illustrated on the Parthenon frieze and is probably modeled on a western Asiatic precedent. His father is Kronos, his mother Rhea, or in alternative tradition Metis (wisdom). His official consort, though barely more so than in name, is Hera. He is a universal deity and through him comes all mortal sovereignty. He earned the finest and most opulent sanctuaries throughout the Greek world. According to tradition, he lives on the mountain in Thessaly that came to be known as Olympus and where the storm clouds are said to gather. Tradition also has it that his grave is on Mount Yuktas, near Knossos on the island of Crete, where he was "buried" by the Kouretes.

Symbolized by the eagle and earning the sacrifice of bulls, Zeus is the strongest among the deities, but in origin he is a weather god paralleling Iškur (Sumerian), Tešub (Hittite) and Hadad (Semitic). He rules the clouds and rain, delivers lightning and hurls thunderbolts forged by the one-eyed Cyclopes, the thunderbolt being his invincible weapon. In the same vein he is said to determine the outcome of battle; victors once draped his statues and other monuments with spoils of war. The great and enduring festival of Zeus is that of Olympia, which became the modern Olympic Games.

The father of gods and men alike, according to tradition, Zeus won his position of authority in a primeval battle against the Titans who had held sway in the time of his father Kronos; Kronos swallowed all his other children, but Zeus's mother Rhea saved him by substituting a stone, which Uranus swallowed, and Zeus eventually overthrew his father. He swallowed Metis, thus combining strength and wisdom in a single godly entity. His *noos*, his ability for pragmatism, became renowned and infallible and his judgment was beyond criticism. Homer pictures him carrying the golden scales of justice. Zeus is surrounded from birth by attendant youthful warriors known as Kouretes or Korybantes.

He is possessed of enormous sexual vigor and sired a vast number of offspring through an incessant parade of goddesses and mortal partners.

In this respect his philandering became an embarrassment in the late Hellenic philosophical age. His fathering of other deities included Apollo and Artemis through Leto, Hermes whose mother is Maia, Persephone and Dionysos by Demeter, and Athena whose mother was said to be Metis, but who emerged in full armor from her father's forehead. Among the more notable of his mortal children are Herakles, Perseus, Zethos and Amphion, Helen and Minos. He was also suspected of homosexuality with the young Trojan Ganymede.

Zhang Kuo-Lao
God. Taoist (Chinese). One of the "eight immortals" of Taoist mythology. Once mortal beings, they achieved immortality through their exemplary lives. According to tradition, Zhang Kuo-Lao was a bat before he took human form. Attributes include a bamboo drum and sticks and his attendant animal is an ass. See Ba Xian.

Zhiwud
Messenger goddess. Kafir [Afghanistan]. A deity connected and possibly syncretizing with the goddess Disani but who, according to legend, carried vital messages to the heroic god Mon during a primordial battle between gods and giants. Mon lives by a lake surrounded by fire, and the goddess's wings (a solitary inference that she can appear in the form of a bird) are scorched in the process until Mon heals them. In some variations Mon lives in the form of a bull that breathes fire. Also Zhuwut.

Zhong-Li Kuan
God. Taoist (Chinese). One of the "eight immortals" of Taoist mythology. Once mortal beings, they achieved immortality through their exemplary lives. Attributes include a fan. See Ba Xian.

Zibelthiurdos
Storm god. Thracian. Believed to send thunder and lightning.

Zipakna
Earthquake god. Mayan (classical Mesoamerican) [Mexico]. Usually coupled with the god Kabrakan

and identified as a creator of mountains that Kabrakan subsequently destroys.

Zoe *(life)*

Goddess of life. Greek and Gnostic Christian. The daughter of Pistis Sophia who, according to Gnostic mythology, became the consort of Sabaoth to create the angels, Israel and Jesus Christ.

Zotz

Tutelary god. Mayan (Zotzil Indian, Mesoamerican) [Guatemala]. Manifest in the form of a bat.

Zurvan

God of temporal time and fate. Persian [Iran]. Once the focus of a cult of Zervanism in which he appeared as the father of Ahura Mazda, the god of light, and Ahriman, god of darkness, in Zoroastrianism. He is perceived as a god of destiny and the controller of all roads that mankind may take, leading ultimately to the otherworld. He was adopted into Manichaean religion. Also Zervan.

CIVILIZATION INDEX

Buddhist *(continued)*
    Citrasena
    Ganapatihrdaya
    Kurukulla
    Locana
    Medha
    Pandara
    Prajna
    Vajradhatvisvari
    Vajrasrnkhala
speech
    Vagisvara
of terrifying aspect
    Dombi
    Gauri
    Ghasmari
undefined
    Bhutadamara
    Camunda
    Candesvari
    Carcika
    Dhupatara
    Dipa Tara
    Gandha Tara
    Garuda
    Jayakara
    Jayatara
    Kakasya
    Kaladuti
    Kalika
    Karttikeya
    Kulisesvari
    Madhukara
    Mahakapi
    Mahaparinirvanamurti
    Maha-Sarasvati
    Puspatara
    Sakra
    Trailokyavijaya
    Vajragandhari
    Vajravidarani
    Vajrayogini
    Yamari
    Yasodhara
vasitas
    Adhimuktivasita
    Ayurvasita
    Buddhabodhiprabhavasita
    Cittavasita
    Dharmavasita
    Jnanavasita
    Karmavasita
    Pariskaravasita
    Pranidhanavasita
    Riddhivasita
    Upapattivasita
Buddhist-Lamaist
    buddhas
        Dipankara
        Sakyamuni
    collective and generic
        Lha

demonic
    Khen-Ma
    Khen-Pa
dharmapalas
    Sri(devi)
fertility and vegetation
    Saraddevi
guardian and tutelary
    Avalokitesvara
    Bi-har
    Chos-Skyon
    Gur-Gyi Mgon-Po
    Mahakala
    Sadaksari (Lokesvara)
    San-Dui
    Yama
    Yamantaka
horse
    Hayagriva
light
    Dipa
local
    Khyung-Gai mGo-Can
mother
    Bhrkuti-Tara
    Dhupa
    Gandha
    Gita
    Lasya
    Mala
    Nrtya
    Puspa
physician
    Abhijnaraja
    Asokottamasri
    Bhaisajyaguru
    Dharmakirtisagaraghosa
    sMan-Bla
    Sikhin
    Sinhanada
    Suparikirtitanamasri
    Survarnabhadravimalar-
        atnaprabhasa
    Svaraghosaraja
primordial
    Adidharma
saktis
    Digambara
seasonal
    Grismadevi
    Hemantadevi
    Vasantadevi
of terrifying aspect
    Candali
    Cauri
    Mahacinatara
    Pukkasi
    Savari
    Vetali
undefined
    Nan-Sgrub
    Phyi-Sgrub

    Sitatara
    Syamatara
war
    Beg-Tse
Buganda
    Kibuka
    Mukasa
Bunyoro
    Kaikara
    Lubanga
    Mugizi
    Muhingo
    Mulindwa
    Munume
    Ndaula
    Ruhanga
    Wamala
Burundi
    Imana

C

Canaanite
    Anat
    Arsay
    Aserah
    Asertu
    Asratum
    Athirat
    Attar
    Baal
    Dagan (2)
    El'eb
    Elkunirsa
    Haurun
    Il
    Kades
    Mot
    Pidray
    Resep(A)mukal
    Sapas
    Sasuratum
Cappadocian
    Ma
Carian
    Aphrodisias
Caribbean (Puerto Rico and Haiti)
    Bugid Y Aiba
    Faraguvol
    Loa
    Yocahu
    Zemi
Carthaginian
    Caelestis
    Gad
    Tanit
Caucasian (pre-Christian)
    Lamaria
    Mirsa
Celtic *See also* Romano-Celtic

Hindu *(continued)*
  Piyusaharana
mother
  Aditi
  Bala
  Bharat Mata
  Brahmani
  Devaki
  Dharti Mata
  Hammu Mata
  Hariti
  Hinglaj(-Mata)
  Karaikkal Ammaiyar
  Karttiki
  Mata
  Narasinhi
  Parvati
  Pattinidevi
  Pradhana
  Prthivi
  Raudri
  Rudracarcika
  Sankari
  Santa
  Santoshi Mata
  Sarasvati
  Sati
  Tripura
mother of evil intent
  Badi Mata
  Camunda
  Gulsilia Mata
  Indrani
  Kankar Mata
  Kaumari
  Krsodari
  Mahesvari
  Malhal Mata
  Pansahi Mata
  Phul Mata
  Sitala(mata)
  Vaisnavi
  Varahi
  Yami
mountain
  Himavan
  Mena
  Vindhya
music and dance
  Narada
  Nataraja
navadurgas
  Aticandika
  Candanayika
  Candarupa
  Candavati
  Candogra
  Pracanda
  Rudracandra
  Ugracandika
navasaktis
  Pitari

phallic
  Linga
primordial
  Ammavaru
  Danu (2)
  Kasyapa
  Prajapati
  Prsni
  Rahu
  Saranyu
  Viraj
sacrificial
  Bharati
  Hotr(a)
  Ila
  Mahi
saktis
  Daya
  Harsa
  Kanti
  Kirti
  Mahakali
  Priti
snake
  Ananta
  Janguli
  Kaliya
  Karkota
  Kulika
  Mahabja
  Mahanaga
  Mahapadma
  Manasa
  Nagaraja
  Padma
  Sankha(pala)
  Sesa(naga)
  Taksaka
speech and writing
  Kubjika
  Vac
sun
  Aditya
  Ansa
  Aryaman
  Bhaga
  Daksa
  Dhanvantari
  Dhatar
  Garuda
  Mitra
  Pusan
  Rbhus
  Savitar
  Surya (1)
  Surya (2)
  Vivasvan
of terrifying aspect
  Bhutamata
  Canda
  Dhumravati
  Pranasakti

Pratyangira
Srividyadevi
Sulini
Svasthavesini
Trikantakidevi
Ugratara
undefined
  Buddhi
  Candrasekhara
  Caturmurti
  Chaya
  Devasena
  Dharani
  Dhumorna
  Dhurjati
  Diksa
  Dipti
  Dirghadevi
  Disa
  Diti
  Gauri
  Ghentu
  Indukari
  Issaki
  Jaya-Vijaya
  Kadru
  Karttikeya
  Katyayani
  Khandoba
  Khasa
  Kollapura-Mahalaksmi
  Ksama
  Kubuddhi
  Kumari
  Laghusyamala
  Laksmana
  Mahakala
  Maharatri
  Maha-Sarasvati
  Mahisasuramardini
  Meghanada
  Mhalsa
  Naigameya
  Niladevi
  Prasuti
  Rajamatangi
  Riddhi
  Rudrani
  Rukmini
  Salagrama
  Sandhya
  Sanjna
  Sanmukha
  Santana
  Santi
  Satarupa
  Satrughna
  Shadanana-Subrahmanya
  Somaskanda
  Sri(devi)
  Subhadra
  Svadha

Indian, American (continued)
  agriculture
    Axo-Mama
    Coca-Mama
    Ganaskidi (Navaho)
    Quinoa-Mama
    Tate Oteganaka (Huichol)
    Zara-Mama
  archetypal
    Snulk'ulxa'ls (Bella Coola)
  chthonic
    Dsahadoldza (Navaho)
  creator
    Awonawilona (Pueblo)
    Kitanitowit (Algonquin)
    Kumokums (Modoc)
    Maheo (Cheyenne)
    Manitu (Algonquin)
    Moma (Uitoto)
    Nainuema (Uitoto)
    Pachacamac
    Pore (Guyanan)
    Qamai'ts (Bella Coola)
    Tate (Sioux)
    Tawa (Pueblo)
    Teharon (Mohawk)
    Tirawa (Pawnee)
    Wakan Tanka (Dakota)
    Wakonda (Omaha)
  death
    Ta'xet (Haida)
    Tia (Haida)
    Tokakami (Huichol)
  fertility and vegetation
    Estsanatlehi (Navaho)
    Takotsi Nakawe (Huichol)
    Yolkai Estan (Navaho)
  fire
    Hastsezini (Navaho)
    Tatevali (Huichol)
    Tatosi (Huichol)
  fishing and hunting
    Hastseoltoi (Navaho)
    Tewi'xilak (Dza'wadenox)
    Toa'lalit (Bella Coola)
    Tsa'qamae (Qwe'gsotenox)
  guardian and tutelary
    Hastehogan (Navaho)
    Koyote (Navaho/Apache)
    Lendix-Tcux (Chilcotin)
    O'meal (Na'kwaxdax)
  medicine and health
    Hatdastsisi (Navaho)
    Xil Sga'nagwai (Haida)
  moon
    Klehanoai (Navaho)
    Metsaka (Huichol)
    Owiot (Luiseno)
  plague
    Haili'laj (Haida)
  racing
    Hastseltsi (Navaho)

  rain and water
    Tate Hautse Kupuri (Huichol)
    Tate Kyewimoka (Huichol)
    Tate Naaliwahi (Huichol)
    Tate Rapawiyema (Huichol)
    Tonenili (Navaho)
  river and sea
    Anaulikutsai'x (Bella Coola)
    Djila'qons (Haida)
    Gonaqade't (Chilkat)
    Sga'na (Haida)
    Ta'ngwania'na (Haida)
    Tienoltsodi
    Navaho
  shamanism
    Lalaia'il (Bella Coola)
  sun
    Alk'unta'm (Bella Coola)
    Senx (Bella Coola)
    Tate Velika Vimali (Huichol)
    Tayau (Huichol)
    Tayau Sakaimoka (Huichol)
    Tsohanoai (Navaho)
    Wi (Sioux)
  supreme
    Menechen (Araucania)
    Qa'wadiliquala (Dza'wadeenox)
    Sins Sga'nagwai (Haida)
  thunder
    Hi'lina (Haida)
    Ku'nkunxuliga (Ma'malelegale)
  war
    Nayenezgani (Navaho)
    Tobadzistsini (Navaho)
  weather
    Acacila (Aymara)
    Pariacaca
  wind
    Tamats Palike Tamoyeke (Huichol)
Islamic
  Allah
Isoko
  Cghene
Italic
  Laverna
  Liber
  Libera
  Mater Matuta
  Neptunus

J

Jain
  Acchupta
  Agnikumara
  Asurakumara
  Bhavanavasi
  Cakresvari
  Devananda

Dhrti
Dikkumara
Dvipakumara
Gandhari
Gauri
Kali (2)
Kulisankusa
Mahakali
Mahamanasika
Manasi
Manavi
Nagakumara
Nagini
Naradatta
Prajnapti
Rohini
Sakti
Sarvastramahajvala
Sasanadevata
Stanitakumara
Suparnakumara
Tripura
Udadhikumara
Vaimanika
Vairotya
Vajrasrnkhala
Vayukumara
Vidyadevi
Vidyutkumara
Janjero
  Hao
Japanese See Shinto
Javan
  Saning Sari
Judaic
  Elim
  Elohim
  Yhwh

K

Kafa
  Atete
  Yaro
Kafir
  Arom
  Bagisht
  Dagan (3)
  Disani
  Dogumrik
  Duzhi
  Gish
  Gujo
  Immat
  Imra
  Indr
  Kshumai
  Lunang
  Maramalik
  Mon

Roman (continued)
   Vesta
   Vulcanus
  fortune
   Fortuna
   Sors
  guardian and tutelary
   Abeona
   Alemona
   Anna Perenna
   Clementia
   Cunina
   Edusa
   Fabulinus
   Janus
   Lares
   Lar Familiaris
   Libertas
   Mandulis
   Penates
   Pilumnus
   Portunus
   Potina
   Priapus
   Securita
   Terminus
   Vagisvara
   Volumna
  horse
   Lupercus
   Pollux
  love and sex
   Amor
   Pudicita
   Venus
  marriage
   Ciuxia
   Juno
   Unxia
  masculinity
   Genius
  medicine and health
   Aesculapius
   Candelifera
   Carmentes
   Decima
   Deverra
   Intercidona
   Lucina
   Meditrina
   Nona
   Partula
   Rumina
   Salus
  messenger
   Mercurius
  mother
   Acca Larentia
   Bellona
   Ceres
  peace and prosperity

   Moneta
   Pax
   Victoria
  sleep
   Somnus
  supreme
   Jupiter
  undefined
   Disciplina
  virtues
   Aequitas
   Fides
   Honus
   Liberalitas
   Pietas
   Providentia
   Spes
   Virtus
  water
   Glaucus
   Hermus
   Iuturna
   Tiberinus
   Tritons
  weather
   Aeolus
   Aquilo
   Corus
   Notus
   Zephyrus
  wine
   Bacchus
  youth
   Juventas
Roman-North African
  Bacax
  Ifru
Romano-Celtic
  agriculture
   Moccus
   Nodotus
  animal
   Mullo
   Rudiobus
   Tarvos Trigaranos
  chthonic
   Aericura
   Alisanos
   Picullus
   Sulis
  collective and generic
   Alaisiagae
  fertility and vegetation
   Abellio
   Abnoba
   Arduinna
   Artio of Muri
   Ialonos
   Nemetona
   Rosmerta
   Sucellos

  guardian and tutelary
   Brigantia
   Britannia
   Coventina
   Mogounos
   Nehalennia
   Proxumae
   Suleviae
   Teutates
  local
   Alaunus
   Anextiomarus
   Contrebis
  medicine and health
   Aveta
   Borvo
   Grannus
   Ocelus
   Sirona
  mother
   Hamavehae
   Matres
  mountain
   Poeninus
   Vosegus
  undefined
   Abandinus
  war
   Andrasta
   Rigisamus
  water
   Ancamna
   Arnemetia
   Icauna
   Nemausius
   Ritona
   Sequana
   Souconna
  weather
   Taranis
Romano-Iberian
  Ataecina
  Candamius
  Cariociecus
  Dercetius
  Duillae
  Eacus
  Endouellicus
  Semnocosus
Ronga
  Mombo Wa Ndhlopfu
Rwanda
  Nyavirezi
  Ryangombe

S

Sabine
  Larunda

SUBJECT INDEX

messenger *(continued)*
  Sasanadevata
  Sogblen
  Yamaduti
  Zhiwud
metallurgy and metalwork
  Hasameli
  Itztapal Totec
  Kinyras
  Ogun
  Xipe Totec
midwifery
  Aveta
  Sasuratum
  Teteoinnan-Toci
military
  Honus
  Mithras
  Virtus
mining
  Kana-Yama-Biko-No-Kami
  Kana-Yama-Hime-No-Kami
misfortune
  Ardra
  Aslesa(s)
  Ate
  Bharani
  Citra
  Dhanistha
  Jyestha
  Shani
mist and fog
  Ganaskidi
  Yina'mna'ut
  Yina'mtilan
moisture *See* water
monkey
  Hanuman
  Sugriva
  Sun Hou-Shi
moon
  Aglibol
  Amm
  Arawa
  Arma
  Avatea
  Caelestis
  Diana
  Gleti
  Hekate
  Hilal
  Hina
  Ix Chel
  Kasku
  Kaumudi
  Khons(u)
  Klehanoai
  Kusuh
  Luna
  Mah
  Mama-Kilya

Mani
Marama
Mawu
Men
Meness
Menulis
Metsaka
Metztli
Moma
Nanna (1)
Napir
Nikkal
Nsongo
Nze
Owiot
Rakib-El
Sahar
Selardi
Selene
Si
Sin
Ta'lab
Tanit
Tecciztecatl
Thoth
Tsuki-Yomi
Wadd
Ya'china'ut
Yah
morality
  Jakomba
morning star
  Attar
  Azizos
  Phosphoros
  Tlahuizcalpantecuhtli
mortuary *See* funerary and
        mortuary
mother
  Aztec
    Coatlicue
    Itzpapalotl
    Itzpapalotl-Itzcueye
    Kundalini
  Buddhist and Buddhist-Lamaist
    Bhrkuti-Tara
    Dhupa
    Gita
    Kotisri
    Lasya
    Mala
    Maya(devi)
    Nrtya
    Puspa
    Yogesvari
  Celtic
    Anu (2)
    Aufaniae
    Don
    Maeve
    Modron

    Sheela Na Gig
  Egyptian
    Hathor
    Ipy
    Isis
    Nekhbet
  Greco-Roman
    Hamavehae
    Matres
    Semele
  Greek
    Artemis
    Demeter
    Gaia
    Leto
    Meter
  Hindu
    Aditi
    Astamatara
    Bala
    Bharat Mata
    Brahmani
    Devaki
    Dharti Mata
    Hammu Mata
    Hariti
    Hinglaj(-Mata)
    Karaikkal Ammaiyar
    Karttiki
    Mata
    Matara
    Narasinhi
    Parvati
    Pattinidevi
    Pradhana
    Prthivi
    Raudri
    Rudracarcika
    Sankari
    Santa
    Santoshi Mata
    Sarasvati
    Sati
    Tripura
  Mesopotamian
    Aya
    Belet-Ili
    Damgalnuna
    Mami
    Ninhursaga
    Ninkurra
    Ninmah
    Ninmena
    Nin-sar
    Nintu
    Nunbarsegunu
    Serida
  other
    Ammavaru
    Anunitu
    Aserah

Y